D1506414

CONCORDANCE

— TO THE —

NEW

ENGLISH

BIBLE

New Testament

A Concordance of words not in,
or not in the same verses as
the King James Version.
A supplement to existing Concordances
of other versions.

CONCORDANCE

—— TO THE ——

NEW

ENGLISH

BIBLE

New Testament

COMPILED BY E. ELDER

ZONDERVAN   PUBLISHING   HOUSE

GRAND RAPIDS · MICHIGAN

65-1490 ✓

NEW ENGLISH BIBLE NEW TESTAMENT — CONCORDANCE
Copyright 1965 by
Zondervan Publishing House
Grand Rapids, Michigan

First printing — 1964
Second printing — 1965

Printed in the United States of America

FOREWORD

The New English Bible — New Testament — created an immediate and wide-spread demand for this *Concordance*. Because many of the words that appear in the New English Bible — New Testament — are different from the words in the Authorized Version, previously existing concordances are of only limited value to the student using this new translation. Thus, this new *Concordance* to the New English Bible — New Testament, is a supplement to existing concordances of other versions — and is offered in the hope that it will prove itself at the study desk.

Arranged in traditional concordance fashion, using bold type for key words, and clear readable type for all references, this volume should prove convenient and easy to use, as well as an important adjunct for Bible students everywhere.

THE PUBLISHERS

CONCORDANCE

— TO THE —

NEW
ENGLISH
BIBLE

New Testament

A

aback
Mark 6:6. he was taken *a.* by their want of faith
John 7:21. once only have I done work on the Sabbath and you are all taken *a.*

abandon-s-ed
John 10:12. the hireling, when he sees the wolf coming, *a.* the sheep
Acts 1:25. apostleship which Judas *a.*
2:27. thou wilt not *a.* my soul to Hades
2:31. he said he was not *a.* to Hades
21:4. urged Paul to *a.* his visit
21:12. implored Paul to *a.* his visit
27:30. the sailors tried to *a.* ship
2 Cor. 4:9. we are never *a.* to our fate
Eph. 4:19. they have *a.* themselves to vice
Heb. 8:9. I *a.* them, says the Lord
2 Pet. 2:15. they have *a.* the straight road
2:21. turn back and *a.* the sacred commandments
Jude 6. *a.* their proper home

A.B.C.
Heb. 5:12. teach you the A.B.C. of God's oracles

abettor
Gal. 2:17. does that mean that Christ is an *a.* of sin

abide
Heb. 8:9. did not *a.* by the terms of that covenant

ability
1 Cor. 12:10. *a.* to distinguish true spirits from false
12:10. *a.* to interpret it
12:28. *a.* to help others
14:13. pray for the *a.* to interpret

abject
1 Cor. 4:9. made us apostles the most *a.* of mankind

abjure
Rev. 9:20. did not *a.* the gods their hands had fashioned

ablaze
Acts 12:7. the cell was *a.* with light
Jam. 3:5. set *a.* by the tiniest spark
2 Pet. 3:12. that day will set the heavens *a.*

able
Mark 9:39. *a.* in the same breath to speak evil of me

14:37. were you not *a.* to keep awake
Luke 8:43. nobody had been *a.* to cure her
John 7:35. we should not be *a.* to find him
Acts 5:39. you will never be *a.* to put them down
8:33. who will be *a.* to speak of his posterity
Rom. 12:2. *a.* to discern the will of God
1 Cor. 14:16. how will the plain man who is present be *a.* to say 'Amen
Heb. 5:2. he is *a.* to bear patiently
2 Pet. 2:9. the Lord is well *a.* to rescue

aboard
John 6:21. ready to take him *a.*
6:24. they themselves went *a.* these boats
21:6. they could not haul the net *a.*
21:11. Simon Peter went *a.*
Acts 20:13. to take Paul *a.*
20:14. we took him *a.*
21:6. we went *a.*
27:6. put us *a.*
27:17. when they had hoisted it *a.*

abolish-ed-ing
Mat. 5:17. to *a.* the law and the prophets
1 Cor. 15:24. *a.* every kind of domination
15:26. the last enemy to be *a.* is death
Heb. 9:26. to *a.* sin by the sacrifice of himself

abominable
2 Pet. 2:10. follow their *a.* lusts

abominate
Rom. 2:22. you *a.* false gods

abounding
2 Cor. 4:15. the *a.* grace of God is shared

about
Mat. 3:1. *a.* that time John the Baptist appeared
5:47. what is there extraordinary *a.* that
6:25. put away anxious thoughts *a.* food and drink
6:28. why be anxious *a.* clothes
6:34. do not be anxious *a.* tomorrow
9:30. see that no one hears *a.* this
9:31. they talked *a.* him
10:19. do not worry *a.* what you are to say
11:7. Jesus began to speak to the people *a.* John

Mat. 14:1. reports *a.* Jesus reached the ears of Prince Herod
15:7. he prophesied *a.* you
16:8. Why do you talk *a.* bringing no bread
16:11. I was not speaking *a.* bread
17:15. he keeps falling *a.*
17:22. they were going *a.* together
17:25. what do you think *a.* this, Simon
18:19. *a.* any request you have to make
19:17. why do you ask me *a.* that
20:6. why are you standing *a.*
21:28. what do you think *a.* this
22:31. *a.* the resurrection of the dead
22:42. what is your opinion *a.* the Messiah
Mark 1:30. they told him *a.* her
5:27. what people were saying *a.* Jesus
5:42. the girl got up and walked *a.*
5:43. to let no one hear *a.* it
7:6. he prophesied *a.* you
8:1. another occasion *a.* this time
8:17. why do you talk *a.* having no bread
8:24. they are walking *a.*
8:30. not to tell anyone *a.* him
8:32. he spoke *a.* it plainly
9:16. what is this argument *a.*
9:20. rolled *a.* foaming
10:10. questioned him *a.* this matter
12:4. whom they beat *a.* the head
12:26. *a.* the resurrection of the dead
13:11. *a.* what you will say
13:32. *a.* that day or that hour no one knows
Luke 1:4. authentic knowledge *a.* the matters
1:39. *a.* this time Mary set out
2:17. told *a.* this child
2:33. what was being said *a.* him
2:38. she talked *a.* the child
3:15. wondering *a.* John
5:15. the talk *a.* him spread
7:3. hearing *a.* Jesus
9:9. who is this I hear such talk *a.*
9:11. spoke to them *a.* the kingdom of God
12:11. do not begin worrying *a.* how
12:22. put away anxious thoughts *a.* food
18:34. they did not grasp what he was talking *a.*
21:7. when will it all come *a.*
23:54. the Sabbath was *a.* to begin
24:7. *a.* the Son of Man
24:19. all this *a.* Jesus of Nazareth
24:36. as they were talking *a.* all this
24:44. everything written *a.* me
John 2:25. no evidence from others *a.* a man
3:12. if you disbelieve me when I talk

to you *a.* things on earth, how are you to believe if I should talk *a.* the things of heaven
5:46. it was *a.* me that he wrote
6:61. his disciples were murmuring *a.* it
6:66. no longer went *a.* with him
7:1. Jesus went *a.* in Galilee
7:12. much whispering *a.* him
7:13. no one talked *a.* him openly
7:32. mutterings of the people *a.* him
8:5. what do you say *a.* it
8:14. though I do bear witness *a.* myself
8:50. I do not care *a.* my own glory
10:41. all that he said *a.* this man was true
12:16. this had been written *a.* him
12:41. he saw his glory and spoke *a.* him
13:18. I am not speaking *a.* all of you
15:15. does not know what his master is *a.*
18:19. questioned Jesus *a.* his disciples and *a.* what he taught
21:7. he wrapped his coat *a.* him
21:8. not far from land, only *a.* a hundred yards
Acts 1:16. *a.* Judas who acted as guide
2:43. marvels and signs were brought *a.*
4:16. a notable miracle has come *a.*
5:20. tell them *a.* this new life
7:58. set *a.* stoning him
8:34. who it is that the prophet is speaking *a.*
9:28. moving *a.* freely in Jerusalem
10:30. four days ago, just *a.* this time
14:13. people were *a.* to offer sacrifice
16:10. set *a.* getting a passage
16:25. *a.* midnight Paul and Silas
17:18. he was preaching *a.* Jesus
17:21. hearing *a.* the latest novelty
18:25. taught accurately the facts *a.* Jesus
19:8. spoke boldly and freely *a.* the kingdom of God
19:15. I know *a.* Paul
20:25. I have gone *a.* among you
21:21. certain information *a.* you
21:24. nothing in the stories they were told *a.* you
22:18. they will not accept your testimony *a.* me
22:29. those who were *a.* to examine him
23:20. more precise information *a.* him
24:22. well informed *a.* the Christian movement
24:24. talk to him *a.* faith in Christ Jesus
25:19. disagreement with him *a.* their peculiar religion

Acts 25:26. I have nothing definite *a.* him

28:22. all we know *a.* this sect is

28:23. sought to convince them *a.* Jesus

28:31. teaching the facts *a.* the Lord Jesus Christ

Rom. 1:3. it is *a.* his Son

1:4. it is *a.* Jesus Christ our Lord

4:1. what, then, are we to say *a.* Abraham

7:13. it used a good thing to bring *a.* my death

9:27. Isaiah makes this proclamation *a.* Israel

10:20. those who never asked *a.* me

11:25. complacent *a.* your own discernment

12:16. go *a.* with humble folk

16:19. this makes me happy *a.* you

1 Cor. 3:18. make no mistake *a.* this

7:1. the matters you wrote *a.*

8:1. *a.* food consecrated to heathen deities

8:4. *a.* eating this consecrated food

12:1. *a.* gifts of the Spirit

16:1. *a.* the collection

2 Cor. 1:15. I felt so confident *a.* all this

2:14. God, who continually leads us *a.*

2:17. we do not go hawking the word of God *a.*

6:16. I will live and move *a.* among them

7:7. greatly comforted *a.* you

8:1. *a.* the grace of generosity

8:23. any question *a.* Titus

9:1. *a.* the provision of aid for God's people

9:3. what we have said *a.* you

10:8. over-boastful *a.* our authority

11:14. there is nothing surprising *a.* that

12:5. *a.* such a man as that I am ready to boast

Gal. 4:20. I am at my wits' end *a.* you

6:7. make no mistake *a.* this

Eph. 6:21. you will want to know *a.* my affairs

6:22. on purpose to let you know all *a.* us

Phil. 1:7. feel like this *a.* you all

1:27. see you for myself or hear *a.* you

4:10. you did care *a.* me before

Col. 2:16. take you to task *a.* what you eat

4:8. let you know all *a.* us

4:10. you have had instructions *a.* him

1 Thess. 3:5. I sent to find out *a.* your faith

3:7. your faith reassures us *a.* you

4:9. *a.* love for our brotherhood

4:13. *a.* those who sleep in death

2 Thess. 1:4. we boast *a.* you ourselves

2:1. *a.* the coming of our Lord Jesus Christ

3:4. we feel perfect confidence *a.* you

1 Tim. 1:7. subjects *a.* which they are so dogmatic

Philem. 10. appeal to you *a.* my child

Heb. 1:3. he had brought *a.* the purgation of sins

6:2. instruction *a.* cleansing rites

Jam. 1:11. so shall the rich man wither away as he goes *a.* his business

1 John 5:16. I do not suggest that he should pray *a.* that

Jude 3. writing to you *a.* our salvation

Rev. 12:4. the woman who was *a.* to give birth

above

Mat. 2:9. it stopped *a.* the place where the child lay

Luke 1:42. God's blessing is on you *a.* all women

23:38. there was an inscription *a.* his head

24:49. until you are armed with the power from *a.*

Rom. 9:5. may God, supreme *a.* all, be blessed for ever

1 Cor. 14:1. *a.* all prophecy

14:12. aspire *a.* all to excel in those which build up the church

2 Cor. 1:12. *a.* all in our dealings with you

Phil. 2:15. show yourselves guileless and *a.* reproach

3:14. God's call to the life *a.*

1 Tim. 3:2. our leader, therefore, or bishop, must be *a.* reproach

4:10. the Saviour *a.* all, of believers

5:7. that the widows may be *a.* reproach

Heb. 1:4. raised as far *a.* the angels

4:5. in the passage *a.* we read

7:26. raised high *a.* the heavens

9:5. *a.* it the cherubim of God's glory

2 Pet. 2:10. *a.* all he will punish those who follow their abominable lusts

3:14. *a.* reproach in his sight

Jude 24. jubilant and *a.* reproach

Rev. 17:1. the great whore, enthroned *a.* the ocean

Abraham

Luke 16:31. *A.* answered

Acts 7:6. *A.*'s descendants

Rom. 4:22. *A.*'s faith

4:23. not for *A.*'s sake alone

9:8. reckoned as *A.*'s descendants

Heb. 6:15. *A.* after patient waiting, attained the promise

abroad

Mat. 21:33. he let it out to vine-growers and went *a.*

Mat. 25:14. a man going *a.* who called his servants

Mark 12:1. let it out to vine-growers and went *a.*

Luke 19:12. a man of noble birth went on a long journey *a.*

20:9. let it out to vine-growers, and went *a.*

2 Cor. 2:14. to reveal and spread *a.* the fragrance of the knowledge of himself

abrogate-d

2 Cor. 3:14. only in Christ is the old covenant *a.*

absence

Acts 24:17. after an *a.* of several years

Rom. 5:13. in the *a.* of law no reckoning is kept of sin

7:8. in the *a.* of law, sin is a dead thing

7:9. in the *a.* of law, I was fully alive

absolute-ly

Rom. 14:14. I am *a.* convinced, as a Christian

Heb. 7:25. that is why he is also able to save *a.*

absorb-ed-ing

2 Cor. 5:4. so that our mortal part may be *a.* into life immortal

1 Tim. 4:15. your business and your *a.* interest

abstain-s

Acts 21:25. *a.* from meat that has been offered to idols

Rom. 14:6. he who *a.* has the Lord in mind no less

14:21. it is a fine thing to *a.* from eating meat

abstinence

1 Cor. 7:5. except when you agree upon a temporary *a.*

1 Tim. 4:3. inculcate *a.* from certain foods

abundantly

Heb. 6:14. I will bless you *a.*

abuse-s-d

Mat. 5:22. if he *a.* his brother he must answer for it

Mat. 27:39. ⎱ the passers-by hurled *a.*
Mark 15:29. ⎰ at him

Acts 13:45. contradicted what Paul and Barnabas said, with violent *a.*

18:6. they opposed him and resorted to *a.*

23:5. you must not *a.* the ruler of your people

1 Tim. 1:13. in the past I had met him with *a.*

Heb. 10:33. some of you were *a.*

1 Pet. 2:23. when he was *a.* he did not retort with *a.*

3:9. do not repay wrong with wrong, or *a.* with *a.*

3:16. when you are *a.*

2 Pet. 2:12. they pour *a.* upon things they do not understand

Jude 10. these men pour *a.* upon things they do not understand

abusive

John 9:28. then they became *a.*

2 Tim. 3:2. they will be arrogant, boastful, and *a.*

abyss

Luke 8:31. they begged him not to banish them to the *a.*

Rom. 10:7. who can go down to the *a.*

Rev. 9:1. the key of the shaft of the *a.*

9:2. he opened the shaft of the *a.*

9:11. they had for their king the angel of the *a.*

11:7. the beast that comes up from the *a.*

17:8. has yet to ascend out of the *a.*

20:1. an angel coming down from heaven with the key of the *a.*

20:3. he threw him into the *a.*

accent

Mat. 26:73. your *a.* gives you away

accept-s-ed-ing

Mat. 5:12. *a.* it with gladness

11:14. John is the destined Elijah, if you will but *a.* it

13:20. hearing the word, *a.* it at once

19:11. something which not everyone can *a.*

19:12. let those *a.* it who can

Mark 4:16. as soon as they hear the word, they *a.* it with joy

10:15. *a.* the kingdom of God like a child

Luke 7:29. they had *a.* John's baptism

14:18 ⎱
14:19 ⎰ please *a.* my apologies

18:17. does not *a.* the kingdom of God like a child

John 3:32. yet no one *a.* his witness

3:33. to *a.* his witness is to attest that God speaks true

10:38. *a.* the evidence of my deeds

12:48. rejects me and does not *a.* my words

14:11. *a.* the evidence of the deeds themselves

Acts 2:36. *a.* as certain that God has made this Jesus, whom you crucified, both Lord and Messiah

2:41. those who *a.* his word were baptized

7:39. our forefathers would not *a.* his leadership

8:14. Samaria had *a.* the word of God

11:1. Gentiles too had *a.* the word of God

Acts 17:25. he *a.* service at men's hands
22:18. they will not *a.* your testimony
23:8. angel, or spirit, but the Pharisees *a.* them
24:15. the hope, which my accusers too *a.*
Rom. 14:1. if a man is weak in his faith you must *a.* him
14:3. God has *a.* him
15:1. *a.* as our own burden the tender scruples
15:7. *a.* one another as Christ *a.* us
1 Cor. 9:2. if others do not *a.* me as an apostle
10:5. most of them were not *a.* by God
2 Cor. 2:9. whether you fully *a.* my authority
6:17. then I will *a.* you, says the Lord
10:18. whom the Lord recommends— he and he alone is to be *a.*
11:8. *a.* support from them to serve you
Gal. 2:9. *a.* Barnabas and myself as partners
Eph. 1:5. *a.* as his sons
Phil. 2:8. in obedience *a.* even death
2 Thess. 3:8. we did not *a.* board and lodging from anyone without paying
Heb. 10:34. cheerfully *a.* the seizure of your possessions
Jam. 1:21. quietly *a.* the message
1 Pet. 2:18. servants, *a.* the authority of your masters
3:1. you women must *a.* the authority of your husbands
1 John 5:9. we *a.* human testimony
5:10. makes him out to be a liar, by refusing to *a.* God's own witness
3 John 7. they would *a.* nothing from pagans
Rev. 2:24. who do not *a.* this teaching
22:17. *a.* the water of life

acceptable
John 8:29. I always do what is *a.* to him
Acts 6:5. this proposal proved *a.*
2 Cor. 5:9. our ambition, wherever we are, here or there, to be *a.* to him

acceptance
Rom. 11:15. if their rejection has meant the reconciliation of the world, what will their *a.* mean

acclaim-ed-ing
Acts. 10:46. *a.* the greatness of God
13:48. thankfully *a.* the word of the Lord

accompany-ied-ing
Mark 4:36. there were other boats *a.* him
5:24. Jesus went with him, *a.* by a great crowd

5:37. after this he allowed no one to *a.* him except
6:1.
Luke 7:11. } *a.* by his disciples
14:25. great crowds were *a.* him, he turned to them
22:39. to the Mount of Olives, *a.* by the disciples
23:49 } the women who had *a.* him
23:55 }
Acts 18:18. *a.* by Priscilla and Aquila
24:1. *a.* by some of the elders
25:23. Agrippa and Bernice came in full state and entered the audience-chamber *a.* by high-ranking officers
1 Cor. 10:4. the supernatural rock that *a.* their travels
2 Cor. 3:9. if splendour *a.* the dispensation under which we are condemned
Jam. 2:18. prove to me that this faith you speak of is real though not *a.* by deeds

accomplice
2 John 11. *a.* in his wicked deeds

accomplish-ed
John 15:24. *a.* what no other man has done
19:30. he said 'It is *a!*' He bowed his head and gave up his spirit

accord-s
John 7:28 } I have not come of my own *a.*
8:42 }
11:51. he did not say this of his own *a.*
Rom. 9:13. that *a.* with the text of Scripture

accordance
John 12:14. Jesus found a donkey and mounted it, in *a.* with the text of Scripture
Acts 15:1. circumcised in *a.* with Mosaic practice
23:3. you sit there to judge me in *a.* with the law

according
John 19:40. *a.* to Jewish burial-customs
1 Cor. 7:17. *a.* to the gift the Lord has granted him
2 Cor. 8:11. give *a.* to your means
Col. 2:19. thus knit together grows *a.* to God's design
Heb. 9:22. *a.* to the Law, it might almost be said, everything is cleansed by blood
12:10. they disciplined us for this short life *a.* to their lights

accordingly
Mat. 13:23. who *a.* bears fruit, and yields a hundredfold
18:32. he *a.* sent for the man 'You scoundrel

Mark 6:32. *a.*, they set off privately by boat

7:5. *a.*, these Pharisees and the lawyers asked him

John 11:54. *a.* Jesus no longer went about publicly

19:32. the soldiers *a.* came to the first of his fellow-victims

Acts 5:21. *a.* they entered the temple at daybreak

24:16. *a.* I, no less than they, train myself

25:26. *a.* I have brought him up before you

Rom. 7:4. *a.* you have found another husband in him who rose from the dead

2 Cor. 9:5. I have *a.* thought it necessary to ask these friends to go on ahead

Philem. 8. *a.*, although in Christ I might make bold to point out your duty

1 Pet. 4:4. they cannot understand it, and they vilify you *a.*

accosted

Mat. 26:69. Peter was sitting outside in the courtyard when a serving-maid *a.* him

Luke 20:1. the priests and lawyers, and the elders with them, came upon him and *a.* him

account-s

Mat. 13:21. persecution on *a.* of the word

14:3. thrown him into prison, on *a.* of Herodias

25:19. their master returned, and proceeded to settle *a.* with them

26:31. you will all fall from your faith on my *a.*

26:33. everyone else may fall away on your *a.* but I never will

27:19. I was much troubled on his *a.* in my dreams

Mark 4:17. persecution on *a.* of the word

13:9. summoned to appear before governor's and kings on my *a.*

Luke 1:1. an *a.* of the events that have happened among us

16:6. here is your *a.* Sit down and make it five hundred

16:7. take your *a.* and make it eight hundred

24:35. they gave their *a.* of the events of their journey

John 1:22. what *a.* do you give of yourself

12:11. on his *a.* many Jews were going over to Jesus

12:42. would not acknowledge him on *a.* of the Pharisees

15:21. it is on my *a.* that they will treat you thus

Rom. 11:25. a deep truth here, my brothers, of which I want you to take *a.*

1 Cor. 4:3. if I am called to *a.* by you

4:6. into this general picture, my friends, I have brought Apollos and myself on your *a.*

2 Cor. 12:5. I will not boast on my own *a.*

Eph. 3:3. I have already written a brief *a.*

2 Thess. 1:6. it is surely just that God should balance the *a.* by sending trouble to those who trouble you

1 Pet. 3:15. called to *a.* for the hope that is in you

accredit-ed

John 5:43. I have come *a.* by my Father

accrue-ing

Phil. 4:17. all I care for is the profit *a.* to you

accurately

Acts 18:25. he taught *a.* the facts about Jesus

accursed

Gal. 3:13. becoming for our sake an *a.* thing

Rev. 22:3. every *a.* thing shall disappear

accusation

Acts 23:29. the *a.* had to do with controversial matters in their law

28:19. not that I had any *a.* to bring against my own people

accuser-s

John 5:45. do not imagine that I shall be your *a.* at God's tribunal

Acts 24:15. I hold the hope, which my *a.* too accept

Rom. 8:33. who will be the *a.* of God's chosen ones

accustomed

John 9:8. those who were *a.* to see him begging said

1 Cor. 8:7. so *a.* to idolatry that even now they eat this food with a sense of its heathen consecration

Gal. 2:2. the gospel which I am *a.* to preach

achieve-d-ing

Acts 27:13. their purpose was as good as *a.*

Rom. 1:13. in the hope of *a.* something among you

9:30. Gentiles, who made no effort after righteousness, nevertheless *a.* it

11:7. what Israel sought Israel has not *a.* but the selected few have *a.* it achievement

Eph. 3:11. his age-long purpose, which he *a.* in Christ Jesus our Lord
Phil. 3:12. it is not to be thought that I have already *a.* all this

achievement
Gal. 6:4. he can measure his *a.* by comparing himself with himself

acknowledge-s-d
Mat. 10:32. whoever then will *a.* me before men, I will *a.* him before my Father in heaven
23:31. you *a.* that you are the sons of the men who killed the prophets
Luke 12:8. everyone who *a.* me before men the Son of Man will *a.* before the angels of God
John 9:22. anyone who *a.* Jesus as Messiah should be banned from the synagogue
12:42. would not *a.* him on account of the Pharisees
Acts 10:22. a good and religious man, *a.* as such by the whole Jewish nation
19:15. Jesus I *a.*, and I know about Paul, but who are you
Rom. 1:28. they have not seen fit to *a.* God
7:15. I do not even *a.* my own actions as mine
11:2. God has not rejected the people which he *a.*
14:11. every knee shall bow and every tongue *a.* God
1 Cor. 8:3. if a man loves, he is *a.* by God
Gal. 2:7. *a.* that I had been entrusted with the Gospel
4:8. when you did not *a.* God you were the slaves
4:9. now that you do *a.* God—or rather, now that he has *a.* you
1 Thess. 5:12. *a.* those who are working so hard among you
2 Thess. 1:8. those who refuse to *a.* God
Tit. 1:16. they profess to *a.* God, but deny him by their actions
Heb. 12:6. he lays the rod on every son whom he *a.*
13:15. the tribute of lips which *a.* his name
John 4:2. every spirit which *a.* that Jesus Christ has come in the flesh is from God
4:3. every spirit which does not thus *a.* Jesus is not from God
4:15. if a man *a.* that Jesus is the Son of God, God dwells in him
2 John 7. who do not *a.* Jesus Christ as coming in the flesh
Rev. 3:5. in the presence of my Father and his angels I will *a.* him as mine

acquaint-ed
John 18:15. this disciple who was *a.* with the High Priest
Rom. 7:7. except through law I should never have become *a.* with sin

acquaintance
John 18:16. the other disciple, the High Priest's *a.*

acquire
Acts 22:28. it cost me a large sum to *a.* this citizenship
1 Tim. 6:19. so *a.* a treasure which will form a good foundation for the future

acquit-s-ted
Mat. 12:37. out of your own mouth you will be *a.*
Luke 6:37. *a.*, and you will be *a.*
18:14. went home *a.* of his sins
Acts 13:39. everyone who has faith is *a.*
Rom. 4:5. he simply puts his faith in him who *a.* the guilty
1 Cor. 4:4. that does not mean I stand *a.*
2 Cor. 3:9. how much richer in splendour must that one be under which we are *a.*

acquittal
Acts 13:39. for which there was no *a.* under the Law of Moses
Rom. 5:16. issued in a verdict of *a.*
5:18. *a.* and life for all men
8:33. it is God who pronounces *a.*

acre
Mat. 27:8. this explains the name 'Blood *a.*', by which that field has been known ever since
Acts 1:19. they named the property in their own language Akeldama, which means 'Blood *a.*

across
Mat. 19:1. came into the region of Judaea *a.* Jordan
John 10:40. Jesus withdrew again *a.* the Jordan
Acts 16:9. come *a.* to Macedonia and help us
18:27. he wished to go *a.* to Achaia
27:5. *a.* the open sea off the coast of Cilicia

act-s-ed-ing
Mat. 6:2. when you do some *a.* of charity, do not announce it with a flourish of trumpets
6:3. when you do some *a.* of charity
7:24. the man who hears these words of mine and *a.* upon them
7:26. hears these words of mine and does not *a.* upon them

Mat. 21:23. by what authority are you *a.* like this

21:24. I will tell you by what authority I *a.*

21:27. neither will I tell you by what authority I *a.*

Mark 7:21. out of a man's heart, come evil thoughts, *a.* of fornication

11:28. by what authority are you *a.* like this? Who gave you authority to *a.*

11:29. I will tell you by what authority I *a.*

11:33. neither will I tell you by what authority I *a.*

Luke 6:47. hears what I say, and *a.* upon it

6:49. he who hears and does not *a.*

8:21. those who hear the word of God and *a.* upon it

16:8. the master applauded the dishonest baillif for *a.* so astutely

20:2. by what authority you are *a.* like this

20:8. neither will I tell you by what authority I *a.*

24:51. in the *a.* of blessing he parted from them

John 5:30. I cannot *a.* by myself

8:40. that is not how Abraham *a.*

10:37. if I am not *a.* as my Father would, do not believe me

13:17. if you know this, happy are you if you *a.* upon it

Acts 1:16. Judas who *a.* as guide

3:17. I know quite well that you *a.* in ignorance

9:36. filled her days with *a.* of kindness

10:4. your prayers and *a.* of charity have gone up to heaven

10:31. your *a.* of charity remembered before God

23:15. *a.* with the Council

23:31. *a.* on their orders, the infantry took Paul

Rom. 1:4. declared Son of God by a mighty *a.*

3:24. God's free grace alone, through his *a.* of liberation

4:6. apart from any specific *a.* of justice

5:15. God's *a.* of grace is out of all proportion to Adam's wrong-doing

5:16. the *a.* of grace, following upon so many misdeeds

5:18. the issue of one just *a.* is acquittal

13:1. there is no authority but bv *a.* of God

1 Cor. 1:30. you are in Christ Jesus by God's *a.*

2 Cor. 2:8. assure him of your love for him by a formal *a.*

13:8. we have no power to *a.* against the truth

Gal. 3:20. an intermediary is not needed for one party *a.* alone

4:7. a son, then also by God's own *a.* an heir

Col. 3:17. whether you speak or *a.*, do everything in the name of the Lord Jesus

2 Thess. 1:11. every *a.* inspired by faith

1 Tim. 1:13. I *a.* ignorantly in unbelief

5:21. *a.* with strict impartiality

Heb. 6:18. two irrevocable *a.* in which God could not possibly play us false

Jam. 1:22. *a.* on the message and do not merely listen

1:23. a man who listens to the message but never *a.* upon it

1:25. does not forget what he hears, but *a.* upon it

2:12. *a.* as men who are to be judged under a law of freedom

1 Pet. 4:11. so *a.* that the glory may be God's

action-s

Luke 12:35. be ready for *a.*

23:51. dissented from their policy and the *a.* they had taken

24:19. a prophet powerful in speech and *a.*

John 2:18. what sign, they asked, can you show as authority for your *a.*

8:38. you are revealing in *a.* what you learned from your father

11:47. a meeting of the Council. 'What *a.* are we taking

Acts 5:17. the Sadducean party as it then was, were goaded into *a.* by jealousy

7:22. Moses was trained in all the wisdom of the Egyptians, a powerful speaker and a man of *a.*

Rom. 5:16. the judicial *a.*, following upon the one offence

7:15. I do not even acknowledge my own *a.* as mine

7:17. it is no longer I who perform the *a.*

14:23. a man who has doubts is guilty if he eats, because his *a.* does not arise from his conviction

2 Cor. 9:11. through our *a.* such generosity will issue in thanksgiving to God

10:11. my *a.* will show the same man as my letters showed

Gal. 2:8. God whose *a.* made Peter an apostle to the Jews

1 Thess. 1:3. your faith has shown itself in *a.*

1 Tim. 6:18. hoard a wealth of noble *a.* by doing good

Tit. 1:16. they profess to acknowledge God, but deny him by their *a.*

Jam. 2:17, faith; if it does not lead to *a.*, it is in itself a lifeless thing

2:21. was it not by his *a.*, in offering his son Isaac upon the altar, that our father Abraham was justified

2:22. you can see that faith was at work in his *a.*, and that by these *a.* the integrity of his faith was fully proved

2:25. the prostitute Rahab also. Was not she justified by her *a.*

1 Pet. 1:13. be like men stripped for *a.*

1 John 3:12. his own *a.* were wrong, and his brother's were right

3:18. it must be genuine, and show itself in *a.*

active

Gal. 5:6. the only thing that counts is faith *a.* in love

Col. 1:10. that you may bear fruit in *a.* goodness

2:12. your faith in the *a.* power of God

2 Tim. 2:4. a soldier on *a.* service

Heb. 4:12. the word of God is alive and *a.*

10:24. arouse others to love and *a.* goodness

actively

Acts 26:9. once thought it my duty to work *a.* against the name of Jesus

activity

Eph. 4:16. the whole frame grows through the due *a.* of each part

actually

John 7:26. can it be that our rulers have *a.* decided that this is the Messiah

Acts 5:15. the sick were *a.* carried out into the streets

Rom. 1:32. they *a.* applaud such practices

5:7. perhaps for a good man one might *a.* brave death

1 Cor. 5:1. I *a.* hear reports of sexual immorality among you

6:8. you *a.* injure and rob

Adam

Rom. 5:15. God's act of grace is out of all proportion to *A.*'s wrongdoing

adapt

Rom. 12:2. *a.* yourselves no longer to the pattern of this present world

add-s-ed-ing

Mat. 19:5. he *a.*, for this reason a man shall leave his father and mother

28:14. they *a.*, If this should reach the Governor's ears

Mark 4:9. he *a.*, 'If you have ears to hear, then hear

6:10. he *a.*, 'stay there until you leave those parts

Luke 11:5. he *a.*, 'Suppose one of you has a friend

John 1:51. he *a.*, 'In truth, in very truth I tell you all, you shall see heaven wide open

11:11. he *a.*, 'Our friend Lazarus has fallen asleep

13:11. he *a.* the words, 'not every one of you

21:19. then he *a.*, 'Follow me

Acts 1:23. known as Barsabbas, and bore the *a.* name of Justus

Rom. 16:22. I Tertius, who took this letter down, *a.* my Christian greetings

Gal. 3:15. no one else can set it aside or *a.* a codicil

Phil. 1:25. to *a.* joy to your faith

1 Tim. 5:7. *a.* these orders to the rest

Tit. 2:10. in all such ways they will *a.* lustre to the doctrine of God our Saviour

Heb. 2:4. God *a.* his testimony by signs

10:17. then he *a.*, 'and their sins and wicked deeds I will remember no more at all

1 Pet. 5:12. *a.* my testimony that this is the true grace of God

3 John. 12. I *a.* my testimony

Rev. 19:9. and he *a.*, 'These are the very words of God

adders

Rom 3:13. *a.* venom is on their lips

address-es-ed-ing

Mat. 5:2. he began to *a.* them

9:6. he now *a.* the paralytic

23:1. Jesus then *a.* the people

23:7. to be *a.* as 'rabbi

28:5. the angel then *a.* the women

Luke 7:1. when he had finished *a.* the people

23:20. Pilate *a.* them again

John 8:12. once again Jesus *a.* the people

Acts 2:14. Peter stood up with the Eleven, raised his voice, and *a.* them

4:1. they were still *a.* the people, when the chief priests came upon them

15:7. after a long debate, Peter rose and *a.* them

19:25. he called a meeting of these men and the workers in allied trades, and *a.* them

20:7. Paul, who was to leave next day, *a.* them

21:40. he *a.* them in the Jewish language

Rom. 3:19. now all the words of the law

are *a*., as we know, to those who are within the pale of the law

1 Cor. 14:28. if there is no interpreter, the speaker had better not *a*. the meeting at all

14:34. women should not *a*. the meeting

14:35. it is a shocking thing that a woman should *a*. the congregation

2 Cor. 1:18. the language in which we *a*. you is not an ambiguous blend of Yes and No

5:11. with this fear of the Lord before our eyes we *a*. our appeal to men

7:14. every word we ever *a*. to you bore the mark of truth

12:19. perhaps you think that all this time we have been *a*. our defence to you

Heb. 12:5. you have forgotten the text of Scripture which *a*. you as sons

1 John 5:13. it is *a*. to those who give their allegiance to the Son of God

adhere-d
Acts 6:7. very many of the priests *a*. to the Faith

Tit. 1:9. he must *a*. to the true doctrine

adherents
2 Pet. 2:2. they will gain many *a*. to their dissolute practices

adjourn-ed
Acts 24:22. Felix, who happened to be well informed about the Christian movement, *a*. the hearing

adjure
1 Thess. 5:27. I *a*. you by the Lord to have this letter read to the whole brotherhood

2 Tim. 2:14. *a*. them before God to stop disputing about mere words

4:1. I *a*. you by his coming appearance and his reign, proclaim the message

administer-ed
Acts 24:10. for many years you have *a*. justice in this province

administration
Rom. 12:7. or the gift of *a*., in *a*.

administrator
Acts 7:10. he appointed him chief *a*. for Egypt

admirable
Rom. 7:16. I agree with the law and hold it to be *a*.

Phil. 4:8. Whatever is excellent and *a*.

admiration
Mat. 6:2. to win *a*. from men

Luke 4:22. there was a general stir of *a*.

9:43. wonder and *a*. at all he was doing

Rev. 13:3. the whole world went after the beast in wondering *a*.

admire-d
Luke 7:9. when Jesus heard this, he *a*. the man

16:15. what sets itself up to be *a*. by men is detestable in the sight of God

admission
2 Pet. 1:11. full and free *a*. into the eternal kingdom of our Lord

admit-s-ted
Mark 6:10. when you are *a*. to a house, he added, stay there

Luke 9:4. when you are *a*. to a house, stay there

John 10:3. the door-keeper *a*. him

Acts 24:14. this much I will *a*.: I am a follower of the new way

Rom. 2:2. it is *a*. that God's judgement is rightly passed

11:25. partial blindness has come upon Israel only until the Gentiles have been *a*.

2 Cor. 11:21. we, you say, have been weak! I *a*. the reproach

admixture
Heb. 4:2. the message they heard did no good, because they brought no *a*. of faith

admonish
Col. 1:28. we *a*. everyone without distinction

3:16. *a*. each other with the utmost wisdom

1 Thess. 5:14. *a*. the careless

adopt-ed
Acts 7:21. Pharoah's daughter herself *a*. him

16:21. customs which it is illegal for us Romans to *a*.

2 Cor. 8:11. be as eager to complete the scheme as you were to *a*. it

adoration
Acts 7:43. the images which you had made for your *a*.

adored
2 Thess. 1:10. *a*. among all believers

adorn-ed-ing
1 Cor. 12:23. our seemly parts need no *a*.

Rev. 21:19. the foundations of the city wall were *a*. with jewels

adornment
1 Pet. 3:3. your beauty should reside, not in outward *a*.

adrift
2 Cor. 11:25. for twenty-four hours I was *a*. on the open sea

advance-d
Luke 2:52. as Jesus grew up he *a.* in wisdom
Acts 10:41. witnesses whom God had chosen in *a.*
Heb. 6:2. let us *a.* towards maturity

advantage
1 Cor. 9:15. earn their living by the Gospel. But I have never taken *a.* of any such right
2 Cor. 7:2. we have wronged no one, ruined no one, taken *a.* of no one
Heb. 13:17. let it be a happy task for them, and not pain and grief, for that would bring you no *a.*

adventurers
2 Tim. 3:4. strangers to all goodness, traitors, *a.*

advice
Acts 5:40. they took his *a.*
27:9. Paul therefore gave them this *a.*
27:21. you should have taken my *a.*
Rom. 15:14. well able to give *a.* to one another
2 Thess. 3:15. I do not mean treat him as an enemy, but give him friendly *a.*
1 Tim. 4:6. by offering such *a.* as this to the brotherhood you will prove a good servant of Christ Jesus

advise-d
John 18:14. the same Caiaphas who had *a.* the Jews
1 Cor. 2:16. who knows the mind of the Lord? who can *a.* him
Rev. 3:18. I *a.* you to buy from me gold refined in the fire

advisers
Acts 25:12. Festus, after conferring with his *a.*, replied

advocate-s-ing
John 14:16. I will ask the Father, and he will give you another to be your *a.*
14:26. your *a.*, the Holy Spirit
15:26. when your *a.* has come
16:7. if I do not go, your *a.* will not come
Acts 16:21. they are *a.* customs which it is illegal for us Romans to adopt
24:1. an *a.* named Tertullus
Gal. 2:12. he was afraid of the *a.* of circumcision
5:11. if I am still *a.* circumcision, why is it I am still persecuted

affair-s
Luke 3:19. rebuked by him over the *a.* of his brother's wife Herodias
Col. 4:7. you will hear all about my *a.* from Tychicus

affect-ed
Acts 17:8. a great commotion in the mob, which *a.* the magistrates also

affection
Rom. 12:10. let love for our brotherhood breed warmth of mutual *a.*
Phil. 1:7. because you hold me in such *a.*
2:1. any sharing of the Spirit, any warmth of *a.*
1 Thess. 5:13. *a.* for the work they do
1 Pet. 1:22. feel sincere *a.* towards your brother Christians
3:8. be full of brotherly *a.*

affirm-s-ed-ing
Acts 10:42. and *a.* that he is the one who has been designated by God as judge
18:5. *a.* before the Jews that the Messiah was Jesus
23:11. you have *a.* the truth about me in Jerusalem
Rom. 10:15. that is what Scripture *a.*
Heb. 7:8. one whom Scripture *a.* to be alive

affliction
Rom. 8:35. what can separate us from the love of Christ? can *a.*

afford-s-ed
Luke 14:28. calculating the cost, to see whether he could *a.* to finish it
2 Cor. 9:13. through the proof which this *a.*, many will give honour to God
Phil. 1:28. a sign of your salvation, and one *a.* by God himself
2 Pet. 1:11. you will be *a.* full and free admission into the eternal kingdom
1 John 2:16. everything the world *a.*

affront-ed
Heb. 10:29. *a.* God's gracious Spirit

afraid
Mat. 1:20. said the angel, 'do not be *a.* to take Mary home with you as your wife
10:26. do not be *a.* of them
14:5. Herod would have liked to put him to death, but he was *a.* of the people
21:26. we are *a.* of the people, for they all take John for a prophet
21:46. they wanted to arrest him, but they were *a.* of the people
Mark 11:18. they were *a.* of him, because the whole crowd was spellbound by his teaching
11:32. they were *a.* of the people, for all held that John was in fact a prophet
12:12. they were *a.* of popular feeling

Luke 1:13. do not be *a.*, Zechariah; your prayer has been heard

1:30. the angel said to her, 'Do not be *a.*, Mary

2:10. the angel said, 'Do not be *a.*; I have good news for you

5:10. do not be *a.*' said Jesus to Simon

8:50. do not be *a.*,' he said 'only show faith and she will be well again

9:34. they were *a.* as they entered the cloud

9:45. they were *a.* to ask him what it meant

19:21. I was *a.* of you, because you are a hard man

20:19 } they were *a.* of the people
22:2 }

John 9:22. his parents gave this answer because they were *a.* of the Jews

Acts 23:10. the commandant was *a.* that Paul would be torn in pieces

27:17. they were *a.* of running on to the shallows of Syrtis

27:24. do not be *a.*, Paul,' he said

2 Cor. 11:3. I am *a.* that your thoughts may be corrupted

12:21. I am *a.* that, when I come again, my God may humiliate me

Gal. 2:12. he was *a.* of the advocates of circumcision

1 John 4:18. anyone who is *a.* has not attained to love in its perfection

Rev. 1:17. do not be *a.* I am the first and the last

2:10. do not be *a.* of the suffering to come

afresh

Phil. 4:10. your care for me has now blossomed *a.*

after

Mat. 3:16. *a.* baptism Jesus came up out of the water

6:32. these are things for the heathen to run *a.*

6:34. tomorrow will look *a.* itself

14:13. came *a.* him in crowds

20:34. they went on *a.* him

Luke 1:5. called *a.* Abijah

10:34. looked *a.* him there

10:35. look *a.* him

John 19:3. time *a.* time they came up to him, crying, 'Hail, King of the Jews

Acts 7:44. he told Moses to make it *a.* the pattern

8:3. he entered house *a.* house, seizing men and women

Rom. 15:5. agree with one another *a.* the manner of Christ Jesus

1 Tim. 3:5. how can he look *a.* a congregation of God's people

4:1. in *a.* times some will desert from the faith

Philem. 13. I should have liked to keep him with me, to look *a.* me

afternoon

Mat. 20:5. at noon he went out again, and at three in the *a.*

27:45. from midday until three in the *a.*

Mark 15:33. darkness fell over the whole land, which lasted till three in the *a.*

Luke 23:44. which lasted until three in the *a.*

John 1:39. it was then about four in the *a.*

4:52. yesterday at one in the *a.* the fever left him

Acts 3:1. one day at three in the *a.*, the hour of prayer

10:3. one day about three in the *a.* he had a vision

10:30. I was in the house here saying the *a.* prayers

afterwards

Mat. 17:19. *a.* the disciples came to Jesus and asked him privately

Mark 8:31. to be put to death, and to rise again three days *a.*

10:34. three days *a.*, he will rise again

16:8. *a.* Jesus himself sent out by them from east to west

John 7:1. *a.* Jesus went about in Galilee

Acts 9:19. *a.* he took food and his strength returned

12:19. *a.* he left Judaea to reside for a time at Caesarea

13:20. *a.* appointed judges for them

16:33. immediately *a.* he and his whole family were baptized

1 Cor. 7:5. *a.* you may come together again

15:5. he appeared to Cephas, and *a.* to the Twelve

15:7. he appeared to James, and *a.* to all the apostles

Gal. 1:17. *a.* returned to Damascus

1 Tim. 2:13. Adam was created first, and Eve *a.*

again

Mat. 8:3. Jesus stretched out his hand, touched him, and said, 'Indeed I will; be clean *a.*

13:15. then they might turn *a.*, and I would heal them

28:6. he is not here; he has been raised *a.*

Mark 4:18. others *a.* receive the seed among thistles

11:14. may no one ever *a.* eat fruit from you

13:19. since the beginning of the world which God created—and will never be *a.*

Mark 14:25. never *a*. shall I drink from the fruit of the vine until that day

Luke 8:50. only show faith and she will be well *a*.

20:37. that the dead are raised to life *a*. is shown by Moses

John 2:20. are you going to raise it *a*. in three days

5:14. now that you are well *a*., leave your sinful ways

11:38. Jesus *a*. sighed deeply

Acts 2:24. God raised him to life *a*.

4:17. we had better caution them never *a*. to speak to anyone in this name

13:42. they were asked to come *a*. and speak on these subjects next Sabbath

20:25. now I know that none of you will see my face *a*.

Rom. 6:9. we know that Christ, once raised from the dead, is never to die *a*.

14:9. this is why Christ died and came to life *a*.

2 Cor. 1:10. and he will deliver us *a*.

Gal. 6:1. you who are endowed with the Spirit must set him right *a*. very gently

1 Tim. 5:14. that young widows shall marry *a*.

Tit. 3:10. a heretic should be warned once, and once *a*.

Heb. 9:25. nor is he there to offer himself *a*. and *a*.

12:26. yet once *a*. I will shake not earth alone, but the heavens also

12:27. the words 'once *a*.'—and only once—imply

2 Pet. 1:12. I will not hesitate to remind you of this *a*. and *a*.

Rev. 7:16. they shall never *a*. feel hunger or thirst

18:14. all the glitter and the glamour are lost, never to be yours *a*.

18:21. thus shall Babylon, the great city, be sent hurtling down, never to be seen *a*.

20:4. these came to life *a*. and reigned with Christ

against

Mat. 5:39. do not set yourself *a*. the man who wrongs you

12:5. the priests in the temple break the Sabbath and it is not held *a*. them

12:10. their aim was to frame a charge *a*. him

12:41. when this generation is on trial, the men of Nineveh will appear *a*. it

16:6. be on your guard *a*. the leaven of the Pharisees and Sadducees

16:12. they were to be on their guard, not *a*. the baker's leaven of the Pharisees and Sadducees, but *a*. their teaching

27:12. the charges laid *a*. him by the chief priests and elders

27:60. he then rolled a large stone *a*. the entrance

Mark 3:2. so that they could bring a charge *a*. him

6:48. seeing them labouring at the oars *a*. a head-wind

15:3. the chief priests brought many charges *a*. him

15:26. the inscription giving the charge *a*. him read

Luke 11:31. the Queen of the South will appear *a*. them

18:3. a widow who constantly came before him demanding justice *a*. her opponent

19:43. your enemies will set up siege-works *a*. you

23:2. they opened the case *a*. him

23:10. pressed the case *a*. him vigorously

John 16:1. to guard you *a*. the break-down of your faith

19:4. I find no case *a*. him

19:6. for my part I find no case *a*. him.

Acts 6:10. could not hold their own *a*. the inspired wisdom with which he spoke

7:51. you always fight *a*. the Holy Spirit

7:60. Lord, do not hold this sin *a*. them

9:23. the Jews hatched a plot *a*. his life

18:13. inducing people to worship God in ways that are *a*. the law

19:37. uttered no blasphemy *a*. our goddess

20:3. a plot was laid *a*. him by the Jews

22:30. what charge the Jews were bringing *a*. Paul

24:13. they cannot make good the charges they bring *a*. me

25:10. *a*. the Jews I have committed no offence

26:9. I myself once thought it my duty to work actively *a*. the name of Jesus

28:18. no capital charge *a*. me

Rom. 2:15. their own thoughts argue the case on either side, *a*. them or even for them

4:8. happy is the man whose sins the Lord does not count *a*. him

7:16. if what I do is *a*. my will, it means that I agree with the law

7:19. what I do is the wrong which is *a*. my will

Rom. 7:20. what I do is *a*. my will
8:3. he has passed judgement *a*. sin
11:24. *a*. all nature grafted into the cultivated olive
13:8. leave no claim outstanding *a*. you
1 Cor. 10:10. do not grumble *a*. God
2 Cor. 5:19. no longer holding men's misdeeds *a*. them
8:20. we want to guard *a*. any criticism
Gal. 2:17. turn out to be sinners *a*. the law
2 Thess. 2:3. the final rebellion *a*. God
2:4. he rises in his pride *a*. every god
1 Tim. 3:10. if there is no mark *a*. them, they may serve
2 Tim. 4:15. you had better be on your guard *a*. him too
4:16. I pray that it may not be held *a*. them
Jam. 5:4. the wages you never paid to the men who mowed your fields are loud *a*. you
1 Pet. 2:7. a stone to trip over, a rock to stumble *a*.
5:5. God sets his face *a*. the arrogant
1 John 3:17. when he sees his brother in need shuts up his heart *a*. him
5:21. my children, be on the watch *a*. false gods
Rev. 13:4. who is like the Beast? Who can fight *a*. it
18:20. in the judgement *a*. her he has vindicated your cause

age-s-ing
Mat. 2:16. the massacre of all children in Bethlehem and its neighbourhood, of the *a*. of two years or less
12:32. for him there is no forgiveness, either in this *a*. or in the *a*. to come
24:3. your coming and the end of the *a*.
24:8. with all these things the birth-pangs of the new *a*. begin
Mark 8:38. this wicked and godless *a*.
10:30. receive in this *a*. a hundred times as much . . . and in the *a*. to come eternal life
13:8. with these things the birth-pangs of the new *a*. begin
Luke 1:70. *a*. after *a*. he proclaimed by the lips of his holy prophets
2:37. then alone as a widow to the *a*. of eighty-four
18:30. repaid many times over in this *a*., and in the *a*. to come have eternal life
Acts 2:40. save yourselves,' he said 'from this crooked *a*.
7:23. he was approaching the *a*. of forty

14:16. in past *a*. he allowed all nations to go their own way
Rom. 16:25. that divine secret kept in silence for long *a*.
16:27. be glory for endless *a*.
1 Cor. 1:20. limited all of them, to this passing *a*.
2:6. not a wisdom belonging to this passing *a*.
3:18. wise, I mean, by the standards of this passing *a*.
10:11. upon us the fulfilment of the *a*. has come
2 Cor. 4:4. their unbelieving minds are so blinded by the god of this passing *a*.
Gal. 1:4. to rescue us out of this present *a*. of wickedness
Eph. 1:21. any title of sovereignty that can be named, not only in this *a*. but in the *a*. to come
2:2. when you followed the evil ways of this present *a*.
3:9. hidden for long *a*. in God the creator
3:11. this is in accord with his *a*.-long purpose
Phil. 4:20. to our God and Father be glory for endless *a*.
2 Tim. 3:1. the final *a*. of this world is to be a time of troubles
Tit. 1:2. eternal life that God, who cannot lie, promised long *a*. ago
2:12. to live a life of temperance, honesty, and godliness in the present *a*.
Heb. 1:2. in this the final *a*. he has spoken to us in the Son
6:5. the spiritual energies of the *a*. to come
8:13. anything that is growing old and *a*. will shortly disappear
Jam. 5:3. you have piled up wealth in an *a*. that is near its close
Jude 18. in the final *a*. there will be men who pour scorn on religion
Rev. 15:3. just and true are thy ways, thou king of the *a*.

agent-s
Luke 20:20. sent secret *a*. in the guise of honest men
Rom. 7:20. clearly it is no longer I who am the *a*.
13:4. they are God's *a*. working for your good . . . God's *a*. of punishment
1 Cor. 3:5. we are simply God's *a*.
2 Cor. 11:15. it is therefore a simple thing for his *a*. to masquerade as *a*. of good

aggressiveness
Jam. 4:1. the *a*. of your bodily desires

agitation
John 13:21. Jesus exclaimed in deep *a*.
of spirit

agitators
Gal. 5:12. as for these *a*., they had better
go the whole way

ago
Acts 5:36. some time *a*. Theudas came
forward
15:18. the Lord whose work it is,
made known long *a*.
Tit. 1:2. God who cannot lie, promised
long ages *a*.
1 Pet. 3:20. they had refused obedience
long *a*.
2 Pet. 3:5. there were heavens and earth
long *a*.
Jude 4. the very men whom Scripture
long *a*. marked down for the doom

agony
Luke 16:24. I am in *a*. in this fire
16:25. now he has his consolation here
and it is you who are in *a*.
Rev. 16:10. men gnawed their tongues
in *a*.

agree-d-ing
Mat. 22:15. the Pharisees went and *a*. on
a plan to trap him
Mark 14:44. the traitor had *a*. with them
upon a signal
Luke 22:6. he *a*., and began to look out
for an opportunity to betray him
Acts 11:29. the disciples *a*. to make a
contribution
Rom. 7:16. I *a*. with the law and hold it
to be admirable
15:5. grant that you may *a*. with one
another after the manner of Christ
Jesus
1 Cor. 1:10. *a*. among yourselves, and
avoid divisions
7:5. except when you *a*. upon a
temporary abstinence
2 Cor. 2:6. the penalty on which the
general meeting has *a*.
6:15. can Christ *a*. with Belial
13:11. *a*. with one another
Gal. 2:9. *a*. that we should go to the
Gentiles
Phil. 3:17. *a*. together, my friends, to
follow my example
4:2. I beg Euodia, and I beg Syntyche,
to *a*. together

agreement
Acts 12:20. who now by common *a*.
presented themselves at his court
15:22. with the *a*. of the whole
church
28:25. without reaching any *a*.
Rom. 4:18. in *a*. with the words which
had been spoken to him

11:26. the whole of Israel will be
saved, in *a*. with the text of Scripture

ahead
Mat. 2:9. the star which they had seen
at its rising went *a*. of them
11:10. here is my herald, whom I send
on *a*. of you
14:22. he made the disciples embark
and go on *a*.
21:9. the crowd that went *a*.
21:31. tax-gatherers and prostitutes
are entering the kingdom of God
a. of you
Mark 1:2. here is my herald whom I
send on *a*. of you
6:45. he made his disciples embark
and cross to Bethsaida *a*. of him
11:9. those who went *a*.
Luke 7:27. here is my herald, whom I
send on *a*. of you
9:52. towards Jerusalem, and sent
messengers *a*.
10:1. sent them on *a*. in pairs to every
town
19:4. he ran on *a*. and climbed a
sycamore tree
John 10:4. he goes *a*. and the sheep
follow
Acts 20:5. these went *a*. and waited for
us at Troas
20:13. we went *a*. to the ship
2 Cor. 9:5. necessary to ask these
friends to go on *a*. to Corinth
Phil. 3:13. reaching out, for that which
lies *a*.
Heb. 11:13. they were not yet in possession of the things promised, but had
seen them far *a*.
12:2. Jesus who, for the sake of the
joy that lay *a*.
2 John 9. anyone who runs *a*. too far

aid
Mat. 26:53. my Father, who would at
once send to my *a*. more than twelve
legions of angels
Acts 7:24. he saw one of them being ill-
treated, so he went to his *a*.
Rom. 8:26. the Spirit comes to the *a*. of
our weakness
1 Cor. 16:1. the collection in *a*. of
God's people
2 Cor. 6:2. on the day of deliverance I
came to your *a*.
9:1. about the provision of *a*. for
God's people

ailment-s
Mat. 9:35. curing every kind of *a*.
10:1. to cure every kind of *a*.
Luke 5:15. to be cured of their *a*.
1 Tim. 5:23. take a little wine for your
digestion, for your frequent *a*.

aim-s-ed

Mat. 12:10. their *a.* was to frame a charge against him

Mark 12:12. they saw that the parable was *a.* at them

Luke 18:9. it was *a.* at those who were sure of their own goodness

20:19. they saw that this parable was *a.* at them

John 5:30. my *a.* is not my own will

7:18. anyone whose teaching is merely his own, *a.* at honour for himself. But if a man *a.* at the honour of him who sent him he is sincere

Rom. 12:17. let your *a.* be such as all men count honourable

1 Cor. 7:28. my *a.* is to spare you

7:32. his *a.* is to please the Lord

7:33. his *a.* is to please his wife

7:34. her *a.* is to be dedicated to him in body as in spirit

12:31. the higher gifts are those you should *a.* at

14:1. there are other gifts of the Spirit at which you should *a.* also

14:26. all of these must *a.* at one thing

2 Cor. 7:12. my *a.* in writing was to help to make plain to you

8:15. the *a.* is equality

8:21. our *a.* are entirely honourable

12:19. our whole *a.*, my own dear people, is to build you up

1 Thess. 5:15. always *a.* at doing the best you can for each other

1 Tim. 1:5. true *a.* and object of this command is the love which springs from a clean heart

1:9. we treat it as law, recognizing that it is not *a.* at good citizens

Heb. 12:14. *a.* at peace with all men

air-s

2 Cor. 11:20. puts on *a.*, and hits you in the face

Col. 2:23. it has an *a.* of wisdom, with its forced piety

alarm-ed

Mat. 24:6. and the news of battles far away; see that you are not *a.*

Mark 13:7. news of battles far away, do not be *a.*

Acts 16:38. the magistrates were *a.* to hear that they were Roman citizens

22:29. the commandant himself was *a.*

24:25. Felix became *a.* and exclaimed

2 Thess. 2:2. do not suddenly lose your heads or *a.* yourselves

alas

Mat. 11:21. 18:7. 23:13, 15, 16, 25, 27, 29. 24:19. 26:24. Mark 13:17.

Luke 6:24, 25, 26. 10:13. 11:42, 43, 44, 47, 52. 21:23. 22:22. Jude 11. Rev. 18:17.

alert

Mark 13:33. be *a.*, be wakeful

Luke 12:37. happy are those servants whom the master finds on the *a.*

12:38. happy they if he finds them *a.*

21:36. be on the *a.*, praying at all times for strength

Acts 20:31. so be on the *a.*

1 Cor. 16:13. be *a.*; stand firm in the faith

1 Pet. 5:8. awake! be on the *a.!* Your enemy the devil

alien

1 John 2:21. lies, one and all, are *a.* to the truth

alien-s

Mat. 17:25. from their own citizens, or from *a.*

17:26. from *a.*,' said Peter

Acts 7:6. Abraham's descendants shall live as *a.* in a foreign land

13:17. they were still living as *a.* in Egypt

Eph. 2:19. thus you are no longer *a.* in a foreign land

Heb. 11:9. by faith he settled as an *a.* in the land promised him

1 Pet. 2:11. dear friends, I beg you, as *a.* in a foreign land

alight

Luke 12:35. be ready for action, with belts fastened and lamps *a.*

alike

Mat. 5:45. who makes his sun rise on good and bad *a.*

22:10. collected all they could find, good and bad *a.*

Acts 8:12. they were baptized, men and women *a.*

20:21. with Jews and pagans *a.* I insisted on repentance

22:4. arresting its followers, men and women *a.*

24:15. there is to be a resurrection of good and wicked *a.*

26:22. to this very day I stand and testify to great and small *a.*

Rom. 3:9. Jews and Greeks *a.* are all under the power of sin

3:12. all *a.* have become debased

3:23. all *a.* have sinned

1 Cor. 1:24. those who have heard his call, Jews and Greeks *a.*

13:9. our knowledge and our prophecy *a.* are partial

2 Cor. 6:8. honour and dishonour, praise and blame, are *a.* our lot

Eph. 2:18. through him we both *a*. have access to the Father

Tit. 1:15. the tainted minds of disbelievers, tainted *a*. in reason and conscience

alive

Mat. 6:25. put away anxious thoughts about food and drink to keep you *a*.

23:30. you say, 'If we had been *a*. in our fathers' time

Luke 12:22. put away anxious thoughts about food to keep you *a*.

16:25. all the good things fell to you while you were *a*.

20:38. for him all are *a*.

John 1:4. all that came to be was *a*. with his life

11:26. no one who is *a*. and has faith shall ever die

Acts 25:24. insisting that he had no right to remain *a*.

27:20. our last hopes of coming through *a*. began to fade

Rom. 7:1. a person is subject to the law so long as he is *a*.

1 Cor. 15:6. most of whom are still *a*.

2 Cor. 4:11. while still *a*., we are being surrendered into the hands of death

Col. 2:13. he has made you *a*. with Christ

2 Tim. 1:5. a faith which was *a*. in Lois your grandmother

Heb. 4:12. the word of God is *a*. and active

7:8. one whom Scripture affirms to be *a*.

9:17. it cannot possibly have force while the testator is *a*.

1 Pet. 4:6. in the spirit be *a*. with the life of God

Rev. 3:1. though you have a name for being *a*., you are dead

17:8. the beast you have seen is he who once was *a*., and is *a*. no longer . . . for he once was *a*., and is *a*. no longer

17:11. the beast that once was *a*. and is *a*. no longer

allegation

Mat. 26:59. the whole council tried to find some *a*. against Jesus

allege-d-ing

Mat. 26:61. finally two men *a*. that he had said

Acts 6:11. *a*. that they had heard him make blasphemous statements

24:9. *a*. that the facts were as he stated

25:19. a dead man whom Paul *a*. to be alive

2. Thess. 2:2. *a*. that the Day of the Lord is already here

allegiance

Mat. 10-22. all will hate you for your *a*. to me

24:9. men of all nations will hate you for your *a*. to me

Mark 13:13. all will hate you for your *a*. to me

Luke 21:12. you will be haled before kings and governors for your *a*. to me

21:17. you will be hated by all for your *a*. to me

John 1:12. those who have yielded him their *a*.

2:23. many gave their *a*. to him when they saw the signs

3:18. he has not given his *a*. to God's only Son

Rom. 15:18. to bring the Gentiles into his *a*.

1 John 3:23. to give our *a*. to his Son Jesus Christ

5:13. those who give their *a*. to the Son of God

allegory

Rev. 11:8. the great city, whose name in *a*. is Sodom

alleys

Luke 14:21. go out quickly into the streets and *a*. of the town

allot-ted

Rom. 12:6. the gifts we possess differ as they are *a*. to us

1 Cor. 3:5. the task which the Lord *a*. to him

1 Pet. 5:3. not tyrannizing over those who are *a*. to your care

allow-ed

Mat. 3:16. John then *a*. him to come

14:36. he was begged to *a*. them simply to touch the edge of his cloak

16:19. what you *a*. on earth shall be *a*. in heaven

18:18. whatever you *a*. on earth shall be *a*. in heaven

Mark 2:26. no one but a priest is *a*. to eat them

5:19. Jesus would not *a*. it

5:37. after this he *a*. no one to accompany him except

11:6. were then *a*. to take it

11:16. he would not *a*. anyone to use the temple court as a thoroughfare

Luke 6:4. priests alone are *a*. to eat them

8:51. he *a*. no one to go in with him except

John 5:10. you are not *a*. to carry your bed on the Sabbath

John 18:31. we are not *a.* to put any man to death

19:38. asked to be *a.* to remove the body of Jesus

Acts 7:46. asked to be *a.* to provide a dwelling-place for the God of Jacob

10:40. God raised him to life on the third day, and *a.* him to appear

14:16. in past ages he *a.* all nations to go their own way

16:7. but the Spirit of Jesus would not *a.* them

27:3. Julius very considerately *a.* Paul to go to his friends

28:16. Paul was *a.* to lodge by himself with a soldier

Rom. 5:2. we have been *a.* to enter the sphere of God's grace

1 Cor. 9:12. if you *a.* others these rights, have not we a stronger claim

10:13. he will not *a.* you to be tested above your powers

2 Cor. 2:11. Satan must not be *a.* to get the better of us

8:4. *a.* to share in this generous service

Col. 2:16. *a.* no one therefore to take you to task about what you eat or drink

1 Thess. 3:10. we pray most earnestly night and day to be *a.* to see you again

Rev. 9:5. these they were *a.* to torment for five months

13:5. the beast was *a.* to mouth bombast

13:7. also *a.* to wage war on God's people

13:14. the miracles it was *a.* to perform

13:15. *a.* to give breath to the image of the beast

13:17. no one was *a.* to buy or sell

16:8. it was *a.* to burn men with its flames

ally-ied-ies
Acts 19:25. the workers in *a.* trades
Rom. 15:30. be my *a.* in the fight; pray to God for me

allud-ing
Phil. 4:11. not that I am *a.* to want

allurement-s
1 John 2:17. that world is passing away with all its *a.*

Almighty
Luke 22:69. the Son of Man will be seated at the right hand of *A.* God

almost
Mark 7:25. *a.* at once a woman whose young daughter was possessed

Luke 24:29. stay with us, for evening draws on, and the day is *a.* over

John 7:10. to the festival, he went up himself, not publicly, but *a.* in secret

aloft
Acts 7:43. you carried *a.* the shrine of Molock

alone
Mat. 4:10. worship him *a.*

15:24. to the lost sheep of the house of Israel, and to them *a.*

17:1. led them up a high mountain where they were *a.*

19:17. one *a.* is good

22:22. they went away and left him *a.*

Mark 9:2. led them up a high mountain where they were *a.*

9:8. Jesus *a.* with themselves

10:18. no one is good except God *a.*

12:12. they left him *a.* and went away

Luke 2:37. then *a.* as a widow

4:8. worship him *a.*

18:19. no one is good except God *a.*

John 5:44. the honour that comes from him who *a.* is God

6:46. he who has come from God has seen the Father and he *a.*

6:63 the spirit *a.* gives life

8:41. God is our Father, and God *a.*

11:52. die not for the nation *a.* but to gather together the scattered children

14:22. you mean to disclose yourself to us *a.*

17:3. know thee who *a.* art truly God

Rom. 3:24. justified by God's free grace *a.*

3:29. do you suppose God is the God of the Jews *a.*

4:12. do not rely upon their circumcision *a.*

4:14. if those who hold by the law, and they *a.* are heirs, then faith is empty

7:25. who is there to rescue me out of this body doomed to death? God *a.*

14:7. no one of us dies for himself *a.*

15:18. those things *a.* in which I have been Christ's instrument

16:4. not I *a.* but all the gentile congregations are grateful to them

16:27. to God who *a.* is wise

1 Cor. 4:15. in Christ Jesus you are my offspring, and mine *a.*

9:6. are Barnabas and I *a.* bound to work for our living

2 Cor. 4:7. such transcendent power does not come from us, but is God's *a.*

2 Cor. 9:4. what a disgrace it will be to us, let *a*. to you

10:18. whom the Lord recommends—he and he *a*. is to be accepted

Gal. 1:10. whose support do I want but God's *a*.

3:20. an intermediary is not needed for one party acting *a*.

Col. 1:18. the first to return from the dead, to be in all things *a*. supreme

1:20. to reconcile all things, whether on earth or in heaven, through him *a*.

1 Thess. 1:8. not in Macedonia and Achaia *a*.

1 Tim. 5:5. one who is *a*. in the world, has all her hope set on God

6:15. God who in eternal felicity *a*. holds sway

6:16. he *a*. possesses immortality

2 Tim. 4:8. award me on that great Day; and it is not for me *a*.

Heb. 12:26. I will shake not earth *a*., but the heavens also

Rev. 14:3. who *a*. from the whole world had been ransomed

15:4. thou *a*. art holy

along

Mat. 13:4. some seed fell *a*. the footpath

13:19. there you have the seed sown *a*. the footpath

Mark 2:14. as he went *a*., he saw Levi

4:4. some seed fell *a*. the footpath

4:15. those *a*. the footpath are people

Luke 8:5. some seed fell *a*. the footpath

8:12. those *a*. the footpath are the men who hear it

8:23. as they sailed *a*. he went to sleep

9:57. as they were going *a*. the road a man said to him

14:23. go out on to the highways and *a*. the hedgerows

17:7. will the master say, 'Come *a*. at once and sit down

24:15. Jesus himself came up and walked *a*. with them

John 6:64. Jesus knew all *a*. who were without faith

Acts 8:36. as they were going *a*. the road, they came to some water

13:43. many Jews and gentile worshippers went *a*. with Paul

15:35. and there, *a*. with many others, they taught and preached

21:16. some of the disciples from Caesarea came *a*. with us

27:13. they sailed *a*. the coast of Crete

Rom. 3:16. ruin and misery lie *a*. their paths

1 Cor. 1:2. *a*. with all men everywhere who invoke the name of our Lord Jesus Christ

aloof

Gal. 2:12. when they came he drew back and began to hold *a*.

2 Thess. 3:6. hold *a*. from every Christian brother who falls into idle habits

aloud

Mat. 3:3. a voice crying *a*. in the wilderness

21:16. children and babes at the breast sound *a*. thy praise

27:46. and about three Jesus cried *a*.

Mark 1:3. a voice crying *a*. in the wilderness

3:11. would fall at his feet and cry *a*., 'You are the Son of God

5:5. night and day, he would cry *a*. among the tombs

9:26. after crying *a*. and racking him fiercely, it came out

15:34. and at three Jesus cried *a*.

Luke 1:42. Elizabeth was filled with the Holy Spirit and cried *a*.

3:4. a voice crying *a*. in the wilderness

17:15. one of them, finding himself cured, turned back praising God *a*.

19:37. his disciples in their joy began to sing *a*. the praises of God

19:40. if my disciples keep silence the stones will shout *a*.

John 1:15. here is John's testimony to him: he cried *a*.

1:23. I am a voice crying *a*. in the wilderness

7:28. Jesus cried *a*. as he taught in the temple

7:37. greatest day of the festival Jesus stood and cried *a*.

12:44. so Jesus cried *a*. when a man believes in me

Acts 7:60. and cried *a*. 'Lord do not hold this sin against them

8:28. reading *a*. the prophet Isaiah

Rev. 5:12. they cried *a*. 'Worthy is the Lamb

7:2. he called *a*. to the four angels

12:10. I heard a voice in heaven proclaiming *a*.

19:17. I saw an angel standing in the sun, and he cried *a*.

already

Mat. 3:10. *a*. the axe is laid to the roots of the trees

6:5. they have their reward *a*.

12:28. be sure the kingdom of God has *a*. come upon you

14:24. the boat was *a*. some furlongs from the shore

Mat. 20:23. it is for those to whom it has *a.* been assigned by my Father

Mark 5:8. Jesus was *a.* saying to him, 'Out, unclean spirit

6:47. the boat was *a.* well out on the water

9:1. before they have seen the kingdom of God *a.* come in power

9:13. Elijah has *a.* come

10:40. for those to whom it has *a.* been assigned

16:4. the stone, huge as it was, had been rolled back *a.*

Luke 3:9. *a.* the axe is laid to the roots of the trees

8:29. Jesus was *a.* ordering the unclean spirit to come out

11:20. be sure the kingdom of God has *a.* come upon you

19:25. but, sir,' they replied, 'he has ten *a.*

John 1:1. when all things began, the word *a.* was

1:15 ⎫
1:30 ⎭ before I was born, he *a.* was

4:23. the time approaches, indeed it is *a.* here

5:24. has *a.* passed from death to life

5:25. a time is coming, indeed it is *a.* here

6:17. darkness had *a.* fallen, and Jesus had not yet joined them

7:14. when the festival was *a.* half over

11:42. I knew *a.* that thou always hearest me

13:2. the devil had *a.* put it into the mind of Judas

15:3. you have *a.* been cleansed by the word

16:32. the hour is coming, has indeed *a.* come, when you are all to be scattered

Acts 3:20. the Messiah he has *a.* appointed

4:3. put in prison for the night, as it was *a.* evening

27:30. they had *a.* lowered the ship's boat

Rom. 3:9. we have *a.* formulated the charge

4:17. things that are not yet in existence as if they *a.* were

5:13. sin was *a.* in the world

8:24. why should a man endure and wait for what he *a.* sees

1 Cor. 3:11. no other foundation beyond that which is *a.* laid

4:8. you have come into your fortune *a.*

6:7. you *a.* fall below your standard

2 Cor. 5:17. a new order has *a.* begun

10:16. never priding ourselves on work *a.* done

11:4. a spirit different from the Spirit *a.* given to you, or a gospel different from the gospel you have *a.* accepted

Gal. 3:17. a testament or covenant, had *a.* been validated by God

Eph. 3:3. I have *a.* written a brief account of this

1 Thess. 4:1. you are indeed *a.* following it

2 Thess. 2:2. alleging that the day of the Lord is *a.* here

2 Tim. 4:6. *a.* my life is being poured out on the altar

Heb. 4:7. he uses the words *a.* quoted

8:4. there are *a.* priests who offer the gifts which the Law prescribes

9:11. now Christ has come, high priest of good things *a.* in being

2 Pet. 1:12. the truth that has *a.* reached you

3:1. I have been recalling to you what you *a.* know

1 John 2:8. the darkness is passing and the real light *a.* shines

Jude 5. you *a.* know it all, but let me remind you

Rev. 17:10. they represent also seven kings, of whom five have *a.* fallen

21:6. indeed,' he said, 'they are *a.* fulfilled

also

Mat. 10:2. Simon *a.* called Peter

27:55. a number of women were *a.* present

Mark 6:38. five, and two fishes *a.*

12:37. how can he *a.* be David's son

16:13. these *a.* went and took the news to the others

Luke 1:5. his wife *a.* was of priestly descent

2:24. *a.* to make the offering as stated in the law

2:36. there was *a.* a prophetess, Anna

14:33. so *a.* none of you can be a disciple of mine without taking leave of all his possessions

John 2:2. Jesus and his disciples were guests *a.*

5:27. as Son of Man, he has *a.* been given the right to pass judgement

Acts 3:4. Peter fixed his eyes on him, as John did *a.*

7:15. there he ended his days, as *a.* our forefathers did

17:34. *a.* a woman named Damaris, and others besides

18:4. he *a.* held discussions in the synagogue

Rom. 9:18. he not only shows mercy as he chooses, but *a.* makes men stubborn as he chooses

9:29. as *a.* he said previously

Rom. 16:23. greetings *a.* from Gaius, my host
2 Cor. 7:14. that *a.* has proved true
Eph. 4:4. there is one body and one Spirit, as there is *a.* one hope
5:23. as Christ *a.* is the head of the Church
Phil. 2:25. I feel *a.* I must send our brother Epaphroditus
3:16. this *a.* God will make plain to you
1 Thess. 5:25. brothers, pray for us *a.*

altar
2 Tim. 4:6. my life is being poured out on the *a.*
Heb. 9:4. here was a golden *a.* of incense

alter
Acts 6:14. we have heard him say that Jesus of Nazareth will destroy this place and *a.* the customs handed down to us

although
Mark 6:20. he liked to listen to him, *a.* the listening left him greatly perplexed
John 4:2. *a.*, in fact, it was only the disciples who were baptizing
4:18. *a.* you have had five husbands
5:37. the Father who sent me, *a.* you never heard his voice
5:39. *a.* their testimony points to me
6:36. you, as I said, do not believe *a.* you have seen
17:25. O righteous Father, *a.* the world does not know thee
20:26. *a.* the doors were locked, Jesus came
Rom. 2:14. *a.* they have no law, they are their own law
8:10. *a.* the body is a dead thing because you sinned
1 Cor. 9:20. *a.* I am not myself subject to it
9:21. *a.* I am not in truth outside God's law
2 Cor. 7:12. *a.* I did send you that letter
Col. 2:13. *a.* you were dead because of your sins
1 Thess. 2:6. *a.* as Christ's own envoys
1 Tim. 1:13. *a.* in the past I had met him with abuse
Heb. 6:9. *a.* we speak as we do, we are convinced
7:5. *a.* they too are descendants of Abraham
10:8. thou didst not desire nor delight in'—*a.* the Law prescribes them
12:17. found no way open for second thoughts, *a.* he strove, to the point of tears
1 Pet. 4:6. *a.* in the body they received the sentence common to men

2 Pet. 1:12. *a.* you know it and are well grounded in the truth
1 John 5:17. *a.* all wrongdoing is sin
Jude 19. *a.* they are themselves wholly unspiritual
Rev. 10:9. it will turn your stomach sour, *a.* in your mouth it will taste sweet

altogether
John 13:10. who has bathed needs no further washing; he is *a.* clean
Acts 7:14. Jacob and all his relatives, seventy-five persons *a.*
19:7. *a.* they were about a dozen men
1 Cor. 14:10. nothing is *a.* soundless

always
Mat. 7:12. *a.* treat others as you would like them to treat you
7:17. a good tree *a.* yields good fruit
13:57. a prophet will *a.* be held in honour, except in his home town
25:29. the man who has will *a.* be given more
Mark 6:4. a prophet will *a.* be held in honour except in his home town
Luke 15:31. 'My boy,' said the father, 'you are *a.* with me
19:26. the man who has will *a.* be given more
John 4:14. an inner spring *a.* welling up for eternal life
6:34. Sir, give us this bread now and *a.*
13:1. he had *a.* loved his own who were in the world
14:1. trust in God *a.*
Acts 22:3. I have *a.* been ardent in God's service
Rom. 1:10. am *a.* asking that by his will I may
1 Cor. 10:33. I *a.* try to meet everyone half way
11:2. I commend you for *a.* keeping me in mind
2 Cor. 9:10. you will *a.* be rich enough to be generous
11:9. I made it a rule, as I *a.* shall, never to be a burden to you
Eph. 4:2. be humble *a.* and gentle, and patient too
1 Thess. 4:17. thus we shall *a.* be with the Lord
5:15. *a.* aim at doing the best you can for each other
5:16. be *a.* joyful
2 Tim. 3:7. who are *a.* wanting to be taught
Heb. 7:7. the lesser is *a.* blessed by the greater
7:25. he is *a.* living to plead on their behalf
13:18. our one desire is *a.* to do what is right
Jam. 2:12. *a.* speak and act as men who

are to be judged under a law of freedom

2 Pet. 3:4. everything continues exactly as it has *a*. been

1 John 2:7. it is the old command which you *a*. had before you

amasses

Luke 12:21. the man who *a*. wealth for himself

amazed

Mat. 21:20. the disciples were *a*. at the sight

Mark 5:20. all that Jesus had done for him; and they were all *a*.

6:2. the large congregation who heard him were *a*.

10:24. they were *a*. that he should say this

Luke 2:47. all who heard him were *a*. at his intelligence

5:9. he and all his companions were *a*. at the catch they had made

Acts 7:31. Moses was *a*. at the sight

amazement

Mat. 9:33. filled with *a*. the onlookers said

13:54. in *a*. they asked, 'Where does he get this wisdom from

15:31. great was the *a*. of the people

Mark 5:42. they were beside themselves with *a*.

Luke 4:36. *a*. fell on them all

5:26. they were all lost in *a*.

ambassador

Philem. 9. I, Paul, *a*. as I am of Christ Jesus

ambiguous

2 Cor. 1:18. the language in which we address you is not an *a*. blend of yes and no

ambition-s

Rom. 2:8. those who are governed by selfish *a*.

15:20. my *a*. to bring the gospel to places where the very name of Christ has not been heard

2 Cor. 5:9. our *a*., wherever we are, here or there, to be acceptable to him

Gal. 5:20. fits of rage, selfish *a*., dissensions

1 Thess. 4:11. let it be your *a*. to keep calm and look after your own business

1 Tim. 3:1. to aspire to leadership is an honourable *a*.

Jam. 3:14. selfish *a*. in your hearts

3:16. with jealousy and *a*. come disorder and evil

4:2. you are envious, and cannot attain your *a*.

ambush

Acts 23:16. the son of Paul's sister heard of the *a*.

25:3. they were planning an *a*. to kill him

amid

Luke 9:43. *a*. the general wonder and admiration

Acts 20:19. I served the Lord in all humility *a*. the sorrows and trials

amiss

John 18:23. Jesus replied, 'If I spoke *a*., state it in evidence

among

Mat. 5:16. you, like the lamp, must shed light *a*. your fellows

7:9. is there a man *a*. you who will offer his son a stone

10:16. I send you out like sheep *a*. wolves

18:20. where two or three have met together in my name, I am there *a*. them

21:25. this set them arguing *a*. themselves

24:51. thus he will find his place *a*. the hypocrites

26:11. you have the poor *a*. you always

27:9. that was his price *a*. the Israelites

Mark 1:13. he was *a*. the wild beasts

5:5. he would cry aloud *a*. the tombs

5:12. the spirits begged him, 'Send us *a*. the pigs

5:25. *a*. them was a woman who had suffered

7:13. your own tradition, handed down *a*. you

9:10. discussed *a*. themselves what this 'rising from the dead' could mean

14:2. we should have rioting *a*. the people

14:51. *a*. those following was a young man

14:54. sitting *a*. the attendants, warming himself at the fire

Luke 3:12. *a*. those who came to be baptized were tax-gatherers

6:13. he called his disciples to him, and from *a*. them he chose twelve

15:10. there is joy *a*. the angels of God over one sinner who repents

17:21. the kingdom of God is *a*. you

23:5. his teaching is causing disaffection *a*. the people

23:34. they divided his clothes *a*. them

24:36. as they were talking about all this, there he was, standing *a*. them

John 12:2. Lazarus sat *a*. the guests with Jesus

John 12:35. the light is *a.* you still but not for long
20:26. although the doors were locked, Jesus came and stood *a.* them
Acts 1:26. the lot fell on Matthias, who was then assigned a place *a.* the twelve apostles
7:37. God will raise up a prophet for you from *a.* yourselves
8:1. Saul was *a.* those who approved of his murder
13:50. the Jews stirred up feeling *a.* the women of standing who were worshippers and *a.* the leading men of the city
15:3. the news caused great rejoicing *a.* all the Christians there
21:20. how many thousands of converts we have *a.* the Jews
26:8. why is it considered incredible *a.* you that God should raise dead men to life
Rom. 1:12. I want to be *a.* you to receive encouragement
1 Cor. 1:10. agree *a.* yourselves
14:25. God is certainly *a.* you
2 Cor. 6:16. I will live and move about *a.* them
13:3. makes his power felt *a.* you
13:5. surely you recognize that Jesus Christ is *a.* you
Eph. 4:18. because ignorance prevails *a.* them
Phil. 2:3. rivalry and personal vanity should have no place *a.* you
Col. 3:16. let the message of Christ dwell *a.* you
1 Tim. 1:15. *a.* them I stand first
3:16. proclaimed *a.* the nations
Heb. 12:15. see to it that there is no one *a.* you who forfeits the grace of God
1 Pet. 3:5. thus it was *a.* God's people in days of old
1 John 2:20. you, no less than they, are *a.* the initiated
2 John 2. for the sake of the truth that dwells *a.* us
Rev. 1:7. every eye shall see him, and *a.* them those who pierced him
21:3. now at last God has his dwelling *a.* men

amount
Mat. 20:10. they expected something extra, but were paid the same *a.* as the others

ample
Acts 1:3. and gave *a.* proof that he was alive
2 Cor. 9:8. *a.* means in yourselves to meet each and every situation
Col. 1:11. may he strengthen you, in his

glorious might, with *a.* power to meet whatever comes

analogy-ies
1 Cor. 9:8. do not suppose I rely on these human *a.*

anarchy
Rom. 6:19. impurity and lawlessness, making for moral *a.*

ancestor-s
Luke 1:32. the Lord God will give him the throne of his *a.* David
John 4:12. are you a greater man than Jacob our *a.*
6:31. our *a.* had manna to eat
Acts 7:2. the God of glory appeared to Abraham our *a.*
7:11. our *a.* could find nothing to eat
7:19. cruelly forced our *a.* to expose their children
Rom. 4:1. Abraham, our *a.* in the natural line
9:10. Rebekah's children had one and the same father, our *a.* Isaac
1 Cor. 10:1. our *a.* were all under the pillar of cloud
Gal. 1:14. my boundless devotion to the traditions of my *a.*
Heb. 7:10. he was still in his *a.* loins when Melchizedek met him

ancestral
Acts 22:3. trained in every point of our *a.* law

anchor
Acts 27:13. weighing *a.*, they sailed along the coast of Crete

ancient
Mark 7:5. why do your disciples not conform to the *a.* tradition
Rom. 15:4. the *a.* scriptures were written for our own instruction

anew
1 Pet. 1:23. you have been born *a.*, not of mortal parentage

angel-s
Acts 10:4. the *a.* said, 'Your prayers and acts of charity have gone up to heaven
Heb. 11:28. so that the destroying *a.* might not touch the first-born of Israel
Jude 7. like the *a.* they committed fornications
14. I saw the Lord come with his myriads of *a.*
Rev. 16:2. the first *a.* went and poured his bowl
19:9. then the *a.* said to me, 'Write this
21:15. the *a.* who spoke with me

angelic
1 Pet. 3:22. after receiving the submission of *a*. authorities

anger-ed
Mat. 5:22. anyone who nurses *a*. against his brother
Luke 6:11. they were beside themselves with *a*.
2 Cor. 7:11. how *a*. you were
Heb. 3:11 ⎱ I vowed in my *a*., they shall
   4:3 ⎰ never enter my rest
11:27. not because he feared the king's *a*.
Jam. 1:20. a man's *a*. cannot promote the justice of God

angrily
Mark 14:4. some of those present said to one another *a*.

angry
Mat. 18:34. so *a*. was the master that he condemned the man
Acts 12:20. he had for some time been furiously *a*.
2 Cor. 12:20. *a*. tempers and personal rivalries
Eph. 4:31. have done with spite and passion, all *a*. shouting
1 Tim. 2:8. excluding *a*. or quarrelsome thoughts
Jam. 1:19. slow to be *a*.

anguish
Mat. 26:38. *a*. and dismay came over him
Luke 22:44. in *a*. of spirit he prayed the more urgently
Rev. 12:2. in the *a*. of her labour she cried out

animal-s
1 Cor. 15:44. sown as an *a*. body, it is raised as a spiritual body. If there is such a thing as an *a*. body
15:46. the *a*. body comes first, and then the spiritual
Heb. 12:20. if even an *a*. touches the mountain
13:11. those *a*. whose blood is brought as a sin-offering

animate
1 Cor. 15:45. the first man, Adam, became an *a*. being

annihilate
2 Thess. 2:8. *a*. by the radiance of his coming

announce-d-ing
Mat. 6:2. do not *a*. it with a flourish of trumpets
9:35. *a*. the good news of the kingdom
Luke 3:18. *a*. the good news
4:18. sent me to *a*. good news

9:60. you must go and *a*. the kingdom of God
Acts 12:14. *a*. that Peter was standing outside
26:23. *a*. the dawn to Israel and to the Gentiles
Rom. 1:2. this gospel God *a*. beforehand
Col. 1:26. to *a*. the secret hidden for long ages
Heb. 2:3. this deliverance was first *a*. through the lips of the Lord himself
1 Pet. 1:12. now it has been openly *a*. to you through preachers

annul-s-led
Eph. 2:15. he *a*. the law with its rules and regulations
Heb. 10:9. he thus *a*. the former to establish the latter

anoint-ed
Luke 23:35. he saved others: now let him save himself, if this is God's *a*.
Heb. 11:26. the stigma that rests on God's *a*.

another
Mat. 4:21. and saw *a*. pair of brothers
12:9. he went on to *a*. place
13:45. here is *a*. picture of the kingdom of Heaven
15:14. if one blind man guides *a*. they will both fall into the ditch
20:6. he went out and found *a*. group
22:46 no one dared ask him *a*. question
23:3. they say one thing and do *a*.
24:12. as lawlessness spreads, men's love for one *a*. will grow cold
26:73. said to Peter, 'Surely you are *a*. of them
Mark 15:31. the chief priests and the doctors of the law jested with one *a*.
Luke 4:40. all who had friends suffering from one disease or *a*.
8:4. they made their way to him from one town after *a*.
24:15. as they talked and discussed it with one *a*.
John 18:17. are you *a*. of this man's disciples
19:24. so they said to one *a*., 'We must not tear this
Acts 5:1. but there was *a*. man called Ananias
Rom. 3:5. *a*. question: if our injustice serves to bring out God's justice
14:20. by his eating causes *a*. to fall
2 Cor. 5:12. this is not *a*. attempt to recommend ourselves to you
13:11. agree with one *a*.

Eph. 5:19. speak to one *a*. in psalms, hymns, and songs
Phil. 2:5. let your bearing towards one *a*. arise out of your life in Christ Jesus
Heb. 4:1. one or *a*. among you should be found to have missed his chance
11:5. by faith Enoch was carried away to *a*. life
Jam. 5:19. and *a*. succeed in bringing him back

answer-ed
Mat. 4:7. Jesus *a*. him, 'Scripture says again
5:22. if he abuses his brother he must *a*. for it to the court; if he sneers at him he will have to *a*. for it in the fires of hell
13:51. have you understood all this? he asked, and they *a*., 'Yes
15:27. true sir,' she *a*.; 'and yet the dogs eat the scraps
17:20. he *a*., 'your faith is too weak
21:24. I have a question to ask too; *a*. it
22:22. this *a*. took them by surprise
27:22. with one voice they *a*., 'Crucify him
Mark 11:6. they *a*. as Jesus had told them
Luke 11:50. this generation will have to *a*. for the blood of all the prophets
23:4. I find no case for this man to *a*.
John 1:23. he *a*. in the words of the prophet Isaiah
7:9. with this *a*. he stayed behind in Galilee
9:22. his parents gave this *a*. because they were afraid of the Jews
Acts 4:10. we are asked by what means he was cured, here is the *a*.
12:13. a maid called Rhoda came to *a*. it
Rom. 9:20. who are you, sir, to *a*. God back
14:12. each of us will have to *a*. for himself
Gal. 3:2. *a*. me one question: did you receive the Spirit by keeping the law
Philem. 22. in *a*. to your prayers, God will grant me to you

answerable
Rom. 6:7. a dead man is no longer *a*. for his sin

Antioch
Acts 15:2. it was arranged that these two and some others from *A*. should go up to Jerusalem

anxiety
Luke 2:48. your father and I have been searching for you in great *a*.

2 Cor. 2:4. that letter I sent you came out of great distress and *a*.
Phil. 4:6. have no *a*., but in everything make your requests known to God
Philem. 20. be generous with me, and relieve my *a*.

anxious-ly
Mat. 6:25. put away *a*. thoughts about food and drink
6:27. who by *a*. thought can add a foot to his height
6:28. why be *a*. about clothes
6:31. do not ask *a*., 'what are we to eat
6:34. do not be *a*. about tomorrow
Luke 9:9. he was *a*. to see him
12:22. put away *a*. thoughts about food
12:25. who by *a*. thought can add a foot to his height
12:26. why are you *a*. about the rest
John 19:31. the Jews were *a*. that the bodies should not remain on the cross
Acts 25:9. Festus, *a*. to ingratiate himself with the Jews
1 Cor. 7:32. I want you to be free from *a*. care
2 Cor. 11:28. my *a*. concern for all our congregations
Gal. 4:21. you who are so *a*. to be under law
1 Thess. 2:17. we were exceedingly *a*. to see you again
3:6. are as *a*. to see us as we are to see you

any
Mat. 10:31. you are worth more than *a*. number of sparrows
12:32. *a*. man who speaks a word against the Son of Man
13:32. when it has grown it is bigger than *a*. garden-plant
15:13. *a*. plant that is not of my heavenly Father's planting
19:3. is it lawful for a man to divorce his wife on *a*. and every ground
21:19. you shall never bear fruit *a*. more
Mark 1:45. Jesus could no longer show himself in *a*. town
6:55. brought the sick on stretchers to *a*. place where he was reported to be
12:43. this widow has given more than *a*. of the others
14:55. tried to find some evidence against Jesus to warrant a death-sentence, but failed to find *a*.
Luke 6:35. lend without expecting *a*. return
16:2. you cannot be manager here *a*. longer

Luke 21:29. look at the fig tree, or *a.*
other tree
John 7:6. *a.* time is right for you
  10:8. the sheep paid no heed to *a.*
who came before me
Acts 15:24. without *a.* instructions from
us
  23:8. the Sadducees deny that there is
a. resurrection
  28:19. not that I had *a.* accusation to
bring against my own people
Rom. 3:26. justifies *a.* man who puts his
faith in Jesus
1 Cor. 8:13. I will never eat meat *a.*
more
2 Cor. 13:9. we are well content to be
weak at *a.* time
Gal. 4:12. it is not that you did me *a.*
wrong
2 Tim. 1:9. not for *a.* merit of ours but
of his own purpose
1 John 4:1. do not trust *a.* and every
spirit

anybody
Luke 5:14. Jesus then ordered him not to
tell *a.*

anyone
Mat. 5:19. *a.* who keeps the law
  5:21. *a.* who commits murder must
be brought to judgement
  5:22. *a.* who nurses anger against his
brother
  5:32. *a.* who marries a woman so
divorced commits adultery
  10:14. if *a.* will not receive you
  10:42. if *a.* gives so much as a cup of
cold water
  12:29. how can *a.* break into a strong
man's house
  12:32. if *a.* speaks against the Holy
Spirit
  16:20. gave his disciples strict orders
not to tell *a.* that he was the
Messiah
  17:9. Jesus enjoined them not to tell
a. of the vision
  19:29. *a.* who has left brothers or
sisters
Mark 7:36. Jesus forbade them to tell
a.
  8:4. how can *a.* provide all these
people with bread
  8:34. *a.* who wishes to be a follower
of mine
  8:38. if *a.* is ashamed of me and mine
  11:23. if *a.* says to this mountain
Luke 3:11. *a.* who has food must do the
same
  4:6. I can give it to *a.* I choose
  12:10. *a.* who speaks a word against
the Son of Man will receive forgiveness

  13:2. greater sinners than *a.* else in
Galilee
John 5:22. the Father does not judge *a.*
  5:24. *a.* who gives heed to what I say
  7:18. *a.* whose teaching is merely his
own
  8:51. if *a.* obeys my teaching he shall
never know what it is to die
  14:9. *a.* who has seen me has seen the
Father
  14:23. *a.* who loves me will heed what
I say
  16:2. *a.* who kills you will suppose
that he is performing a religious
duty
Acts 3:23. *a.* who refuses to listen to
that prophet
  4:17. caution them never again to
speak to *a.* in this name
  8:19. so that when I lay my hands on
a., he will receive the Holy Spirit
  10:26. stand up; I am a man like *a.*
else
  20:33. I have not wanted *a.* money
Rom. 10:15. how could *a.* spread the
news without a commission
1 Cor. 11:27. *a.* who eats the bread or
drinks the cup of the Lord un-
worthily
Gal. 5:19. *a.* can see the kind of behaviour that belongs to the lower
nature
  6:4. comparing himself with himself
and not with *a.* else
Heb. 11:6. *a.* who comes to God must
believe that he exists
  12:7. can *a.* be a son, who is not
disciplined by his father
1 John 4:18. *a.* who is afraid has not
attained to love in its perfection
2 John 9. *a.* who runs ahead too far, and
does not stand by the doctrine of
the Christ

anything
Mat. 5:37. plain 'Yes' or 'No' is all you
need to say; *a.* beyond that comes
from the devil
  14:7. he took an oath to give her *a.*
she cared to ask
  15:5. *a.* of mine which might have
been used for your benefit
  25:40. *a.* you did for one of my
brothers
  25:45. *a.* you did not do for one of
these
Mark 7:11. *a.* of mine
  7:12. no longer permitted to do *a.* for
his father or mother
  8:23. asked whether he could see *a.*
Luke 15:16. no one gave him *a.*
John 14:13. *a.* you ask in my name I will
do

John 16:23. if you ask the Father for *a.* in my name, he will give it you

Acts 15:29. from *a.* that has been strangled

17:21. had no time for *a.* but talking or hearing

28:6. without seeing *a.* extraordinary happen to him

28:17. I, who never did *a.* against our people

Rom. 3:19. no one may have *a.* to say in self-defence

4:2. if Abraham was justified by *a.* he had done

14:20. *a.* is bad for the man who by his eating causes another to fall

14:23. *a.* which does not arise from conviction is sin

1 Cor. 6:12. I am free to do *a.* you say . . . I am free to do *a.*, but I for one will not let *a.* make free with me

10:23. 'we are free to do *a.*'; you say . . . 'we are free to do *a.*

10:25. you may eat *a.* sold in the meat market

2 Cor. 11:9. *a.* I needed was fully met by our friends

12:13. is there *a.* in which you were treated worse than the other congregations

Gal. 6:14. God forbid, that I should boast of *a.* but the cross

Phil. 3:3. who put no confidence in *a.* external

4:13. I have strength for *a.* through him

1 Tim. 6:7. when we leave it we cannot take *a.* with us

Tit. 3:13. see that they are not short of *a.*

Heb. 7:13. no member of which has ever had *a.* to do with the altar

8:13. *a.* that is growing old and ageing will shortly disappear

1 John 2:15. do not set your hearts on the godless world or *a.* in it

anywhere
Luke 13:33. unthinkable for a prophet to meet his death *a.* but in Jerusalem

apart
Mat. 15:5. might have been used for your benefit is set *a.* for God

Mark 7:11. Corban (meaning, set *a.* for God

John 15:5. *a.* from me you can do nothing

Acts 13:2. set Barnabas and Saul *a.* for me

24:21. *a.* from this one open assertion

26:29. might become what I am, *a.* from these chains

Rom. 1:1. set *a.* for the service of the Gospel

3:28. a man is justified by faith quite *a.* from success in keeping the law

4:6. *a.* from any specific acts of justice

1 Cor. 9:17. since I do it *a.* from my own choice

2 Cor. 11:28. *a.* from these external things

Gal. 1:15. God, who had set me *a.* from birth

Jam. 2:10. if a man keeps the whole law *a.* from one single point

2 Pet. 3:12. that day will set the heavens ablaze until they fall *a.*

apologize-d
Acts 16:39. alarmed to hear that they were Roman citizens, and came and *a.* to them

apology-ies
Luke 14:18, 19. please accept my *a.*

apostle-s
Acts 2:6. each one heard the *a.* talking in his own language

4:7. they brought the *a.* before the court

5:41. the *a.* went out from the Council rejoicing

apostleship
2 Cor. 11:12. to put their vaunted *a.* on the same level as ours

apostolate
1 Cor. 9:2. you are yourselves the very seal of my *a.*, in the Lord

appal-ling
Heb. 12:21. so *a.* was the sight, that Moses said

appeal-s-ed-ing
Mat. 18:32. I remitted the whole of your debt when you *a.* to me

26:53. do you suppose that I cannot *a.* to my Father

Luke 3:18. in this and many other ways he made his *a.* to the people

Acts 16:9. a Macedonian stood there *a.* to him

28:23. sought to convince them about Jesus by *a.* to the law of Moses

1 Cor. 1:10. I *a.* to you, my brothers, in the name of our Lord Jesus Christ

4:13. they slander us, and we humbly make our *a.*

4:16. I *a.* to you therefore to follow my example

2 Cor. 1:23. I *a.* to God to witness

5:11. we address our *a.* to men

5:20. it is as if God were *a.* to you through us

6:1. sharing in God's work, we urge this *a.* upon you

2 Cor. 10:1. I, Paul, *a.* to you by the gentleness and magnanimity of Christ
13:11. take our *a.* to heart
1 Thess. 2:3. the *a.* we make never springs from error
2:11. *a.* to you by encouragement
4:10. we *a.* to you, brothers, to do better still
2 Thess. 3:12. we *a.* to them in the name of the Lord Jesus Christ to work quietly
1 Tim. 5:1. *a.* to him as if he were your father
2 Tim. 4:2. and *a.*, with all the patience that the work of teaching requires
Philem. 9. because of that same love, I would rather *a.* to you
10. *a.* to you about my child
Heb. 12:5. *a.* to you in these words
1 Pet. 3:21. the *a.* made to God by a good conscience
5:1 I *a.* to the elders of your community
Jude 3. *a.* to you to join the struggle in defence of the faith

appear-s-ed
Mat. 3:1. John the Baptist *a.* as a preacher
4:11. angels *a.* and waited on him
11:11. never has there *a.* on earth a mother's son greater than John the Baptist
11:13. things to come until John *a.*
12:41. the men of Nineveh will *a.* against it
12:42. the Queen of the South will *a.* at the Judgement
12:46. his mother and brothers *a.*
18:24. there *a.* before him a man whose debt ran into millions
24:32. when its tender shoots *a.*
26:47. Judas, one of the Twelve, *a.*
Mark 1:4. John the Baptist *a.* in the wilderness
9:7. then a cloud *a.*, casting its shadow
13:9. you will be summoned to *a.* before governors
13:28. when its tender shoots *a.*
14:43. Judas, one of the Twelve, *a.*
15:8. the crowd *a.* asking for the usual favour
Luke 1:80. until the day when he *a.* publicly
5:18. some men *a.* carrying a paralysed man
8:41. then a man *a.*—Jairus was his name
11:31. the Queen of the South will *a.* against them
11:32. the men of Nineveh will *a.* at the Judgement

21:25. portents will *a.* in sun, moon, and stars
22:47. a crowd *a.* with the man called Judas
23:10. the chief priests and lawyers *a.* and pressed the case
24:11. the story *a.* to them to be nonsense
John 1:6. there *a.* a man named John
7:27. when the Messiah *a.* no one is to know where he comes from
8:2. at daybreak he *a.* again in the temple
21:14. this makes the third time that Jesus *a.* to his disciples
Acts 1:3. over a period of forty days he *a.* to them
6:15. his face *a.* to them like the face of an angel
8:40. Philip *a.* at Azotus
10:40. God raised him to life on the third day, and allowed him to *a.*
13:31. there was a period of many days during which he *a.*
17:18. he would *a.* to be a propagandist for foreign deities
19:30. Paul wanted to *a.* before the assembly
23:11. the following night the Lord *a.* to him
25:7. when he *a.*, the Jews who had come
27:24. it is ordained that you shall *a.* before the Emperor
1 Cor. 15:5. he *a.* to Cephas
15:6. he *a.* to over five hundred of our brothers
15:7. he *a.* to James
15:8. in the end he *a.* even to me
2 Cor. 10:10. when he *a.* he has no presence
Phil. 1:7. when I lie in prison or *a.* in the dock
Tit. 2:13. when the splendour of our great God and Saviour Christ Jesus will *a.*
1 John 2:18. now many antichrists have *a.*
3:5. Christ *a.*, as you know, to do away with sins
3:8. the Son of God *a.* for the very purpose
Rev. 13:3. one of its heads *a.* to have received a death-blow
14:14. then as I looked there *a.* a white cloud
16:2. foul malignant sores *a.* on those men
17:8. is alive no longer, and has still to *a.*

appearance
Mark 12:40. they say long prayers for *a.* sake

Luke 9:29. while he was praying the *a.*
of his face changed
12:56. you know how to interpret the
a. of earth and sky
20:47. they say long prayers for *a.*
sake
1 Thess. 1:10. the *a.* from heaven of his
Son Jesus
1 Tim. 6:15. that *a.* God will bring to
pass in his own good time
2 Tim. 1:10. by the *a.* on earth of our
Saviour Jesus Christ
4:1. I adjure you by his coming *a.* and
his reign
4:8. all who have set their hearts on
his coming *a.*
Rev. 4:3. whose *a.* was like the gleam of
jasper
9:7. in *a.* the locusts were like horses

appetite-s
Rom. 13:14. give no more thought to
satisfying the bodily *a.*
16:18. servants not of Christ our
Lord but of their own *a.*
Phil. 3:19. *a.* is their god
1 John 2:16. all that panders to the *a.*

applaud-ed
Luke 16:8. the master *a.* the dishonest
bailiff
Rom. 1:32. they actually *a.* such
practices

apply-ies-ied
Acts 9:2. *a.* for letters to the synagogues
at Damascus
17:3. he expounded and *a.* to show
that the Messiah
23:15. to *a.* to the commandant to
bring him down to you
Rom. 14:22. if you have a clear conviction, *a.* it to yourself
Eph. 5:33. it *a.* also individually

appoint-ed-ing
Mat. 19:11. only those for whom God
has *a.* it
26:18. the Master says, 'My *a.* time is
near
26:24. the Son of Man is going the
way *a.* for him
Mark 3:14. he *a.* twelve as his companions
3:15. so he *a.* the Twelve
14:21. the Son of Man is going the
way *a.* for him
Luke 12:42. sensible man whom his
master will *a.* as his steward
19:12. to be *a.* king and then return
22:22. the Son of Man is going his
a. way
John 7:30. because his *a.* hour had not
yet come
15:16. I *a.* you to go on and bear fruit

19:28. Jesus, aware that all had now
come to its *a.* end
Acts 3:20. the Messiah he has already *a.*
7:10. he *a.* him chief administrator
for Egypt
12:21. on an *a.* day, attired in his
royal robes
13:20. *a.* judges for them until the
time of the prophet Samuel
13:47. I have *a.* you to be a light for
the Gentiles
14:23. they also *a.* elders for them in
each congregation
22:14. the God of our fathers *a.* you
to know his will
26:16. to *a.* you my servant and
witness
Rom. 4:17. I have *a.* you to be father of
many nations
1 Cor. 12:18. God *a.* each limb and
organ to its own place.
12:28. God has *a.*, in the first place
apostles
2 Cor. 8:19. they have duly *a.* him to
travel with us
Eph. 1:22. *a.* him as supreme head to
the church
1 Tim. 1:12. *a.* me to his service
2:7. I was *a.* herald and apostle
Heb. 5:1. *a.* their representative before
God
7:23. other priests are *a.* in numerous
succession
7:28. the priest *a.* by the words of the
oath
8:3. every high priest is *a.* to offer
gifts
Rev. 11:3. two witnesses, whom I will
a. to prophesy

appointment
Acts 25:1. three days after taking up his
a. Festus went up
Gal. 1:1. Paul, an apostle, not by
human *a.*
2 Tim. 1:11. of this Gospel I, by his *a.*,
am herald

apprehensive
2 Cor. 7:11. how angered you were, how
a.

approach-es-ed-ing
Mat. 4:3. the tempter *a.* him and said
8:2. a leper *a.* him, bowed low, and
said
15:1. Jesus was *a.* by a group of
Pharisees
21:34. when the vintage season *a.*
27:58. he *a.* Pilate, and asked for the
body of Jesus
Mark 1:40. once he was *a.* by a leper
6:35. as the day wore on, his disciples
a. him

Mark 10:35. James and John, the sons of Zebedee, *a.* him
11:1. they were now *a.* Jerusalem
Luke 7:4. they *a.* Jesus
7:7. I did not presume to *a.* you in person
7:12. as he *a.* the gate of the town he met a funeral
9:12. the Twelve *a.* him
9:51. as the time *a.* when he was to be taken up to heaven
14:32. long before the enemy *a.*, he sends envoys
15:25. as he *a.* the house, he heard music
18:35. as he *a.* Jericho a blind man sat
19:29. as he *a.* Bethphage and Bethany
19:37. as he *a.* the descent from the Mount of Olives
22:1. the Festival of Unleavened Bread, known as Passover, was *a.*
23:52. this man now *a.* Pilate
John 4:23. the time *a.*, indeed it is already here, when those who are real worshippers
6:19. saw Jesus walking on the sea and *a.* the boat
14:30. the Prince of this world *a.*
19:38. Pilate was *a.* by Joseph of Arimathaea
Acts 7:17. the time *a.* for God to fulfil the promise
7:23. he was *a.* the age of forty
7:31. as he *a.* to look closely, the voice of the Lord was heard
10:9. and *a.* the city, about noon Peter went up on the roof
16:7. when they *a.* the Mysian border
18:3. Paul *a.* them and, because he was of the same trade
25:24. the whole body of the Jews *a.* me
Heb. 4:16. let us therefore boldly *a.* the throne of our gracious God
7:25. able to save absolutely those who *a.* God through him
10:22. let us make our *a.* in sincerity of heart
1 John 3:21. if our conscience does not condemn us, then we can *a.* God with confidence
5:14. we can *a.* God with confidence for this reason

approval
Acts 13:22. set up David as their king, giving him his *a.*
15:8. showed his *a.* of them by giving the Holy Spirit
Rom. 13:3. continue to do right and you will have their *a.*
Eph. 5:10. make sure what would have the Lord's *a.*

2 Tim. 2:15. try hard to show yourself worthy of God's *a.*
Heb. 11:4. his offerings had God's *a.*

approve-s-d-ing
Luke 11:48. so testify that you *a.* of the deeds your fathers did
Acts 8:1. Saul was among those who *a.* of his murder
12:3. when he saw that the Jews *a.*, proceeded to arrest Peter also
22:20. when the blood of Stephen thy witness was shed I stood by, *a.*
Rom. 7:23. a different law, fighting against the law that my reason *a.*
1 Cor. 16:3. letters of introduction to persons *a.* by you
1 Thess. 2:4. God has *a.* us as fit to be entrusted with the Gospel
1 Tim. 2:3. such prayer is right, and *a.* by God
Heb. 13:16. such are the sacrifices which God *a.*
1 John 3:22. keeping his commands and doing what he *a.*

arbiter
Col. 3:15. let Christ's peace be *a.* in your hearts

arbitrate
Luke 12:14. who set me over you to judge or *a.*

archdeceiver
2 John 7. persons described as the Antichrist, the *a.*

architect
Heb. 11:10. whose *a.* and builder is God

ardent
Acts 22:3. I have always been *a.* in God's service

ardour
Rom. 12:11. in *a.* of spirit, serve the Lord

arena
1 Cor. 4:9. we are like men condemned to death in the *a.*

Areopagus
Acts 17:22. Paul stood up before the Court of *a.*

argue-d-ing
Mat. 21:25. this set them *a.* among themselves
27:6. taking up the money, the chief priests *a.*
Mark 9:14. lawyers *a.* with them
9:33. what were you *a.* about on the way
11:31. } this set them *a.* among
Luke 20:5. } themselves

Acts 6:9. came forward and *a.* with Stephen

17:2. for the next three Sabbaths he *a.* with them

17:17. he *a.* in the synagogue with the Jews

24:12. they did not find me *a.* with anyone

Rom. 2:15. their own thoughts *a.* the case on either side

1 Cor. 11:16. however, if you insist on *a.*

Tit. 2:15. these, then, are your themes; urge them and *a.* them

argument-s

Mat. 12:27. if this is your *a.*, they themselves will refute you

Mark 9:16. he asked them, 'What is this *a.* about

Luke 11:19. if this is your *a.*, they themselves will refute you

Acts 19:8. using *a.* and persuasion, spoke boldly

28:24. some were won over by his *a.*

Rom. 3:28. our *a.* is that a man is justified by faith

1 Cor. 2:4. did not sway you with subtle *a.*

3:20. the Lord knows that the *a.* of the wise are futile

Eph. 5:6. let no one deceive you with shallow *a.*

Col. 2:4. talked into error by specious *a.*

2 Tim. 4:2. use *a.*, reproof, and appeal

Heb. 7:15. the *a.* becomes still clearer

arise-s-ing

Mat. 18:7. alas for the world that such causes of stumbling *a.*

24:11. many false prophets will *a.*

Luke 17:1. Causes of stumbling are bound to *a.*

Rom. 14:23. because his action does not *a.* from his conviction

Phil. 2:5. let your bearing towards one another *a.* out of your life in Christ Jesus

Heb. 7:11. what further need would there have been to speak of another priest *a.*

Jam. 1:14. temptation *a.* when a man is enticed

arm-s

Mat. 4:6. they will support you in their *a.*

12:10. a man was there with a withered *a.*

12:13. stretch out your *a.*

16:22. Peter took him by the *a.*

Mark 3:1. a man in the congregation who had a withered *a.*

3:3. he said to the man with the withered *a.*

3:5. stretch out your *a.*

8:32. at this Peter took him by the *a.*

Luke 4:11. they will support you in their *a.*

6:6. whose right *a.* was withered

6:8. said to the man with the withered *a.*

6:10. stretch out your *a.*

11:22. overpowers him, he carries off the *a.*

15:20. he ran to meet him, flung his *a.* round him

John 21:18. when you are old you will stretch out your *a.*

Acts 20:10. Paul went down, threw himself upon him, seizing him in his *a.*

20:37. they folded Paul in their *a.* and kissed him

23:19. the commandant took him by the *a.*

Heb. 12:12. come, then, stiffen your drooping *a.*

arm-ed

Mat. 26:47. a great crowd *a.* with swords

Mark 14:43. with him was a crowd *a.* with swords and cudgels

Luke 4:14. Jesus, *a.* with the power of the Spirit

24:49. until you are *a.* with the power from above

Acts 23:23. seventy cavalrymen and two hundred light-*a.* troops

1 Thess. 5:8. *a.* with faith and love for breastplate

1 Tim. 1:19. fight gallantly, *a.* with faith and a good conscience

armful

Acts 28:3. Paul had got together an *a.* of sticks

armour

Rom. 13:14. let Christ Jesus himself be the *a.* that you wear

army

1 Cor. 9:7. serving in the *a.* at his own expense

aromatic

Mark 16:1. bought *a.* oils intending to go and anoint him

arose

Acts 19:34. a single cry *a.* from them all

around

Mark 9:8. when they looked *a.*, there was nobody to be seen but Jesus

Acts 2:10. and the districts of Libya *a.* Cyrene

9:3. suddenly a light flashed from the sky all *a.* him

22:6. suddenly about midday a great light flashed from the sky all *a.* me

Acts 26:13. more brilliant than the sun, shining all *a.* me

Heb. 12:1. all these witnesses to faith *a.* us like a cloud

Rev. 14:20. for two hundred miles *a.* blood flowed from the press

arouse

Heb. 10:24. we ought to see how each of us may best *a.* others

arrange-d

Acts 15:2. it was *a.* that these two and some others from Antioch

23:15. we have *a.* to do away with him before he arrives

1 Cor. 11:34. the other matters I will *a.* when I come

arrangement-s

Mat. 20:5. at three in the afternoon, and made the same *a.* as before

Luke 9:52. went into a Samaritan village to make *a.* for him

Acts 20:13. he had made this *a.*, as he was going to travel by road

Heb. 9:6. under this *a.*, the priests are always entering the first tent

array

Col. 2:5. your orderly *a.* and the firm front which your faith in Christ presents

arrest-ed-ing

Mat. 4:11. when he heard that John had been *a.*

10:19. when you are *a.*, do not worry about what you are to say

14:3. Herod had *a.* John

21:46. they wanted to *a.* him, but they were afraid of the people

26:4. they conferred together on a scheme to have Jesus *a.*

26:55. you have come out with swords and cudgels to *a.* me

26:57. Jesus was led off under *a.*

Mark 1:14. after John had been *a.*

6:17. this same Herod had sent and *a.* John

12:12. then they began to look for a way to *a.* him

13:11. When you are *a.* and taken away

14:48 ⎱ come out with swords and
Luke 22:52 ⎰ cudgels to *a.* me

22:54. then they *a.* him and led him away

John 7:32. the Pharisees sent temple police to *a.* him

8:20. yet no one *a.* him, because his hour had not yet come

11:57. anyone who knew where he was should give information, so that they might *a.* him

18:12. the Jewish police, now *a.* Jesus

18:36. my followers would be fighting to save me from *a.*

Acts 1:16. Judas who acted as guide to those who *a.* Jesus

4:3. they were *a.*

5:18. they proceeded to *a.* the apostles

9:2. authorizing him to *a.* anyone he found

9:14. to *a.* all who invoke thy name

9:21. did he not come here for the sole purpose of *a.* them

12:3. proceeded to *a.* Peter also

21:33. the commandant stepped forward, *a.* him

22:4. I began to persecute this movement to the death *a.* its followers

24:6. made an attempt to profane the temple, and then we *a.* him

24:23. to keep Paul under open *a.*

1 Cor. 11:23. the Lord Jesus, on the night of his *a.*, took bread

2 Cor. 11:32. King Aretas kept the city under observation so as to have me *a.*

arrival

Mat. 17:24. on their *a.* at Capernaum the collectors of the temple tax

Luke 8:51. on *a.* at the house he allowed no one to go in with him except

John 4:45. on his *a.* in Galilee the Galileans gave him a welcome

11:17. on his *a.* Jesus found that Lazarus had already been four days in the tomb

Acts 17:10. on *a.*, they made their way to the synagogue

18:27. from the time of his *a.*, he was very helpful

2 Cor. 7:6. comforted us by the *a.* of Titus

7:7. not merely by his *a.*, but by his being so greatly comforted

Gal. 3:19. pending the *a.* of the 'issue' to whom the promise was made

arrive-s-d-ing

Mat. 2:1. astrologers from the east *a.* in Jerusalem

3:13. Jesus *a.* at the Jordan from Galilee

9:23. when Jesus *a.* at the president's house

24:50. the master will *a.* on a day that servant does not expect

25:10. while they were away the bridegroom *a.*

Mark 3:31. then his mother and his brothers *a.*

6:33. from all the towns towards the place, and *a.* there first

8:22. they *a.* at Bethsaida

Luke 8:19. his mother and his brothers *a.*

Luke 12:36. ready to let him in the moment he *a.*

12:46. the master will *a.* on a day that servant does not expect

Acts 5:21. when the High Priest *a.* with his colleagues

5:25. then a man *a.* with the report

9:39. when he *a.* they took him upstairs to the room

10:17. to Simon's house, and now *a.* at the entrance

10:24. he *a.* at Caesarea

10:25. when Peter *a.*, Cornelius came to meet him

11:11. *a.* at the house where I was staying

11:20. when they *a.* at Antioch, began to speak

11:23. when he *a.* and saw the divine grace at work

13:5. *a.* at Salamis, they declared the word of God

14:27. when they *a.* and had called the congregation together

18:2. he had recently *a.* from Italy

18:24. there *a.* at Ephesus a Jew named Apollos

20:15. *a.* opposite Chios

21:10. a prophet named Agabus *a.* from Judaea

21:22. they are sure to hear that you have *a.*

23:15. we have arranged to do away with him before he *a.*

23:35. when your accusers *a.*

25:13. King Agrippa and Bernice *a.* at Caesarea

28:13. then we sailed round and *a.* at Rhegium

28:21. *a.* with any report or gossip to your discredit

Rom. 15:29. when I *a.* I shall come to you with a full measure of the blessing of Christ

1 Cor. 16:3. when I *a.*, I will give letters of introduction

16:17. Stephanas, Fortunatus, and Achaicus have *a.*

Phil. 3:11. if only I may finally *a.* at the resurrection from the dead

1 Thess. 3:6. Timothy has just *a.* from Thessalonica

1 Tim. 4:13. until I *a.* devote your attention to the public reading of the scriptures

arrogance

Mark 7:22. slander, *a.*, and folly

2 Cor. 12:20. *a.* and general disorder

arrogant

Luke 1:51 the *a.* of heart and mind he has put to rout

Rom. 1:30. insolent *a.*, and boastful

2 Tim. 3:2. they will be *a.*, boastful and abusive

Jam. 4:6. God opposes the *a.*

1 Pet. 5:5. God sets his face against the *a.*

arrogate-s

Heb. 5:4. nobody *a.* the honour to himself

arrow-s

Eph. 6:16. you will be able to quench all the flaming *a.* of the evil one

artfully

2 Pet. 1:16. it was not on tales *a.* spun that we relied

arts

Acts 8:9. swept the Samaritans off their feet with his magical *a.*

ascend-s-ed

Acts 7:18. another king who knew nothing of Joseph, *a.* the throne

2 Cor. 4:15. the chorus of thanksgiving that *a.* to the glory of God

ascent

Luke 19:28. Jesus went forward and began the *a.* to Jerusalem

ascertain-ed

Mat. 2:7. *a.* from them the time when the star had appeared

2:16. the time he had *a.* from the astrologers

Acts 23:28. I wished to *a.* the charge

24:8. you can *a.* from him the truth of all the charges

24:11. you can *a.* the facts for yourself

ash-es

Rev. 17:16. they will batten on her flesh and burn her to *a.*

ashamed

Rev. 16:15. he will not have to go naked and *a.*

ashore

Mat. 13:48. when it was full, it was dragged *a.*

14:14. when he came *a.*, he saw a great crowd

Mark 5:2. as he stepped *a.*, a man possessed by an unclean spirit came up to him

6:34. when he came *a.*, he saw a great crowd

6:54. when they came *a.*, he was immediately recognized

Luke 5:2. the fishermen had come *a.*, and were washing their nets

8:27. as he stepped *a.* he was met by a man from the town

John 6:23. boats from Tiberias, however, came *a.* near the place

John 21:9. when they came *a.*, they saw a charcoal fire there

Acts 21:5. when our time *a.* was ended, we left and continued our journey

27:26. though we have to be cast *a.* on some island

27:29. we might be cast *a.* on a rugged coast

27:39. on which they planned, if possible, to run the ship *a.*

Asia

Rom. 16:5. the first convert to Christ in *A.*

aside

Mat. 1:19. Joseph desired to have the marriage contract set *a.* quietly

5:19. if any man therefore sets *a.* even the least of the Law's demands

20:17. on the way he took the Twelve *a.*

Mark 7:9. how well you set *a.* the commandment of God

10:32. he took the Twelve *a.* and began to tell them

Luke 18:31. he took the Twelve *a.* and said

John 10:35. Scripture cannot be set *a.*

11:28. she went to call her sister Mary, and taking her *a.*, she said

Acts 7:39. they thrust him *a.*

Rom. 3:12. all have swerved *a.*, all alike have become debased

1 Cor. 16:2. every Sunday each of you is to put *a.* and keep by him a sum

Gal. 3:15. no one else can set it *a.* or add a codicil

Eph. 4:22. you must lay *a.* that old human nature

Col. 2:14. he has set it *a.*, nailing it to the cross

Col. 3:8. you yourselves must lay *a.* all anger

ask-s-ed-ing

Mat. 6:31. do not *a.* anxiously, 'What are we to eat

8:5. a centurion came up to *a.* his help

12:39. a wicked, godless generation that *a.* for a sign

16:1. to test him they *a.* him to show them a sign

19:17. why do you *a.* me about that

19:18. which commandments? he *a.*

21:10. who is this? people *a.*

21:16. they *a.* him indignantly, 'Do you hear what they are saying

27:58. he approached Pilate, and *a.* for the body of Jesus

Mark 3:31. sent in a message *a.* him to come out to them

11:24. whatever you *a.* for in prayer,

believe that you have received it and it will be yours

15:11. the chief priests incited the crowd to *a.* him to release Barabbas

Luke 9:40. I *a.* your disciples to cast it out, but they could not

14:8. when you are *a.* by someone to a wedding-feast

14:12. they will only *a.* you back again

14:13. when you give a party, *a.* the poor

14:32. he sends envoys, and *a.* for terms

John 11:28. the Master is here; he is *a.* for you

14:8. Lord, show us the Father and we *a.* no more

14:16. I will *a.* the Father, and he will give you another to be your Advocate

Acts 4:9. we are *a.* by what means he was cured

7:46. David found favour with God and *a.* to be allowed to provide a dwelling-place

8:15. *a.* that they might receive the Holy Spirit

8:31. he *a.* Philip to get in and sit beside him

9:11. *a.* for a man from Tarsus named Saul

10:17. *a.* the way to Simon's house

13:21. they *a.* for a king and God gave them Saul

13:28. they *a.* Pilate to have him executed

13:42. they were *a.* to come again and speak on these subjects

18:20. he was *a.* to stay longer, but declined

21:33. he then *a.* who the man was

21:39. I *a.* your permission to speak to the people

25:11. I do not *a.* to escape the death penalty

28:20. that is why I have *a.* to see you

Rom. 1:10. am always *a.* that by his will I may

1 Cor. 15:35. but, you may *a.*, how are the dead raised

2 Cor. 7:15. how ready you all were to do what he *a.*

8:12. God accepts what a man has; he does not *a.* for what he has not

Phil. 4:3. I *a.* you to help these women, who shared my struggles

Col. 1:9. we *a.* God that you may receive from him all wisdom

Philem. 21. I know that you will in fact do better than I *a.*

Heb. 13:19. all the more earnestly I *a.* for your prayers

asleep

Mat. 9:24. the girl is not dead: she is *a.*

  13:25. while everyone was *a.* his enemy came

  28:13. stole the body while we were *a.*

Mark 5:39. the child is not dead: she is *a.*

  13:36. if he comes suddenly, he must not find you *a.*

  14:37. he came back and found them *a.*

Luke 8:52. weep no more; she is not dead: she is *a.*

  22:45. and came to the disciples he found them *a.*

John 11:11. our friend Lazarus has fallen *a.*

  11:12. if he has fallen *a.* he will recover

1 Thess. 5:10. he died for us so that we, awake or *a.*, might live in company with him.

aspire

1 Cor. 14:12. *a.* above all to excel in those which build up the church

Col. 3:1. *a.* to the realm above, where Christ is

1 Tim. 3:1. a popular saying: 'To *a.* to leadership is an honourable ambition

assail

Luke 11:53. began to *a.* him fiercely

assayer

1 Pet. 1:7. even gold passes through the *a.* fire

assemble-d-ing

Mat. 22:41. turning to the *a.* Pharisees Jesus asked them

  27:17. when they were *a.* Pilate said to them

Mark 14:53. the chief priests, elders, and doctors of the law were all *a.*

Luke 22:66. the elders of the nation, chief priests, and doctors of the law *a.*

  23:48. the crowd who had *a.* for the spectacle

  24:33. the Eleven and the rest of the company had *a.*

Acts 1:15. Peter stood up before the *a.* brotherhood

  7:38. when they were *a.* there in the desert

  20:8. many lamps in the upper room where we were *a.*

  22:30. ordered the chief priests and the entire council to *a.*

  28:17. the local Jewish leaders; and when they were *a.*

1 Cor. 5:4. you all being *a.* in the name of our Lord Jesus

  14:23. if the whole congregation is *a.*

Rev. 16:16. so they *a.* the kings at the place called in Hebrew Armageddon

assembly

Luke 23:1. the whole *a.* rose, and they brought him before Pilate

Acts 17:5. the intention of bringing Paul and Silas before the town *a.*

  17:33. so Paul left the *a.*

  19:30. Paul wanted to appear before the *a.*

  19:33. attempted to make a defence before the *a.*

  20:7. in our *a.* for the breaking of bread

  23:7. the *a.* was divided

Heb. 2:12. in full *a.* I will sing thy praise

assert

Acts. 17:7. and *a.* that there is a rival king, Jesus

  26:22. I *a.* nothing beyond what was foretold by the prophets

assertion

Acts 24:21. apart from this one open *a.* which I made

assessment

Luke 3:13. exact no more than the *a.*

assets

Phil. 3:7. all such *a.* I have written off

assign-ed

Mat. 20:23. it is for those to whom it has already been *a.* by my Father

Mark 10:40. for those to whom it has already been *a.*

Acts 1:26. was then *a.* a place among the twelve apostles

  20:24. and complete the task which the Lord Jesus *a.* to me

Eph. 3:2. God has *a.* the gift of his grace to me

Col. 1:25. by virtue of the task *a.* to me by God

assistant

Acts 13:5. they had John with them as their *a.*

  19:22. two of his *a.*, Timothy and Erastus

2 Tim. 4:11. bring him with you, for I find him a useful *a.*

assize-s

Acts 19:38. *a.* are held and there are such people as proconsuls

1 Pet. 2:12. glory to God on the day when he comes to hold *a.*

associate-d

Acts 10:28. a Jew is forbidden by his religion to visit or *a.*

Rom. 16:15. all God's people *a.* with them

2 Cor. 8:23. Titus, he is my partner and my *a.*

assume-d-ing
Acts 16:27. *a.* that the prisoners had escaped
21:29. *a.* that Paul had brought him into the temple
Phil. 2:7. made himself nothing, *a.* the nature of a slave

assurance
Heb. 2:6. a solemn *a.* which runs: 'What is man

assure-s-ed
Mat. 28:20. and be *a.*, I am with you always
Acts 20:23. the Holy Spirit *a.* me that imprisonment and hardships await me
27:24. be *a.*, God has granted you the lives of all who are sailing with you
Rom. 9:1. enlightened by the Holy Spirit, *a.* me it is no lie
2 Cor. 1:12. our conscience *a.* us that in our dealings
2:8. *a.* him of your love for him
1 John 5:13. this letter is to *a.* you that you have eternal life

assuredly
Mat. 10:42. that man will *a.* not go unrewarded
Mark 9:41. that man *a.* will not go unrewarded
Luke 6:23. *a.* you have a rich reward in heaven

astonish-ed-ing
Mat. 8:27. the men were *a.* at what had happened
Luke 2:18. all who heard were *a.* at what the shepherds said
2:48. his parents were *a.* to see him there
11:14. the people were *a.*
20:26. *a.* by his reply, they fell silent
John 3:7. you ought not to be *a.*
4:27. *a.* to find him talking with a woman
7:15. began to teach. The Jews were *a.*
Gal. 1:6. I am *a.* to find you turning so quickly away
Rev. 15:1. I saw another great and *a.* portent in heaven
17:6. I was greatly *a.*
17:7. the angel said to me, 'Why are you so *a.*
17:8. will all be *a.* to see the beast

astonishment
Mat. 8:10. Jesus heard him with *a.*
27:14. to the Governor's great *a.*
Mark 7:37. their *a.* knew no bounds
12:17. they heard him with *a.*
15:5. to Pilate's *a.*, Jesus made no further reply

Luke 1:63. to the *a.* of all wrote down, 'His name is John
8:25. in fear and *a.*, they said to one another, 'Who can this be
Acts 2:7. in their *a.* exclaimed, 'Why, they are all Galileans
3:11. the people came running in *a.*

astound-ed
Mat. 7:28. the people were *a.* at his teaching
22:33. the people heard what he said, and were *a.* at his teaching
Mark 1:22. the people were *a.* at his teaching
2:12. so that they were *a.* and praised God
Luke 4:32. they were *a.* at his teaching
8:56. her parents were *a.*
24:22. some women of our company have *a.* us
Acts 9.21. 'This' he said 'is the Son of God.' All who heard were *a.*
12:16. when they opened the door and saw him, they were *a.*

astray
Mat. 5:29. if your right eye leads you *a.*, tear it out
Mark 9:42. as for the man who leads *a.* one of these little ones
9:45. if it is your foot that leads you *a.*, cut it off
John 7:12. he is leading the people *a.*
Rom. 16:17. those who stir up quarrels and lead others *a.*
1 Tim. 1:6. some people have gone *a.* into a wilderness of words
Tit. 1:10. they talk wildly and lead men's minds *a.*
3:3. in our folly and obstinacy were all *a.*
Heb. 3:10. I said, Their hearts are for ever *a.*
Rev. 12:9. that serpent of old that led the whole world *a.*

astrologer-s
Mat. 2:1. *a.* from the east arrived in Jerusalem
2:7. Herod next called the *a.* to meet him
2:16. Herod saw how the *a.* had tricked him

astute-ly
Luke 16:8. the dishonest bailiff for acting so *a.* For the worldly are more *a.* than the other-worldly

ate
Mat. 12:4. went into the house of God and *a.* the consecrated loaves
13:4. the birds came and *a.* it up
14:20 ⎱ they all *a.* to their hearts'
15:37 ⎰ content

Mat. 24:38. in the days before the flood they *a*. and drank and married
Mark 2:26. and *a*. the consecrated loaves
4:4. the birds came and *a*. it up
6:42. they all *a*. to their hearts' content
6:44. those who *a*. the loaves numbered five thousand men
8:8. they all *a*. to their hearts' content
Luke 8:5. the birds *a*. it up
9:17. they all *a*. to their hearts' content
17:27. they *a*. and drank and married
17:28. they *a*. and drank
John 6:26. your hunger was satisfied with the loaves you *a*.
6:58. it is not like the bread which our fathers *a*.
Acts 20:11. he then went upstairs, broke bread and *a*.
1 Cor. 10:3. they all *a*. the same supernatural food

athlete
1 Cor. 9:25. every *a*. goes into strict training
2 Tim. 2:5. no *a*. can win a prize unless he has kept the rules

atrophy-ied
1 Tim. 6:5. men who have let their reasoning powers become *a*.

attach-ed
Luke 15:15. he went and *a*. himself to one of the local landowners
Eph. 6:2. the first commandment with a promise *a*.

attack-s-ed-ing
Mat. 22:6. the others seized the servants, *a*. them brutally
Mark 9:18. whenever it *a*. him, it dashes him to the ground
Acts 7:19. he made a crafty *a*. on our race
12:1. King Herod *a*. certain members of the church
16:22. the mob joined in the *a*.
18:17. there was a general *a*. on Sosthenes
21:28. *a*. our people, our law, and this sanctuary
24:9. the Jews supported the *a*.

attain-ed-ing
2 Cor. 10:15. we may *a*. a position among you greater than ever before
Gal. 4:5. that we might *a*. the status of sons
5:5. our hope of *a*. that righteousness
Eph. 3:19. so may you *a*. to fullness of being
4:13. at last *a*. to the unity inherent in our faith

2 Tim. 2:10. *a*. the glorious and eternal salvation
Heb. 6:15. Abraham, after patient waiting, *a*. the promise
12:9. submit even more readily to our spiritual Father, and so *a*. life
Jam. 4:2. you are envious, and cannot *a*. your ambition
1 John 4:18. anyone who is afraid has not *a*. to love in its perfection

attainable
Heb. 7:11. if perfection had been *a*. through the Levitical priesthood

attainment
1 Thess. 5:9. to the full *a*. of salvation through our Lord Jesus Christ

attempt-ed-ing
Luke 12:47. knew his master's wishes, yet made no *a*. to carry them out
20:26. their *a*. to catch him out in public failed
John 10:39. one more *a*. to seize him
Acts 18:10. no one shall *a*. to do you harm
19:33. he, motioning for silence, *a*. to make a defence
23:30. informed of an *a*. to be made on the man's life
24:6. he even made an *a*. to profane the temple
Rom. 14:1. accept him without *a*. to settle doubtful points
2 Cor. 5:12. this is not another *a*. to recommend ourselves to you
10:13. no *a*. to boast beyond our proper sphere
1 Thess. 2:3. there is no *a*. to deceive
2 Tim. 4:18. the Lord will rescue me from every *a*. to do me harm
Heb. 11:29. the Egyptians, when they *a*. the crossing, were drowned

attend-s-ed
Acts 19:8. during the next three months he *a*. the synagogue
21:18. we were with him, and all the elders *a*.
2 Cor. 12:12. was *a*. by signs, marvels and miracles
Col. 4:17. *a*. to the duty entrusted to you
2 Thess. 2:9. it will be *a*. by all the powerful signs and miracles of the Lie
1 Tim. 5:5. regularly *a*. the meetings for prayer and worship
2 Pet. 1:19. the message of the prophets, to which you will do well to *a*.

attendance
Luke 1:19. I stand in *a*. upon God
Acts 2:46. kept up their daily *a*. at the temple

attendant-s

Mat. 14:2. 'This is John the Baptist,' he said to his *a*.

22:13. the king then said to his *a*.

26:58. he sat down there among the *a*.

Mark 14:54. there he remained, sitting among the *a*.

Luke 4:20. he rolled up the scroll, gave it back to the *a*.

19:24. turning to his *a*. he said

Acts 23:2. ordered his *a*. to strike him on the mouth

23:4. the *a*. said, 'Would you insult God's high priest

attention

Mat. 23:3. do what they tell you, pay *a*. to their words

Acts 3:5. expecting a gift from them, the man was all *a*.

21:40. with a gesture called for the *a*. of the people

27:11. the centurion paid more *a*. to the captain

1 Tim. 4:13. devote your *a*. to the public reading of the scriptures

Jam. 2:3. suppose you pay special *a*. to the well-dressed man

attest-s-ed

John 3:33. to accept his witness is to *a*. that God speaks true

John 21:24. it is this same disciple who *a*. what has here been written

1 Cor. 2:1. I declared the *a*. truth of God

Heb. 11:4. through faith his goodness was *a*.

1 John 4:14. we *a*. that the Father sent the Son

attired

Mat. 6:29. Solomon in all his splendour was not *a*.

Luke 12:27. even Solomon in all his splendour was not *a*.

Acts 12:21. *a*. in his royal robes

attitude

Phil. 3:5. in my *a*. to the law, a Pharisee

attributes

Rom. 1:20. his invisible *a*., that is to say his everlasting power

audience

Acts 25:23. Agrippa and Bernice came in full state and entered the *a*.-chamber

authentic

Luke 1:4. to give you *a*. knowledge about the matters

authenticates

2 Thess. 3:17. this *a*. all my letters

author

Luke 1:1. the *a*. to Theophilus

authorities

Luke 12:11. when you are brought before synagogues and state *a*.

John 9:22. the Jewish *a*. had already agreed

Acts 14:5. the connivance of the city *a*.

16:19. dragged them to the city *a*.

Rom. 13:1. submit to the supreme authorities . . . the existing *a*. are instituted by him

13:3. you wish to have no fear of the *a*.

13:6. the *a*. are in God's service

Eph. 3:10. the rulers and *a*. in the realms of heaven

6:12. *a*. and potentates of this dark world

Col. 1:16. the invisible orders of thrones, sovereignties, *a*.

2:15. he discarded the cosmic powers and *a*.

Tit. 3:1. submissive to the government and the *a*.

authority

Mat. 5:41. if a man in *a*. makes you go one mile

9:8. praised God for granting such *a*. to men

10:1. gave them *a*. to cast out unclean spirits

28:18. full *a*. in heaven and on earth has been committed to me

Mark 6:7. he gave them *a*. over unclean spirits

11:33. neither will I tell you by what *a*. I act.

Luke 2:51. continued to be under their *a*.

4:32. for what he said had the note of *a*.

12:5. fear him who, after he has killed, has *a*. to cast into hell

John 2:18. 'What sign,' they asked, 'can you show as *a*. for your actions

3:35. the Father loves the Son and has entrusted him with all *a*.

6:27. upon whom the Father has set the seal of his *a*.

8:28. I do nothing on my own *a*.

12:42. even among those in *a*. a number believed in him

12:49. I do not speak on my own *a*.

16:13. he will not speak on his own *a*.

18:36. my kingly *a*. comes from elsewhere

19:10. 'Surely you know that I have *a*. to release you, and I have *a*. to crucify you

19:11. 'You would have no *a*. at all over me,' Jesus replied

Rom. 13:1. there is no *a*. but by act of God

13:2. anyone who rebels against *a*. is resisting a divine institution

1 Cor. 11:10. it is woman's duty to have a sign of *a*. on her head

14:37. let him recognize that what I write has the Lord's *a*.

2 Cor. 2:9. whether you fully accepted my *a*.

13:10. any sharp exercise of *a*.—*a*. which the Lord gave me

Eph. 1:21. far above all government and *a*.

Col. 2:10. every power and *a*. in the universe

Tit. 2:5. respecting the *a*. of their own husbands

2:9. tell slaves to respect their masters' *a*.

1 Pet. 2:18. servants, accept the *a*. of your masters

3:1. you women must accept the *a*. of your husbands

2 Pet. 2:10. they flout *a*.; reckless and headstrong

Jude 8. their dreams lead them to defile the body, to flout *a*.

24. to the only God our Saviour, be glory and majesty, might and *a*.

Rev. 2:26. I will give *a*. over the nations —that same *a*. which I received from my Father

13:4. the dragon because he had conferred his *a*. upon the beast

13:7. was granted *a*. over every tribe and people

13:12. it wielded all the *a*. of the first beast

14:18. the angel who has *a*. over fire

17:12. share with the beast the exercise of royal *a*.

17:13. will confer their power and *a*. upon the beast

18:1. another angel coming down from heaven; he came with great *a*.

authorize-ing

Acts 9:2. *a*. him to arrest anyone he found

avail-ed

John 6:63. the spirit alone gives life; the flesh is of no *a*.

1 Cor. 9:12. I have *a*. myself of no such right

avoid-ed-ing

John 3:20. bad men all hate the light and *a*. it

7:1. he wished to *a*. Judaea

7:23. if a child is circumcised on the Sabbath to *a*. breaking the law of Moses

18:28. the Jews themselves stayed outside the headquarters to *a*. defilement

Acts 20:16. so *a*. having to spend time in the province of Asia

27:21. then you would have *a*. this damage and loss

1 Cor. 1:10. agree among yourselves, and *a*. divisions

5:10. to *a*. them you would have to get right out of the world

2 Cor. 6:3. we *a*. giving offence in anything

1 Thess. 5:22. keep what is good in them and *a*. the bad

1 Tim. 3:3. of a forbearing disposition, *a*. quarrels

2 Tim. 2:16. *a*. empty and wordly chatter

avow-ed

John 1:20. he confessed without reserve and *a*., 'I am not the Messiah

await-s-ed-ing

Mat. 6:1. if you do, no reward *a*. you in your Father's house

Mark 15:43. a man who was eagerly *a*. the kingdom of God

John 1:21. are you the prophet we *a*.

Acts 20:23. the Holy Spirit assures me that imprisonment and hardships *a*. me

2 Cor. 2:12. where an opening *a*. me for the Lord's work

9:5. it will then be *a*. me as a bounty indeed

Gal. 5:5. our hope of attaining that righteousness which we eagerly *a*.

2 Tim. 4:8. now the prize *a*. me, the garland of righteousness

Heb. 4:9. a sabbath rest still *a*. the people of God

1 Pet. 1:10. those who prophesied about the grace of God *a*. you

awake

Mat. 24:42. keep *a*., then; for you do not know on what day your Lord is to come

24:43. he would have kept *a*.

25:13. keep *a*., then; for you never know the day or the hour

26:38. stay *a*. with me

26:40. could none of you stay *a*. with me one hour

26:41. stay *a*., and pray

Mark 13:34. he has ordered the doorkeeper to stay *a*.

13:35. keep *a*., then, for you do not know when the master of the house is coming

13:37. what I say to you, I say to everyone: Keep *a*.

14:34. my heart is ready to break with grief; stop here, and stay *a*.

Mark 14:37. were you not able to keep
a. for one hour
14:38. stay a., all of you
Col. 4:2. persevere in prayer, with
mind a.
1 Thess. 5:6. we must not sleep like the
rest, but keep a.
5:10. that we, a. or asleep, might live
in company with him
1 Pet. 5:8. a.! be on the alert
Rev. 16:15. I come like a thief! Happy
the man who stays a.

awaken-s-ed-ing

Acts 3:16. The name of Jesus, by a.
faith, has strengthened this man
Rom. 10:17. we conclude that faith is a.
by the message, and the message
that a. it comes through the word
of Christ

award

2 Tim. 4:8. the all-just Judge, will a. me
on that great day

aware

Mat. 12:15. Jesus was a. of it and withdrew
22:18. Jesus was a. of their malicious
intention
26:10. Jesus was a. of this, and said to
them
Mark 5:30. Jesus, a. that power had
gone out of him
John 5:6. Jesus saw him lying there and
was a. that he had been ill a long
time
6:15. Jesus, a. that they meant to
come and seize him
6:61. Jesus was a. that his disciples
were murmuring about it
13:2. Jesus, well a. that the Father
had entrusted everything to him
19:28. Jesus, a. that all had now come
to its appointed end
Acts 23:6. Paul was well a. that one
section of them were Sadducees
Rom. 2:18. you are a. of moral distinctions
1 Cor. 6:3. are you not a. that we are to
judge angels
2 Thess. 2:6. you must now be a. of the
restraining hand

away

Mat. 2:13. Herod is going to search for
the child to do a. with him
2:14. taking mother and child by
night he went a. with them
4:1. Jesus was then led a. by the Spirit
into the wilderness
5:13. it is now good for nothing but
to be thrown a.
6:25. I bid you put a. anxious thoughts
8:17. He took a. our illnesses and
lifted our diseases from us

9:15. the time will come when the
bridegroom will be taken a. from
them
12:14. laid a plot to do a. with him
13:21. persecution on account of the
word he falls a. at once
14:12. John's disciples came and took
a. the body, and buried it
16:23. Jesus turned and said to Peter,
'A. with you, Satan
21:43. the kingdom of God will be
taken a. from you
24:6. the noise of battle near at hand
and the news of battles far a.
25:10. while they were a. the bridegroom arrived
26:56. the disciples all deserted him
and ran a.
26:73. said to Peter, 'Surely you are
another of them; your accent gives
you a.
28:8. they hurried a. from the tomb
Mark 1:12. thereupon the Spirit sent
him a. into the wilderness
1:35. he went a. to a lonely spot and
remained there in prayer
3:6. to see how they could make a.
with him
4:17. persecution on account of the
word, they fall a. at once
7:33. he took the man aside, a. from
the crowd
8:23. he took the blind man by the
hand and led him a. out of the
village
8:33. 'a. with you, Satan,' he said
11:18. sought some means of making
a. with him
13:7. the news of battles far a.
13:34. it is like a man a. from home
14:29. Peter answered, 'Everyone else
may fall a., but I will not
14:50. the disciples all deserted him
and ran a.
14:52. he slipped out of the linen
cloth and ran a. naked
16:8. ran a. from the tomb, beside
themselves with terror
Luke 19:13. trade with this while I am
a.
19:20. I kept it put a. in a handkerchief
22:42. Father, if it be thy will, take
this cup a. from me
John 6:37. the man who comes to me I
will never turn a.
7:33. Jesus said, 'For a little longer I
shall be with you; then I am going
a. to him who sent me
10:5. they will not follow a stranger;
they will run a. from him
10:12. the hireling, when he sees the
wolf coming, abandons the sheep
and runs a.

John 10:13. the man runs *a.* because he is a hireling
  12:10. resolved to do *a.* with Lazarus as well
  12:36. after these words Jesus went *a.* from them into hiding
Acts 1:8. *a.* to the ends of the earth
  2:39. the promise is to you, and to your children, and to all who are far *a.*
  12:7. the chains fell *a.* from his wrists
  22:21. 'Go, for I am sending you far *a.* to the Gentiles
  23:15. we have arranged to do *a.* with him
  23:21. not to eat or drink until they have done *a.* with him
  26:21 tried to do *a.* with me
Rom. 4:7. whose lawless deeds are forgiven, whose sins are buried *a.*
  11:20. put *a.* your pride
2 Cor. 4:18. what is seen passess *a.*; what is unseen is eternal
  10:1. so brave when I am *a.*
Gal. 1:6. astonished to find you turning so quickly *a.* from him
Col. 1:13. brought us *a.* into the kingdom of his dear Son
1 Tim. 6:18. to be ready to give *a.* and to share
Heb. 1:11. they shall pass *a.*, but thou endurest
  9:28. will appear a second time, sin done *a.*, to bring salvation
  10:25. not staying *a.* from our meetings
Jam. 1:21. *a.* then with all that is sordid
1 Pet. 2:1. *a.* with all malice and deceit, *a.* with all pretence

awe
Mat. 9:8. the people were filled with *a.* at the sight

27:54. they were filled with *a.*, and they said, 'Truly this man was a son of God
  28:8. they hurried away from the tomb in *a.* and great joy
Mark 6:20. Herod went in *a.* of John
  9:15. as soon as they saw Jesus the whole crowd were overcome with *a.*
  10:32. Jesus leading the way; and the disciples were filled with *a.*
Luke 1:65. all the neighbours were struck with *a.*
  5:26. filled with *a.* they said, 'You would never believe the things we have seen today
  7:16. Jesus gave him back to his mother. Deep *a.* fell upon them all
  9:43. they were all struck with *a.* at the majesty of God
Acts 2:43. a sense of *a.* was everywhere
  5:11. a great *a.* fell upon the whole church
Heb. 12:28. so worship him as he would be worshipped, with reverence and *a.*
1 Pet. 1:17. you must stand in *a.* of him while you live out your time on earth

awestruck
Mark 4:41. they were *a.* and said to one another, 'Who can this be
Acts 5:5. he dropped dead; and all the others who heard were *a.*
  19:17. they were all *a.*, and the name of the Lord Jesus gained in honour

awoke
Luke 9:32. when they *a.*, they saw his glory
2 Cor. 7:11. how your longing for me *a.*

B

babble-ing
Mat. 6:7. 'In your prayers do not go *b.* on like the heathen

babes, babies
Luke 18:15. they even brought *b.* for him to touch
1 Cor. 14:20. be as innocent of evil as *b.*

back-s
Mat. 2:12. warned in a dream not to go *b.* to Herod
  5:24. make your peace with your brother, and only then come *b.* and offer your gift

5:42. do not turn your *b.* on a man who wants to borrow
  7:2. whatever measure you deal out to others will be dealt *b.* to you
  12:44. 'I will go *b.* to the home I left
  16:26. what can he give that will buy that self *b.*
  25:27. I should have got it *b.* with interest
Mark 8:24. the man's sight began to come *b.*
  8:37. what can he give to buy that self *b.*

Mark 9:25. 'I command you, come out of him and never go *b*.

10:51. I want my sight *b*.

11:3. 'Our Master needs it, and will send it *b*. here without delay

12:23. at the resurrection, when they come *b*. to life

15:13. they shouted *b*., 'Crucify him

16:4. the stone, huge as it was, had been rolled *b*. already

Luke 1:16. he will bring *b*. many Israelites to the Lord their God

7:15. Jesus gave him *b*. to his mother

8:39. 'Go *b*. home,' he said, 'and tell them everything that God has done for you

9:8 ⎱that one of the old prophets
9:19 ⎰had come *b*. to life

9:42. cured the boy, and gave him *b*. to his father

10:35. if you spend any more, I will repay you on my way *b*.

15:24. this son of mine was dead and has come *b*. to life

15:27. he has him *b*. safe and sound

15:32. your brother here was dead and has come *b*. to life

17:18. could none be found to come *b*. and give praise to God

18:41. Sir, I want my sight *b*.

18:42. Jesus said to him, 'Have *b*. your sight

19:15. *b*. he came as king

23:26. put the cross on his *b*., and made him walk behind Jesus

John 13:3. he had come from God and was going *b*. to God

13:25. that disciple, as he reclined, leaned *b*. close to Jesus

21:20. the one who at supper had leaned *b*. close to him

Acts 21:21. you teach all the Jews in the gentile world to turn their *b*. on Moses

Rom. 8:15. not a spirit of slavery leading you *b*. into a life of fear

9:20.' Who are you, sir, to answer God *b*.

12:17. never pay *b*. evil for evil

1 Cor. 15:34. come *b*. to a sober and upright life

1 Thess. 5:15. see to it that no one pays *b*. wrong for wrong

Tit. 1:14. men who turn their *b*. upon the truth

2:9. comply with their demands without answering *b*.

Heb. 7:21. 'The Lord has sworn and will not go *b*. on his word

11:19. from the dead, he did, in a sense, receive him *b*.

Jam. 5:19. stray from the truth and another succeed in bringing him *b*.

5:20. any man who brings a sinner *b*. from his crooked ways

2 Pet. 2:21. better never to have known the right way, than, having known it, to turn *b*.

bad

Mat. 5:45. your heavenly Father, who makes his sun rise on good and *b*. alike

6:23. if the eyes are *b*., your whole body will be in darkness

7:11. if you, then, *b*. as you are, know how to give your children what is good

7:17. a poor tree *b*. fruit

7:18. a good tree cannot bear *b*. fruit

9:10. many *b*. characters—tax-gatherers and others—were seated with him

12:33. or make the tree *b*. and its fruit *b*.

17:15. he is an epileptic and has *b*. fits

21:41. 'He will bring those *b*. men to a *b*. end

24:48. if he is a *b*. servant and says to himself

Mark 2:15. many *b*. characters—tax-gatherers and others—were seated with him

2:16. Pharisees noticed him eating in this *b*. company

Luke 11:13. if you, then, *b*. as you are, know how to give your children what is good

11:34. when the eyes are *b*., you are in darkness

15:1. *b*. characters were all crowding in to listen to him

16:25. all the *b*. to Lazarus

John 3:20. *b*. men all hate the light

Acts 8:20. 'May you come to a *b*. end, for thinking God's gift is for sale

Rom. 14:20. anything is *b*. for the man who by his eating causes another to fall

1 Cor. 11:5. it is as *b*. as if her head were shaved

15:33. '*b*. company is the ruin of a good character

Eph. 4:29. no *b*. language must pass your lips

4:31. have done with spite and passion, all angry shouting and cursing, and *b*. feeling

1 Thess. 5:22. avoid the *b*. of whatever kind

2 Tim. 3:13. wicked men and charlatans will make progress from *b*. to worse

3 John 11. do not imitate *b*. examples

bade

Acts 21:6. *b*. each other goodbye

bag-s
Mat. 25:15. five *b*. of gold
   25:16. five *b*.
   25:17. two *b*.
   25:18. one *b*. of gold
   25:20. five *b*. of gold
   25:22. two *b*.
   25:24. one *b*.
   25:28. take the *b*. of gold from him, and give it to the one with the ten *b*.

baggage
Acts 21:15. we packed our *b*. and took the road up to Jerusalem

bailiff
Luke 16:1. there was a rich man who had a *b*.
   16:3. the *b*. said to himself, 'What am I to do now
   16:8. the master applauded the dishonest *b*. for acting so astutely

bait
2 Pet. 2:18. make of sensual lusts and debauchery a *b*. to catch

bake-ing
1 Cor. 5:7. purge it out, and then you will be bread of a new *b*.

baker
Mat. 16:12. on their guard, not against the *b*. leaven of the Pharisees and Sadducees, but against their teaching

balance-d
2 Thess. 1:6. it is surely just that God should *b*. the account
Jam. 1:4. you will go on to complete a *b*. character

ban-ned
Luke 6:22. *b*. your very name as infamous, because of the Son of Man
John 9:22. anyone who acknowledged Jesus as Messiah should be *b*. from the synagogue
   12:42. for fear of being *b*. from the synagogue
   16:2. they will *b*. you from the synagogue

band-s
John 11:44. the dead man came out, his hands and feet swathed in linen *b*.

bandage-d
Luke 10:34. moved to pity. He went up and *b*. his wounds

bandit-s
Mat. 26:55. Jesus spoke to the crowd. 'Do you take me for a *b*.
   27:38. two *b*. were crucified with him
   27:44. even the *b*. who were crucified with him taunted him

Mark 14:48. then Jesus spoke: 'Do you take me for a *b*.
   15:27. two *b*. were crucified with him
Luke 22:52. do you take me for a *b*.
John 18:40. Barabbas was a *b*.

banish-es
Luke 8:31. they begged him not to *b*. them to the Abyss
John 14:27. set your troubled hearts a rest, and *b*. your fears
Acts 7:43. I will *b*. you beyond Babylon
1 John 4:18. perfect love *b*. fear

bank-ing
Luke 12:54. when you see cloud *b*. up in the west, you say at once, 'It is going to rain

banquet
Mark 6:21. Herod on his birthday gave a *b*.
Luke 14:24. not one of those who were invited shall taste my *b*.

baptism
Mat. 3:16. after *b*. Jesus came up out of the water at once
Mark 16:16. those who believe it and receive *b*. will find salvation
Luke 3:21. during a general *b*. of the people
   7:30. the Pharisees and lawyers, who refused his *b*., had rejected God's purpose for themselves
John 3:23. people were constantly coming for *b*.
1 Cor. 12:13. we were all brought into one body by *b*.
   15:29. there are those who receive *b*. on behalf of the dead

Baptist
Mark 1:4. John the *B*. appeared in the wilderness

baptize-d
1 Tim. 3:6. he must not be a convert newly *b*.

bar-s
Gal. 4:17. what they really want is to *b*. the door to you
Heb. 11:36. had to face jeers and flogging, even fetters and prison *b*.

bare
Luke 2:35. the secret thoughts of many will be laid *b*.
1 Cor. 14:24. the secrets of his heart are laid *b*.
2 Pet. 3:10. the earth with all that is in it will be laid *b*.

barefoot
Luke 10:4. carry no purse or pack and travel *b*.

Luke 22:35. I sent you out *b.* without purse or pack

bare-headed
1 Cor. 11:5. brings shame on her head if she prays or prophesies *b.*
11:13. is it fitting for a woman to pray to God *b.*

barely
Acts 14:18. they *b.* managed to prevent the crowd from offering sacrifice to them
2 Pet. 2:18. those who have *b.* begun to escape from their heathen environment

Barnabas
Acts 14:3. for some time Paul and *B.* stayed on and spoke boldly

barracks
Acts 21:34. because of the hubbub, he ordered him to be taken into *b.*
21:37. just before Paul was taken into the *b.*
22:24. the commandant ordered him to be brought into the *b.*
23:10. pull him out of the crowd, and bring him into the *b.*
23:16. the son of Paul's sister heard of the ambush; he went to the *b.*
23:32. next day they returned to their *b.*

barren
Mat. 13:22. worldly cares and the false glamour of wealth choke it, and it proves *b.*
Mark 4:19. all kinds of evil desire come in and choke the word, and it proves *b.*
John 15:2. every *b.* branch of mine he cuts away
Eph. 5:11. take no part in the *b.* deeds of darkness
Jam. 2:20. faith divorced from deeds is *b.*

barter-ed
Rom. 1:25. they have *b.* away the true God for a false one

base-d
Mat. 26:59. tried to find some allegation against Jesus on which a death sentence could be *b.*
Rom. 8:13. by the Spirit you put to death all the *b.* pursuits of the body
9:11. *b.* not upon men's deeds but upon the call of God
9:30. a righteousness *b.* on faith
9:32. their efforts were not *b.* on faith
12:3. a sober estimate *b.* on the measure
Phil. 3:4. if anyone thinks to *b.* his claims on externals

Col. 2:8. *b.* on traditions of man-made teaching
1 Thess. 2:3. the appeal we make never springs from error or *b.* motive
1 Tim. 6:4. slander, *b.* suspicions, and endless wrangles

base-born
John 8:41. they said, 'We are not *b.*; God is our father

baseless
3 John 10. he lays *b.* and spiteful charges against us

basin
Luke 8:16. nobody lights a lamp and then covers it with a *b.*
John 13:5. he poured water into a *b.*, and began to wash his disciples' feet

basis
Heb. 7:11. the Levitical priesthood (for it is on this *b.* that the people were given the Law

bathe-d-ing
Luke 10:34. his wounds, *b.* them with oil and wine
John 13:10. a man who has *b.* needs no further washing

batten
Rev. 17:16. they will *b.* on her flesh and burn her to ashes

batter-ed
Acts 19:16. they ran out of the house stripped and *b.*

battle-s-ing
Mat. 14:24. the boat was already some furlongs from the shore, *b.* with a head-wind
24:6. you will hear the noise of *b.* near at hand and the news of *b.* far away
Mark 13:7. when you hear the noise of *b.* near at hand and the news of *b.* far away, do not be alarmed
Luke 14:31. what king will march to *b.* against another king, without first sitting down to consider
2 Cor. 10:3. weak men we may be, but it is not as such that we fight our *b.*
Rev. 19:19. their armies mustered to do *b.* with the Rider and his army

bay
Acts 27:39. they noticed a *b.* with a sandy beach

beach
Mark 4:1. there he sat, with the whole crowd on the *b.*
John 21:4. morning came, and there stood Jesus on the *b.*
Acts 21:5. we knelt down on the *b.* and prayed

Acts 27:39. they noticed a bay with a sandy *b.*
27:40. set the foresail to the wind, and let her drive to the *b.*

beam
Acts 21:3. we came in sight of Cyprus, and leaving it on our port *b.*

bear-s-ing
Mat. 1:21. she will *b.* a son; and you shall give him the name Jesus
1:23. 'The virgin will conceive and *b.* a son
3:8. prove your repentance by the fruit it *b.*
7:16. you will recognize them by the fruits they *b.*
7:18. a good tree cannot *b.* bad fruit
11:30. my yoke is good to *b.*, my load is light
13:23. who accordingly *b.* fruit, and yields a hundredfold
21:19. he said to the tree, 'You shall never *b.* fruit any more
23:36. this generation will *b.* the guilt of it all
Mark 4:20. they *b.* fruit thirtyfold
Luke 1:31. you shall conceive and *b.* a son
1:32. he will *b.* the title 'Son of the Most High
3:8. prove your repentance by the fruit it *b.*
20:24. a silver piece. 'Whose head does it *b.*
22:26. the highest among you must *b.* himself like the youngest
John 3:31. He who comes from heaven *b.* witness
12:24. if it dies, it *b.* a rich harvest
15:5. he who dwells in me, as I dwell in him, *b.* much fruit
15:16. I appointed you to go on and *b.* fruit
15:26. the Spirit of truth that issues from the Father—he will *b.* witness to me
Acts 1:8. when the Holy Spirit comes upon you; and you will *b.* witness for me
2:32. the Jesus we speak of has been raised by God, as we can all *b.* witness
10:39. we can *b.* witness to all that he did
15:14. to choose from among them a people to *b.* his name
16:18. she did this day after day, until Paul could *b.* it no longer
17:23. an altar *b.* the inscription 'To an Unknown God
20:24. *b.* my testimony to the gospel of God's grace

Rom. 2:17. you may *b.* the name of Jew
3:21. the Law and the prophets both *b.* witness to it
7:4. so that we may *b.* fruit for God
7:5. sinful passions evoked by the law worked in our bodies, to *b.* fruit for death
8:18. the sufferings we now endure *b.* no comparison with the splendour
1 Cor. 3:15. if it burns, he will have to *b.* the loss
9:23. the Gospel, to *b.* my part in proclaiming it
10:13. you have faced no trial beyond what man can *b.*
2 Cor. 1:8. the burden of it was far too heavy for us to *b.*
7:9. you bore the smart as God would have you *b.* it
11:19. how gladly you *b.* with fools
Gal. 4:24. the one *b.* children into slavery is the covenant
Eph. 1:15. the love you *b.* towards all God's people
Phil. 2:5. let your *b.* towards one another arise out of your life in Christ Jesus
2:8. *b.* the human likeness
Col. 1:4. the love you *b.* towards all God's people
1:6. everywhere it is growing and *b.* fruit
1:10. we pray that you may *b.* fruit in active goodness
1 Thess. 3:1. when we could *b.* it no longer, we decided to remain alone at Athens
3:5. when I could *b.* it no longer, I sent to find out about your faith
Tit. 2:3. the older women, similarly, should be reverent in their *b.*
Heb. 3:5. to *b.* witness to the words that God would speak
5:2. he is able to *b.* patiently with the ignorant
12:20. they could not *b.* the command, 'If even an animal touches the mountain
13:22. I beg you, brothers, *b.* with this exhortation
2 Pet. 3:15. *b.* in mind that our Lord's patience with us is our salvation
Jude 12. trees that in season *b.* no fruit
Rev. 19:10. you and your brothers who *b.* their testimony . . . those who *b.* testimony to Jesus
22:4. they shall see him face to face, and *b.* his name on their foreheads

bearable
Mat. 10:15. on the day of judgement it will be more *b.* for the land of Sodom and Gomorrah
11:22. it will be more *b.*, I tell you, for

Tyre and Sidon on the day of judgement

Mat. 11:24. it will be more *b*., I tell you, for the land of Sodom

Luke 10:12. it will be more *b*. for Sodom on the great Day

 10:14. it will be more *b*. for Tyre and Sidon at the Judgement

bearer-s

Luke 7:14. laid his hand on the bier; and the *b*. halted

beast-s

Mat. 21:5. riding on the foal of a *b*. of burden

 22:4. I have had my bullocks and fatted *b*. slaughtered

2 Pet. 2:16. the dumb *b*. spoke with a human voice

beat-en-ing

Mat. 26:67. they spat in his face and *b*. him with their fists

 27:30. used the cane to *b*. him

Mark 12:4. another servant, whom they *b*. about the head

 12:5. they *b*. some, and killed others

 15:19. they *b*. him about the head with a cane

Luke 10:30. robbers, who stripped him, *b*. him

 12:48. one who did not know them and earned a *b*. will be flogged less severely

 18:13. *b*. upon his breast, saying, 'O God, have mercy on me

 22:63. they *b*. him, they blindfolded him

 23:48. when they saw what had happened, went home *b*. their breasts

Acts 16:23. after giving them a severe *b*. they flung them into prison

 18:17. they gave him a *b*. in full view of the bench

1 Pet. 2:20. when you have done wrong and are *b*. for it

Rev. 7:16. the sun shall not *b*. on them nor any scorching heat

beauty

1 Pet. 3:3. your *b*. should reside, not in outward adornment

became

Mat. 9:26. this story *b*. the talk of all the country round

 17:2. his clothes *b*. white as the light

 28:15. this story *b*. widely known

Luke 1:65. in the uplands of Judaea the whole story *b*. common talk

 9:29. the appearance of his face changed and his clothes *b*. dazzling white

 23:12. that same day Herod and Pilate *b*. friends

John 1:14. the Word *b*. flesh

 4:41. many more *b*. believers because of what they heard

 9:28. then they *b*. abusive

 21:23. that saying of Jesus *b*. current in the brotherhood

Acts 4:4. many of those who had heard the message *b*. believers

 11:21. a great many *b*. believers

 13:12. when the Governor saw what had happened he *b*. a believer

 13:48. those who were marked out for eternal life *b*. believers

 14:1. a large body both of Jews and Greeks *b*. believers

 17:12. many of them therefore *b*. believers

 18:8. Crispus, who held office in the synagogue, now *b*. a believer

 19:17. this *b*. known to everybody in Ephesus

 24:25. Felix *b*. alarmed

Rom. 15:8. Christ *b*. a servant of the Jewish people

1 Cor. 15:45. the first man Adam *b*. an animate being

Eph. 1:13. and had believed it, *b*. incorporate in Christ

Col. 1:24. the church. I *b*. its servant

Jude 3. it *b*. urgently necessary to write at once

because

Mat. 8:13. *b*. of your faith, so let it be

 10:41. whoever receives a good man *b*. he is a good man will be given a good man's reward

 10:42. a cup of cold water to one of these little ones, *b*. he is a disciple of mine

 22:29. you are mistaken, *b*. you know neither the scriptures nor the power of God

 24:44. hold yourselves ready, therefore, *b*. the Son of Man will come

Mark 2:4. *b*. of the crowd they could not get him near

 10:5. it was *b*. you were so unteachable that he made this rule for you

Luke 4:41. forbade them to speak, *b*. they knew that he was the Messiah

 6:19. trying to touch him, *b*. power went out from him

 6:22. ban your very name as infamous, *b*. of the Son of Man

 6:48. the river burst upon that house, but could not shift it, *b*. it had been soundly built

 8:30. this was *b*. so many devils had taken possession of him

 8:42. he begged him to come to his house, *b*. he had an only daughter

Luke 9:53. the villagers would not have him *b*. he was making for Jerusalem

19:48. but found they were helpless, *b*. the people all hung upon his words

20:36. they are sons of God, *b*. they share in the resurrection

21:15. *b*. I myself will give you power of utterance

John 4:39. many Samaritans of that town came to believe in him *b*. of the woman's testimony

4:45. the Galileans gave him a welcome, *b*. they had seen all that he did

5:28. *b*. the time is coming when all who are in the grave shall hear his voice

6:57. I live *b*. of the Father, so he who eats me shall live *b*. of me

7:8. I am not going up to this festival *b*. the right time for me has not yet come

8:20. no one arrested him, *b*. his hour had not yet come

8:43. it is *b*. my revelation is beyond your grasp

10:4. the sheep follow, *b*. they know his voice

10:12. abandons the sheep and runs away, *b*. he is no shepherd

12:41. Isaiah said this *b*. he saw his glory

13:11. he added the words 'not every one of you' *b*. he knew who was going to betray him

Acts 9:26. all afraid of him *b*. they did not believe that he was really a convert

16:6. *b*. they were prevented by the Holy Spirit

21:35. carried by the soldiers *b*. of the violence of the mob

22:15. hear his very voice, *b*. you are to be his witness

Rom. 1:8. *b*. all over the world they are telling the story of your faith

1:25. *b*. they have bartered away the true God for a false one

2:24. *b*. of you the name of God is dishonoured

3:25. *b*. in his forbearance he had overlooked the sins of the past

5:3. *b*. we know that suffering trains us to endure

10:12. there is no distinction between Jew and Greek, *b*. the same Lord is Lord of all

1 Cor. 10:17. *b*. there is one loaf, we, many as we are, are one body

2 Cor. 3:14. *b*. only in Christ is the old covenant abrogated

9:14. their hearts will go out to you *b*.

of the richness of the grace which God has imparted

Gal. 3:5. is it *b*. you keep the law, or is it *b*. you have faith in the gospel message

Eph. 5:29. how Christ treats the church, *b*. it is his body

Phil. 1:5. my prayers are always joyful, *b*. of the part you have taken in the work of the Gospel

1:19. *b*. you are praying for me

Col. 2:13. although you were dead *b*. of your sins and *b*. you were morally uncircumcised, he has made you alive with Christ

2 Thess. 1:3. *b*. your faith increases mightily

1:4. *b*. your faith remains so steadfast

Tit. 3:5. *b*. he was merciful, he saved us

Heb. 4:2. the message they heard did no good, *b*. they brought no admixture of faith

5:7. *b*. of his humble submission his prayer was heard

Jam. 4:2. you do not get what you want, *b*. you do not pray for it

1 Pet. 1:5. *b*. you put your faith in God, are under the protection of his power

2 Pet. 3:9. he is very patient with you, *b*. it is not his will for any to be lost

Rev. 1:9. I was on the island called Patmos *b*. I had preached God's word

4:11. to receive glory and honour and power, *b*. thou didst create all things

18:11. the merchants of the earth also will weep and mourn for her, *b*. no one any longer buys their cargoes

becloud-ed

Eph. 4:18. their wits are *b*., they are strangers to the life that is in God

become-s-ing

Mat. 4:3. tell these stones to *b*. bread

5:13. if salt *b*. tasteless, how is its saltness to be restored

13:32. it *b*. a tree, big enough for the birds to come and roost

13:52. a teacher of the law has *b*. a learner in the kingdom of heaven

19:5. the two shall *b*. one flesh

19:27. here are we who left everything to *b*. your followers

27:57. a man of means, and had himself b. a disciple of Jesus

Mark 10:8. the two shall *b*. one flesh

10:28. we here' he said, 'have left everything to *b*. your followers

Luke 1:66. what will this child *b*.

4:3. tell this stone to *b*. bread

8:17. there is nothing hidden that will not *b*. public

Luke 14:34. if salt itself *b.* tasteless, what will you use to season it

18:28. here are we who gave up our belongings to *b.* your followers

John 1:7. that all might *b.* believers through him

8:33. what do you mean by saying, 'You will *b.* free men

9:27. do you also want to *b.* his disciples

12:36. trust to the light, that you may *b.* men of light

Acts 5:24. the chief priests were wondering what could have *b.* of them

15:5. some of the Pharisaic party who had *b.* believers

18:27. those who had by God's grace *b.* believers

19:18. many of those who had *b.* believers came and openly confessed

26:29. might *b.* what I am apart from these chains

Rom. 6:5. if we have *b.* incorporate with him in a death like his

7:4. have died to the law by *b.* identified with the body of Christ

7:7. except through law I should never have *b.* acquainted with sin

9:29. we should have *b.* like Sodom

14:16. a good thing must not *b.* an occasion for slanderous talk

1 Cor. 5:6. your self-satisfaction ill *b.* you

6:16. Scripture says, 'The pair shall *b.* one flesh

7:23. you were bought at a price; do not *b.* slaves

10:20. I will not have you *b.* partners with demons

15:45. the last Adam has *b.* a life-giving spirit

2 Cor. 8:9. through his poverty you might *b.* rich

Gal. 3:13. Christ bought us freedom from the curse of the law by *b.* for our sake an accursed thing

Eph. 5:31. the two shall *b.* a single body

Phil. 1:13. my imprisonment in Christ's cause has *b.* common knowledge

Col. 1:23. I, Paul, have *b.* its minister

1 Thess. 1:7. you have *b.* a model for all believers

1 Tim. 2:9. women again must dress in *b.* manner

Philem. 10. appeal to you about my child, whose father I have *b.* in this prison

Heb. 3:14. we have *b.* Christ's partners

4:3. we who have *b.* believers

5:5. the glory of *b.* high priest

6:12. we want you not to *b.* lazy

6:20. having *b.* a high priest for ever in the succession of Melchisedek

7:15. the argument *b.* still clearer

Jam. 3:1. my brothers, not many of you should *b.* teachers

1 Pet. 2:5. *b.* a holy priesthood, to offer spiritual sacrifices

2:7. the stone which the builders rejected has *b.* not only the cornerstone

3:6. her children you have now *b.* if you do good

4:18. what will *b.* of the impious and sinful

bed

Mat. 8:14. found Peter's mother-in-law in bed with fever

Mark 1:30. Simon's mother-in-law was ill in *b.* with fever

4:27. he goes to *b.* at night and gets up in the morning, and the seed sprouts

7:30. when she returned home, she found the child lying in *b.*

Luke 5:19. let him down through the tiling, *b.* and all

5:24. stand up, take your *b.,* and go home

5:25. took up the *b.* he had been lying on, and went home

Acts 28:8. this man's father was in *b.* suffering from recurrent bouts of fever

Jam. 5:15. the Lord will raise him from his *b.*

bedizened

Rev. 17:4. the woman was clothed in purple and scarlet and *b.* with gold

18:16. alas for the great city, that was clothed in fine linen and purple and scarlet, *b.* with gold

bed-ridden

Acts 9:33. Aeneas, who had been *b.* with paralysis for eight years

befit-s

John 1:14. such glory as *b.* the Father's only Son

Rom. 13:13. let us behave with decency as *b.* the day

Eph. 5:3. must not be so much as mentioned among you as *b.* the people of God

1 Tim. 2:10. with good deeds, as *b.* women who claim to be religious

before

Mat. 6:33. set your mind on God's kingdom and his justice *b.* everything else

9:18. there came a president of the synagogue who bowed low before him

10:18. you will be brought *b.* governors and kings

Mat. 12:45. in the end the man's plight
is worse than *b*.

13:24. here is another parable that he
put *b*. them

15:2. they do not wash their hands *b*.
meals

16:28. who will not taste death *b*. they
have seen the Son of Man coming

17:14. a man came up to Jesus, fell
on his knees *b*. him

20:20. the mother of Zebedee's sons
then came *b*. him

26:44. he prayed the third time, using
the same words as *b*.

28:17. when they saw him, they fell
prostrate *b*. him

Mark 1:40. a leper, who knelt *b*. him
begging his help

10:17. a stranger ran up, and, kneeling
b. him, asked

13:10. *b*. the end the Gospel must be
proclaimed to all nations

Luke 2:9. suddenly there stood *b*. them
an angel

22:66. he was brought *b*. their
Council

24:26. was the Messiah not bound to
suffer thus *b*. entering upon his
glory

John 4:49. the officer pleaded with him,
'Sir, come down *b*. my boy dies

9:38. 'Lord, I believe,' he said, and
bowed *b*. him

13:38. *b*. the cock crows you will have
denied me three times

18:35. your own nation and their
chief priests have brought you *b*. me

Acts 4:7. they brought the apostles *b*.
the court

17:5. with the intention of bringing
Paul and Silas *b*. the town assembly

18:5. preaching, affirming *b*. the Jews
that the Messiah was Jesus

20:21. repentance *b*. God and trust in
our Lord Jesus

22:15. you are to be his witness *b*. the
world

Rom. 1:19. all that may be known of
God by men lies plain *b*. their eyes

1 Cor. 9:26. I run with a clear goal *b*. me

2 Cor. 5:11. with this fear of the Lord *b*.
our eyes

Gal. 3:11. no one is ever justified *b*. God
in terms of law

Col. 1:22. so that he may present you *b*.
himself as dedicated men

1 Thess. 2:19. when we stand *b*. our
Lord Jesus at his coming

2 Tim. 1:13. keep *b*. you an outline of
the sound teaching

4:1. *b*. God, and *b*. Christ Jesus who is
to judge men living and dead

Heb. 2:17. as their high priest *b*. God

4:1. we must have *b*. us the fear

9:24. to appear now *b*. God on our
behalf

12:22. you stand *b*. Mount Zion . . .
b. myriads of angels

Jam. 4:10. humble yourselves *b*. God

1 John 3:3. everyone who has this hope
b. him purifies himself

Jude 24. Jesus Christ our Lord, *b*. all
time, now, and for evermore

Rev. 4:1. *b*. my eyes was a door opened
in heaven

14:10. *b*. the holy angels and *b*. the
Lamb

16:18. a violent earthquake, like none
b. it in human history

beforehand

Mark 14:8. she is *b*. with anointing my
body for burial

Luke 21:14. make up your minds not to
prepare your defence *b*.

John 14:29. I have told you now, *b*., so
that when it happens you may have
faith

Rom. 1:2. this gospel God announced *b*.
in sacred scriptures

Gal. 3:8. declared the Gospel to
Abraham

beforehand

Eph. 1:9. his will and pleasure determined *b*. in Christ

beg-ged-ging

Mat. 8:31. the devils *b*. him: 'If you
drive us out, send us into that herd
of pigs.

8:34. they *b*. him to leave the district
and go

9:38. you must therefore *b*. the owner
to send labourers

14:36. he was *b*. to allow them simply
to touch the edge of his cloak

18:29. the man fell at his fellow-
servant's feet, and *b*. him

20:20. she bowed low and *b*. a favour

Mark 1:40. a leper, who knelt before
him *b*. his help

5:10. he *b*. hard that Jesus would not
send them out of the country

5:12. the spirits *b*. him, 'Send us
among the pigs

5:17. they *b*. Jesus to leave the district

5:18. the man who had been possessed
b. to go with him

5:23. I *b*. you to come and lay your
hands on her

6:56. *b*. him to let them simply touch
the edge of his cloak

7:26. she *b*. him to drive the spirit out
of her daughter

8:22. brought a blind man to Jesus
and *b*. him to touch him

Luke 5:12. seeing Jesus, he bowed to
the ground and *b*. his help

Luke 8:31. they *b*. him not to banish them to the Abyss

8:32. the spirits *b*. him to let them go into these pigs

8:38. *b*. leave to go with him

8:41. he *b*. him to come to his house

10:2. you must therefore *b*. the owner to send labourers

John 4:47. *b*. him to go down and cure his son

9:8. those who were accustomed to see him *b*. said, 'Is not this the man who used to sit and *b*.

Acts 3:2. by the gate of the temple called 'Beautiful Gate,' to *b*. from people

3:10. they recognized him as the man who used to sit *b*.

3:14. you *b*. as a favour the release of a murderer

16:15. I *b*. you to come and stay in my house

21:12. we and the local people *b*. and implored Paul to abandon his visit

26:3. I *b*. you to give me a patient hearing

27:34. I *b*. you to have something to eat

2 Cor. 8:4. they *b*. us most insistently

10:2. spare me, I *b*. you, the necessity of such bravery

12:8. three times I *b*. the Lord to rid me of it

12:18. I *b*. Titus to visit you

Gal. 4:12. put yourselves in my place, my brothers, I *b*. you

Eph. 3:13. I *b*. you, then, not to lose heart over my sufferings

Phil. 4:2. I *b*. Euodia, and I beg Syntyche, to agree together

1 Thess. 4:1. we have one thing to *b*. and pray of you . . . live to please God . . . we *b*. you to do so yet more thoroughly

5:12. we *b*. you, brothers, to acknowledge those who are working so hard among you

2 Thess. 2:1. I *b*. you, do not suddenly lose your heads

Heb. 12:19. the oracular voice, which they heard, and *b*. to hear no more

13:22. I *b*. you, brothers, bear with this exhortation

1 Pet. 2:11. I *b*. you, as aliens in a foreign land, to abstain from the lusts of the flesh

began

Mat. 5:2. when his disciples had gathered round him, he *b*. to address them

13:26. the corn sprouted and *b*. to fill out

16:7. they *b*. to say among themselves

16:22. Peter took him by the arm and *b*. to rebuke him

19:8. it was not like that when all *b*.

23:32. go on then, finish off what your fathers *b*.

26:7. as he sat at table she *b*. to pour it over his head

26:16. he *b*. to look for a good opportunity to betray him

Mark 1:21. he went to synagogue and *b*. to teach

1:27. and *b*. to ask one another, 'What is this

3:6. the Pharisees, on leaving the synagogue, *b*. plotting against him

8:15. he *b*. to warn them

8:24. the man's sight *b*. to come back

8:32. Peter took him by the arm and *b*. to rebuke him

12:12. they *b*. to look for a way to arrest him

14:11. he *b*. to look for a good opportunity to betray him

Luke 1:64. his lips and tongue were freed and he *b*. to speak

6:20. turning to his disciples he *b*. to speak

8:23. they *b*. to ship water and were in grave danger

11:14. the dumb man *b*. to speak

13:13. at once she straightened up and *b*. to praise God

19:28. with that Jesus went forward and *b*. the ascent to Jerusalem

22:6. *b*. to look out for an opportunity to betray him

22:41. withdrew from them about a stone's throw, knelt down, and *b*. to pray

24:27. then he *b*. with Moses and all the prophets

John 1:1. when all things *b*., the Word already was

5:9. the man recovered instantly, took up his stretcher, and *b*. to walk

6:41. at this the Jews *b*. to murmur disapprovingly

7:14. Jesus went up to the temple and *b*. to teach

7:25. people of Jerusalem *b*. to say

17:5. the glory which I had with thee before the world *b*.

17:24. thou didst love me before the world *b*.

Acts 4:7. they brought the apostles before the court and *b*. the examination

4:13. they *b*. to wonder, then recognized them as former companions of Jesus

5:27. the High Priest *b*. his examination

6:8. Stephen, who was full of grace and power, *b*. to work great miracles

8:5. Philip came down to a city in

Samaria and *b*. proclaiming the Messiah

Acts 8:35. then Philip *b*. Starting from this passage

10:34. Peter *b*. 'I now see how true it is that God has no favourites

11:4. Peter *b*. by laying before them the facts

11:20. when they arrived at Antioch, *b*. to speak to pagans

13:16. Paul rose, made a gesture with his hand, and *b*.

15:1. certain persons who had come down from Judaea *b*. to teach the brotherhood

22:4. so I *b*. to persecute this movement

22:22. they *b*. shouting, 'Down with him

24:10. the Governor motioned to Paul to speak, and he *b*. his reply

26:1. Paul stretched out his hand and *b*. his defence

27:7. we *b*. to sail under the lee of Crete

27:18. they *b*. to lighten the ship

27:20. our last hopes of coming through alive *b*. to fade

28:25. without reaching any agreement among themselves they *b*. to disperse

Rom. 1:20. his everlasting power and deity, have been visible, ever since the world *b*.

Gal. 2:12. when they came he drew back and *b*. to hold aloof

2 Pet. 3:4. everything continues exactly as it has always been since the world *b*.

beggar

Mark 10:46. a blind *b*., was seated at the roadside

begin-s-ning

Mat. 24:8. with all these things the birth-pangs of the new age *b*.

24:49. *b*. to bully the other servants

Mark 1:1. Here *b*. the Gospel of Jesus Christ

13:8. with these things the birth-pangs of the new age *b*.

Luke 2:44. only then did they *b*. looking for him among their friends

12:11. do not *b*. worrying about how you will conduct your defence

14:9. you will look foolish as you *b*. to take the lowest place

23:54. it was Friday, and the Sabbath was about to *b*.

24:47. *b*. from Jerusalem

Acts 1:1. I wrote of all that Jesus did and taught from the *b*.

8:1. this was the *b*. of a time of violent persecution

26:4. the life I led from the *b*. among my people

Rom. 1:8. let me *b*. by thanking my God

1 Cor. 2:7. his secret purpose framed from the very *b*.

11:18. to *b*. with, I am told that when you meet as a congregation you fall into sharply divided groups

2 Cor. 3:1. are we *b*. all over again to produce our credentials

8:10. you made a good *b*. last year

2 Tim. 4:18. keep me safe until his heavenly reign *b*.

1 Pet. 2:24. that we might cease to live for sin and *b*. to live for righteousness

begone

Mat. 4:10. Jesus said, '*B*., Satan

8:32. '*b*.' he said. Then they came out and went into the pigs

Acts 13:41. see this, you scoffers, wonder, and *b*.

begun

Luke 11:38. noticed with surprise that he had not *b*. by washing before the meal

1 Cor. 5:7. indeed our Passover has *b*.

2 Cor. 5:17. the old order has gone, and a new order has already *b*.

2 Pet. 2:18. those who have barely *b*. to escape from their heathen environment

Rev. 17:12. ten kings who have not yet *b*. to reign

behalf

John 5:31. if I testify on my own *b*., that testimony does not hold good

1 Cor. 15:29. those who receive baptism on *b*. of the dead . . . what do they mean by being baptized on their *b*.

2 Cor. 8:16. I thank God that he has made Titus as keen on your *b*. as we are

9:14. they join in prayer on your *b*.

Eph. 5:2. Christ loved you, and gave himself up on your *b*.

Col. 1:7. a trusted worker for Christ on our *b*.

Heb. 6:20. Jesus has entered on our *b*. as forerunner

7:25. he is always living to plead on their *b*.

9:7. the blood which he offers on his own *b*. and for the people's sins

9:24. to appear now before God on our *b*.

1 Pet. 2:21. Christ suffered on your *b*.

behave-d-ing

Rom. 1:27. males *b*. indecently with males

1:32. those who *b*. like this deserve to die

Rom. 13:13. let us *b.* with decency as befits the day

1 Cor. 7:36. if a man has a partner in celibacy and feels that he is not *b.* properly towards her

Gal. 5:21. those who *b.* in such ways will never inherit the kingdom of God

Col. 2:20. why *b.* as though you were still living the life of the world

4:5. *b.* wisely towards those outside your own number

1 Pet. 2:20. when you have *b.* well and suffer for it

2 Pet. 1:10. if you *b.* so, you will never come to grief

behaviour

Rom. 13:3. a terror to crime, has no terrors for good *b.*

2 Cor. 6:6. we recommend ourselves by the innocence of our *b.*

Gal. 5:19. anyone can see the kind of *b.* that belongs to the lower nature

1 Thess. 2:10. just and blameless was our *b.* towards you

1 Tim. 1:10. all whose *b.* flouts the wholesome teaching

4:12. make yourself an example to believers in speech and *b.*

1 Pet. 1:15. like him, be holy in all your *b.*

2:12. let all your *b.* be such as even pagans can recognize as good

3:2. by observing the chaste and reverent *b.* of their wives

behead-ed

Acts 12:2. he *b.* James, the brother of John

behind

Mat. 16:24. if anyone wishes to be a follower of mine, he must leave self *b.*

21:9. the crowd that went ahead and the others that came *b.* raised the shout

Mark 8:34. anyone who wishes to be a follower of mine must leave self *b.*

10:32. those who followed *b.* were afraid

11:9. the others who came *b.* shouted

Luke 5:28. he rose to his feet, left everything *b.*, and followed him

9:23. if anyone wishes to be a follower of mine, he must leave self *b.*

12:3. what you have whispered *b.* closed doors will be shouted from the house-tops

23:26. put the cross on his back, and made him walk *b.* Jesus carrying it

John 7:9. with this answer he stayed *b.* in Galilee

20:19. when the disciples were together *b.* locked doors

Acts 17:14. Silas and Timothy both stayed *b.*

2 Tim. 4:20. Erastus stayed *b.* at Corinth

Rev. 6:8. its rider's name was Death, and Hades came close *b.*

being-s

John 1:10. the world, though it owed its *b.* to him, did not recognize him

8:42. God is the source of my *b.*, and from him I come

Acts 14:15. we are only human *b.*

Rom. 2:9. there will be grinding misery for every human *b.* who is an evil-doer

3:20. no human *b.* can be justified in the sight of God

7:25. I myself, subject to God's law as a rational *b.*

8:27. God who searches our inmost *b.* knows what the Spirit means

11:5. in just the same way at the present time a 'remnant' has come into *b.*

1 Cor. 8:6. one God, the Father, from whom all *b.* comes

15:45. the first man, Adam, became an animate *b.*

15:53. this perishable *b.* must be clothed with the imperishable

2 Cor. 6:18. the Lord, the Ruler of all *b.*

Gal. 1:16. without consulting any human *b.*

4:8. the slaves of *b.* which in their nature are no gods

Eph. 3:16. strength and power through his Spirit in your inner *b.*

3:19. may you attain to fullness of *b.*

Col. 1:19. in him the complete *b.* of God, by God's own choice, came to dwell

2:9. it is in Christ that the complete *b.* of the Godhead dwells

Heb. 1:3. the Son who is the effulgence of God's splendour and the stamp of God's very *b.*

9:11. Christ has come, high priest of good things already in *b.*

Jam. 3:2. the man who never says a wrong thing is a perfect character, able to bridle his whole *b.*

3:6. it pollutes our whole *b.*

1 Pet. 3:4. in the inmost centre of your *b.*

2 Pet. 1:4. come to share in the very *b.* of God

2:11. they are not afraid to insult celestial *b.*

Jude 8. to flout authority, and to insult celestial *b.*

Rev. 4:11. by thy will they were created, and have their *b.*

belief

Tit. 1:13. pull them up sharply, so that they may come to a sane *b.*

believe-d-ing
Mat. 9:29. as you have *b*., so let it be
23:36. *b*. me, this generation will bear
the guilt of it all
Luke 5:26. you would never *b*. the
things we have seen today
12:5. *b*. me, he is the one to fear
Acts 26:26. I do not *b*. that he can be
unaware of any of these facts
Rom. 11:1. has God rejected his people?
I cannot *b*. it
1 Cor. 7:40. that is my opinion, and I
b. that I too have the Spirit of God
Gal. 3:2. did you receive the Spirit by
keeping the law or by *b*. the gospel
message
2. Thess. 2:13. the truth that you *b*.
Jam. 2:1. *b*. as you do in our Lord Jesus
Christ

believer-s
Mark 16:17. *b*. will cast out devils in my
name
Luke 8:13. when they hear it, but have
no root; they are *b*. for a while
John 1:7. that all might become *b*.
through him
4:41. many more became *b*. because of
what they heard from his own lips
4:53. he and all his household became
b.
6:47. in truth, in very truth I tell you,
the *b*. possesses eternal life
7:5. even his brothers were not *b*. in
him
7:39. the Spirit which *b*. in him would
receive
Acts 4:4. many of those who had heard
the message became *b*.
4:32. the whole body of *b*. was united
in heart and soul
10:45. the *b*. who had come with
Peter, men of Jewish birth
11:21. the power of the Lord was with
them, and a great many became *b*.
13:12. when the Governor saw what
had happened he became a *b*.
13:48. those who were marked out for
eternal life became *b*.
14:1. a large body both of Jews and
Greeks became *b*.
15:5. some of the Pharisaic party who
had become *b*.
16:15. if you have judged me to be a
b. in the Lord
17:12. many of them therefore
became *b*.
18:8. Crispus, who held office in the
synagogue, now became a *b*. in the
Lord
18:27. those who had by God's grace
become *b*.
19:2. did you receive the Holy Spirit
when you became *b*.

19:18. many of those who had become
b. came and openly confessed
1 Cor. 14:22. these 'strange tongues' are
not intended as a sign for *b*.
2 Cor. 6:15. can Christ agree with
Belial, or a *b*. join hands with an
unbeliever
Eph. 1:1. to God's people at Ephesus, *b*.
incorporate in Christ Jesus
1 Thess. 1:7. thus you have become a
model for all *b*.
2:10. just and blameless was our
behaviour towards you who are *b*.
2 Thess. 1:10. he comes to be glorified
among his own and adored among
all *b*.
1 Tim. 4:3. God created them to be
enjoyed with thanksgiving by *b*.
4:10. the Saviour of all men—the
Saviour, above all, of *b*.
Tit. 1:6. the father of children who are
b.
Heb. 4:3. it is we, we who have become
b., who enter the rest

belong-s-ed-ing
Mat. 19:14. the kingdom of Heaven *b*.
to such as these
25:25. here it is—you have what *b*.
to you
Mark 10:14. the kingdom of God *b*. to
such as these
Luke 2:23. every first-born male shall
be deemed to *b*. to the Lord
5:3. he got into one of the boats,
which *b*. to Simon
16:12. if you have proved untrustworthy with what *b*. to another
18:16. the kingdom of God *b*. to such
as these
John 3:29. it is the bridegroom to whom
the bride *b*.
3:31. he who is from the earth *b*. to the
earth
8:23. you *b*. to this world below, I to
the world above
8:35. the slave has no permanent
standing in the household, but the
son *b*. to it for ever
10:16. other sheep of mine, not *b*. to
this fold
15:19. if you *b*. to the world, the
world would love its own; but
because you do not *b*. to the world
17:9. those whom thou hast given me,
because they *b*. to thee
18:36. my kingdom does not *b*. to
this world
Acts 1:25. apostleship which Judas
abandoned to go where he *b*.
21:11. thus will the Jews in Jerusalem
bind the man to whom this belt *b*.
23:9. doctors of the law *b*. to the
Pharisaic party

Acts 26:5. I *b.* to the strictest group in our religion

28:7. there were lands *b.* to the chief magistrate

Rom. 1:6. you who have heard the call and *b.* to Jesus Christ

14:8. whether therefore we live or die, we *b.* to the Lord

1 Cor. 2:6. not a wisdom *b.* to this passing age

2:14. a man who is unspiritual refuses what *b.* to the Spirit of God

3:22. everything *b.* to you . . . all of them *b.* to you

3:23. yet you *b.* to Christ

6:19. you do not *b.* to yourselves; you were bought at a price

7:14. the heathen husband now *b.* to God through his Christian wife

12:15. because I am not a hand, I do not *b.* to the body, it does *b.* to the body

12:16. because I am not an eye, I do not *b.* to the body, it does still *b.* to the body

15:23. afterwards, at his coming, those who *b.* to Christ

2 Cor. 1:21. if you and we *b.* to Christ, guaranteed as his and anointed

10:7. someone is convinced, is he, that he *b.* to Christ? Let him think again, and reflect that we *b.* to Christ

Gal. 3:29. if you thus *b.* to Christ, you are the 'issue' of Abraham

5:19. anyone can see the kind of behaviour that *b.* to the lower nature

5:24. those who *b.* to Christ Jesus have crucified the lower nature

Eph. 6:4. the instruction, and the correction, which *b.* to a Christian upbringing

Phil. 3:21. he will transfigure the body *b.* to our humble state

4:22. those who *b.* to the imperial establishment

Col. 3:5. put to death those parts of you which *b.* to the earth

1 Thess. 1:1. to the congregation of Thessalonians who *b.* to God

5:5. we do not *b.* to night or darkness

5:8. we, who *b.* to daylight

2 Thess. 1:1. to the congregation of Thessalonians who *b.* to God

2 Tim. 3:17. so that the man who *b.* to God may be efficient

Heb. 7:13. the One here spoken of *b.* to a different tribe

9:11. not made by men's hand that is, not *b.* to this created world

1 Pet. 5:14. peace to you all who *b.* to Christ

1 John 2:19. they went out from our company, but never really *b.* to us

3:19. we may know that we *b.* to the realm of truth

4:6. we *b.* to God, and a man who knows God listens to us, while he who does not *b.* to God refuses us a hearing

Rev. 19:1. victory and glory and power *b.* to our God

belongings

Luke 17:31. his *b.* in the house

18:28. we who gave up our *b.* to become your followers

beloved

Rev. 3:9. they shall know that you are my *b.* people

below

John 8:23. you belong to this world *b.*

Acts 2:19. signs on the earth *b.*

1 Cor. 6:7. you already fall *b.* your standard in going to law

belt-s

Mat. 3:4 ⎱ with a leather *b.* round his
Mark 1:6 ⎰ waist

6:8. no bread, no pack, no money in their *b.*

Luke 12:35 be ready for action, with *b.* fastened

12:37. he will buckle his *b.*, seat them at table, and come and wait on them

17:8. prepare my supper, buckle your *b.*, and then wait on me

John 21:18. when you were young you fastened your *b.*

Acts 12:8. the angel then said to him, 'Do up your *b.*

21:11. took Paul's *b.*, bound his own feet and hands . . . the man to whom this *b.* belongs

Eph. 6:14. buckle on the *b.* of truth

bench

Acts 18:17. they gave him a beating in full view of the *b.*

bend

Mat. 11:29. *b.* your necks to my yoke, and learn from me

beneath

Rom. 16:20. the God of peace will soon crush Satan *b.* your feet

2 Cor. 10:10. as a speaker he is *b.* contempt

Eph. 1:22. he put everything in subjection *b.* his feet

Heb. 2:8. thou didst put all things in subjection *b.* his feet

Jude 6. bound *b.* the darkness in everlasting chains

Rev. 12:1. a woman robed with the sun, *b.* her feet the moon

beneficent

2 Cor. 8:19. help in this *b.* work

benefit-s
Mat. 15:5. anything of mine which might have been used for your *b.*, is set apart for God
Mark 7:11. anything of mine which might have been used for your *b.* is Corban
Rom. 15:26. a common fund for the *b.* of the poor among God's people
1 Cor. 10:11. were recorded for our *b.* as a warning
14:19. I would rather speak five intelligible words, for the *b.* of others
Eph. 3:2. God has assigned the gift of his grace to me for your *b.*
Col. 1:25. the task assigned to me by God for your *b.*
1 Tim. 4:8. the training of the body does bring limited *b.*, but the *b.* of religion are without limit

benevolence
2 Cor. 9:9. his *b.* stands fast for ever
9:10. he will multiply it and swell the harvest of your *b.*

benighted
Rom. 2:19. you are confident that you are the one to guide the blind, to enlighten the *b.*

bent
Luke 13:11. she was *b.* double
19:47. the chief priests and lawyers were *b.* on making an end of him
John 8:6. Jesus *b.* down and wrote with his finger on the ground
8:8. once again he *b.* down
8:37. you are *b.* on killing me because my teaching makes no headway with you
8:40. you are *b.* on killing me, a man who told you the truth
Phil. 2:21. they are all *b.* on their own ends, not on the cause of Christ Jesus
Jam. 4:2. you want something which you cannot have, and so you are *b.* on murder

bereavement
Rev. 18:8. plagues shall strike her in a single day—pestilence, *b.*, famine

bereft
John 14:18. I will not leave you *b.*; I am coming back to you

beset
Heb. 5:2. he is able to bear patiently with the ignorant and erring, since he too is *b.* by weakness

beside
Mat. 13:1. Jesus went out and sat *b.* the lake

21:2. you will at once find a donkey tethered with her foal *b.* her
Mark 5:42. they were *b.* themselves with amazement
6:51. he climbed into the boat *b.* them
12:32. God is one and *b.* him there is no other
16:8. ran away from the tomb, *b.* themselves with terror
Luke 6:11. they were *b.* themselves with anger
9:32. they saw his glory and the two men who stood *b.* him
John 13:23. the disciple he loved, was reclining close *b.* Jesus
19:26. Jesus saw his mother, with the disciple whom he loved standing *b.* her
Acts 1:10. all at once there stood *b.* them two men in white
5:10. they carried her out and buried her *b.* her husband
8:31. he asked Philip to get in and sit *b.* him
22:13. stood *b.* me and said, 'Saul, my brother, recover your sight
Rev. 15:2. *b.* the sea of glass

besides
Mark 4:24. the measure you give is the measure you will receive, with something more *b.*
10:30. and persecutions *b.*
12:5. so he sent another, and that one they killed; and many more *b.*
Acts 17:34. a woman named Damaris, and others *b.*
2 Cor. 7:13. *b.* being encouraged ourselves we have also been delighted
1 Tim. 5:18. and *b.*, the workman earns his pay

best
Mat. 27:65. go and make it secure as *b.* you can
Luke 10:42. the part that Mary has chosen is *b.*
John 2:10. everyone serves the *b.* wine first . . . you have kept the *b.* wine till now
1 Cor. 7:26. this is the *b.* way for a man to live—it is *b.* for a man to be as he is
12:31. now I will show you the *b.* way of all
Col. 4:6. study how *b.* to talk with each person you meet
1 Thess. 5:15. aim at doing the *b.* you can for each other
Heb. 10:24. we ought to see how each of us may *b.* arouse others to love

bestow-s-ed
Luke 7:21. on many blind people he *b.* sight

Acts 8:18. the Spirit was *b.* through the laying on of the apostles' hands

Gal. 2:9. recognizing, then, the favour thus *b.* upon me

3:18. it was by promise that God *b.* it as a free gift

3:21. if a law had been given which had power to *b.* life

Eph. 1:3. who has *b.* on us in Christ every spiritual blessing

1:6. his gracious gift, so graciously *b.* on us in his Beloved

3:7. God's gift, *b.* unmerited on me in the working of his power

Phil. 2:9. *b.* on him the name above all names

1 Thess. 4:8. God who *b.* upon you his Holy Spirit

2 Pet. 1:3. his divine power has *b.* on us everything that makes for life

Bethany

Mat. 21:1. they reached *B.* at the Mount of Olives

John 1:28. this took place at *B.* beyond Jordan

betide

Mat. 18:7. woe *b.* the man through whom they come

Luke 17:1. causes of stumbling are bound to arise; but woe *b.* the man through whom they come

betray

Mat. 10:21. brother will *b.* brother to death

26:15. what will you give me to *b.* him to you

betrayer

Mark 14:42. my *b.* is upon us

Luke 22:21. my *b.* is here, his hand with mine on the table

John 18:2. the place was known to Judas, his *b.*

betroth-ed

Mat. 1:18. Mary his mother was *b.* to Joseph

Luke 1:27. a girl *b.* to a man named Joseph

2:5. with him went Mary who was *b.* to him

2 Cor. 11:2. I *b.* you to Christ, thinking to present you as a chaste virgin

better

Mat. 5:20. unless you show yourselves far *b.* men than the Pharisees

5:29. it is *b.* for you to lose one part of your body

19:10. if that is the position with husband and wife, it is *b.* to refrain from marriage

25:9. you had *b.* go to the shop and buy some

26:24 ⎫ it would be *b.* for that man
Mark 14:21 ⎭ if he had never been born

Luke 11:46. yes, you lawyers, it is no *b.* with you

22:36. whoever has a purse had *b.* take it with him

John 4:52. he asked them what time it was when he got *b.*

Acts 4:17. we had *b.* caution them never again to speak to anyone in this name

22:22. down with him! A scoundrel like that is *b.* dead

27:42. the soldiers thought they had *b.* kill the prisoners

Rom. 9:29. we should have become like Sodom, and no *b.* than Gomorrah

1 Cor. 7:40. she is *b.* off as she is; that is my opinion

13:3. even give my body to be burnt, but if I have no love, I am none the *b.*

14:5. but *b.* pleased for you to prophesy

14:28. if there is no interpreter, the speaker had *b.* not address the meeting at all

2 Cor. 2:11. Satan must not be allowed to get the *b.* of us

4:7. we are no *b.* than pots of earthenware to contain this treasure

Gal. 4:1. so long as the heir is a minor, he is no *b.* off than a slave

5:12. they had *b.* go the whole way and make eunuchs of themselves

1 Thess. 4:10. yet we appeal to you, brothers, to do *b.* still

1 Tim. 5:13. gossips and busybodies, speaking of things *b.* left unspoken

6:2. they must be all the *b.* servants

2 Tim. 1:18. the many services he rendered at Ephesus you know *b.* than I could tell you

4:15. you had *b.* be on your guard against him too

Philem. 21. I know that you will in fact do *b.* than I ask

Rev. 2:19. of late you have done even *b.* than at first

between

Mat. 14:25. *b.* three and six in the morning he came to them, walking over the lake

Mark 6:48. somewhere *b.* three and six in the morning, seeing them labouring at the oars

Luke 15:12. so he divided his estate *b.* them

John 19:18. they crucified him, and with him two others, one on the right, one on the left, and Jesus *b.* them

Acts 27:41. caught *b*. cross-currents and ran the ship aground
2 Cor. 6:16. can there be a compact *b*. the temple of God and the idols
Eph. 2:14. has broken down the enmity which stood like a dividing wall *b*. them
Heb. 5:14. their perceptions are trained by long use to discriminate *b*. good and evil
1 John 3:10. the distinction *b*. the children of God and the children of the devil
Rev. 9:13. I heard a voice coming from *b*. the horns of the golden altar

beware
Mat. 16:6 ⎱ *b*., be on your guard against
Mark 8:15 ⎰ the leaven of the Pharisees
1 Cor. 10:12. if you feel sure that you are standing firm, *b*.
2 John 8. *b*. of them, so that you may not lose all that we worked for

bewilder-ed
Acts 2:6. *b*. because each one heard the apostles talking in his own language
2 Cor. 4:8. *b*., we are never at our wits' end
1 Pet. 4:12. do not be *b*. by the fiery ordeal that is upon you

bewilderment
John 13:22. the disciples looked at one another in *b*.

beyond
Mat. 5:37. anything *b*. that comes from the devil
12:31 ⎱ no sin, no slander, is *b*.
Mark 3:28 ⎰ forgiveness for men
6:8. take nothing for the journey *b*. a stick
Luke 23:47. *b*. all doubt,' he said, 'this man was innocent
John 8:43. my revelation is *b*. your grasp
Acts 15:28. to lay no further burden upon you *b*. these essentials
19:36. since these facts are *b*. dispute
26:22. I assert nothing *b*. what was foretold by the prophets
1 Cor. 2:9. things *b*. our seeing, things *b*. our hearing, things *b*. our imagining, all prepared by God
3:11. there can be no other foundation *b*. that which is already laid
10:13. you have faced no trial *b*. what man can bear
2 Cor. 7:13. delighted *b*. everything by seeing how happy Titus is
9:15. thanks be to God for his gift *b*. words
10:13. there will be no attempt to boast *b*. our proper sphere

10:15. where others have laboured, work *b*. our proper sphere
12:6. I should not like anyone to form an estimate of me which goes *b*. the evidence of his own eyes
Eph. 3:19. the love of Christ, and to know it, though it is *b*. knowledge
Phil. 4:7. the peace of God, which is *b*. our utmost understanding
Col. 2:20. pass *b*. reach of the elemental spirits of the world
1 Tim. 3:16. great *b*. all question is the mystery of our religion
Heb. 7:7. *b*. all dispute the lesser is always blessed by the greater
9:3. *b*. the second curtain was the tent called the Most Holy Place
2 Pet. 1:4. he has given us his promises, great *b*. all price

bickering
Acts 18:15. some *b*. about words and names and your Jewish law

bid-den-ding
Mat. 2:9. they set out at the king's *b*.
6:25 ⎱ I *b*. you put away anxious
Luke 12:22 ⎰ thoughts about food
John 5:30. I judge as I am *b*., and my verdict is just

bide-ing
Luke 4:13. the devil departed, *b*. his time

big-ger
Mat. 9:16. the patch tears away from the coat, and leaves a *b*. hole
13:32. when it has grown it is *b*. than any garden plant; it becomes a tree *b*. enough for the birds to come and roost
17:20. if you have faith no *b*. even than a mustard seed
25:21, 23. I will now put you in charge of something *b*.
Mark 2:2. the space in front of the door was not *b*. enough to hold them
2:21. the new from the old, and leaves a *b*. hole
Luke 2:40. the child grew *b*. and strong
5:6. made a *b*. haul of fish
5:29. Levi held a *b*. reception in his house for Jesus
12:18. I will pull down my storehouses and build them *b*.
14:16. a man was giving a *b*. dinner party
17:6. if you had faith no *b*. even than a mustard-seed
John 21:11. dragged the net to land, full of *b*. fish
Gal. 6:11. you see these *b*. letters? I am now writing to you
2 Pet. 2:18. they utter *b*., empty words

Jude 16. *b*. words come rolling from their lips

bind-s
John 21:18. you will stretch out your arms, and a stranger will *b*. you fast
Col. 3:14. there must be love, to *b*. all together
1 John 2:6. whoever claims to be dwelling in him, *b*. himself to live as Christ lived

bird-s
Mat. 6:26. look at the *b*. of the air
Mark 13:4 / 4:3 { some seed fell along the footpath; and the *b*. came and ate it up
4:32. forms branches so large that the *b*. can settle in its shade
Luke 8:5. the *b*. ate it up
12:24. you are worth far more than the *b*.
13:19. the *b*. came to roost among its branches
Rev. 19:17. he cried aloud to all the *b*. flying in mid-heaven
19:21. all the *b*. gorged themselves on their flesh

birth
Mat. 1:16. Mary, who gave *b*. to Jesus called Messiah
2:1. after his *b*. astrologers from the east arrived in Jerusalem
24:8. with all these things the *b*.-pangs of the new age begin
Mark 13:8. with these things the *b*.-pangs of the new age begin
Luke 1:15. from his very *b*. he will be filled with the Holy Spirit
1:57. the time came for Elizabeth's child to be born, and she gave *b*. to a son
2:7. the time came for her child to be born, and she gave *b*. to a son
19:12. a man of noble *b*. went on a long journey
John 3:6. flesh can give *b*. only to flesh; it is spirit that gives *b*. to spirit
Acts 3:2. a man who had been a cripple from *b*.
4:36. Barnabas (which means 'Son of Exhortation') a Levite, by *b*. a Cypriot
10:45. the believers who had come with Peter, men of Jewish *b*.
11:2. those who were of Jewish *b*. raised the question with him
14:8. at Lystra sat a crippled man, lame from *b*.
18:24. a Jew named Apollos, an Alexandrian by *b*.
22:28. Paul said, 'But it was mine by *b*.
1 Cor. 15:8. this *b*. of mine was mon-

strous, for I had persecuted the church
Gal. 1:15. God, who had set me apart from *b*.
2:15. we ourselves are Jews by *b*.
Jam. 1:15. then lust conceives, and gives *b*. to sin
1:18. he gave us *b*. to be a kind of first fruits of his creatures
1 Pet. 1:3. who in his mercy gave us new *b*. into a living hope
Rev. 12:4. the woman who was about to give *b*.
12:5. she gave *b*. to a male child
12:13. he went in pursuit of the woman who had given *b*. to the male child

bishop-s
1 Tim. 3:10. no less than *b*., they must first undergo a scrutiny

bit-s
Rev. 2:27. smashing them to *b*. like earthenware

bitter
Acts 8:23. you are doomed to taste the *b*. fruit and wear the fetters of sin

black-est
2 Pet. 2:17. the place reserved for them is *b*. darkness
2 John 12. I do not care to put it down in *b*. and white
Jude 13. the place for ever reserved for them is *b*. darkness

blackmail
Luke 3:14. no bullying; no *b*.; make do with your pay

blame-d
Rom. 9:19. you will say, 'Then why does God *b*. a man
1 Cor. 10:30. why am I *b*. for eating food over which I have said grace
2 Cor. 6:8. praise and *b*., are alike our lot
7:3. I do not want to *b*. you
7:11. at every point you have cleared yourselves of *b*.
Phil. 1:10. on the Day of Christ you will be flawless and without *b*.
Jam. 5:9. do not *b*. your troubles on one another

blameless
1 Thess. 2:10. *b*. was our behaviour towards you

blast
Mat. 24:31. with a trumpet *b*. he will send out his angels
Heb. 12:19. the trumpet-*b*. and the oracular voice, which they heard

blaze-ing

Mat. 13:42. all whose deeds are evil, and these will be thrown into the *b.* furnace

13:50. separate the wicked from the good, and throw them into the *b.* furnace

20:12. who have sweated the whole day long in the *b.* sun

2 Cor. 11:29. if anyone is made to stumble, does my heart not *b.* with indignation

2 Thess. 1:7. Christ is revealed from heaven with his mighty angels in *b.* fire

Heb. 12:18. remember where you stand: not before the palpable, *b.* fire of Sinai

Rev. 8:8. what looked like a great *b.* mountain was hurled into the sea

bleacher

Mark 9:3. his clothes became dazzling white, with a whiteness no *b.* on earth could equal

blemish

Eph. 1:4. to be dedicated, to be without *b.* in his sight

Col. 1:22. that he may present you before himself as dedicated men, without *b.*

Heb. 9:14. he offered himself without *b.* to God, a spiritual and eternal sacrifice

blend

2 Cor. 1:18. the language in which we address you is not an ambiguous *b.* of Yes and No

1:19. was never a *b.* of Yes and No

blessing-s

Acts 13:34. I will give you the *b.* promised to David

16:36. now you may go free, and *b.* on your journey

Gal. 3:22. faith in Jesus Christ may be the ground on which the promised *b.* is given

Eph. 4:29. no bad language must pass your lips, but only what is good and helpful to the occasion, so that it brings a *b.*

Philem. 6. all the *b.* that our union with Christ brings

blew

Rev. 8:7. the first *b.* his trumpet; and there came hail

8:8. the second angel *b.* his trumpet

8:10. the third angel *b.* his trumpet

8:12. the fourth angel *b.* his trumpet

9:1. then the fifth angel *b.* his trumpet

9:13. the sixth angel then *b.* his trumpet

11:15. then the seventh angel *b.* his trumpet

blind-ed

Luke 6:42. when you are *b.* to the plank in your own

John 9:3. he was born *b.* that God's power might be displayed

Acts 9:9. he was *b.* for three days

22:11. I had been *b.* by the brilliance of that light

Rom. 11:8. he gave them *b.* eyes and deaf ears

1 John 2:11. the darkness has made him *b.*

blindfold-ed

Mark 14:65. *b.* him, and struck him with their fists

blindness

Mat. 23:19. what *b*! Which is the more important, the offering, or the altar

bloated

Rev. 18:3. merchants the world over have grown rich on her *b.* wealth

blood

Eph. 2:14. in his own body of flesh and *b.* has broken down the enmity

Col. 1:22. by Christ's death in his body of flesh and *b.* God has reconciled you to himself

blossom-ed

Phil. 4:10. after so long your care for me has now *b.* afresh

blot

2 Pet. 2:13. they are an ugly *b.* on your company

Jude 12. these men are a *b.* on your love-feasts

blow-s-ing

Mark 14:65. the High Priest's men set upon him with *b.*

John 6:18. a strong wind was *b.*

Rev. 8:6. the seven angels that held the seven trumpets prepared to *b.* them

8:13. when the trumpets sound which the three last angels must now *b.*

13:3. one of its heads appeared to have received a death-*b.*

blue

Rev. 9:17. they wore breastplates, fiery red, *b.*, and sulphur-yellow

board

Acts 27:31. unless these men stay on *b.* you can none of you come off safely

27:37. there were on *b.* two hundred and seventy-six of us

28:10. when we were leaving they put on *b.* provision for our needs

2 Thess. 3:8. we did not accept *b.* and

lodging from anyone without paying for it

boast-ing

Rom. 1:22. they *b.* of their wisdom
1 Cor. 9:15. no one shall make my *b.* an empty *b.*
2 Cor. 10:17. if a man must *b.*, let him *b.* of the Lord
   11:30. if *b.* there must be, I will *b.* of the things that show up my weakness
   12:1. I am obliged to *b.*
   12:5. about such a man as that I am ready to *b.*; but I will not *b.* on my own account
   12:6. if I should choose to *b.*, it would not be the *b.* of a fool
Gal. 6:13. they only want you to be circumcised in order to *b.*
   6:14. God forbid that I should *b.* of anything but the cross of our Lord Jesus Christ
2 Thess. 1:4. we *b.* about you ourselves among the congregations

boastful

1 Cor. 13:4. love is never *b.*

boat

the word '*b.*' frequently occurs in the Gospels

bodily

Rom. 7:23. I perceive that there is in my *b.* members a different law
   13:14. give no more thought to satisfying the *b.* appetites
1 Cor. 6:15. shall I then take from Christ his *b.* parts and make them over to a harlot
   7:28. those who marry will have pain and grief in this *b.* life
Gal. 2:20. my present *b.* life is lived by faith
   4:13. it was *b.* illness that originally led to my bringing you the Gospel
   6:12. those who want to make a fair outward and *b.* show who are trying to force circumcision upon you
Jam. 2:16. does nothing to supply their *b.* needs
   4:1. do they not spring from the aggressiveness of your *b.* desires
1 Pet. 3:21. baptism is not the washing away of *b.* pollution
   4:1. Christ endured *b.* suffering . . . when a man has thus endured *b.* suffering

body-ies

Mat. 27:62. the chief priests and the Pharisees came in a *b.* to Pilate
   27:64. his disciples may come, steal the *b.*

28:13. his disciples came by night and stole the *b.*
Mark 6:29. when John's disciples heard the news, they came and took his *b.*
   12:8. flung his *b.* out of the vineyard
John 7:23. giving health on the Sabbath to the whole of a man's *b.*
   12:12. the great *b.* of pilgrims who had come to the festival
Acts 4:32. the whole *b.* of believers
   5:6. covered his *b.*, then carried him out
   6:2. the whole *b.* of disciples
   6:5. this proposal proved acceptable to the whole *b.*
   9:26. he tried to join the *b.* of disciples
   9:37. they washed her *b.*
   14:1. a large *b.* both of Jews and Greeks became believers
   18:12. the Jews set upon Paul in a *b.*
   20:30. from your own *b.* there will be men coming forward who will distort the truth
   25:24. the whole *b.* of the Jews approached me
Rom. 6:13. yield your *b.* to him as implements for doing right
   6:19. you once yielded your *b.* to the service of impurity
   7:5. the sinful passions evoked by the law worked in our *b.*
1 Cor. 5:5. this man is to be consigned to Satan for the destruction of the *b.*
   15:46. the animal *b.* comes first, and then the spiritual
2 Cor. 4:11. that the life of Jesus also may be revealed in this mortal *b.* of ours
   5:2. in this present *b.* we do indeed groan
   5:4. we do not want to have the old *b.* stripped off. Rather our desire is to have the new *b.* put on over it
   7:5. there was still no relief for this poor *b.* of ours
   12:7. I was given a sharp pain in my *b.*
Gal. 4:14. you resisted any temptation to show scorn or disgust at the state of my poor *b.*
Eph. 2:14. in his own *b.* of flesh and blood has broken down the enmity
   4:25. all of us are the parts of one *b.*
   5:29. no one ever hated his own *b.*
   5:31. the two shall become a single *b.*
Phil. 1:22. what if my living on in the *b.* may serve some good purpose
   1:24. for your sake there is greater need for me to stay on in the *b.*
Col. 1:28. to present each one of you as a mature member of Christ's *b.*
   2:5. though absent in *b.*, I am with you in spirit

1 Thess. 4:4. each one of you must learn to gain mastery over his *b.*

1 Tim. 3:16. he who was manifested in the *b.*

4:8. the training of the *b.* does bring limited benefit

4:14. the laying on of the hands of the elders as a *b.*

Heb. 3:17. whose *b.* lay where they fell in the desert

1 Pet. 3:7. pay honour to the woman's *b.*

3:18. in the *b.* he was put to death

4:6. in the *b.* they received the sentence common to men

2 Pet. 1:13. I think it right to keep refreshing your memory so long as I still lodge in this *b.*

Jude 8. their dreams lead them to defile the *b.*

boldly

2 Cor. 3:12. with such a hope as this we speak out *b.*

Heb. 10:19. the blood of Jesus makes us free to enter *b.* into the sanctuary

bombast

Rev. 13:5. the beast was allowed to mouth *b.* and blasphemy

bond-ed

2 Cor. 3:6. a covenant expressed not in a written document, but in a spiritual *b.*

Eph. 2:21. in him the whole building is *b.* together

4:16. *b.* and knit together by every constituent joint

Col. 2:14. he has cancelled the *b.* which pledged us to the decrees of the law

Heb. 13:4. marriage is honourable; let us all keep it so, and the marriage-*b.* inviolate

bonfire

Acts 28:2. they lit a *b.* and made us all welcome

book

Rom. 9:25. as it says in the *B.* of Hosea

border-ing

John 11:54. left that region for the country *b.* on the desert

Acts 16:7. when they approached the Mysian *b.* they tried to enter Bithynia

borderlands

Luke 17:11. he was travelling through the *b.* of Samaria and Galilee

bore

Mat. 13:8. some of the seed fell into good soil, where it *b.* fruit

Mark 4:8. good soil, where it came up and grew, and *b.* fruit

Luke 23:29. happy are the barren, the wombs that never *b.* a child

Acts 1:21. one of those who *b.* us company all the while we had the Lord Jesus with us

1:23. Joseph, who was known as Barsabbas, and *b.* the added name of Justus

4:33. the apostles *b.* witness with great power

13:18. for some forty years he *b.* with their conduct in the desert

1 Cor. 15:15. we *b.* witness that he raised Christ to life

2 Cor. 7:9. you *b.* the smart as God would have you bear it

7:11. you *b.* your hurt in God's way

7:14. every word we ever addressed to you *b.* the mark of truth

Gal. 4:27. rejoice, O barren woman who never *b.* child

Eph. 2:4. God, rich in mercy, for the great love he *b.* us

Heb. 13:13. let us then go to him outside the camp, bearing the stigma that he *b.*

Jam. 5:18. down came the rain and the land *b.* crops once more

Rev. 6:9. slaughtered for God's word and for the testimony they *b.*

13:17. no one was allowed to buy or sell unless he *b.* this beast's mark

born

Mat. 1:25. had no intercourse with her until her son was *b.*

8:12. those who were *b.* to the kingdom will be driven out into the dark

Luke 1:14. many will be glad that he was *b.*

1:57. the time came for Elizabeth's child to be *b.*

2:6. while they were there the time came for her child to be *b.*

2:7. she gave birth to a son, her first-*b.*

2:23. every first-*b.* male shall be deemed to belong to the Lord

John 1:15, 30. before I was *b.*, he already was

8:58. I tell you, before Abraham was *b.*, I am

9:3. he was *b.* blind that God's power might be displayed

Acts 7:8. after Isaac was *b.*, he circumcised him

7:29. there two sons were *b.* to him

23:6. I am a Pharisee, a Pharisee *b.* and bred

Rom. 1:3. he was *b.* of David's stock

9:8. it is not those *b.* in the course of nature who are children of God; it is the children *b*. through God's promise

1 Cor. 1:26. few are powerful or highly *b*.

Gal. 2:14. you, a Jew *b*. and bred

4:4. God sent his own son, *b*. of a woman, born under the law

4:22. two sons, one by his slave and the other by his free-*b*. wife

Eph. 3:12. confidence *b*. of trust in him

Phil. 3:5. a Hebrew *b*. and bred

1 Tim. 1:2. Timothy his true-*b*. son in the faith

2 Tim. 2:8. Jesus Christ, risen from the dead, *b*. of David's line

Tit. 1:4. to Titus my true-*b*. son in the faith

1 Pet. 1:4. the inheritance to which we are *b*.

2 Pet. 2:12. beasts, *b*. in the course of nature to be caught and killed

Rev. 1:5. Jesus Christ, the faithful witness, the first-*b*. from the dead

borne

John 1:34. I saw it myself and I have *b*. witness

Acts 13:35. this is *b*. out by another passage

2 Cor. 7:10. the wound which is *b*. in God's way . . . the hurt which is *b*. in the world's way

1 John 5:9. the witness he has *b*. to his son

Rev. 1:2. John, who, in telling all that he saw, has *b*. witness

1:9. *b*. my testimony to Jesus

17:6. those who had *b*. their testimony to Jesus

both

Mat. 5:25. while you are *b*. on your way to court

17:27. it will meet the tax for us *b*.

18:9. than to keep *b*. eyes and be thrown into the fires of hell

23:20. to swear *b*. by the altar and by whatever lies on it

23:21. to swear *b*. by the sanctuary and by him who dwells there

25:9. there will never be enough for us *b*.

Mark 2:22. then wine and skins are *b*. lost

9:43. than to keep *b*. hands and go to hell

9:45. than to keep *b*. your feet and be thrown into hell

9:47. than to keep *b*. eyes and be thrown into hell

Acts 2:18. my slaves, *b*. men and women

5:9. why did you *b*. conspire to put the Spirit of the Lord to the test

Rom. 3:26. showing that he is *b*. himself just and justifies

3:30. he will therefore justify *b*.

11:9. *b*. stumbling-block and retribution

2 Cor. 8:10. *b*. in the work you did and in your willingness to undertake it

12:18. have we not *b*. been guided by the same Spirit

Eph. 6:9. remember you *b*. have the same Master in heaven

Col. 1:5. *b*. spring from the hope stored up for you in heaven

Tit. 1:9. so that he may be well able *b*. to move his hearers

Philem. 11. now useful indeed, *b*. to you and to me

20. we are *b*. in Christ

Jam. 3:11. does a fountain gush with *b*. fresh and brackish water

1 John 2:22. he is Antichrist, for he denies *b*. the Father and the Son

bother

Luke 11:7. do not *b*. me. The door is shut for the night

bottle

Mat. 26:7. a woman came to him with a small *b*. of fragrant oil

Mark 14:3. carrying a small *b*. of very costly perfume

bought

Mat. 13:44. sold everything he had, and *b*. that field

Gal. 3:13. Christ *b*. us freedom from the curse of the law

1 Pet. 1:18. no perishable stuff, like gold or silver, that *b*. your freedom

bound-s

Mat. 18:33. were you not *b*. to show your fellow-servant the same pity

23:16 ⎫
23:18 ⎭ he is *b*. by his oath

24:6. such things are *b*. to happen

24:31. from the farthest *b*. of heaven

Mark 7:37. their astonishment knew no *b*.

13:7. such things are *b*. to happen

13:27. from the farthest *b*. of earth to the farthest *b*. of heaven

Luke 2:49. did you not know that I was *b*. to be in my Father's house

17:1. causes of stumbling are *b*. to arise

21:9. these things are *b*. to happen first

24:26. was the Messiah not *b*. to suffer

24:44. everything written about me in the Law of Moses and in the prophets and psalms was *b*. to be fulfilled

Acts 1:16. the prophecy in Scripture was *b*. to come true

Acts 13:47. a means of salvation to earth's farthest *b*.

17:9. they *b*. over Jason and the others

21:2. there we found a ship *b*. for Phoenicia

27:2. we embarked in a ship of Adramyttium *b*. for ports

27:6. an Alexandrian vessel *b*. for Italy

Rom. 6:22. *b*. to the service of God

7:6. having died to that which held us *b*.

10:18. their words to the *b*. of the inhabited world

1 Cor. 9:2. if others do not accept me as an apostle, you at least are *b*. to do so

9:6. are Barnabas and I alone *b*. to work for our living

Eph. 5:28. men also are *b*. to love their wives

1 Thess. 3:4. we were *b*. to suffer hardship

Heb. 2:1. we are *b*. to pay all the more heed

5:3. he is *b*. to make sin-offerings for himself

7:16. owing his priesthood not to a system of earth-*b*. rules

Jam. 3:15. this is not the wisdom that comes from above; it is earth-*b*., sensual, demonic

1 John 3:16. we in our turn are *b*. to lay down our lives for our brothers

4:11. we in turn are *b*. to love one another

3 John 8. we are *b*. to support such men

Jude 6. *b*. beneath the darkness in everlasting chains

Rev. 13:10. by the sword he is *b*. to be killed

boundless

Gal. 1:14. my *b*. devotion to the traditions of my ancestors

bounty

Eph. 4:7. each of us has been given his gift, his due portion of Christ's *b*.

bout-s

Acts 28:8. suffering from recurrent *b*. of fever and dysentery

Gal. 5:21. drinking *b*., orgies, and the like

bow-s-ed

Mat. 2:11. saw the child with Mary his mother, and *b*. to the ground

8:2. a leper approached him, *b*. low, and said

9:18. a president of the synagogue, who *b*. low before him

20:20. she *b*. low and begged a favour

Luke 5:12. he *b*. to the ground and begged his help

John 9:38. Lord, I believe,' he said, and *b*. before him

Acts 10:25. Cornelius came to meet him, and *b*.

27:30. pretending they were going to lay out anchors from the *b*.

27:41. ran the ship aground, so that the *b*. stuck fast

bowels

Mat. 12:40. the Son of Man will be three days and three nights in the *b*. of the earth

bowl-s

Mat. 26:23. one who has dipped his hand into this *b*. with me will betray me

Mark 7:4. washing of cups and jugs and copper *b*.

14:20. who is dipping into the same *b*. with me

Rev. 5:8. they held golden *b*. full of incense

15:7. seven golden *b*. full of the wrath of God

16:1. pour out the seven *b*. of God's wrath

16:2. poured his *b*. on the earth

16:3. poured his *b*. on the sea

16:4. poured his *b*. on the rivers and springs

16:8. poured his *b*. on the sun

16:10. poured his *b*. on the throne of the beast

16:12. poured his *b*. on the great river Euphrates

16:17. poured his *b*. on the air

17:1 ⎱ one of the seven angels that
21:9 ⎰ held the seven *b*.

boxer

1 Cor. 9:26. I am like a *b*. who does not beat the air

boy-s

Mat. 8:6. a *b*. of mine lies at home paralysed

8:8. say the word and the *b*. will be cured

8:13. at that moment the *b*. recovered

17:18. Jesus then spoke sternly to the *b*.

21:15. heard the *b*. in the temple shouting

21:28. my *b*., go and work today in the vineyard

21:29. I will sir' the *b*. replied

Mark 9:20. so they brought the *b*. to him; and as soon as the spirit saw him it threw the *b*. into convulsions

9:24. I have faith,' cried the *b*. father

9:26. the *b*. looked like a corpse

Mark 10:20. I have kept all these since
I was a *b*.
Luke 2:43. the *b*. Jesus stayed behind in
Jerusalem
9:42. before the *b*. could reach him
the devil dashed him to the ground
and threw him into convulsions.
Jesus rebuked the unclean spirit,
cured the *b*.
15:31. my *b*.,' said the father, 'you
are always with me
18:21. I have kept all these since I was
a *b*.
John 4:49. Sir, come down before my *b*.
dies
4:51. your *b*. is going to live
6:9. there is a *b*. here who has five
barley loaves and two fishes
Acts 20:12. they took the *b*. away alive

brackish
Jam. 3:11. does a fountain gush with
both fresh and *b*. water

brag-ging
2 Cor. 11:17. I am not speaking here as
a Christian, but like a fool, if it
comes to *b*.
11:18. so many people *b*. of their
earthly distinctions
Jam. 4:16. you boast and *b*., and all
such boasting is wrong

braiding
1 Pet. 3:3. not in outward adornment—
the *b*. of the hair

brand-ed
Gal. 6:17. I bear the marks of Jesus
b. on my body
1 Tim. 4:2. whose own conscience is *b*.
with the devil's sign
Rev. 13:16. to be *b*. with a mark on his
right hand

bravado
2 Cor. 11:21. if there is to be *b*.

brave-ly-ry
Mark 15:43. *b*. went in to Pilate and
asked for the body of Jesus
Rom. 5:7. perhaps for a good man one
might actually *b*. death
2 Cor. 10:1. so *b*. when I am away
10:2. spare me, I beg you, the necessity
of such *b*.

brawler
Tit. 1:7. he must be no drinker, no *b*.

breach
Rom. 4:15. where there is no law there
can be no *b*. of law

bread
Mark 8:6. he broke the *b*. and gave it to
his disciples to distribute
John 13:26. it is the man to whom I give
this piece of *b*.

13:30. Judas, then, received the *b*. and
went out
1 Cor. 5:7. then you will be *b*. of a new
baking, as it were unleavened
Passover *b*.
Heb. 9:2. the table with the *b*. of the
Presence

break-ing
Mat. 5:33. do not *b*. your oath
8:24. the waves were *b*. right over the
boat
12:5. the priests in the temple *b*. the
Sabbath
12:29. how can anyone *b*. into a strong
man's house
15:2. why do your disciples *b*. the
old-established tradition
15:3. why do you *b*. God's commandment
24:32. when its tender shoots appear
and are *b*. into leaf, you know that
summer is near
26:38. my heart is ready to *b*. with
grief
Mark 3:27. no one can *b*. into a strong
man's house
13:28. when its tender shoots appear
and are *b*. into leaf
14:34. my heart is ready to *b*. with
grief
John 5:18. he was not only *b*. the
Sabbath
7:19. did not Moses give you the
law? Yet you all *b*. it
7:23. a child is circumcised on the
Sabbath to avoid *b*. the law of
Moses
Acts 2:42. to share the common life, to
b. bread
20:30. who will distort the truth to
induce the disciples to *b*. away
Rom. 1:28. this leads them to *b*. all
rules of conduct
2:27. he will pass judgement on you
who *b*. it
5:20. law intruded into this process to
multiply law-*b*.
1 Tim. 5:12. stand condemned for *b*. their
troth
Heb. 2:14. *b*. the power of him who had
death at his command
Jam. 2:10. he is guilty of *b*. all of it
2 Pet. 1:19. until the day *b*.
3:11. the whole universe is to *b*. up in
this way
1 John 3:4. to commit sin is to *b*. God's
law
Rev. 5:2. who is worthy to open the
scroll and to *b*. its seals
5:5. the right to open the scroll and *b*.
its seven seals
5:9. thou art worthy to take the scroll
and to *b*. its seals

breakdown
John 16:1. to guard you against the *b.* of your faith

breakers
Acts 27:41. the stern was being pounded to pieces by the *b.*

breakfast
John 21:12. Jesus said, 'Come and have *b.*
21:15. after *b.,* Jesus said to Simon Peter

breast-s
Mat. 21:16. babes at the *b.* sound aloud thy praise
24:19 ⎱ those who have children
Mark 13:17 ⎰ at the *b.*
Luke 11:27. happy the womb that carried you and the *b.* that suckled you
21:23. alas for women who are with child in those days, or have children at the *b.*
23:29. happy are the barren, the wombs that never bore a child, the *b.* that never fed one
Rev. 1:13. with a golden girdle round his *b.*

breath
Mark 9:39. will be able in the same *b.* to speak evil of me
1 Thess. 3:8. it is the *b.* of life to us that you stand firm in the Lord
2 Thess. 2:8. whom the Lord Jesus will destroy with the *b.* of his mouth
Jam. 2:26. as the body is dead when there is no *b.* left in it
Rev. 11:11. at the end of the three days and a half the *b.* of life from God came into them
13:15. it was allowed to give *b.* to the image of the beast

breathe-d
Mat. 27:50. Jesus again gave a loud cry, and *b.* his last
Luke 8:42. while Jesus was on his way he could hardly *b.* for the crowds

bred
John 9:34. born and *b.* in sin as you are
Acts 23:6. I am a Pharisee, a Pharisee born and *b.*
Gal. 2:14. if you, a Jew born and *b.,* live like a Gentile
Phil. 3:5. of the tribe of Benjamin, a Hebrew born and *b.*
1 Tim. 4:6. a good servant of Christ Jesus, *b.* in the precepts of our faith

breed-s
Rom. 12:10. let love for our brotherhood *b.* warmth of mutual affection

1 Cor. 8:1. this 'knowledge' *b.* conceit
2 Tim. 2:23. foolish and ignorant speculations. You know they *b.* quarrels
Jam. 1:3. such testing of your faith *b.* fortitude
1:15. sin full-grown *b.* death

breeze
Acts 27:13. a southerly *b.* sprang up

briars
Mat. 7:16. can grapes be picked from *b.*

bribe
Mat. 28:12. the chief priests offered the soldiers a substantial *b.*
Acts 24:26. he had hopes of a *b.* from Paul

bride
Rev. 19:7. his *b.* has made herself ready

brief-ly
Mark 16:8. they delivered all these instructions *b.* to Peter
Acts 24:4. I crave your indulgence for a *b.* statement
Eph. 3:3. I have already written a *b.* account
1 Pet. 5:10. after your *b.* suffering, restore, establish, and strengthen you

bright-ly
Mat. 13:43. the righteous will shine as *b.* as the sun
John 5:35. John was a lamp, burning *b.*
2 Cor. 3:7. made the face of Moses so *b.*
2 Thess. 2:16. given us such unfailing encouragement and such *b.* hopes
Rev. 4:3. round the throne was a rainbow, *b.* as an emerald
21:18. the city itself was of pure gold, *b.* as clear glass

brightness
1 Cor. 15:41. star differs from star in *b.*

brilliance
Acts 22:11. I had been blinded by the *b.* of that light

brilliant
Acts 26:13. I saw a light from the sky, more *b.* than the sun

brim
Mat. 23:28. inside you are *b.*-full of hypocrisy

bring-s-ing
Mat. 6:13. do not *b.* us to the test
10:34. you must not think that I have come to *b.* peace to the earth; I have not come to *b.* peace
15:30. crowds flocked to him, *b.* with them the lame, blind

Mat. 16:8. why do you talk about *b*. no bread

21:41. he will *b*. those bad men to a bad end

26:62. have you no answer to the charge that these witnesses *b*. against you

Mark 3:2. so that they could *b*. a charge against him

4:21. do you *b*. in the lamp to put it under the meal-tub

6:26. he could not *b*. himself to refuse her

6:27. with orders to *b*. John's head

13:19. those days will *b*. distress such as never has been

15:4. you see how many charges they are *b*. against you

16:17. faith will *b*. with it these miracles

Luke 1:16. he will *b*. back many Israelites to the Lord

1:19. sent to speak to you and *b*. you this good news

6:7. so that they could find a charge to *b*. against him

8:15. *b*. a good and honest heart to the hearing of the word

11:4. do not *b*. us to the test

12:51. I have come to *b*. division

19:44. they will *b*. you to the ground

22:43. an angel from heaven *b*. him strength

24:47. repentance *b*. the forgiveness of sins

John 6:33. the bread that God gives comes down from heaven and *b*. life to the world

Acts 3:26. he sent him to you first, to *b*. you blessing

7:26. tried to *b*. them to make up their quarrel

7:42. did you *b*. me victims and offerings those forty years

8:25. *b*. the good news to many Samaritan villages

9:15. my chosen instrument to *b*. my name before the nations

10:21. what *b*. you here

11:14. words that will *b*. salvation to you

11:19. *b*. the message to Jews only

12:6. the very night before Herod had planned to *b*. him forward

13:40. beware, then, lest you *b*. down upon yourselves the doom

14:15. the good news we *b*. tells you to turn from these follies

14:21. after *b*. the good news to that town

15:41. *b*. new strength to the congregations

16:10. God had called us to *b*. them the good news

16:20. *b*. them before the magistrates

18:23. *b*. new strength to all the converts

19:38. let the parties *b*. their charges

21:16. *b*. a certain Mnason of Cyprus

22:30. wishing to be quite sure what charge the Jews were *b*. against Paul

24:8. the truth of all the charges we *b*.

24:13. they cannot make good the charges they *b*. against me

25:7. stood round *b*. many grave charges

25:11. the charges which these men *b*. against me

27:43. the centurion wanted to *b*. Paul safely through

28:19. not that I had any accusation to *b*. against my own people

Rom. 1:11. I want to *b*. you some spiritual gift

3:5. is it unjust of God (I speak of him in human terms) to *b*. retribution upon us

3:7. if the truth of God *b*. him all the greater honour

4:15. law can *b*. only retribution

5:4. endurance *b*. proof that we have stood the test

7:13. it used a good thing to *b*. about my death

10:4. Christ ends the law and *b*. righteousness

14:15. do not by your eating *b*. disaster to a man

15:18. Christ's instrument to *b*. the Gentiles into his allegiance

15:20. to *b*. the gospel to places where the very name of Christ has not been heard

16:26. all nations, to *b*. them to faith and obedience

1 Cor. 2:7. framed from the very beginning to *b*. us to our full glory

3:5. we are simply God's agents in *b*. you to the faith

4:14. I am not writing thus to shame you, but to *b*. you to reason

8:8. food will not *b*. us into God's presence

14:24. something that searches his conscience and *b*. conviction

15:2. which is now *b*. you salvation

2 Cor. 1:6. it is to help us to *b*. you comfort

2:16. a vital fragrance that *b*. life

4:4. cannot dawn upon them and *b*. them light

6:10. poor ourselves, we *b*. wealth to many

7:6. God, who *b*. comfort to the downcast

7:10. the wound which is borne in God's way *b*. a change of heart too

salutary to regret; but the hurt
which is borne in the world's way
b. death
2 Cor. 8:6. *b*. this work of generosity
also to completion
9:4. if I *b*. with me men from
Macedonia
Gal. 4:13. my *b*. you the Gospel
6:8. the Spirit will *b*. him a harvest of
eternal life
Eph. 3:9. *b*. to light how this hidden
purpose was to be put into effect
4:29. so that it *b*. a blessing to those
who hear it
Phil. 1:6. the One who started the good
work in you will *b*. it to completion
1:10. may thus *b*. you the gift of true
discrimination
Col. 2:2. the full wealth of conviction
which understanding *b*.
1 Thess. 3:6. *b*. good news of your faith
and love
3:11. *b*. us direct to you
5:21. *b*. them all to the test
2 Thess. 1:5. this *b*. out the justice of
God's judgement
1:11. mightily *b*. to fulfilment every
good purpose
1 Tim. 3:6. for fear the sin of conceit
should *b*. upon him a judgement
4:8. the training of the body does *b*.
limited benefit
6:15. that appearance God will *b*. to
pass
Philem. 6. blessings that our union with
Christ *b*. us
Heb. 6:6. it is impossible to *b*. them
again to repentance
9:15. a death to *b*. deliverance from
sins
9:28. sin done away, to *b*. salvation
10:1. it can never *b*. the worshippers
to perfection
13:17. that would *b*. you no advantage
Jam. 1:21. the message planted in your
hearts, which can *b*. you salvation
4:14. yet you have no idea what tomorrow will *b*.
5:19. succeed in *b*. him back
5:20. any man who *b*. a sinner back
1 Pet. 3:21. it *b*. salvation through the
resurrection
2 Pet. 2:1. *b*. swift disaster on their own
heads
1 John 4:9. he sent his only Son into the
world to *b*. us life
4:18. fear *b*. with it the pains of
judgement
3 John 10. I will *b*. up the things he is
doing
Jude 15. to *b*. all men to judgement
Rev. 22:12. I am coming soon, and *b*.
my recompense with me

broad
Mat. 10:27. what I say to you in the dark
you must repeat in *b*. daylight
Luke 12:3. everything you have said in
the dark will be heard in *b*. daylight
2 Pet. 2:13. to carouse in *b*. daylight is
their idea of pleasure

broke-n
Mat. 12:20. he will not snap off the *b*.
reed
26:74. at this he *b*. into curses
Mark 4:37. the waves *b*. over the boat
14:71. at this he *b*. out into curses
Luke 4:18. to let the *b*. victims go free
4:42. when day *b*. he went out and
made his way to a lonely spot
6:13. when day *b*. he called his
disciples
22:24. then a jealous dispute *b*. out
22:66. when day *b*., the elders of the
nation, chief priests, and doctors
of the law assembled
Acts 5:36. his whole following was *b*. up
23:9. a great uproar *b*. out
23:12. when day *b*., the Jews banded
together
2 Tim. 1:10. he has *b*. the power of
death
Rev. 6:1. the Lamb *b*. the first of the
seven seals
6:3. when the Lamb *b*. the second seal
6:5. when he *b*. the third seal
6:7. when he *b*. the fourth seal
6:9. when he *b*. the fifth seal
6:12. I watched as he *b*. the sixth seal
8:1. now when the Lamb *b*. the
seventh seal
12:7. then war *b*. out in heaven

bronze
Rev. 9:20. idols made from gold, silver,
b.
18:12. costly woods, *b*., iron, or
marble

brood
Mat. 3:7. ⎫
12:34 ⎬ you vipers' *b*.
23:33 ⎭
23:37. as a hen gathers her *b*. under
her wings

brother-s
Mat. 20:22. Jesus turned to the *b*. and
said
1 Cor. 15:31. I swear it by my pride in
you, my *b*.

brotherhood
John 21:23. that saying of Jesus became
current in the *b*.
Acts 1:15. Peter stood up before the
assembled *b*.
15:1. began to teach the *b*.

Acts 18:18. Paul stayed on for some time and then took leave of the *b*.

18:27. the *b*. gave him their support

21:7. we greeted the *b*. and spent one day with them

21:17. Jerusalem, where the *b*. welcomed us gladly

Rom. 12:10. let love for our *b*. breed warmth of mutual affection

1 Thess. 4:9. about love for our *b*. you need no words of mine

5:27. have this letter read to the whole *b*.

1 Tim. 4:6. offering such advice as this to the *b*.

brotherly

1 Pet. 3:8. be full of *b*. affection

brought

Mat. 5:21. anyone who commits murder must be *b*. to judgement

5:22. who nurses anger against his brother must be *b*. to judgement

12:48. Jesus turned to the man who *b*. the message

16:7. it is because we have *b*. no bread

27:4. I have *b*. an innocent man to his death

27:11. Jesus was now *b*. before the Governor

27:13. do you not hear all this evidence that is *b*. against you

27:18. it was out of spite that they had *b*. Jesus before him

Mark 2:3. a man was *b*. who was paralysed

3:32. word was *b*. to him

6:55. and *b*. the sick on stretchers

7:32. they *b*. to him a man who was deaf

8:22. the people *b*. a blind man to Jesus

15:3. the chief priests *b*. many charges against him

15:10. it was out of spite that they had *b*. Jesus before him

15:22. they *b*. him to the place called Golgotha

Luke 8:17. nothing under cover that will not be made known and *b*. into the open

10:15. *b*. down to the depths

12:11. when you are *b*. before synagogues

21:12. you will be *b*. before synagogues

22:66. he was *b*. before their Council

23:1. they *b*. him before Pilate

John 8:31. Jesus said, 'If you dwell within the revelation I have *b*.

10:4. when he has *b*. them all out he goes ahead

12:3. Mary *b*. a pound of very costly perfume

18:30. if he were not a criminal,' they replied, 'we should not have *b*. him before you

18:35. your own nation and their chief priests have *b*. you before me

Acts 2:43. many marvels and signs were *b*. about through the apostles

4:7. they *b*. the apostles before the court

7:21. Pharoah's daughter herself adopted him and *b*. him up as her own son

13:23. God, as he promised, has *b*. Israel a saviour, Jesus

15:2. that *b*. them into fierce dissension

15:31. they all rejoiced at the encouragement it *b*.

19:27. is *b*. down from her divine preeminence

24:20. say what crime they discovered when I was *b*. before the Council

25:2. *b*. before him the case against Paul

26:2. the charges *b*. against me by the Jews

Rom. 3:21. God's justice has been *b*. to light

5:15. the wrongdoing of that one man *b*. death upon so many

11:8. God *b*. upon them a numbness of spirit

16:25. according to the Gospel I *b*. you

1 Cor. 3:13. the work that each man does will at last be *b*. to light

4:6. into this general picture, my friends, I have *b*. Apollos and myself

12:13. we were all *b*. into one body by baptism

15:21. it was a man who *b*. death into the world, a man also *b*. resurrection of the dead

15:22. in Christ all will be *b*. to life

2 Cor. 6:3. in order that our service may not be *b*. into discredit

Eph. 1:10. that the universe, all in heaven and on earth, might be *b*. into a unity in Christ

2:5. the great love he bore us, *b*. us to life with Christ

2:13. you who once were far off have been *b*. near

Phil. 4:12. I know what it is to be *b*. low

Col. 1:8. *b*. us the news of your God-given love

1:13. *b*. us away into the kingdom of his dear Son

2:10. in him you have been *b*. to completion

3:10. *b*. to know God

1 Thess. 1:5. when we *b*. you the Gospel, we *b*. it not in mere words

bruise

1 Thess. 3:9. what thanks for all the joy you have *b*. us

2 Thess. 1:10. you did indeed believe the testimony we *b*. you

2:12. so that they may all be *b*. to judgement

2:14. he called you through the gospel we *b*.

1 Tim. 6:1. so that the name of God and the Christian teaching are not *b*. into disrepute

2 Tim. 1:9. it is he who *b*. us salvation

1:10. has now at length been *b*. fully into view

Tit. 2:5. thus the Gospel will not be *b*. into disrepute

Heb. 1:3. when he had *b*. about the purgation of sins

4:2. *b*. no admixture of faith to the hearing of it

7:19. the Law *b*. nothing to perfection

10:3. in these sacrifices year after year sins are *b*. to mind

Jam. 1:10. the wealthy brother must find his pride in being *b*. low

1 Pet. 1:12. preachers who *b*. you the Gospel

3:18. in the spirit he was *b*. to life

3:21. the water of baptism through which you are now *b*. to safety

2 Pet. 2:2. through whom the true way will be *b*. into disrepute

2:5. *b*. the deluge upon that world of godless men

1 John 4:12. his love is *b*. to perfection within us

Rev. 21:26. the wealth and splendour of the nations shall be *b*. into it

bruise

1 Cor. 9:27. I *b*. my own body and make it know its master

2 Cor. 12:7. which came as Satan's messenger to *b*. me

brushwood

Mark 11:8. carpeted the road with their cloaks, while others spread *b*.

brutally

Mat. 22:6. seized the servants, attacked them *b*.

brute-s

Tit. 1:12. Cretans were always liars, vicious *b*., lazy gluttons

bucket

John 4:11. you have no *b*. and this well is deep

buckle

Luke 12:37. he will *b*. his belt, seat them at table, and come and wait on them

17:8. prepare my supper, *b*. your belt, and then wait on me

Eph. 6:14. *b*. on the belt of truth

bud-s

Luke 21:30. as soon as it *b*., you can see for yourselves that summer is near

build-s, built

Acts 9:31. the church, throughout Judaea, Galilee, and Samaria, was left in peace to *b*. up its strength

Rom. 14:19 } *b*. up the common life
15:2 }

1 Cor. 2:5. that your faith might be *b*. not upon human wisdom but upon the power of God

8:1. it is love that *b*.

14:3. his words have power to *b*.

14:4. it is prophecy that *b*. up a Christian community

14:5. so help to *b*. up the community

14:12. aspire above all to excel in those which *b*. up the church

14:26. all of these must aim at one thing: to *b*. up the church

2 Cor. 10:8. an authority given by the Lord to *b*. you up

12:19. our whole aim, my own dear people, is to b. you up

Eph. 4:16. *b*. itself up in love

Heb. 11:7. took good heed and *b*. an ark to save his household

Rev. 21:16. the city was *b*. as a square

building-s

Mat. 24:2. you see all these *b*.

Acts 4:31. the *b*. where they were assembled rocked

1 Cor. 10:23. does everything help the *b*. of the community

2 Cor. 13:10. authority which the Lord gave me for *b*. up

Eph. 4:12. to the *b*. up of the body of Christ

1 Pet. 3:20. God waited patiently in the days of Noah and the *b*. of the ark

bull

Acts 7:41. when they made the *b*.-calf, and offered sacrifice to the idol

bullock-s

Mat. 22:4. I have had my *b*. and fatted beasts slaughtered

bully-ing

Mat. 24:49. and begins to *b*. the other servants

Luke 3:14. no *b*.; no blackmail

12:45. and begins to *b*. the men-servants and maids

bulwark

1 Tim. 3:15. the church of the living God, the pillar and *b*. of the truth

burden-ed

Mat. 21:5. riding on the foal of a beast of *b*.

John 16:12. the *b.* would be too great for you now

Rom. 15:1. must accept as our own *b.* the tender scruples of weaker men

2 Cor. 1:8. the *b.* of it was far too heavy for us to bear

11:9. I made it a rule, as I always shall, never to be a *b.* to you

Phil. 4:14. it was kind of you to share the *b.* of my troubles

1 Thess. 2:9. we worked for a living night and day, rather than be a *b.* to anyone

2 Thess. 3:8. we worked for a living night and day, rather than be a *b.* to any of you

1 Tim. 5:16. the congregation must be relieved of the *b.*

2 Tim. 3:6. women *b.* with a sinful past

Heb. 9:28. Christ was offered once to bear the *b.* of men's sins

burdensome

1 John 5:3. to love God is to keep his commands; and they are not *b.*

burglar

Mat. 24:43. if the householder had known at what time of night the *b.* was coming, he would have kept awake

Luke 12:39. if the householder had known what time the *b.* was coming he would not have let his house be broken into

burial

Mat. 27:7. they used it to buy the Potter's Field, as a *b.*-place for foreigners

Mark 14:8. she is beforehand with anointing my body for *b.*

John 12:7. let her keep it till the day when she prepares for my *b.*

19:40. in strips of linen cloth according to Jewish *b.*-customs

19:41. a new tomb, not yet used for *b.*

Rev. 11:9. gaze upon their corpses and refuse them *b.*

burn-ed-ing-t

Mat. 7:19. when a tree does not yield good fruit it is cut down and *b.*

Mark 12:26. in the Book of Moses, in the story of the *b.* bush

Luke 9:54. Lord, may we call down fire from heaven to *b.* them up

20:37. shown by Moses himself in the story of the *b.* bush

John 15:6. the withered branches are heaped together, thrown on the fire, and *b.*

Acts 7:30. an angel appeared to him in the flame of a *b.* bush

2 Pet. 2:6. the cities of Sodom and Gomorrah God *b.* to ashes

3:7. the present heavens and earth, again by God's word, have been kept in store for *b.*

Rev. 16:8. it was allowed to *b.* men with its flames

16:9. they were fearfully *b.*

burnish-ed

Rev. 1:15. his feet gleamed like *b.* brass

2:18. whose feet gleam like *b.* brass

burst-ing

Mat. 9:17. the skins *b.*, and then the wine runs out

Mark 14:72. he *b.* into tears

Luke 6:48. when the flood came, the river *b.* upon that house

6:49. as soon as the river *b.* upon it, the house collapsed

Acts 16:26. the foundations of the jail were shaken; all the doors *b.* open

Col. 2:18. such people, *b.* with the futile conceit of worldly minds

bury-ied

Mat. 13:44. the kingdom of heaven is like treasure lying *b.* in a field. The man who found it, *b.* it again

Acts 7:16. *b.* in the tomb which Abraham had bought

Rom. 4:7. whose lawless deeds are forgiven, whose sins are *b.* away

bushel-s

Luke 16:7. he said, 'A thousand *b.* of wheat

business

Mat. 22:5. one went off to his farm, another to his *b.*

25:16. the man who had the five bags went at once and employed them in *b.*

Acts 18:3. they carried on *b.* together

19:27. our line of *b.* will be discredited

26:26. this has been no hole-and-corner *b.*

Rom. 14:4. whether he stands or falls is his own Master's *b.*

15:28. when I have finished this *b.*

1 Cor. 5:12. what *b.* of mine is it to judge outsiders

6:3. how much more, mere matters of *b.*

6:4. if therefore you have such *b.* disputes

7:32. the unmarried man cares for the Lord's *b.*

7:34. the unmarried or celibate woman cares for the Lord's *b.*

Gal. 2:10. which was the very thing I made it my *b.* to do

Phil. 1:12. the work of the Gospel has been helped on, rather than hindered, by this *b.* of mine

2 Thess. 3:11. idling their time away,

minding everybody's *b*. but their own

1 Tim. 4:15. make these matters your *b*. and your absorbing interest

Jam. 1:11. so shall the rich man wither away as he goes about his *b*.

busy

Tit. 2:5. mothers, temperate, chaste, and kind, *b*. at home

buy-ing

Mat. 16:26. what can he give that will *b*. that self back

21:12. drove out all who were *b*. and selling in the temple precincts

27:7. they used it to *b*. the Potter's Field

Mark 8:37. what can he give to *b*. that self back

John 6:7. twenty pounds would not *b*.

enough bread for every one of them to have a little

Acts 1:18. Judas, be it noted, after *b*. a plot of land with the price of his villainy

buyers

1 Cor. 7:30. *b*. must not count on keeping what they buy

bystanders

Mat. 12:23. the *b*. were all amazed

26:73. the *b*. came up and said to Peter

27:47. some of the *b*., on hearing this, said, 'He is calling Elijah

Mark 11:5. the *b*. asked, 'What are you doing, untying that colt

14:69. began to say to the *b*., 'He is one of them

14:70. the *b*. said to Peter, 'Surely you are one of them

C

calamity

1 Thess. 5:3. while they are talking of peace and security, all at once *c*. is upon them

calculate-ing

Luke 14:28. *c*. the cost

call-s-ed-ing

Mat. 2:4. he *c*. a meeting of the chief priests

7:21. not everyone who *c*. me 'Lord, Lord

14:28. Peter *c*. to him: 'Lord, if it is you

17:5. a voice *c*. from the cloud

26:65. need we *c*. further witnesses

Mark 6:12. *c*. publicly for repentance

14:32. they reached a place *c*. Gethsemane

14:63. need we *c*. further witnesses

15:21. a man *c*. Simon, from Cyrene

Luke 1:5. the division of the priesthood *c*. after Abijah

1:26. a town in Galilee *c*. Nazareth

1:72. *c*. to mind his solemn covenant

2:25. in Jerusalem a man *c*. Simeon

8:8. he *c*. out, 'If you have ears to hear

9:54. may we *c*. down fire from heaven to burn them up

11:27. a woman in the crowd *c*. out

16:24. Abraham, my father,' he *c*. out, 'take pity on me

17:13. *c*. out to him, 'Jesus, Master, take pity on us

23:50. a man *c*. Joseph, a member of the council

John 4:6. the spring *c*. Jacob's well

5:18. by *c*. God his own Father, he claimed equality with God

6:20. he *c*. out, 'It is I; do not be afraid

14:26. will *c*. to mind all that I have told you

21:5. he *c*. out to them, 'Friends, have you caught anything

Acts 4:24. they raised their voices as one man and *c*. upon God

5:1. there was another man, *c*. Ananias

5:34. a Pharisee *c*. Gamaliel

7:5. he gave him nothing in it to *c*. his own

8:10. that power of God which is *c*. 'The Great Power

11:13. Simon also *c*. Peter

14:27. *c*. the congregation together

15:30. *c*. the congregation together, and delivered the letter

21:40. with a gesture *c*. for the attention of the people

22:12. a man *c*. Ananias, a devout observer of the Law

23:6. he *c*. out in the Council

25:19. about their peculiar religion, and about someone *c*. Jesus

26:20. sounded the *c*. to repent

Rom. 2:15. their conscience is *c*. as witness

12:14. *c*. down blessings on your persecutors

16:13. his mother, whom I *c*. mother too

1 Cor. 1:22. Jews *c*. for miracles, Greeks look for wisdom
4:3. if I am *c*. to account by you
10:29. is my freedom to be *c*. in question
2 Cor. 2:7. something very different is *c*. for now
2:16. who is equal to such a *c*.
12:12. the work I did among you, which *c*. for such constant fortitude
Eph. 4:24. devout life *c*. for by the truth
Phil. 3:2. 'circumcision' I will not *c*. it
1 Thess. 1:3. we *c*. to mind, before our God and Father
2:10. we *c*. you to witness
2 Tim. 4:5. do all the duties of your *c*.
1 Pet. 3:15. your defence whenever you are *c*. to account for the hope
Rev. 2:24. what they like to *c*. the deep secrets of Satan
6:16. they *c*. out to the mountains and the crags
7:2. he *c*. aloud to the four angels
8:13. I heard an eagle *c*. with a loud cry
14:15. another angel came out of the temple and *c*. in a loud voice

calm

1 Thess. 4:11. let it be your ambition to keep *c*.
2 Tim. 4:5. keep *c*. and sane at all times

calumny

Mat. 5:11. every kind of *c*. for my sake

came

Mat. 3:16. after baptism Jesus *c*. up out of the water
14:13. *c*. after him in crowds
14:14. he *c*. ashore
14:25. he *c*. to them, walking over the lake
20:8. pay, beginning with those who *c*. last
20:34. at once their sight *c*. back
21:9. the others that *c*. behind raised the shout
26:58. till he *c*. to the High Priest's courtyard
27:19. a message *c*. to him from his wife
Mark 1:21. they *c*. to Capernaum
2:13. all the crowd *c*. to him, and he taught them
3:10. sick people of all kinds *c*. crowding
3:17. then *c*. the sons of Zebedee
4:8. it *c*. up and grew, and bore fruit
4:37. a heavy squall *c*. on
5:2. a man possessed by an unclean spirit *c*. up to him
5:13. the unclean spirits *c*. out
5:14. the people *c*. out to see what had happened

11:9. the others who *c*. behind shouted
12:2. when the vintage season *c*., he sent a servant
14:34. horror and dismay *c*. over him
15:1. when morning *c*. the chief priests
Luke 2:6. the time *c*. for her child to be born
2:21. the time *c*. to circumcise him
4:39. he *c*. and stood over her and rebuked the fever
6:48. when the flood *c*., the river burst upon that house
7:44. I *c*. to your house: you provided no water
8:33. the devils *c*. out of the man
10:17. the seventy-two *c*. back jubilant
10:25. a lawyer *c*. forward to put this test question
11:37. he *c*. in and sat down
19:44. you did not recognize God's moment when it *c*.
22:47. he *c*. up to Jesus to kiss him
23:44. there *c*. a darkness over the whole land
24:15. Jesus himself *c*. up and walked along with them
John 1:3. through him all things *c*. to be
10:41. crowds *c*. to him
10:42. many *c*. to believe in him there
11:54. *c*. to a town called Ephraim
19:3. time after time they *c*. up to him
19:4. once more Pilate *c*. out
19:24. thus the text of Scripture *c*. true
Acts 3:11. all the people *c*. running in astonishment
5:36. Theudas *c*. forward, claiming to be somebody
6:9. *c*. forward and argued with Stephen
7:26. he *c*. upon two of them fighting
8:5. Philip *c*. down to a city in Samaria
9:42. many *c*. to believe in the Lord
10:44. Peter was still speaking when the Holy Spirit *c*. upon all
11:15. hardly had I begun speaking, when the Holy Spirit *c*. upon them
12:18. when morning *c*., there was consternation among the soldiers
13:4. sent out on their mission by the Holy Spirit, *c*. down to Seleucia
13:11. mist and darkness *c*. over him
16:35. when daylight *c*. the magistrates sent their officers
19:12. the evil spirits *c*. out of them
19:19. it *c*. to fifty thousand pieces of silver
20:19. the sorrows and trials that *c*. upon me
21:3. we *c*. in sight of Cyprus
21:16. some of the disciples from Caesarea *c*.

Acts 21:30. people *c.* running from all directions

21:32. *c.* down on the rioters at the double

24:1. the High Priest Ananias *c.* down

Rom. 4:13. the righteousness that *c.* from faith

5:15. the gift that *c.* to so many by the grace of the one man

14:9. Christ died and *c.* to life again

1 Cor. 2:3. I *c.* before you weak

8:6. Jesus Christ, through whom all things *c.* to be

11:23. I handed on to you *c.* to me from the Lord himself

2 Cor. 2:4. that letter I sent you *c.* out of great distress

6:2. on the day of deliverance I *c.* to your aid

12:7. a sharp pain in my body which *c.* as Satan's messenger

Phil. 2:30. in Christ's cause he *c.* near to death

Col. 1:6. when the message of the true Gospel first *c.* to you

1:19. the complete being of God, by God's own choice, *c.* to dwell

2 Tim. 1:17. took pains to search me out when he *c.* to Rome

Heb. 11:3. the visible *c.* forth from the invisible

Jam. 5:18. down *c.* the rain and the land bore crops once more

Rev. 1:16. out of his mouth *c.* a sharp two-edged sword

2:8. who was dead and *c.* to life again

6:4. out *c.* another horse, all red

6:8. Hades *c.* close behind

9:17. out of their mouths *c.* fire, smoke, and sulphur

9:18. the sulphur that *c.* from their mouths

11:11. the breath of life from God *c.* into them

11:19. there *c.* flashes of lightning

12:16. the earth *c.* to her rescue and opened its mouth

18:1. he *c.* with great authority

20:4. these *c.* to life again

cancel-s-led-ling

Rom. 3:3. will their faithlessness *c.* the faithfulness of God

Col. 2:14. he has *c.* the bond which pledged us

Heb. 7:19. the earlier rules are *c.* as impotent

Jam. 5:20. rescuing his soul from death and *c.* innumerable sins

1 Pet. 4:8. love *c.* innumerable sins

cane

Mat. 27:29. with a *c.* in his right hand

27:30. used the *c.* to beat him about the head

27:48. held it to his lips on the end of a *c.*

Mark 15:19. they beat him about the head with a *c.*

15:36. a sponge, soaked in sour wine, on the end of a *c.*

Rev. 11:1. I was given a long *c.*, a kind of measuring-rod

canvassing

Gal. 1:10. as if I were *c.* for men's support

capacity

Mat. 25:15. each according to his *c.*

capital

Mat. 25:14. put his *c.* in their hands

Luke 23:22. I have not found him guilty of any *c.* offence

Acts. 25:11. if I am guilty of any *c.* crime

25:25. it was clear to me that he had committed no *c.* crime

28:18. there was no *c.* charge against me

captain-s

Acts 27:11. the centurion paid more attention to the *c.*

Rev. 18:17. all the sea-*c.* and voyagers, the sailors

captive-s

2 Cor. 2:14. *c.* in Christ's triumphal procession

Col. 2:15. a public spectacle of them and led them as *c.*

4:10. Aristarchus, Christ's *c.* like myself

Philem. 23. Epaphras, Christ's *c.* like myself

captivity

Rom. 16:7. comrades in *c.*

capture-d

Col. 2:8. do not let your minds be *c.* by hollow and delusive speculations

care-s-d-ing

Mat. 10:37. who *c.* more for father or mother than for me; no man is worthy of me who *c.* more for son or daughter

14:7. took an oath to give her anything she *c.* to ask

16:25. whoever *c.* for his own safety is lost

24:4. take *c.* that no one misleads you

Mark 8:35. whoever *c.* for his own safety is lost

13:5. take *c.* that no one misleads you

Luke 4:10. he will give his angels orders to take *c.* of you

7:16. God has shown his *c.* for his people

8:18. take *c.*, then, how you listen

Luke 9:24. whoever *c.* for his own safety is lost
11:42. but have no *c.* for justice and the love of God
18:2. a judge who *c.* nothing for God or man
18:4. I *c.* nothing for God or man
21:8. take *c.* that you are not misled
John 5:44. and *c.* nothing for the honour that comes from him who alone is God
7:49. this rabble, which *c.* nothing for the Law
8:50. I do not *c.* about my own glory; there is one who does *c.*
10:28. no one shall snatch them from my *c.*
10:29. no one can snatch them out of the Father's *c.*
Acts 24:2. it is due to your provident *c.*
27:3. allowed Paul to go to his friends to be *c.* for
1 Cor. 3:10. let each take *c.* how he builds
10:27. if an unbeliever invites you to a meal and you *c.* to go
Eph. 5:29. he provides and *c.* for it
Phil. 2:2. and a common *c.* for unity
3:10. all I *c.* for is to know Christ
4:17. all I *c.* for is the profit accruing to you
1 Thess. 2:7. as a nurse *c.* fondly for her children
1 Tim. 5:10. showing whether she has had the *c.* of children
1 Pet. 5:3. not tyrannizing over those who are allotted to your *c.*
2 Pet. 3:17. take *c.*, then, not to let these unprincipled men
2 John 12. I do not *c.* to put it down in black and white
3 John 13. I do not *c.* to set it down with pen and ink
Jude 12. shepherds who take *c.* only of themselves

careful
Mat. 2:8. go and make a *c.* enquiry for the child
6:1. be *c.* not to make a show of your religion
1 Cor. 8:9. be *c.* that this liberty of yours
Eph. 5:15. be most *c.* then how you conduct yourselves

careless
1 Thess. 5:14. admonish the *c.*

cargo-es
Acts 21:3. there the ship was to unload her *c.*
Acts 27:10. loss not only of ship and *c.* but also of life

Rev. 18:11. no one any longer buys their *c.*
18:12. *c.* of gold and silver

carouse
2 Pet. 2:13. to *c.* in broad daylight is their idea of pleasure

carpet-ed
Mat. 21:8. crowds of people *c.* the road with their cloaks
Mark 11:8. people *c.* the road with their cloaks
Luke 19:36. they *c.* the road with them

carriage
Acts. 8:28. sitting in his *c.* and reading aloud
8:29. go and join the *c.*
8:38. he ordered the *c.* to stop

carry-ies-ied-ing
Mat. 13:19. the evil one comes and *c.* off what has been sown
14:11. she *c.* it to her mother
22:24. marry the widow and *c.* on his brother's family
27:32. pressed him into service to *c.* his cross
Mark 2:3. four men were *c.* him
4:15. Satan comes and *c.* off the word
5:14. *c.* the news to the town
11:16. to use the temple court as a thoroughfare for *c.* goods
12:19. marry the widow and *c.* on his brother's family
14:3. a woman came in *c.* a small bottle
14:13. a man will meet you *c.* a jar of water
15:21. they pressed him into service to *c.* his cross
16:10. *c.* the news to his mourning and sorrowful followers
Luke 5:18. some men appeared *c.* a paralysed man
8:12. the devil comes and *c.* off the word
8:34. they *c.* the news to the town
11:22. he *c.* off the arms and armour
11:27. happy the womb that *c.* you
12:47. yet made no attempt to *c.* them out
14:22. sir, your orders have been *c.* out
14:27. no one who does not *c.* his cross
17:9. is he grateful to the servant for *c.* out his orders
17:10. when you have *c.* out all your orders
20:28. *c.* on his brother's family
21:24. they will be *c.* captive into all countries
22:10. a man will meet you *c.* a jar of water

Luke 23:26. made him walk behind Jesus *c.* it
John 8:44. you choose to *c.* out your father's desires
9:4. while daylight lasts we must *c.* on the work
19:17. *c.* his own cross
Acts 5:15. the sick were actually *c.* out into the streets
8:11. they had for so long been *c.* away by his magic
8:13. he was *c.* away when he saw the powerful signs
13:22. who will *c.* out all my purposes
13:29. when they had *c.* out all that the scriptures said
18:3. they *c.* on business together
19:12. scarves which had been in contact with his skin were *c.* to the sick
21:35. he had to be *c.* by the soldiers
27:43. prevented them from *c.* out their plan
Rom. 2:14. *c.* out its precepts by the light of nature
1 Cor. 2:4. it *c.* conviction by spiritual power
16:3. send them to *c.* your gift to Jerusalem
2 Cor. 4:10. we *c.* death with us in our body
10:16. *c.* the Gospel to lands that lie beyond you
Gal. 6:2. help one another to *c.* these heavy loads
Heb. 10:35. your confidence, for it *c.* a great reward
11:5. Enoch was *c.* away to another life
1 Pet. 2:24. he *c.* our sins to the gallows
Rev. 7:2. *c.* the seal of the living God
17:17. God has put it into their heads to *c.* out his purpose
21:15. the angel who spoke with me *c.* a gold measuring-rod

case
Luke 23:2. they opened the *c.* against him
23:4. I find no *c.* for this man to answer
23:7. he remitted the *c.* to him
23:10. pressed the *c.* against him vigorously
John 18:38. I find no *c.* against him
19:4. I find no *c.* against him'; and Jesus came out
19:6. for my part I find no *c.* against him
Acts 2:40. he pressed his *c.* and pleaded with them
19:38. if therefore Demetrius and his craftsmen have a *c.* against anyone

23:15. a closer investigation of his *c.*
23:30. instructed his accusers to state their *c.*
23:35. I will hear your *c.*
24:2. Tertullus opened the *c.*
24:4. a brief statement of our *c.*
24:22. I will go into your *c.*
25:2. brought before him the *c.* against Paul
25:14. Festus laid Paul's *c.* before the king
Rom. 2:15. their own thoughts argue the *c.* on either side
1 Cor. 4:6. so that you may take our *c.* as an example
6:2. are you incompetent to deal with these trifling *c.*
7:15. in such *c.* the Christian husband or wife is under no compulsion
2 Cor. 3:14. in any *c.* their minds had been made insensitive
Gal. 5:11. in that *c.*, my preaching of the cross is a stumbling-block no more
Phil. 3:4. I could make a stronger *c.* for myself
1 Tim. 3:14. I write this in *c.* I am delayed
2 Tim. 4:16. at the first hearing of my *c.*
Heb. 6:9. we are convinced that you, my friends, are in the better *c.*

cash
Luke 15:13. the younger son turned the whole of his share into *c.*

cast-ing
Mark 9:7. a cloud appeared, *c.* its shadow over them
9:29. there is no means of *c.* out this sort but prayer
Luke 9:34. there came a cloud which *c.* a shadow over them
24:5. they were terrified, and stood with eyes *c.* down
Acts 26:10. when they were condemned to death, my vote was *c.* against them

castle
Luke 11:21. on guard over his *c.* his possessions are safe

casual
Acts 17:17. in the city square every day with *c.* passers-by

catch-ing
Mat. 12:11. who would not *c.* hold of it and lift it out
18:28. *c.* hold of him he gripped him by the throat
22:18 ⎱ why are you trying to *c.* me
Mark 12:15 ⎰ out
Luke 5:4. let down your nets for a *c.*
5:9. were amazed at the *c.* they had made

Luke 20:26. their attempt to *c.* him out in public failed

John 21:6. shoot the net to starboard, and you will make a *c.*

21:10. bring some of your *c.*

2 Cor. 12:16. use a trick to *c.* you

2 Pet. 2:18. a bait to *c.* those who have barely begun to escape

cattle

John 2:14. he found in the temple the dealers in *c.*

2:15. drove them out of the temple, sheep, *c.*, and all

Jam. 5:5. wanton luxury, fattening yourselves like *c.*

Rev. 18:13. sheep and *c.*, horses, chariots

Cauda

Acts 27:16. the lee of a small island called *C.*

caught

Mat. 13:47. fish of every kind were *c.* in it

Luke 5:5. we were hard at work all night and *c.* nothing

John 8:4. this woman was *c.* in the very act of adultery

11:32. as soon as she *c.* sight of him she fell at his feet

21:5. friends, have you *c.* anything

21:21. when he *c.* sight of him, Peter asked

Acts 8:27. he *c.* sight of an Ethiopian

27:41. found themselves *c.* between cross-currents

1 Tim. 3:7. get *c.* in the devil's snare

2 Tim. 2:26. the devil's snare, in which they have been *c.*

2 Pet. 2:12. born in the course of nature to be *c.*

Rev. 1:10. I was *c.* up by the Spirit

4:1. at once I was *c.* up by the Spirit

cause-s-d-ing

Mat. 5:10. suffered persecution for the *c.* of right

13:41. everything that *c.* offence

17:27. we do not want to *c.* difficulty for these people

18:6. if a man is a *c.* of stumbling to one of these little ones

18:7. alas for the world that such *c.* of stumbling arise

19:9. for any *c.* other than unchastity

Luke 17:1. *c.* of stumbling are bound to arise

17:2. than to *c.* one of these little ones to stumble

23:5. his teaching is *c.* disaffection among the people

John 7:43 thus he *c.* a split among the people

8:13. you are witness in your own *c.*

8:18. a witness in my own *c.*

10:19. these words once again *c.* a split

Acts 4:26. the rulers made common *c.*

4:27. they did indeed make common *c.*

4:30. *c.* signs and wonders to be done

7:11. *c.* great hardship

14:3. by *c.* signs and miracles to be worked

15:26. devoted themselves to the *c.* of our Lord Jesus Christ

16:20. these men are *c.* a disturbance

17:8. these words *c.* a great commotion

Rom. 8:34. and indeed pleads our *c.*

13:4. then you will have *c.* to fear them

14:20. who by his eating *c.* another to fall

14:21. doing anything which *c.* your brother's downfall

1 Cor. 3:21. never make mere men a *c.* for pride

6:5. a decision in a brother-Christian's *c.*

8:13. I will not be the *c.* of my brother's downfall

2 Cor. 2:2. if I *c.* pain to you, who is left to cheer me up

2:4. I never meant to *c.* you pain

4:6. has *c.* his light to shine within us

6:10. in our sorrows we have always *c.* for joy

7:8. I saw that the letter had *c.* you pain

9:8. enough and to spare for every good *c.*

Eph. 1:12. should *c.* his glory to be praised

Phil. 1:13. my imprisonment in Christ's *c.*

1:20. I shall have no *c.* to be ashamed

2:21. all bent on their own ends, not on the *c.* of Christ Jesus

2:30. in Christ's *c.* he came near to death

4:3. my struggles in the *c.* of the Gospel

Col. 3:13. forgiving, where any of you has *c.* for complaint

1 Thess. 2:5. never been flattering words, as you have *c.* to know

Jam. 4:1. what *c.* conflicts and quarrels among you

1 Pet. 1:6. this is *c.* for great joy

2:23. committed his *c.* to the One who judges justly

4:13. that is *c.* for joy

1 John 2:1. one to plead our *c.* with the Father

Rev. 2:3. you have borne up in my *c.*

2:13. you are holding fast to my *c.*

17:17. by making common *c.*

18:20. he has vindicated your *c.*

caution
Acts 4:17. *c.* them never again to speak
    to anyone in this name
    4:21. the court repeated the *c.*

cautious
Acts 5:35. be *c.* in deciding what to do
    with these men

cavalry-men
Acts 23:23. together with seventy *c.*
    23:32. leaving the *c.* to escort him
    23:33. the *c.* entered Caesarea
Rev. 9:16. and their squadrons of *c.*

cave
Mat. 21:13. you are making it a robbers'
    c.
Mark 11:17 ⎱ you have made it a
Luke 19:46 ⎰ robbers' *c.*
Rev. 6:15. all men, slave or free, hid
    themselves in *c.*

cease-d
John 5:17. my Father has never yet *c.*
    his work
Acts 19:27. the great goddess Diana will
    c. to command respect
Rom. 11:6. or grace would *c.* to be
    grace
    14:13. let us therefore *c.* judging one
    another
2 Cor. 5:6. therefore we never *c.* to be
    confident
    5:15. should *c.* to live for them-
    selves
    5:16. worldly standards have *c.* to
    count
Heb. 13:1. never *c.* to love your fellow-
    Christians
1 Pet. 2:24. so that we might *c.* to live
    for sin
Rev. 9:20. nor *c.* their worship of devils

celebrate-ing
Luke 15:23. let us have a feast to *c.* the
    day
    15:32. how could we help *c.* this happy
    day
Heb. 11:28. by faith he *c.* the Passover

celebrations
Mat. 14:6. at his birthday *c.* the daughter
    of Herodias

celestial
Mat. 24:29 ⎱
Mark 13:25 ⎰ the *c.* powers will be shaken
Luke 21:26 ⎰
2 Pet. 2:10. they are not afraid to insult
    c. beings
Jude 8. to flout authority, and to insult *c.*
    beings

celibacy
1 Cor. 7:25. on the question of *c.*, I have
    no instructions from the Lord
    7:36. if a man has a partner in *c.*

celibate
1 Cor. 7:34. *c.* woman cares for the
    Lord's business

cell
Acts 12:7. the *c.* was ablaze with light

cellar
Luke 11:33. no one lights a lamp and
    puts it in a *c.*

census
Acts 5:37. came Judas the Galilean at
    the time of the *c.*

centre-d
Col. 2:8. *c.* on the elemental spirits of
    the world
1 Pet. 3:4. in the inmost *c.* of your being
Rev. 4:6. in the *c.*, round the throne it-
    self

centurion
Acts 23:18. the *c.* took him and brought
    him to the commandant

Cephas
Gal. 1:18. I did go up to Jerusalem to
    get to know *C.*
    2:11. when *C.* came to Antioch
    2:14. I said to *C.*, before the whole
    congregation

certain-ly-ty
Mat. 26:18. go to a *c.* man in the city
John 7:40. this must *c.* be the expected
    prophet
    8:52. now we are *c.* that you are
    possessed
    16:30. we are *c.* now that you know
    everything
    17:8. they know with *c.* that I came
    from thee
Acts 2:36. let all Israel then accept as *c.*
    8:2. Stephen was given burial by *c.*
    devout men
    19:40. we *c.* run the risk of being
    charged with riot
    21:16. bringing a *c.* Mnason of
    Cyprus
    21:21. given *c.* information about you
Rom. 3:4. *c.* not! God must be true
    3:6. *c.* not! If God were unjust
    3:29. *c.*, of Gentiles also
    5:9. we shall all the more *c.* be saved
1 Cor. 4:18. *c.* persons who are filled
    with self-importance
    8:8. *c.* food will not bring us into
    God's presence
    11:22. on this point, *c.* not
    14:25. God is *c.* among you
Gal. 2:4. a concession to *c.* sham-
    Christians
Phil. 1:6. of one thing I am *c.*
    1:25. this indeed I know for *c.*: I shall
    stay

1 Thess. 1:4. we are c., brothers beloved by God

1 Tim. 1:3. command c. persons to give up teaching erroneous doctrines

1:19. c. persons made shipwreck of their faith

4:3. inculcate abstinence from c. foods

Heb. 11:1. makes us c. of realities we do not see

Jam. 1:19. of that you may be c., my friends

3:1. c. that we who teach shall ourselves be judged

certify

Mat. 8:4 ⎫
Mark 1:44 ⎬ that will c. the cure
Luke 5:14 ⎭

chain-s-ed

Mat. 14:3. had arrested John, put him in c.

27:2. put him in c. and led him off

Mark 15:1. put Jesus in c.

Acts 22:4. arresting its followers, men and women alike, and putting them in c.

26:29. might become what I am, apart from these c.

Eph. 6:20. for which I am an ambassador—in c.

Rev. 20:2. c. him up for a thousand years

chair

Mat. 23:2. the Pharisees sit in the c. of Moses

challenge-d-ing

John 2:18. the Jews c. Jesus

Gal. 5:26. c. one another to rivalry

Heb. 10:32. you met the c. of great sufferings

chamber

Acts 25:23. came in full state and entered the audience-c.

chance

Mark 3:20. a crowd collected round them that they had no c. to eat

John 7:1. the Jews were looking for a c. to kill him

1 Cor. 7:21. if a c. of liberty should come, take it

16:17. because they have done what you had no c. to do

2 Cor. 5:12. giving you a c. to show yourselves proud of us

11:12. any c. to put their vaunted apostleship

Heb. 4:1. should be found to have missed his c.

change-d

Mat. 21:30. afterwards he c. his mind and went

21:32. you did not c. your minds and believe him

Luke 9:29. while he was praying the appearance of his face c.

Rom. 2:4. meant to lead you to a c. of heart

2 Cor. 1:17. that was my intention; did I lightly c. my mind

7:9. but that the wound led to a c. of heart

7:10. a c. of heart too salutary to regret

2 Tim. 2:25. the Lord may grant them a c. of heart

chant-ed

Rev. 13:4. they worshipped the beast also, and c.

15:3. the song of the Lamb, as they c.

character-s

Mat. 9:10. many bad c.—tax-gatherers and others—were seated with him

Mark 2:15. when Jesus was at table in his house, many bad c.

Luke 15:1. other bad c. were all crowding in

Rom. 7:13. thereby sin exposed its true c.

1 Cor. 8:10. if a weak c. sees you sitting down

15:33. bad company is the ruin of a good c.

Tit. 1:6. of unimpeachable c., faithful to his one wife

1:7. a bishop must be a man of unimpeachable c.

Jam. 1:4. to complete a balanced c.

3:2. the man who never says a wrong thing is a perfect c.

1 Pet. 1:14. not let your c. be shaped any longer

charcoal

John 18:18. the police had made a c. fire

21:9. a c. fire there, with fish laid on it

charge-s-d

Mat. 8:33. the men in c. of them took to their heels

10:8. you received without cost; give without c.

12:10. to frame a c. against him

24:45. the sensible man c. by his master

24:47. put in c. of all his master's property

25:21 ⎫
25:23 ⎬ put you in c. of something big

26:62. have you no answer to the c.

26:63. by the living God I c. you to tell us

27:12. the c. laid against him

27:37. placed the inscription giving the c.

Mat. 27:66. and left the guard in *c.*
Mark 3:2. so that they could bring a *c.* against him
3:21. they set out to take *c.* of him
5:14. the men in *c.* of them took to their heels
13:34. put his servants in *c.*
14:60. have you no answer to the *c.*
15:3. the chief priests brought many *c.*
15:26. the inscription giving the *c.*
Luke 6:7. find a *c.* to bring against him
8:29. with the devil in *c.* made off
8:34. the men in *c.* of them saw what had happened
12:44. put in *c.* of all his master's property
19:17. you shall have *c.* of ten cities
19:19. take *c.* of five cities
23:14. on a *c.* of subversion . . . your *c.*
John 5:19. to this *c.* Jesus replied
8:6. hoping to frame a *c.* against him
10:2. the shepherd in *c.* of the sheep
10:18. this *c.* I have received from my Father
10:36. why do you *c.* me with blasphemy
12:6. the common purse, which was in his *c.*
13:29. Judas was in *c.* of the common purse
18:29. what *c.* do you bring against this man
19:16. Jesus was now taken in *c.*
Acts 1:20. let another take over his *c.*
11:30. sent it off in the *c.* of Barnabas
19:38. let the parties bring their *c.*
19:40. *c.* with riot for this day's work
20:28. of which the Holy Spirit has given you *c.*
22:30. what *c.* the Jews were bringing
23:28. the *c.* on which they were accusing him
24:8. the truth of all the *c.* we bring
24:13. they cannot make good the *c.*
24:19. if they had any *c.* against me
25:7. bringing many grave *c.*
25:9. stand trial on these *c.*
25:11. if there is no substance in the *c.*
25:16. given an opportunity of answering the *c.*
25:18. none of the *c.* I was expecting
25:27. without indicating the *c.* against him
26:2. my defence today upon all the *c.*
28:16. with a soldier in *c.* of him
28:18. there was no capital *c.* against me
Rom. 3:9. the *c.* that Jews and Greeks alike are all under the power of sin

7:3. she will incur the *c.* of adultery
9:14. is God to be *c.* with injustice
2 Cor. 10:2. *c.* us with moral weakness
11:7. I made no *c.* for preaching
Gal. 3:24. a kind of tutor in *c.* of us
3:25. the tutor's *c.* is at an end
1 Tim. 5:19. do not entertain a *c.* against an elder
2 Tim. 1:12. keep safe what he has put into my *c.*
1:14. guard the treasure put into our *c.*
2:2. into the *c.* of men you can trust
Jam. 3:8. an intractable evil, *c.* with deadly venom
1 Pet. 5:7. cast all your cares on him, for you are his *c.*
3 John 10. he lays baseless and spiteful *c.* against us

charitable
Acts 24:17. I came to bring *c.* gifts to my nation
Eph. 4:2. be forbearing with one another and *c.*

charity
Mat. 6:2. act of *c.*, do not announce it with a flourish of trumpets
6:3. when you do some act of *c.*
Luke 11:41. let what is in the cup be given in *c.*
12:33. sell your possessions and give in *c.*
19:8. I give half my possessions to *c.*
Acts 3:3. he asked for *c.*
9:36. who filled her days with acts of kindness and *c.*
10:4. your prayers and acts of *c.*
10:31. your acts of *c.* remembered before God
Rom. 12:8. if you give to *c.*, give with all your heart

charlatan-s
Acts 13:10. you utter imposter and *c.*
17:18. what can this *c.* be trying to say
2 Tim. 3:13. wicked men and *c.*

chasm
Luke 16:26. there is a great *c.* fixed between us

chaste
Rev. 14:4. they have kept themselves *c.*

chatter
1 Tim. 6:20. turn a deaf ear to empty and worldly *c.*
2 Tim. 2:16. avoid empty and worldly *c.*

cheap
2 Tim. 2:20. the former are valued, the latter held *c.*

cheat-ed
Luke 19:8. if I have *c.* anyone, I am ready to repay

cheer
Acts 14:17. gives you food and good *c*.
2 Cor. 2:2. who is left to *c*. me up
Phil. 2:19. it will *c*. me to hear news of you

cheerful-ly
Rom. 12:8. helping others in distress, do it *c*.
Eph. 6:7. the *c*. service of those who serve the Lord
Heb. 10:34. you *c*. accepted the seizure of your possessions

cherish-ed
1 Pet. 1:14. the desires you *c*. in your days of ignorance

chest
Mark 12:41. as people dropped their money into the *c*.
Luke 21:1. the rich people dropping their gifts into the *c*.

chief
Mat. 28:12. the *c*. priests offered the soldiers a substantial bribe
Acts 4:1. the *c*. priests came upon them
7:10. appointed him *c*. administrator for Egypt

child
Mat. 1:20. by the Holy Spirit that she has conceived this *c*.
1:25. he named the *c*. Jesus
2:2. the *c*. who is born to be king of the Jews
Mark 5:39. the *c*. is not dead
5:40. he took the *c*. father and mother
5:41. which means, 'Get up, my *c*.
7:30. she found the *c*. lying in bed
12:19. one dies leaving a wife but no *c*.
13:12. betray brother to death, and the father his *c*.
Luke 1:17. to reconcile father and *c*.
1:35. the holy *c*. to be born will be called 'Son of God
1:57. for Elizabeth's *c*. to be born
2:6. the time came for her *c*. to be born
2:33. the *c*. father and mother were full of wonder
2:38. she talked about the *c*. to all
8:51. and the *c*. father and mother
8:54. called her: 'Get up, my *c*.
16:25. remember, my *c*., that all the good things
20:28. one dies leaving a wife but no *c*.
23:29. the wombs that never bore a *c*.
John 7:23. if a *c*. is circumcised on the Sabbath
Acts 7:20. Moses was born. He was a fine *c*.

Gal. 4:27. barren woman who never bore *c*.
Philem. 10. appeal to you about my *c*.
1 John 2:29. every man who does right is his *c*.
3:8. the man who sins is a *c*. of the devil
3:9. a *c*. of God does not commit sin . . . he is God's *c*.
3:10. no one who does not do right is God's *c*.
3:12. Cain, who was a *c*. of the evil one
4:7. everyone who loves is a *c*. of God
5:1. is a *c*. of God, and to love the parent means to love his *c*.
5:4. every *c*. of God is victor
5:18. no *c*. of God is a sinner
3 John 11. the well-doer is a *c*. of God

childbirth
Rom. 8:22. as if in the pangs of *c*.

childhood
Mark 9:21. how long has he been like this?' 'From *c*.
2 Tim. 3:15. from early *c*. you have been familiar

childish
1 Cor. 14:20. do not be *c*., my friends

childless
Mat. 22:24. if a man should die *c*.
Luke 20:29. the first took a wife and died *c*.
Acts 7:5. though he was then *c*.

children
Mat. 19:15. he laid his hands on the *c*.
21:16. and babes at the breast sound aloud thy praise
24:19 ⎱ those who have *c*. at the
Mark 13:17 ⎰ breast
Luke 1:55. mercy to Abraham and his children's *c*.
21:23. or have *c*. at the breast
John 1:12. he gave the right to become *c*. of God
8:47. you are not God's *c*.
1 Cor. 4:14. you are my dear *c*.
Gal. 4:18. not only when I am present with you, dear *c*.
4:24. the one bearing *c*. into slavery
Phil. 2:15. above reproach, faultless *c*. of God
1 Pet. 3:6. her *c*. you have now become
1 John 3:1. we were called God's *c*., and such we are
3:2. here and now, dear friends, we are God's *c*.

choice
Mat. 11:26 ⎱ yes, Father, such was thy *c*.
Luke 10:21 ⎰
Rom. 8:20. it was made the victim of frustration, not by its own *c*.

Rom. 11:28. God's *c*. stands, and they are his friends

1 Cor. 7:37. has complete control of his own *c*.

9:17. I did it of my own *c*. . . . I do it apart from my own *c*.

15:38. God clothes it with the body of his *c*.

2 Cor. 5:14. the love of Christ leaves us no *c*.

Col. 1:19. by God's own *c*., came to dwell

2 Thess. 2:12. make sinfulness their deliberate *c*.

1 Pet. 2:4. *c*. and precious in the sight of God

2:6. I lay in Zion a *c*. corner-stone

2 Pet. 1:10. God's *c*. and calling of you

choose-s-ing

Mat. 11:27. to whom the Son may *c*. to reveal him

20:14. I *c*. to pay the last man the same

Luke 4:6. I can give it to anyone I *c*.

10:22 to whom the Son may *c*. to reveal him

John 8:44. you *c*. to carry out your father's desires

Acts 15:14. to *c*. from among them a people

17:31. justly judged, by a man of his *c*.

Rom. 9:18. shows mercy as he *c*., but also makes men stubborn as he *c*.

1 Cor. 4:21. *c*., then: am I to come to you with a rod

2 Cor. 12:6. if I should *c*. to boast

Jam. 3:4. whatever course the helmsman *c*.

4:4. whoever *c*. to be the world's friend

chorus

2 Cor. 4:15. the greater maybe the *c*. of thanksgiving

chose-n

Mat. 24:22. for the sake of God's *c*. it will be cut short

24:24. to mislead even God's *c*.

24:31. gather his *c*. from the four winds

27:15. release one prisoner *c*. by the people

Mark 13:22. to mislead God's *c*.

13:27. gather his *c*. from the four winds

Luke 9:35. this is my Son, my *C*.

12:32. your Father has *c*. to give you the Kingdom

18:7. will not God vindicate his *c*.

John 1:34. this is God's *C*. One

21:18. walked where you *c*.

Rom. 8:33. who will be the accuser of God's *c*. ones

1 Cor. 1:21. he *c*. to save those who have faith

12:18. to its own place in the body, as he *c*.

Gal. 1:16. *c*. to reveal his Son to me

Phil. 2:13. for his own *c*. purpose

Col. 1:20. through him God *c*. to reconcile

3:12. the garments that suit God's *c*. people

1 Thess. 1:4. brothers beloved by God, that he has *c*. you

2:8. we *c*. to impart to you

1 Tim. 5:21. the angels who are his *c*.

2 Tim. 2:10. I endure it all for the sake of God's *c*. ones

Tit. 1:1. the faith of God's *c*. people

1 Pet. 1:2. *c*. of old in the purpose of God

5:13. *c*. by God like you

2 John 13. the children of your Sister, *c*. by God

Christ-'s

Rom. 5:9. *C*. sacrificial death

6:6. has been crucified with *C*.

10:17. comes through the word of *C*.

16:2. in the fellowship of *C*., a welcome

1 Cor. 6:17. links himself with *C*. is one with him

11:11. in *C*. fellowship woman is as essential

2 Cor. 1:20. it is through *C*. Jesus that we say 'Amen

5:21. *C*. was innocent of sin

Eph. 1:7. in *C*. our release is secured

1:9. determined beforehand in *C*.

1:11. in *C*. indeed we have been given our share

5:21. be subject to one another out of reverence for *C*.

5:29. that is how *C*. treats the church

Col. 1:22. *C*. death in his body of flesh and blood

1:29. the energy and power of *C*.

2:13. he has made you alive with *C*.

3:15. let *C*. peace be arbiter in your hearts

4:10. *C*. captive like myself

2 Thess. 1:7. when our Lord Jesus *C*. is revealed from heaven

Philem. 20. we are both in *C*.

Heb. 10:12. *C*. offered for all time one sacrifice for sins

1 Pet. 3:15. hold the Lord *C*. in reverence

1 John 2:6. to live as *C*. himself lived

2:8. *C*. has made this true

3:3. purifies himself, as *C*. is pure

3:5. *C*. appeared, as you know, to do away with sins

3:16. *C*. laid down his life for us

1 John 4:21. this command comes to us from *C.* himself
3 John 7. it was on *C.* work that they went out
Rev. 6:11. all their brothers in *C.* service
14:13. happy are the dead who die in the faith of *C.*

Christian-s
Acts 11:29. for the relief of their fellow-*C.*
14:2. poisoned their minds against the *C.*
15:3. great rejoicing among all the *C.*
16:1. the son of a Jewish *C.* mother
16:2. he was well spoken of by the *C.*
16:40. where they met their fellow-*C.*
19:23. the *C.* movement gave rise to a serious disturbance
19:30. the other *C.* would not let him
20:2. speaking words of encouragement to the *C.*
21:16. Mnason of Cyprus, a *C.* from the early days
22:5. to bring the *C.* there to Jerusalem as prisoners
24:22. well informed about the *C.* Movement
28:14. there we found fellow-*C.*
28:15. the *C.* there had had news of us
Rom. 8:9. if a man does not possess the Spirit of Christ, he is no *C.*
9:1. I am speaking the truth as a *C.*
14:14. I am absolutely convinced, as a *C.*
15:27. if the Jewish *C.* shared
16:1. Phoebe, a fellow *C.*
16:7. they were *C.* before I was
16:22. add my *C.* greetings
1 Cor. 4:10. you are such sensible *C.*
4:17. a most trustworthy *C.*
5:11. so-called *C.* who leads a loose life
6:5. a decision in a brother-*C.* cause
7:12. if a *C.* has a heathen wife
7:14. belongs to God through his *C.* wife, and the heathen wife through her *C.* husband
7:15. the *C.* husband or wife
7:22. received the call to be a *C.*
9:5. take a *C.* wife about with me
14:4. builds up a *C.* community
2 Cor. 8:4. generous service to their fellow-*C.*
11:17. I am not speaking here as a *C.*
12:2. I know a *C.* man who fourteen years ago
12:19. speaking in God's sight and as *C.* men
Gal. 1:2. the *C.* congregations of Galatia
2:4. a concession to certain sham-*C.*
2:12. taking his meals with Gentile *C.*
2:13. the other Jewish *C.*

Eph. 4:21. were you not as *C.* taught the truth
5:8. now as *C.* you are light
6:4. which belong to a *C.* upbringing
Phil. 1:14. confidence to most of our fellow-*C.*
Col. 3:18. that is your *C.* duty
3:20. and is the *C.* way
4:11. Jewish *C.*, these are the only ones who work with me
1 Thess. 4:10. your fellow-*C.* throughout Macedonia
4:14. those who died as *C.*
4:16. first the *C.* dead will rise
2 Thess. 3:6. *C.* brother who falls into idle habits
1 Tim. 3:7. a good reputation with the non-*C.* public
3:13. on matters of the *C.* faith
5:16. if a *C.* man or woman
6:1. the *C.* teaching are not brought into disrepute
6:2. being their *C.* brothers
2 Tim. 3:12. all who want to live a godly life as *C.*
Philem. 16. both as man and as *C.*
20. as a *C.*, be generous with me
Heb. 13:1. never cease to love your fellow-*C.*
1 Pet. 1:22. affection towards your brother *C.*
3:16. those who malign your *C.* conduct
5:9. your brother *C.* are going through the same kinds of suffering
3 John 5. everything that you do for these our fellow-*C.*

Christianity
Heb. 6:1. stop discussing the rudiments of *C.*

church
Acts 11:1. members of the *c.* in Judaea
12:17. report this to James and the members of the *c.*
1 Cor. 14:26. aim at one thing: to build up the *c.*

circle-s
Mat. 28:15. is current in Jewish *c.* to this day
Mark 3:34. those who were sitting in the *c.* about him
Rev. 4:4. in a *c.* about this throne
5:6. inside the *c.* of living creatures and the *c.* of elders.

circumstance-s
Rom. 4:10. in what *c.* was it so counted
2 Cor. 6:4. to recommend ourselves in all *c.*
Phil. 4:11. resources in myself whatever my *c.*
Jam. 1:9. the brother in humble *c.*

cite

1 Pet. 1:11. to find out what was the time, and what the *c.*

cite

Rom. 10:19. in reply, I first *c.* Moses

citizen-s

Mat. 17:25. from their own *c.*, or from aliens

17:26. the *c.* are exempt

Luke 19:47. bent on making an end of him, with the support of the leading *c.*

Acts 16:37. though we are Roman *c.*

16:38. alarmed to hear that they were Roman *c.*

22:25. flog a man who is a Roman *c.*

22:26. this man is a Roman *c.*

22:27. tell me, are you a Roman *c.*

22:29. he realized that Paul was a Roman *c.*

23:27. I discovered that he was a Roman *c.*

25:23. high-ranking officers and prominent *c.*

Phil. 3:20. we, by contrast, are *c.* of heaven

1 Tim. 1:9. it is not aimed at good *c.*

Heb. 8:11. saying to brother and fellow-*c.*, 'Know the Lord

12:23. assembly of the first-born *c.* of heaven

citizenship

Acts 22:28. it cost me a large sum to acquire this *c.*

city

Mat. 23:37. Jerusalem, the *c.* that murders the prophets

Mark 1:5. country-side and the *c.* of Jerusalem

Luke 13:34. Jerusalem, the *c.* that murders the prophets

19:1. entering Jericho he made his way through the *c.*

21:21. those who are in the *c.* itself must leave it

21:37. leave the *c.* and spend the night on the hill called Olivet

23:5. has spread as far as this *c.*

John 11:19. people had come from the *c.* to Martha and Mary

Acts 1:13. entering the *c.* they went to the room upstairs

4:27. make common cause in this very *c.*

9:24. kept watch on the *c.* gates

14:5. with the connivance of the *c.* authorities

16:19. dragged them to the *c.* authorities

17:17. also in the *c.* square every day

Rom. 15:28. set out for Spain by way of your *c.*

Rev. 2:13. Antipas, my faithful witness, was killed in your *c.*

21:22. I saw no temple in the *c.*

21:25. the gates of the *c.* shall never be shut

22:1. down the middle of the *c.* street

civilian

2 Tim. 2:4. will not let himself be involved in *c.* affairs

civilize-d

Acts 19:27. she who is worshipped by all Asia and the *c.* world

claim-s-ed-ing

Mat. 24:5. many will come *c.* my name

24:24. *c.* to be messiahs

Mark 13:6. *c.* my name

13:22. *c.* to be messiahs

Luke 19:23. I could have *c.* it with interest

21:8. many will come *c.* my name

23:2. *c.* to be Messiah, a king

John 5:18. he *c.* equality with God

8:53. what do you *c.* to be

10:33. you, a mere man, *c.* to be a god

19:7. he has *c.* to be Son of God

19:12. any man who *c.* to be a king is defying Caesar

19:21. he *c.* to be king of the Jews

Acts 4:32. not a man of them *c.* any of his possessions

5:36. Theudas came forward, *c.* to be somebody

8:9. *c.* to be someone great

15:17. the Gentiles, whom I have *c.* for my own

Rom. 8:12. our lower nature has no *c.* upon us

13:8. leave no *c.* outstanding against you . . . has satisfied every *c.* of the law

1 Cor. 1:2. dedicated to him in Christ Jesus, *c.* by him

7:4. the wife cannot *c.* her body as her own . . . the husband cannot *c.* his body

9:12. have not we a stronger *c.*

9:13. *c.* their share of the sacrifice

9:15. nor do I intend to *c.* it in this letter

9:16. I can *c.* no credit for it

14:37. if anyone *c.* to be inspired

2 Cor. 3:4. through Christ, that we make such *c.*

10:12. those who put forward their own *c.*

Phil. 3:4. thinks to base his *c.* on externals

2 Thess. 2:4. *c.* to be a god himself

1 Tim. 2:10. as befits women who *c.* to be religious

3:13. may *c.* a high standing and the right to speak

1 Tim. 6:21. who lay *c.* to it have shot far wide of the faith

2 Tim. 2:6. has first *c.* on the crop

Heb. 6:18. who have *c.* his protection

11:7. made good his own *c.* to the righteousness

12:17. he wanted afterwards to *c.* the blessing

Jam. 2:7. the honoured name by which God has *c.* you

2:18. one who *c.* to have faith

3:5. it is a small member but it can make huge *c.*

3:14. consider whether your *c.* are not false

1 Pet. 2:9. a people *c.* by God for his own

1 John 1:6. if we *c.* to be sharing in his life

1:8. if we *c.* to be sinless, we are self-deceived

2:6. whoever *c.* to be dwelling in him

Rev. 2:2. those who *c.* to be apostles but are not

2:9. those who *c.* to be Jews but are not

2:20. the woman who *c.* to be a prophetess

3:9. who *c.* to be Jews but are lying frauds

20:6. upon such the second death has no claim

clamour-ing

John 18:40. again the *c.* rose: 'Not him; we want Barabbas

Acts 21:31. while they were *c.* for his death

clan

Acts 7:16. had bought and paid for from the *c.* of Emmor

clang-ing

1 Cor. 13:1. I am a sounding gong or a *c.* cymbal

clasp-ed

Mat. 28:9. they came up and *c.* his feet

class

Luke 18:18. a man of the ruling *c.* put this question to him

2 Cor. 10:12. we should not dare to *c.* ourselves

clean-s

Mat. 12:44. the house unoccupied, swept *c.*

27:24. my hands are *c.* of this man's blood

Mark 7:19. he declared all foods *c.*

Luke 11:25. the house swept *c.*, and tidy

John 15:2. every fruiting branch he *c.*

1 Tim. 1:5. the love which springs from a *c.* heart

5:22. keep your own hands *c.*

Heb. 10:22. our guilty hearts sprinkled *c.*

Rev. 15:6. they were robed in fine linen, *c.* and shining

22:14. happy are those who wash their robes *c.*

cleanse-d-ing

Mat. 8:4. the offering laid down by Moses for your *c.*

2 Tim. 2:21. a man must *c.* himself from all those evil things

Heb. 6:2. instruction about *c.* rites

9:10. various rites of *c.*

9:14. his blood will *c.* our conscience

9:22. everthing is *c.* by blood

9:23. these sacrifices *c.* the copies of heavenly things

10:2. the worshippers, *c.* once for all

2 Pet. 1:9. he has forgotten how he was *c.*

clear-er

Mat. 3:3. *c.* a straight path for him

16:21. Jesus began to make it *c.* to his disciples

Mark 1:3 }
Luke 3:4 } *c.* a straight path for him

Acts 2:30. it is *c.* therefore that he spoke as a prophet

5:38. keep *c.* of these men

18:6. my conscience is *c.*

23:1. with a perfectly *c.* conscience before God

24:16. keep at all times a *c.* conscience

25:25. it was *c.* to me that he had committed no capital crime

Rom. 14:22. if you have a *c.* conviction . . . a *c.* conscience

15:27. the Gentiles have a *c.* duty to contribute

1 Cor. 9:26. I run with a *c.* goal before me

14:8. if the trumpet-call is not *c.*

2 Cor. 8:24. give them *c.* expression of your love

Gal. 1:11. I must make it *c.* to you, my friends

1 Tim. 3:9. a *c.* conscience with a firm hold

2 Tim. 3:5. keep *c.* of men like these

Tit. 3:9. steer *c.* of foolish speculations

Heb. 7:15. the argument becomes still *c.*

13:18. we are convinced that our conscience is *c.*

1 Pet. 3:16. keep your conscience *c.*

1 John 2:19. *c.* that not all in our company truly belong to it

clearly

Luke 23:15. *c.* he has done nothing to deserve death

John 3:21. *c.* seen that God is in all he does

Acts 10:3. he *c.* saw an angel of God

Acts 10:28. God has shown me *c.* that I must not call any man profane

Rom. 7:20. *c.* it is no longer I who am the agent

10:20. I was *c.* shown to those who never asked about me

1 Cor. 9:10. or is the reference *c.* to ourselves

14:22. *c.* then these 'strange tongues

15:27. it *c.* means to exclude God

Gal. 2:11. because he was *c.* in the wrong

Phil. 1:20. the greatness of Christ will shine out *c.* in my person

Heb. 2:10. it was *c.* fitting that God

6:17. so God, desiring to show even more *c.*

clever-ness

1 Cor. 1:19. bring to nothing the *c.* of the clever

Jam. 3:13. who among you is wise or *c.*

climax

Heb. 9:26. at the *c.* of history to abolish sin

climbed

Mat. 14:32. they then *c.* into the boat

Mark 6:51. he *c.* into the boat beside them

Luke 19:6. he *c.* down as fast as he could

clinch

2 Pet. 1:10. to *c.* God's choice and calling of you

cling-s-ing

Luke 10:11. dust of your town that *c.* to our feet

John 20:17. do not *c.* to me, for I have not yet ascended

Rom. 12:9. loathing evil and *c.* to the good

Heb. 12:1. every sin to which we *c.*

cloak-s

Mat. 9:20. touched the edge of his *c.*

9:21. if I can only touch his *c.*

14:36. to allow them simply to touch the edge of his *c.*

21:7. they laid their *c.* on them

21:8. carpeted the road with their *c.*

Mark 5:27. behind in the crowd and touched his *c.*

6:56. simply touch the edge of his *c.*

10:50. threw off his *c.*, sprang up, and came to Jesus

11:7. spread their *c.* on it

11:8. people carpeted the road with their *c.*

13:16. he must not turn back for his *c.*

Luke 5:36. tears a piece from a new *c.* . . . he will have made a hole in the new *c.*

8:44. touched the edge of his *c.*

19:35. they threw their *c.* on the colt

22:36. let him sell his *c.* to buy one

John 19:1. robed him in a purple *c.*

19:5. wearing the crown of thorns and the purple *c.*

Acts 12:8. wrap your *c.* round you and follow me

18:6. he shook out the skirts of his *c.*

22:23. waving their *c.* and flinging dust

Heb. 1:12. thou shalt fold them up like a *c.*

cloister

John 10:23. in the temple precincts, in Solomon's *C.*

Acts 3:11. towards them in Solomon's *C.*

5:12. meet by common consent in Solomon's *C.*

close-ly-r

Luke 10:9. the kingdom of God has come *c.* to you

10:11. the kingdom of God has come *c.*

12:1. packed so *c.* that they were treading on one another

14:1. they were watching him *c.*

16:23. with Lazarus *c.* beside him

19:11. he was now *c.* to Jerusalem

John 7:2. the Jewish Feast of Tabernacles was *c.* at hand

13:23. reclining *c.* beside Jesus

13:25. leaned back *c.* to Jesus and asked

21:20. who at supper had leaned back *c.* to him

Acts 7:31. he approached to look *c.*

10:24. called together his relatives and *c.* friends

12:19. Herod made *c.* search

16:23. the jailer to keep them under *c.* guard

23:15. the pretext of a *c.* investigation

Gal. 3:23. before this faith came, we were *c.* prisoners

1 Tim. 4:16. *c.* watch on yourself and your teaching

Jam. 1:25. the man who looks *c.* into the perfect law

4:8. come *c.* to God, and he will come *c.* to you

Rev. 6:8. Hades came *c.* behind

close-s-d-ing

Mark 6:52. their minds were *c.*

8:17. are your minds *c.*

9:25. the crowd was *c.* in upon them

Luke 12:3. whispered behind *c.* doors

21:34. the great Day *c.* upon you suddenly

Jam. 5:3. in an age that is near its *c.*

clot-s

Luke 22:44. his sweat was like *c.* of blood

cloth-s
John 11:44. his face wrapped in a *c*.
  19:40. with the spices, in strips of linen *c*.
Acts 10:11. looked like a great sheet of sail-*c*.
  11:5. sheet of sail-*c*., slung by the four corners
Rev. 18:12. *c*. of purple and scarlet, silks and fine linens

clothed
1 Cor. 15:53. this perishable being must be *c*. with the imperishable, and what is mortal must be *c*. with immortality
  15:54. our mortality has been *c*. with immortality
Rev. 17:4. the woman was *c*. in purple

clothes
Mat. 6:25. *c*. to cover your body . . . the body more than *c*.
  6:28. why be anxious about *c*.
  17:2. his *c*. became white as the light
  22:12. come to be here without your wedding *c*.
  27:31. dressed him in his own *c*.
  27:35. they divided his *c*. among them
Mark 9:3. his *c*. became dazzling white
  15:24. they divided his *c*. among them
Luke 7:25. you must look in palaces for grand *c*.
  9:29. his *c*. became dazzling white
  12:22. *c*. to cover your body
  12:23. the body more than *c*.
  23:34. they divided his *c*. among them
John 19:23. took possession of his *c*.
Acts 20:33. I have not wanted anyone's money or *c*.
  22:20. I looked after the *c*. of those who killed him
1 Cor. 15:38. God *c*. it with the body of his choice
1 Tim. 2:9. or expensive *c*., but with good deeds
Heb. 1:11. like *c*. they shall all grow old
Jam. 2:2. a poor man in shabby *c*.
  5:2. your fine *c*. are moth-eaten
Rev. 3:18. white *c*. to put on
  16:15. stays awake and keeps on his *c*.

clothing
Mat. 3:4. John's *c*. was a rough coat
John 19:24. cast lots for my *c*.
Jude 23. hate the very *c*. that is contaminated
Rev. 3:4. who have not polluted their *c*.

cloud
Luke 1:79. live in darkness, under the *c*. of death

clue
Acts 8:31. unless someone will give me the *c*.

14:17. he has not left you without some *c*. to his nature
Rev. 17:9. the *c*. for those who can interpret it

clutch-es-ing
John 10:39. he escaped from their *c*.
Acts 3:11. as he was *c*. Peter and John
  12:11. rescued me from Herod's *c*.
2 Cor. 11:20. exploits you, gets you in his *c*.
  11:33. through a window in the wall, and so escaped his *c*.
2 Tim. 3:6. get miserable women into their *c*.

coarse
Eph. 5:4. no *c*., stupid, or flippant talk

coast
Acts 16:7. reached the *c*. at Troas
  17:14. sent Paul off at once to go down to the *c*.
  27:5. off the *c*. of Cilicia
  27:8. hugging the *c*.
  27:13. sailed along the *c*. of Crete
  27:29. we might be cast ashore on a rugged *c*.

coat-s
Mat. 3:4. a rough *c*. of camel's hair
  5:40. let him have your *c*. as well
  9:16. on to an old *c*.; for then the patch tears away from the *c*.
  24:18. he must not turn back for his *c*.
Mark 1:6. a rough *c*. of camel's hair
  2:21. unshrunk cloth on to an old *c*.
Acts 7:58. laid their *c*. at the feet of a young man
Eph. 6:14. for *c*. of mail put on integrity

code
Rom. 2:27. your written *c*.
  7:6. the way of a written *c*.

codicil
Gal. 3:15. no one else can set it aside or add a *c*.

cogent
Acts 9:22. *c*. proofs that Jesus was the Messiah

cohort
Acts 10:1. a centurion in the Italian *C*.
  21:31. the officer commanding the *c*.
  27:1. Julius, of the Augustan *C*.

coin-s
Mat. 17:27. open its mouth, and you will find a silver *c*.
Mark 12:42. widow who dropped in two tiny *c*.
Luke 21:2. poor widow putting in two tiny *c*.
John 2:15. the money-changers, scattering their *c*.
Rev. 18:6. pay her back in her own *c*.

collapse-d
Luke 6:49. the river burst upon it, the house *c.*
Acts 5:38. of human origin, it will *c.*

colleague-s
Acts 5:17. the High Priest and his *c.*
  5:21. the High Priest arrived with his *c.*
Rom. 16:21. greetings to you from my *c.* Timothy
1 Cor. 1:1. our *c.* Sosthenes
2 Cor. 1:1. our *c.* Timothy
  2:13. my *c.* Titus was not there
Col.   1:1 ⎫
Philem. 1 ⎭ our *c.* Timothy

collect-s-ed-ing
Mat. 12:45. *c.* seven other spirits more wicked
  13:30. *c.* the wheat into my barn
  13:48. *c.* the good fish into pails
  17:25. from whom do earthly monarchs *c.* tax
  21:34. to *c.* the produce due to him
  22:10. *c.* all they could find, good and bad
  27:27. they *c.* the whole company round him
Mark 2:2. he was at home; and such a crowd *c.*
  3:20. such a crowd *c.* round them
  8:1. a huge crowd had *c.*
  12:2. to *c.* from them his share
Luke 11:26. *c.* seven other spirits
  12:18. I will *c.* in them all my corn
  20:10. a servant to the tenants to *c.* from them
  22:6. to betray him to them without *c.* a crowd
John 6:12. *c.* the pieces left over
Acts 19:19. *c.* their books and burnt them
  24:12. not find me arguing with anyone, or *c.* a crowd
1 Cor. 16:2. that there may be no *c.* when I come

collector-s
Mat. 17:24. the *c.* of the temple-tax

colonnade-s
John 5:2. a place with five *c.*
  5:3. in these *c.* there lay a crowd of sick people

combat-ing
Col. 2:23. of no use at all in *c.* sensuality

combine-d
1 Cor. 12:24. God has *c.* the various parts of the body
1 Tim. 3:9. men who *c.* a clear conscience with a firm hold

come-s-ing
Mat. 4:19. *c.* with me, and I will make you fishers of men

5:25. if someone sues you, *c.* to terms with him
6:33. all the rest will *c.* to you as well
7:22. when that day *c.*, many will say to me
10:11. when you *c.* to any town or village
10:19. when the time *c.*, the words you need will be given
11:12. since the *c.* of John the Baptist
11:13. the prophets and the Law foretold things to *c.*
12:34. the words that the mouth utters *c.* from the overflowing of the heart
12:36. a thoughtless word that *c.* from men's lips
12:43. when an unclean spirit *c.* out of a man
12:45. they all *c.* in and settle down
13:27. where has the darnel *c.* from
15:23. see how she *c.* shouting after us
20:28. the Son of Man; he did not *c.* to be served
21:41. his share of the crop when the season *c.*
22:38. the greatest commandment. It *c.* first
24:24. impostors will *c.* claiming to be messiahs
25:1. when that day *c.*
25:5. the bridegroom was late in *c.*
25:23. *c.* and share your master's delight
25:43. you did not *c.* to my help
Mark 1:15. the time has *c.*
  3:3. *c.* and stand out here
  3:23. he called them to *c.* forward
  3:31. asking him to *c.* out to them
  4:11. everything *c.* by way of parables
  4:19. all kinds of evil desire *c.* in
  8:24. the man's sight began to *c.* back
  12:23. at the resurrection, when they *c.* back to life
  13:7. the end is still to *c.*
  13:11. when the time *c.* say whatever is given you
  13:18. pray that it may not *c.* in winter
  13:25. the stars will *c.* falling from the sky
  14:11. when they heard what he had *c.* for
  15:32. let the Messiah, the king of Israel, *c.* down now from the cross
  16:18. they will *c.* to no harm
Luke 1:22. when he did *c.* out he could not speak
  2:10. great joy *c.* to the whole people
  4:13. having *c.* to the end of all his temptations
  4:21. this text has *c.* true
  5:2. the fishermen had *c.* ashore

Luke 8:6. after *c.* up, withered for lack of moisture

9:8. one of the old prophets had *c.* back to life

12:12. when the time *c.* the Holy Spirit will instruct you

13:5. you will all of you *c.* to the same end

13:25. I do not know where you *c.* from

15:24. this son of mine was dead and has *c.* back to life

16:17. easier for heaven and earth to *c.* to an end

17:18. could none be found to *c.* back and give praise

17:24. will the Son of Man be when his day *c.*

18:31. will *c.* true for the Son of Man

22:32. when you have *c.* to yourself

22:49. when his followers saw what was *c.*

John 1:32. I saw the Spirit *c.* down from heaven

1:33. the Spirit *c.* down

3:18. does not *c.* under judgement

6:46. he who has *c.* from God has seen the Father

7:17. know whether my teaching *c.* from him

7:52. prophets do not *c.* from Galilee

9:16. how could such signs *c.* from a sinful man

9:29. we do not know where he *c.* from

10:9. anyone who *c.* into the fold through me

11:4. it has *c.* for the glory of God

11:25. though he die, he shall *c.* to life

12:43. the honour which *c.* from God

17:7. all thy gifts have *c.* to me from thee

18:36. my kingly authority *c.* from elsewhere

19:28. all had now *c.* to its appointed end

Acts 3:21. until the time of universal restoration *c.*

8:16. until then the Spirit had not *c.* upon any of them

13:42. they were asked to *c.* again and speak

27:20. our last hopes of *c.* through alive

27:29. prayed for daylight to *c.*

Rom. 6:8. we shall also *c.* to life with him

8:23. first fruits of the harvest to *c.*

8:26. the Spirit *c.* to the aid of our weakness

10:6. the righteousness that *c.* by faith

11:5. a 'remnant' has *c.* into being

11:12. how much more their *c.* to full strength

1 Cor. 1:5. the enrichment that has *c.* to you in Christ

4:8. *c.* into your fortune already. You have *c.* into your kingdom

6:2. if the world is to *c.* before you for judgement

6:9. the unjust will never *c.* into possession

7:21. if a chance of liberty should *c.*, take it

8:6. the Father, from whom all being *c.*

9:12. I put up with all that *c.* my way

10:13. when the test *c.* he will at the same time provide

11:12. through woman that man now *c.* to be

13:8. love will never *c.* to an end

13:10. the partial vanishes when wholeness *c.*

15:34. *c.* back to a sober and upright life

15:36. not *c.* to life unless it has first died

15:46. the spiritual does not *c.* first; the animal body *c.* first

15:54. the saying of Scripture will *c.* true

16:22. *c.*, O Lord

2 Cor. 1:22. a pledge of what is to *c.*

3:3. a letter that has *c.* from Christ

3:5. such qualification as we have *c.* from God

4:7. power does not *c.* from us

5:20. we *c.* therefore as Christ's ambassadors

6:2. the hour of favour has now *c.*

7:3. *c.* death, *c.* life, we meet it together

11:5. have I in any way *c.* short

12:9. power *c.* to its full strength in weakness

Gal. 3:21. righteousness would have *c.* from keeping the law

3:24. until Christ should *c.*

4:24. the covenant that *c.* from Mount Sinai

Eph. 1:17. by which there *c.* the knowledge of him

6:17. the words that *c.* from God

Phil. 1:11. righteousness that *c.* through Jesus Christ

3:9. righteousness which *c.* from faith in Christ

3:20. from heaven we expect our deliverer to *c.*

Col. 1:11. ample power to meet whatever *c.*

1:27. Christ in you, the hope of glory to *c.*

2:2. to *c.* to the full wealth of conviction

2 Tim. 1:8. the strength that *c.* from God

4:1. his *c.* appearance

Tit. 1:13. that they may *c.* to a sane belief

Heb. 9:27. after death *c.* judgement

11:26. the *c.* day of recompense

Jam. 3:10. out of the same mouth *c.* praises and curses

4:8. *c.* close to God, and he will *c.* close to you

1 Pet. 1:5. until salvation *c.*

1:7. trials *c.* so that your faith

1 John 2:5. the divine love has indeed *c.* to its perfection

4:21. this command *c.* to us from Christ himself

Rev. 20:5. the rest of the dead did not *c.* to life

21:10. *c.* down out of heaven from God

command-s-ed-ing

Mark 9:25. I *c.* you, come out of him

John 14:31. I love the Father, and do exactly as he *c.*

17:6. they have obeyed thy *c.*

Acts 7:44. as God *c.* when he told Moses

19:27. goddess Diana will cease to *c.* respect

21:31. the officer *c.* the cohort

24:22. Lysias the *c.* officer

Rom. 5:14. by disobeying a direct *c.*

6:22. freed from the *c.* of sin

1 Thess. 4:12. *c.* the respect of those outside

4:16. at the word of *c.*

1 Tim. 1:3. *c.* certain persons to give up teaching erroneous doctrines

2 Tim. 2:4. wholly at his *c.* officer's disposal

Heb. 2:14. break the power of him who had death at his *c.*

Rev. 3:8. yet you have observed my *c.*

3:10. you have kept my *c.* and stood fast

commandant

Acts 21:32. as soon as they saw the *c.*

21:33. the *c.* stepped forward

21:37. before Paul was taken into the barracks he said to the *c.*, 'May I say something to you?' The *c.* said

22:24. the *c.* ordered him to be brought

22:26. reported it to the *c.*

22:27. the *c.* came to Paul

22:28. the *c.* rejoined

22:29. the *c.* himself was alarmed

23:10. the *c.* was afraid that Paul would be torn in pieces

23:15. apply to the *c.* to bring him down

23:17. take this young man to the *c.*

23:18. brought him to the *c.*

23:19. the *c.* took him by the arm

23:22. the *c.* dismissed the young man

24:7. Lysias the *c.*

commander-s

Mark 6:21. a banquet to his chief officials and *c.*

John 18:12. with their *c.* and the Jewish police

Eph. 2:2. you obeyed the *c.* of the spiritual powers

Rev. 19:18. to eat the flesh of kings and *c.*

commandment-s

Mat. 19:18. which *c.*?' he asked

John 15:17. this is my *c.* to you: love one another

Rom. 8:4. that the *c.* of the law may find fulfilment

Gal. 5:14. the whole law can be summed up in a single *c.*

Heb. 9:19. Moses had recited all the *c.*

commemorate-d

Heb. 11:39. one and all, are *c.* for their faith

commend-ed

Acts 7:10. *c.* him to Pharoah

14:26. been *c.* to the grace of God

15:40. *c.* by the brothers to the grace of the Lord

1 Cor. 11:2. I *c.* you for always keeping me in mind

11:17. a practice which I cannot *c.*

11:22. can I *c.* you? on this point, certainly not

commendation

Rom. 2:29. his *c.* not from men but from God

1 Pet. 2:14. the *c.* of those who do right

commission-ed

Mark 3:15. with a *c.* to drive out devils

Acts 7:35. this very man was *c.* as ruler

Rom. 1:5. the privilege of a *c.* in his name

10:15. how could anyone spread the news without a *c.*

2 Cor. 4:1. we have been entrusted with this *c.*

10:14. we are not overstretching our *c.*

Gal. 1:1. or human *c.*, but by *c.* from Jesus Christ

Eph. 1:1. *c.* by the will of God

Phil. 2:25. *c.* to minister to my needs

Col. 1:1. Paul, apostle of Christ Jesus *c.*

commissioner

2 Cor. 11:32. the *c.* of King Aretas

commit-s-ted-ting

Mat. 5:21. do not *c.* murder; anyone who *c.* murder

Mat. 18:15. brother *c.* a sin, go and take the matter up

28:18. full authority in heaven and on earth has been *c.* to me

Luke 11:48. they *c.* the murders and you provide the tombs

23:46. Father, into thy hands I *c.* my spirit

Acts 3:13. Jesus, whom you *c.* for trial

14:23. *c.* them to the Lord

19:37. have *c.* no sacrilege

25:.8 Paul's plea was: 'I have *c.* no offence

25:10. against the Jews I have *c.* no offence

Rom. 2:3. *c.* the same crimes yourself

7:3. and she does not *c.* adultery

1 Tim. 5:20. those who *c.* sins you must expose publicly

Heb. 9:15. to bring deliverance from sins *c.*

1 Pet. 2:22. he *c.* no sin, he was convicted of no falsehood

1 John 1:10. if we say we have *c.* no sin

2:1. my purpose is that you should not *c.* sin. But should anyone *c.* a sin

5:16. *c.* a sin which is not a deadly sin

Jude 7. like the angels, they *c.* fornication

Rev. 20:4. sat those to whom judgement was *c.*

common

Luke 1:65. the whole story became *c.* talk

John 4:9. do not use vessels in *c.*

9:31. it is *c.* knowledge that God does not listen to sinners

12:6. the money put into the *c.* purse

13:29. Judas was in charge of the *c.* purse

Acts 2:42. to share the *c.* life

4:16. it is *c.* knowledge in Jerusalem

4:26. and the rulers made *c.* cause

4:27. make *c.* cause in this very city

5:12. meet by *c.* consent in Solomon's Cloister

12:20. by *c.* agreement presented themselves

Rom. 9:21. one to be treasured, the other for *c.* use

14:19. build up the *c.* life

15:2. for his good and will build up the *c.* life

15:26. a *c.* fund for the benefit of the poor

1 Cor. 16:16. labours hard at our *c.* task

2 Cor. 4:2. the *c.* conscience of our fellow-men

Phil. 1:13. my imprisonment in Christ's cause has become *c.* knowledge

2:1. our *c.* life in Christ

2:2. a *c.* care for unity

2 Tim. 2:9. shut up like a *c.* criminal

Philem. 6. our *c.* faith

1 Pet. 4:6. they received the sentence *c.* to men

1 John 1:3. together may share in a *c.* life

1:7. we share together a *c.* life

Rev. 17:17. carry out his purpose, by making *c.* cause

commotion

Mat. 9:23. saw the flute-players and the general *c.*

Mark 5:38. where he found a great *c.*

5:39. why this crying and *c.*

Acts 17:8. these words caused a great *c.*

20:10. stop this *c.*: there is still life in him

communication

Acts 28:21. we have had no *c.* from Judaea

community

Acts 15:22. chose two leading men in the *c.*

1 Cor. 5:13. root out the evil-doer from your *c.*

6:1. the *c.* of God's people

6:4. men who count for nothing in our *c.*

10:23. help the building of the *c.*

12:28. within our *c.* God has appointed

14:4. prophecy that builds up a Christian *c.*

14:5. so help to build up the *c.*

Eph. 2:12. strangers to the *c.* of Israel

1 Pet. 5:1. I appeal to the elders of your *c.*

compact

2 Cor. 6:16. can there be a *c.* between the temple of God and the idols

companion-s

Mark 1:36. Simon and his *c.* searched him out

3:14. he appointed twelve as his *c.*

5:40. the child's father and mother and his own *c.*

16:8. to Peter and his *c.*

Luke 5:9. he and all his *c.* were amazed

8:45. Peter and his *c.* said

9:32. Peter and his *c.* had been in a deep sleep

John 11:33. and the Jews her *c.* weeping

Acts 4:13. as former *c.* of Jesus

11:12. my six *c.* here came with me

13:13. Paul and his *c.* went by sea

20:34. enough for the needs of me and my *c.*

22:9. my *c.* saw the light

22:11. my *c.* led me by the hand

26:13. shining all around me and my travelling-*c.*

Gal. 2:3. even my *c.* Titus

company
Mat. 22:11. the king came in to see the *c.* at table
  22:16. in *c.* with men of Herod's party
  27:27. collected the whole *c.* round him
Mark 2:16. noticed him eating in this bad *c.*
  15:16. called together the whole *c.*
Luke 2:13. with the angel a great *c.* of the heavenly host
  5:19. the middle of the *c.* in front of Jesus
  9:13. buy provisions for all this *c.*
  14:15. one of the *c.,* after hearing all this
  19:37. the whole *c.* of his disciples
  24:33. the Eleven and the rest of the *c.*
John 2:12. to Capernaum in *c.* with his mother
  9:40. some Pharisees in his *c.* asked
Acts 1:4. while he was in their *c.* he told them
  8:13. was constantly in Philip's *c.*
  12:12. a large *c.* was at prayer
  15:12. the whole *c.* fell silent
  15:39. dispute was so sharp that they parted *c.*
  16:3. Paul wanted to have him in his *c.*
  26:30. the Governor, Bernice, and the rest of the *c.*
Rom. 16:14. and all friends in their *c.*
1 Cor. 5:2. should have been rooted out of your *c.*
  15:33. bad *c.* is the ruin of a good character
2 Cor. 8:18. one of our *c.* whose reputation is high
  8:22. sending another of our *c.*
1 Thess. 5:10. awake or asleep, might live in *c.* with him
Heb. 11:40. in *c.* with us should they reach their perfection
Jam. 1:25. who lives in its *c.*
2 Pet. 2:13. they are an ugly blot on your *c.*
1 John 2:19. they went out from our *c.*
  . . . not all in our *c.* truly belong to it

compare-d-ing
Luke 13:18. what shall I *c.* it with
  13:20. what shall I *c.* the kingdom of God with
Rom. 5:16. the gift of God is not to be *c.* in its effect
Gal. 6:4. *c.* himself with himself

compassion
Luke 1:78. the tender *c.* of our God
Phil. 2:1. any warmth of affection or *c.*
Col. 3:12. *c.,* kindness, humility

Jam. 5:11. the Lord is full of pity and *c.*

compassionate
Luke 6:36. be *c.* as your Father is *c.*

compel
2 Cor. 10:5. we *c.* every human thought to surrender in obedience to Christ

competent
2 Tim. 2:2. *c.* to teach others

complacent
Rom. 11:25. not be *c.* about your own discernment

complain-ed-ing
Luke 5:30. their sect *c.* to his disciples
Acts 6:1. *c.* that their widows were being overlooked
1 Pet. 4:9. be hospitable to one another without *c.*

complaint-s
Luke 16:1. *c.* that this man was squandering
Phil. 2:14. without *c.* or wrangling
Col. 3:13. where any of you has cause for *c.*

complete-d-ing
Mat. 5:17. I did not come to abolish, but to *c.*
Luke 1:23. his period of duty was *c.*
  2:22. after their purification had been *c.*
  6:40. when his training is *c.*
  14:29. laid its foundation and then is not able to *c.* it
John 15:11. joy may be in you, and your joy *c.*
  16:24. that your joy may be *c.*
  17:4. by *c.* the work which thou gavest me
Acts 14:26. the task which they had now *c.*
  20:24. *c.* the task which the Lord Jesus assigned to me
Rom. 11:11. did their failure mean *c.* downfall
  15:19. I have *c.* the preaching of the gospel of Christ
1 Cor. 7:37. *c.* control of his own choice
2 Cor. 7:1. in the fear of God *c.* our consecration
  7:16. have *c.* confidence in you
  8:11. be as eager to *c.* the scheme
Gal. 4:4. when the term was *c.,* God sent his own Son
Eph. 6:13. to *c.* every task and still to stand
Col. 1:19. in him the *c.* being of God
  1:24. this is my way of helping to *c.*
  2:9. the *c.* being of the Godhead
  3:14. bind all together and *c.* the whole

2 Tim. 1:4. to make my happiness c.
Jam. 1:4. go on to c. a balanced character
1 John 1:4. that the joy of us all may be c.
2 John 12. so that our joy may be c.
Rev. 3:2. not found any work of yours c.
   6:11. until the tally should be c.
   11:7. when they have c. their testimony
   15:8. until the seven plagues of the seven angels were c.

completely
Mat. 14:36. everyone who touched it was c. cured
Mark 6:51. at this they were c. dumbfounded
Acts 3:16. this faith has made him c. well
   20:9. he was c. overcome by sleep
2 Cor. 7:13. set his mind c. at rest
Gal. 5:4. your relation with Christ is c. severed

completion
2 Cor. 8:6. this work of generosity also to c.
Phil. 1:6. will bring it to c.

comply
Tit. 2:9. and to c. with their demands

comprise-ing
Acts 6:9. the Synagogue of Freedmen, c. Cyrenians

compulsion
1 Cor. 7:15. Christian husband or wife is under no c.
   7:37. steadfast in his purpose being under no c.
2 Cor. 9:7. no reluctance, no sense of c.
Philem. 14. not of c., but of your own free will
1 Pet. 5:2. and do it, not under c.

comrade-s
Rom. 16:7. c. in captivity
   16:9. Urban my c. in Christ
Phil. 2:25. Epaphroditus, my fellow-worker and c.
   4:3. yes, and you too, my loyal c.
Philem. 2. Archippus our c.-in-arms

conceal-ed
Luke 18:34. its meaning was c. from them
1 Tim. 5:25. they cannot be c. for ever

conceit-ed
Rom. 12:3. do not be c. or think too highly of yourself
1 Cor. 8:1. this 'knowledge' breeds c.
   13:4. love is never boastful nor c.
Gal. 5:26. we must not be c.
Col. 2:18. people, bursting with the futile c.

1 Tim. 3:6. for fear the sin of c.

conceive
Mat. 1:23. the virgin will c. and bear a son
Eph. 3:20. more than all we can ask or c.

concern-s-ed
John 2:4. your c., mother, is not mine
Acts 17:22. in everything that c. religion
1 Cor. 9:9. do you suppose God's c. is with oxen
   12:25. feel the same c. for one another
2 Cor. 7:12. or his victim that most c. me
   11:28. my anxious c. for all our congregations
   13:7. not c. to be vindicated ourselves
Phil. 2:20. takes a genuine interest in your c.
Heb. 6:11. show the same eager c.
   13:17. tireless in their c. for you

concert-ed
Acts 19:29. a c. rush with them into the theatre

concession
1 Cor. 7:6. by way of c., not command
Gal. 2:4. as a c. to certain sham-Christians

conclude-ing
Acts 16:10. c. that God had called us
Rom. 10:17. we c. that faith is awakened
Heb. 8:8. I will c. a new covenant

conclusion
Rom. 8:1. the c. of the matter is this
2 Cor. 5:14. reached the c. that one man died for all

concourse
Luke 6:17. a large c. of his disciples
Heb. 12:23. the full c. and assembly of the first-born

condemn-s-ed
Mat. 18:34. he c. the man to torture
   23:33. how can you escape being c. to hell
Mark 16:16. those who do not believe will be c.
John 16:11. the Prince of this world stands c.
Act 13:46. c. yourselves as unworthy
   26:10. when they were c. to death
Rom. 3:7. why should I any longer be c. as a sinner
   3:8. to c. such men as these is surely no injustice
1 Cor. 4:9. men c. to death in the arena
2 Cor. 3:6. the written law c. to death

1 Tim. 5:12. stand *c.* for breaking their troth
Jude 9. did not presume to *c.* him
Rev. 19:2. he has *c.* the great whore

condemnation
Acts 25:15. demanding his *c.*

condition-s
Acts 7:23. to look into the *c.* of his fellow-countrymen
1 Cor. 7:17. his *c.* when God called him
7:20. remain in the *c.* in which he was called
7:24. to remain before God in the *c.*
Eph. 2:3. in our natural *c.* we
2:11. remember then your former *c.*
Heb. 7:26. such a high priest does indeed fit our *c.*

condole-ing
John 11:19. to *c.* with them on their brother's death
11:31. in the house *c.* with Mary

conduct
Luke 12:11. how you will *c.* your defence
Acts 13:18. he bore with their *c.* in the desert
Rom. 1:20. no possible defence for their *c.*
1:28. leads them to break all rules of *c.*
8:4. *c.*, no longer under the control of our lower nature
14:15. your *c.* is no longer guided by love
2 Cor. 1:12. our *c.* has been governed by a devout
5:10. his *c.* in the body, good or bad
Gal. 2:14. their *c.* did not square with the truth
6:4. examine his own *c.* for himself
Eph. 5:15. be most careful then how you *c.* yourselves
Phil. 1:27. let your *c.* be worthy of the gospel
3:16. let our *c.* be consistent
1 Tim. 3:15. *c.* themselves in God's household
Jam. 3:13. let his right *c.* give practical proof
1 Pet. 2:15. the will of God that by your good *c.*
3:7. *c.* your married life with understanding
3:16. those who malign your Christian *c.*

confer-red-ring
Mat. 26:4. there they *c.* together on a scheme
27:7. after *c.* they used it to buy
28:12. meeting with the elders and *c.* together

Heb. 5:5. he did not *c.* upon himself the glory
Rev. 13:2. the dragon *c.* upon it his power
13:4. he had *c.* his authority upon the beast
17:13. will *c.* their power and authority
17:17. *c.* their sovereignty upon the beast

conference
Mat. 27:1. met in *c.* to plan the death of Jesus

confess-ed
2 Cor. 9:13. you *c.* the gospel of Christ
1 Tim. 6:12. you *c.* your faith nobly
1 Pet. 4:16. *c.* that name

confession
Heb. 10:23. unswerving in the *c.* of our hope

confidence
Acts 24:10. I make my defence with *c.*
1 John 4:17. have *c.* on the day of judgement

confident
Phil. 2:24. I am *c.*, under the Lord
2 Tim. 1:5. which, I am *c.*, lives in you also
1:12. am *c.* of his power to keep

confine-d
Rom. 4:9. is this happiness *c.* to the circumcised

confirm-s-ed
Acts 14:3. he *c.* the message of his grace
15:27. will themselves *c.* this by word of mouth
2 Pet. 1:19. *c.* for us the message

conflagration
Rev. 18:9. they see the smoke of her *c.*
18:18. her *c.*: 'Was there ever a city

conflict-s
Gal. 5:17. they are in *c.* with one another
Jam. 4:1. what causes *c.* and quarrels among you

conform-s
Mat. 3:15. we do well to *c.* in this way
Mark 7:5. your disciples not *c.* to the ancient tradition
Phil. 3:17. whose way of life *c.* to it
1 Tim. 1:11. teaching which *c.* with the gospel

confront-ed
Acts 25:16. *c.* with his accusers

confusion
Luke 13:17. all his opponents were covered with *c.*

confute-ing
John 16:8. he will *c.* the world
Acts 18:28. indefatigable in *c.* the Jews
Tit. 1:9. to *c.* objectors

congregate
John 18:20. the temple, where all Jews *c.*

congregation-s
Mat. 18:17. report the matter to the *c:*
 and if he will not listen even to the *c.*
Mark 3:1. a man in the *c.* who had a
 withered arm
 6:2. the large *c.* who heard him
Luke 1:10. the whole *c.* was at prayer
 4:28. the whole *c.* were infuriated
 6:6. there happened to be a man in
 the *c.*
 13:14. intervened and said to the *c.*
Acts 9:41. he called the members of the
 c.
 10:23. accompanied by some members of the *c.*
 11:26. in fellowship with the *c.*
 13:1. in the *c.* there, certain prophets
 14:23. appointed elders for them in
 each *c.*
 14:27. called the *c.* together
 15:3. sent on their way by the *c.*
 15:30. the *c.* together, and delivered
 the letter
 15:41. new strength to the *c.*
 16:5. the *c.* grew stronger in faith
 17:6. members of the *c.* before the
 magistrates
 17:10. the *c.* sent Paul and Silas off
 17:14. the *c.* sent Paul off at once
 18:27. wrote to the *c.*
 19:9. speaking evil of the new way
 before the whole *c.*
 20:17. summon the elders of the *c.*
Rom. 16:1. the *c.* at Cenchreae
 16:4. the gentile *c.*
 16:5. the *c.* at their house
 16:16. Christ's *c.*
 16:23. host of the whole *c.*
1 Cor. 1:2. the *c.* of God's people
 4:17. I teach everywhere in all our *c.*
 7:17. I teach in all our *c.*
 11:16. in any of the *c.*
 11:18. as a *c.* you fall into sharply
 divided
 11:20. when you meet as a *c.*
 14:19. in the *c.* I would rather speak
 14:23. if the whole *c.* is assembled
also 1 Cor. 14:31, 34, 35. 16:1, 19. 2 Cor.
 1:1. 8:1, 18, 23. 11:8, 28. 12:13.
 Gal. 1:2, 22. 2:14. Phil. 4:15. Col.
 4:15, 16. 1 Thess. 1:1. 2:14. 2 Thess.
 1:1, 4. 1 Tim. 2:8. 3:5. 5:16.
 Philem. 2. Jam. 5:14. 3 John 6,9, 10.

connect-ed
Luke 1:3. write a *c.* narrative for you

connexion-s
Acts 7:13. his family *c.* were disclosed

connivance
Acts 14:5. with the *c.* of the city authorities

conquer-ed
John 16:33. I have *c.* the world
Rom. 12:21. do not let evil *c.* you
Rev. 12:11. by the sacrifice of the Lamb
 they have *c.* him

conscience
Acts 18:6. my *c.* is clear
Rom. 1:31. no *c.*, no fidelity
 14:22. make his decision with a clear
 c.
 15:1. those of us who have a robust
 c.
1 Cor. 4:3. I have nothing on my *c.*
 14:24. something that searches his *c.*
1 John 3:20. if our *c.* condemns us, God
 is greater than our *c.*
 3:21. if our *c.* does not condemn us

consciousness
Rom. 3:20. law brings only the *c.* of sin

consecrate-s-ed-ing
Mat. 12:4 ⎱ate the *c.* loaves
Mark 2:26 ⎰
Luke 6:4. took the *c.* loaves to eat
John 10:36. I, *c.* and sent into the world
 by the Father
 17:17. *c.* them by the truth
 17:19. for their sake I now *c.* myself,
 that they too may be *c.*
Rom. 11:16. if the first portion of dough
 is *c.*, so is the whole lump. If the
 root is *c.*
 15:16. *c.* by the Holy Spirit
1 Cor. 1:30. in him we are *c.* and set free
 8:1. food *c.* to heathen deities
 8:4. about eating this *c.* food
 8:10. food *c.* to the heathen deity
Eph. 5:26. *c.* it, cleansing it by water and
 word
2 Thess. 2:13. in the Spirit that *c.* you
Heb. 2:11. a *c.* priest and those whom
 he *c.*
 10:10. by the will of God that we have
 been *c.*
 10:14. those who are thus *c.*
 10:29. the covenant by which he was
 c.
 13:12. to *c.* the people by his own
 blood
1 Pet. 1:2. *c.* with the sprinkled blood

consecration
1 Cor. 8:7. a sense of its heathen *c.*
2 Cor. 7:1. in the fear of God complete
 our *c.*

consent-ed
Acts 5:12. meet by common *c.*
23:21. wait only for your *c.*
Philem. 14. do nothing without your *c.*
2 Pet. 2:15. *c.* to take pay for doing wrong

consequence
Rom. 1:26. in *c.*, I say, God has given them up to

consequent-ly
Rom. 1:24. the *c.* degradation of their bodies
4:11. *c.*, he is the father of all who have faith
13:2. *c.* anyone who rebels

consider-s-ed
Luke 14:31. first sitting down to *c.*
John 7:22. but *c.*: Moses gave you the law
Acts 26:2. I *c.* myself fortunate, King Agrippa
26:8. why is it *c.* incredible
Rom. 4:9. *c.*: we say, 'Abraham's faith
14:14. if a man *c.* a particular thing impure
15:1. not *c.* ourselves
15:2. each of us must *c.* his neighbour
15:3. Christ too did not *c.* himself
2 Cor. 8:10. my *c.* opinion on the matter
Heb. 11:26. he *c.* the stigma
Jam. 3:14. *c.* whether your claims are not false

considerate-ly
Acts 27:3. Julius very *c.* allowed Paul
Jam. 3:17. peace-loving, *c.*
1 Pet. 2:18. not only when they are kind and *c.*

consideration
Acts 16:3. out of *c.* for the Jews
1 Cor. 10:28. out of *c.* for him
2 Cor. 1:23. it was out of *c.* for you

consign-ed
1 Cor. 5:5. this man is to be *c.* to Satan
1 Tim. 1:20. whom I *c.* to Satan
2 Pet. 2:4. *c.* them to the dark pits of hell

consistent-ly
Phil. 3:16. let our conduct be *c.*
Tit. 3:2. a *c.* gentle disposition

consolation
Mat. 2:18. refusing all *c.*, because they were no more
5:4. the sorrowful ; they shall find *c.*
Luke 16:25. Lazarus; now he has his *c.*
2 Cor. 1:3. the God whose *c.* never fails us
1:4. the *c.* we ourselves receive
7:4. my cup is full of *c.*

console
1 Thess. 4:18. *c.* one another

consolidated
Col. 2:7. be *c.* in the faith

consort-s-ing
Rom. 7:3. in her husband's lifetime she *c.* with another man . . . by *c.* with another man
2 Cor. 6:14. can light *c.* with darkness

conspire-d
Acts 4:27. Pontius Pilate *c.* with the Gentiles
5:9. why did you both *c.*

constable
Mat. 5:25. and the judge to the *c.*
Luke 12:58. to the *c.*, and the *c.* put you in jail

constant-ly
Luke 18:3. a widow who *c.* came
John 3:23. *c.* coming for baptism
Acts 1:14. these were *c.* at prayer together
2:42. met *c.* to hear the apostles teach
8:13. was *c.* in Philip's company
12:5. kept in prison under *c.* watch
2 Cor. 11:26. I have been *c.* on the road
12:12. which called for such *c.* fortitude
Col. 3:10. which is being *c.* renewed
2 Tim. 1:3. this I do *c.* night and day

consternation
Acts 12:18. there was *c.* among the soldiers

constituent
Eph. 4:16. knit together by every *c.* joint

constraint
Acts 20:22. under the *c.* of the Spirit
2 Cor. 6:12. on our part there is no *c.*; any *c.* there may be is in yourselves

consult-ing
Gal. 1:16. without *c.* any human being

consultation
Gal. 2:6. did not prolong the *c.*

consume-s-d
Heb. 10:27. fire which will *c.* God's enemies
Jam. 5:3. *c.* your flesh like fire
Rev. 11:5. and *c.* their enemies
20:9. from heaven and *c.* them

consummate-d
Rev. 15:1. the wrath of God is *c.*

contact
Acts 15:20. things polluted by *c.* with idols
19:12. scarves which had been in *c.* with his skin

contain-s-ed-ing
1 Cor. 14:6. *c.* something by way of revelation
2 Cor. 4:7. earthenware to *c.* this treasure
Heb. 9:4. a golden jar *c.* the manna
10:1. the law *c.* but a shadow
2 Pet. 3:16. they *c.* some obscure passages
Rev. 22:7. the words of prophecy *c.* in this book

contaminated
Jude 23. clothing that is *c.* with sensuality

contemplate-d
Rom. 4:19. he *c.* his own body

contemporary-ies
Gal. 1:14. outstripping many of my Jewish *c.*

contempt-ible
Mark 9:12. to be treated with *c.*
Luke 23:11. treated him with *c.* and ridicule
Rom. 14:3. the man who eats must not hold in *c.*
14:10. why do you hold your brother in *c.*
1 Cor. 1:28. chosen things low and *c.*
2 Cor. 10:10. as a speaker he is beneath *c.*
12:10. weakness, *c.*, persecution
Jam. 2:7. pour *c.* on the honoured name

contemptuous-ly
Acts 2:13. said *c.*, 'They have been drinking
1 Cor. 11:22. are you so *c.* of the church

contending
Phil. 1:27. *c.* as one man for the gospel faith

content
Mat. 10:25. pupil should be *c.* to share his teacher's lot
14:20 } they all ate to their heart's *c.*
15:37 }
Mark 6:42. they all ate to their heart's *c.*
7:29. for saying that, you may go home *c.*
8:8 } they all ate to their hearts' *c.*
Luke 9:17 }
Acts 8:39. went on his way well *c.*
2 Cor. 12:10. hence I am well *c.*, for Christ's sake
13:9. we are well *c.* to be weak
Jude 6. the angels, how some of them were not *c.*

contentious
Gal. 5:20. quarrels, a *c.* temper, envy

contest
Phil. 1:30. you and I are engaged in the same *c.*

continually
Mat. 18:10. *c.* on the face of my heavenly Father
John 6:56. dwells *c.* in me and I dwell in him
Rom. 1:9. *c.* I make mention of you in my prayers
2 Cor. 2:14. God, who *c.* leads us about
4:11. for *c.*, while still alive
1 Thess. 1:2. mention you in our prayers *c.*
2:4. God, who is *c.* testing our hearts
2:13. this is why we thank God *c.*
5:17. pray *c.*

continue-s-d
Luke 2:51. *c.* to be under their authority
13:18. what is the kingdom of God like?' he *c.*
13:22. he *c.* his journey
24:28. he made as if to *c.* his journey
John 8:22. where I am going you cannot come?' So Jesus *c.*
9:17. they *c.* to question him
12:34. the Messiah *c.* for ever
Acts 1:20. the text I have in mind,' Peter *c.*
12:24. the word of God *c.* to grow
13:14. from Perga they *c.* their journey
14:7. they *c.* to spread the good news
19:9. *c.* to hold discussions daily
21:3. *c.* our voyage to Syria
21:5. we left and *c.* our journey
22:10. *c.* your journey to Damascus
27:7. the wind *c.* against us
Rom. 5:1. let us *c.* at peace with God
11:23. if they do not *c.* faithless, will be grafted in
13:3. *c.* to do right
2 Cor. 1:11. yes, he will *c.* to deliver us
Col. 2:2. *c.* in good heart and in the unity of love
2 Thess. 3:4. will *c.* to do what we order
Heb. 11:4. *c.* to speak after his death
Jude 20. *c.* to pray in the power of the Holy Spirit

contract
Mat. 1:19. have the marriage *c.* set aside

contradict
Gal. 3:21. does the law, then, *c.* the promises

contradiction-s
1 Tim. 6:20. the *c.* of so-called 'knowledge'

contrary
Mark 5:26. on the *c.*, she had grown worse

Luke 8:16. on the *c.*, he puts it on a lamp-stand

22:26. on the *c.*, the highest among you must bear himself like the youngest

1 Cor. 9:12. on the *c.*, I put up with all that comes my way.

11:5. a woman, on the *c.*, brings shame on her head

12:22. quite the *c.*: those organs of the body

15:10. on the *c.*, in my labours

Eph. 5:29. on the *c.*, he provides and cares for it

1 Tim. 6:2. quite the *c.*; they must be all the better servants

contrast

Rom. 7:6. the way of the spirit, in *c.*

Phil. 3:20. we, by *c.*, are citizens of heaven

Jude 9. in *c.*, when the archangel Michael

contribute-s-d

Rom. 12:13. *c.* to the needs of God's people

15:27. the Gentiles have a clear duty to *c.*

1 Cor. 14:26. each of you *c.* a hymn

Phil. 4:16. at Thessalonica you *c.* to my needs

contribution

Acts 11:29. the disciples agreed to make a *c.*

2 Cor. 9:12. a *c.* towards the needs

9:13. your liberal *c.* to their need

contrive-d

1 Tim. 3:6. a judgement *c.* by the devil

control-led

Mark 5:3. he could no longer be *c.*

Acts 1:7. which the Father has set within his own *c.*

24:25. morals, self-*c.*

27:16. get the ship's boat under control

Rom. 6:20. free from the *c.* of righteousness

8:4. no longer under the *c.* of our lower nature

1 Cor. 7:5. for lack of self-*c.*

7:9. if they cannot *c.* themselves

7:37. complete *c.* of his own choice

14:32. to *c.* prophetic inspiration

Gal. 5:22. gentleness, and self-*c.*

1 Tim. 3:5. how to *c.* his own family

Tit. 1:6. are not out of *c.*

1:8. devout, and self-*c.*

1:10. converts, who are out of all *c.*

Jam. 1:26. if he has no *c.* over his tongue

1 Pet. 1:13. perfectly self-*c.*

2 Pet. 1:6. knowledge with self-*c.*, self-*c.* with fortitude

Controller

Acts 4:1. together with the *C.* of the Temple

5:24. The *C.* of the Temple

5:26. the *C.*

controversial

Acts 23:29. *c.* matters in their law

controversy-ies

Acts 15:2. *c.* with Paul and Barnabas

Tit. 3:9. *c.* over the Law

convene-d

John 11:47. the Pharisees *c.* a meeting

convenient

2 Tim. 4:2. press it home on all occasions, *c.*

conversation

Luke 9:28. eight days after this *c.*

Acts 20:11. after much *c.*

Col. 4:6. let your *c.* be always gracious

converse-d-ing

Mat. 17:3. saw Moses and Elijah appear, *c.* with him

Mark 9:4. there they were, *c.* with Jesus

Acts 7:38. in the desert, *c.* with the angel

conversion

1 Cor. 15:2. if not, your *c.* was in vain

convert-s

Mat. 23:15. over sea and land to win one *c.*

Luke 1:17. to *c.* the rebellious

Acts 6:5. a former *c.* to Judaism

8:15. prayed for the *c.*

9:25. his *c.* took him one night

9:26. they did not believe that he was really a *c.*

13:52. the *c.* were filled with joy

14:20. the *c.* formed a ring round him

14:21. they gained many *c.*

14:22. heartening the *c.*

15:10. on the shoulders of these *c.* a yoke

18:23. bringing new strength to all the *c.*

19:1. there he found a number of *c.*

19:9. he left them, withdrew his *c.*

21:20. how many thousands of *c.* we have

21:25. the gentile *c.*

Rom. 16:5. the first *c.* to Christ in Asia

1 Cor. 16:15. the first *c.* in Achaia

1 Tim. 3:6. must not be a *c.* newly baptized

Tit. 1:10. Jewish *c.*

convict-ed

John 16:9. *c.* them of wrong, by their refusal to believe

Jam. 2:9. you stand *c.* by that law

1 Pet. 2:22. he was *c.* of no falsehood
Jude 15. to *c.* all the godless

conviction
Rom. 4:21. in the firm *c.* of his power
  14:5. reached *c.* in his own mind
  14:22. if you have a clear *c.*
  14:23. does not arise from his *c.*, and anything which does not arise from *c.* is sin
1 Cor. 2:4. it carried *c.* by spiritual power
Col. 2:2. to the full wealth of *c.*
  4:12. ripe in *c.* and wholly devoted
1 Thess. 1:5. in the power of the Holy Spirit, and with strong *c.*

convince-d
Mat. 9:6. to *c.* you that the Son of Man has the right on earth
Mark 2:10 ⎱ to *c.* you that the Son of Man
Luke 5:24 ⎰
  20:6. they are *c.* that John was a prophet
John 16:10. he will *c.* them that right is on my side
  16:11. he will *c.* them of divine judgement
Acts 17:4. were *c.* and joined Paul and Silas
  18:4. to *c.* both Jews and pagans
  28:23. sought to *c.* them about Jesus
Rom. 8:38. I am *c.* that there is nothing
  14:14. I am absolutely *c.*, as a Christian
2 Cor. 10:7. *c.*, is he, that he belongs to Christ
Heb. 6:9. we are *c.* that you, my friends
1 John 3:19. *c.* ourselves in his sight

convulsion-s
Mark 1:26. the unclean spirit threw the man into *c.*
  9:20. it threw the boy into *c.*
Luke 9:39. *c.* with foaming at the mouth
  9:42. threw him into *c.*

cooked
Luke 24:42. a piece of fish they had *c.*

co-operate-s
Rom. 8:28. he *c.* for good with those who love God
2 Cor. 1:11. if you will *c.* by praying for us

copper
Mat. 10:9. provide no gold, silver, or *c.*
Mark 7:4. washing of cups and jugs and *c.* bowls

copy-ies
2 Thess. 3:7. you ought to *c.* our example
Heb. 8:5. a sanctuary which is only a *c.*
  9:23. cleanse the *c.* of heavenly things

Corinth
1 Cor. 4:18. they think I am not coming to *C.*
  16:5. I shall come to *C.*
  16:12. urged him strongly to go to *C.*
2 Cor. 9:5. ask these friends to go on ahead to *C.*
  10:13. to come as far as *C.*
  10:14. we were the first to reach *C.*

corn
Mat. 13:6. the young *c.* was scorched
  13:7. and choked the *c.*
  13:26. the *c.* sprouted
Mark 4:6. when the sun rose the young *c.* was scorched
  4:7. thistles shot up and choked the *c.*
Luke 12:18. I will collect in them all my *c.*
  17:35. two women together grinding *c.*
Acts 27:38. dumping the *c.* in the sea

cornelian
Rev. 4:3. the gleam of jasper and *c.*
  21:20. the sixth *c.*

corner
Luke 3:5. the *c.* shall be straightened
  15:8. look in every *c.*

corpse-s
Mat. 24:28. wherever the *c.* is, there the vultures
Mark 9:26. the boy looked like a *c.*
Luke 17:37. where the *c.* is, there the vultures
1 Cor. 10:5. the desert was strewn with their *c.*
Jam. 2:26. faith divorced from deeds is lifeless as a *c.*
Rev. 11:8. their *c.* will lie in the street
  11:9. gaze upon their *c.*
  16:3. like the blood from a *c.*

correct-s
Heb. 12:5. nor lose heart when he *c.* you

correction
Eph. 6:4. the instruction, and the *c.*

correspond-ing
Mat. 2:16. *c.* with the time

corruption
1 Cor. 5:7. the old leaven of *c.*
  5:8. the leaven of *c.* and wickedness

Cos
Acts 21:1. a straight run and came to *C.*

cosmic
Eph. 6:12. against *c.* powers
Col. 2:15. on that cross he discarded the *c.* powers

cost-ly
Mat. 10:8. you received without *c.*
  16:26. at the *c.* of his true self

Mat. 26:7. a small bottle of fragrant oil, very *c*.
Mark 8:36. at the *c*. of his true self
14:3. a small bottle of very *c*. perfume
Luke 9:25. at the *c*. of his true self
Acts 22:28. it *c*. me a large sum to acquire
2 Cor. 8:13. at the *c*. of hardship to yourselves
Rev. 18:12. made of *c*. woods

Council
Mark 15:43. a respected member of the *C*.
Luke 23:50. Joseph, a member of the *C*.
John 3:1. a member of the Jewish *C*.
Acts 22:5. the whole *C*. of Elders

councillor-s
Luke 23:13. called together the chief priests, *c*.

counsel
Acts 20:31. I never ceased to *c*. each of you

counsellor-s
1 Thess. 5:12. your leaders and *c*.

count-s-ed
Mat. 10:30. the hairs of your head have all been *c*.
Luke 1:48. all generations will *c*. me blessed
12:7. the hairs of your head have all been *c*.
22:37. he was *c*. among the outlaws
Acts 10:15 ⎱ not for you to call profane
11:9 ⎰ what God *c*. clean
Rom. 4:4. his wages are not '*c*.' as a favour
4:6. whom God '*c*.' as just
4:8. whose sins the Lord does not *c*.
4:9. Abraham's faith was *c*. as righteousness
4:10. in what circumstances was it so *c*.
4:11. righteousness is '*c*.' to them
4:22. *c*. to him as righteousness
4:24. '*c*.' in the same way to us
12:17. be such as all men *c*. honourable
1 Cor. 1:27. what the world *c*. folly, and to shame what is strong, God has chosen what the world *c*. weakness
3:7. not the gardeners with their planting and watering who *c*.
6:4. men who *c*. for nothing
7:30. *c*. on keeping what they buy
2 Cor. 5:16. ceased to *c*. in our estimate of any man; even if once they *c*.
Gal. 3:6. *c*. to him as righteousness
5:6. the only thing that *c*. is faith
6:15. the only thing that *c*. is new creation
Jam. 2:23. *c*. to him as righteousness

1 Pet. 3:14. you may *c*. yourselves happy
4:14. *c*. yourselves happy
Rev. 7:9. a vast throng, which no one could *c*.
9:16. cavalry, whose *c*. I heard

countercharge-s
Acts 19:38. bring their charges and *c*.

countless
Rom. 9:27. though the Israelites be *c*.
Heb. 11:12. as the *c*. grains of sand
Rev. 5:11. the voices of *c*. angels
20:8. *c*. as the sands of the sea

country-ies
Mat. 9:26. the talk of all the *c*. round
25:15. then he left the *c*.
Mark 1:38. let us move on to the *c*. towns
1:45. stayed outside in the open *c*.
3:13. went up into the hill-*c*.
Luke 4:25. famine lay hard over the whole *c*.
15:14. a severe famine fell upon that *c*.
21:24. carried captive into all *c*.
22:25. their *c*. 'Benefactors'
Acts 7:29. Moses fled the *c*.
8:1. scattered over the *c*. districts
8:4. they went through the *c*. preaching
8:40. toured the *c*., preaching
13:17. brought them out of that *c*.
13:19. in the Canaanite *c*.
14:6. and the surrounding *c*.
20:2. through those parts of the *c*.
26:20. all the *c*. of Judaea
2 Cor. 11:26. dangers in the *c*.

countryman-men
Acts 7:23. his fellow-*c*. the Israelites
7:25. he thought his fellow-*c*. would understand
28:21. nor has any *c*. of ours arrived
Rom. 16:7. Andronicus and Junias my fellow-*c*.
16:11. my *c*. Herodion
16:21. Lucius, Jason and Sosipater my fellow-*c*.
Tit. 1:12. one of their own *c*., who said

country-side
Mark 1:5. the whole Judaean *c*.
6:55. scoured that whole *c*.
Luke 4:14. reports about him spread through the whole *c*.
Acts 10:39. all that he did in the Jewish *c*.

couple
Acts 23:23. he called a *c*. of his centurions

courage
John 16:33. but *c*.! The victory is mine
Acts 23:11 ⎱ keep up your *c*,
27:25 ⎰

Acts 27:36. then they all plucked up *c*.
Phil. 1:14. fearlessly and with extraordinary *c*.
Heb. 13:6. we can take *c*. and say

course-s
Luke 1:3. the whole *c*. of these events
  12:57. judge for yourselves what is the right *c*.
  17:11. in the *c*. of his journey to Jerusalem
  21:24. until their day has run its *c*.
  22:59. of *c*. this fellow was with him
Acts 2:1. the day of Pentecost was running its *c*.
  9:32. a general tour, in the *c*. of which
  18:14. of *c*., have given you Jews a patient hearing
  19:36. your proper *c*. is to keep quiet
Rom. 6:15. of *c*. not. You know well enough
  7:7. is the law identical with sin? Of *c*. not
  9:8. those born in the *c*. of nature
  10:18. never heard it? Of *c*. they did
1 Cor. 5:10. I was not, of *c*., referring to pagans
  8:1. of *c*. we all 'have knowledge
  8:4. of *c*., as you say, 'a false god
  9:10. is the reference clearly to ourselves? Of *c*.
2 Cor. 12:18. and followed the same *c*.
  13:5. unless of *c*. you prove unequal to the test
Gal. 2:4. that *c*. was urged only as a concession
  4:23. slave-woman's son was born in the *c*. of nature
  5:25. let the Spirit also direct our *c*.
1 Tim. 6:6. of *c*. religion does yield high dividends
2 Tim. 2:16. further and further into godless *c*.
Heb. 2:1. for fear of drifting from our *c*.
  13:9. do not be swept off your *c*.
Jam. 1:8. never can keep a steady *c*.
  3:4. whatever *c*. the helmsman chooses
2 Pet. 2:8. their evil *c*. tortured that good man's heart
  2:12. brute beasts, born in the *c*. of nature
Jude 13. stars that have wandered from their *c*.

court-s
Mat. 5:22. he must answer for it to the *c*.
  5:25. both on your way to *c*.
  10:17. men will hand you over to their *c*.
  27:19. while Pilate was sitting in *c*.
Mark 11:16. use the temple *c*. as a thoroughfare

11:27. as he was walking in the temple *c*.
13:9. you will be handed over to the *c*.
Luke 12:58. going with your opponent to *c*.
Acts 3:13. repudiated in Pilate's *c*.
  4:7. brought the apostles before the *c*.
  4:15. ordered them to leave the *c*.
  4:21. the *c*. repeated the caution
  12:20. presented themselves at his *c*.
  13:1. Manaen, who had been at the *c*. of Prince Herod
  17:19. brought him before the *C*. of Areopagus
  17:22. Paul stood up before the *C*. of Areopagus
  17:34. Dionysius, a member of the *C*. of Areopagus
  18:12. brought him into *c*.
  18:16. he had them ejected from the *c*.
  24:19. ought to have been in *c*. to state it
  25:6. took his seat in *c*.
  25:17. I took my seat in *c*.
1 Cor. 4:3. or by any human *c*. of judgement
  6:1. the face to take it to pagan law-*c*.
1 Tim. 5:24. they run before them into *c*.
2 Tim. 4:16. no one came into *c*. to support me
Jam. 2:6. they who drag you into *c*.
Jude 16. they *c*. favour to gain their ends

courteous
1 Tim. 3:2. temperate, *c*., hospitable

courtesy
Acts 25:13. on a *c*. visit to Festus

courtyard
Mat. 26:58. he came to the High Priest's *c*.
  26:69. Peter was sitting outside in the *c*.
Mark 14:54. right into the High Priest's *c*.
  14:66. Peter was still in the *c*. downstairs
  15:16. the soldiers took him inside the *c*.
Luke 22:55. lit a fire in the middle of the *c*.
John 18:15. went with Jesus into the High Priest's *c*.

cousin
Col. 4:10. Mark, the *c*. of Barnabas

covenant
Mat. 26:28. this is my blood, the blood of the *c*.

Mark 14:24. my blood of the *c.*, shed for
  many
1 Cor. 11:25. the new *c.* sealed by my
  blood
2 Cor. 3:6. his new *c.*—a *c.* expressed
  not in a written document
  3:14. the old *c.*; and it is never lifted,
  because only in Christ is the old
  c. abrogated
Heb. 7:22. far superior must the *c.* also
  be
  9:15. a new *c.*, or testament, under
  which, now that there has been a
  death to bring deliverance from
  sins committed under the former *c.*
  9:18. the former *c.* itself
  9:20. this is the blood of the *c.*
Rev. 11:19. was seen the ark of his *c.*

cover-ed-ing
Mat. 6:25. clothes to *c.* your body
  23:27. like tombs *c.* with whitewash
Mark 4:22. nothing put under *c.*
Luke 5:12. a man *c.* with leprosy
  8:17. under *c.* that will not be made
  known
  12:22. clothes to *c.* your body
  13:17. his opponents were *c.* with
  confusion
  16:20. *c.* with sores, lay a poor man
  named Lazarus
Acts 5:6. *c.* his body, then carried him
  out
1 Tim. 6:8. we have food and *c.*
Rev. 4:6. living creatures, *c.* with eyes
  17:3. *c.* with blasphemous names

coward-s-ly
Mat. 8:26 ⎰ why are you such *c.*
Mark 4:40 ⎱
Rev. 21:8. as for the *c.*, the faithless

crafty
Mark 12:15. he saw how *c.* their
  question was
Acts 7:19. he made a *c.* attack on our
  race

craftsmanship
Acts 17:29. shaped by human *c.*

crag
Rev. 6:15. hid themselves in caves and
  mountain *c.*
  6:16. they called out to the mountains
  and the *c.*

crash
Mat. 7:27. down it fell with a great *c.*
Luke 6:49. the house collapsed, and
  fell with a great *c.*

crave-ings
Acts 24:4. I *c.* your indulgence for a
  brief statement
2 Cor. 12:13. I *c.* forgiveness
Col. 3:5. lust, foul *c.*

1 Pet. 2:2. *c.* for pure milk (spiritual
  milk

craven
2 Tim. 1:7. God gave us no *c.* spirit

crawl
Acts 10:12. whatever walks or *c.* or
  flies
  11:6. things that *c.* or fly
Jam. 3:7. creatures that *c.* on the ground

crazy
Acts 12:15. you are *c.*', they told her

create-d
John 1:3. no single thing was *c.* without
  him
Acts 17:24 the God who *c.* the world
  17:26. he *c.* every race of men
Rom. 1:25. worship to *c.* things
  8:19. the *c.* universe waits with eager
  expectation
  8:22. the whole *c.* universe groans
Eph. 2:15. to *c.* out of the two a single
  new humanity
Col. 1:15. his is the primacy over all *c.*
  things
1 Tim. 2:13. Adam was *c.* first
  4:4. everything that God *c.* is good
Heb. 1:2. through whom he *c.* all
  orders of existence
  4:3. ever since the world was *c.*
  9:11. not belonging to this *c.* world
  12:27. the shaking of these *c.* things
2 Pet. 3:5. *c.* by God's word out of water

creation
Mark 16:15. proclaim the Good News
  to the whole *c.*
Rom. 8:39. nothing in all *c.* that can
  separate us
Gal. 6:15. the only thing that counts is
  new *c.*
Col. 1:23. proclaimed in the whole *c.*
Heb. 4:13. there is nothing in *c.* that
  can hide from him

Creator
Mat. 19:4. have you never read that the
  C. made them
Eph. 3:9. God the *c.* of the universe
Col. 3:10. renewed in the image of its
  C.

creature-s
Acts 10:12. he saw *c.* of every kind
  11:6. four-footed *c.* of the earth
Rom. 7:24. miserable *c.* that I am
Jam. 3:7. *c.* that crawl on the ground
  4:4. you false, unfaithful *c.*
Rev. 4:6. round the throne itself were
  four living *c.*
  4:7. the first *c.* was like a lion
  4:8. four living *c.*
  4:9. the living *c.* give glory
  5:6. inside the circle of living *c.*
  5:8. the four living *c.*

Rev. 5:11. and the living *c*. and the elders
5:14. the four living *c*. said
6:1. one of the four living *c*. say
6:3. I heard the second *c*. say
6:5. the third *c*. say
6:6. the midst of the living *c*.
6:7. the voice of the fourth *c*.
7:11. the elders and the four living *c*.
14:3. the four living *c*.
15:7. one of the four living *c*.
19:4. the four living *c*. fell down

credentials
John 10:25. my deeds done in my Father's name are my *c*.
2 Cor. 3:1. over again to produce our *c*.
12:11. my *c*. should have come from you

credit
Luke 6:32⎤
    6:33⎦ what *c*. is that to you
6:34. expect to be repaid, what *c*. is that
17:10. we are servants and deserve no *c*.
Rom. 4:5. without any work to his *c*.
1 Cor. 4:7. why take the *c*. to yourself
9:16. even if I preach the Gospel, I can claim no *c*. for it
1 Pet. 2:20. what *c*. is there in fortitude

credulity
2 Pet. 2:3. they will trade on your *c*.

crime-s
Mat. 23:28. you are brim-full of hypocrisy and *c*.
Acts 18:14. if it had been a question of *c*.
24:20. to say what *c*. they discovered
25:11. if I am guilty of any capital *c*.
25:25. clear to me that he had committed no capital *c*.
Rom. 2:2. all who commit such *c*. as these
2:3. committing the same *c*. yourself
13:3. government, a terror to *c*.
Rev. 18:5. God has not forgotten her *c*.

criminal-s
Luke 23:32. two others with him, *c*.
23:33. and the *c*. with him
23:39. one of the *c*. who hung there
John 18:30. if he were not a *c*.
2 Tim. 2:9. shut up like a common *c*.
1 Pet. 2:12. they malign you as *c*.
2:14. for the punishment of *c*.

cripple-s-d
Mat. 15:30. blind, dumb, and *c*.
21:14. blind men and *c*. came to him
Mark 9:45. better to enter into life a *c*.
Luke 13:11. a spirit that had *c*. her for eighteen years

14:13. ask the poor, the *c*.
14:21. bring me in the poor, the *c*.
John 5:5. *c*. for thirty eight-years
5:13. the *c*. who had been cured
Acts 3:2. a *c*. from birth
8:7. *c*. folk were cured

critical
Rom. 13:11. remember how *c*. the moment is

criticism
2 Cor. 8:20. *c*. of our handling of this generous gift

crooked
Acts 2:40. save yourselves', he said 'from this *c*. age
2 Cor. 11:13. *c*. in all their practices
Jam. 5:20. brings a sinner back from his *c*. ways

crop-s-ped
Mat. 9:37. the *c*. is heavy
9:38. labourers to harvest his *c*.
21:41. his share of the *c*.
Mark 4:7. it yielded no *c*.
4:28. the ground produces a *c*.
4:29. as soon as the *c*. is ripe
Luke 10:2. the *c*. is heavy . . . to harvest his *c*.
12:16. whose land yielded heavy *c*.
John 4:36. gathering a *c*. for eternal life
4:38. a *c*. for which you have not toiled
Acts 14:17. *c*. in their seasons
1 Cor. 9:11. if we have sown a spiritual *c*.
11:6. a disgrace for her to be *c*.
2 Tim. 2:6. has first claim on the *c*.
Heb. 6:7. yields a useful *c*.
Jam. 5:7. the farmer looking for the precious *c*.
5:18. the land bore *c*. once more
Rev. 14:15. earth's *c*. is over-ripe
22:2. which yields twelve *c*. of fruit

cross-ed-ing
Mat. 8:18. Jesus gave word to *c*. to the other shore
9:1. he got into the boat and *c*. over
14:34. they finished the *c*.
16:5. in *c*. to the other side
27:35. after fastening him to the *c*.
Mark 4:35. let us *c*. over to the other side
6:45. embark and *c*. to Bethsaida
6:53. they finished the *c*.
15:24. they fastened him to the *c*.
15:46. took him down from the *c*.
Luke 8:22. let us *c*. over to the other side
16:26. no one from our side who wants to reach you can *c*. it
23:53. taking it down from the *c*.
John 6:17. pushed off to *c*. the water
18:1. *c*. the Kedron ravine

Acts 27:41. found themselves caught between *c.*-currents
1 Cor. 1:23. Christ nailed to the *c.*
  2:2. nothing but Jesus Christ— Christ nailed to the *c.*
2 Cor. 13:4. he died on the *c.* in weakness
Gal. 3:1. Jesus Christ was openly displayed upon his *c.*
Col. 2:15. on that *c.* he discarded the cosmic powers
Heb. 11:29. by faith they *c.* the Red Sea . . . the Egyptians, when they attempted the *c.*
1 John 3:14. have *c.* over from death to life

crowd-s-ed-ing
Mat. 4:25. great *c.* also followed him
  8:18. the *c.* surrounding him
  12:46. speaking to the *c.*
  13:34. this teaching to the *c.*
  14:13. came after him in *c.*
  15:10. he called the *c.*
  15:33. bread enough to feed such a *c.*
  21:11. the *c.* replied, 'This is the prophet Jesus
Mark 2:4. because of the *c.* they could not get him near
  3:9. save him from being crushed by the *c.*
  5:30. turned round in the *c.* and asked, 'Who touched my clothes
  8:1. a huge *c.* had collected
  9:15. the whole *c.* were overcome with awe
  11:18. the whole *c.* was spellbound by his teaching
2 Tim. 4:3. a *c.* of teachers to tickle their ears
also Matt. 14:14. 15:30, 39. 17:14. 19:2. 20:29. 21:8,9. 26:47, 55. 27:20. Mark 2:2, 13. 3:10, 20, 32. 4:1, 36. 5:21, 24, 27, 31. 6:34. 7:33. 9:14, 17. 10:1, 46. 12:38. 14:43. 15:8. Luke 3:7. 5:1, 3, 15, 19. 6:19. 7:9, 11, 24. 8:19, 42, 45. 9:11, 37, 38. 11:27, 29. 12:1, 13. 14:25. 15:1. 18:36. 19:3, 39. 22:6, 47. 23:4, 48. John 3:26. 5:3, 13. 6:2, 5, 22. 7:12, 20. 10:41. 12:18, 29. Acts 2:6. 8:6. 14:11, 14, 18, 19. 19:26, 33, 35. 21:27, 34, 36. 23:10. 24:12, 18. Rev. 19:6.

crown-ed
Luke 3:20. misdeeds, *c.* them all by shutting John up in prison
Phil. 2:17. if my life-blood is to *c.* that sacrifice
Col. 3:14. to *c.* all, there must be love

crucifixion
Mat. 26:2. the Son of Man is to be handed over for *c.*

Mark 15:25. the hour of the *c.* was nine in the morning

cruelly
Acts 7:19. *c.* forced our ancestors to expose their children
Rev. 2:10. for ten days you will suffer *c.*

crush-ed
Mark 3:9. save him from being *c.* by the crowd
Luke 20:18. if it falls on a man he will be *c.* by it
Rom. 16:20. the God of peace will soon *c.* Satan

cry-ies-ied-ing
Mat. 8:25. woke him up, *c.*
  15:25. fell at his feet and *c.*
  27:25. with one voice the people *c.*
  27:40. they wagged their heads and *c.*
  27:50. Jesus again gave a loud *c.*
Mark 5:38. with loud *c.* and wailing
  5:39. why this *c.* and commotion
  14:65. *c.* out, 'Prophesy
  15:29. aha!' they *c.*, wagging their heads
  15:37. Jesus gave a loud *c.* and died
Luke 1:41. was filled with the Holy Spirit and *c.* aloud
  8:24. roused him, *c.*, 'Master
  15:6. he *c.* 'I have found my lost sheep
  23:46. Jesus gave a loud *c.* and said
John 19:3. *c.*, 'Hail, King of the Jews
  20:2. they have taken the Lord out of his tomb' she *c.*
Acts 20:37. there were loud *c.* of sorrow
1 Cor. 14:25. *c.*, 'God is certainly among you
Rev. 5:12. they *c.* aloud: 'Worthy is the Lamb
  5:13. *c.*: 'Praise and honour
  7:12. *c.*: 'Amen! Praise and glory
  14:8. he *c.*, 'Fallen, fallen is Babylon the great
  14:9. *c.* out loud, 'Whoever worships the beast
  16:7. I heard the altar *c.*
  19:4. they too *c.*: 'Amen! Alleluia
  19:6. and they *c.*: 'Alleluia

cudgel-s
Mat. 26:47. a great crowd armed with swords and *c.*
  26:55. with swords and *c.* to arrest me
Mark 14:43. a crowd armed with swords and *c.*
  14:48. with swords and *c.* to arrest me
Luke 22:52. you have come out with swords and *c.*

culprit-s
Acts 19:37. you have brought here as *c.*

cultivate-d
Rom. 11:24. grafted into the *c*. olive
Heb. 6:7. a useful crop to those for whom it is *c*.

cunning
Mark 14:1. some *c*. plan to seize him
1 Cor. 3:19. he traps the wise in their own *c*.
2 Cor. 4:2. we neither practise *c*. nor distort the word of God
　11:3. the serpent in his *c*. seduced Eve

cup
Luke 11:41. let what is in the *c*. be given in charity
2 Cor. 1:5. Christ's *c*. of suffering over-flows
　7:4. my *c*. is full of consolation
Phil. 2:2. fill up my *c*. of happiness

curb-ed
Tit. 1:11. such men must be *c*.

cure-s-d-ing
Mat. 4:23. *c*. whatever illness or infirmity
　4:24. all brought to him, and he *c*. them
　8:3. his leprosy was *c*. immediately
　8:4. that will certify the *c*.
　8:7. I will come and *c*. him
　8:8. only say the word and the boy will be *c*.
　9:21. touch his cloak, I shall be *c*.
　9:22. your faith has *c*. you
　9:35. *c*. every kind of ailment
　12:15. he *c*. all who were ill
Mark 3:10. he *c*. so many that sick people of all kinds came
John 9:3. that God's power might be displayed in *c*. him
also Mat. 10:1. 12:22. 14:14, 36. Mark 1:44. 3:2. 5:16, 23, 28, 29, 34. 6:13, 56. 8:25. 10:52. Luke 4:40. 5:14, 15. 6:7, 17, 18, 19. 7:7. 8:36, 43, 47, 48. 9:11, 42. 13:14. 14:3, 4. 17:15, 19. 18:42. John 4:47. 5:10, 11, 13, 15. Acts 4:9. 14. 5:16. 8:7. 9:34. 14:9. 28:9.

current-s
Mat. 28:15. is *c*. in Jewish circles to this day
John 21:23. that saying of Jesus became *c*.
Acts 27:41. caught between cross-*c*.

curry-ing
Acts 24:27. wishing to *c*. favour with the Jews
Gal. 1:10. do you think I am *c*. favour with men
Eph. 6:6 ⎫
Col. 3:22 ⎬ to *c*. favour with men
1 Thess. 2:4. we do not *c*. favour with men

curse-d-ing
1 Cor. 4:12. they *c*. us, and we bless
　12:3. no one who says 'A *c*. on Jesus!' can be speaking under the influence of the Spirit of God
Eph. 4:31. have done with spite and passion, all angry shouting and *c*.
Col. 3:8. lay aside all anger, passion, malice, *c*.
Rev. 16:9. they only *c*. the name of God
　16:11. they only *c*. the God of heaven
　16:21. they *c*. God for the plague of hail

curtain
Mat. 27:51 ⎫
Mark 15:38 ⎬ the *c*. of the temple was torn in two
Luke 23:45 ⎭
Heb. 9:3. beyond the second *c*. was the tent
　10:20. which he has opened for us through the *c*.

cushion
Mark 4:38. he was in the stern asleep on a *c*.

custody
Mat. 27:16. in *c*. a man of some notoriety
Mark 6:20. so he kept him in *c*.
　15:7. Barabbas was then in *c*.
Acts 5:18. the apostles, and put them in official *c*.
　23:35. ordered him to be held in *c*.
　24:27. Felix left Paul in *c*.
　25:4. Paul is in safe *c*.
　25:14. left in *c*. by Felix
　25:21. Paul appealed to be remanded in *c*.
Gal. 3:23. close prisoners in the *c*. of law

custom-s
Mat. 27:15. the Governor's *c*. to release one prisoner
John 19:40. according to Jewish burial-*c*.

cut-s
Mat. 3:10. fails to produce good fruit is *c*. down
　7:19. it is *c*. down and burnt
　24:22. if that time of troubles were not *c*. short
　26:51. the High Priest's servant and *c*. off his ear
　27:60. which he had *c*. out of the rock
Mark 13:20. if the Lord had not *c*. short that time of troubles . . . he has *c*. short the time
　15:46. a tomb *c*. out of the rock
Luke 3:9. *c*. down and thrown on the fire
　23:53. a tomb *c*. out of the rock
John 15:2. every barren branch of mine he *c*. away

Acts 2:37. they were c. to the heart
   8:33. his life is c. off and he is gone
      from the earth
   18:18. at Cenchreae he had his hair
      c. off

1 Cor. 11:6. she might as well have her
   hair c. off
2 Thess. 1:9. c. off from the presence of
   the Lord
Heb. 4:12. c. more keenly than any two-
   edged sword

D

damage
Acts 27:21. then you would have avoid-
   ed this d.
Rev. 7:3. do no d. to sea or land or
   trees

dance
Luke 6:23. on that day be glad and d.
   for joy

danger-s
Luke 8:23. to ship water and were in
   grave d.
1 Cor. 15:30. face these d. hour by hour
2 Cor. 11:26. d. from rivers, d. from
   robbers, d. from my fellow-countrymen, d. from foreigners, d. in
   towns, d. in the country, d. at sea,
   d. from false friends
Jude 4. it is in d. from certain persons

dangerously
Phil. 2:27. he was indeed d. ill

dare-d-ing
Mat. 8:28. no one d. pass that way
   22:46. no one d. ask him another
      question
John 21:12. none of the disciples d. to
   ask 'Who are you
Acts 7:32. Moses was terrified and d. not
   look
Rom. 10:20. Isaiah is still more d.

dark
Mat. 4:16. the land of death's d.
   shadow
   6:23. the darkness is doubly d.
   8:12. driven out into the d.
   10:27. what I say to you in the d.
   22:13. turn him out into the d.
   25:30. fling the useless servant out
      into the d.
John 8:12. no follower of mine shall
   wander in the d.
Eph. 6:12. authorities and potentates of
   this d. world
Phil. 2:15. you shine like stars in a d.
   world
2 Pet. 2:4. the d. pits of hell

darkness
Acts 17:10. as soon as d. fell

Rom. 1:21. their misguided minds are
   plunged in d.

darnel
Mat. 13:25. sowed d. among the wheat
   13:26. the d. could be seen
   13:27. where has the d. come from
   13:28. gather the d.
   13:30. gather the d. first
   13:36. explain to us the parable of the
      d.
   13:38. the d. for the children of the
      evil one
   13:39. sowed the d. is the devil
   13:40. as the d., then, is gathered up
      and burnt

dash-es-ed
Mark 9:18. it d. him to the ground
Luke 9:42. the devil d. him to the ground
   20:18. falls on that stone will be d. to
      pieces

date-s
Acts 1:7. it is not for you to know about
   d.
   21:26. the d. when the period of
      purification would end
Gal. 4:2. until the d. fixed by his father
1 Thess. 5:1. about d. and times, my
   friends, we need not write

dawn-s-ed
Mat. 4:16. light d. on the dwellers in the
   land
Mark 13:35. cock-crow or early d.
Luke 12:38. or before d. when he comes
   19:11. the reign of God might d. at
      any moment
Acts 20:11. much conversation, which
   lasted until d.
   26:23. announce the d. to Israel
   28:23. this went on from d. to dusk
1 Cor. 3:13. that day d. in fire
2 Cor. 4:4. the gospel of the glory of
   Christ, who is the very image of
   God, cannot d. upon them
   6:2. on the day of deliverance I came
      to your aid . . . now, I say, has the
      day of deliverance d.
Tit. 2:11. the grace of God has d. upon
   the world

Tit. 3:4. generosity of God our Saviour
d. upon the world

day-s
Mat. 4:17. from that *d.* Jesus began to
proclaim the message
14:15. the *d.* has gone
20:9. were paid the full *d.* wage
20:13. the usual wage for the *d.*
24:42. you do not know on what *d.*
your Lord is to come
25:1. when that *d.* comes
26:55. *d.* after *d.* I sat teaching
Mark 11:12. the following *d.*, after they
had left Bethany
14:49. *d.* after *d.* I was within your
reach
Luke 1:48. from this *d.* forth, all
generations
2:29. this *d.*, Master, thou givest thy
servant his discharge
5:1. one *d.* as he stood by the Lake
9:18. one *d.* when he was praying
alone
9:23. *d.* after *d.* he must take up his
cross
10:35. next *d.* he produced two silver
pieces
14:14. repaid on the *d.* when good
men rise
15:23. a feast to celebrate the *d.*
15:32. celebrating this happy *d.*
16:22. one *d.* the poor man died
19:47. *d.* by *d.* he taught in the temple
21:8. the *D.* is upon us
21:24. until their *d.* has run its course
22:53. *d.* after *d.*, when I was in the
temple
John 13:7. not understand now what I
am doing, but one *d.* you will
13:36. you cannot follow me now, but
one *d.* you will
Acts 2:47. *d.* by *d.* the Lord added to
their number
3:1. one *d.* at three in the afternoon
3:2. laid every *d.* by the gate
5:42. every *d.* they went steadily on
with their teaching
7:15. there he ended his *d.*
9:36. filled her *d.* with acts of kindness
10:9. next *d.*, while they were still on
their way
10:23. next *d.* he set out with them
10:24. the *d.* after that, he arrived
15:7. in the early *d.*, as you yourselves know
16:5. *d.* by *d.*, the congregations grew
17:11. studying the scriptures every
d.
17:17. in the city square every *d.*
21:16. a Christian from the early *d.*
22:30. the following *d.*

23:32. next *d.* they returned to their
barracks
25:17. the very next *d.* I took my seat
in court
1 Cor. 4:11. to this *d.* we go hungry and
thirsty
12:2. in the *d.* when you were still
pagan
15:31. every *d.* I die
2 Cor. 8:14. one *d.* your need may be
met
Gal. 4:29. in those *d.* the natural-born
son persecuted the spiritual son
Eph. 5:20. give thanks every *d.* for
everything to our God
Phil. 4:15. in the early *d.* of my mission
Tit. 3:3. our *d.* were passed in malice
and envy
Heb. 3:15. as in those *d.* of rebellion
11:26. the coming *d.* of recompense
1 Pet. 1:14. in your *d.* of ignorance
3:5. among God's people in *d.* of old
4:2. the rest of his *d.* on earth
2 Pet. 2:6. an object-lesson for godless
men in future *d.*
Jude 21. look forward to the *d.*
Rev. 6:6. a whole *d.* wage for a quart of
flour, a whole *d.* wage for three
quarts of barley-meal
11:18. thy *d.* of retribution has come
16:15. that is the *d.* when I come like
a thief
19:7. the wedding-*d.* of the Lamb has
come

daybreak
Mat. 28:1. about *d.* on Sunday
John 8:2. at *d.* he appeared again in the
temple
Acts 5:21. they entered the temple at
d.
27:33. shortly before *d.* Paul urged
them all to take some food

daylight
Mat. 10:27. you must repeat in broad *d.*
Luke 12:3. said in the dark will be
heard in broad *d.*
John 9:4. while *d.* lasts we must carry
on the work.
11:9. are there not twelve hours of *d.*
Acts 16:35. when *d.* came the magistrates
sent their officers
27:29. prayed for *d.* to come
Eph. 5:8. live like men who are at
home in *d.*
1 Thess. 5:8. we, who belong to *d.*, must
keep sober
2 Pet. 2:13. carouse in broad *d.*

day-time
John 11:9. walk in *d.* without stumbling

dazzling
Mark 9:3 } his clothes became *d.* white
Luke 9:29 }

Luke 24:4. two men in *d*. garments

dead

Mat. 8:26 ⎱
Mark 4:39 ⎰ there was a *d*. calm

    15:45. he gave Joseph leave to take
the *d*. body

    16:9. when he had risen from the *d*.

    16:14. those who had seen him risen
from the *d*.

Luke 14:14. when good men rise from
the *d*.

Acts 5:5. when Ananias heard these
words he dropped *d*.

    13:33. by raising Jesus from the *d*.

    22:22. a scoundrel like that is better *d*.

Rom. 8:34. died, and, more than that,
was raised from the *d*.

1 Cor. 6:14. raised our Lord from the *d*.

Eph. 4:19. *d*. to all feeling

Rev. 2:23. her children I will strike *d*.

deadly

2 Cor. 2:16. a *d*. fume that kills

Jam. 3:8. charged with *d*. venom

1 John 5:16. a sin which is not a *d*. sin
    . . . when men are not guilty of
    d. sin. There is such a thing as *d*.
    sin

    5:17. not all sin is *d*. sin

deadness

Heb. 6:1. the *d*. of our former ways

    9:14. cleanse our conscience from the
d. of our former ways

deaf

John 18:37. all who are not *d*. to truth
listen to my voice

Acts 7:51. heathen still at heart and *d*.
to the truth

Rom. 11:8. he gave them blind eyes
and *d*. ears

1 Tim. 6:20. turn a *d*. ear to empty and
worldly chatter

deal-s-ing-t

Mat. 7:2. measure you *d*. out to others
will be *d*. back to you

    18:35. how my heavenly Father will
d. with you

    21:40. how do you think he will *d*.
with those tenants

Luke 1:49. so wonderfully has he *d*.
with me

    1:72. *d*. mercifully with our fathers

    6:38. measure you *d*. out to others
will be *d*. to you

    16:8. in *d*. with their own kind

Acts 6:3. appoint them to *d*. with these
matters

    19:24. provided a great *d*. of employ-
ment

    19:39. it will be *d*. with in the statutory
assembly

    28:23. he *d*. at length with the whole
matter

1 Cor. 3:1. to *d*. with you on the merely
natural plane

    6:2. incompetent to *d*. with these
trifling cases

Gal. 5:23. no law *d*. with such things

1 Thess. 2:11. we *d*. with you one by one,
as a father *d*. with his children

1 Tim. 1:13. I was *d*. with mercifully

    1:16. I was mercifully *d*. with

2 Tim. 4:14. the copper-smith did me a
great *d*. of harm

Rev. 9:19. with them too they *d*.
injuries

dealer-s

Mat. 21:12 ⎱
Mark 11:15 ⎰ *d*. in pigeons

John 2:14. *d*. in cattle, sheep, and pigeons

    2:16. he turned on the *d*. in pigeons

Acts 16:14. Lydia, a *d*. in purple fabric

dealings

Rom. 9:17. my power in my *d*. with you

2 Cor. 1:12. in our *d*. with our fellow-
men, and above all in our *d*. with
you

    8:23. my associate in *d*. with you

2 Thess. 3:14. have no *d*. with him until
he is ashamed

Rev. 15:4. thy just *d*. stand revealed

dear

Mark 12:6. his own *d*. son

Luke 6:42. my *d*. brother, let me take
the speck out of your eye

    20:13. I will send my own *d*. son

1 Cor. 4:14. you are my *d*. children

    4:17. Timothy, who is a *d*. son to me

Rev. 12:11. they did not hold their lives
too *d*. to lay them down

also Rom. 16:5, 8, 9, 12. 1 Cor. 10:14.
2 Cor. 12:19. Gal. 4:18. Eph. 6:21.
Col. 4:7, 9, 14. Philem. 1. 1 John
2:7. 3:2, 21. 4:7, 11. 3 John 1, 2, 5,
11.

dearly

John 11:36. the Jews said, 'How *d*. he
must have loved him

death

Mat. 16:18. the forces of *d*. shall never
overpower it

    16:21. to be put to *d*. and to be raised
again

    26:4. Jesus arrested by some trick and
put to *d*.

    27:4. brought an innocent man to his
d.

    27:20. to have Jesus put to *d*.

Mark 8:31. put to *d*., and to rise again

    12:9. put the tenants to *d*.

Luke 7:2. this servant was ill and near
to *d*.

    9:22. to be put to *d*. and to be raised
again

Luke 13:33. unthinkable for a prophet to meet his *d.* anywhere but in Jerusalem

15:17. here am I, starving to *d.*

20:16. put these tenants to *d.*

20:36. they are not subject to *d.* any longer

22:15. I have longed to eat this Passover with you before my *d.*

John 7:25. is not this the man they want to put to *d.*

11:19. to condole with them on their brother's *d.*

Acts 1:3. he showed himself to these men after his *d.*

5:28. make us responsible for that man's *d.*

5:30. Jesus whom you had done to *d.*

5:33. they wanted to put them to *d.*

10:39. he was put to *d.* by hanging on a gibbet

21:31. they were clamouring for his *d.*

Rom. 3:25. expiating sin by his sacrificial *d.*

4:25. delivered to *d.* for our misdeeds

5:7. for a good man one might actually brave *d.*

5:9. justified by Christ's sacrificial *d.*

5:15. the wrongdoing of that one man brought *d.*

8:13. put to *d.* all the base pursuits of the body

8:36. we are being done to *d.* for thy sake

2 Cor. 3:6. the written law condemns to *d.*

4:10. we carry *d.* with us in our body, the *d.* that Jesus died

6:9. disciplined by suffering, we are not done to *d.*

7:3. come *d.*, come life, we meet it together

Eph. 4:22. deluded by its lusts, is sinking towards *d.*

Phil. 1:21. life is Christ, and *d.* gain

Col. 3:5. put to *d.* those parts of you which belong to the earth

1 Thess. 4:13. those who sleep in *d.*

Heb. 6:6. making mock of his *d.*

9:17. a testament is operative only after a *d.*

10:28. he is put to *d.* without pity

11:34. escaped *d.* by the sword

11:35. others were tortured to *d.*

Rev. 13:15. all who would not worship the image to be put to *d.*

18:24. all who had been done to *d.*

debased

Rom. 3:12. all alike have become *d.*

debate-d-ing

Luke 12:17. he *d.* with himself

24:17. what is it you are *d.* as you walk

Acts 9:29. *d.* with the Greek-speaking Jews

15:7. after a long *d.*, Peter rose

Jude 9. archangel Michael was in *d.* with the devil

debater

1 Cor. 1:20. your subtle *d.*

debauchery

Rom. 13:13. no *d.* or vice

1 Pet. 4:3. then you lived in licence and *d.*

2 Pet. 2:18. *d.* a bait to catch

debt

Mat. 18:24. a man whose *d.* ran into millions

18:25. ordered him to be sold to meet the *d.*

18:34. pay the *d.* in full

Luke 7:41. two men were in *d.* to a money-lender

Philem. 18. done you any wrong or is in your *d.*

decay

2 Cor. 4:16. our outward humanity is in *d.*

deceit

1 Pet. 2:1. away with all malice and *d.*

3:10. and his lips from *d.*

Rev. 22:15. all who love and practise *d.*

deceitful

Eph. 4:14. crafty rogues and their *d.* schemes

deceive

1 Thess. 2:3. there is no attempt to *d.*

Jam. 1:16. do not *d.* yourselves, my friends

decency

Rom. 13:13. behave with *d.* as befits the day

deception-s

Mat. 27:64. the final *d.* will be worse than the first

2 Thess. 2:10. all the *d.* that sinfulness can impose

2 Pet. 2:13. they revel in their own *d.*

decide-d-ing

Mat. 18:23. a king who *d.* to settle accounts

Mark 15:24. casting lots to *d.* what each should have

Luke 1:3. have *d.* to write a connected narrative

23:24. Pilate *d.* that they should have their way

John 1:43. Jesus *d.* to leave for Galilee

John 7:26. actually *d.* that this is the Messiah
Acts 3:14. Pilate had *d.* to release him
  5:35. be cautious in *d.* what to do
  20:3. he *d.* to return by way of Macedonia
  20:16. Paul had *d.* to pass by Ephesus
  25:25. I *d.* to send him
  27:1. it was *d.* that we should sail for Italy
1 Cor. 7:37. if he has *d.* in his own mind
2 Cor. 9:7. each person should give as he has *d.*
1 Thess. 3:1. we *d.* to remain alone at Athens

decision-s

Acts 15:28. it is the *d.* of the Holy Spirit, and our *d.*, to lay no further burden upon you
  16:4. the *d.* taken by the apostles
  21:25. the gentile converts, we sent them our *d.*
  25:21. for His Imperial Majesty's *d.*
Rom. 14:22. make his *d.* with a clear conscience
1 Cor. 6:5. a *d.* in a brother-Christian's cause
Col. 2:18. the *d.* of people who go in for self-mortification

deck-ed

1 Tim. 2:9. not *d.* out with gold or pearls

declare-s-d-ing

Mat. 1:22. what the Lord *d.* through the prophet
  2:15. the Lord had *d.* through the prophet
  25:12. he answered, 'I *d.*, I do not know you
  26:74. *d.* with an oath: 'I do not know the man
Mark 3:30. they had *d.* that he was possessed
  7:19. thus he *d.* all foods clean
John 4:44. Jesus himself *d.* that a prophet
Acts 1:24. *d.* which of these two thou hast chosen
  10:43. *d.* that everyone who trusts in him
  13:5. they *d.* the word of God
  13:34. he *d.* in these words
  13:46. that the word of God should be *d.* to you first
  16:17. *d.* to you a way of salvation
  20:26. *d.* that no man's fate can be laid at my door
  23:9. *d.*, 'We can find no fault with this man
Rom. 1:15. my eagerness to *d.* the Gospel to you
  2:16. so my gospel *d.*

2 Cor. 2:17. when we *d.* the word we do it in sincerity
  4:2. *d.* the truth openly
  6:7. by *d.* the truth
Gal. 3:8. *d.* the Gospel to Abraham
  3:22. Scripture has *d.* the whole world to be prisoners
1 Thess. 2:2. we *d.* the gospel of God to you frankly
Tit. 1:3. in his own good time he has openly *d.* himself
Jam. 1:18. of his set purpose, by *d.* the truth
1 John 1:2. we here *d.* to you the eternal life

decline-d-ing

Acts 18:20. he was asked to stay longer, but *d.*
1 Cor. 2:6. governing powers, which are *d.* to their end

decree-s-d

Acts 4:28. by thy *d.*, were foreordained
Rom. 1:32. the just *d.* of God
Eph. 1:11. as was *d.* in his design
Col. 2:14. pledged us to the *d.* of the law
2 Pet. 2:3. the judgement long *d.* for them

dedicate-d

Acts 20:32. your heritage among all who are *d.* to him
Rom. 1:7. called to be his *d.* people
  12:1. *d.* and fit for his acceptance
1 Cor. 1:2. *d.* to him in Christ Jesus
  6:11. *d.* to God and justified
  7:34. *d.* to him in body as in spirit
2 Cor. 1:1. together with all who are *d.* to him
Eph. 1:4. to be *d.*, to be without blemish
  3:5. his *d.* apostles and prophets
Col. 1:22. present you before himself as *d.* men
2 Tim. 1:9. brought us salvation and called us to a *d.* life
  2:21. those which are valued and *d.*
1 Pet. 2:9. a royal priesthood, a *d.* nation
2 Pet. 3:11. what devout and *d.* lives you should live
Rev. 11:18. thy *d.* people
  22:11. the *d.* man

dedication

Rev. 22:11. be true to his *d.*

deed-s

Mat. 6:4. your good *d.* must be secret
  13:41. all whose *d.* are evil
Luke 1:51. the *d.* his own right arm has done
John 2:11. this *d.* at Cana-in-Galilee
  10:25. my *d.* done in my Father's name

John 10:32. I have set before you many good *d.*

10:33. not going to stone you for any good *d.*

10:38. accept the evidence of my *d.*

14:11. accept the evidence of the *d.* themselves

Acts 13:41. I am doing a *d.* in your days, a *d.* which you will never believe

26:20. prove their repentance by *d.*

Rom. 4:7. whose lawless *d.* are forgiven

7:18. the will to do good is there, the *d.* is not

9:11. based not upon men's *d.* but upon the call of God

9:32. their efforts were not based on faith, but (as they supposed) on *d.*

11:6. if it is by grace, then it does not rest on *d.*

13:12. throw off the *d.* of darkness

2 Cor. 4:2. the *d.* that men hide for very shame

11:15. meet the end their *d.* deserve

Gal. 2:16. not through *d.* dictated by law; for by such *d.*, Scripture says, no mortal man

Eph. 2:10. the good *d.* for which God has designed us

5:11. take no part in the barren *d.* of darkness

Phil. 2:13. inspiring both the will and the *d.*

Col. 1:21. your *d.* were evil

2 Thess. 2:17. fortify you in every good *d.*

1 Tim. 2:10. good *d.*, as befits women who claim to be religious

5:10. evidence of good *d.* performed

5:25. good *d.* are obvious

Tit. 3:5. not for any good *d.* of our own

Heb. 8:12. I will be merciful to their wicked *d.*

10:17. wicked *d.* I will remember no more

Jam. 2:18. real though not accompanied by *d.*, and by my *d.* I will prove to you my faith

2:20. faith divorced from *d.* is barren

2:24. a man is justified by *d.*

2:26. faith divorced from *d.* is lifeless

3:17. kindly *d.* that are its fruit

1 Pet. 1:17. impartially on the record of his *d.*

Jude 13. foaming shameful *d.*

Rev. 2:23. each one of you according to his *d.*

14:13. take with them the record of their *d.*

15:3. great and marvellous are thy *d.*, O Lord God

18:6. repay her twice over for her *d.*

19:8. the righteous *d.* of God's people

20:12. judged upon the record of their *d.*

20:13. each man on the record of his *d.*

22:12. everyone according to his *d.*

deem-ed

Luke 2:23. shall be *d.* to belong to the Lord

Heb. 3:3. *d.* worthy of greater honour than Moses

deep-er-est

Mat. 23:5. wear *d.* fringes on their robes

Luke 7:16. *d.* awe fell upon them all

9:32. Peter and his companions had been in a *d.* sleep

John 13:21. Jesus exclaimed in *d.* agitation

19:11. the *d.* guilt lies with the man

Acts 10:25. bowed to the ground in *d.* reverence

Rom. 10:1. my *d.* desire and my prayer to God

11:25. there is a *d.* truth here

1 Cor. 12:8. put the *d.* knowledge into words

Eph. 3:17. with *d.* roots and firm foundations

Phil. 1:8. with the *d.* yearning of Christ Jesus

1 Tim. 3:9. the *d.* truths of our faith

Rev. 2:24. the *d.* secrets of Satan

14:2. the *d.* roar of thunder

18:3. all nations have drunk *d.* of the fierce wine

19:6. *d.* roars of thunder

deepen

Philem. 6. may *d.* the understanding

deeply

Mat. 14:9. the king was *d.* distressed when he heard it

18:31. the other servants were *d.* distressed

20:34. Jesus was *d.* moved

Luke 1:29. she was *d.* troubled by what he said

1:66. all who heard it were *d.* impressed

John 11:33. he sighed heavily and was *d.* moved

11:38. Jesus again sighed *d.*

Acts 13:12. *d.* impressed by what he learned

defeat

Rom. 12:21. use good to *d.* evil

1 John 5:4. the victory that *d.* the world is our faith

Rev. 11:7. will *d.* and kill them

13:7. wage war on God's people and to *d.* them

17:14. the Lamb will *d.* them

defence
Mark 15:4. have you nothing to say in your *d.*
Luke 12:11. how you will conduct your *d.*
   21:14. not to prepare your *d.* before-hand
Acts 24:10. I make my *d.* with confidence
   26:1. began his *d.*
   26:2. I am to make my *d.* today
   26:24. Paul was thus making his *d.*
Rom. 1:20. no possible *d.* for their conduct
   2:1. you therefore have no *d.*
   3:19. anything to say in self-*d.*
2 Cor. 12:19. we have been addressing our *d.* to you
1 Pet. 3:15. be always ready with your *d.*
Jude 3. the struggle in *d.* of the faith

defend-ed
John 5:17. he *d.* himself by saying
Phil. 1:16. to *d.* the Gospel that I am where I am

defer
Heb. 13:17. obey your leaders and *d.* to them

deference
Luke 20:21. you pay *d.* to no one

defiance-defiant
Acts 23:3. in *d.* of the Law you order me
Jam. 3:14. false, and a *d.* of the truth
Jude 15. *d.* words which godless sinners had spoken

defile-d
Mark 7:5. eat their food with *d.* hands
2 Cor. 7:1. all that can *d.* flesh or spirit
Heb. 9:13. those who have been *d.*

defilement-s
John 18:28. outside the headquarters to avoid *d.*
2 Pet. 2:20. escaped the world's *d.*
1 John 2:2. the remedy for the *d.* of our sins
   4:10. his Son as the remedy for the *d.*

definite
Acts 25:26. nothing *d.* about him to put in writing
1 Cor. 14:7. unless their notes mark *d.* intervals

defraud
2 Cor. 12:17. was used by me to *d.* you
   12:18. did Titus *d.* you

defy-ied-ing
John 19:12. any man who claims to be a king is *d.* Caesar
1 Cor. 10:22. can we *d.* the Lord
2 Tim. 3:8. as Jannes and Jambres *d.* Moses, so these men *d.* the truth

degradation
Rom. 1:24. the consequent *d.* of their bodies

deigned
Luke 1:25. he has *d.* to take away my reproach

deity-ies
Acts 17:18. a propagandist for foreign *d.*
   17:29. we ought not to suppose that the *d.*
Rom. 1:20. his everlasting power and *d.*
1 Cor. 8:1. food consecrated to heathen *d.*
   8:10. food consecrated to the heathen *d.*

delay-ed
Mark 8:10. without *d.*, got into the boat with his disciples
   11:3. will send it back here without *d.*
Luke 24:33. without a moment's *d.* they set out
Acts 22:16. and now why *d.*
   22:18. leave Jerusalem without *d.*
1 Tim. 3:15. I write this in case I am *d.*
Heb. 10:37. he who is to come will come; he will not *d.*
Rev. 10:6. there shall be no more *d.*

delegate-s
2 Cor. 8:23. they are *d.* of our congregations

delegation
Luke 19:14. they sent a *d.* on his heels

deliberate
Acts 2:23. by the *d.* will and plan of God
2 Thess. 2:12. make sinfulness their *d.* choice

delight-s-ed
Mat. 14:6. Herod was so *d.*
   18:13. he is more *d.* over that sheep
   25:21 } come and share your master's
   25:23 } *d.*
Mark 6:22. so *d.* Herod and his guests
Luke 1:58. they were as *d.* as she was
   13:17. the people were *d.* at all the wonderful things
   15:5. he has found it'? How *d.* he is
1 Cor. 13:6. *d.* in the truth
2 Cor. 7:13. *d.* beyond everything by seeing how happy Titus is
Phil. 2:29. with whole-hearted *d.*
Philem. 7. *d.* and encouraged by your love
Heb. 10:6. sin-offerings thou didst not *d.* in
   10:8. thou didst not desire nor *d.* in
2 John 4. I was *d.* to find that
3 John 3. I was *d.* when friends came

deliver-s-ed-ing
Mark 5:36. Jesus, overhearing the message as it was *d.*

Mark 16:8. they *d.* all these instructions
Luke 1:71. *d.* us from our enemies
John 10:35. to whom the word of God
was *d.*
17:14. I have *d.* thy word to them
Acts 15:23. gave them this letter to *d.*
16:6. prevented by the Holy Spirit
from *d.* the message
20:20. I *d.* the message to you
Rom. 15:28. *d.* the proceeds under my
own seal
2 Cor. 3:3. a letter that has come from
Christ, given to us to *d.*
Col. 1:25. to *d.* his message in full
2:6. Jesus was *d.* to you as Christ and
Lord
Heb. 2:10. the leader who *d.* them
5:7. God who was able to *d.* him
Jude 5. the Lord, having once *d.* the
people

deliverance
Luke 2:30. the *d.* which thou hast made
3:6. all mankind shall see God's *d.*
Rom. 13:11. wake out of sleep, for *d.* is
nearer
2 Cor. 1:11. many people praying for
our *d.*
6:2. on the day of *d.* I came . . . the
day of *d.* dawned
Phil. 1:19. the issue of it all will be my
d.
Heb. 2:3. if we ignore a *d.* so great? For
this *d.*
9:12. secured an eternal *d.*
9:15. *d.* from sins committed

deliverer
Luke 1:69. a *d.* of victorious power
2:11. in the city of David a *d.* has
been born
Phil. 3:20. we expect our *d.* to come
1 Thess. 1:10. Jesus our *d.* from the
terrors

delude-d-ing
Gal. 6:3. somebody, when he is nothing,
he is *d.* himself
Eph. 4:22. old human nature which, *d.*
by its lusts
Rev. 13:14. it *d.* the inhabitants of the
earth
19:20. *d.* those that had received the
mark

deluge
2 Pet. 2:5. the *d.* upon that world of
godless men
3:6. the water of the *d.*

delusive
Col. 2:8. hollow and *d.* speculations

demand-s-ed-ing
Mat. 5:19. the least of the Laws *d.*
23:23. the weightier *d.* of the Law

Luke 6:30. takes what is yours, do not
d. it back
11:16. *d.* of him a sign from heaven
11:29. a wicked generation. It *d.* a
sign
18:3. *d.* justice against her opponent
23:23. they insisted on their *d.*
Acts 25:15. *d.* his condemnation
Gal. 2:16. by doing what the law *d.*
Tit. 2:9. to comply with their *d.*

demolish-ed
2 Cor. 5:1. if the earthly frame that
houses us today should be *d.*
10:4. potent to *d.* strongholds
10:5. we *d.* sophistries

demons
1 Cor. 10:20. offered (in the words of
Scripture) 'to *d.* and to that which
is not God'; and I will not have you
become partners with *d.*
10:21. you cannot drink the cup of the
Lord and the cup of *d.* You cannot
partake of the Lord's table and the
table of *d.*
Rev. 18:2. she has become a dwelling for
d.

demonic
Jam. 3:15. it is earth-bound, sensual,
d.

demonstrate-ing
Acts 18:28. *d.* publicly from the scriptures
Rom. 3:25. God meant by this to *d.* his
justice
3:26. to *d.* his justice now

demur
Acts 10:29. I came here without *d.*

denial
2 Tim. 3:5. a standing *d.* of its reality

denounce-d
Mat. 11:20. *d.* them for their impenitence

deny
John 5:23. to *d.* honour to the Son is to
deny it to the Father
Acts 23:8. the Sadducees *d.* that there is
any resurrection
1 Cor. 7:5. do not *d.* yourselves to one
another

departure
Luke 9:31. spoke of his *d.*

depend-s
Acts 19:25. living *d.* on this industry
27:34. your lives *d.* on it
Rom. 9:16. does not *d.* on man's will
or effort
Eph. 4:16. on him the whole body *d.*
Heb. 12:2. Jesus, on whom faith *d.*

deportation
Mat. 1:11. the *d.* to Babylon
  1:12. after the *d.*
  1:17. from David until the *d.* to Babylon, and fourteen from the *d.* until the Messiah

deposit
Mat. 25:27. you ought to have put my money on *d.*
Luke 19:23. put my money on *d.*

depraved
Rom. 1:28. given them up to their own *d.* reason

deprived
Rom. 3:23. *d.* of the divine splendour

depth-s
Mat. 11:23. brought down to the *d.*
  13:5. it had no *d.* of earth
Luke 10:15. brought down to the *d.*
Acts 25:20. out of my *d.* in such discussions
1 Cor. 2:10. even the *d.* of God's own nature
2 Cor. 8:2. from the *d.* of their poverty
Phil. 2:10. in heaven, on earth, and in the *d.*

deputation
John 1:19. sent a *d.* of priests and Levites
  1:24. some Pharisees who were in the *d.*

deputy
1 Pet. 2:14. to the governor as his *d.*

descend-ed-ing
Mat. 10:13. your peace may *d.* on it
John 8:37. you are *d.* from Abraham
Jam. 5:1. the miserable fate *d.* on you

descendant-s
Luke 1:27. Joseph, a *d.* of David
John 8:33. we are Abraham's *d.*
Acts 2:30. one of his own direct *d.* should sit on his throne
  7:5. in possession to him and his *d.*
  7:6. Abraham's *d.* shall live
Rom. 9:6. not all *d.* of Israel are truly Israel
  9:8. reckoned as Abraham's *d.*
2 Cor. 11:22. Abraham's *d.*? So am I
Heb. 6:14. multiply your *d.*
  7:5. the *d.* of Levi . . . they too are *d.* of Abraham
  11:12. *d.* numerous as the stars

descent
Mat. 1:1. a table of the *d.* of Jesus Christ
Luke 1:5. his wife also was of priestly *d.*
  2:5. of the house of David by *d.*
Rom. 9:5. in natural *d.*, sprang the Messiah

Jude 14. the seventh in *d.* from Adam

describe-d
Mat. 11:16. how can I *d.* this generation
Mark 4:30. by what parable shall we *d.* it
Luke 7:31. how can I *d.* the people
Acts 9:27. he *d.* to them how Saul had seen
  21:19. *d.* in detail all that God had done
2 John 7. the persons *d.* as the Antichrist
Rev. 22:18. the plagues *d.* in this book
  22:19. *d.* in this book

desecrate-ing
1 Cor. 11:27. *d.* the body and blood of the Lord

desert-s-ed
Mat. 12:43. it wanders over the *d.*
  26:56. the disciples all *d.* him and ran away
Mark 14:50. the disciples all *d.* him
Luke 8:13. in the time of testing they *d.*
  11:24. over the *d.* seeking a resting-place
John 6:49. ate the manna in the *d.*
  11:54. the country bordering on the *d.*
Acts 7:30. a burning bush in the *d.*
  7:36. forty years in the *d.*
  7:38. assembled there in the *d.*
  7:42. those forty years in the *d.*
  7:44. the Tent of the Testimony in the *d.*
  13:18. he bore with their conduct in the *d.*
  15:38. the man who had *d.* them
1 Cor. 10:5. the *d.* was strewn with their corpses
Gal. 4:27. the *d.* wife shall have more children
1 Tim. 4:1. some will *d.* from the faith
2 Tim. 1:15. everyone in the province of Asia *d.* me
  4:10. Demas has *d.* me
Heb. 3:8. that time of testing in the *d.*
  3:17. whose bodies lay where they fell in the *d.*
  13:5. I will never leave you or *d.* you
Rev. 16:6. they have their *d.*

deserter
Heb. 3:12. a *d.* from the living God

deserve-s
Mat. 22:8. did not *d.* the honour
Luke 7:4. he *d.* this favour from you
  17:10. we are servants and *d.* no credit
  23:15. clearly he has done nothing to *d.* death
Acts 26:31. doing nothing that *d.* death
Rom. 1:32. who behave like this *d.* to die

1 Cor. 4:5. such praise as he *d.*
 16:18. such men *d.* recognition
2 Cor. 11:15. the end their deeds *d.*
Gal. 4:18. a fine thing to *d.* an honest envy
Heb. 10:29. a penalty that man will *d.*
Rev. 3:4. walk with me in white, for so they *d.*

design-ed
Acts 17:29. by human craftsmanship and *d.*
Rom. 3:25. God *d.* him to be the means of expiating sin
1 Cor. 14:22. prophecy is *d.* not for unbelievers
Eph. 1:11. decreed in his *d.*
 2:10. good deeds for which God has *d.* us
Col. 2:19. grows according to God's *d.*

designated
Acts 10:42. *d.* by God as judge

desire-s-d-ing
Mat. 1:19. *d.* to have the marriage contract set aside
Mark 4:19. all kinds of evil *d.* come in
 15:15. in his *d.* to satisfy the mob
Luke 23:20. in his *d.* to release Jesus
John 1:13. by the fleshly *d.* of a human father
 8:44. to carry out your father's *d.*
 17:24. Father, I *d.* that these men
Rom. 1:24. the vileness of their own *d.*
 6:12. obedience to the body's *d.*
 7:8. all kinds of wrong *d.*
 9:22. God, *d.* to exhibit his retribution
1 Cor. 4:8. have everything you could *d.*
 7:9. better be married than burn with vain *d.*
 10:6. not to set our *d.* on evil things
 14:17. prayer of thanksgiving may be all that could be *d.*
2 Cor. 5:4. our *d.* is to have the new body put on
 8:12. an eager *d.* to give
 8:17. by his own *d.* he is now leaving
Gal. 5:16. the *d.* of your lower nature
 5:17. sets its *d.* against the Spirit
 5:24. the lower nature with its passions and *d.*
Eph. 4:19. to satisfy their foul *d.*
1 Tim. 2:8. it is my *d.*, therefore, that everywhere prayers
 6:9. foolish harmful *d.*
2 Tim. 3:6. led on by all kinds of *d.*
Tit. 2:12. godless ways and worldly *d.*
Heb. 6:17. God, *d.* to show
 10:5. sacrifice and offering thou didst not *d.*
 10:8. sin-offerings, thou didst not *d.*

13:18. our one *d.* is always to do what is right
Jam. 4:1. the aggressiveness of your bodily *d.*
 4:5. turns towards envious *d.*
1 Pet. 1:14. the *d.* you cherished in your days of ignorance
 4:2. the things that men *d.*
Rev. 22:17. a free gift to all who *d.* it

desist
Acts 5:28. to *d.* from teaching in that name

destined
Mat. 11:14. John is the *d.* Elijah
Luke 2:34. this child is *d.* to be a sign
1 Cor. 15:25. he is *d.* to reign
Eph. 1:5. he *d.* us—such was his will and pleasure
1 Thess. 5:9. God has not *d.* us to the terrors
Heb. 11:8. a land *d.* for himself and his heirs
Rev. 12:5. a male child, who is *d.* to rule all nations

destiny
Luke 9:31. the *d.* he was to fulfil in Jerusalem

destroy-ed
Luke 12:33. no moth *d.* it
John 2:17. zeal for thy house shall *d.* me
 11:50. than that the whole nation should be *d.*
Gal. 1:13. the church of God, and tried to *d.* it
2 Thess. 2:10. *d.* they shall be, because they did not open their minds
Heb. 7:16. the power of a life that cannot be *d.*
1 Pet. 1:4. one that nothing can *d.*
2 Pet. 3:6. by water that first world was *d.*
 3:7. the godless will be *d.*

Destroyer
Rev. 9:11. Apollyon, or the *D.*

destruction
Luke 21:20. be sure that her *d.* is near
Rom. 6:6. for the *d.* of the sinful self
Gal. 5:15. all you can expect is mutual *d.*
2 Thess. 2:10. those doomed to *d.*
2 Pet. 2:6. condemned them to total *d.*

detachment
John 18:3. Judas took a *d.* of soldiers

detail
Luke 1:3. the whole course of these events in *d.*
John 21:25. if it were all to be recorded in *d.*
Acts 18:26. expounded the new way to him in greater *d.*

Acts 21:19. described in *d.* all that God had done

detained
Acts 25:21. I ordered him to be *d.*

detecte-d
Luke 8:47. the woman, seeing that she was *d.*
John 8:3. a woman *d.* in adultery

determine-d
John 5:18. still more *d.* to kill him
1 Cor. 16:12. he was quite *d.* not to go at present
2 Cor. 10:13. *d.* by the limit God laid down for us
Gal. 2:5. I was *d.* that the full truth of the Gospel
Eph. 1:9. *d.* beforehand in Christ

detest
Rom. 7:15. what I do is not what I want to do, but what I *d.*

detestable
Luke 16:15. *d.* in the sight of God
Tit. 1:16. their *d.* obstinacy disqualifies them

device-s
Eph. 6:11. firm against the *d.* of the devil

devil
Mat. 5:37. anything beyond that comes from the *d.*
1 Tim. 4:2. conscience is branded with the *d.* sign
5:15. taken the wrong turning and gone to the *d.*

devise
Mark 14:1. *d.* some cunning plan to seize him
Luke 22:2. *d.* some means of doing away with him

devote-d
Mat. 6:24. he will be *d.* to the first
Luke 16:13. *d.* to the first and think nothing of the second
Acts 6:4. we *d.* ourselves to prayer
15:26. who have *d.* themselves to the cause
18:5. Paul *d.* himself entirely to preaching
Rom. 13:6. to these duties they *d.* their energies
1 Cor. 7:5. to *d.* yourselves to prayer
2 Cor. 7:12. how truly you are *d.* to us
Eph. 2:10. to *d.* ourselves to the good deeds
Col. 4:12. wholly *d.* to doing God's will
1 Tim. 4:13. *d.* your attention to the public reading
1 Pet. 3:13. if you are *d.* to what is good

devotion
Acts 26:7. worshipping with intense *d.*
2 Cor. 7:11. your *d.* and your eagerness
11:3. your single-hearted *d.* to Christ
Gal. 1:14. *d.* to the traditions of my ancestors
1 Pet. 5:2. not for gain but out of sheer *d.*

devour-ing
Mark 9:48. the *d.* worm never dies
Heb. 12:29. our God is a *d.* fire

devout
Luke 1:6. both of them were upright and *d.*
John 9:31. he listens to anyone who is *d.*
2 Cor. 1:12. a *d.* and godly sincerity
Eph. 4:24. in the just and *d.* life
1 Thess. 2:10. how *d.* and just and blameless
Tit. 1:8. just, *d.*, and self-controlled
Heb. 7:26. *d.*, guileless, undefiled
2 Pet. 3:11. what *d.* and dedicated lives you should live

diadem-s
Rev. 12:3. on his heads were seven *d.*
13:1. on its horns were ten *d.*
19:12. on his head were many *d.*

dictate-d-ing
2 Cor. 1:24. *d.* the terms of your faith
Gal. 2:16. not through deeds *d.* by law
Col. 2:20. why let people *d.* to you

dictation
Gal. 2:5. not for one moment did I yield to their *d.*

die-d
Mat. 22:25. the first married and *d.*
26:52. all who take the sword *d.* by the sword
26:66. they answered; 'he should *d.*
Mark 15:37. Jesus gave a loud cry and *d.*
15:39. saw how he *d.*
Luke 23:46. with these words he *d.*
John 3:16. may not *d.* but have eternal life
Acts 7:60. and with that he *d.*
12:23. he was eaten up with worms and *d.*
13:36. he *d.*, and was gathered to his fathers
1 Cor. 10:8. twenty-three thousand *d.* in one day
11:30. a number have *d.*
15:6. though some have *d.*
15:18. those who have *d.* within Christ's fellowship
15:51. we shall not all *d.*, but we shall all be changed
2 Cor. 4:9. struck down, we are not left to *d.*

2 Cor. 4:10. the death that Jesus *d.*
   13:4. he *d.* on the cross in weakness
1 Thess. 4:15. shall not forestall those
   who have *d.*
1 Pet. 3:18. Christ also *d.* for our sins
Rev. 11:5. thus shall the man *d.* who
   seeks to do them harm

difference
Gal. 5:6. circumcision makes no *d.*
Heb. 7:20. how great a *d.* it makes

different-ly
Mark 16:12. he appeared in a *d.* guise
Luke 22:36. it is *d.* now,' he said
John 5:42. with you it is *d.*
   9:16. so they took *d.* sides
Rom. 7:23. in my bodily members a *d.*
   law
   12:4. limbs and organs, all with *d.*
   functions
1 Cor. 12:10. ecstatic utterance of *d.*
   kinds
   12:20. many *d.* organs, but one body
   14:10. how many *d.* kinds of sound
   there are
   15:39. flesh of beasts, of birds, and of
   fishes—all *d.*
2 Cor. 2:7. something very *d.* is called
   for now
   11:4. a spirit *d.* from the Spirit already
   given to you, or a gospel *d.* from
   the gospel
   12:20. find you *d.* from what I wish
   you to be, and that you may find
   me also *d.*
Gal. 1:6. following a *d.* gospel
Phil. 3:15. any point on which you think
   d.
Heb. 7:13. belongs to a *d.* tribe
Jam. 2:25. sending them away by a *d.*
   route

difficult-ies-y
Mat. 17:27. we do not want to cause *d.*
1 Thess. 3:7. in all our *d.* and hardships
Heb. 5:11. much that is *d.* to explain

digestion
1 Tim. 5:23. take a little wine for your *d.*

dignitary-ies
Acts 19:31. some of the *d.* of the
   province

diligent-ly
John 5:39. study the scriptures *d.*

dill
Mat. 23:23. you pay tithes of mint and
   d.

dine-ing
Luke 7:37. Jesus was *d.* in the Pharisee's
   house

dinner
Luke 7:36. one of the Pharisees invited
   him to *d.*
   11:37. a Pharisee invited him to *d.*
   14:16. a man was giving a big *d.* party
   14:17. at *d.*-time he sent his servant

dire
2 Cor. 6:4. in hardships and *d.* straits

direct-s-ed
Mat. 1:24. Joseph did as the angel had
   d. him
   21:6. did as Jesus had *d.*
   26:19. the disciples did as Jesus *d.*
   27:10. as the Lord *d.* me
Acts 2:30. one of his own *d.* descendants
   should sit on his throne
   10:22. he was *d.* by a holy angel
Rom. 2:29. *d.* not by written precepts
   5:14. who had not sinned as Adam
   did, by disobeying a *d.* command
   8:4. *d.* by the Spirit
1 Cor. 14:34. keep their place as the law
   d.
Gal. 5:25. let the Spirit also *d.* our
   course
Heb. 9:19. as the Law *d.*, Moses had
   recited
Jam. 3:3. we can *d.* their whole body
   3:4. they can be *d.* by a tiny rudder
Jude 14. *d.* his prophecy when he said

directions
Acts 21:30. people came running from
   all *d.*
1 Cor. 16:1. my *d.* to our congregations

disabled
Heb. 12:13. the *d.* limb will not be put
   out of joint

disaffection
Luke 23:5. his teaching is causing *d.*

disagreement
Acts 6:1. when disciples were growing in
   number, there was *d.*
   25:19. *d.* with him about their
   peculiar religion

disappear-s-ed
Mat. 5:18. not a letter, not a stroke, will
   d. from the Law
Acts 5:36. his whole following was
   broken up and *d.*
2 Thess. 2:7. until the Restrainer *d.*
Heb. 8:13. growing old and ageing will
   shortly *d.*
Jam. 1:10. the rich man will *d.*
2 Pet. 3:10. on that day the heavens will
   d.
Rev. 22:3. every accursed thing shall *d.*

disapproval
Luke 19:7. there was a general murmur
   of *d.*

disapprovingly
John 6:41. the Jews began to murmur *d.*

disaster
Rom. 14:15. do not by your eating bring *d.*
1 Cor. 8:11. this 'knowledge' of yours is utter *d.* to the weak

disastrous
Acts 27:10. this voyage will be *d.*
2 Pet. 2:1. they will import *d.* heresies

disbelieve-s
John 3:12. *d.* me when I talk to you about things on earth
1 Pet. 2:8. they stumble when they *d.* the Word
3:1. who *d.* the Gospel
1 John 5:10. he who *d.* God, makes him out to be a liar

disbelievers
Tit. 1:15. the tainted minds of *d.*

discard-ed
Col. 2:15. on that cross he *d.* the cosmic powers
3:9. you have *d.* the old nature

discern
Rom. 12:2. able to *d.* the will of God
Heb. 3:10. they would not *d.* my ways

discernment
Rom. 11:25. not be complacent about your own *d.*

discharge-d-ing
Matt. 15:17. is *d.* into the drain
Luke 2:29. thou givest thy servant his *d.*
Acts 4:21. repeated the caution and *d.* them
4:23. as soon as they were *d.*
5:40. give up speaking in the name of Jesus, and *d.* them
26:32. *d.*, if he had not appealed
Rom. 7:2. if her husband dies, she is *d.*
7:6. we are *d.* from the law
13:7. *d.* your obligations
1 Cor. 9:17. I am simply *d.* a trust
Col. 4:17. *d.* it to the full
Heb. 9:6. in the *d.* of their duties

disciple-s
Mat. 26:20. he sat down with the twelve *d.*
28:19. make all nations my *d.*
Mark 10:32. the *d.* were filled with awe
14:50. the *d.* all deserted him
Luke 9:36. the *d.* kept silence
19:40. if my *d.* keep silence

discipline-s-d-ing
1 Cor. 11:32. *d.* us, to save us
2 Cor. 6:9. *d.* by suffering
1 Tim. 1:20. through this *d.* they might learn

2 Tim. 2:25. when *d.* is needed
3:16. *d.* in right living
Tit. 2:12. *d.* to renounce godless ways
Heb. 12:5. the Lord's *d.*
12:6. the Lord *d.*
12:7. endure it as *d.* . . . . *d.* by his father
12:8. if you escape the *d.*
12:9. fathers who *d.* us
12:10. *d.* us for this short life
12:11. *d.*, no doubt, is never pleasant
Rev. 3:19. all whom I love I reprove and *d.*

disclaimed
Luke 8:45. who was it that touched me?' All *d.*

disclose-d
Mark 4:22. nothing is hidden unless it is to be *d.*
Luke 1:51. *d.* his might
2:26. *d.* to him by the Holy Spirit
John 14:21. *d.* myself to him
14:22. you mean to *d.* yourself to us alone
15:15. *d.* to you everything that I heard
Acts 7:13. his family connexions were *d.*
20:27. *d.* to you the whole purpose of God
Rom. 1:19. God himself has *d.* it
16:26. in silence for long ages but now *d.*
1 Cor. 4:5. *d.* men's inward motives
Eph. 3:5. not *d.* to the human race
Col. 1:26. now *d.* to God's people
1 Pet. 1:12. *d.* to them that the matter
1 John 3:2. not yet been *d.*, but we know that when it is *d.* we shall be like him
4:9. his love was *d.* to us

discord
Acts 24:5. a fomenter of *d.* among the Jews

discourse-s
Mat. 7:28. when Jesus had finished this *d.*
19:1
26:1 } finished this *d.*
Acts 18:25. in his *d.* he taught
24:25. when the *d.* turned to questions

discover-ed
Acts 23:27. I *d.* that he was a Roman
24:20. say what crime they *d.*
Rom. 7:21. I *d.* this principle

discredit-ed
Acts 19:27. our line of business will be *d.*
28:21. gossip to your *d.*
2 Cor. 6:3. service may not be brought into *d.*

2 Cor. 13:7. even if we should seem to be *d.*
Tit. 2:8. not a word to say to our *d.*

discriminate
Heb. 5:14. *d.* between good and evil

discrimination
Phil. 1:10. the gift of true *d.*

discuss-ed-ing
Mark 9:10. *d.* among themselves
9:34. who was the greatest
Luke 6:11. *d.* among themselves what
they could do to Jesus
22:4. to *d.* ways and means
24:15. *d.* it with one another
John 16:19. are you *d.* what I said
Acts 4:15. *d.* the matter among them-
selves
Heb. 6:1. stop *d.* the rudiments of
Christianity

discussion-s
Mark 8:11. engaged him in *d.*
12:28. listening to these *d.*
Acts 18:4. held *d.* in the synagogue
18:19. he held a *d.* with the Jews
19:9. to hold *d.* daily
25:20. out of my depth in such *d.*

disdaining
Heb. 11:35. tortured to death, *d.* release

disease-s
Mat. 8:17. lifted our *d.* from us
Luke 7:21. cured many sufferers from *d.*

disgrace
1 Cor. 4:10. we are in *d.*; you are
honoured
11:6. if it is a *d.* for her to be cropped
11:14. flowing locks *d.* a man
2 Cor. 9:4. not prepared, what a *d.* it
will be to us
Heb. 12:2. making light of its *d.*
1 Pet. 4:16. he should feel it no *d.*

disgust
Gal. 4:14. temptation to show scorn or
d.

dish
Mat. 14:8. on a *d.* the head of John the
Baptist
14:11. brought in on a *d.*
23:25. clean the outside of cup and *d.*
Mark 6:25. on a *d.*, the head of John the
Baptist
6:28. brought the head on a *d.*
John 13:26. when I have dipped it in the
d.' Then, after dipping it in the *d.*

dishearten-ed
Col. 3:21. for fear they grow *d.*

dishonest
Mat. 5:45. sends the rain on the honest
and the *d.*
Luke 16:8. applauded the *d.* bailiff

16:10. *d.* in little things is *d.* also in
great things
18:11. greedy, *d.*, adulterous
Acts 8:21. you are *d.* with God

dishonesty
Col. 3:25. *d.* will be requited

dishonoured
Rom. 2:24. the name of God is *d.*

disintegrate
2 Pet. 3:10. the elements will *d.* in flames

dislodge-d
Col. 1:23. never to be *d.* from the hope

dismay-ed
Mat. 26:37. anguish and *d.* came over
him
Mark 14:19. at this they were *d.*
14:34. horror and *d.* came over him

dismiss-ed-ing
Mat. 13:36. he then *d.* the people
15:39. he then *d.* the crowds
Mark 1:43. *d.* him with this stern
warning
8:9. he *d.* them; and, without delay
Luke 16:3. my employer is *d.* me
Acts 15:33. were *d.* with the good wishes
23:22. the commandant *d.* the young
man

dismissal
Mat. 5:31. must give her a note of *d.*
19:7 ⎫
Mark 10:4 ⎭ divorce his wife by note of *d.*

disobedience-t
Rom. 11:30, 31, 32. you were *d.* to God,
but now have received mercy in the
time of their *d.*, so now, when you
receive mercy, they have proved *d.*,
but only in order that they too may
receive mercy. For in making all
mankind prisoners to *d.*

disobey-s-ed-ing
Luke 15:29. I never once *d.* your orders
John 3:36. he who *d.* the Son shall not
see that life
Rom. 5:14. sinned as Adam did, by *d.*
2 Thess. 3:14. if anyone *d.* our instructions
1 John 2:4. while he *d.* his commands

disorder
1 Cor. 14:33. not a God of *d.* but of
peace
2 Cor. 12:20. arrogance and general *d.*
Jam. 3:16. with jealousy and ambition
come *d.*

disown-s-ed-ing
Mat. 10:33. *d.* me before men, I will *d.*
him
26:34. you will *d.* me three times
26:35. I will never *d.* you

Mat. 26:75. before the cock crows you will *d.* me
Mark 14:30. you yourself will *d.* me
14:31. I will never *d.* you
14:72. you will *d.* me three times
Luke 12:9. who *d.* me before men will be *d.*
22:61. you will *d.* me three times
2 Pet. 2:1. *d.* the very Master who bought them
Jude 4. *d.* Jesus Christ, our only Master
Rev. 3:8. have not *d.* my name

disparage-s
Jam. 4:11. you must never *d.* one another. He who *d.* a brother or passes judgment on his brother *d.* the law

dispensation
2 Cor. 3:8. the divine *d.* of the Spirit
3:9. the *d.* under which we are condemned

dispense-d-ing
2 Cor. 3:6. to *d.* his new covenant
3:7. *d.* death
1 Pet. 4:10. *d.* the grace of God

disperse-d-ing
Acts 2:3. flames of fire, *d.* among them
13:43. after the congregation had *d.*
28:25. they began to *d.*
Jam. 1:1. the Twelve Tribes *d.* throughout the world
4:14. seen for a little while and then *d.*

display-ed-ing
John 9:3. that God's power might be *d.*
Rom. 2:15. they *d.* the effect of the law
1 Cor. 2:1. without *d.* of fine words
Gal. 3:1. openly *d.* upon his cross
Eph. 2:7. *d.* in the ages to come
1 Tim. 1:16. occasion for *d.* all his patience

disposal
Acts 5:4. was it not still at your own *d.*
Rom. 6:13. at sin's *d.*, as implements for doing wrong. No: put yourselves at the *d.* of God
6:16. yourselves at the *d.* of a master
2 Tim. 2:4. at his commanding officer's *d.*

disposition
1 Tim. 3:3. of a forbearing *d.*
Tit. 3:2. gentle *d.* towards all men

dispossess-ed
Acts 7:45. they *d.* the nations

dispute-s-ing
Luke 9:46. a *d.* arose among them
22:24. a jealous *d.* broke out
John 3:25. John's disciples had fallen into a *d.* with Jews
6:52. a fierce *d.* among the Jews

Acts 15:39. the *d.* was so sharp that they parted company
19:36. these facts are beyond *d.*
26:3. both our customs and our *d.*
1 Cor. 6:1. one of your number has a *d.* with another
6:4. such business *d,*
2 Tim. 2:14. stop *d.* about mere words
Heb. 6:16. a confirmation to end all *d.*
7:7. beyond all *d.* the lesser is always blessed by the greater

disqualify-ies-ied
Col. 2:18. not to be *d.* by the decision of people
Tit. 1:16. their detestable obstinacy *d.* them

disregard-s
Heb. 10:28. if a man *d.* the Law of Moses

disrepute
1 Tim. 6:1. Christian teaching are not brought into *d.*
Tit. 2:5. the Gospel will not be brought into *d.*
2 Pet. 2:2. the true way will be brought into *d.*

dissension-s
1 Cor. 11:19. *d.* are necessary
Gal. 5:20. selfish ambitions, *d.*

dissent-ed
Luke 23:51. who had *d.* from their policy

dissipation
Luke 21:34. do not let your minds be dulled by *d.*
Eph. 5:18. do not give way to drunkenness and the *d.*
1 Pet. 4:4. all this reckless *d.*

dissolute
2 Pet. 2:2. adherents to their *d.* practices
2:7. the *d.* habits of the lawless society

dissolution. dissolved
1 Cor. 7:27. do not seek a *d.* Has your marriage been *d.*

dissuade
Mat. 3:14. John tried to *d.* him

distance
Mat. 8:30. in the *d.* a large herd of pigs
26:58. Peter followed him at a *d.*
27:55. watching from a *d.*
Mark 5:6. he saw Jesus in the *d.*
8:3. some of them have come from a *d.*
11:13. noticing in the *d.* a fig-tree
14:54. Peter followed him at a *d.*
15:40. women were also present, watching from a *d.*
Luke 18:13. the other kept his *d.*
22:54. Peter followed at a *d.*

Luke 23:49. his friends had all been standing at a *d.*

Phil. 1:27. hear about you from a *d.*

Rev. 18:10. they will stand at a *d.*

18:15. stand at a *d.* for horror at her torment

18:17. who traded by sea, stood at a *d.*

distant
Luke 15:13. left home for a *d.* country

distinction-s
Rom. 2:18. you are aware of moral *d.*

3:22. all who have such faith—all, without *d.*

10:12. there is no *d.* between Jew and Greek

2 Cor. 11:18. people brag of their earthly *d.*

Gal. 2:6. God does not recognize these personal *d.*

Col. 1:28. we admonish everyone without *d.*

1 John 3:10. the *d.* between the children of God and the children of the devil

distinguish-ed
Luke 14:8. some person more *d.*

1 Cor. 12:10. *d.* true spirits from false

1 John 4:6. *d.* the spirit of truth from the spirit of error

distort-ed
Acts 20:30. who will *d.* the truth

2 Cor. 4:2. nor *d.* the word of God

Gal. 1:7. trying to *d.* the gospel of Christ

Tit. 3:11. a man of that sort has a *d.* mind

distracted
Luke 10:40. Martha was *d.* by her many tasks

distress-ed
Mat. 14:9. the king was deeply *d.*

18:31. the other servants were deeply *d.*

24:21. it will be a time of great *d.*

24:29. the *d.* of those days

26:22. in great *d.* they exclaimed

Mark 6:26. the king was greatly *d.*

13:19. those days will bring *d.*

13:24. in those days, after that *d.*

Acts 20:38. what *d.* them most

Rom. 12:8. helping others in *d.*, do it cheerfully

2 Cor. 1:6. if *d.* be our lot, it is the price we pay

2:4. great *d.* and anxiety

Phil. 2:26. *d.* that you heard he was ill

1 Tim. 5:10. supported those in *d.*

Heb. 11:37. in poverty, *d.*, and misery

Jam. 1:27. widows in their *d.*

distribute-ing
Mark 6:41. gave them to the disciples to *d.*

8:6. gave it to his disciples to *d.*

8:7. ordered them to *d.*

Luke 9:16. to *d.* to the people

1 Cor. 12:11. *d.* them separately

Heb. 2:4. *d.* the gifts of the Holy Spirit

distribution
Acts 2:45. a general *d.* as the need

6:1. overlooked in the daily *d.*

district-s
Mat. 4:13. in the *d.* of Zebulun

8:34. they begged him to leave the *d.*

Mark 1:28. spoken of all over the *d.* of Galilee

5:17. begged Jesus to leave the *d.*

8:10. went to the *d.* of Dalmanutha

9:30. they now left that *d.*

Luke 2:8. in this same *d.* there were shepherds

4:37. he was the talk of the whole *d.*

8:37. population of the Gergesene *d.* asked him to go

John 7:3. leave this *d.* and go into Judaea

Acts 2:10. *d.* of Libya

8:1. the country *d.* of Judaea

13:50. they were expelled from the *d.*

16:12. a city of the first rank in that *d.*

disturb-ed
John 5:7. when the water is *d.*

Acts 15:24. have *d.* you with their talk

disturbance
Acts 16:20. causing a *d.* in our city

19:23. gave rise to a serious *d.*

20:1. when the *d.* had ceased

24:18. no crowd with me, and there was no *d.*

ditch
Mat. 12:11. fell into a *d.* on the Sabbath

divest-ed
Col. 2:11. being *d.* of the lower nature

divided-ing
Mat. 27:35 ⎫
Mark 15:24 ⎬ they *d.* his clothes among them
Luke 23:34 ⎭

John 19:23. and *d.* them into four parts

1 Cor. 7:33. he has a *d.* mind

11:18. you fall into sharply *d.* groups

Eph. 2:14. stood like a *d.* wall between them

dividends
1 Tim. 6:5. they think religion should yield *d.*

6:6. of course religion does yield high *d.*

divine
Mark 9:39. a work of *d.* power in my name
Luke 1:8. take part in *d.* service
John 16:11. convince them of *d.* judgement
Acts 11:23. saw the *d.* grace at work
19:27. brought down from her *d.* preeminence
28:4. *d.* justice has not let him live
Rom. 1:18. *d.* retribution revealed from heaven
3:23. deprived of the *d.* splendour
5:2. hope of the *d.* splendour
9:4. the splendour of the *d.* presence
11:22. *d.* kindness to you
12:19. *d.* retribution
13:2. a *d.* institution
16:25. the revelation of that *d.* secret
1 Cor. 1:25. *d.* folly is wiser than the wisdom of man, and *d.* weakness stronger
2 Cor. 1:7. the *d.* consolation
3:7. *d.* splendour
3:8. *d.* dispensation of the Spirit
11:2. I am jealous for you, with a *d.* jealousy
Phil. 2:6. the *d.* nature was his from the first
1 Tim. 2:6. proof of the *d.* purpose
Heb. 9:21. all the vessels of *d.* service
1 John 2:5. the *d.* love has indeed come to its perfection
3:9. the *d.* seed remains in him
3:17. how can it be said that the *d.* love dwells in him
5:9. *d.* testimony is stronger

divinely
2 Cor. 10:4. *d.* potent to demolish strongholds
Heb. 11:7. Noah, *d.* warned

division
Luke 1:5. the *d.* of the priesthood
1:8. it was the turn of his *d.*
1 Cor. 12:25. no sense of *d.* in the body

divorce-s-d
Mat. 19:3. *d.* his wife on any and every ground
19:8. Moses gave you permission to *d.*
19:9. if a man *d.* his wife
Mark 10:2. is it lawful for a man to *d.* his wife
10:11. whoever *d.* his wife
10:12. if she *d.* her husband
Luke 16:18. a man who *d.* his wife
1 Cor. 7:11. the husband must not *d.* his wife
7:12. willing to live with him, he must not *d.* her
7:13. must not *d.* her husband
Jam. 2:20. faith *d.* from deeds is barren
2:26. faith *d.* from deeds is lifeless

Doberian
Acts 20:4. Gaius the *D.*

dock
Acts 26:6. I stand in the *d.* today
1 Cor. 9:3. those who put me in the *d.*
Phil. 1:7. appear in the *d.* to vouch for the truth

doctor-s
Mat. 5:20. the Pharisees and the *d.* of the law
9:12. not the healthy that need a *d.*
Mark 1:22. unlike the *d.* of the law, he taught with a note of authority
2:17. it is not the healthy that need a *d.*
5:26. in spite of long treatment by *d.*
Luke 5:31. it is not the healthy that need a *d.*
Col. 4:14. our dear friend Luke, the *d.*
also—*d.* of the law. Mat. 8:19. 12:38. 20:18. 21:15. 23:2. Mark 2:16. 3:22. 7:1. 8:31. 10:33. 11:18. 12:38. 14:1, 53. 15:31. Luke 9:22. 15:2. 22:2, 66. John 8:3. Acts 4:5. 6:12. 23:9.

doctrine
Acts 21:28. spreads his *d.* all over the world
1 Cor. 1:18. this *d.* of the cross is sheer folly

document
2 Cor. 3:6. a covenant expressed not in a written *d.*

doer
1 Cor. 5:13. root out the evil-*d.*
Rev. 22:11. let the evil-*d.* go on doing evil

dogmatic
1 Tim. 1:7. the subjects about which they are so *d.*

doing
Luke 1:25. this is the Lord's *d.*
Eph. 2:8. through trusting him; it is not your own *d.*

dole
1 Cor. 13:3. I may *d.* out all I possess

domain
Gal. 5:4. fallen out of the *d.* of God's grace
Col. 1:13. rescued us from the *d.* of darkness

domination
1 Cor. 15:24. *d.*, authority, and power

domineer
1 Tim. 2:12. nor must woman *d.* over man

dominion
Luke 4:6. all this *d.* will I give to you
Acts 26:18. from the *d.* of Satan to God
Jude 6. not content to keep the *d.* given
to them

donkey
Mat. 21:2. a *d.* tethered with her foal
21:7. brought the *d.* and her foal
Luke 13:15. does not loose his ox or his *d.*
14:5. if one of you has a *d.* or an ox
John 12:14. Jesus found a *d.* and mounted it

doom-ed
John 5:29. who have done wrong will
rise to hear their *d.*
Acts 8:23. you are *d.* to taste the bitter
fruit
13:40. the *d.* proclaimed by the
prophets
Rom. 7:24. this body *d.* to death
Phil. 1:28. a sure sign to them that their
d. is sealed
2 Thess. 2:3. the man *d.* to perdition
2:10. *d.* to destruction
Heb. 11:31. escaped the *d.* of the unbelievers
Jude 4. the *d.* they have incurred
11. like Korah, and they share his *d.*
Rev. 18:8. the Lord God who has pro-
nounced her *d.*
18:10. in a single hour your *d.* has
struck

door-s
Mat. 7:7. knock, and the *d.* will be
opened
7:8. the *d.* will be opened
23:13. you shut the *d.* of the kingdom of Heaven
25:11. sir, sir,' they cried, 'open the *d.*
Mark 5:23. my little daughter,' he said,
'is at death's *d.*
Luke 11:9. knock, and the *d.* will be
opened
11:10. to him who knocks, the *d.* will
be opened
12:3. what you have whispered behind
closed *d.*
13:24. struggle to get in through the
narrow *d.*
Acts 12:14. instead of opening the *d.* she
ran in
18:7. who lived next *d.* to the synagogue
20:26. no man's fate can be laid at my
d.
Gal. 4:17. what they really want is to
bar the *d.* to you

door-keeper
Mark 13:34. ordered the *d.* to stay
awake
John 10:3. the *d.* admits him

dot
Luke 16:17. one *d.* or stroke of the Law

double
Luke 13:11. she was bent *d.*
Acts 21:32. came down on the rioters at
the *d.*
2 Cor. 1:15. the benefit of a *d.* visit

doubly
Mat. 6:23. the darkness is *d.* dark

doubt-s-ed-ing
Luke 4:23. no *d.* you will quote the
proverb
23:47. beyond all *d.*,' he said, 'this man
was innocent
John 7:28. no *d.* you know me; no *d.*
you know where I come from
Acts 11:18. their *d.* were silenced
Rom. 4:20. never *d.* God's promise
15:14. I have no *d.* in my own mind
1 Cor. 4:8. all of you, no *d.*, have everything you could desire
6:12. no *d.* I am free to do anything
14:2. he is no *d.* inspired
16:18. relieved my mind—and no *d.*
yours too
Heb. 12:11. discipline, no *d.*, is never
pleasant
Jam. 1:6. without a *d.* in his mind
Jude 22. there are some *d.* souls

doubter
Jam. 1:6. the *d.* is like a heaving sea

dough
Rom. 11:16. the first portion of *d.* is
consecrated
1 Cor. 5:6. a little leaven leavens all the
d.
Gal. 5:9. a little leaven,' remember,
'leavens all the *d.*

down
Mat. 7:25⎱
7:27⎰ the rain came *d.*
12:45. they all come in and settle *d.*
19:7. Moses lay it *d.* that a man might
divorce
26:61. I can pull *d.* the temple of God
Mark 4:1. crowd on the beach right *d.*
to the water's edge
5:6. flung himself *d.* before him
15:32. come *d.* now from the cross
Luke 4:2. led by the Spirit up and *d.* the
wilderness
18:9. looked *d.* on everyone else
20:46. lawyers who love to walk up
and *d.*
24:5. stood with eyes cast *d.*
John 10:11. lays *d.* his life for the sheep
19:31. and the bodies taken *d.*
Acts 5:39. you will never be able to
put them *d.*
18:11. so he settled *d.* for eighteen
months

2 Cor. 10:8. to build you up, not pull you *d.*
Eph. 4:9. *d.* to the very earth
Rev. 3:20. I will come in and sit *d.* to supper with him
21:10. coming *d.* out of heaven from God

downcast
2 Cor. 7:6. God, who brings comfort to the *d.*

downfall
Rom. 11:11. did their failure mean complete *d.*
14:21. causes your brother's *d.*
1 Cor. 8:13. if food be the *d.* of my brother, I will never eat meat any more, for I will not be the cause of my brother's *d.*

downs
Phil. 4:12. the human lot with all its ups and *d.*

downstairs
Mark 14:66. Peter was still in the courtyard *d.*
Acts 10:20. make haste and go *d.*

doze-d
Mat. 25:5. they all *d.* off to sleep

dozen
Acts 19:7. altogether they were about a *d.* men

drag-ged
Mat. 13:48. it was *d.* ashore
Luke 12:58. he may *d.* you before the judge
John 21:11. *d.* the net to land
Acts 14:19. *d.* him out of the city
16:19. *d.* them to the city authorities
17:6. they *d.* Jason himself
21:30. seized Paul and *d.* him out of the temple
Jam. 2:6. who *d.* you into court

drain
Mat. 15:17. discharged into the *d.*
Mark 7:19. passes out into the *d.*

draught
Mat. 27:34. they offered him a *d.* of wine
Rev. 21:6. a *d.* from the water-springs of life

draw-s-n-ing
Luke 1:1. *d.* up an account of the events
9:12. when evening was *d.* on
19:21. you *d.* out what you never put in
19:22. I *d.* out what I never put in
24:29. stay with us, for evening *d.* on
John 4:36. the reaper is *d.* his pay
16:14 ⎫
16:15 ⎭ he will *d.* from what is mine

Acts 2:5. devout Jews *d.* from every nation
2:44. all whose faith had *d.* them together
1 Tim. 5:11. when their passions *d.* them away from Christ
Heb. 10:25. you see the Day *d.* near
Jude 19. *d.* a line between spiritual and unspiritual

dreadful
Eph. 2:3. the *d.* judgement of God
5:6. God's *d.* judgement is coming
Col. 3:6. God's *d.* judgement is impending

dregs
Acts 17:5. from the *d.* of the populace
1 Cor. 4:13. the *d.* of humanity

drench-ed
Rev. 19:13. in a garment *d.* in blood

dress-ed
Mat. 7:15. *d.* up as sheep
11:8. a man *d.* in silks and satins
22:11. who was not *d.* for a wedding
27:28. *d.* him in a scarlet mantle
27:31. *d.* him in his own clothes
Mark 1:6. John was *d.* in a rough coat
15:17. they *d.* him in purple
15:20. *d.* him in his own clothes
Luke 7:25. *d.* in silks and satins
16:19. *d.* in purple and the finest linen
23:11. *d.* in a gorgeous robe
1 Tim. 2:9. must *d.* in becoming manner
Heb. 11:37. *d.* in skins of sheep or goats
Jam. 2:2. a well-*d.* man with gold rings
2:3. special attention to the well-*d.* man
1 Pet. 3:3. or *d.*—but in the inmost centre of your being
Rev. 11:3. *d.* in sackcloth
19:8. for her *d.* she has been given fine linen

drew
Mat. 11:7. what was the spectacle that *d.* you
Luke 7:24. *d.* you to the wilderness
John 18:6. they *d.* back and fell to the ground
Acts 1:26. they *d.* lots
12:20. their country *d.* its supplies
23:19. *d.* him aside, and asked him

drift-ing
Luke 9:45. that they should not perceive its *d.*
Acts 2:19. fire and *d.* smoke
27:27. still *d.* in the Sea of Adria
Heb. 2:1. for fear of *d.* from our course

drink-ing
John 4:34. meat and *d.* for me to do the will of him

Acts 2:13. they have been *d.*
1 Cor. 3:2. so I gave you milk to *d.*
Gal. 5:21. *d.* bouts
1 Tim. 3:3. he must not be given to *d.*
   3:8. given neither to excessive *d.*
Tit. 2:3. slaves to strong *d.*
Jude 12. eat and *d.* without reverence
Rev. 16:19. made her *d.* the cup

drinker
Mat. 11:19. a glutton and a *d.*
Luke 7:34. look at him! a glutton and a *d.*
Tit. 1:7. he must be no *d.*, no brawler

drive-s-n-ing
Mat. 8:12. born to the kingdom will be *d.* out into the dark
   8:31. if you *d.* us out, send us into that herd of pigs
   12:24. this man *d.* the devils out
   12:27. by whom do your own people *d.* them out
   12:28. by the Spirit of God that I *d.* out the devils
Mark 3:15. a commission to *d.* out devils
   3:22. he *d.* out devils by the prince of devils
   3:23. how can Satan *d.* out Satan
   7:26. to *d.* the spirit out of her daughter
   9:38. we saw a man *d.* out devils
   11:15. *d.* out those who bought and sold
Luke 11:14. *d.* out a devil which was dumb
   11:15. that he *d.* the devils out
   11:18. I *d.* out the devils by Beelzebub
   11:19. by whom do your own people *d.* them out
   11:20. by the finger of God that I *d.* out the devils
   19:45. he went into the temple and began *d.* out the traders
John 12:31. now shall the Prince of this world be *d.* out
Acts 2:2. a noise like that of a strong *d.* wind
   26:24. too much study is *d.* you mad
   27:40. let her *d.* to the beach
   28:3. a viper, *d.* out by the heat
Gal. 4:30. *d.* out the slave-woman and her son
2 Tim. 2:15. *d.* a straight furrow
2 Pet. 2:17. mists *d.* by a storm

drooping
Heb. 12:12. stiffen your *d.* arms

drop-ped-ping
Mat. 14:32 ⎫
Mark 4:39 ⎬ the wind *d.*
   6:51 ⎭
   12:41. people *d.* their money into the chest

   12:42. a poor widow who *d.* in two tiny coins
Luke 21:1. the rich people *d.* their gifts
Acts 5:5. he *d.* dead
   5:10. she *d.* dead at his feet
   27:29. they *d.* four anchors
   27:32. cut the ropes of the boat and let her *d.* away
   28:6. he would swell up or *d.* down dead
Jam. 5:17. not a *d.* fell on the land for three years and a half

drove
Mat. 8:16. he *d.* the spirits out
   21:12. *d.* out all who were buying
Mark 1:34. *d.* out many devils
   6:13. they *d.* out many devils
2 Cor. 12:11. very foolish, but it was you who *d.* me to it
1 Thess. 2:15. and the prophets and *d.* us out

drown-ed
Mark 5:13. into the lake and were *d.*
Luke 8:33. over the edge into the lake and were *d.*

drudge-d
2 Cor. 11:27. I have toiled and *d.*
1 Thess. 2:9. how we toiled and *d.*
2 Thess. 3:8. we toiled and *d.*

drug-ged
Mark 15:23. he was offered *d.* wine

drunkards
1 Thess. 5:7. *d.* are drunk at night

drunkenness
Eph. 5:18. do not give way to *d.*
1 Pet. 4:3. *d.*, riot, and tippling

due
Mat. 16:27. the *d.* reward for what he has done
   21:34. collect the produce *d.* to him
   22:21 ⎫ pay Caesar what is *d.* to
Mark 12:17 ⎬ Caesar, and pay God
Luke 20:25 ⎭ what is *d.* to God
   21:7. the sign when it is *d.* to happen
Acts 12:23. usurped the honour *d.* to God
   24:2. *d.* to your provident care
Rom. 9:22. retribution *d.* for destruction
1 Cor. 16:16. give their *d.* position to such persons
2 Cor. 5:10. *d.* to him for his conduct in the body
Eph. 4:7. his *d.* portion of Christ's bounty
   4:16. the *d.* activity of each part
2 Thess. 1:3. our thanks are always *d.* to God for you
1 Tim. 2:11. listening quietly and with *d.* submission
Heb. 2:2. met with *d.* retribution

Heb. 12:9. we paid *d.* respect to the earthly fathers

1 Pet. 2:17. give *d.* honour to everyone

2:18. with all *d.* submission

dull-ed

Mat. 15:16. are you still as *d.* as the rest

Mark 7:18. are you as *d.* as the rest

Luke 21:34. do not let your minds be *d.* by dissipation

24:25. how *d.* you are!' he answered

John 12:40. blinded their eyes and *d.* their minds

dullness

Mark 16:14. their incredulity and *d.*

duly

Mat. 18:16. all facts may be *d.* establish-ed

2 Cor. 8:19. *d.* appointed him to travel with us

Gal. 3:15. testament has been *d.* executed

dumb

Luke 1:22. making signs to them, and remained *d.*

dumbfounded

Mark 1:27. all *d.* and began to ask

6:51. at this they were completely *d.*

16:5. wearing a white robe; and they were *d.*

dump-ing

Acts 27:38. *d.* the corn in the sea

dungeon

Rev. 20:7. Satan will be let loose from his *d.*

dupe-s

Eph. 4:14. *d.* of crafty rogues

during

Mat. 2:1. at Bethlehem in Judaea *d.* the reign of Herod

26:5. it must not be *d.* the festival

26:21. *d.* supper he said

26:26. *d.* supper Jesus took bread

Mark 14:2. it must not be *d.* the festival

14:22. *d.* supper he took bread

Luke 3:21. *d.* a general baptism of the people

6:12. *d.* this time he went out one day

John 13:3. *d.* supper, Jesus, well aware

Acts 1:15. *d.* this time that Peter stood up

5:19. opened the prison doors *d.* the night

6:1. *d.* this period, when disciples were growing in numbers

11:27. *d.* this period some prophets came

12:3. *d.* the festival of Unleavened Bread

13:31. many days *d.* which he appear-ed

16:9. *d.* the night a vision came to Paul

19:8. *d.* the next three months he attended

25:14. *d.* this time Festus laid Paul's case

Gal. 4:3. *d.* our minority we were slaves

2 Thess. 3:10. *d.* our stay with you

Rev. 9:6. *d.* that time these men will seek death

11:6. no rain may fall *d.* the time of their prophesying

dusk

Acts 28:23. this went on from dawn to *d.*

dust

1 Cor. 15:47. the first man was made 'of the *d.*

15:48. the man made of *d.* is the pattern of all men of *d.*

15:49. the likeness of the man made of *d.*

duty-ies

Luke 1:23. his period of *d.* was com-pleted

John 16:2. performing a religious *d.*

18:17. the maid on *d.* at the door

Acts 20:35. our *d.* to help the weak

26:9. my *d.* to work actively against the name of Jesus

Rom. 13:6. to these *d.* they devote their energies

1 Cor. 11:10. woman's *d.*

Eph. 6:20. as it is my *d.* to speak

Col. 3:18. subject to your husbands: that is your Christian *d.*

4:4. make the secret plain, as it is my *d.* to do

4:17. attend to the *d.* entrusted to you

1 Tim. 5:4. *d.* to show loyalty to the family

2 Tim. 4:5. do all the *d.* of your calling

Philem. 8. bold to point out your *d.*

Heb. 9:6. in the discharge of their *d.*

dwell-s-t-ing

John 1:1. the Word *d.* with God

8:31. if you *d.* within the revelation

14:2. many *d.*-places in my Father's house

14:23. make our *d.* with him

15:4. *d.* in me, as I in you

15:5. he who *d.* in me, as I *d.* in him

15:6. he who does not *d.* in me

15:7. if you *d.* in me, and my words *d.* in you

15:9. *d.* in my love

15:10. you will *d.* in my love . . . and *d.* in his love

Acts 2:26. my flesh shall *d.* in hope

7:46. a *d.*-place for the God of Jacob

Rom. 8:10. if Christ is *d.* within you

2 Cor. 1:22. the Spirit to *d.* in our hearts

Eph. 2:22. a spiritual *d.* for God

Col. 3:2. thoughts *d.* on that higher realm

1 Pet. 5:13. greetings from her who *d.* in Babylon

1 John 1:2. eternal life which *d.* with the Father

2:6. claims to be *d.* in him

2:10. the man who loves his brother *d.* in light

2:24. if what you heard then still *d.* in you, you will yourselves *d.* in the Son

2:27. *d.* in him

2:28. my children, *d.* in him

3:6. no man therefore who *d.* in him is a sinner

Rev. 18:2. she has become a *d.* for demons

21:3. God has his *d.* among men

dweller-s
Mat. 4:16. *d.* in the land of death's dark shadow

dying
John 11:37. have done something to keep Lazarus from *d.*

Rom. 6:10. in *d.* as he died, he died to sin

2 Cor. 5:15. his purpose in *d.* for all

dysentery
Acts 28:8. bouts of fever and *d.*

E

each
Mat. 6:34. *e.* day has troubles enough of its own

11:16. shouting at *e.* other

25:15. *e.* according to his capacity

Mark 6:40. a hundred rows of fifty *e.*

15:24. to decide what *e.* should have

Luke 6:34. even sinners lend to *e.* other

8:29. *e.* time he broke loose

9:3. nor are you *e.* to have a second coat

11:3 give us *e.* day our daily bread

19:13 gave them a pound *e.*

19.15. to see what profit *e.* had made

Acts 12:4. four squads of four men *e.*

1 Cor. 3:5. *e.* of us performed the task

3:8. *e.* will get his own pay

12:27. *e.* of you a limb or organ of it

Gal. 6:1. look to yourself, *e.* one of you

Eph. 4:16. the due activity of *e.* part

4:25. speak the truth to *e.* other

6:8. whatever good *e.* man may do

Phil. 2:4. you must look to *e.* other's interest

4:21. to *e.* one of God's people.

Col. 4:6. study how best to talk with *e.* person

1 Thess. 5:15. aim at doing the best you can for *e.* other

Heb. 10:24. see how *e.* of us may best arouse others

11.21. blessed *e.* of Joseph's sons

1 Pet. 5:5. humility towards *e.* other

Rev. 13:1. on *e.* head a blasphemous name

22:2. one for *e.* month of the year

eager-ly
Mark 12:38. they listened *e.*

15.43. *e.* awaiting the kingdom of God

Luke 19:3. *e.* to see what Jesus looked like

Acts 8:6. listened *e.* to what Philip said

8:10. listened *e.* to him

20:16. he was *e.* to be in Jerusalem

Rom. 8:19. waits with *e.* expectation.

1 Cor. 14:12. *e.* for gifts of the Spirit

14:39. be *e.* to prophesy

2 Cor. 7:7. how *e.* to take my side

8:11. *e.* to complete the scheme

8:12. an *e.* desire to give

8:17. he is so *e.* that by his own desire

9:2. I know how *e.* you are to help

Gal. 5:5. that righteousness which we *e.* await

Phil. 2:28. I am all the more *e.* to send him

Tit. 2:14. *e.* to do good

Heb. 6:11. show the same *e.* concern

2 Pet. 3:12. look *e.* for the coming of the Day of God

eagerness
Acts 17:11. received the message with great *e.*

Rom. 1:15. my *e.* to declare the Gospel

2 Cor. 7:11. your *e.* to see justice done

8:19. show our own *e.* to serve

eagle
Rev. 8:13. an *e.* calling with a loud cry

ear-s
Mat. 14:1. reached the *e.* of Prince Herod

2 Cor. 12:6. the evidence of his own eyes and *e.*

1 Thess. 1:8. your faith in God has reached men's *e.*

1 Tim. 6:20. turn a deaf *e.* to empty and worldly chatter

Tit. 1:14. lending their *e.* to Jewish myths
Heb. 3:13. that word 'Today' still sounds in your *e.*

early-ier
Mark 1:35. very *e.* next morning he got up
11.20 *e.* next morning, as they passed by
13:35. cock-crow or *e.* dawn.
John 10:40. where John had been baptizing *e.*
Acts 15:7. in the *e.* days, as you yourselves know
21:16. a Christian from the *e.* days.
Phil. 4:15. in the *e.* days of my mission
2 Tim. 3:15. from *e.* childhood you have been familiar
Heb. 7:19. the *e.* rules are cancelled
9:8. the *e.* tent still stands
Rev. 2:4. you have lost your *e.* love

earn-s-ed-ing
Mat. 10:10. the worker *e.* his keep
Luke 10:7. the worker *e.* his pay
12.48. *e.* a beating
Acts 20:34. these hands of mine *e.*
1 Cor. 9:14. should *e.* their living by the Gospel
9:17. I should be *e.* my pay
1 Tim. 5:18. the workman *e.* his pay

earnest-ly
Luke 7:4. pressed their petition *e.*
2 Cor. 8:22. more *e.* because of the great confidence
1 Thess. 3:10. we pray most *e.* night and day
Heb. 13:19. all the more *e.* I ask for your prayers

earth-ly
Mat. 11:11. never has there appeared on *e.*
24.14. proclaimed throughout the *e.*
Luke 17:24. the lightning-flash that lights up the *e.*
1 Cor. 15:40. heavenly bodies and *e.* bodies; and the splendour of the heavenly bodies is one thing, the splendour of the *e.*, another
15:42. sown in the *e.*
2 Cor. 5:4. enclosed within this *e.* frame
11:18. people brag of their *e.* distinctions.
Eph. 6:5. slaves, obey your *e.* masters
Col 3:22. give entire obedience to your *e.* masters
2 Tim. 1:10. the appearance on *e.* of our Saviour
Heb. 5:7. in the days of his *e.* life
12:9. we paid due respect to the *e.* fathers
1 Pet. 1:17. live out your time on *e.*
4:2. the rest of his days on *e.*

earth-bound
Heb. 7:16. not to a system of *e.* rules

earthenware
2 Cor. 4:7. we are no better than pots of *e.*
2 Tim. 2:20. others of wood or *e.*
Rev. 2:27. smashing them to bits like *e.*

earthquake
Mat. 27:51. there was an *e.*

ease
Mat. 26:45 ⎫
Mark 14:41 ⎬ still taking your *e.*
1 Cor. 16:10. see that you put him at his *e.*

east
Mark 16:8. from *e.* to west the sacred and imperishable message

easter
Acts 27:14. a fierce wind, the 'north-*e.*'

easy
Luke 12:19. take life *e.*, eat, drink

eat-en-ing
Mat. 25:42. you gave me nothing to *e.*
Mark 2:25. hungry and had nothing to *e.*
12:40. who *e.* up the property of widows
Luke 8:55. to give her something to *e.*
15:17. more food than they can *e.*
20:47. men who *e.* up the property of widows
24:41. have you anything here to *e.*
Acts 7:11. our ancestors could find nothing to *e.*
27:33. you have *e.* nothing whatever
27:34. I beg you to have something to *e.*
Rom. 14:15. outraged by what you *e.*— Do not by your *e.* bring disaster
14:17. the kingdom of God is not *e.*
1 Cor. 9:13. *e.* the temple offerings
10:30. why am I blamed for *e.* food
Col. 2:16. take you to task about what you *e.*
Heb. 13:9. not from scruples about what we *e.*
Jam. 2:16. keep yourselves warm, and have plenty to *e.*
Jude 12. they *e.* and drink without reverence

eclipse
Luke 23:45. the sun was in *e.*

ecstasy
Acts 10:46. speaking in tongues of *e.*
19:6. they spoke in tongues of *e.*
1 Cor. 12:30. do all speak in tongues of *e.*
13:8. are there tongues of *e.*
14:2. using the language of *e.*

1 Cor. 14:4. *e.* is good for the speaker himself
14:5. all to use the tongues of *e.*
14:19. in the language of *e.*
14:23. 'strange tongues' of *e.*

ecstatic
1 Cor. 12:10. *e.* utterance of different kinds
12:28. the gift of *e.* utterance
14:6. I use *e.* language
14:9. your *e.* utterance yields no precise meaning
14:13. the man who falls into *e.* utterance
14:18. gifted in *e.* utterance
14:26. a revelation, an *e.* utterance
14:27. a matter of *e.* utterance
14:39. do not forbid *e.* utterance

edge
Mat. 8:32. rushed over the *e.* into the lake
9:20. touched the *e.* of his cloak
14:36. simply to touch the *e.* of his cloak
Mark 4:1. on the beach right down to the water's *e.*
5:13. about two thousand, rushed over the *e.*
6:56. let them simply touch the *e.* of his cloak
Luke 4:29. meaning to hurl him over the *e.*
5:2. two boats lying at the water's *e.*
8:33. the herd rushed over the *e.*
8:44. touched the *e.* of his cloak

edict
Acts 18:2. an *e.* that all Jews should leave Rome
Heb. 11:23. were not afraid of the king's *e.*

effect
Acts 23:25. he wrote a letter to this *e.*
Rom. 2:14. they display the *e.* of the law
5:15. its *e.* is vastly exceeded by the grace of God
5:16. not to be compared in its *e.*
Eph. 1:10. to be put into *e.* when the time was ripe
3:9. this hidden purpose was to be put into *e.*
1 Thess. 1:9. our visit to you and its *e.*
Jam. 3:6. the tongue is in *e.* a fire

effective-ly
Acts 19:20. spreading more and more widely and *e.*
Rom. 3:22. *e.* through faith in Christ
3:25. *e.* through faith
1 Cor. 16:9. opportunity has opened for *e.* work
Jam. 5:16. prayer is powerful and *e.*

efficient
2 Tim. 3:17. that the man who belongs to God may be *e.*

effort-s
Luke 12:58. make an *e.* to settle with him
Rom. 9:16. does not depend on man's will or *e.*
9:30. Gentiles, who made no *e.* after righteousness
9:31. Israel made great *e.* after a law
9:32. their *e.* were not based on faith
Gal. 6:9. not slacken our *e.*
Eph. 4:3. spare no *e.*
Heb. 4:11. make every *e.* to enter that rest

effulgence
Heb. 1:3. the Son who is the *e.* of God's splendour

Egypt
Acts 7:18. ascended the throne of *E.*
Heb. 11:22. the departure of Israel from *E.*

eight
Luke 16:7. make it *e.* hundred
Acts 25:6. after spending *e.* or ten days

eighteen
Acts 18:11. he settled down for *e.* months

eighty
Luke 2:37. as a widow to the age of *e.*-four

ejected
Acts 18:16. he had them *e.* from the court

elaborate
1 Tim. 2:9. not with *e.* hair-styles

elated
2 Cor. 12:7. keep me from being unduly *e.* . . . save me from being unduly *e.*

elders
1 Tim. 4:14. laying on of the hands of the *e.*

eldest
Rom. 8:29. the *e.* among a large family of brothers

elected
Acts 6:5. they *e.* Stephen

elemental
Gal. 4:3. slaves to the *e.* spirits of the universe
Col. 2:8. the *e.* spirits of the world
2:20. beyond reach of the *e.* spirits

Elijah
Mat. 11:14. John is the destined *E.*
Mark 15:35. hark, he is calling *E.*

Elisha
Luke 4:27. the time of the prophet *E.*

elsewhere
John 18:36. my kingly authority comes from *e.*
Acts 12:17. and went off *e.*
Jam. 2:23. *e.* he is called 'God's friend

elude
Rev. 9:6. death will *e.* them

emancipated
Rom. 6:18. *e.* from sin

embark-ed-ing
Mat. 14:22. he made the disciples *e.*
Mark 6:45. *e.* and cross to Bethsaida
John 6:22. had not *e.* with his disciples
Acts 20:3. on the point of *e.* for Syria.
   27:2. we *e.* in a ship of Adramyttium

embellish
Mat. 23:29. *e.* the monuments of the saints

embody-ied
Col. 2:9. the Godhead dwells *e.*

eminent
Rom. 16:7. *e.* among the apostles

Emperor
Mat. 22:17 ⎫
Mark 12:14 ⎬ pay taxes to the Roman *E.*
Luke 2:1: the *E.* Augustus
   3:1. the *E.* Tiberius
   20.22 taxes to the Roman *E.*
Acts 17:7. they all flout the *E.* laws
   25:8. or against the *E.*
   25:10. the *E.* tribunal
   25:21. send him to the *E.*
   26:32. appealed to the *E.*
   27:24. appear before the *E.*
   28:19. no option but to appeal to the *E.*

emphasis
1 Thess. 4:6. we told you before with all *e.*

employ-ed
Mat. 25:16. *e.* them in business
Rom. 12:7. a teacher should *e.* his gift
2 Pet. 2:11. *e.* no insults

employer
Mat. 20:11. they grumbled at their *e.*
Luke 16:3. my *e.* is dismissing me

employment
Acts 19:24. *e.* for the craftsmen
Tit. 3:14. taught to engage in honest *e.*

empty
Luke 20:10. sent him away *e.*-handed
   20:11. sent away *e.*-handed
Mark 12:4. sent him away *e.*-handed
Rom. 4:14. then faith is *e.*

1 Cor. 9:15. no one shall make my boast an *e.* boast
2 Cor. 9:3. prove to be an *e.* boast.
1 Tim. 6:20. turn a deaf ear to *e.* and worldly chatter
2 Tim. 2:16. avoid *e.* and worldly chatter
1 Pet. 1:18. the *e.* folly of your traditional ways
2 Pet. 2:18. they utter big, *e.* words

emulation
Rom. 11:11. to stir Israel to *e.*

enable-s-ing
Acts 4:29. *e.* thy servants to speak thy word
Rom. 8:15. *e.* us to cry 'Abba! Father
   14:4. his Master has power to *e.* him
1 Cor. 10:13. *e.* you to sustain it
Phil. 3:21. by the very power which *e.* him
2 Pet. 1:3. *e.* us to know the One who called us

encircle-d
Luke 19:43. they will *e.* you and hem you in
   21:20. Jerusalem *e.* by armies
Heb. 11:30. *e.* on seven successive days

enclose-d
2 Cor. 5:4. *e.* within this earthly frame

encourage-d-ing
Acts 11:23. *e.* them all to hold fast
   14:22. *e.* them to be true to their religion
   15:32. much to *e.* and strengthen the members
   20:1. after *e.* them, said good-bye
1 Cor. 14:3. they stimulate and they *e.*
2 Cor. 7:13. we have been so *e.* But besides being *e.* ourselves
1 Thess. 3:2. to *e.* you to stand firm
   5:14. *e.* the faint-hearted
2 Thess. 2:17. *e.* and fortify you
Philem. 7. *e.* by your love
Heb. 3:13. *e.* one another
   10:25. *e.* one another
Rev. 2:14. *e.* them to eat food sacrificed to idols

encouragement
Acts 15:31. rejoiced at the *e.*
   16:40. spoke words of *e.* to them
   20:2. *e.* to the Christians there
Rom. 1:12. to receive *e.* myself
   15:4. through the *e.* they give us
   15:5. God, the source of all fortitude and all *e.*
1 Cor. 14:31. receive instruction and *e.*
1 Thess. 2:11. appealing to you by *e.*
2 Thess. 2:16. given us such unfailing *e.*
Heb. 6:18. to give powerful *e.* to us

encumbrance
Heb. 12:1. we must throw off every *e.*

end-s-ed-ing

Mat. 4:2. at the *e*. of them he was famished

12:42. she came from the *e*. of the earth

12:45. in the *e*. the man's plight is worse

20:8. *e*. with the first

21:41. he will bring those bad men to a bad *e*.

24:33. you may know that the *e*. is near

27:48. held it to his lips on the *e*. of a cane

Mark 9:22. it has tried to make an *e*. of him.

12:6. in the *e*. he sent him

13:10. before the *e*. the Gospel must be proclaimed

13:29. you may know that the *e*. is near

15:36. a sponge, soaked in sour wine, on the *e*. of a cane

Luke 11:26. in the *e*. the man's plight is worse

11:31. she came from the *e*. of the earth

13:3 ⎱ you will all of you come to the
13:5 ⎰ same end

16:17. easier for heaven and earth to come to an *e*.

17:24. that lights up the earth from *e*. to *e*.

17:27. the flood came and made an *e*. of them

17:29. sulphur from heaven and made an *e*. of them all

18:4. in the *e*. he said to himself

19:47. were bent on making an *e*. of him

John 11:4. this sickness will not *e*. in death

19:28. all had now come to its appointed *e*.

Acts 1:8. and away to the *e*. of the earth

4:31. when they had *e*. their prayer

5:15. in the *e*. the sick were actually carried out

7:15. there he *e*. his days

8:20. may you come to a bad *e*.

13:25. John was nearing the *e*. of his course

21:5. our time ashore was *e*.

21:15. at the *e*. of our stay

21:26. the period of purification would *e*.

27:20. for days on *e*. there was no sign of either sun or stars

Rom. 1:17. starts from faith and *e*. in faith

1:21. all their thinking has *e*. in futility

1 Cor. 2:6. governing powers, which are declining to their *e*.

6:13. one day God will put an *e*. to both

13:8. love will never come to an *e*.

15:8. in the *e*. he appeared even to me

2 Cor. 4:8. we are never at our wits' *e*.

5:5. God himself has shaped us for this very *e*.

Gal. 3:25. the tutor's charge is at an *e*.

4:20. I am at my wit's *e*. about you

Eph. 6:18. to this *e*. keep watch

Phil. 2:21. they are all bent on their own *e*.

Col. 1:29. to this *e*. I am toiling

2 Tim. 2:10. with this *e*. in view

Heb. 1:12. thy years shall have no *e*.

11:22. by faith Joseph, at the *e*. of his life

12:11. in the *e*. it yields for those who have been trained by it

1 Pet. 1:5. will be revealed at the *e*. of time

Jude 16. they court favour to gain their *e*.

Rev. 11:11. at the *e*. of the three days and a half

21:4. there shall be an *e*. to death

endless

Rom. 16:27. be glory for *e*. ages

Phil. 4:20. to our God and Father be glory for *e*. ages

1 Tim. 6:4. *e*. wrangles

endow-s-ed

Gal. 6:1. you who are *e*. with the Spirit

1 Tim. 6:17. God, who *e*. us richly

endowment

1 Tim. 4:14. the spiritual *e*. you possess

endue

Acts 2:18. I will *e*. even my slaves

endurance

Rom. 5:4. *e*. brings proof that we have stood the test

8:25. in waiting for it, we show our *e*.

1 Cor. 13:7. its hope, and its *e*.

2 Cor. 6:4. by our steadfast *e*.

Tit. 2:2. sound in faith, in love, and in *e*.

Heb. 10:36. you need *e*., if you are to do God's will

Rev. 1:9. the *e*. which is ours in Jesus

endure-s-d-ing

Mat. 5:18. so long as heaven and earth *e*.

17:17. how much longer must I *e*. you

Mark 9:12. he is to *e*. great sufferings

9:19. how long must I *e*. you

Luke 9:41. how long shall I be with you and *e*. you all

17:25. first he must *e*. much suffering

Rom. 5:3. suffering trains us to *e*.

8:18. the sufferings we now *e*.

8:24. *e*. and wait

2 Cor. 1:6. the same sufferings we now *e*.

3:11. the splendour of that which *e*.

Col. 1:24. Christ's afflictions still to be *e*.
2 Thess. 1:4. all the troubles you *e*.
2 Tim. 2:12. if we *e*., we shall reign with him
Heb. 1:11. they shall pass away, but thou *e*.
1 Pet. 1:23. *e*. word of God
    4:1. Christ *e*. bodily suffering . . . when a man has thus *e*.
Rev. 2:2. you cannot *e*. evil men

enemy-ies
Mat. 10:36. find his *e*. under his own roof
Luke 14:31. whether with ten thousand men he can face an *e*.
    14:32. before the *e*. approaches
Acts 2:35. make your *e*. your footstool
1 Thess. 2:15. *e*. of their fellow-men
2 Thess. 2:4. he is the *E*.
Heb. 10:27. which will consume God's *e*.
1 Pet. 5:8. your *e*. the devil
Jude 4. they are the *e*. of religion.

energy-ies
Rom. 12:11. with unflagging *e*.
    13:6. to these duties they devote their *e*.
Col. 1:29. the *e*. and power of Christ
Heb. 6:5. spiritual *e*. of the age to come

engage-d
Mark 8:11. *e*. him in discussion
John 8:2. was *e*. in teaching them
Acts 24:18. purified and *e*. in this service
1 Cor. 16:10. it is the Lord's work that he is *e*. upon
Phil. 1:30. you and I are *e*. in the same contest
Tit. 3:8. *e*. in honourable occupations
    3:14. *e*. in honest employment
Jude 3. *e*. in writing to you about our salvation

enjoin-ed
Mat. 17:9. Jesus *e*. them not to tell anyone
Mark 9:9. on their way down the mountain, he *e*. them
Acts 16:4. *e*. their observance

enjoy-s-ed
Luke 12:19. eat, drink, and *e*. yourself
Acts 2:47. *e*. the favour of the whole people
Rom. 15:24. having *e*. your company
    15:32. *e*. a time of rest with you
Gal. 2:4. the liberty we *e*.
1 Tim. 4:3. to be *e*. with thanksgiving
Heb. 3:3. *e*. more honour than his household
2 Pet. 1:1. *e*. equal privilege with ourselves
3 John 2. I pray that you may *e*. good health

enlarge
Heb. 9:5. on these we cannot now *e*.

enlighten-s-ed
John 1:9. the real light which *e*. every man
Rom. 2:19. to *e*. the benighted
    9:1. conscience, *e*. by the Holy Spirit
Heb. 10:32. newly *e*., you met the challenge

enlightenment
1 Cor. 14:6. revelation, or *e*.

enlisted
2 Cor. 5:18. he has *e*. us in this service

enough
Mat. 6:34. each day has troubles *e*. of its own
    7:26. foolish *e*. to build his house on sand
    13:12. till he has *e*. and to spare
    13:32. big *e*. for the birds to come
    14:20. *e*. to fill twelve great baskets
    15:33. bread *e*. to feed such a crowd
    15:37. *e*. to fill seven baskets
    25:29. till he has *e*. and to spare
Mark 2:2. in front of the door was not big *e*.
    5:4. no one was strong *e*. to master him
    12:44. had more than *e*., but she, with less than *e*.
Luke 12:15. when a man has more than *e*.
    12:19. *e*. for many years
    16:3. I am not strong *e*. to dig
    18:8. he will vindicate them soon *e*.
    21:4. more than *e*., but she, with less than *e*.
John 1:27. I am not good *e*. to unfasten his shoes
    5:36. *e*. to testify that the Father has sent me
    6:7. *e*. bread for every one of them
    6:12. when everyone had had *e*.
Acts 20:34. earned *e*. for the needs
    26:5. they have known me long *e*.
Rom. 1:32. they know well *e*. the just decree of God
    6:16. you know well *e*.
    10:12. is rich *e*. for the need of all
    14:2. faith *e*. to eat all kinds of food
1 Cor. 13:2. faith strong *e*. to move mountains
2 Cor. 1:24. your hold on the faith is secure *e*.
    2:6. met the offence well *e*.
    8:15. had no more than *e*.
    9:8. *e*. and to spare for every good cause
    9:11. rich *e*. to be generous
    11:4. you manage to put up with that well *e*.
    12:16. I was unscrupulous *e*.

Jam. 2:15. not *e.* food for the day
2:19. faith *e.* to believe
1 Pet. 4:3. you had time *e.* in the past
4:18. hard *e.* for the righteous to be
saved
1 John 3:17. if a man has *e.* to live on

enrichment
Rom. 11:12. if their offence means the
e. of the world, and if their falling-
off means the *e.* of the Gentiles
1 Cor. 1:5. the *e.* that has come to you
in Christ

enrol-led
Luke 10:20. that your names are *e.* in
heaven

ensure-s-d
Mat. 12:41 ⎫
      12:42 ⎬ *e.* its condemnation
Luke 11:31 ⎫
      11:32 ⎬ *e.* their condemnation
John 18:32. they *e.* the fulfilment of the
words
2 Cor. 9:3. to *e.* that what we have said
about you
2 Thess. 2:6. which *e.* that he shall be
revealed

enter-s-ed-ing
Mat. 2:11. *e.* the house, they saw the
child
10:5. do not *e.* any Samaritan town
10:12. wish the house peace as you
e. it
12:9. *e.* their synagogue
21:10. when he *e.* Jerusalem
21:23. he *e.* the temple
21:31. tax-gatherers and prostitutes
are *e.* the kingdom of God
25:34. *e.* and possess the kingdom
25:46. the righteous will *e.* eternal life
Mark 3:20. he *e.* a house
14:14. when he *e.* a house give this
message
Luke 1:9. to *e.* the sanctuary of the Lord
John 1:11. he *e.* his own realm
20:5. saw the linen wrappings lying
there, but did not *e.*
Acts 1:13. *e.* the city
Rom. 3:18. reverence for God does not
e. their thoughts
5:2. allowed to *e.* the sphere of God's
grace
8:21. *e.* upon the liberty and splendour
Gal. 4:9. to *e.* their service all over again
Eph. 1:14. we shall *e.* upon our heritage
Col. 2:18. try to *e.* into some vision of
their own
Heb. 9:6. the priests are always *e.* the
first tent
11:39. they did not *e.* upon the promised inheritance
12:1. the race for which we are *e.*

Jam. 2:2. two visitors may *e.* your place
of worship
1 Pet. 3:22. Jesus Christ who *e.* heaven
Rev. 11:17. *e.* upon thy reign
19:6. has *e.* on his reign

entertain-ed
Acts 28:7. *e.* us hospitably
1 Tim. 5:19. do not *e.* a charge against
an elder

enthrone-d
Eph. 1:20. *e.* him at his right hand
2:6. *e.* us with him in the heavenly
realms
Rev. 17:1. the great whore, *e.* above the
ocean

enthusiasm
2 Cor. 8:22. whose *e.* we have had many
opportunities of testing

entice-s
1 John 2:16. panders to the appetites, or
e. the eyes

entire-ly
Acts 18:5. devoted himself *e.* to preaching
22:30. the *e.* Council to assemble
2 Cor. 4:1. we owe *e.* to God's mercy
8:21. our aims are *e.* honourable
Gal. 5:3. obligation to keep the *e.* law
Eph. 1:23. receives the *e.* fullness of God
Col. 1:10. *e.* pleasing to him
3:22. slaves, give *e.* obedience

entrails
Acts 1:18. so that his *e.* poured out

entrance
Mat. 27:60. rolled a large stone against
the *e.*
Mark 15:46. rolled a stone against the *e.*
16:3. roll away the stone for them
from the *e.*
John 20:1. moved away from the *e.*
Acts 10:17. now arrived at the *e.*

entreat-y
Eph. 4:1. I *e.* you, then—I, a prisoner
6:18. wholly to prayer and *e.*

entrust-ed
Mat. 11:27 ⎫ everything is *e.* to me by
Luke 10:22 ⎭ my Father
12:48. the more a man has had *e.* to
him
John 3:35. *e.* him with all authority
13:3. the Father had *e.* everything to
him
Rom. 3:2. the Jews were *e.* with the
oracles of God
1 Cor. 6:4. *e.* jurisdiction to outsiders
2 Cor. 4:1. *e.* with this commission
5:19. *e.* us with the message
Gal. 2:7. *e.* with the Gospel for Gentiles
as surely as Peter had been *e.* with
the Gospel for Jews

Col. 4:17. attend to the duty *e.* to you
1 Thess. 2:4. as fit to be *e.* with the Gospel
1 Tim. 1:11. the gospel *e.* to me
6:20. keep safe that which has been *e.* to you
Tit. 1:3. *e.* to me by ordinance of God
Jude 3. the faith which God *e.* to his people

entry
Acts 23:16. he went to the barracks, obtained *e.*

envious
Gal. 4:17. the persons I have referred to are *e.*
Jam. 4:2. *e.*, and cannot attain your ambition

environment
2 Pet. 2:18. escape from their heathen *e.*

envoy-s
Luke 14:32. he sends *e.*, and asks for terms
1 Thess. 2:6. as Christ's own *e.*

envy
Mark 7:22. *e.*, slander, arrogance
Rom. 10:19. to stir your *e.*
Gal. 4:17. not with an honest *e.*: what they really want is to bar the door to you so that you may come to *e.* them
4:18. to deserve an honest *e.*

epileptic
Mat. 4:24. *e.*, or paralysed
17:15. he is an *e.*

epoch-s
Acts 17:26. he fixed the *e.* of their history

equal-ly
Mark 9:3. no bleacher on earth could equal
Luke 11:18. *e.* if Satan is divided against himself
Rom. 2:1. you, the judge, are *e.* guilty
2:26 *e.*, if an uncircumcised man
12:16. have equal regard for one another
14:7. *e.* no one of us dies
1 Cor. 7:3. the wife *e.* must give the husband his due
7:4. *e.*, the husband cannot claim his body as his own
7:22. *e.*, the free man who received the call
2 Cor. 2:16. who is *e.* to such a calling
8:7. *e.* lavish in this generous service
1 Tim. 1:12. has made me *e.* to the task
3:11. wives, *e.*, must be women of high principle
2 Pet. 1:1. *e.* privilege with ourselves

equality
2 Cor. 8:15. the aim is *e.*

equip-ped
John 18:3. the Pharisees, *e.* with lanterns
Rom. 15:14. *e.* with knowledge of every kind
Eph. 4:12. *e.* God's people for work in his service
2 Tim. 3:17. *e.* for good work of every kind
Rev. 9:7. like horses *e.* for battle

erect
Heb. 8:5. Moses, about to *e.* the tent
Rev. 13:14. made them *e.* an image

errand
Luke 19:32. went on their *e.* and found it
Rom. 15:25. on an *e.* to God's people
15:31. that my *e.* to Jerusalem may find acceptance

err-ing
Heb. 5:2. bear patiently with the ignorant and *e.*

erroneous
1 Tim. 1:3. teaching *e.* doctrines

error
Col. 2:4. being talked into *e.*
1 Thess. 2:3. never springs from *e.*
2 Tim. 3:16. teaching the truth and refuting *e.*

escape-d
Mat. 2:13. *e.* with them to Egypt
3:7. who warned you to *e.*
24:20. not be winter when you have to make your *e.*
Luke 3:7. *e.* from the coming retribution
Acts 14:6. made their *e.* to the Lycaonian cities
16:27. assuming that the prisoners had *e.*
25:11. to *e.* the death penalty
1 Cor. 3:15. *e.* with his life, as one might from a fire
Gal. 6:12. their sole object is to *e.* persecution
2 Tim. 2:26. *e.* from the devil's snare
Heb. 11:31. Rahab *e.* the doom
12:8. if you *e.* the discipline

escort-ed
Acts 9:30. they *e.* him to Caesarea
16:30. *e.* them out and said, 'Masters
16:37. come in person and *e.* us out
16:39. then they *e.* them out
17:15. Paul's *e.* brought him as far as Athens
20:38. they *e.* him to his ship
21:5. their wives and children all *e.* us out
23:24. under safe *e.* to Felix
23:32. leaving the cavalry to *e.* him.

especially
1 Tim. 5:8. *e.* for members of his own household
Tit. 1:10. *e.* among Jewish converts

essential-s
Acts 15:28. no further burden upon you beyond these *e.*
1 Cor. 11:11. in Christ's fellowship woman is as *e.* to man

establish-ed
Mat. 15:2. your disciples break the old-*e.* tradition
Mark 7:3. in obedience to an old-*e.* tradition
Luke 12:51. do you suppose I came to *e.* peace.
Acts 1:6. *e.* once again the sovereignty of Israel
Rom. 5:17. death *e.* its reign
5:21. sin *e.* its reign by way of death, so God's grace might *e.* its reign
14:9. to *e.* his lordship over dead and living
Heb. 9:16. the death of the testator to be *e.*
11:33. overthrew kingdoms, *e.* justice
1 Pet. 5:10. restore, *e.*, and strengthen you

establishment
Phil. 4:22. who belong to the imperial *e.*

estate
Luke 15:12. he divided his *e.* between them
Acts 4:37. owned an *e.*, which he sold
Gal. 4:1. even though the whole *e.* is his

esteem
Acts 4:33. they were all held in high *e.*
Rom. 12:10. give pride of place to one another in *e.*

estimate
Rom. 12:3. a sober *e.* based on the measure of faith
2 Cor. 5:16. to count in our *e.* of any man
12:6. an *e.* of me which goes beyond

estrange-d
Col. 1:21. yourselves *e.* from God

eternal
Mat. 18:8. thrown into the *e.* fire
19:29. and gain *e.* life
25:41. the *e.* fire that is ready for the devil
Mark 3:29. guilty of *e.* sin
16:8. message of *e.* salvation
Luke 16:9. received into an *e.* home
18:30. in the age to come have *e.* life
John 3:16. not die but have *e.* life
3:36. has hold of *e.* life
6:27. the food of *e.* life
6:40. possess *e.* life

6:47. the believer possesses *e.* life
Rom. 16:26. by *e.* God's command
2 Thess. 1:9. the punishment of *e.* ruin
1 Tim. 1:11. God in his *e.* felicity
also **eternal**—John 4:14, 5:24, 6:47, 12:50, 20:31; Acts 13:46; Rom. 6:22; Gal. 6:8; 2 Thess. 1:9; 1 Tim. 1:16, 6:15; Heb. 13:20; 2 Pet. 1:11; Rev. 14:6.

eternity
2 Tim. 1:9. granted to us in Christ Jesus from all *e.*
2 Pet. 3:18. glory now and for all *e.*

eunuch-s
Gal. 5:12. make *e.* of themselves

eve
John 19:14 ⎫ it was the *e.* of Passover
    19:31 ⎭
19:42. it was the *e.* of the Jewish Sabbath

even
Mat. 24:36. no one knows, not *e.* the angels in heaven, not *e.* the Son
Mark 1:45. *e.* so, people kept coming to him
2:28. the Son of Man is sovereign *e.* over the Sabbath
4:8. *e.* a hundredfold
5:28. if I touch *e.* his clothes, I shall be cured
7:37. he *e.* makes the deaf hear
13:32. no one knows, not *e.* the angels in heaven, not *e.* the Son.
Luke 12:26. you cannot do *e.* a very little thing
18:15. they *e.* brought babies for him to touch
John 1:9. was *e.* then coming into the world
6:39. I should not lose *e.* one
12:42. *e.* among those in authority a number believed
Acts 2:18. I will endue *e.* my slaves
5:15. that *e.* the shadow of Peter might fall on one
15:16. *e.* from its ruins I will rebuild
19:2. we have not *e.* heard that there is a Holy Spirit
1 Cor. 2:10. *e.* the depths of God's own nature
Gal. 2:13. *e.* Barnabas was carried away
Heb. 11:11. by faith *e.* Sarah herself received strength

evening
Luke 9:12. when *e.* was drawing on

event-s
Luke 1:1. draw up an account of the *e.*
1:3. the whole course of these *e.*
24:35. their account of the *e.* of their journey

John 13:19. I tell you this now, before the *e.*
Acts 5:11. all who heard of these *e.*
1 Cor. 10:6. these *e.* happened as symbols

eventually
Mark 12:22. *e.* the seven of them died

ever
Mark 5:34. free for *e.* from this trouble

everlasting
Rom. 1:20. his *e.* power and deity

evermore
Eph. 3:21. from generation to generation *e.*

every
Mat. 4:24. sufferers from *e.* kind of illness
24:31. the farthest bounds of heaven on *e.* side
John 13:10. you are clean, though not *e.* one of you
13:11. not *e.* one of you' because he knew who was going to betray him
Acts 10:12. in it he saw creatures of *e.* kind
17:26. he created *e.* race of men
22:3. trained in *e.* point of our ancestral law
Rom. 15:14. equipped with knowledge of *e.* kind
1 Cor. 11:26. *e.* time you eat this bread
15:24. after abolishing *e.* kind of domination
2 Cor. 1:20. God's promises, *e.* one of them
Eph. 1:3. *e.* spiritual blessing
6:18. pray on *e.* occasion
Col. 2:10. *e.* power and authority in the universe
Heb. 4:11. let us then make *e.* effort to enter that rest
1 John 5:4. *e.* child of God is victor

everybody
Acts 19:17. became known to *e.* in Ephesus
2 Thess. 3:11. minding *e.* business but their own
3 John 12. a good testimonial from *e.*

everyone
Mat. 5:15. light to *e.* in the house
6:5. at the street-corners, for *e.* to see them
9:25. when *e.* had been turned out
14:36. *e.* who touched it was completely cured
19:11. something which not *e.* can accept
22:9. invite *e.* you can find
26:33. *e.* else may fall away
Mark 13:37. I say to *e.*: Keep awake

14:29. *e.* else may fall away
Luke 6:19. *e.* in the crowd was trying to touch him
6:47. *e.* who comes to me
12:8. *e.* who acknowledges me
12:41. specially for us or is it for *e.*
18:9. looked down on *e.* else
John 3:15 ⎫ *e.* who has faith in him
3:16 ⎭
6:12. when *e.* had had enough
8:34. *e.* who commits sin is a slave
Acts 2:17. upon *e.* a portion of my spirit
2:21. *e.* who invokes the name of the Lord
10:43. *e.* who trusts in him receives forgiveness
13:39. *e.* who has faith is acquitted of everything
16:32. spoke the word of the Lord to him and to *e.* in his house
Rom. 10:11. *e.* who has faith in him will be saved
10:13. *e.*, as it says again—'*e.* who invokes the name of the Lord will be saved
1 Cor. 14:24. hears from *e.* something that searches his conscience
2 Tim. 3:9. recognized by *e.* for the fools they are
1 John 5:1. *e.* who believes that Jesus is the Christ

everything
Mat. 6:33. his justice before *e.* else
11:27. *e.* is entrusted to me by my Father
17:11. Elijah will come and set *e.* right
19:26. *e.* is possible for God
19:27. left *e.* to become your followers
22:4. *e.* is ready
22:40. *e.* in the Law and the prophets
Mark 4:11. *e.* comes by way of parables
4:34. to his disciples he explained *e.*
9:12. Elijah does come first to set *e.* right
9:23. *e.* is possible to one who has faith
10:27: to God *e.* is possible
10:28. left *e.* to become your followers
Luke 2:39. *e.* prescribed in the law of the Lord
5:11. left *e.* and followed him
5:28. left *e.* behind, and followed him
8:39. tell them *e.* that God has done for you
10:22. *e.* is entrusted to me by my Father
12:3. *e.* you have said in the dark
15:31. *e.* I have is yours
24:44. *e.* written about me
John 4:25. when he comes he will tell us *e.*
13:3. the Father had entrusted *e.* to him

John 14:26. will teach you *e*.
　15:15. *e*. that I heard from my Father
　16:15. *e*. that he makes known to you
　16:30. we are certain now that you know *e*.
　21:17. you know *e*.; you know I love you
Acts 13:39. everyone who has faith is acquitted of *e*.
　17:22. *e*. that concerns religion
1 Cor. 2:10. the Spirit explores *e*.
　3:22. *e*. belongs to you
　9:22. I have become *e*. in turn
　10:23. is *e*. good for us
　10:26. the earth is the Lord's and *e*. in it
2 Cor. 7:13. delighted beyond *e*.
Gal. 3:10. *e*. that is written in the Book of the Law
1 Tim. 4:4. *e*. that God created is good
2 Tim. 4:15. he violently opposed *e*. I said
Heb. 7:2. a tithe of *e*. as his portion
2 Pet. 1:3. *e*. that makes for life and true religion
1 John 2:16. *e*. the world affords
3 John 5. you show a fine loyalty in *e*. that you do
Rev. 3:17. I have *e*. I want in the world

everywhere
Mat. 28:19. baptize men *e*.
Luke 1:65. *e*. in the uplands of Judaea
Acts 2:43. a sense of awe was *e*.
Rom. 16:19. the fame of your obedience has spread *e*.
1 Cor. 1:2. all men *e*. who invoke the name
2 Cor. 2:14. *e*. uses us to reveal
　8:18. our congregations *e*.
Eph. 1:11. whose purpose is *e*. at work
Col. 1:6. *e*. it is growing and bearing fruit
1 Thess. 1:8. *e*. your faith in God has reached
2 Thess. 3:1. *e*. the swift and glorious course

evidence
Mat. 18:16. the *e*. of two or three witnesses
　19:18. do not give false *e*.
　26:60. came forward with false *e*.
　27:13. this *e*. that is brought against you
Mark 10:19. do not give false *e*.
　14:55. some *e*. against Jesus
　14:56. many gave false *e*.
　14.57. false *e*. against him
　14:59. their *e*. did not agree
Luke 18:20. do not give false *e*.
John 2:25. he needed no *e*. from others
　10:38. accept the *e*. of my deeds
　14:11. the *e*. of the deeds themselves
　18:23. if I spoke amiss, state it in *e*.

　19:35. an eyewitness, whose *e*. is to be trusted
1 Cor. 1:6. the *e*. for the truth of Christ
2 Cor. 12:6. beyond the *e*. of his own eyes
　13:1. the *e*. of two or three
1 Tim. 5:10. produce *e*. of good deeds
Heb. 10:28. on the *e*. of two or three witnesses
Jam. 5:3. their very rust will be *e*.

evil
Matt. 13:19. the *e*. one comes and carries off
　13:38. the darnel for the children of the *e*. one
　13:41. all whose deeds are *e*.
Mark 4:19. all kinds of *e*. desire
John 10:21. no one possessed by an *e*. spirit could speak like this. Could an *e*. spirit open blind men's eyes
1 Cor. 5:13. root out the *e*.-doer
　14:20. be as innocent of *e*. as babes
Eph. 2:2. the *e*. ways of this present age
　6:12. forces of *e*. in the heavens
　6:16. the flaming arrows of the *e*. one
Col. 1:21. your deeds were *e*.
2 Tim. 2:21. Cleanse himself from all those *e*. things
Heb. 4:11. this *e*. example of unbelief
2 Pet. 2:8. every sound, of their *e*. courses
1 John 2:13 ⎱ you have mastered the *e*.
　　2:14 ⎰ one
　5:18. the *e*. one cannot touch him
　5:19. in the power of the *e*. one
Rev. 22:11. let the *e*.-doer go on doing *e*.

evoked
Rom. 7:5. the sinful passions *e*. by the law

exact-ing-ly
John 4:53. this was the *e*. time when Jesus had said
　14:31. do *e*. as he commands
Rom. 6:12. *e*. obedience to the body's desires
　11:8. *e*. as it stands written
2 Pet. 3:4. *e*. as it has always been

examination
Acts 4:7. began the *e*.
　5:27. the High Priest began his *e*.

examine-d
1 Cor. 11:31. if we *e*. ourselves
Gal. 6:4. each man should *e*. his own conduct

example-s
Mark 7:4. for *e*., washing of cups and jugs
Rom. 7:2. for *e*., a married woman is by law bound
　7:7. for *e*., I should never have known

Rom. 12:6. the gift of inspired utterance,
for *e*.
1 Cor. 4:6. you may take our case as
an *e*.
4:16. follow my *e*.
11:1. follow my *e*. as I follow Christ's
Phil. 3:17. agree together, my friends,
to follow my *e*.
1 Thess. 1:6. the *e*. set by us and by the
Lord
2 Thess. 3:7. to copy our *e*.
3:9. an *e*. for you to imitate
Tit. 2:7. set them a good *e*.
Heb. 13:7. follow the *e*. of their faith
1 Pet. 5:3. setting an *e*. to the flock.
3 John 11. do not imitate bad *e*.

exasperate-d
Acts 4:2. *e*. at their teaching the people
17:16. *e*. to see how the city was full
of idols
Col. 3:21. do not *e*. your children

exceed-ed
Rom. 5:15. vastly *e*. by the grace of God
5:20. grace immeasurably *e*. it

exceedingly
1 Thess. 2:17. *e*. anxious to see you
again

Excellency
Mat. 27:63. your *E*.,' they said, 'we
recall how that impostor
Luke 1:3. your *E*., as one who has gone
over the whole course
Acts 23:26. to His *E*. the Governor
Felix
24:2. your *E*.,' he said, 'we owe it
to you
26:25. I am not mad, Your *E*.

excellent
Phil. 4:8. whatever is *e*. and admirable
1 Tim. 1:8. the law is an *e*. thing
Jam. 2:8. love your neighbour as
yourself,' that is *e*.
2:19. believe that there is one God. *E*.

except
Mat. 12:31. *e*. slander spoken against
the Spirit
13:57 ⎫
Mark 6:4 ⎬ *e*. in his home town
6:5. *e*. that he put his hands on a few
sick people
10.18. no one is good *e*. God alone
Luke 8:51. no one to go in with him *e*.
Peter, John, and James
17:18. give praise to God *e*. this
foreigner
John 3:13. *e*. the one who came down
from heaven
14:6. no one comes to the Father *e*.
by me
17:12. *e*. the man who must be lost

Acts 20:23. *e*. that in city after city
Rom. 13:8. *e*. that of mutual love
1 Cor. 1:14. I never baptized one of you
—*e*. Crispus and Gaius
12:3. *e*. under the influence of the
Holy Spirit
2 Cor. 2:2. *e*. you, whom I have offended
12:5. *e*. of my weaknesses
Gal. 1:19. *e*. James the Lord's brother
2 Pet. 2:5. *e*. for Noah
Rev.13:8. *e*. those whose names
14:3. that song no one could learn *e*.
the hundred and forty-four thousand

exception
Tit. 2:8. speech to which none can take
e.

excess
Jam. 1:21. the malice that hurries to *e*.

excessive
1 Tim. 3:8. given neither to *e*. drinking

exchange-d-ing
Luke 10:4. *e*. no greetings
Rom. 1:23. *e*. the splendour of immortal
God
1:26. women have *e*. natural inter-
course
2 Cor. 6:13. in fair *e*.
Rev. 11:10. make merry, and *e*. presents

excitement
Mat. 21:10. the whole city went wild
with *e*.

exclaim-ed-ing
Mat. 8:27. *e*., 'What sort of man is this
14:33 *e*., 'Truly you are the Son of
God
26:22. *e*. one after the other, 'Can you
mean me, Lord
26:65. *e*., 'Blasphemy
Mark 13:1. *e*., 'Look, Master, what
huge stones
John 1:46. Nazareth!' Nathaniel *e*.
6:60. *e*., 'This is more than we can
stomach
13:21. Jesus *e*. in deep agitation
18:22. *e*., 'Is that the way to answer
Acts 2:7. *e*., 'Why, they are all Galileans
24:25. Felix became alarmed and *e*.

exclude-ing
1 Cor. 15:27. *e*. God who subordinates
them
1 Tim. 2:8. *e*. angry or quarrelsome
thoughts

excuse
John 15:22. they have no *e*. for their sin

execute-d
Acts 13:28. they asked Pilate to have
him *e*.
Gal. 3:15. testament has been duly *e*.

execution
Mat. 24:9. handed over for punishment and *e.*
Luke 23:26. led him away to *e.*
  23.32. criminals who were being led away to *e.*
Acts 5:38. this idea of theirs or its *e.*
  12:19. interrogated the guards and ordered their *e.*

exempt
Mat. 17:26. the citizens are *e.*

exercise-d
Rom. 12:6. must be *e.* accordingly
1 Cor. 14:29. the rest *e.* their judgement
2 Cor. 13:10. sharp *e.* of authority
Rev. 17:12. the *e.* of royal authority

exert-ed
Rom. 12:8. if you are a leader, *e.* yourself to lead
Eph. 1:20. the might which he *e.* in Christ
2 Pet. 1:10. *e.* yourselves to clinch God's choice.

exertions
Col. 2:1. how strenuous are my *e.* for you

exhibit
Rom. 9:17. to *e.* my power in my dealings
  9.22. desiring to *e.* his retribution

exhortation
Acts 4:36. Barnabas (which means 'Son of *E.*

exiles
2 Cor. 5:6. we are *e.* from the Lord

exist-s-ing
Acts 17:28. we live and move, in him we *e.*
Rom. 13:1. *e.* authorities are instituted by him
1 Cor. 1:28. to overthrow the *e.* order
Col. 1:17. he *e.* before everything
Heb. 2:10. through whom all things *e.*
  11:6. must believe that he *e.*

existence
Rom. 4:17. not yet in *e.* as if they already were
1 Cor. 8:4. a false god has no *e.*
Heb. 1:2. he created all orders of *e.*
Jam. 3:6. it keeps the wheel of our *e.* red-hot

expect-ed-ing
Mat. 5:46. what reward can you *e.*
  9.15. can you *e.* the bridegroom's friends
  11:3. are we to *e.* some other
  20:10. they *e.* something extra
  24.44. at the time you least *e.* him

24:50. on a day that servant does not *e.*
Mark 2:19. can you *e.* the bridegroom's friends
Luke 6:34. only where you *e.* to be repaid
  6:35. without *e.* any return
  7:19 ⎱ or are we to *e.* some other
  7:20 ⎰
  8:40. they were all *e.* him
  12:40. at the time you least *e.* him
  12:46. on a day that servant does not *e.*
  12:48. much will be *e.* of him.
John 7:40. this must certainly be the *e.* prophet
Acts 10:24. Cornelius was *e.* them
  25:18. none of the charges I was *e.*
  28:6. *e.* that any moment he would swell
1 Cor. 4:2. *e.* to show themselves trustworthy
  9:11. *e.* from you a material harvest
Gal. 5.15. all you can *e.* is mutual destruction
Phil. 3:20. from heaven we *e.* our deliverer
Jam. 1:7. must not *e.* the Lord to give him anything

expectantly
1 Cor. 1:7. you wait *e.* for our Lord Jesus Christ
1 Thess. 1:10. wait *e.* for the appearance from heaven

expectation-s
2 Cor. 8:5. their giving surpassed our *e.*
Heb. 10:27. a terrifying *e.* of judgement

expel-led
John 9:34. they *e.* him from the synagogue
  9:35. Jesus heard that they had *e.* him
3 John 10. tries to *e.* them from the congregation

expense-s
Acts 21:24. paying their *e.*
  28:30. stayed there two full years at his own *e.*
1 Cor. 9:7. serving in the army at his own *e.*
  9:18. preaching the Gospel without *e.*

expensive
1 Tim. 2:9. gold or pearls, or *e.* clothes

experience-s-d
Rom. 7:10. proved in my *e.* to lead to death
Gal. 3:4. have all your great *e.* been in vain
Phil. 3:10. *e.* the power of his resurrection
Heb. 6:5. *e.* the goodness of God's word
1 John 2:8. true in your own *e.*

Rev. 2:24. no *e.* of what they like to call the deep secrets of Satan

experts
Rom. 16:19. *e.* in goodness

expiate-ing
Rom. 3:25. *e.* sin by his sacrificial death
Heb. 2:17. to *e.* the sins of the people

expiation
Heb. 9:5. overshadowing the place of *e.*

explain-s-ed
Mat. 13:36. *e.* to us the parable
27:8. this *e.* the name 'Blood Acre
Mark 4:34. to his disciples he *e.* everything
Luke 8:47. she *e.* why she had touched him
24:27. *e.* to them the passages
24:32. *e.* the scriptures to us
Acts 19.33. the crowd *e.* the trouble
1 Cor. 14:5. unless indeed he can *e.* its meaning
Heb. 5:11. much that is difficult to *e.*

explanation
Acts 19:40. unable to give any *e.*

exploits
2 Cor. 11:20. tyrannizes over you, *e.* you

explores-d
1 Cor. 2:10. the Spirit *e.* everything
1 Pet. 1:10. the prophets pondered and *e.*

expose-d-ing
John 7:7. *e.* the wickedness of its ways
Acts 7:19. forced our ancestors to *e.* their children
7:21. when he was *e.*, Pharoah's daughter
27:12. a Cretan harbour *e.* south-west
Rom. 3:19. *e.* to the judgement of God
7:13. sin *e.* its true character
1 Cor. 3:13. the day of judgement will *e.* it
1 Tim. 3:7. so that he may not be *e.* to scandal
5:20. those who commit sins you must *e.*
2 Tim. 2:9 in whose service I am *e.* to hardship
Heb. 4:13. *e.* to the eyes of the One with whom we have to reckon
Jam. 5:12. for fear that you *e.* yourselves to judgement

exposure
Mat. 1:19. wanting to save her from *e.*
2 Cor. 11:27. suffered from cold and *e.*

expound-ed
Acts 17:2. texts of Scripture which he *e.*

express-ed
2 Cor. 3:6. *e.* not in a written document

expression
1 Cor. 1:5. you can give full *e.* to it
2 Cor. 8:24. clear *e.* of your love

expressly
Acts 5:28. we *e.* ordered you

extend-ed
Acts 26:11. *e.* my persecution to foreign cities
2 Cor. 10:14. if it did not *e.* to you, for we were the first to reach Corinth
Gal. 3:14. be *e.* to the Gentiles

extent
John 13:1. show the full *e.* of his love
2 Cor. 2:5. to some *e.*

external-s
Rom. 2:28. the true Jew is not he who is such in *e.*, neither is the true circumcision the *e.* mark
2 Cor. 11:28. apart from these *e.* things
Phil. 3:3. no confidence in anything *e.*
3:4. base his claims on *e.*
Heb. 9:13. restore their *e.* purity

extirpate-d
Acts 3:23. refuses to listen to that prophet must be *e.*

extortion
2 Cor. 9:5. as a bounty indeed, and not as an *e.*

extra
Mat. 20:10. they expected something *e.*

extraordinary
Mat. 5:47. what is there *e.* about that
John 9:30. what an *e.* thing
Acts 28:6. without seeing anything *e.* happen
Phil. 1:14. with *e.* courage
1 Pet. 4:12. as though it were something *e.*

exuberantly
2 Cor. 8:2. they have been so *e.* happy

exult-ed
Luke 10:21. Jesus *e.* in the Holy Spirit
John 5:35. you were ready to *e.* in his light
Rom. 5:2. let us *e.* in the hope
5:3. *e.* in our present sufferings
5:11. *e.* in God through our Lord Jesus
Rev. 18:20. let heaven *e.* over her; *e.*, apostles and prophets
19:7. *e.* and shout for joy

exultation
Mat. 5:12. accept it with gladness and *e.*
Heb. 1:9. anointing with the oil of *e.*

eye-s
Mat. 2:6. in the *e.* of the rulers of Judah
5:28. looks on a woman with a lustful *e.*

Mat. 14:5. in whose *e.* John was a prophet
Luke 1:15. he will be great in the *e.* of the Lord.
5:25. he rose to his feet before their *e.*
24:5. stood with *e.* cast down
24:43. he took and ate before their *e.*
John 7:4. hope to be in the public *e.*
Acts 4:19. is it right in God's *e.* for us to obey you
6:15. fixed their *e.* on him
23:1. Paul fixed his *e.* on the Council
Rom. 1:19. lies plain before their *e.*
1:20. to the *e.* of reason
16:17. keep your *e.* on those who stir up quarrels
2 Cor. 4:18. our *e.* are fixed, not on the things that are seen
5:11. this fear of the Lord before our *e.*
8:21. not only in the Lord's *e.*, but also in the *e.* of men

12:6. the evidence of his own *e.* and ears
Phil. 3:18. now tell you with tears in my *e.*
Col. 2:1. all who have never set *e.* on me
Heb. 11:26. his *e.* were fixed upon the coming day
12:2. our *e.* fixed on Jesus.
Jam. 2:5. poor in the *e.* of the world
2 Pet. 2:3. perdition waits for them with unsleeping *e.*
Rev. 3:2. completed in the *e.* of my God
4:1. before my *e.* was a door opened in heaven
6:2. before my *e.* was a white horse
13:13. fire come down from heaven to earth before men's *e.*

eyewitness
John 19:35. vouched for by an *e.*

F

fabric
Acts 16:14. Lydia, a dealer in purple *f.*

fabrications
2 Pet. 2:3. trade on your credulity with sheer *f.*

face-d-s
Mat. 7:23. I will tell them to their *f.*
19:26. Jesus looked them in the *f.*
23:13. you shut the door of the kingdom of heaven in men's *f.*
26:70. Peter denied it in *f.* of them all
28:3. his *f.* shone like lightning
Mark 10:22. his *f.* fell and he went away
10:27. Jesus looked them in the *f.*
14:67. she looked into his *f.* and said
Luke 9:29. the appearance of his *f.* changed
14:31. he can *f.* an enemy
24:18. they halted, their *f.* full of gloom
John 1:42. Jesus, who looked him in the *f.*
18:22. one of the police struck him on the *f.*
19:3. struck him on the *f.*
Acts 13:9. looked him in the *f.* and said
14:9. Paul looked him in the *f.*
1 Cor. 6:1. has he the *f.* to take it to pagan law-courts
10:13. *f.* no trial beyond what man can bear
13:7. there is nothing love cannot *f.*
15:30. why do we *f.* these dangers
2 Cor. 1:6. to *f.* with fortitude the same sufferings

10:1. so feeble (you say) when I am *f.* to *f.* with you
10:2. as bold a *f.* as you please
10:7. look facts in the *f.*
11:23. many a time *f.* to *f.* with death
2 Tim. 3:1. you must *f.* the fact
4:5. *f.* hardship
Heb. 11:36. had to *f.* jeers and flogging
Jam. 1:2. whenever you have to *f.* trials
1 Pet. 5:5. God sets his *f.* against the arrogant
Rev. 1:16. his *f.* shone like the sun

facing
Mark 13:3. on the Mount of Olives *f.* the temple

fact-s
Mat. 13:34. in *f.* he never spoke to them without a parable
18:16. so that all *f.* may be duly established
Mark 9:26. in *f.*, many said, 'He is dead
11:32. all held that John was in *f.* a prophet
Luke 17:21. in *f.* the kingdom of God is among you
John 4:2. in *f.*, it was only the disciples who were baptizing
7:51. learned the *f.*
21:23. in *f.* Jesus did not say that he would not die
21:24. it is in *f.* he who wrote it
Acts 11:4. the *f.* as they had happened
11:28. which in *f.* occurred in the reign of Claudius

Acts 18:25. he taught accurately the *f.* about Jesus

19:36. these *f.* are beyond dispute

24:9. alleging that the *f.* were as he stated

24:11. ascertain the *f.* for yourself

26:26. unaware of any of these *f.*

28:31. teaching the *f.* about the Lord Jesus Christ

1 Cor. 1:17. the *f.* of Christ on his cross

7:14. your children would not belong to God, whereas in *f.* they do

12:18. in *f.*, God appointed each limb and organ

12:20. in *f.*, however, there are many different organs

15:3. I handed on to you the *f.*

2 Cor. 10:7. look *f.* in the face

13:1. all *f.* must be established

Gal. 1:7. not that it is in *f.* another gospel

Phil. 3:8. for whose sake I did in *f.* lose everything

1 Thess. 4:10. you are in *f.* practising this rule

1 Tim. 1:10. in *f.* all whose behaviour flouts

5:15. there have in *f.* been widows

2 Tim. 3:1. you must face the *f.*

Philem. 21. you will in *f.* do better than I ask

Heb. 2:8. in *f.* we do not yet see all things in subjection to man

4:6. the *f.* remains that someone must enter it

8:6. but in *f.* the ministry which has fallen to Jesus

2 Pet. 3:5. the *f.* that there were heavens and earth long ago

1 John 3:4. sin, in *f.*, is lawlessness

Rev. 3:17. in *f.*, though you do not know it, you are the most pitiful wretch

fade-s-ing

Acts 27:20. our last hopes of coming through alive began to *f.*

1 Cor. 9:25. they do it to win a *f.* wreath; we, a wreath that never *f.*

2 Cor. 3:7. that splendour, though it was soon to *f.*

3:11. that which was soon to *f.*

3:13. from gazing on that *f.* splendour

fail-s-ed-ing

Mat. 3:10. every tree that *f.* to produce good fruit

13:19. *f.* to understand it

16:11. *f.* to see that I was not speaking about bread

17:12. they *f.* to recognize him

26:60. they *f.* to find one

Mark 9:18. I asked your disciples to cast it out, but they *f.*

14:55. to warrant a death-sentence, but *f.* to find any

Luke 1:37. God's promises can never *f.*

3:9. *f.* to produce good fruit is cut down

20:26. attempt to catch him out in public *f.*

24:23. *f.* to find his body

John 11:10. he stumbles, because the light *f.* him

Acts 5:22. went to the prison *f.* to find them

12:19. Herod made close search, but *f.* to find him

13:28. they *f.* to find grounds for the sentence of death

17:6. *f.* to find them, they dragged Jason himself

24:20. *f.* that, it is for these persons here present

Rom. 2:21. do you *f.* to teach yourself

7:19. the good which I want to do, I *f.* to do

8:32. how can he *f.* to lavish upon us

10:19. can it be that Israel *f.* to recognize the message

1 Cor. 1:21. the world *f.* to find him by its wisdom

2 Cor. 1:3. God whose consolation never *f.* us

Heb. 4:6. *f.* to enter through unbelief

1 Pet. 4:19. their Maker will not *f.* them

Rev. 8:12. a third of the light of the day *f.*

failure

Rom. 11:11. did their *f.* mean complete downfall

faint

Luke 21:26. men will *f.* with terror at the thought

1 Thess. 5:14. encourage the *f.*-hearted

fair

Mat. 20:4. I will pay you a *f.* wage

Mark 7:27. it is not *f.* to take the children's bread

Acts 17:12. so did a *f.* number of Greeks

2 Cor. 6:13. in *f.* exchange then

Col. 4:1. masters, be just and *f.* to your slaves

faith

Mat. 8:13. because of your *f.*, so let it be

13:58. such was their want of *f.*

18:6. these little ones who have *f.* in me

21:22. whatever you pray for in *f.* you will receive

24:10. many will lose their *f.*

26:31. fall from your *f.* on my account

Mark 5:36. do not be afraid; only have *f.*

6:6. he was taken aback by their want of *f.*

9:23. everything is possible to one who has *f.*

Mark 9:24. I have *f.*', cried the boy's father; 'help me where *f.* falls short
9:42. one of these little ones who have *f.*
14:27. you will all fall from your *f.*
16:17. *f.* will bring with it these miracles
Luke 1:45. *f.* that the Lord's promise would be fulfilled
8:50. only show *f.* and she will be well again
John 1:50. is this the ground of your *f.*
3:15. *f.* in him may in him possess eternal life
3:16. has *f.* in him may not die
3:18. *f.* in him does not come under judgement
3:36. *f.* in the Son has hold of eternal life
5:44. how can you have *f.* so long as you receive honour
6:40. puts his *f.* in him shall possess eternal life
6:64. some of you who have no *f.*' For Jesus knew all along who were without *f.*
6:69. we have *f.*, and we know that you are the Holy One of God
8:30. many put their *f.* in him
9:35. have you *f.* in the Son of Man
9:36. that I should put my *f.* in him
11:15. for the good of your *f.*
11:25. if a man has *f.* in me
11:26. no one who is alive and has *f.*
11:40. if you have *f.* you will see the glory of God
11:45. seen what Jesus did, put their *f.* in him
12:11. putting their *f.* in him
12:46. no one who has *f.* in me should remain in darkness
14:12. he who has *f.* in me will do what I am doing
14:29. when it happens you may have *f.*
16:1. guard you against the breakdown of your *f.*
17:8. *f.* to believe that thou didst send me
17:20. through their words put their *f.* in me
20:29. you have found *f.* Happy are they who never saw me and yet have found *f.*
20:31. the *f.* that Jesus is the Christ, the Son of God, and that through this *f.*
Acts 2:44. all whose *f.* had drawn them together
13:39. everyone who has *f.* is acquitted
14:23. in whom they had put their *f.*
16:34. his new-found *f.* in God
26:11. to make them renounce their *f.*
Rom. 1:16. for everyone who has *f.*

3:26. justifies any man who puts his *f.* in Jesus
4:3. Abraham put his *f.* in God, and that *f.*
4:17. the God in whom he put his *f.*
4:18. without any weakening of *f.*
4:22. *f.* was 'counted to him as righteousness
4:24. *f.* in the God who raised Jesus
9:33. *f.* in him will not be put to shame
10:4. righteousness for everyone who has *f.*
10:9. in your heart the *f.*
10:10. the *f.* that leads to righteousness
10:11. *f.* in him will be saved from shame
10:14. invoke one in whom they had no *f.*? And how could they have *f.*
14:2. *f.* enough to eat all kinds of food
15:13. all joy and peace by your *f.* in him
1 Cor. 1:21. to save those who have *f.*
3:5. God's agents in bringing you to the *f.*
13:7. there is no limit to its *f.*
14:22. those who hold the *f.*
Gal. 3:6. he put his *f.* in God, and that *f.* was counted to him as righteousness
6:6. under instruction in the *f.*
1 Thess. 2:13. you who hold the *f.*
1 Tim. 1:16. in future to have *f.* in him
Philem: 17. partner in the *f.*
Heb. 10:39. we have the *f.* to make life our own
11:2. for their *f.* that the men of old stand on record
12:1. these witnesses to *f.* around us
Jam. 2:19. *f.* enough to believe that there is one God. Excellent! The devils have *f.* like that
2:23. Abraham put his *f.* in God, and that *f.* was counted to him as righteousness
1 Pet. 2:6. *f.* in it will not be put to shame
2:7. for you who have *f.* For those who have no *f.*
Rev. 14:13. happy are the dead who die in the *f.*

faithful
1 Tim. 3:2. *f.* to his one wife
3:12. a deacon must be *f.* to his one wife
5:9. she must have been *f.* in marriage
Heb. 3:6. Christ is *f.* as a son

faithfully
2 Cor. 9:13. how *f.* you confess the gospel

faithfulness
Rom. 3:3. the *f.* of God

faithless
Luke 12:46. he will find his place among
   the *f.*
Rom. 11:23. if they do not continue *f.*
2 Tim. 2:13. if we are *f.*, he keeps faith
Heb. 3:12. *f.* heart of a deserter
Rev. 21:8. the cowardly, the *f.*

faithlessness
Rom. 3:3. will their *f.* cancel the faithfulness of God

fall-s-en-ing
Mat. 13:21. he *f.* away at once
   19:20. where do I still *f.* short
   23:35. on you will *f.* the guilt of all
   the innocent blood
   26:31. all *f.* from your faith on my
   account
   26:33. everyone else may *f.* away
   27:29. *f.* on their knees before him
   they jeered at him
   28:9. *f.* prostrate before him
Mark 4:17. they *f.* away at once
   9:24. help me where faith *f.* short
   14:27. you will all *f.* from your faith
   14:29. everyone else may *f.* away
Luke 2:35. will stand or *f.* because of
   him
   4:22. words of such grace should *f.*
   from his lips
   21:9. do not *f.* into a panic
John 3:25. *f.* into a dispute with Jews
   6:17. darkness had already *f.*
   11:1. Lazarus who had *f.* ill
   11:2. whose brother Lazarus had *f.* ill
   11:11. Lazarus has *f.* asleep
   11:12. if he has *f.* asleep
Acts 1:20. let his homestead *f.* desolate
   5:15. the shadow of Peter might *f.* on
   one
   8:24. things you have spoken of may
   f. upon me
Rom. 1:18. *f.* upon all the godless
   14:20. causes another to *f.*
   15:16. it *f.* to me to offer
1 Cor. 6:7. *f.* below your standard
   11:18. you *f.* into sharply divided
   groups
   11:31. we should not thus *f.* under
   judgement
   11:32. we do *f.* under the Lord's
   judgement
   11:34. you may not *f.* under judgement
   14:13. *f.* into ecstatic utterance
2 Cor. 12:11. in no respect did I *f.* short
1 Thess. 3:10. mend your faith where it
   f. short
2 Thess. 3:6. Christian brother who *f.*
   into idle habits

1 Tim. 1:6. *f.* short of these, some
   people have gone astray
2 Tim. 4:14. retribution will *f.* upon him
Heb. 6:7. the rain that *f.* upon it
   8:6. the ministry which has *f.* to Jesus
   13:4. God's judgement will *f.* on
   fornicators
Jam. 1:4. character that will *f.* short in
   nothing
   1:5. if any of you *f.* short in wisdom
   5:7. until the winter and spring rains
   have *f.*
   5:9. you will *f.* under judgement
2 Pet. 3:12. the heavens ablaze until they
   f. apart
Rev. 3:10. the ordeal that is to *f.* upon
   the whole world

fallow
1 Cor. 14:14. my intellect lies *f.*

false
Mat. 13:22. the *f.* glamour of wealth
Mark 4:19. worldly cares and the *f.*
   glamour of wealth
John 1:47 ⎫
   7:18 ⎭ there is nothing *f.* in him
Rom. 1:25. they have bartered away the
   true God for a false one
   2:22. you abominate *f.* gods
   9:6. impossible that the word of God
   should have proved *f.*
1 Cor. 8:4. a *f.* god has no existence
   12:10. distinguish true spirits from *f.*
Gal. 2:13. even Barnabas was carried
   away and played *f.*
Heb. 6:18. God could not possibly play
   us *f.*
Jam. 2:4. judge by *f.* standards
   3:14. consider whether your claims
   are not *f.*
   4:4. you *f.*, unfaithful creatures
1 John 4:4. mastery over these *f.*
   prophets
   5:21. be on the watch against *f.* gods
Rev. 2:2. have found them *f.*
   21:27. nor anyone whose ways are *f.*

falsehood-s
Rom. 3:7. the greater honour because
   of my *f.*
Eph. 4:25. throw off *f.*
1 Tim. 4:2. the specious *f.* of men
1 Pet. 2:22. he was convicted of no *f.*

falsifying
Acts 13:10. will you never stop *f.* the
   straight ways of the Lord

fame
Mark 6:14. the *f.* of Jesus had spread
Rom. 9:17. to spread my *f.* over all the
   world
   16:19. the *f.* of your obedience has
   spread everywhere

familiar
Acts 26:4. is *f.* to all Jews
2 Tim. 3:15. *f.* with the sacred writings

family-ies
Mat. 13:57. except in his home town, and in his own *f.*
22:24. carry on his brother's *f.*
Mark 3:21. when his *f.* heard of this
6:4. among his kinsmen and *f.*
12:19. carry on his brother's *f.*
Luke 1:61. nobody in your *f.* who has that name
12:13. divide the *f.* property
12:52. members of a *f.* will be divided
20:28. carry on his brother's *f.*
John 7:42. Messiah is to be of the *f.* of David
Acts 3:25. all the *f.* on earth shall find blessing
4:6. of the high-priestly *f.*
7:13. his *f.* connexions were disclosed
10:2. his whole *f.* joined in the worship of God
16:33. his whole *f.* were baptized
Rom. 8:29. a large *f.* of brothers
1 Cor. 16:15. the Stephanas *f.* were the first converts
2 Thess. 3:15. friendly advice, as one of the *f.*
1 Tim. 3:5. control his own *f.*
5:4. loyalty to the *f.*
5:16. has widows in the *f.*
Tit. 1:11. they are ruining whole *f.*
Heb. 2:14. a *f.* share the same flesh and blood
3:1. brothers in the *f.* of God
1 John 4:4. you, my children, are of God's *f.*
5:19. we know that we are of God's *f.*

famine
Acts 7:11. *f.* struck the whole of Egypt
11:28. A severe and world-wide *f.*
Rev. 6:8. to kill by sword and by *f.*

famish-ed
Mat. 4:2. at the end of them he was *f.*
Luke 4:2. at the end of it he was *f.*

famous
John 3:10. this *f.* teacher of Israel

fancy-ies
1 Cor. 3:18. who *f.* himself wise
8:2. *f.* that he knows
2 Tim. 4:3. will follow their own *f.*

far
Mat. 2:6. *f.* from least in the eyes of the rulers
5:20. *f.* better men than the Pharisees
11:9. *f.* more than a prophet
12:12. a man is worth *f.* more than a sheep
24:6. news of battles *f.* away
24:27. flashing as *f.* as the west

Mark 1:45. he spread it *f.* and wide
4:33. so *f.* as they were able to receive it
13:7. news of battles *f.* away
Luke 12:24. you are worth *f.* more than the birds
16:23. there, *f.* away, was Abraham
23:5. has spread as *f.* as this city
John 16:24. so *f.* you have asked nothing in my name
19:20. the place where Jesus was crucified was not *f.* from the city
Acts 13:49. the word of the Lord spread *f.* and wide
Rom. 5:17. receive in *f.* greater measure God's grace
2 Cor. 1:8. the burden of it was *f.* too heavy for us
1 Tim. 6:21. shot *f.* wide of the faith
Heb. 7:22. how *f.* superior must the covenant also be
8:6. the ministry which has fallen to Jesus is as *f.* superior to theirs
2 John 9. anyone who runs ahead too *f.*

fare-d-ing
Acts 15:36. to see how our brothers are *f.*
1 Thess. 2:14. you have *f.* like the congregations in Judaea

farewell
Phil. 3:1. and now, friends, *f.*
4:4. *f.*; I wish you all joy in the Lord

farm-s
Mark 6:36: send the people off to the *f.*
Luke 9:12. into the villages and *f.* round about
15:15. sent him on to his *f.* to mind the pigs.
15:25. the elder son was out on the *f.*

farmer
Mat. 13:27. the *f.* men went to their master
2 Tim. 2:6. the *f.* who gives his labour
Jam. 5:7. the *f.* looking for the precious crop

farmstead-s
Mark 6:56. wherever he went, to *f.*

farther
John 6:1. Jesus withdrew to the *f.* shore
Acts 1:12. no *f.* than a Sabbath days' journey

farthest
Mat. 24:31. from the *f.* bounds of heaven
Mark 13:27. from the *f.* bounds of earth to the *f.* bounds of heaven
Acts 13:47. a means of salvation to earth's *f.* bounds

farthing
Luke 12:59. till you have paid the last *f.*

fashion-ed
Heb. 1:1. he spoke in fragmentary and varied *f.*
11:3. the universe was *f.* by the word of God
Rev. 9:20. the gods their hands had *f.*

fast
Mat. 26:50. seized Jesus, and held him *f.*
Mark 6:53. to land at Gennesaret, where they made *f.*
14:46. they seized him and held him *f.*
Luke 8:15. the hearing of the word, hold it *f.*
19:6. he climbed down as *f.* as he could
John 21:18. a stranger will bind you *f.*
Acts 11:23. hold *f.* to the Lord
13:43. hold *f.* to the grace of God
1 Cor. 15:2. do you still hold *f.* the Gospel
2 Cor. 9:9. his benevolence stands *f.* for ever
Eph. 4:3. make *f.* with bonds of peace
Col. 4:12. that you may stand *f.*
1 Pet. 5:12. the true grace of God. In this stand *f.*
Rev. 3:10. you have kept my command and stood *f.*

fasten-ed-ing
Mat. 27:35. *f.* him to the cross
Mark 15:24. then they *f.* him to the cross
Luke 12:35. be ready for action, with belts *f.*
John 19:19. an inscription to be *f.* to the cross
21:18. when you were young you *f.* your belt

fate
Luke 13:2. these Galileans suffered this *f.*
Acts 20:26. no man's *f.* can be laid at my door
2 Cor. 4:9. we are never abandoned to our *f.*
Jam. 5:1. the miserable *f.* descending on you

fateful
Luke 12:56. how is it you cannot interpret this *f.* hour

father
Mat. 1:2. Abraham was the *f.* of Isaac
1:6. Jesse was the *f.* of King David
1:11. Josiah was the *f.* of Jeconiah
1:12. Jeconiah was the *f.* of Shealtiel
21:30. the *f.* came to the second
Luke 2:33. the child's *f.* and mother
John 1:13. or by the fleshly desire of a human *f.*
6:40. it is my *F.* will
8:47. he who has God for his *f.*

2 Cor. 6:13. may a *f.* speak so to his children
Tit. 1:6. the *f.* of children who are believers
Philem. 10. whose *f.* I have become in this prison

fatten-ing
Jam. 5:5. *f.* yourselves like cattle

fault
Acts 7:27. the man who was at *f.* pushed him away
23:9. we can find no *f.* with this man
1 Thess. 5:23. without *f.* when our Lord Jesus Christ comes
1 Tim. 6:14. irreproachably and without *f.*
Jam. 1:27. without stain or *f.* in the sight of God

faultless
John 8:7. who is *f.* shall throw the first stone
Phil. 2:15. *f.* children of God
3:6. in legal rectitude, *f.*
1 Thess. 3:13. holy and *f.*
Rev. 14:5. no lie was found in their lips; they are *f.*

favour-ed
Mat. 3:17. my Beloved, on whom my *f.* rests
12:18. my beloved, on whom my *f.* rests
16:17. Simon son of Jonah, you are *f.*
17:5. on whom my *f.* rests
20:20. she bowed low and begged a *f.*
Mark 1:11. on thee my *f.* rests
10:35. Master, we should like you to do us a *f.*
15:8. asking for the usual *f.*
Luke 1:58. great *f.* the Lord had shown her
2:14. for men on whom his *f.* rests
2:40. God's *f.* was upon him
3:22. on thee my *f.* rests
4:19. the year of the Lord's *f.*
7:4. he deserves this *f.* from you
Acts 3:14. as a *f.* the release of a murderer
24:27. wishing to curry *f.* with the Jews
27:12. in *f.* of putting out to sea
Rom. 4:4. his wages are not 'counted' as a *f.*
2 Cor. 1:11. the gracious *f.* God has shown towards us
6:2. in the hour of my *f.* . . . the hour of *f.*
Gal. 1:10. *f.* with men? If I still sought men's *f.*
2:9. the *f.* thus bestowed upon me
Eph. 6:6. to curry *f.* with men
Col. 3:22. outward show of service, to curry *f.*

1 Thess. 2:4. not curry *f.* with men; we
  seek only the *f.* of God
1 Pet. 5:5. *f.* the humble
2 Pet. 1:17. on whom my *f.* rests
Jude 4. the free *f.* of our God
  16. they court *f.* to gain their ends
Rev. 2:6. you have this in your *f.*

favourite-s
Acts 10:34 ⎱ God has no *f.*
Rom. 2:11 ⎰
Eph. 6:9. Master in heaven, and he has
  no *f.*
Col. 3:25. dishonesty will be requited,
  and he has no *f.*

fear-s-ing
Mat. 4:6. for *f.* you should strike your
  foot
  14:30. saw the strength of the gale he
  was seized with *f.*
Mark 16:6. *f.* nothing
Luke 4:11. for *f.* you should strike your
  foot
  8:12. for *f.* they should believe
  8:25. in *f.* and astonishment
  12:4. do not *f.* those who kill the body
John 3:20. for *f.* their practices should
  be shown up
  12:42. for *f.* of being banned from the
  synagogue
  14:27. banish your *f.*
Acts 16:29. trembling with *f.*
  18:9. have no *f.*; go on with your
  preaching
  27:42. for *f.* that any should swim
  away
Rom. 13:3. no *f.* of the authorities
  13:4. then you will have cause to *f.*
  them
  13:5. not merely by *f.* of retribution
1 Cor. 9:27. for *f.* that after preaching
  to others
2 Cor. 5:11. with this *f.* of the Lord
  before our eyes
Gal. 4:11. *f.* that all the pains I spent on
  you
Col. 3:21. for *f.* they grow disheartened
1 Thess. 3:5. *f.* that the tempter might
  have tempted you
1 Tim. 3:6. for *f.* the sin of conceit
Heb. 2:1. for *f.* of drifting from our
  course
Jam. 5:12. for *f.* that you expose yourselves to judgement
1 Pet. 3:6. if you do good and show no *f.*
  3:14. have no *f.* of them

fearfully
Rev. 16:9. they were *f.* burned

fearless-ly
Phil. 1:14. to speak the word of God *f.*
1 Thess. 2:2. declared the gospel of God
  to you frankly and *f.*
Heb. 3:6. *f.* and keep our hope high

feast-ed
Mat. 8:11. to *f.* with Abraham
  22:2. a king who prepared a *f.*
  22:4. I have prepared this *f.* for you
  22:8. the wedding-*f.* is ready
Luke 13:29. the *f.* in the kingdom of
  God
  14:8. asked by someone to a wedding-*f.*
  14:15. the *f.* in the kingdom of God
  15:23. let us have a *f.* to celebrate the
  day
  15:29. for a *f.* with my friends
  16:19. *f.* in great magnificence every
  day
Acts 7:41. a *f.* in honour of the thing
  their hands had made
1 Cor. 10:7. the people sat down to *f.*

feeble
1 Cor. 11:30. that is why many of you
  are *f.* and sick
2 Cor. 10:1. *f.* (you say) when I am face
  to face with you

feed-fed
Mat. 7:6. do not *f.* your pearls to pigs
  15:33. bread enough to *f.* such a
  crowd
Mark 1:6. he *f.* on locusts and wild
  honey
Luke 6:25. alas for you who are well-*f.*
  now
  23:29. the breasts that never *f.* one
John 6:5. where are we to buy bread to
  f. these people
Jam. 3:6. its flames are *f.* by hell

feel-s-ing-ings-felt
Mat. 12:1. his disciples *f.* hungry
  20:25. make them *f.* the weight of
  authority
  21:18. he *f.* hungry
Mark 8:2. I *f.* sorry for all these people
  10:42. make them *f.* the weight of
  authority
  11:12. he *f.* hungry
  12:12. they were afraid of popular *f.*
Luke 8:46. I *f.* that power had gone out
  from me
  15:14. he began to *f.* the pinch
  24:32. *f.* our hearts on fire as he talked
  with us
Acts 13:50. the Jews stirred up *f.* among
  the women
  27:27. the sailors *f.* that land was
  getting nearer
1 Cor. 7:36. *f.* that he is not behaving
  properly
  10:12. if you *f.* sure that you are
  standing firm, beware
  12:25. *f.* the same concern for one
  another
2 Cor. 1:9. we *f.* in our hearts
  1:15. I *f.* so confident about all this
  7:9. your *f.* were wounded

2 Cor. 13:3. makes his power *f.* among you
Eph. 4:31. and bad *f.* of every kind
Phil. 1:7. I should *f.* like this about you all
2:2. thinking and *f.* alike
2:25. I *f.* also I must send our brother
1 Thess. 2:6. we might have made our weight *f.*
2 Thess. 3:4. we *f.* perfect confidence about you
1 Pet. 1:22. you *f.* sincere affection
3:8. be one in thought and *f.*
4:16. he should *f.* it no disgrace
1 John 1:1. *f.* it with our own hands
Rev. 7:16. they shall never again *f.* hunger or thirst

feet
Mat. 14:33. the men in the boat fell at his *f.*
15:25. the woman came and fell at his *f.*
18:26. the man fell prostrate at his master's *f.*
22:44. until I put your enemies under your *f.*
Mark 1:31. helped her to her *f.*
3:11. fall at his *f.* and cry aloud
5:33. fell at his *f.* and told him
9:27. raised him to his *f.*
Luke 5:25 ⎫ he rose to his *f.*
5:28 ⎭
8:28. fell at his *f.* shouting
8:47. came trembling and fell at his *f.*
10:11. dust of your town that clings to our *f.*
John 5:8. rise to your *f.*
Acts 3:8. stood on his *f.*
5:34. rose to his *f.*, a Pharisee called Gamaliel
8:9. swept the Samaritans off their *f.*
9:41. helped her to her *f.*
10:26. Peter raised him to his *f.*
14:20. he got to his *f.* and went into the city
Rom. 6:4. set our *f.* upon the new path of life

felicity
1 Tim. 1:11. the glory of God in his eternal *f.*
6:15. God who in eternal *f.* alone holds sway

fell
Mat. 2:16. he *f.* into a passion
8:16. when evening *f.*
13:23. seed that *f.* into good soil
13:57. they *f.* foul of him
14:33. *f.* at his feet, exclaiming
17:14. *f.* on his knees before him
18:26. the man *f.* prostrate at his master's feet
20:8. when evening *f.*
27:45. darkness *f.* over the whole land

27:57. when evening *f.*
28:17. they *f.* prostrate before him
Mark 6:3. so they *f.* foul of him
10:22. at these words his face *f.*
15:33. darkness *f.* over the whole land
Luke 1:9. it *f.* to his lot, by priestly custom
7:16. deep awe *f.* upon them all
15:14. a severe famine *f.*
16:25. good things *f.* to you while you were alive
20:26. they *f.* silent
Acts 5:11. great awe *f.* upon the whole church
9:37. she *f.* ill and died
15:12. the whole company *f.* silent
17:10. as soon as darkness *f.*
18:2. he *f.* in with a Jew named Aquila
23:7. *f.* out among themselves
1 Tim. 2:14. yielding to deception, *f.* into sin
Jam. 5:17. not a drop *f.* on the land

fellow-s
Mat. 5:16. shed light among your *f.*
Luke 5:21. who is this *f.* with his blasphemous talk
7:39. if this *f.* were a real prophet
14:10. your *f.*-guests will see the respect
15:2. this *f.*,' they said, 'welcomes sinners
16:15. impress your *f.*-men with your righteousness
19:14. his *f.*-citizens hated him
John 9:16. this *f.* is no man of God
9:24. we know that this *f.* is a sinner
19:32. the first of his *f.*-victims
Acts 2:14. *f.* Jews
7:23. the conditions of his *f.*-countrymen
7:25. he thought his *f.*-countrymen would understand
11:29. for the relief of their *f.*-Christians
16:40. they met their *f.*-Christians
19:26. hear how this *f.* Paul
21:28. this is the *f.* who spreads his doctrine.
22:5. our *f.*-Jews at Damascus
26:32. the *f.* could have been discharged
28:14. there we found *f.*-Christians
Rom. 2:1. judging your *f.*-man
2:21. who teach your *f.*-man
8:17. Christ's *f.*-heirs
16:1. Phoebe, a *f.*-Christian
16:3. Prisca and Aquila, my *f.*-workers
16:7 ⎫ my *f.*-countrymen
16:21 ⎭
1 Cor. 2:15. judgement by his *f.*-men
3:9. we are God's *f.*-workers

2 Cor. 1:12. dealings with our *f.*-men
4:2. common conscience of our *f.*-men
8:4. service to their *f.*-Christians
11:26. dangers from my *f.*-country-men
Phil. 1:14. confidence to most of our *f.*-Christians
1 Thess. 2:15. enemies of their *f.*-men
4:10. love towards all your *f.*-Christians
Tit. 3:8. useful to their *f.*-men
Heb. 8:11. saying to brother and *f.*-citizen
13:1. never cease to love your *f.*-Christians
Jam. 3:9. our *f.*-men who are made in God's likeness
1 Pet. 5:1. as a *f.*-elder
3 John 5. our *f.*-Christians

fellowship
John 13:8. you are not in *f.* with me
Acts 11:26. in *f.* with the congregation there
Rom. 15:17. in the *f.* of Christ Jesus
16:2. in the *f.* of Christ
16:8. in the *f.* of the Lord
16:11. who are in the Lord's *f.*
1 Cor. 5:12. you are judges within the *f.*
7:39. the marriage is within the Lord's *f.*
10:2. baptism into the *f.* of Moses
11:11. in Christ's *f.*
15:18. who have died within Christ's *f.*
2 Cor. 13:14. *f.* in the Holy Spirit
Gal. 2:4. in the *f.* of Christ Jesus
Phil. 2:29. in the *f.* of the Lord
4:2. agree together in the Lord's *f.*
4:21. in the *f.* of Christ
1 Thess. 4:1. by our *f.* with the Lord Jesus
5:12. in the Lord's *f.* are your leaders
Philem. 6. your *f.* with us in our common faith

fervently
Acts 12:5. the church kept praying *f.* for him

fervour
Acts 18:25. full of spiritual *f.*

festival-s
Mat. 26:5. it must not be during the *f.*
27:15. at the *f.* season
Mark 14:1. the *f.* of Passover
14:2. it must not be during the *f.*
15:6. at the *f.* season
Luke 2:41. every year for the Passover *f.*
22:1. the *f.* of Unleavened Bread
John 4:45. all that he did at the *f.* in Jerusalem; they had been at the *f.*
5:1. for one of the Jewish *f.*
6:4. Passover, the great Jewish *f.*
7:8. go to the *f.* yourselves. I am not going up to this *f.*

7:10. his brothers had gone to the *f.*
7:11. the Jews were looking for him at the *f.*
7:14. the *f.* was already half over
7:37. and greatest day of the *f.*
11:55. to purify themselves before the *f.*
11:56. perhaps he is not coming to the *f.*
12:1. before the Passover *f.*
12:12. the great body of pilgrims who had come to the *f.*
12:20. to worship at the *f.*
13:1. it was before the Passover *f.*
13:29. what was needed for the *f.*
Acts 12:3. during the *f.* of Unleavened Bread
1 Cor. 5:8. we who observe the *f.*
Col. 2:16. or over the observance of *f.*

festive
Luke 2:43. when the *f.* season was over

festivity-ies
Luke 15:24. and the *f.* began

fetch-ed
Mat. 24:17. he must not come down to *f.* his goods
27:48. *f.* a sponge
Mark 12:15. *f.* me a silver piece
13:15. into the house to *f.* anything
Luke 15:22. *f.* a robe, my best one
Acts 5:21. sent to the jail to *f.* the prisoners
5:26. with the police and *f.* them

fetters
Acts 8:23. wear the *f.* of sin
16:26. found their *f.* unfastened
Heb. 11:36. even *f.* and prison bars

feud
Luke 23:12. a standing *f.* between them

few
Mat. 18:28. owed him a *f.* pounds
Luke 15:13. a *f.* days later the younger son
24:18. happened there in the last *f.* days
Acts 1:5. within the next *f.* days
Rom. 11:7. the selected *f.* have achieved it
1 Cor. 1:26. *f.* of you are men of wisdom, by any human standard; *f.* are powerful

fidelity
Rom. 1:31. no *f.* to their plighted word
Gal. 5:22. goodness, *f.*, gentleness
1 Tim. 4:12. in love, *f.*, and purity
6:11. pursue justice, piety, *f.*

field-s
Mark 11:8. brushwood which they had cut in the *f.*

Gal. 6:8. sows seed in the *f.* of his lower nature, he will reap from it a harvest of corruption, but if he sows in the *f.* of the Spirit

Jam. 1:10. disappear like the flower of the *f.*

1 Pet. 1:24. their splendour like the flower of the *f.*

fierce-ly

Mark 9:26. crying aloud and racking him *f.*

Luke 11:53. Pharisees began to assail him *f.*

John 6:52. a *f.* dispute among the Jews

Acts 15:2. *f.* dissension and controversy

27:14. a *f.* wind, the 'North-easter'

Heb. 10:27. a *f.* fire which will consume God's enemies

Jude 13. *f.* waves of the sea

Rev. 14:8 ⎱ the *f.* wine of her fornica-
18:3 ⎰ tion

fiery

Heb. 1:7. his ministers a *f.* flame

Rev. 9:17. they wore breastplates, *f.* red

fight-s-ing

Acts 7:26. the next day he came upon two of them *f.*

7:51. you always *f.* against the Holy Spirit

Rom. 7:23. *f.* against the law that my reason approves

15:30. be my allies in the *f.*

2 Cor. 10:3. we *f.* our battles

Gal. 5:15. *f.* one another, tooth and nail

5:17. the Spirit *f.* against it

Eph. 6:12. our *f.* is not against human foes

1 Tim. 1:18. so *f.* gallantly, armed with faith

Rev. 13:4. who can *f.* against it

19:18. commanders and *f.* men

figure-s

John 16:25. I have been using *f.* of speech; a time is coming when I shall no longer use *f.*

16:29. this is no *f.* of speech

fill-ed

Mat. 9:8. people were *f.* with awe at the sight

9:33. *f.* with amazement the on-lookers said

10:9. provide no gold, silver, or copper to *f.* your purse

13:26. the corn sprouted and began to *f.* out

17:23. they were *f.* with grief

27:54. they were *f.* with awe

Mark 10:32. the disciples were *f.* with awe

John 5:20. greater yet, to *f.* you with wonder

20:20. saw the Lord, they were *f.* with joy

1 Cor. 4:18. persons who are *f.* with self-importance

Phil. 2:2. *f.* up my cup of happiness

4:8. *f.* all your thoughts with these things

Col. 3:15. be *f.* with gratitude

Rev. 16:19. the cup which was *f.* with the fierce wine of his vengeance

filth

Mat. 23:27. all kinds of *f.*

final-ly

Mat. 26:60. *f.* two men alleged

27:31. *f.*, when the mockery was over

27:64. the *f.* deception will be worse than the first

Mark 12:22. *f.* the woman died

Rom. 5:9. saved through him from *f.* retribution

9:28. the Lord's sentence on the land will be summary and *f.*

Eph. 4:30. the day of our *f.* liberation

Phil. 3:11. I may *f.* arrive at the resurrection

2 Thess. 2:3. the *f.* rebellion against God

2 Tim. 3:1. the *f.* age of this world

Heb. 1:2. in this the *f.* age he has spoken

6:11. until your hope is *f.* realized

Jude 18. in the *f.* age there will be men

find-s-ing

Mat. 5:4. they shall *f.* consolation

10:36. *f.* his enemies under his own roof

11:6. happy is the man who does not *f.* me a stumbling-block

15:33. *f.* bread enough to feed such a crowd

19:23. a rich man will *f.* it hard to enter

24:51. he will *f.* his place among the hypocrites

26:59. tried to *f.* some allegation against Jesus

Mark 16:16. will *f.* salvation

Luke 7:23. happy is the man who does not *f.* me a stumbling-block

9:12. to *f.* food and lodging

12:46. *f.* his place among the faithless

14:6. they could *f.* no reply

17:15. *f.* himself cured

22:16. *f.* its fulfilment in the kingdom of God

22:37. must *f.* fulfilment in me

John 4:27. to *f.* him talking with a woman

7:52. you will *f.* that prophets do not come from Galilee

16:33. in me you may *f.* peace

Acts 3:25. all the families on earth shall *f.* blessing

9:11. you will *f.* him at prayer

Acts 12:19. failed to *f.* him.
22:24. *f.* out what reason there was for such an outcry
24:25. when I *f.* it convenient
25:20. *f.* myself out of my depth
Rom. 8:4. the commandment of the law may *f.* fulfilment
15:31. may *f.* acceptance with God's people
1 Cor. 1:21. the world failed to *f.* him by its wisdom
9:27. I should *f.* myself rejected
2 Cor. 4:3. our gospel be found veiled, the only people who *f.* it so
10:12. to *f.* in themselves their own standard
12:9. prefer to *f.* my joy
Gal. 1:6. to *f.* you turning so quickly away
3:8. in you all nations shall *f.* blessing
Eph. 4:26. do not let sunset *f.* you still nursing it
6:10. *f.* your strength in the Lord
Phil. 3:9. *f.* myself incorporate in him
4:11. learned to *f.* resources in myself
1 Thess. 3:5. to *f.* out about your faith
2 Thess. 2:10. love of the truth, so as to *f.* salvation
2:13. God chose you to *f.* salvation
1 Tim. 1:16. Jesus Christ might *f.* in me the first occasion for displaying all his patience
2:4. whose will it is that all men should *f.* salvation
5:22. *f.* yourself responsible for other people's misdeeds
2 Tim. 4:11. I *f.* him a useful assistant
Tit. 2:8. when he *f.* not a word to say to our discredit
Heb. 9:18. thus we *f.* that the former covenant
10:38. by faith my righteous servant shall *f.* life
11:16. we *f.* them longing for a better country
12:17. he strove, to the point of tears, to *f.* one
Jam. 1:10. the wealthy brother must *f.* his pride in being brought low
1:25. that is the man who by acting will *f.* happiness
1 Pet. 1:11. they tried to *f.* out what was the time

fine-st
Mat. 13:45. looking out for *f.* pearls
26:10. it is a *f.* thing she has done for me
Mark 13:1. what *f.* buildings
14:6. it is a *f.* thing she has done for me
Luke 21:5. the temple and the *f.* stones
Acts 7:20. Moses was born. He was a *f.* child

Rom. 14:21. it is a *f.* thing to abstain
1 Cor. 2:1. without display of *f.* words
3:12. gold, silver, and *f.* stone
Gal. 4:18. a *f.* thing to deserve an honest envy
Heb. 7:4. a tithe of the *f.* of the spoil
11:23. they saw what a *f.* child he was
Jam. 5:2. your *f.* clothes are moth-eaten
1 Pet. 2:19. it is a *f.* thing if a man endure
2:20. your fortitude is a *f.* thing
3 John 5. you show a *f.* loyalty
Rev. 15:6. they were robed in *f.* linen

finger
Luke 15:22. put a ring on his *f.*

finish-ed
Mat. 7:28. when Jesus had *f.* this discourse
11:1. when Jesus had *f.* giving his twelve disciples
14:34. they *f.* the crossing
23:32. *f.* off what your fathers began
Mark 6:53. so they *f.* the crossing
15:20. when they had *f.* their mockery
Luke 5:4. when he had *f.* speaking
7:1. when he had *f.* addressing
11:37. when he had *f.* speaking
Acts 15:13. when they had *f.* speaking
20:36. as he *f.* speaking, he knelt down
Rom. 15:28. when I have *f.* this business
1 Cor. 13:11. I had *f.* with childish things
2 Cor. 8:11. go on and *f.* it
1 Pet. 4:1. he has *f.* with sin

fire-d
Mat. 22:7. set their town on *f.*
Luke 16:24. I am in agony in this *f.*
24:32. did we not feel our hearts on *f.*
2 Cor. 9:2. most of them have been *f.* by your zeal
Heb. 10:27. a fierce *f.* which will consume God's enemies

firelight
Luke 22:56. saw him sitting in the *f.*

firm-er-ly
Luke 1:54. *f.* in his promise to our forefathers
21:19. by standing *f.* you will win true life
22:28. stood *f.* by me in my times of trial
Rom. 3:31. placing law itself on a *f.* footing
4:21. the *f.* conviction of his power
12:12. in trouble stand *f.*
1 Cor. 1:8. he will keep you *f.*
1:10. be *f.* joined in unity
10:12. if you feel sure that you are standing *f.*
15:58. stand *f.* and immovable
16:13. stand *f.* in the faith

2 Cor. 1:7. our hope for you is *f.* grounded
Gal. 5:1. free men. Stand *f.*
Eph. 3:17. with deep roots and *f.* foundations
 6:11. stand *f.* against the devices of the devil
 6:14. stand *f.,* I say
 6:15. to give you *f.* footing
Phil. 1:27. standing *f.,* one in spirit
 4:1. stand thus *f.* in the Lord
Col. 1:23. *f.* on your foundations
 2:5. the *f.* front which your faith in Christ presents
1 Thess. 3:2. stand *f.* for the faith
 3:8. stand *f.* in the Lord
 3:13. may he make your hearts *f.*
2 Thess. 2:15. stand *f.,* then, brothers
1 Tim. 3:9. a *f.* hold on the deep truths
2 Tim. 2:19. a foundation, and it stands *f.*
Heb. 3:14. original confidence *f.* to the end
 10:23. let us be *f.* and unswerving
 10:32. great sufferings and held *f.*
 11:10. the city with *f.* foundations
Jam. 5:11. those happy who stood *f.'* You have all heard how Job stood *f.*
1 Pet. 5:9. stand up to him, *f.* in faith
 5:10. strengthen you on a *f.* foundation

first
Mat. 6:24. either he will hate the *f.* and love the second, or he will be devoted to the *f.*
 15:20. eat without *f.* washing his hands, that cannot defile him
 20:27. whoever would be *f.* must be the willing slave of all
 27:28. *f.* they stripped him
Mark 6:33. arrived there *f.*
 7:4. they never eat without *f.* washing
 10:44. whoever wants to be *f.* must be the willing slave of all
Luke 2:36. after she was *f.* married
 16:13. he will hate the *f.* and love the second, or will be devoted to the *f.*
 19:13. *f.* he called ten of his servants
John 2:10. everyone serves the best wine *f.*
 2:11. this deed at Cana-in-Galilee is the *f.* of the signs
 7:51. unless we have *f.* given him a hearing
 8:9. one by one they went away, the eldest *f.*
 15:18. if the world hates you, it hated me *f.*
 15:27. you have been with me from the *f.*
 16:4. I did not tell you this at *f.*
Acts. 1:1. in the *f.* part of my work
 16:12. a city of the *f.* rank

Rom. 3:2. in the *f.* place, the Jews were entrusted
 9:23. from the *f.* had been prepared
 13:11. when *f.* we believed
1 Cor. 14:1. put love *f.*
 15:36. unless it has *f.* died
2 Cor. 1:15. intended to come *f.* of all to you
 5:18. from *f.* to last this has been the work of God
 10:14. we were the *f.* to reach Corinth in preaching
Phil. 2:6. the divine nature was his from the *f.*
Col. 1:5. the true Gospel *f.* came to you
1 Tim. 1:15. among them I stand *f.*
 1:18. which *f.* pointed you out to me
Heb. 10:8. *f.* he says
 10:15. he *f.* says
 13:7. who *f.* spoke God's message to you
2 Pet. 3:6. by water that *f.* world was destroyed
1 John 3:8. the devil has been a sinner from the *f.*
Rev. 6:1. the Lamb broke the *f.* of the seven seals
 9:12. the *f.* woe has now passed

first-born
Luke 2:23. every *f.*-born male shall be deemed to belong to the Lord

fish
Mat. 13:47. *f.* of every kind were caught
 13:48. the good *f.* into pails

fist-s
Mat. 26:67. beat him with their *f.*
Mark 14:65. struck him with their *f.*

fit-s-ting
Mat. 3:11. I am not *f.* to take off his shoes
 17:15. he is an epileptic and has bad *f.*
 23:15. twice as *f.* for hell as you are
Mark 1:7. I am not *f.* to unfasten his shoes
Luke 1:17. *f.* for the Lord
 3:16. I am not *f.* to unfasten his shoes
 15:19 ⎰ no longer *f.* to be called your
 15:21 ⎱ son
Acts 4:10. stands here before you *f.* and well
 13:25. whose shoes I am not *f.* to unfasten
Rom. 1:28. they have not seen *f.* to acknowledge God
 12:1. *f.* for his acceptance
1 Cor. 7:25. by God's mercy is *f.* to be trusted.
 11:13. is it *f.* for a woman to pray to God bare-headed?
 15:9. not *f.* to be called an apostle
2 Cor. 6:14. they are no *f.* mates for you
Gal. 5:20. *f.* of rage

Col. 1:12. *f.* to share the heritage
1 Thess. 2:4. *f.* to be entrusted with the Gospel
1 Tim. 2:6. at the *f.* time, proof of the divine purpose
   4:7. godless myths, *f.* only for old women
2 Tim. 2:21. *f.* for any honourable purpose
Heb. 2:10. it was clearly *f.* that God
   7:26. such a high priest does indeed *f.* our condition
   9:14. *f.* us for the service of the living God

five
Mat. 25:11. the other *f.* came back
Luke 16:6. make it *f.* hundred
Acts 7:14. seventy-*f.* persons altogether

fix-es-ed
Luke 4:20. all eyes in the synagogue were *f.* on him
John 19:29. a sponge with the wine, *f.* it on a javelin
Acts 3:4. Peter *f.* his eyes on him
   6:15. the Council *f.* their eyes on him
   17:26. he *f.* the epochs of their history
   17:31. he has *f.* the day on which he will have the world judged
   23:1. Paul *f.* his eyes on the Council
   28:23. so they *f.* a day
Rom. 9:9. at the time *f.* I will come
2 Cor. 1:10. he on whom our hope is *f.*
   4:18. meanwhile our eyes are *f.*
Gal. 4:2. until the date *f.* by his father
1 Tim. 6:17. not to *f.* their hopes on so uncertain a thing as money
Heb. 2:13. I will keep my trust *f.* on him
   4:7. God *f.* another day
   11:26. his eyes were *f.* upon the coming day
   12:2. our eyes *f.* on Jesus
1 Pet. 1:13. *f.* your hopes on the gift of grace
   1:21. your faith and hope are *f.* on God
   3:5. women who *f.* their hopes on him

flag-ged
Rev. 2:3. borne up in my cause and never *f.*

flame-s-ing
Acts 2:3. tongues like *f.* of fire
Eph. 6:16. the *f.* arrows of the evil one
2 Tim. 1:6. stir into *f.* the gift of God
Jam. 3:6. its *f.* are fed by hell
2 Pet. 3:10. the elements will disintegrate in *f.*
   3:12. melt the elements in *f.*
Jude 23. snatch them from the *f.*
Rev. 4:5. seven *f.* torches
   8:10. *f.* like a torch
   14:10. tormented in sulphurous *f.*
   16:8. to burn men with its *f.*

   19:20. the lake of fire with its sulphurous *f.*
   21:8. the lake that burns with sulphurous *f.*

flash-es-ed-ing
Mat. 24:27. *f.* as far as the west
Luke 4:5. in a *f.* all the kingdoms of the world
   11:36. when a lamp *f.* its rays upon you
   17:24. the lightning-*f.* that lights up
Acts 9:3. a light *f.* from the sky
   22:6. a great light *f.* from the sky
1 Cor. 15:52. we shall all be changed in a *f.*
Rev. 4:5. from the throne went out *f.* of lightning
   11:19. there came *f.* of lightning
   16:18. there followed *f.* of lightning

flask-s
Mat. 25:4. took *f.* of oil with their lamps
Luke 7:37. oil of myrrh in a small *f.*

flawless
Phil. 1:10. on the day of Christ you will be *f.*

flesh-ly
John 1:13. the *f.* desire of a human father
Eph. 2:14. in his own body of *f.* and blood

flew
Acts 19:16. the man with the evil spirit *f.* at them

flight
Rev. 4:7. like an eagle in *f.*

fling-ing
Mat. 5:29. tear it out and *f.* it away
   5:30 }
   18:8 } cut it off and *f.* it away
   18:9. tear it out and *f.* it away
   25:30. *f.* the useless servant out into the dark
Acts 7:58. *f.* him out of the city
   22:23. *f.* dust in the air

flippant
Eph. 5:4. no coarse, stupid, or *f.* talk

flock-ed-ing
Mat. 3:5. they *f.* to him from Jerusalem
   15:30. crowds *f.* to him
Mark 1:5. they *f.* to him
Luke 21:38. the people *f.* to listen to him
John 3:26. crowds are *f.* to him
   10:12. the wolf harries the *f.*
   10:16. one *f.*, one shepherd
   10:26. you are not sheep of my *f.*
Acts 5:16. *f.* in, bringing those who were ill

flog-ged-ging
Mat. 10:17. they will *f.* you in the synagogues
20:19. to be mocked and *f.*
23:34. others you will *f.*
27:26. he had Jesus *f.*
Mark 10:34. *f.* and killed
13:9. you will be *f.* in synagogues
15:15. he had Jesus *f.*
Luke 12:47. will be *f.* severely
12:48. will be *f.* less severely
18:33. they will *f.* him and kill him
23:16⎤
23:22⎦ let him off with a *f.*
John 19:1. Pilate now took Jesus and had him *f.*
Acts 5:40. sent for the apostles and had them *f.*
16:22. ordered them to be *f.*
16:37. they gave us a public *f.*
22:19. *f.* them in every synagogue
22:24. to examine him by *f.*
22:25. *f.* a man who is a Roman citizen
2 Cor. 6:5. *f.*, imprisoned, mobbed
Heb. 11:36. had to face jeers and *f.*

flood-ed
Rom. 5:5. God's love has *f.* our inmost heart
2 Cor. 9:12. a *f.* of thanksgiving to God

floor
Acts 20:9. fell from the third *f.* to the ground
Jam. 2:3. you may sit here on the *f.*

flour
Mat. 13:33. half a hundredweight of *f.*
Luke 13:21. *f.* till it was all leavened
Rev. 6:6. a whole day's wage for a quart of *f.*

flourish-es
Mat. 6:2. with a *f.* of trumpets
1 Cor. 12:26. if one *f.*, they all rejoice together

flout-s-ing
Acts 17:7. they all *f.* the Emperor's laws
1 Cor. 4:6. patronize one and *f.* the other
1 Thess. 4:8. who *f.* these rules is *f.*, not man, but God
1 Tim. 1:10. *f.* the wholesome teaching
2 Pet. 2:10. they *f.* authority
Jude 8. to *f.* authority

flow-s-ing
John 19:34. there was a *f.* of blood and water
Acts 2:33. all that you now see and hear *f.* from him
1 Cor. 11:14. *f.* locks disgrace a man
Rev. 14:20. for two hundred miles around blood *f.*
22:1. *f.* from the throne of God

flung
Mat. 15:30. they *f.* them down at his feet
21:39. *f.* him out of the vineyard
Mark 5:6. *f.* himself down before him
12:8. *f.* his body out of the vineyard
Luke 15:20. ran to meet him, *f.* his arms round him
20:12. they wounded and *f.* out
20:15. they *f.* him out of the vineyard
Acts 16:23. they *f.* them into prison
1 Pet. 4:14. if Christ's name is *f.* in your teeth as an insult
Rev. 12:4. *f.* them to the earth
20:10. *f.* into the lake of fire and sulphur, where the beast and the false prophet had been *f.*
20:14. Death and Hades were *f.* into the lake of fire
20:15. into it were *f.* any whose names

flute
Mat. 9:23. saw the *f.*-players
1 Cor. 14:7. that produce sounds—a *f.*
Rev. 18:22. *f.*-players and trumpeters

fly-ies-ing
Acts 10:12. whatever walks or crawls or *f.*
11:6. things that crawl or *f.*
1 Cor. 16:7. I do not want this to be a *f.* visit

foal
Mat. 21:2. with her *f.* beside her
21:7. brought the donkey and her *f.*

foes
Eph. 6:12. our fight is not against human *f.*

fold-ed
John 10:9. who comes into the *f.* through me
Acts 20:37. they *f.* Paul in their arms

folk
Mark 5:19. go home to your own *f.*
Acts 8:7. crippled *f.* were cured
Rom. 12:16. go about with humble *f.*

follow-s-ed-ing
Mat. 10:5. with the *f.* instructions
19:6. it *f.* that they are no longer two
23:3. do not *f.* their practice
Mark. 1:20. they went off to *f.* him
10:1. he *f.* his usual practice
10:8. it *f.* that they are no longer two individuals
11:12. on the *f.* day
Luke 1:2. *f.* the traditions handed down
21:8. do not *f.* them
21:9. the end does not *f.* immediately
John 15:20. they will *f.* your teaching as little as they have *f.* mine
Acts 5:36. his whole *f.* was broken up
5:37. his whole *f.* was scattered
9:2. who *f.* the new way

Acts 13:44. on the *f.* Sabbath
16:21. to adopt and *f.*
17:2. *f.* his usual practice Paul
20:15. on the *f.* day
20:18. he spoke as *f.*
20:30. break away and *f.* them
21:21. *f.* our way of life
22:30. the *f.* day
27:44. the rest were to *f.*
Rom. 5:12. mark what *f.*
5:16. *f.* upon the one offence . . . the act of grace, *f.* upon so many misdeeds
5:18. it *f.*, then
7:7. what *f.*
8:12. it *f.*, my friends
11:7. what *f.*
1 Cor. 4:17. the way of life in Christ which I *f.*
10:33. *f.* my example as I *f.* Christ's
11:27. it *f.* that
15:16. it *f.* that Christ was not raised
15:18. it *f.* also that those who have died
16:1. you should *f.* my directions
2 Cor. 12:18. followed the same course
Gal. 1:6. *f.* a different gospel
5:7. hindered you from *f.* the truth
Eph. 2:2. you *f.* the evil ways
Col. 2:22. to *f.* merely human injunctions
3:7. the ways you yourselves *f.*
1 Thess. 4:1. already *f.* it
2 Thess. 3:6. does not *f.* the tradition
1 Tim. 1:18. *f.* that prophetic utterance
4:6. the sound instruction which you have *f.*
2 Tim. 3:10. have *f.*, step by step, my teaching
4:3. will *f.* their own fancy
Heb. 4:11. *f.* this evil example
2 Pet. 2:10. *f.* their abominable lusts
1 John 5:2. it *f.* that when we love God
2 John 6. *f.* the commands of God
Jude 7. *f.* unnatural lusts
16. they *f.* their lusts
18. *f.* their own godless lusts
Rev. 16:18. there *f.* flashes of lightning

follower-s
Mat. 22:16. some of their *f.*
Mark. 8:34. anyone who wishes to be a *f.* of mine
9:41. *f.* of the Messiah
16:10. his mourning and sorrowful *f.*
Luke 9:23. wishes to be a *f.* of mine
22:49. When his *f.* saw what was coming
John 18:36. my *f.* would be fighting to save me
Acts 22:4. arresting its *f.*
24:14. I am a *f.* of the new way
Rom. 16:13. an outstanding *f.* of the Lord

Rev. 17:14. his *f.*, called and chosen and faithful

folly-ies
Mark 7:22. arrogance, and *f.*
Acts 14:15. turn from these *f.* to the living God
1 Cor. 1:18. *f.* to those on their way to ruin
1:21. the *f.* of the Gospel
1:23. *f.* to Greeks
1:25. divine *f.* is wiser
1:27. what the world counts *f.*
2:14. it is *f.* to him; he cannot grasp it
3:19. *f.* in God's sight
1 Pet. 1:18. empty *f.* of your traditional ways

fomenter
Acts 24:5. A *f.* of discord among the Jews

fondly
1 Thess. 2:7. a nurse caring *f.* for her children

food-s
Mat. 3:4. his *f.* was locusts and wild honey
6:25. anxious thoughts about *f.* and drink
14:15. to buy themselves *f.*
25:35. when I was hungry, you gave me *f.*
Mark 7:2. eating their *f.* with 'defiled' hands
7:5. eat their *f.* with defiled hands
7:19. thus he declared all *f.* clean
8:1. they had no *f.*
Luke 3:11. anyone who has *f.*
9:12. to find *f.* and lodging
10:7. sharing their *f.* and drink
10:8. eat the *f.* provided for you
12:22. put away anxious thoughts about *f.*
12:23. life is more than *f.*
12:29. you are not to set your mind on *f.*
15:17. more *f.* than they can eat
John 4:8. to the town to buy *f.*
4:32. *f.* to eat of which you know nothing
4:33. can someone have brought him *f.*
6:27. not for this perishable *f.*, but for the *f.* that lasts, the *f.* of eternal life. 'This *f.* the Son of Man will give you.
6:55. my flesh is real *f.*
Acts 7:12. Jacob heard that there was *f.* in Egypt
9:9. took no *f.* or drink
9:19. afterwards he took *f.*
23:14. not to taste *f.* until we have killed Paul
27:21. for a long time without *f.*
27:33. Paul urged them all to take some *f.*

Acts 27:36. took *f*. themselves
Rom. 14:2. eat all kinds of *f*.
    14:20. do not ruin the work of God
      for the sake of *f*.
1 Cor. 3:2. instead of solid *f*.
    6:13. *f*. is for the belly and the belly
      for *f*.
    8:1. *f*. consecrated to heathen deities
    8:4. eating this consecrated *f*.
    8:7. this *f*. with a sense of its heathen
      consecration
    8:8. *f*. will not bring us into God's
      presence
    8:10. *f*. consecrated to the heathen
      deity
    8:13. if *f*. be the downfall of my
      brother
    10:3. all ate the same supernatural *f*.
    10:19. or *f*. offered to it anything
      more than *f*.
    10:28. this *f*. has been offered in
      sacrifice
    10:30. *f*. over which I have said grace
1 Tim. 4:3. abstinence from certain *f*.
Heb. 5:12. you need milk instead of
    solid *f*.
    5:14. grown men can take solid *f*.
    9:10. a matter of *f*. and drink
Rev. 2:14. *f*. sacrificed to idols
    2:20. eating *f*. sacrificed to idols

fool-s-ed
2 Cor. 10:12. what *f*. they are to measure
    themselves
    11:17. not speaking here as a Chris-
    tian, but like a *f*.
Gal. 6:7. God is not to be *f*.
Eph. 5:17. do not be *f*., but try to
    understand
2 Tim. 3:9. recognised by everyone for
    the *f*. they are

foolish
Luke 14:9. then you will look *f*.

foot
Mat. 6:27 ⎫ by anxious thought can
Luke 12:25 ⎭ add a *f*. to his height
    22:10. as soon as you set *f*. in the city
Acts 20:18. I first set *f*. in the province
    of Asia

foothold
2 Pet. 3:17. do not lose your own safe *f*.
Rev. 12:8. no *f*. was left them in heaven

footing
Rom. 3:31. placing law itself on a
    firmer *f*.

footpath
Mat. 13:4. some seed fell along the *f*.
    13:19. the seed sown along the *f*.
Mark 4:3. some seed fell along the *f*.
    4:15. those along the *f*.
Luke 8:5. some seed fell along the *f*.
    8:12. those along the *f*. are the men

footprint-s
Rom. 4:12. walk in the *f*. of the faith

footstep-s
Mat. 10:38. walk in my *f*.
Acts 5:9. at the door are the *f*. of those

forbade
Mark 7:36. Jesus *f*. them to tell anyone
Luke 4:41. *f*. them to speak
    8:56. he *f*. them to tell anyone

forbear-ing
1 Tim. 3:3. of a *f*. disposition

forbearance
Tit. 3:2. to show *f*.

forbid-den
Mat. 12:2. *f*. on the Sabbath
    16:19. what you *f*. on earth shall be
    f. in heaven
    16:22. heaven *f*.
    18:18. whatever you *f*. on earth shall
    be *f*. in heaven
Mark 2:24 ⎫ what is *f*. on the Sabbath
Luke 6:2 ⎭
Acts 10:28. a Jew is *f*. by his religion
1 Pet. 4:3. *f*. worship of idols

force-s-d
Mat. 16:18. the *f*. of death shall never
    overpower
Luke 10:19. all the *f*. of the enemy
    16:16. everyone *f*. his way in
    16:17. dot or stroke of the Law to lose
    its *f*.
Acts 5:26. without using *f*.
    7:19. *f*. our ancestors to expose their
    children
    21:32. took a *f*. of soldiers
    21:38. a *f*. of four thousand terrorists
    24:7. took him by *f*.
Rom. 8:39. the *f*. of the universe
    15:19. the *f*. of miraculous signs
Gal. 6:12. trying to *f*. circumcision upon
    you
Eph. 6:12. superhuman *f*. of evil in the
    heavens
Col. 2:23. with its *f*. piety
Heb. 2:2. word spoken through angels
    had such *f*.
    9:10. outward ordinances in *f*.

forceful
Acts 9:22. Saul grew more and more *f*.

forebodings
2 Cor. 7:5. *f*. in our heart

forefathers
Mat. 5:21. our *f*. were told
Luke 1:54. his promise to our *f*.
John 6:49. your *f*. ate the manna
Acts 7:15. ended his days, as also our
    f. did
    7:38. spoke to him on Mount Sinai,
    and with our *f*.

foreign-ers

Acts 7:39. our *f.* would not accept
  7:44. our *f.* had the Tent
  26:6. God's promise to our *f.*
  28:17. the customs of our *f.*
Heb. 1:1. God spoke to our *f.*
  3:9. your *f.* tried me
  8:9. the covenant I made with their *f.*

foreign-ers

Mat. 20:19. hand him over to the *f.* power
  27:7. a burial-place for *f.*
Mark 10:33. hand him over to the *f.* power
Luke 17:18. give praise to God except this *f.*
  18:32. handed over to the *f.* power
  21:24. Jerusalem will be trampled down by *f.*
Acts 7:6. live as aliens in a *f.* land
  17:18. a propagandist for *f.* deities
  17:21. Athenians in general and the *f.*
  26:11. persecution to *f.* cities
1 Cor. 14:21. by the lips of *f.*
2 Cor. 11:26. dangers from *f.*
Heb. 11:34. put *f.* armies to rout
1 Pet. 2:11. as aliens in a *f.* land

foreknowledge

Acts 2:31. with *f.* of the resurrection

foremost

1 Cor. 15:3. first and *f.*

foreordained

Acts 4:28. by the decree, were *f.*
Rom. 8:30. *f.*, whom he has also called

forerunner

Luke 1:17. he will go before him as *f.*
  1:76. the Lord's *f.*
John 3:28. I have been sent as his *f.*

foresail

Acts 27:40. set the *f.* to the wind

foreshadows

Rom. 5:14. *f.* the Man who was to come

forestall-ed

Mat. 17:25. Jesus *f.* him by asking
1 Thess. 4:15. shall not *f.* those who have died

foretell-ing

1 Pet. 1:11. *f.* the sufferings

foretold

Mat. 11:13. the Law *f.* things to come
Acts 3:18. God fulfilled what he had *f.*
  7:52. *f.* the coming of the Righteous One
  26:22. *f.* by the prophets

forewarned

Mat. 24:25. I have *f.* you
Mark 13:23. I have *f.* you of it all
2 Pet. 3:17. you, my friends, are *f.*

forfeit-s

Mat. 13:12 ⎫ will *f.* even what he has
  25:29 ⎭
Mark 4:25. the man who has not will *f.*
Luke 8:18. *f.* even what he thinks he has
  19:26. *f.* even what he has
Heb. 12:15. who *f.* the grace of God

forget-s

John 16:21. when the child is born she *f.* the anguish
Rev. 16:19. God did not *f.* Babylon the great

forgive-n

John 20:23. if you *f.* any man's sins, they stand *f.*
Heb. 10:18. where these have been *f.*

forgiveness

Mat. 26:28. shed for many for the *f.* of sins
Mark 1:4. repentance, for the *f.* of sins
Luke 1:77. by the *f.* of their sins
  3:3. repentance for the *f.* of sins
  24:47. the *f.* of sins is to be proclaimed
Acts 2:38. for the *f.* of your sins
  10:43. everyone who trusts in him receives *f.*
Heb. 9:22. without the shedding of blood there is no *f.*

forgotten

Mark 8:18. have you *f.*? When I broke the five loaves
Luke 1:55. he has not *f.* to show mercy
Rom. 6:3. have you *f.* that when we were baptized
Gal. 4:15. have you *f.* how happy you thought yourselves
Rev. 18:5. God has not *f.* her crimes

form-s-ed

Mark 4:32. *f.* branches so large
Luke 3:22. in bodily *f.* like a dove
John 5:37. never heard his voice, or saw his *f.*
Acts 14:11. the gods have come down to us in human *f.*
  14:20. the converts *f.* a ring round him
Rom. 8:3. his own Son in a *f.* like that of our own sinful nature
  8:5. have their outlook *f.* by it
  12:5. united with Christ, *f.* one body
1 Cor. 10:15. *f.* your own judgement
  12:6. there are many *f.* of work
2 Cor. 12:6. to *f.* an estimate of me
Eph. 3:10. the wisdom of God in all its varied *f.*
Phil. 3:21. a *f.* like that of his own resplendent body
2 Thess. 2:3. wickedness will be revealed in human *f.*
1 Tim. 6:19. which will *f.* a good foundation

Tit. 3:1. any honourable *f.* of work
1 Pet. 4:10. the grace of God in its varied *f.*

formal
2 Cor. 2:8. assure him of your love for him by a *f.* act

former
Acts 4:13. *f.* companions of Jesus
6:1. the *f.* party complained
6:5. a *f.* convert to Judaism
2 Cor. 2:16. to the *f.* a vital fragrance
Gal. 1:23. our *f.* persecutor is preaching
Eph. 2:11. remember then your *f.* condition
3:5. in *f.* generations this was not disclosed
2 Tim. 2:20. the *f.* are valued
Heb. 1:1. when in *f.* times God spoke
6:1 ⎫
9:14 ⎬ the deadness of our *f.* ways
9:15. sins committed under the *f.* covenant
9:18. we find that the *f.* covenant
10:9. annuls the *f.* to establish the latter
12:13. regain its *f.* powers
2 Pet. 1:9. he was cleansed from his *f.* sins

formerly
Mark 16:9. from whom he had *f.* cast out seven devils
Acts 19:19. those who *f.* practised magic
Rom. 11:30. *f.* you were disobedient to God
Gal. 4:8. *f.*, when you did not acknowledge God
Col. 1:21. *f.* you were yourselves estranged from God

formulate-d
Rom. 3:9. already *f.* the charge

fornication
Eph. 5:5. no one given to *f.*

fornicator
1 Cor. 6:18. the *f.* sins against his own body
1 Tim. 1:10. murderers and *f.*
Heb. 13:4. God's judgement will fall on *f.*
Rev. 21:8. *f.*, sorcerers
22:15. sorcerers and *f.*

forsake-n
Mat. 23:38 ⎫
Luke 13:35 ⎬ your temple, *f.* by God
2 Tim. 2:19. must *f.* wickedness

forswear
Rev. 2:22. unless they *f.* what she is doing

forth
Mat. 28:19. go *f.* therefore and make all nations my disciples

Mark 16:15. go *f.* to every part of the world
Phil. 1:18. Christ is set *f.*
Heb. 11:3. the visible came *f.* from the invisible

fortify
1 Thess. 5:11. *f.* one another
2 Thess. 2:17. encourage and *f.* you
3:3. *f.* you and guard you
Jude 20. *f.* yourselves in your most sacred faith

fortitude
Rom. 15:4. maintain our hope with *f.*
15:5. God, the source of all *f.*
2 Cor. 1:6. strength to face with *f.*
12:12. called for such constant *f.*
Col. 1:11. meet whatever comes with *f.*
1 Thess. 1:3. your hope of our Lord Jesus Christ in *f.*
1 Tim. 6:11. *f.*, and gentleness
2 Tim. 3:10. my *f.* under persecutions
Jam. 1:3. testing of your faith breeds *f.*
1:4. give *f.* full play
1 Pet. 2:20. what credit is there in *f.* . . . . your *f.* is a fine thing in the sight of God
2 Pet. 1:6. self-control with *f.*, *f.* with piety
Rev. 2:2. your toil and your *f.*
2:3. *f.* you have
2:19. your good service and your *f.*
13:10. *f.* and faithfulness
14:12. the *f.* of God's people

fortnight
Gal. 1:18. I stayed with him for a *f.*

fortunate
Acts 26:2. I consider myself *f.*

fortune-s
Acts 16:16. profits to her owners by telling *f.*
1 Cor. 4:8. you have come into your *f.* already

forward
Mat. 20:9. came *f.*, and were paid
26:46. let us go *f.*; the traitor is upon us
26:49. stepping *f.* at once
26:50. they then came *f.*, seized Jesus
26:60. many came *f.* with false evidence
Mark 1:31. he came *f.*, took her by the hand
3:23. he called them to come *f.*
9:15. they ran *f.* to welcome him
12:28. came *f.* and asked him
14:42. let us go *f.*! My betrayer is upon us
14:45. stepped *f.* at once and said to Jesus
Luke 7:13. stepped *f.* and laid his hand on the bier

Luke 10:25. a lawyer came *f.*
  19:28. Jesus went *f.* and began the ascent
  20:27. some Sadducees came *f.*
  23:36. came *f.* offering him their sour wine
  23:51. one who looked *f.* to the kingdom of God
John 14:31. up, let us go *f.*
Acts 1:18. fell *f.* on the ground
  1:23. two names were put *f.*
  5:36. some time ago Theudas came *f.*
  6:9 came *f.* and argued with Stephen
  12:6. Herod had planned to bring him *f.*
  15:5 who had become believers came *f.*
  20:30. men coming *f.* who will distort the truth
  21:33. the commandant stepped *f.*
2 Cor. 10:12. those who put *f.* their own claims
Phil. 1:25. to help you *f.*
Heb. 11:10. looking *f.* to the city with firm foundations
2 Pet. 3:14. with this to look *f.* to
Jude 21. look *f.* to the day
Rev. 22:17. come *f.*, you who are thirsty

foster
2 Pet. 1:8. these are gifts which, if you possess and *f.* them

foul
Mat. 13:57 ⎱ they fell *f.* of him
Mark 6:3 ⎰
Eph. 4:19. to satisfy their *f.* desires
Col. 3:5. *f.* cravings
Rev. 16:2. *f.* malignant sores appeared
  16:13. three *f.* spirits like frogs
  21:27. anyone whose ways are false or *f.*

foulness
Rev. 17:4. the *f.* of her fornication

found
Mat. 8:14. *f.* Peter's mother-in-law in bed
Mark 5:38. he *f.* a great commotion
  6:21. Herodias *f.* her opportunity
  6:38. they *f.* out and told him
  7:24. he *f.* a house to stay in
Luke 9:11. the crowds *f.* out and followed him
John 5:38. his word has *f.* no home in you
  19:33. they *f.* that he was already dead
  20:29. you have *f.* faith. Happy are they who never saw me and yet have *f.* faith
  21:6. *f.* they could not haul the net
Acts 5:41. *f.* worthy to suffer
  16:1. he *f.* a disciple named Timothy
  16:26. the prisoners *f.* their fetters unfastened
  16:34. his new-*f.* faith in God

  16:37. have not been *f.* guilty
  22:25. has not been *f.* guilty
  23:29. I *f.* that the accusation
  27:41. *f.* themselves caught between cross-currents
Rom. 7:4. you have *f.* another husband in him
  7:8 ⎱ sin *f.* its opportunity
  7:11 ⎰
1 Cor. 1:6. the truth of Christ has *f.* confirmation
  2:13. in words *f.* for us not by our human wisdom
2 Cor. 4:3. if indeed our gospel be *f.* veiled
Heb. 4:1. should be *f.* to have missed his chance
  12:25. who refused to hear the oracle speaking on earth *f.* no escape
1 John 5:11. this life is *f.* in his Son
Rev. 12:13. the dragon *f.* that he had been thrown down

foundation-s
Eph. 3:17. deep roots and firm *f.*
Col. 1:23. firm on your *f.*
1 Pet. 5:10. strengthen you on a firm *f.*

founder-ed
Heb. 3:3. the *f.* of a house
  3:4. every house has its *f.*; and the *f.* of all is God
Rev. 8:9. a third of the ships on it *f.*

four
John 1:39. then about *f.* in the afternoon
  6:19. they had rowed about three or *f.* miles
Acts 21:26. so Paul took the *f.* men

fragmentary
Heb. 1:1. he spoke in *f.* and varied fashion

fragrance
John 12:3. the house was filled with the *f.*
2 Cor. 2:14. the *f.* of the knowledge of himself
  2:16. a vital *f.* that brings life
Eph. 5:2. whose *f.* is pleasing to God

fragrant
Mat. 26:7. a small bottle of *f.* oil
Phil. 4:18. it is a *f.* offering

frail-ties-ty
1 Cor. 12:22. those organs of the body which seem to be more *f.*
Heb. 7:28. men in all their *f.*
Jam. 5:17. Elijah was a man with human *f.*

frame-d
Mat. 12:10. to *f.* a charge against him.
John 8:6. hoping to *f.* a charge against him
Rom. 15:32. in a happy *f.* of mind
1 Cor. 2:7. *f.* from the very beginning

1 Cor. 7:31. the whole *f.* of this world is passing away

2 Cor. 1:17. When I *f.* my plans, *f.* them as a worldly man might

5:1. the earthly *f.* that houses us

5:4. enclosed within this earthly *f.*

Eph. 4:16. the whole *f.* grows

frank-ly

2 Cor. 6:11. men of Corinth, we have spoken very *f.* to you

7:4. I am perfectly *f.* with you

1 Thess 2:2. we declared the gospel of God to you *f.*

fraud-s

Mark 7:22. *f.*, indecency, envy

Rev. 3:9. claim to be Jews but are lying *f.*

free-d-ly

Mat. 20:15. *f.* to do what I like with my own money

Mark 5:34. *f.* for ever from this trouble

Luke 1:64. his lips and tongue were *f.*

1:68. saved them and set them *f.*

1:74. grant us, *f.* from fear, to worship him

4:18. to let the broken victims go *f.*

8:2. set *f.* from evil spirits

13:16. was it wrong for her to be *f.* from her bonds on the Sabbath

John 2:10. until the guests have drunk *f.*

10:18. I am laying it down of my own *f.* will

Acts 2:24. setting him *f.* from the pangs of death

7:7. after that they shall come out *f.*

9:28. moving about *f.* in Jerusalem

15:29. keep yourselves *f.* from these things

16:36. so now you may go *f.*

19:8. spoke boldly and *f.* about the kingdom

Rom. 6:23. God gives *f.*, and his gift is eternal life

8:21. *f.* from the shackles of mortality

8:23. set our whole body *f.*

9:21. is he not *f.* to make out of the same lump two vessels

1 Cor. 1:30. in him we are consecrated and set *f.*

6:12. I am *f.* to do anything,' you say. Yes, but not everything is for my good. No doubt I am *f.* to do anything, but I for one will not let anything make *f.* with me.

7:32. *f.* from anxious care

7:39. if the husband die, she is *f.* to marry whom she will

10:23. we are *f.* to do anything

Gal. 3:18. God bestowed it as a *f.* gift on Abraham

5:13. you, my friends, were called to be *f.* men

Eph. 1:7. God's *f.* grace

6:19. boldly and *f.* make known his hidden purpose

1 Tim. 5:16. that it may be *f.* to support those who are widows

Tit. 2:14. to set us *f.* from all wickedness

Philem. 14. of your own *f.* will

Heb. 10:19. Jesus makes us *f.* to enter boldly

Jam. 1:25. the law that makes us *f.*

1 Pet. 5:2. of your own *f.* will

2 Pet. 1:11. *f.* admission into the eternal kingdom

Jude 4. they pervert the *f.* favour of our God

Rev. 1:5. *f.* us from our sins

freedmen

Acts 6:9. the Synagogue of *f.*

freedom

1 Cor. 7:35. *f.* to wait upon the Lord

10:29. is my *f.* to be called in question

Gal. 3:13. Christ bought us *f.*

4:5 to purchase *f.* for the subjects of the law

5:13. do not turn your *f.* into licence

Eph. 3:12. we have access to God with *f.*

1 Tim. 2:6. to win *f.* for all mankind

Jam. 2:12. to be judged under a law of *f.*

1 Pet. 1:18 *f.* from the empty folly

2:16. as though your *f.* were there to provide a screen

2 Pet. 2:19. they promise them *f.*

frequent

1 Tim. 5:23. for your *f.* ailments

fresh

Mat. 9:17. you put new wine into *f.* skins

Mark 2:22 } *f.* skins for new wine
Luke 5:38 }

Eph. 4:14. every *f.* gust of teaching

6:22. to put *f.* heart into you

Phil. 1:17. to stir up *f.* trouble for me

Col. 4:8. to put *f.* heart into you

Jam. 3:11. both *f.* and brackish water

fret-ting

Luke 10:41. Martha, you are *f.* and fussing

Friday

Mat. 27:62. the morning after that *F.*

Luke 23:54. it was *F.*, and the Sabbath was about to begin

friend-s

Mat. 9:15. the bridegroom's *f.*

24:49. drink with his drunken *f.*

Luke 2:44. looking for him among their *f.*

4:40. all who had *f.* suffering

7:5. he is a *f.* of our nation

23:49. his *f.* had all been standing at a distance

John 11:3. your *f.* lies ill

21:5. *f.*, have you caught anything

Acts 4:23. they went back to their *f*.
24:23. not to prevent any of his *f*.
Rom. 11:28. God's choice stands, and
they are his *f*.
16:2. a good *f*. to many
2 Cor. 11:26. dangers from false *f*.
Col. 4:14. our dear *f*. Luke
Heb. 13:24. greetings to you from our
Italian *f*.
2 Pet. 3:15. Paul, our *f*. and brother
also Mark 2:19 ; Luke 5:34; Acts
1:16, 2:29, 37, 3:17, 6:3, 13:15,
15:13; Rom. 7:1, 4, 8:12, 12:19,
15:14, 16:5, 8, 14, 17; 1 Cor. 4:6, 7,
7:24, 29, 10:14, 14:6, 20, 26, 39,
16:11, 12; 2 Cor. 1:8, 7:1, 8:1, 9:3, 5,
11:9, 12:18, 13:11; Gal. 1:2, 11,
5:11, 13; Phil. 1:12, 2:12, 3:1, 13,
17, 4:1, 8; 1 Thess. 2:17, 4:1, 5:1, 4;
2 Thess. 3:13; Tit. 3:15; Philem.
1:1; Heb. 6:9, 13:23; Jam. 1:16, 19,
2:5; 1 Pet. 2:11, 3:1, 8, 17; 1 John
2:7, 3:2, 21, 4:1, 7, 11; 3 John 3, 5,
10, 11; Jude 3, 17.

friendly
Acts 19:31. dignitaries of the province,
who were *f*.
2 Thess. 3:15. give him *f*. advice

fringe-s
Mat. 23:5. wear deep *f*. on their robes

front
Mat. 18:2. a child, set him in *f*. of them
Mark 2:2. the space in *f*. of the door
9:36. took a child, set him in *f*. of
them
Luke 4:35. throwing the man down in
f. of the people
5:18. set him down in *f*. of Jesus
5:19. into the middle of the company
in *f*. of Jesus
14:2. in *f*. of him, was a man suffering
from dropsy
18:39. the people in *f*. told him
sharply to hold his tongue
Acts 19:33. whom the Jews had pushed
to the *f*.
27:35. gave thanks to God in *f*. of
them all
Col. 2:5. the firm *f*. which your faith in
Christ presents
Rev. 4:6. in *f*. of it stretched what
seemed a sea of glass
7:9. standing in *f*. of the throne
8:3. the golden altar in *f*. of the throne
12:4. the dragon stood in *f*. of the
woman

fruit
Acts 8:23. doomed to taste the bitter *f*.

fruitless
1 Thess. 2:1. our visit to you was not *f*.

frustration
Rom. 8:20. it was made the victim of *f*
2 Cor. 12:10. hardship, and *f*.

fulfil-led-ling
Luke 1:45. faith that the Lord's promise
would be *f*.
2:29. thy promise is *f*.
9:31. the destiny he was to *f*.
22:37. all that is written of me is
being *f*.
Acts 7:17. for God to *f*. the promise
2 Tim. 1:1. whose promise of life is *f*.
Heb. 11:33. saw God's promises *f*.
2 Pet. 3:9. not that the Lord is slow in
f. his promise
Rev. 10:7. the hidden purpose of God
will have been *f*.
21:6. they are already *f*.

fulfilment
Luke 22:37. these words, I tell you, must
find *f*. in me
Acts 26:7. our twelve tribes hope to see
the *f*.
1 Cor. 10:11. the *f*. of the ages has come
Tit. 2:13. the happy *f*. of our hopes
Rev. 1:3 } the hour of *f*. is near
22:10 }

full
Mat. 18:26. I will pay in *f*.
18:34. he should pay the debt in *f*
20:9. were paid the *f*. day's wage
27:24. washed his hands in *f*. view of
the people
28:18. *f*. authority in heaven and on
earth
Mark 2:12. went out in *f*. view of them
all
Luke. 2:31. in *f*. view of all the nations
2:33. the child's father and mother
were *f*. of wonder
6:34. if they are to be repaid in *f*.
24:18. their faces *f*. of gloom
John 5:22. given *f*. jurisdiction to the Son
13:1. the *f*. extent of his love
17:13. my joy within them in *f*.
measure
21:8. towing the net *f*. of fish
Acts 5:2. with the *f*. knowledge of his
wife
5:21. Sanhedrin,' that is, the *f*. senate
of the Israelite nation
15:3. the *f*. story of the conversion of
the Gentiles
17:16. the city was *f*. of idols
18:17. gave him a beating in *f*. view
of the bench
18:25. *f*. of spiritual fervour
25:23. Agrippa and Bernice came in *f*.
state
28:30. he stayed there two *f*. years
Rom. 9:23. the *f*. wealth of his
splendour

1 Cor. 1:5. you possess *f.* knowledge and you can give *f.* expression to it
1:17. the fact of Christ on his cross might have its *f.* weight
2:7. to bring us to our *f.* glory
7:31. the world's wealth on using it to the *f.*
2 Cor. 3:4. in *f.* reliance upon God
11:6. made known to you the *f.* truth
12:9. power comes to its *f.* strength
Gal. 2:5. the *f.* truth of the Gospel
Eph. 1:4. to be *f.* of love
1:8. imparting *f.* wisdom
5:16. use the present opportunity to the *f.*
Phil. 1:11. the *f.* harvest of righteousness
Col. 1:25. to deliver his message in *f.*
4:5. use the present opportunity to the *f.*
1 Thess. 5:9. the *f.* attainment of salvation
1 Tim. 1:15. words that merit *f.* acceptance
2:2. in *f.* observance of religion
4:9. words that merit *f.* acceptance
5:3. widows who are such in the *f.* sense
5:5. a widow, however, in the *f.* sense
5:16. widows in the *f.* sense of the term
2 Tim. 2:7. the Lord will help you to *f.* understanding
Heb. 2:12. in *f.* assembly I will sing thy praise
12:23. the *f.* concourse and assembly of the first-born citizens of heaven
Jam. 1:4. give fortitude *f.* play
1:15. sin *f.*-grown breeds death
5:11. the Lord is *f.* of pity
1 Pet. 3:8. be *f.* of brotherly affection
4:8. keep your love for one another at *f.* strength
2 Pet. 1:11. *f.* and free admission into the eternal kingdom
Rev. 1:16. his face shone like the sun in *f.* strength
11:12. in *f.* view of their enemies

fullest
1 Pet. 1:2. grace and peace to you in *f.* measure
Jude 2. mercy, peace, and love be yours in *f.* measure

fullness
John 10:10. have life, and may have it in all its *f.*

fully
Luke 11:21. a strong man *f.* armed
Rom. 7:9. in the absence of law, I was *f.* alive
2 Cor. 1:14. come to understand *f.*

2:9. whether you *f.* accepted my authority
11:9. anything I needed was *f.* met
Eph. 4:15. so shall we *f.* grow up into Christ
2 Tim. 1:10. now at length been brought *f.* into view
Jude 3. I was *f.* engaged in writing

function-s
Rom. 12:4. all with different *f.*

fund
Mat. 27:6. this cannot be put into the temple *f.*
Rom. 15:26. a common *f.* for the benefit of the poor

funeral
Luke 7:12. he met a *f.*
Rev. 6:12. the sun turned black as a *f.* pall

fume
2 Cor. 2:16. a deadly *f.* that kills

furious-ly
Mat. 22:7. the king was *f.*
Acts 12:20. *f.* angry with the people of Tyre
Rev. 12:17. the dragon grew *f.* with the woman

furlong-s
Mat. 14:24. the boat was already some *f.* from the shore

furrow
2 Tim. 2:15. driving a straight *f.*

further
Mark 15:5. Jesus made no *f.* reply
Luke 7:6. do not trouble *f.*, sir
8:14. their *f.* growth is choked by cares
8:49. trouble the Rabbi no *f.*
10:1. the Lord appointed a *f.* seventy-two
20:40. no *f.* question that they ventured
John 1:32. John testified *f.*
13:10. bathed needs no *f.* washing
21:18. and *f.*, I tell you this in very truth
Acts 13:3. after *f.* fasting and prayer
15:28. to lay no *f.* burden upon you
19:39. some *f.* questions to raise
Rom. 15:23. I have no *f.* scope in these parts
1 Tim. 4:16. you will *f.* the salvation of yourself
2 Tim. 2:16. will stray *f.* and *f.* into godless courses
Rev. 2:24. on you I will impose no *f.* burden

fury
Mark 14:5. they turned upon her with *f.*
Acts 7:54. they ground their teeth with *f.*

Acts 19:28. roused to *f.* and shouted
26:11. my *f.* rose to such a pitch
Rom. 2:8. the *f.* of retribution
Heb. 11:34. quenched the *f.* of fire
Rev. 12:12. the Devil has come down
to you in great *f.*

fuss-ing
Luke 10:41. *f.* about so many things

futile
1 Cor. 3:20. the arguments of the wise
are *f.*
Col. 2:18. the *f.* conceit of worldly minds
Jam. 1:26. that man's religion is *f.*

futility
Rom. 1:21. their thinking has ended in *f.*

future
1 Cor. 3:22. the present and the *f.*, all
of them belong to you
Gal. 6:17. in *f.* let no one make trouble
for me
1 Tim. 1:16. who were in *f.* to have faith
6:19. a good foundation for the *f.*
Heb. 11:7. divinely warned about the
unseen *f.*
2 Pet. 2:6. object-lesson for godless men
in *f.* days

G

Gadarenes
Mat. 8:28. in the country of the *G.*

gaiety
Jam. 4:9. your *g.* into gloom

gain-s-ed-ing
Mat. 10:39. by *g.* his life a man will lose
it; by losing his life for my sake, he
will *g.* it
19:16. what good must I do to *g.*
eternal life
19:29. be repaid many times over, and
g. eternal life
27:24. Pilate could see that nothing
was being *g.*
John 9:11. washed, and *g.* my sight
9:15. by what means he had *g.* his
sight
9:18. been blind and had *g.* his sight
Acts 14:21. they *g.* many converts
19:17. the name of the Lord Jesus *g.*
in honour
Rom. 1:17. he shall *g.* life who is justified
6:21. what was the *g.*
6:22. your *g.* are such as make for
holiness
10:5. the man who does this shall *g.*
life
1 Cor. 3:18. must become a fool to *g.*
true wisdom
15:32. what have I *g.* by it
15:56. sin *g.* its power from the law
16:2. a sum in proportion to his *g.*
Gal. 3:11. he shall *g.* life who is justified
3:12. shall *g.* life by what he does
Eph. 5:5. the greed which makes an idol
of *g.*
Phil. 3:8. the *g.* of knowing Christ . . .
for the sake of *g.* Christ.
1 Thess. 4:4. *g.* mastery over his body
1 Tim. 1:16. faith in him and *g.* eternal
life

Tit. 1:11. all for sordid *g.*
Heb. 13:9. our souls should *g.* their
strength
1 Pet. 5:2. not for *g.* but out of sheer
devotion
2 Pet. 2:2. *g.* many adherents to their
dissolute practices
Jude 16. court favour to *g.* their ends
Rev. 18:15. who *g.* their wealth from her

gale-s
Mat. 14:30. when he saw the strength
of the *g.*
Jam. 3:4. when driven by strong *g.*
Rev. 6:13. like figs shaken down by a *g.*

Galilee
Mat. 4:13. settled at Capernaum on the
Sea of *G.*

gallant-ly
1 Tim. 1:18. fight *g.*, armed with faith

gallon-s
Luke 16:6. a thousand *g.* of olive oil
John 2:6. each held from twenty to
thirty *g.*

gallows
1 Pet. 2:24. he carried our sins to the *g.*

gangrene
2 Tim. 2:17. their teaching will spread
like a *g.*

garbage
Phil. 3:8. I count it so much *g.*

garden-er-ers
Mat. 13:32. bigger than any *g.*-plant
Luke 11:42. rue and every *g.*-herb
John 15:1. my Father is the *g.*
18:3. made his way to the *g.*
1 Cor. 3:7. it is not the *g.* with their
planting

1 Cor. 3:9. you are God's *g.*
Rev. 2:7. the tree of life that stands in the *G.* of God

garland
2 Tim. 4:8. the *g.* of righteousness
1 Pet. 5:4. the unfading *g.* of glory

garment-s
Mat. 28:3. his *g.* were white as snow
John 19:24. they shared my *g.* among them
Gal. 3:27. you have all put on Christ as a *g.*
Col. 2:15. discarded the cosmic powers and authorities like a *g.*
3:12. the *g.* that suit God's chosen people
1 Pet. 5:5. wrap yourselves in the *g.* of humility
Rev. 19:13. robed in a *g.* drenched in blood

gate-s
Acts 14:27. thrown open the *g.* of faith to the Gentiles
16:13. we went outside the city *g.*

gateway
Mat. 26:71. he then went out to the *g.*

gather-s-ed-ing
Mat. 5:1. when his disciples had *g.* round him
Mark 10:1. a crowd *g.* round him
Luke 5:15. great crowds *g.* to hear him
John 8:2. the people *g.* round him
10:24. the Jews *g.* round him
Acts 2:6. at this sound the crowd *g.*
10:27. found a large *g.*
13:36. was *g.* to his fathers
13:44. almost the whole city *g.* to hear
16:13. the women who had *g.* there
2 Tim. 4:3. *g.* a crowd of teachers

gave
Mat. 1:16. who *g.* birth to Jesus
2:16. *g.* orders for the massacre of all children in Bethlehem
5:2. this is the teaching he *g.*
15:31. they *g.* praise to the God of Israel
19:8. Moses *g.* you permission to divorce
25:43. a stranger you *g.* me no home
27:58. Pilate *g.* orders that he should have it
28:9. he *g.* them his greeting
Mark 3:16. to Simon he *g.* the name Peter
3:17. John, to whom he *g.* the name Boanerges
5:43. he *g.* them strict orders
6:21. Herod on his birthday *g.* a banquet
14:57. *g.* this false evidence against him

Luke 1:57. she *g.* birth to a son
2:47. and the answers he *g.*
7:15. Jesus *g.* him back to his mother
8:32. he *g.* them leave
9:42. *g.* him back to his father
18:28. *g.* up our belongings to become your followers
19:13. *g.* them a pound each
23:25. and *g.* Jesus up to their will
23:47. the centurion saw it all, and *g.* praise to God
24:35. they *g.* their account of the events
John 1:19. the testimony which John *g.*
2:3. the wine *g.* out
2:23. many *g.* their allegiance to him
9:22. his parents *g.* this answer
20:18. and *g.* them his message
Acts 7:53. the Law as God's angels *g.* it
7:57. they *g.* a great shout
11:18. they *g.* praise to God
13:19. lands he *g.* them
18:27. the brotherhood *g.* him their support
19:4. the baptism that John *g.*
19:23. the Christian movement *g.* rise to a serious disturbance
27:9. Paul therefore *g.* them this advice
1 Cor. 9:14. the Lord *g.* instructions
2 Cor. 6:2. I *g.* heed to you
1 Tim. 6:13. *g.* his testimony to it before Pontius Pilate
Jam. 1:23. the face nature *g.* him
1 John 2:25. the promise that he himself *g.* us
Jude 18. the warning they *g.* you
Rev. 12:5. she *g.* birth to a male child
21:23. the glory of God *g.* it light

gaze-ing
Luke 21:6. these things which you are *g.* at
Acts 1:10. *g.* intently into the sky
7:55. *g.* intently up to heaven
2 Cor. 3:7. the Israelites could not *g.* steadily at him
3:13. to keep the Israelites from *g.*
Rev. 11:9. *g.* upon their corpses

gazelle
Acts 9:36. in Greek, Dorcas, meaning a *g.*

gear
Acts 27:19. they jettisoned the ship's *g.*

general
Mat. 9:23. the flute-players and the *g.* commotion
Mark 7:3. the Jews in *g.* never eat without washing the hands
Luke 2:1. a *g.* registration throughout the Roman world
3:21. a *g.* baptism of the people
4:22. there was a *g.* stir of admiration

Luke 9:43. amid the *g.* wonder
19:7. a *g.* murmur of disapproval
23:18. a *g.* outcry, 'Away with him
Acts 2:45. make a *g.* distribution
5:13. people in *g.* spoke highly of them
9:32. Peter was making a *g.* tour
17:21. the Athenians in *g.*
18:17. a *g.* attack on Sosthenes
1 Cor. 4:6. into this *g.* picture, my friends, I have brought Apollos and myself
2 Cor. 2:6. the *g.* meeting has agreed
9:13. contribution to their need and to the *g.* good
12:20. arrogance and *g.* disorder

generation-s
Acts 7:45. our fathers of the next *g.*
15:21. in every town for *g.* past
Eph. 3:5. in former *g.* this was not disclosed
3:21. from *g.* to *g.* evermore
Phil. 2:15. a warped and crooked *g.*

generosity
2 Cor. 8:1. the grace of *g.*
8:6. this work of *g.*
9:11. such *g.* will issue in thanksgiving
Tit. 3:4. *g.* of God our Saviour

generous-ly
Acts 10:2. gave *g.* to help the Jewish people
2 Cor. 8:4. share in this *g.* service
8:7. lavish in this *g.* service
8:9. how *g.* our Lord Jesus Christ has been
8:20. our handling of this *g.* gift
9:10. rich enough to be *g.*
Eph. 4:32. be *g.* to one another
Philem. 20. as a Christian, be *g.* with me
Jam. 1:5. God is a *g.* giver

Gentile
Mat. 10:5. do not take the road to *g.* lands
Mark 7:26. she was a *G.*, a Phoenician
Acts 4:25. why did the *G.* rage
13:43. many Jews and *g.* worshippers
17:17. with the Jews and *g.* worshippers
1 Cor. 9:21. to win *G.*, who are outside the Law
Gal. 1:16. proclaim him among the *G.*
2:7. entrusted with the Gospel for *G.*
2:9. agreeing that we should go to the *G.*
2:17. we ourselves no less than the *G.*
3:8. God would justify the *G.* through faith
Eph. 2:14. *G.* and Jews, he has made the two one

gentle-y
Mat. 5:5. how blest are those of a *g.* spirit
11:29. I am *g.* and humble-hearted
1 Cor. 4:21. in love and a *g.* spirit
Gal. 6:1. set him right again very *g.*
Eph. 4:2. be humble always and *g.*
1 Pet. 3:4. a *g.*, quiet spirit, which is of high value

gentlemen
Acts 25:24. all you *g.* here present
27:10. I can see, *g.*,' he said
27:21. you should have taken my advice, *g.*

gentleness
Mat. 21:5. here is your king, who comes to you in *g.*
Col. 3:12. humility, *g.*, patience
1 Tim. 6:11. love, fortitude, and *g.*

genuine
Phil. 2:20. takes a *g.* interest in your concerns
1 Tim. 1:5. faith that is *g.*
1 John 3:18. love must not be a matter of words or talk; it must be *g.*

Gerasene-s
Mark 5:1. into the country of the *G.*

Gergesene-s
Luke 8:26. in the country of the *G.*
8:37. population of the *G.* district

germ
Rom. 9:29. the mere *g.* of a nation

gesture
Acts 13:16. made a *g.* with his hand
21:40. with a *g.* called for the attention

get-s-ting
Mat. 13:2. he had to *g.* into a boat
Mark 5:41. *g.* up, my child
6:2. where does he *g.* it from
6:35. it is *g.* very late
Luke 6:8. *g.* up and stand out here
11:7. I cannot *g.* up and give you
11:8. will make him *g.* up and give him
13:24. struggle to *g.* in through the narrow door
18:12. I pay tithes on all that I *g.*
23:9. without *g.* any reply
Acts 9:34. *g.* up and make your bed
12:7. quick! *G.* up,' he said
21:34. he could not *g.* at the truth
22:10. *g.* up and continue your journey
27:16. *g.* the ship's boat under control
Jam. 4:3. you do not *g.* what you want ... spend what you *g.* on your pleasures
3 John 12. Demetrius *g.* a good testimonial

ghost
Mat. 14:26. cried out in terror: 'It is a *g*.
Mark 6:49. they thought it was a *g*.
Luke 24:37. thought they were seeing a *g*.
24:39. no *g*. has flesh and bones

gibberish
1 Cor. 14:11. his words will be *g*. to me

gibbet
Acts 5.30. hanging him on a *g*.
10:39. put to death by hanging on a *g*.
13:29. they took him down from the *g*.

gift-s
Luke 24:49. my Father's promised *g*.
John 14:27. peace is my parting *g*. to you
Acts 3:5. expecting a *g*. from them
21:9. who possessed the *g*. of prophecy
24:17. to bring charitable *g*.
Rom. 8:32. with this *g*. how can he fail to lavish upon us
12:7. the *g*. of administration . . . his *g*. in teaching
12:8. the *g*. of stirring speech
15:15. in virtue of the *g*. I have from God
1 Cor. 2:13. we speak of these *g*. of God
4:7. received it all as a *g*.
6:19. the Spirit is God's *g*. to you
7:17. the *g*. the Lord has granted him
12:10. the *g*. of prophecy . . . the *g*. of ecstatic utterance
12:11. these *g*. are the work of one and the same Spirit
16:3. to carry your *g*. to Jerusalem
2 Cor. 6:6. *g*. of the Holy Spirit
8:20. this generous *g*.
9:8. provide you richly with every good *g*.
9:9. he has lavished his *g*. on the needy
Gal. 3:18. God bestowed it as a free *g*. on Abraham
Eph. 1:6. the glory of his gracious *g*.
Phil. 1:10. the *g*. of true discrimination
Jam. 1:12. the *g*. of life promised to those who love God
1 Pet. 1:13. fix your hopes on the *g*. of grace
2 Pet. 1:8. these are *g*. which, if you possess
1 John 2:20. this is the *g*. of the Holy One
Rev. 21:6. my free *g*. to the thirsty

gifted
1 Cor. 2:15. a man *g*. with the Spirit
14:18. I am more *g*. in ecstatic utterance

girl-s
Mat. 9:24. the *g*. is not dead
9:25. took the *g*. by the hand

14:11. brought in on a dish and given to the *g*.
25:1. there were ten *g*.
25:7. the *g*. all got up
26:71. another *g*., seeing him
Mark 5:42. the *g*. got up and walked about
6:22. the king said to the *g*.
6:25. the *g*. hastened back at once to the king
6:28. gave it to the *g*.
Luke 1:27. a *g*. betrothed to a man named Joseph . . . the *g*. name was Mary
Acts 16:19. the *g*. owners saw that their hope of gain had gone

give-s-en-ing
Mat. 1:21. *g*. him the name Jesus
5:16. they may *g*. praise to your Father
10:41. *g*. a prophet's reward . . . *g*. a good man's reward
11:1. *g*. his twelve disciples their instructions
17:22. the Son of Man is to be *g*. up
19:18. do not *g*. false evidence
20:18. the Son of Man will be *g*. up to the chief priests
20:21. I want you,' she said, 'to *g*. orders
22:17. *g*. us your ruling on this
25:18. the man who had been *g*. one bag of gold
25:20. the man who had been *g*. the five bags
25:24. the man who had been *g*. one bag
27:37. the inscription *g*. the charge
Mark 1:27. when he *g*. orders, even the unclean spirits submit
4:33. with many such parables he would *g*. them his message
5:43. told them to *g*. her something to eat
Mark 9:31. the Son of Man is now to be *g*. up
10:33. the Son of Man will be *g*. up
12:41. rich people were *g*. large sums
12:43. this widow has *g*. more
12:44. others who have *g*. had more than enough, but she, . . . has *g*. all that she had to live on
14:13. *g*. this message to the householder
15:26. the inscription *g*. the charge
16:7. *g*. this message to his disciples and Peter
Luke 1:4. to *g*. you authentic knowledge
1:31. you shall *g*. him the name Jesus
2:21. he was *g*. the name Jesus, the name *g*. by the angel
4:36. he *g*. orders to the unclean spirits

Luke 4:43. I must *g*. the good news of the kingdom of God
5:33. John's disciples are much *g*. to fasting
8:25. he *g*. his orders to wind and waves
9:39. *g*. a sudden scream
9:44. the Son of Man is going to be *g*. up
12:15. his wealth does not *g*. him life
14:16. *g*. a big dinner party
16:4. people to *g*. me house and home
18:29. *g*. up home, or wife
21:3. *g*. more than any of them
21:4. who have *g*. had more than enough, but she, with less than enough, has *g*. all
23:18. *g*. us Barabbas
24:7. the Son of Man: how he must be *g*. up
John 1:22. what account do you *g*. of yourself
3:6. flesh can *g*. birth only to flesh; it is spirit that *g*. birth to spirit
3:18. has not *g*. his allegiance to God's only Son
5:21. *g*. them life, so the Son *g*. life to men
5:22. *g*. full jurisdiction to the Son
5:24. anyone who *g*. heed to what I say
5:37. this testimony to me was *g*. by the Father
6:63. the spirit alone *g*. life
7:16. the teaching that I *g*. is not my own
7:23. *g*. health on the Sabbath
9:34. who are you to *g*. us lessons
12:2. a supper was *g*. in his honour
Acts 2:23. when he had been *g*. up to you
3:13. *g*. the highest honour to his servant Jesus
4:9. help *g*. to a sick man
4:20. we cannot possibly *g*. up speaking
4:21. all *g*. glory to God
8:31. unless someone will *g*. me the clue
19:3. what baptism were you *g*.
20:28. the Holy Spirit has *g*. you charge
Rom. 8:2. the life-*g*. law of the Spirit
8:11. *g*. new life to your mortal bodies
8:23. the Spirit is *g*. as first fruits
8:30. he has also *g*. his splendour
12:10. *g*. pride of place to one another
15:14. well able to *g*. advice to one another
1 Cor. 16:16. *g*. their due position to such persons
2 Cor. 8:12. an eager desire to *g*.
Eph. 1:11. we have been *g*. our share in the heritage

4:3. the unity which the Spirit *g*.
4:17. *g*. up living like pagans
5:18. do not *g*. way to drunkenness
5:20. *g*. thanks every day for everything
6:7. *g*. the cheerful service
6:9. *g*. up using threats
6:15. to *g*. you firm footing
6:17. take that which the Spirit *g*. you
6:18. *g*. yourselves wholly to prayer
Phil. 1:19. the Spirit of Jesus Christ is *g*. me for support
4:14. him who *g*. me power
2 Thess. 3:15. *g*. him friendly advice
1 Tim. 6:3. *g*. his mind to wholesome precepts
6:13. God, who *g*. life to all things
6:18. ready to *g*. away and to share
Heb. 7:6. *g*. his blessing to the man
11:31. she had *g*. the spies a kindly welcome
1 Pet. 4:7. sober life, *g*. to prayer
2 Pet. 3:2. the commands *g*. by the Lord
1 John 5:13. *g*. their allegiance to the Son of God
Rev. 15:2. the harps which God had *g*. them
19:8. for her dress she had been *g*. fine linen
22:20. who *g*. this testimony speaks

giver
Heb. 10:23. the *G*. of the promise may be trusted
Jam. 1:5. God is a generous *g*.

glad-ly
Luke 6:23. on that day be *g*.
15:16. *g*. to fill his belly with the pods
16:21. *g*. to satisfy his hunger
19:6. welcomed him *g*.
John 14:28. *g*. to hear that I was going to the Father
16:20. the world will be *g*.
Phil. 2:17. I am *g*. of it

gladness
Acts 2:28. thou wilt fill me with *g*.
Phil. 2:17. I share my *g*. with you all

glamour
Mat. 13:22 } the false *g*. of wealth
Mark 4:19 }
1 John 2:16. all the *g*. of its life
Rev. 18:14. all the glitter and the *g*. are lost

glances
Jam. 1:24. he *g*. at himself

gleam-ed
Rev. 1:15. his feet *g*. like burnished brass
2:18. whose feet *g*.
4:3. appearance was like the *g*. of jasper

glitter
Rev. 18:14. all the *g.* and the glamour
   are lost

gloat
1 Cor. 13:6. not *g.* over other men's sins
Rev. 11:10. all men on earth *g.* over
   them

gloom-y
Mat. 6:16. do not look *g.* like the
   hypocrites
Luke 24:16. their faces full of *g.*
Heb. 12:18. darkness, *g.*, and whirlwind
Jam. 4:9. your gaiety into *g.*

glorify-ies-ied
John 8:54. Jesus replied, 'If I *g.* myself,
   . . . It is the Father who *g.* me
1 Tim. 3:16. *g.* in high heaven

glorious
Eph. 1:17. the all-*g.* Father
   Col. 1:27. how rich and *g.* it is
2 Thess. 3:1. the swift and *g.* course
2 Tim. 2:10. the *g.* and eternal salvation
1 Pet. 4:14. that *g.* Spirit

glory
John 8:54. that *g.* of mine is worthless

glutton-s
Mat. 11:19. a *g.* and a drinker
Tit. 1:12. vicious brutes, lazy *g.*

goad-ed
Acts 5:17. *g.* into action by jealousy
   26:14. this kicking against the *g.*
Eph. 6:4. must not *g.* your children

goal
Luke 13:32. on the third day I reach
   my *g.*
Rom. 11:36. Source, Guide, and *G.* of all
1 Cor. 9:26. with a clear *g.* before me
Phil 3:14. I press towards the *g.*

God
Mat. 19:11. only those for whom *G.* has
   appointed it
   21:25. was it from *G.* . . .If we say,
   'from *G.*
   24:22 ⎫
   24:24 ⎭ *G.*'s chosen
   26:27. offered thanks to *G.*
   26:64 the Son of Man seated at the
   right hand of *G.*
   27:52. many of *G.*'s people arose
Mark 4:12. turn to *G.* and be forgiven
   7:11. Corban' (meaning, set apart
   for *G.*
   8:6. giving thanks to *G.*
   11:30. was it from *G.*
   11:31. if we say, 'from *G.*
   13:22. to mislead *G.*'s chosen
   14:23. offered thanks to *G.*
   14:62. the Son of Man seated on the
   right hand of *G.*

Luke 1:42. *G.*'s blessing is on you above
   all women
   2:38. returned thanks to *G.*
   7:35. *G.*'s wisdom is proved right
   13:35. your temple, forsaken by *G.*
   15:21. Father, I have sinned against *G.*
   19:44. you did not recognize *G.*'s
   moment
   20:4. was the baptism of John from *G.*
   20:5. if we say, 'from *G.*
John 3:27. a man can have only what
   G. gives him
   5:45. *G.*'s tribunal
   12:13. *G.* bless the king of Israel
Acts 7:4. *G.* led him to migrate
   7:38. the living utterances of *G.*
   7:44. *G.* commanded when he told
   Moses
   18:27. who had by *G.*'s grace become believers
Rom. 3:24. justified by *G.*'s free grace
   5:16. the gift of *G.*
   5:17. *G.*'s grace
   7:6. serve *G.* in a new way
   8:11. *G.* who raised Christ Jesus
   12:6. allotted to us by *G.*'s grace
   14:10. *G.*'s tribunal
1 Cor. 7:14. belongs to *G.* . . . belong
   to *G.*
   13:12. like *G.*'s knowledge of me
   15:25. until *G.* has put all enemies
   under his feet
   15:27. it clearly means to exclude *G.*
2 Cor. 1:11. the gracious favour *G.* has
   shown
Gal. 2:8. *G.* whose action made Peter
   an apostle
   4:23. through *G.*'s promise
   4:28. children of *G.*'s promise
   5:4. fallen out of the domain of *G.*'s
   grace
   5:8. *G.* who is calling you
   5:10. bear *G.*'s judgement
Eph. 1:23. the entire fullness of *G.*
   2:2. *G.*'s rebel subjects
   2:3. the dreadful judgement of *G.*
   3:12. we have access to *G.*
   4:1. as *G.* has called you
   5:4. rather be thanking *G.*
   Phil. 1:14. to speak the word of *G.*
   fearlessly
Col. 1:8. *G*-given love
   1:9. we ask *G.* that you may receive
   1:19. the complete being of *G.*, by
   G.'s own choice
   1:20. *G.* chose to reconcile
   1:21. estranged from *G.*
   1:22. *G.* has reconciled you.
   2:3. *G.*'s treasures of wisdom and
   knowledge
   3:10. brought to know *G.*
2 Thess. 2:3. the final rebellion against *G.*
1 Tim. 1:4. *G.*'s plan for us
Heb. 1:3. *G.*'s splendour

Heb. 3:1. the family of *G.*
  3:2. Moses also was faithful in *G.*'s household
  3:5. a servitor in *G.*'s whole household...the words that *G.* would speak
  4:7. *G.* fixes another day
  4:8. *G.* would not thus have spoken
  4:16. the throne of our gracious *G.*
  6:8. *G.*'s curse hangs over it
  8:8. *G.*, finding fault with them
  9:5. cherubim of *G.*'s glory
  9:15. those whom *G.* has called
  11:21. worshipped *G.*
  11:26. *G.*'s Anointed
  11:33. saw *G.*'s promises fulfilled
  13:5. *G.* himself has said
  13:9. strength from the grace of *G.*
2 Pet. 2:6. Sodom and Gomorrah *G.* burned to ashes
  2:14. *G.*'s curse is on them
  3:2. the predictions made by *G.*'s own prophets
  3:7. the present heavens and earth, again by *G.*'s word
1 John 3:4. to commit sin is to break *G.*'s law
  3:7. righteous, as *G.* is righteous
  5:14. we can approach *G.* with confidence
  5:16. he should pray to *G.* for him
3 John 6. the *G.* we serve
Jude 3. the faith which *G.* entrusted to his people
  6. *G.* has reserved them for judgement also 1 Cor. 11:24, 14:16; Eph. 5:3; Phil. 4:21, 22; Col. 1:4, 26; 1 Tim. 5:10; 2 Tim. 2:1; Philem. 5, 7; Heb. 13:24; Jam. 1:9, 12; 2:7; 2 John 13

god-s
Rom. 2:22. you abominate false *g.*
1 Cor. 12:2. those dumb heathen *g.*
1 John 5:21. be on the watch against false *g.*
Rev. 9:20. the *g.* their hands had fashioned

godfearing
Acts 10:35. the man who is *g.*
  17:4. a great number of *g.* Greeks

godless
Mat. 12:39. a wicked, *g.* generation
Mark 8:38. this wicked and *g.* age
Rom. 1:18. the *g.* wickedness of men
1 Tim. 4:7. have nothing to do with those *g.* myths
2 Tim. 2:16. stray further and further into *g.* courses
Tit. 2:12. renounce *g.* ways
2 Pet. 2:5. that world of *g.* men
  2:6. *g.* men in future days
  3:7. the *g.* will be destroyed

1 John 2:15. do not set your hearts on the *g.* world
  2:16. from the *g.* world
  3:1. the *g.* world does not recognize us
  4:4. he who inspires the *g.* world
  5:4. victor over the *g.* world
  5:19. the whole *g.* world
Jude 15. convict all the *g.* of all the *g.* deeds they had committed, and of all the defiant words which *g.* sinners had spoken against him
  18. follow their own *g.* lusts

godliness
Acts 3:12. power of *g.* of our own
Tit. 2:12. *g.* in the present age

gold
Mat. 25:15. five bags of *g.*
  25:18. one bag of *g.*
  25:20. five bags of *g.*
  25:25. hid your *g.* in the ground
  25:28. take the bag of *g.* from him

gong
1 Cor. 13:1. I am a sounding *g.*

good
Mat. 5:48. your heavenly Father is all *g.*
  6:4. your *g.* deed must be secret
  8:17. to make *g.* the prophecy of Isaiah
  9.35. the *g.* news of the Kingdom
  10:41. receives a *g.* man because he is a *g.* man will be given a *g.* man's reward
  11:5. the poor are hearing the *g.* news
  11:30 my yoke is *g.* to bear
  12:12. permitted to do *g.* on the Sabbath
  13:35. making *g.* the prophecy of Isaiah
  13:49. separate the wicked from the *g.*
  23:23. mercy, and *g.* faith
  26:9. it could have been sold for a *g.* sum
  26.16. a *g.* opportunity to betray him
Mark 6:20. knowing him to be a *g.* and holy man
  14:11. a *g.* opportunity to betray him
  16:15. proclaim the *G.* News
Luke 1:19. bring you this *g.* news
  3:18. announced the *g.* news
  4:18. sent me to announce *g.* news
  4:43. the *g.* news of the kingdom of God
  5:39. the old wine is *g.*
  7:10. found the servant in *g.* health
  7:22. the poor are hearing the *g.* news
  8:1. proclaiming the *g.* news
  9:6. they told the *g.* news
  12:14. my *g.* man, who set me over you
  14:14. when *g.* men rise from the dead

Luke 16:16. the *g.* news of the Kingdom of God

20:1. telling them the *g.* news

24:41. it seemed too *g.* to be true

John 1:27. I am not *g.* enough to unfasten his shoes

5:31. that testimony does not hold *g.*

11:15. it will be for your *g.* and for the *g.* of your faith

12:19. you see you are doing no *g.* at all

16:7. it is for your *g.* that I am leaving you

18:9. this was to make *g.* his words

Acts 5:42. telling the *g.* news of Jesus the Messiah

6:3. seven men of *g.* reputation

8:12. Philip with his *g.* news

8:25. bringing the *g.* news to many Samaritan villages

8:35. he told him the *g.* news of Jesus

10:36. the *g.* news of peace through Jesus Christ

11:20. the *g.* news of the Lord Jesus

13:32. to give you the *g.* news

14:7. continued to spread the *g.* news

14:15. the *g.* news we bring

14:17. *g.* cheer in plenty

14:21. bringing the *g.* news to that town

15:33. with the *g.* wishes of the brethren

16:10. God had called us to bring them the *g.* news

20:20. I kept back nothing that was for your *g.*

24:2. for the *g.* of this province

24:13. they cannot make *g.* the charges

24:15. a resurrection of *g.* and wicked alike

Rom. 10:16. not all have responded to the *g.* news

15:8. making *g.* his promises to the patriarchs

16:2. been a *g.* friend to many

1 Cor. 6:12. not everything is for my *g.*

7:35. I am thinking simply of your own *g.*

10:33. regarding not my own *g.* but the *g.* of the many

11:17. your meetings tend to do more harm than *g.*

15:33. bad company is the ruin of a *g.* character

2 Cor. 9:13. contribution to their need and to the general *g.*

10:8. I shall make my boast *g.*

Gal. 1:15. in his *g.* pleasure God

1:23. our former persecutor is preaching the *g.* news

5:2. if you receive circumcision Christ will do you no *g.*

6:9. let us never tire of doing *g.*

Eph. 1:13. the *g.* news of your salvation

2:17. proclaimed the *g.* news

3:8. proclaiming to the Gentiles the *g.* news

4:17. pagans with their *g.*-for-nothing notions

Phil. 1:22. if my living on in the body may serve some *g.* purpose

1 Thess. 2:9. the *g.* news of God

2:16. retribution has overtaken them for *g.* and all

1 Tim. 3:12. *g.* at managing his children

6:3. *g.* religious teaching

Tit. 1:3. now in his own *g.* time

Heb. 4:2. we have heard the *g.* news, as they did. But in them the message they heard did no *g.*

4:6. those who first heard the *g.* news

11:7. took *g.* heed and built an ark

11:38. they were too *g.* for this world

12:23. the spirits of *g.* men made perfect

Jam. 2:16. *g.* luck to you . . . what is the *g.* of that

5:13. is anyone in *g.* heart

5:16. a *g.* man's prayer is powerful

1 Pet. 2:3. surely you have tasted that the Lord is *g.*

2:15. by your *g.* conduct you should put ignorance and stupidity to silence

3:6. if you do *g.* and show no fear

2 Pet. 2:7. Lot, who was a *g.* man

2:8. their evil courses tortured that *g.* man's heart

3 John 2. I pray that you may enjoy *g.* health

Rev. 2:19. your *g.* service and your fortitude

good-bye

Luke 9:61. first say *g.* to my people

Acts 20:1. said *g.* and set out on his journey

21:6. prayed, then bade each other *g.*

goodness

Mat. 5:48. you must therefore be all *g.*

Luke 18:9. those who were sure of their own *g.*

Acts 13:10. enemy of all *g.*

2 Cor. 5:21. made one with the *g.* of God

Heb. 11:4. through faith his *g.* was attested

Rev. 22:11. let the good man persevere in his *g.*

goods

Mat. 24:17. he must not come down to fetch his *g.*

Mark 11:16. as a thoroughfare for carrying *g.*

1 Tim. 6:17. rich in this world's *g.*

gorged
Rev. 19:21. the birds *g*. themselves on their flesh

gospel
Mark 3:14. he would send out to proclaim the *G*.
Luke 1:2. servants of the *G*.
4:44. he proclaimed the *G*. in the synagogues
Rom. 1:2. this *G*. God announced beforehand
1 Cor. 1:21. by the folly of the *G*.
2:4. the *G*. I proclaimed
15:2. the *G*. as I preached it to you
15:14. then our *g*. is null and void
Gal. 3:2. by believing the *g*. message
3:5. have faith in the *g*. message
2 Tim. 1:11. of this *G*. I, by his appointment, am herald
4:5. work to spread the *G*.
4:17. the full proclamation of the *G*.
Tit. 2:5. the *G*. will not be brought into disrepute
1 Pet. 3:1. any of them who disbelieve the *G*.

gossip-s
Acts 28:21. *g*. to your discredit
2 Cor. 12:20. backbiting and *g*.
1 Tim. 5:13. *g*. and busybodies

govern-ed-ing
Rom. 2:8. *g*. by selfish ambition
15:12. raised up to *g*. the Gentiles
1 Cor. 2:6. its *g*. powers, which are declining
2 Cor. 1:12. *g*. by a devout and godly sincerity
Heb. 13:9. never done any good to those who were *g*. by them

government
Rom. 13:3. *g*., a terror to crime
Eph. 1:21. heavenly realms, far above all *g*.
Tit. 3:1. submissive to the *g*.

governor-s
Mark 13:9. appear before *g*. and kings on my account
15:6. the *G*. used to release one prisoner
15:16. took him inside the courtyard (the *G*. headquarters
Luke 21:12. haled before kings and *g*.
John 18:28. Jesus was led into the *G*. headquarters
Acts 13:7. the *G*., Sergius Paulus, an intelligent man
13:8. trying to turn the *G*. away from the Faith
13:12. when the *G*. saw what had happened

grabber-s
1 Cor. 5:10. *g*. and swindlers
6:10. thieves or *g*. or drunkards

grace
Acts 6:8. Stephen, who was full of *g*. and power
Rom. 5:16. but the act of *g*.
15:16. his *g*. has made me a minister
1 Cor. 2:12. all that God of his own *g*. gives us

gracious
Luke 1:30. God has been *g*. to you
Rom. 11:29. the *g*. gifts of God
2 Cor. 1:11. the *g*. favour God has shown
Phil. 4:8. all that is lovable and *g*.

grain-s
John 12:24. a *g*. of wheat remains a solitary *g*. unless it falls into the ground
Heb. 11:12. countless *g*. of sand on the sea-shore

granary
Mat. 3:12. the wheat he will gather into his *g*.
Luke 3:17. gather the wheat into his *g*.

grand
Luke 7:25. look in palaces for *g*. clothes

grandchildren
1 Tim. 5:4. if a widow has children or *g*.

grandparents
1 Tim. 5:4. parents and *g*.

grant-ed-ing
Mat. 9:8. praised God for *g*. such authority to men
13:11. *g*. to you to know the secrets
14:9. ordered the request to be *g*.
18:19. that request will be *g*.
20:23 ⎱ to sit at my right or left is
Mark 10:40 ⎰ not for me to *g*.
Luke 8:10. *g*. to you to know the secrets
John 6:65. unless it has been *g*. to him by the Father
11:22. whatever you ask of God, God will *g*. you
19:11. if it had not been *g*. you from above
Acts 3:19. the Lord may *g*. you a time of recovery
4:12. no other name under heaven *g*. to men
5:31. to *g*. Israel repentance
27:24. God has *g*. you the lives of all
Rom. 5:11. we have now been *g*. reconciliation
11:27. this is the covenant I will *g*. them
1 Cor. 7:7. the gift God has *g*. him
7:17. the gift the Lord has *g*. him

1 Cor. 12:9. another, by the same Spirit, is *g*. faith
2 Cor. 12:1. revelations *g*. by the Lord
12:16. *g*. that I did not prove a burden to you
Eph. 3:8. he has *g*. of his grace
6:19. that I may be *g*. the right words
Phil. 1:29. you have been *g*. the privilege
1 Tim. 5:3. the status of widow is to be *g*.
2 Tim. 1:9. *g*. to us in Christ Jesus
2:25. the Lord may *g*. them a change of heart
Philem. 22. God will *g*. me to you
Heb. 5:5. it was *g*. by God
Jam. 4:3. your requests are not *g*.
1 John 5:16. pray to God for him, and he will *g*. him life
Rev. 13:7. *g*. authority over every tribe

grape-s
Rev. 14:19. gathered in its *g*.

grasp-ed-ing
Mark 5:33. when she *g*. what had happened
Luke 18:34. they did not *g*. what he was talking about
John 8:43. my revelation is beyond your *g*.
Acts 3:7. he *g*. him by the right hand
1 Cor. 2:14. it is folly to him; he cannot *g*. it
5:11. so-called Christian who leads a loose life, or is *g*.
2 Cor. 6:6. our *g*. of truth
Eph. 3:18. may you be strong to *g*.
Col. 2:2. *g*. God's secret
1 Tim. 6:19. *g*. the life which is life indeed
Heb. 6:18. *g*. the hope set before us

grateful-ly
Luke 17:9. is he *g*. to the servant
Acts 24:3. we welcome this, sir, most *g*.
Rom. 16:4. the gentile congregations are *g*.

gratitude
Col. 3:15. be filled with *g*.
2 Tim. 3:2. no *g*., no piety

grave
Mat. 27:61. Mary, sitting opposite the *g*.
27:64. for the *g*. to be made secure
27:66. made the *g*. secure
28:1. came to look at the *g*.
Luke 8:23. were in *g*. danger
Acts 6:2. a *g*. mistake for us to neglect the word of God
18:14. *g*. misdemeanour
25:7. bringing many *g*. charges
27:10. it will mean *g*. loss
Rom. 3:13. their throat is an open *g*.
1 Thess. 1:6. meant *g*. suffering for you
Heb. 5:7. God who was able to deliver him from the *g*.

great-er-ly
Mat. 2:3. King Herod was *g*. perturbed
7:3. the *g*. plank in your own
14:20. twelve *g*. baskets
15:31. *g*. was the amazement of the people
20:26. whoever wants to be *g*. must be your servant
26:22. in *g*. distress they exclaimed
Mark 5:21. a *g*. crowd once more gathered
5:24. accompanied by a *g*. crowd
6:20. listening left him *g*. perplexed
6:26. the king was *g*. distressed
6:43. twelve *g*. basketfuls of scraps
8:31. the Son of Man had to undergo *g*. sufferings
9:12. he is to endure *g*. sufferings
12:37. there was a *g*. crowd
14:11. they were *g*. pleased
Luke 2:13. a *g*. company of the heavenly host
2:48. searching for you in *g*. anxiety
6:41. the *g*. plank in your own
7:47. her *g*. love proves that her many sins
9:17. they filled twelve *g*. baskets
9:22. the Son of Man has to undergo *g*. sufferings
10:12. more bearable for Sodom on the *g*. Day
13:2. *g*. sinners than anyone else
15:7. *g*. joy in heaven over one sinner who repents
16:10. trusted in little things can be trusted also in *g*.; and the man who is dishonest in little things is dishonest also in *g*. things
16:19. feasted in *g*. magnificence
18:5. this widow is so *g*. a nuisance
19:42. if only you had known, on this *g*. day
20:46. have a *g*. liking for respectful greetings
21:34. the *g*. Day closes upon you suddenly
22:5. they were *g*. pleased and undertook to pay him
23:8. when Herod saw Jesus he was *g*. pleased
John 3:30. as he grows *g*., I must grow less
6:4. Passover, the *g*. Jewish festival
7:3. may see the *g*. things you are doing
11:43. raised his voice in a *g*. cry: 'Lazarus come forth
12:9. a *g*. number of the Jews heard that he was there
12:12. the *g*. body of pilgrims who had come to the festival
16:12. the burden would be too *g*. for you now

John 19:31. that Sabbath was a day of *g.* solemnity

Acts 2:11. telling in our own tongues the *g.* things God has done

8:7. the unclean spirits came out with a *g.* outcry

17:11. they received the message with *g.* eagerness

18:26. expounded the new way to him in *g.* detail

19:24. provided a *g.* deal of employment

27:20. a *g.* storm was raging

Rom. 3:2. what is the value of circumcision? *G.*

3:7. brings him all the *g.* honour because of my falsehood

5:17. receive in far *g.* measure God's grace

9:31. Israel made *g.* efforts after a law of righteousness

2 Cor. 2:4. letter I sent you came out of *g.* distress

3:8. must not even *g.* splendour

3:10. outshone by a splendour *g.* still

3:11. how much *g.* is the splendour of that which endures

4:15. the *g.* may be the chorus of thanksgiving

7:4. I have *g.* pride in you

7:7. *g.* comforted about you

10:15. a position among you *g.* than ever before

Gal. 3:4. have all your *g.* experiences been in vain

Eph. 2:7. how *g.* his kindness to us in Christ Jesus

6:16. take up the *g.* shield of faith

2 Thess. 1:3. the love you have, each for all and all for each, grows ever *g.*

1:10. when on that *g.* Day he comes

1 Tim. 6:12. run the *g.* race of faith

2 Tim. 1:12. put into my charge, until the *g.* Day

1:18. find mercy from the Lord on the *g.* Day

4:7. I have run the *g.* race

4:8. award me on that *g.* Day

Heb. 3:3. worthy of *g.* honour than Moses

7:7. the lesser is always blessed by the *g.*

7:20. how *g.* a difference it makes that an oath was sworn

9:14. how much *g.* is the power of the blood of Christ

10:21. a *g.* priest set over the household of God

11:4. Abel offered a sacrifice *g.* than Cain's

Jam. 5:1. you who have *g.* possessions

1 Pet. 1:8. a joy too *g.* for words

2:6. a choice corner-stone of *g.* worth

2:7. the *g.* worth of which it speaks

1 John 3:1. how *g.* is the love that the Father has shown to us

Rev. 8:3. he was given a *g.* quantity of incense

8:11. men in *g.* numbers died

10:3. then he gave a *g.* shout

greatness

Luke 1:46. tell out, my soul, the *g.* of the Lord

Acts 10:46. acclaiming the *g.* of God

Phil. 1:20. the *g.* of Christ will shine out clearly in my person

greed-y

Mark 7:22. ruthless *g.*, and malice

Luke 11:39. inside you there is nothing but *g.*

12:15. be on your guard against *g.*

18:11. I am not like the rest of men, *g.*

Eph. 5:3. ruthless *g.*, must not be so much as mentioned

5:5. the *g.* which makes an idol of gain

Col. 3:5. the ruthless *g.* which is nothing less than idolatry

1 Thess. 2:5. a cloak for *g.*

2 Pet. 2:3. their *g.* for money

2:14. past masters in mercenary *g.*

Greek-s

John 7:35. will he go to the Dispersion among the *G.*, and teach the *G.*

Acts 6:1. those of them who spoke *G.*

9:29. debating with the *G.*-speaking Jews

9:36. Tabitha (in *G.*, Dorcas

Rom. 2:9. grinding misery for every human being who is an evil-doer, for the Jew first and for the *G.* also; and for every well-doer there will be glory, honour, and peace, for the Jew first and also for the *G.*

3:9. Jews and *G.* alike are all under the power of sin

1 Cor. 10:32. give no offence to Jews, or *G.*

12:13. in the one Spirit, whether we are Jews or *G.*

greet-ed-ing-ings

Mat. 5:47. if you *g.* only your brothers

28:9. Jesus was there in their path. He gave them his *g.*

Mark 12:38. respectful *g.* in the street

Luke 1:28. the angel went in and said to her, '*G.*, most favoured one

1:29. wondered what this *g.* might mean

1:40. went into Zechariah's house and *g.* Elizabeth

1:41. Elizabeth heard Mary's *g.*

1:44. when your *g.* sounded in my ears

10:4. exchange no *g.* on the road

also Acts 21:7, 19; Rom. 1:7, 16:10,
13 to 16, 21, 22, 23; 1 Cor. 16:19,
21; 2 Cor. 13:13; Gal. 1:2; Phil.
4:21; Col. 4:10, 12, 18; 2 Thess.
3:17; 2 Tim. 4:19, 21; Philm. 23;
Heb. 13:24; Jam. 1:1; 1 Pet. 5:13;
2 John 10, 11

grew
Mat. 14:15. when it *g.* late the disciples
came
14:23. it *g.* late, and he was there by
himself
Mark 4:8. *g.*, and bore fruit
6:47. it *g.* late and the boat was
already well out
Luke 2:52. as Jesus *g.* up he advanced
in wisdom
8:7. the thistles *g.* up with it and
choked it
8:8. *g.*, and yielded a hundredfold
John 6:18. the sea *g.* rough
Acts 3:7. his feet and ankles *g.* strong
9:22. Saul *g.* more and more forceful
9:31. the church . . . *g.* in numbers
10:10. Peter went up on the roof to
pray. He *g.* hungry
16:5. the congregations *g.* stronger in
faith
20:9. *g.* more and more sleepy as Paul
went on
1 Cor. 13:11. When I *g.* up, I had finished
with childish things
Heb. 11:24. Moses, when he *g.* up,
refused to be called the son of
Pharoah's daughter
11:34. they *g.* powerful in war
Rev. 12:17. the dragon *g.* furious
18:19. *g.* rich on her wealth

grief-s
Mat. 17:23. they were filled with *g.*
Mark 26:38 ⎱ my heart is ready to break
14:34 ⎰ with *g.*
Luke 22:45. worn out by *g.*
John 16:6. you are plunged into *g.*
16:20. plunged in *g.*, your *g.* will be
turned to joy
Rom. 9:2. in my heart there is great *g.*
1 Cor. 7:28. *g.* in this bodily life
1 Tim. 6:10. spiked themselves on many
thorny *g.*
2 Pet. 1:10. you will never come to *g.*
Rev. 18:7. mete out *g.* and torment

grievance
Mat. 5:23. your brother has a *g.* against
you
Mark 11:25. have a *g.* against anyone

grieve
1 Cor. 7:30. nothing to *g.* them
1 Thess. 4:13. you should not *g.* like the
rest of men

grind-s-ing
Mat. 8:12. place of wailing and *g.* of
teeth
13:42 ⎤
13:50 ⎥
22:13 ⎬ grinding of teeth
24:51 ⎥
25:30 ⎦
Mark 9:18. foams at the mouth, *g.* his
teeth
Luke 13:28. *g.* of teeth there
Rom. 2:9. *g.* misery

grip-ped
Mat. 18:28. he *g.* him by the throat
Luke 4:38. in the *g.* of a high fever
8:37. in the *g.* of a great fear
Acts 2:24. that death should keep him
in its *g.*
1 Tim. 6:5. lost *g.* of the truth

grope-d
Acts 13:11. he *g.* about for someone

ground-s-ed
Mat. 2:11. bowed to the *g.* in homage
13:5. some seed fell on rocky *g.*
13:20. sown on rocky *g.*
19:3. to divorce his wife on any and
every *g.*
23:35. innocent blood spilt on the *g.*
25:18. dug a hole in the *g.*
25:25. hid your gold in the *g.*
Mark 4:28. the *g.* produces a crop
4:31. seed in the *g.*
9:18 dashes him to the *g.*
Luke 5:12. he bowed to the *g.*
6:17. took his stand on level *g.*
9:42. the devil dashed him to the *g.*
John 1:50. is this the *g.* of your faith
Acts 1:18. fell forward on the *g.*
7:54. they *g.* their teeth
9:4. he fell to the *g.* and heard a voice
9:8. Saul got up from the *g.*
10:11. lowered to the *g.*
10:25. bowed to the *g.*
13:28. find *g.* for the sentence of death
20:9. fell from the third floor to the *g.*
26:14. we all fell to the *g.*
Rom. 4:2. he has a *g.* for pride. But he
has no such *g.* before God
4:16. on the *g.* of faith
5:4. the *g.* of hope
15:17. *g.* for pride in the service of
God
2 Cor. 1:7. our hope for you is firmly *g.*
11:12. cut the *g.* from under
Gal. 3:22. faith in Jesus Christ may be
the *g.*
Eph. 6:13. able to stand your *g.*
Phil. 3:4. not that I am without *g.*
Heb. 11:38. hiding in caves and holes in
the *g.*
Jam. 3:7. creatures that crawl on the *g.*
2 Pet. 1:12. are well *g.* in the truth

group-s

Mat. 15:1. a *g.* of Pharisees and lawyers
  20:6. another *g.* standing there
  25:32. separate men into two *g.*
Mark 6:39. in *g.* on the green grass
  7:1. a *g.* of Pharisees
Luke 9:14. sit down in *g.* of fifty
Acts 1:14. with them a *g.* of women
  26:5. the strictest *g.* in our religion
1 Cor. 11:18. you fall into sharply
  divided *g.*
Gal. 1:2. I and the *g.* of friends now with
  me

grow-s-n-ing

Mat. 6:19. it *g.* rusty and moth-eaten
  13:15. *g.* gross at heart
  24:12. love for one another will *g.*
  cold
Mark 4:28. full-*g.* corn in the ear
Luke 12:28. *g.* in the field today
  13:6. a fig-tree *g.* in his vineyard
John 3:30. as he *g.* greater, I must *g.* less
Acts 6:1. disciples were *g.* in number
  28:27. this people has *g.* gross at heart
1 Cor. 3:6. God made it *g.*
  3:7. God, who makes it *g.*
  14:20. be *g.*-up in your thinking
2 Cor. 10:15. as your faith *g.*
Eph. 4:16. the whole frame *g.*
  4:18. their minds have *g.* hard as
  stone
Phil. 1:9. that your love may *g.* ever
  richer
  3:10. in *g.* conformity with his death
Col. 1:6. *g.* and bearing fruit
  1:10. *g.* in the knowledge of God
  2:19. *g.* according to God's design
  3:21. for fear they *g.* disheartened
Heb. 1:11. like clothes they shall all
  g. old
  3:8 ⎫
  3:15 ⎬ do not *g.* stubborn
  4:7 ⎭
  5:11. you have *g.* so dull of hearing
  5:14. *g.* men can take solid food
  8:13. anything that is *g.* old
  12:3. not to lose heart and *g.* faint
  12:15. no bitter, noxious weed *g.* up
Jam. 1:15. sin full-*g.* breeds death
Rev. 18:3. *g.* rich on her bloated wealth

growth

Luke 8:14. their further *g.* is choked

grub-ber-ing

1 Tim. 3:8. nor to money-*g.*
Tit. 1:7. no brawler, no money-*g.*

grudge

Mark 6:19. Herodias nursed a *g.* against
  him

grumble-d-ing-rs

Mat. 20:11. they *g.* at their employer
Luke 15:2. doctors of the law began *g.*

1 Cor. 10:10. do not *g.* against God
Jude 16. *g.* and malcontents

guaranteed

2 Cor. 1:21. *g.* as his and anointed
Heb. 6:17. *g.* it by oath

guarantor

Heb. 7:22. Jesus is the *g.*

guard-s-ing

Mat. 10:17. be on your *g.*
  16:6. be on your *g.* against the leaven
  16:11. be on your *g.*, I said, against
  the leaven
  16:12. they were to be on their *g.*
  27:65. you may have your *g.*
  27:66. left the *g.* in charge
  28:4. the *g.* shook with fear
  28:11. some of the *g.* went into the
  city
Mark 6:27. sent a soldier of the *g.*
  8:15. be on your *g.* against the leaven
  13:9. as for you, be on your *g.*
  13:23. be on your *g.*; I have forewarned you
Luke 11:21. on *g.* over his castle
  12:15. be on your *g.* against greed
  22:63. the men who were *g.* Jesus
  mocked
John 16:1. to *g.* you against the break-
  down of your faith
Acts 12:4. under a military *g.*
  12:6. sentries kept *g.*
  12:10. they passed the first *g.*-post
  12:19. he interrogated the *g.*
  16:23. keep them under close *g.*
Rom. 11:20. be on your *g.*
2 Cor. 8:20. we want to *g.* against any
  criticism
Phil. 4:7. will keep *g.* over your hearts
Col. 2:8. be on your *g.*
2 Thess. 3:3. *g.* you from the evil one
2 Tim. 1:14. *g.* the treasure put into our
  charge
  4:15. be on your *g.* against him too

guardian-s

Mat. 18:10. their *g.* angels in heaven
Acts 12:15. it must be his *g.* angel
Gal. 4:2. he is under *g.* and trustees
1 Pet. 2:25. the Shepherd and *G.* of
  your souls

guest-s

Mat. 14:6. Herodias danced before the *g.*
  14:9. out of regard for his oath and
  for his *g.*
  22:3. summon the *g.* he had invited
  22:4. telling them to say to the *g.*
  22:8. the *g.* I invited did not deserve
Mark 6:22. delighted Herod and his *g.*
  6:26. regard for his oath and for his *g.*
Luke 5:29. among the *g.* was a large
  party
  7:49. the other *g.* began to ask

guidance

Luke 14:7. the *g.* were trying to secure
14:10. all your fellow-*g.* will see
14:17. a message for his *g.*
John 2:2. Jesus and his disciples were *g.*
2:10. until the *g.* have drunk freely
12:2. Lazarus sat among the *g.*
Acts 28:23. large numbers as his *g.*

guidance

1 Tim. 4:14. under the *g.* of prophecy

guide-s-d

Mat 15:14. they are blind *g.*, and if one
blind man *g.* another
Luke 2:27. *g.* by the Spirit
6:39. can one blind man be *g.* to
another
Rom. 2:8. take the wrong for their *g.*
11:36. Source, *G.* and Goal of all
14:15. no longer *g.* by love
1 Cor. 12:28. power to *g.* them
2 Cor. 5:7. faith is our *g.*
12:18. have we not both been *g.*
Gal. 5:16. if you are *g.* by the Spirit
6:16. take this principle for their *g.*
Rev. 7:17. *g.* them to the springs of the
water of life

guileless

Phil. 2:15. show yourselves *g.*
Heb. 7:26. devout, *g.*

guilt-y

Mat. 23:35. the *g.* of all the innocent
blood
23:36. this generation will bear the *g.*
of it all
Mark 3:29. he is *g.* of eternal sin

Luke 13:4. more *g.* than all the other
people
23:22. I have not found him *g.*
John 9:41. said Jesus, 'you would not
be *g.* . . . . your *g.* remains
15:22 }
15:24 } they would not be *g.* of sin
19:11. the deeper *g.* lies with the man
Acts 16:37. have not been found *g.*
22:25. moreover has not been found *g.*
25:11. if I am *g.* of any capital crime
Rom. 2:1. you, the judge, are equally *g.*
2:3. who pass judgement on the *g.*
4:5. him who acquits the *g.*
14:23. a man who has doubts is *g.* if
he eats
1 Cor. 6:9. *g.* either of adultery
1 Thess. 2:16. the full measure of their *g.*
Heb. 10:22. our *g.* hearts sprinkled clean
1 John 5:16. when men are not *g.* of
deadly sin
Jude 5. *g.* of unbelief

guise

Mark 16:12. appeared in a different *g.*
Luke 20:20. secret agents in the *g.* of
honest men

gulp

Mat. 23:24. *g.* down a camel

gush

Jam. 3:11. *g.* with both fresh and
brackish water

gust

Eph. 4:14. whirled about by every fresh
g. of teaching

H

habit-s

2 Thess. 3:6. Christian brother who falls
into idle *h.*
2 Pet. 2:7. shocked by the dissolute *h.*

habitation

2 Cor. 5:2. we yearn to have our
heavenly *h.*

Hades

Luke 16:23. *H.*, where he was in torment
Acts 2:27. thou wilt not abandon my
soul to *H.*
2:31. he was not abandoned to *H.*
Rev. 1:18. I hold the keys of death
and *H.*
6:8. *H.* came close behind
20:13. Death and *H.* gave up the dead
20:14. Death and *H.* were flung into
the lake of fire

haemorrhage-s

Mat. 9:20 } a woman who had suffered
Mark 5:25 } from *h.*
5:29. the source of her *h.* dried up
Luke 8:43. suffered from *h.* for twelve
years
8:44. at once her *h.* stopped

Hagar

Gal. 4:24. the covenant that comes from
Mount Sinai: that is *H.*

hail-ed

John 2:9. he *h.* the bridegroom
Heb. 11:13. had seen them far ahead
and *h.* them

hailstone-s

Rev. 16:21. huge *h.* . . . . fell on men from
the sky

hair
Acts 18:18. at Cenchreae he had his *h.* cut off
1 Cor. 11:6. she might as well have her *h.* cut off
1 Tim. 2:9. not with elaborate *h.*-styles

hale-d
Luke 21:12. you will be *h.* before kings

half
Mat. 13:33 ⎱ mixed with *h.* a hundred-
Luke 13:21 ⎰ weight of flour
John 7:14. when the festival was already *h.* over
19:39. myrrh and aloes, more than *h.* a hundredweight
1 Cor. 10:33. I always try to meet everyone *h.*-way
Jam. 5:17. not a drop fell on the land for three years and a *h.*

hall
Mat. 22:10. the *h.* was packed with guests
Acts 19:9. discussions daily in the lecture-*h.*
Rom. 4:11. *h.*-mark of the righteousness

hallow-ed
1 Thess. 4:4. his body, to *h.* and honour it
1 Tim. 4:5. it is *h.* by God's own word
Heb. 9:13. power to *h.* those who have been defiled
1 Pet. 1:2. *h.* to his service by the Spirit

halt-ed
Luke 7:14. the bearers *h.*
24:17. they *h.*, their faces full of gloom
John 18:16. Peter *h.* at the door outside

hamper-ed
Luke 12:50. how *h.* I am until the ordeal is over

hand-s-ed-ing
Mat. 5:25. he may *h.* you over to the judge
10:17. men will *h.* you over to their courts
17:12. the Son of Man is to suffer at their *h.*
20:19. *h.* him over to the foreign power
21:41. *h.* the vineyard over to other tenants
22:19. they *h.* him a silver piece
24:6. hear the noise of battle near at *h.*
24:9. you will then be *h.* over for punishment
25:14. put his capital in their *h.*
26:2. the Son of Man is to be *h.* over for crucifixion
26:55. and you did not lay *h.* on me
27:2. to *h.* him over to Pilate

27:26. *h.* him over to be crucified
Mark 7:13. tradition, *h.* down among you
10:33. *h.* him over to the foreign power
13:4. when the fulfilment of all this is at *h.*
13:7. the noise of battle near at *h.*
13:9. you will be *h.* over to the courts
14:49. you did not lay *h.* on me
15:1. *h.* him over to Pilate
15:15. *h.* him over to be crucified
Luke 1:2. the traditions *h.* down to us
4:6. it has been put in my *h.*
4:17. was *h.* the scroll of the prophet Isaiah
9:47. he took a child by the *h.*
10:36. the man who fell into the *h.* of the robbers
10:40. tell her to come and lend a *h.*
18:32. he will be *h.* over to the foreign power
20:20. a pretext for *h.* him over to the authority
24:20. *h.* him over to be sentenced to death
John 5:36. the very works I have in *h.*
19:11. the man who *h.* me over to you
19:16. he *h.* Jesus over to be crucified
Acts 6:14. the customs *h.* down to us by Moses
9:27. Barnabas, however, took him by the *h.*
16:4. they *h.* on the decisions
19:13. tried their *h.* at using the name of the Lord Jesus
23:33. *h.* Paul over to him
25:11. not open to anyone to *h.* me over as a sop to them
25:16. not Roman practice to *h.* over any accused man
27:1. *h.* over to a centurion
1 Cor. 4:21. am I to come to you with a rod in my *h.*
11:2. the tradition I *h.* on to you
11:23. the tradition which I *h.* on to you
15:3. I *h.* on to you the facts
2 Cor. 4:11. we are being surrendered into the *h.* of death
6:15. a believer join *h.* with an unbeliever
10:6. when once you have put yourselves in our *h.*
1 Thess. 2:13. when we *h.* on God's message, you received it
2 Thess. 2:6. you must now be aware of the restraining *h.*
Heb. 6:6. with their own *h.* they are crucifying the Son of God
2 Pet. 1:17. at the *h.* of God the Father he was invested with honour
Rev. 11:17. thou hast taken thy great power into thy *h.*

handiwork
1 Cor. 9:1. my own *h.*, in the Lord
Eph. 2:10. we are God's *h.*

handkerchief
Luke 19:20. I kept it put away in a *h.*

handle-d-ing
Mark 16:18. if they handle snakes
Acts 19:16. *h.* them with such violence
1 Cor. 4:11. we are roughly *h.*
2 Cor. 8:20. our *h.* of this generous gift

hang-s-ing
Acts 10:39. he was put to death by *h.* on
a gibbet
Heb. 6:8. God's curse *h.* over it

hanker
1 Tim. 5:11. they *h.* after marriage

happen-s-ed-ing
Mat. 1:22. all this *h.* in order to fulfil
5:18. until all that must *h.* has *h.*
8:27. were astonished at what had *h.*
8:33. what had *h.* to the madmen
14:13. when he heard what had *h.*
16:22. no, Lord, this shall never *h.*
to you
18:31. deeply distressed when they
saw what had *h.*
22:26. the same thing *h.* with the
second
24:3. tell us,' they said, 'when will this *h.*
24:6. such things are bound to *h.*
26:56. this has all *h.* to fulfil
27:54. saw the earthquake and all that
was *h.*
28:11. reported to the chief priests
everything that had *h.*
Mark 1:9. it *h.* at this time that Jesus
came
4:4. it *h.* that as he sowed
5:11. there *h.* to be a large herd of pigs
5:14. to see what had *h.*
5:16. what had *h.* to the pigs
5:33. when she grasped what had *h.*
to her
11:21. Peter, recalling what had *h.*
11:23. believes that what he says is *h.*
13:4. tell us,' they said, 'when will
this *h.*
13:7. such things are bound to *h.*
13:29. when you see all this *h.*, you
may know that the end is near
15:7. as it *h.*, the man known as
Barabbas was then in custody
Luke 1:1. the events that have *h.* among
us
1:20. remain silent until the day when
these things *h.* to you
2:15. go straight to Bethlehem and see
this thing that has *h.*
2:20. it had all *h.* as they had been told
5:8. when Simon saw what had *h.*

8:34. the men in charge of them saw
what had *h.*
8:56. he forbade them to tell anyone
what had *h.*
9:7. Prince Herod heard of all that
was *h.*
18:36. he asked what was *h.*
21:7. the sign when it is due to *h.*
21:9. these things are bound to *h.* first
21:12. before all this *h.*
21:28. when all this begins to *h.*
21:31. when you see all this *h.*
23:31. what will *h.* when it is dry
23:48. when they saw what had *h.*,
went home beating their breasts
24:18. staying in Jerusalem not to
know what has *h.* there
24:21. this is the third day since it *h.*
John 12:16. that this had *h.* to him
13:19. that when it *h.* you may believe
14:22. Lord, what can have *h.*
14:29. when it *h.* you may have faith
16:4. when the time comes for it to *h.*
19:36. *h.* in fulfilment of the text of
Scripture
21:21. Peter asked, 'Lord, what will
h. to him
Acts 2:17. this will *h.* in the last days
4:21. giving glory to God for what
had *h.*
5:7. unaware of what had *h.*
5:28. what has *h.*
10:16. this *h.* three times
10:37. tell you what *h.* lately
11:4. the facts as they had *h.*
11:10. this *h.* three times
12:3. this *h.* during the festival of
Unleavened Bread
13:12. saw what had *h.* he became a
believer
15:14. how it first *h.* that God took
notice of the Gentiles
22:6. this is what *h.*
24:22. Felix, who *h.* to be well
informed about the Christian movement
28:6. without seeing anything extraordinary *h.*
28:8. it so *h.* that this man's father was
in bed
Rom. 11:26. when that has *h.*, the whole
of Israel will be saved
1 Cor. 10:6. these events *h.* as symbols
12:2. however you *h.* to be led
Gal. 1:16. when that *h.*
1 Thess. 5:18. give thanks whatever *h.*
Rev. 1:1. what must shortly *h.*
4:1. what must *h.* hereafter
22:6. what must shortly *h.*

happier
2 Cor. 7:7. that has made me *h.* still

happily
1 Cor. 16:11. send him *h.* on his way

happiness
Luke 6:24. you have had your time of *h*.
  14:14. and so find *h*.
Acts 20:35. *h*. lies more in giving than
  in receiving
Rom. 4:6. *h*. of the man whom God
  'counts' as just
  4:9. is this *h*. confined to the circumcised
2 Cor. 1:24. working with you for your
  own *h*.
Phil. 2:2. fill up my cup of *h*.
  2:28. the *h*. of seeing him again
Col. 1:24. my *h*. to suffer for you
2 Tim. 1:4. to make my *h*. complete
Jam. 1:25. who by acting will find *h*.

happy
Mat. 11:6. *h*. is the man who does not
  find me a stumbling-block
  13:16. *h*. are your eyes because they see
  24:46. *h*. that servant who is found at
  his task
Luke 1:45. *h*. is she who has had faith
  7:23. *h*. is the man who does not find
  me a stumbling-block
  10:23. *h*. the eyes that see what you
  are seeing
  11:27. *h*. the womb that carried you
  11:28. no, *h*. are those who hear the
  word of God
  12:37. *h*. are those servants
  12:38. *h*. they if he finds them alert
  12:43. *h*. that servant who is found at
  his task
  14:15. *h*. the man who shall sit at the
  feast
  15:32. celebrating this *h*. day
  23:29. *h*. are the barren
John 20:29. *h*. are they who never saw
  me and yet have found faith
Rom. 4:7. *h*. are they,' he says, 'whose
  lawless deeds are forgiven
  4:8. *h*. is the man whose sins the Lord
  does not count
  16:19. this makes me *h*. about you
2 Cor. 2:3. the very people who ought
  to have made me *h*. . . . for me to
  be *h*. is for all of you to be *h*.
  7:9. but now I am *h*.
  7:13. seeing how *h*. Titus is
  7:16. how *h*. I am now
  8:2. they have been so exuberantly *h*.
Gal. 4:15. have you forgotten how *h*.
  you thought yourselves
Tit. 2:13. the *h*. fulfilment of our hopes
Heb. 13:17. let it be a *h*. task for them
Jam. 1:2. count yourselves supremely *h*.
  1:12. *h*. the man who remains steadfast
Rev. 1:3. *h*. is the man who reads, and
  h. those who listen
  14:13. *h*. are the dead who die in the
  faith

  16:15. *h*. the man who stays awake
  19:9. *h*. are those who are invited to
  the wedding supper
  20:6. *h*. indeed, and one of God's own
  people
  22:7. *h*. is the man who heeds the
  words
  22:14. *h*. are those who wash their
  robes

harangue-d
Acts 12:21. Herod *h*. them

harassed
Mat. 9:36. without a shepherd, *h*. and
  helpless
Acts 5:16. *h*. by unclean spirits

harbour-ed-ing
Mat. 9:4. why do you *h*. these evil
  thoughts
Mark 2:8 ⎱ why do you *h*. thoughts like
Luke 5:22 ⎰ these
Acts 17:7. Jason has *h*. them
  27:12. the *h*. was unsuitable for
  wintering . . . a Cretan *h*.
Jam. 3:14. if you are *h*. bitter jealousy

hard-est-ly
Mat. 11:28. come to me, all whose work
  is *h*.
Mark 5:10. he begged *h*. that Jesus
  would not send them out of the
  country
  8:25. he looked *h*., and now he was
  cured
Luke 4:25. famine lay *h*. over the whole
  country
  5:5. we were *h*. at work all night
  8:42. he could *h*. breathe for the
  crowds
  19:21. because you are a *h*. man
  19:22. you knew, did you, that I am
  a *h*. man
John 19:12. Pilate tried *h*. to release him
Acts 20:35. to help the weak in this way,
  by *h*. work
  27:7. put to it to reach Cnidus
Rom. 5:7. even for a just man one of us
  would *h*. die
  16:6. Mary, who toiled *h*. for you
1 Cor. 16:16. labours *h*. at our common
  task
2 Cor. 4:8. *h*.-pressed on every side
  8:2. the troubles they have been
  through have tried them *h*.
Eph. 4:18. their minds have grown *h*.
  as stone
  4:28. give up stealing, and instead
  work *h*.
Col. 4:12. he prays *h*. for you all the
  time
1 Thess. 2:3. a *h*. struggle it was
  5:12. those who are working so *h*.
2 Tim. 2:15. try *h*. to show yourself
  worthy

1 Pet. 4:18. it is *h*. enough for the righteous to be saved
2 Pet. 1:5. try your *h*. to supplement your faith
Rev. 2:9. I know how *h*. pressed you are

hardship-s
Acts 7:11. famine struck the whole of Egypt and Canaan, and caused great *h*.
14:22. we must pass through many *h*.
20:23. *h*. await me
Rom. 8:35. can affliction or *h*.
2 Cor. 6:4. in *h*. and dire straits
8:13. at the cost of *h*. to yourselves
12:10. *h*., and frustration
1 Thess. 3:3. under all these *h*., not to be shaken
3:4. we were bound to suffer *h*.
3:7. in all our difficulties and *h*.
2 Tim. 2:9. in whose service I am exposed to *h*.
4:5. face *h*., work to spread the Gospel
Heb. 11:25. preferring to suffer *h*.

hark
Mark 15:35. *h*., he is calling Elijah
Acts 5:9. *h*! there at the door are the footsteps

harm-ed
Mat. 27:23. what *h*. has he done
Mark 15:14. why, what *h*. has he done
16:18. they will come to no *h*.
Luke 10:19. nothing will ever *h*. you
Acts 9:13. the *h*. he has done to thy people
18:10. no one shall attempt to do you *h*.
1 Cor. 11:17. your meetings tend to do more *h*. than good
2 Tim. 4:14. the copper-smith did me a great deal of *h*.
4:18. every attempt to do me *h*.
Rev. 2:11. cannot be *h*. by the second death
11:5. if anyone seeks to do them *h*. . . . shall the man die who seeks to do them *h*.

harmful
1 Tim. 6:9. foolish *h*. desires

Harran
Acts 7:2. before he had settled in *H*.
7:4. settled in *H*.

harry-ies-ing
John 10:12. the wolf *h*. the flock
Acts 8:3. Saul, meanwhile, was *h*. the church

harsh
Col. 3:19. love your wives and do not be *h*. with them
1 Tim. 5:1. never be *h*. with an elder

harvest
Luke 8:15. by their perseverence yield a *h*.
John 4:38. the *h*. of their toil
12:24. if it dies, it bears a rich *h*.
Rom. 8:23. firstfruits of the *h*. to come
1 Cor. 9:11. to expect from you a material *h*.
15:20. the firstfruits of the *h*. of the dead
2 Cor. 9:10. swell the *h*. of your benevolence
Gal. 5:22. the *h*. of the Spirit is love, joy, peace
6:8. a *h*. of corruption . . . a *h*. of eternal life
6:9. in due time reap our *h*.
Phil. 1:11. the full *h*. of righteousness
Heb. 12:11. the peaceful *h*. of an honest life
Jam. 3:18. the *h*. reaped by peace-makers
1 Pet. 1:9. reap the *h*. of your faith
Rev. 14:16. its *h*. was reaped
14:18. gather in earth's grape-*h*.

haste
Acts 10:20. make *h*. and go downstairs
Tit. 3:12. make *h*. to join me

hasten
Rom. 3:15. their feet *h*. to shed blood

hastily
Acts 22:29. about to examine him withdrew *h*.

hasty
1 Tim. 5:22. do not be over-*h*. in laying on hands

hatched
Acts 9:23. *h*. a plot against his life

hateful
Rom. 1:30. *h*. to God

hatreds
2 Tim. 3:3. implacable in their *h*.

haughty
Rom. 12:16. do not be *h*.

haul
Luke 5:6. made a big *h*. of fish
14:5. will he hesitate to *h*. it up on the Sabbath day
John 21:6. they could not *h*. the net aboard

haunt
Rev. 18:2. a *h*. for every unclean spirit

hawking
2 Cor. 2:17. we do not go *h*. the word of God about

head-s
Mat. 14:24. battling with a *h*.-wind
22:20. Jesus asked, 'Whose *h*. is this

Mat. 27:9. the price set on a man's *h.*
Mark 12:16. he said to them, 'Whose *h.* is this
Luke 20:24. whose *h.* does it bear
22:47. Judas, one of the Twelve, at their *h.*
23:38. an inscription above his *h.*
Acts 27:15. impossible to keep *h.* to wind
2 Cor. 10:5. rears its proud *h.* against the knowledge of God
2 Thess. 2:2. do not suddenly lose your *h.*
1 Pet. 5:4. when the *H.* Shepherd appears
2 Pet. 2:1. swift disaster on their own *h.*
Rev. 17:17. God has put it into their *h.* to carry out his purpose

heading
Phil. 3:19. they are *h.* for destruction

headquarters
Mat. 27:27. took Jesus into the Governor's *h.*
Mark 15:16. inside the courtyard (the Governor's *h.*
John 18:28. Jesus was led into the Governor's *h.* . . . the Jews themselves stayed outside the *h.*
18:33. Pilate then went back into his *h.*
19:9. going back into his *h.* he asked Jesus
Acts 23:35. held in custody at his *h.*
Phil. 1:13. common knowledge to all at *h.*

headstrong
2 Pet. 2:10. reckless and *h.*

headway
John 8:37. my teaching makes no *h.* with you
Acts 27:7. for a good many days we made little *h.*

head-wind
Mark 6:48. labouring at the oars against a *h.*

heal-ed-ing
Luke 4:27. not one of them was *h.*, but only Naaman
John 6:2. the signs he performed in *h.* the sick
Tit. 2:11. with *h.* for all mankind

health-y
Mat. 9:12. it is not the *h.* that need a doctor
15:28. her daughter was restored to *h.*
Mark 2:17 ⎱ it is not the *h.* that need a
Luke 5:31 ⎰ doctor
7:10. found the servant in good *h.*
John 7:23. giving *h.* on the Sabbath
1 Pet. 2:2. thrive upon it to your souls' *h.*

heap-ed-ing
Luke 22:65. went on *h.* insults upon him
John 15:6. withered branches are *h.* together

hear-s-d-ing
Mat. 3:17. a voice from heaven was *h.*
9:30. see that no one *h.* about this
14:9. deeply distressed when he *h.* it
15:28. *h.* this Jesus replied
21:15. *h.* the boys in the temple shouting
25:6. at midnight a cry was *h.*
Mark 5:43. strict orders to let no one *h.* about it
12:17. they *h.* him with astonishment
Luke 4:21. in your very *h.* this text has come true
20:45. in the *h.* of all the people Jesus said
John 4:41. what they *h.* from his own lips
5:29. rise to *h.* their doom
Acts 2:42. met constantly to *h.* the apostles teach
7:31. the voice of the Lord was *h.*
9:27. Saul had seen the Lord on his journey, and *h.* his voice
18:14. given you Jews a patient *h.*
22:22. they had given him a *h.*
Rom. 1:6. you who have *h.* the call
15:20. where the very name of Christ has not been *h.*
1 Cor. 1:24. those who have *h.* his call
5:6. have you never *h.* the saying
Gal. 1:11. the gospel you *h.* me preach
2 Tim. 4:16. at the first *h.* of my case
Heb. 4:6. those who first *h.* the good news
12:25. do not refuse to *h.* the voice that speaks. Those who refused to *h.* the oracle speaking on earth found no escape; still less shall we escape if we refuse to *h.* the One who speaks from heaven
Rev. 11:15. voices were *h.* in heaven shouting

hearer-s
Rom. 12:8. use it to stir his *h.*
2 Cor. 3:15. a veil lies over the minds of the hearers
Tit. 1:9. move his *h.* with wholesome teaching

heart-s-ed
Mat. 9:2. take *h.*, my son; your sins are forgiven
11:29. I am gentle and humble-*h.*
14:14. his *h.* went out to them
14:20. they all ate to their *h.* content
14:27. take *h*! it is I
15:37. they all ate to their *h.* content
19:22. he went away with a heavy *h.*

Mat. 26:38. my heart is ready to break with grief
Mark 6:34. his *h.* went out to them
  6:42. they all ate to their *h.* content
  6:50. take *h*! It is I
  8:8. they all ate to their *h.* content
  10:21. his *h.* warmed to him
  10:22. he went away with a heavy *h.*
  10:49. take *h.*; stand up; he is calling you
  14:34. my *h.* is ready to break
Luke 1:14. your *h.* will thrill with joy
  1:75 with uprightness of *h.*
  7:13. his *h.* went out to her
  9:17. they all ate to their *h.* content
  15:20. his *h.* went out to him
  18:1. keep on praying and never lose *h.*
  18:23. at these words his *h.* sank
John 1:18. he who is nearest to the Father's *h.*
Acts 27:22. I urge you not to lose *h.*
Rom. 2:4. God's kindness is meant to lead you to a change of *h.*
  2:16. God judges the secrets of human *h.*
  12:1. the worship offered by mind and *h.*
  12:8. if you give to charity, give with all your *h.*
2 Cor. 1:9. felt in our *h.* that we had received a death-sentence
  2:7. put *h.* into him
  4:1. we never lose *h.*
  4:16. no wonder we do not lose *h.*
  5:11. to you in your *h.* of *h.*
  6:13. open wide your *h.* to us
  7:2. a place for us in your *h.*
  7:5. forebodings in our *h.*
  7:9. the wound led to a change of *h.*
  7:10. the wound which is borne in God's way brings a change of *h.*
  7:15. his *h.* warms all the more to you
  9:14. their *h.* will go out to you
  11:3. your single-*h.* devotion to Christ
  11:29. does my *h.* not blaze with indignation
  13:11. take our appeal to *h.*
Eph. 3:13. not to lose *h.* over my sufferings
Phil. 2:1. anything to stir the *h.*
  4:17. do not think I set my *h.* upon the gift
Col. 1:21. you were his enemies in *h.*
  2:7. let your *h.* overflow with thankfulness
  4:2. with mind awake and thankful *h.*
2 Tim. 2:25. the Lord may grant them a change of *h.*
  4:8. set their *h.* on his coming appearance
  4:10. because his *h.* was set on this world
Heb. 11:15. if their *h.* had been in the country they had left

12:3. not to lose *h.*
12:5. nor lose *h.* when he corrects you
Jam. 1:21. the message planted in your *h.*
  5:13. is anyone in good *h.*
2 Pet. 2:8. tortured that good man's *h.*
1 John 2:15. do not set your *h.* on the godless world
  2:24. keep in your *h.* that which you heard
  3:17. shuts up his *h.* against him
  5:10. has this testimony in his own *h.*
Rev. 7:17. the Lamb who is at the *n.* of the throne

hearten-ing
Acts 14:22. *h.* the converts
1 Thess. 5:11. *h.* one another

heathen
Mat. 4:15. *h.* Galilee
  5:47. even the *h.* do as much
  6:32. all these are things for the *h.* to run after
  10:18. to testify before them and the *h.*
Luke 2:32. a revelation to the *h.*
  12:30. things for the *h.* to run after
Acts 2:23. you used *h.* men to crucify
  7:51. *h.* still at heart
1 Cor. 7:12. if a Christian has a *h.* wife
  7:13. a woman who has a *h.* husband
  7:14. the *h.* husband now belongs to God through his Christian wife, and the heathen wife through her Christian husband
  7:15. the *h.* partner
  8:1. food consecrated to *h.* deities
  8:7. with a sense of its *h.* consecration
  8:10. a meal in a *h.* temple . . . food consecrated to the *h.* deity
  10:20. the sacrifices the *h.* offer
  12:2. dumb *h.* gods
2 Cor. 6:16. the idols of the *h.*
2 Pet. 2:18. their *h.* environment

heave-ing
Jam. 1:6. the doubter is like a *h.* sea

heaven-s
Mat. 16:22. *H.* forbid!' he said. 'No, Lord, this shall never happen to you
Mat. 21:9 ⎱ Hosanna in the *h.*
Mark 11:10 ⎰
Luke 1:78. the morning sun from *h.* will rise upon us
  2:14. glory to God in highest *h.*
  9:51. when he was to be taken up to *h.*
Acts 1:2. he was taken up to *h.*
  10:4. your prayers and acts of charity have gone up to *h.*
  19:35. that symbol of her which fell from *h.*
Eph. 6:12. forces of evil in the *h.*
1 Tim. 3:16. glorified in high *h.*
Jam. 1:17. the Father of the lights of *h.*

heavenly
Mat. 19:28. his throne in *h*. splendour
1 Cor. 15:40. there are *h*. bodies and earthly bodies; and the splendour of the *h*. bodies
Gal. 4:26. the *h*. Jerusalem is the free woman

heavily
John 11:33. he sighed *h*.

heavy
Mat. 9:37. the crop is *h*.
19:22. he went away with a *h*. heart
Mark 4:37. a *h*. squall came on
10:22. he went away with a *h*. heart
Luke 8:23. a *h*. squall struck the lake
10:2. the crop is *h*.
12:16. whose land yielded *h*. crops
Acts 27:18. we were making very *h*. weather
2 Cor. 1:8. the burden of it was far too *h*. for us to bear, so *h*. that we even despaired of life
Gal. 6:2. help one another to carry these *h*. loads

Hebrew
John 1:41. Messiah' (which is the *H*. for 'Christ
20:16. Rabbuni!' (which is *H*. for 'My Master

heed-s-ed
Luke 16:31. they will pay no *h*.
22:31. Simon, Simon, take *h*.
John 5:24. anyone who gives *h*. to what I say
10:8. the sheep paid no *h*.
14:23. anyone who loves me will heed what I say
14:24. he who does not love me does not *h*.
15:10. if you heed my commands, you will dwell in my love, as I have *h*. my Father's commands
1 Cor. 14:21. even so they will not *h*. me, says the Lord
2 Cor. 6:2. in the hour of my favour I gave *h*. to you
Heb. 11:7. took good *h*. and built an ark
Rev. 1:3. *h*. what is written in it
22:7. who *h*. the words of prophecy
22:9. those who *h*. the words of this book

heedless
1 Thess. 2:15. the Jews who are *h*. of God's will

heel-s
Mat. 8:33 ⎱ the men in charge of them
Mark 5:14 ⎰ took to their *h*.
Luke 8:34. taking to their *h*.
19:14 sent a delegation on his *h*.
Acts 21:36. at their *h*. yelling, 'Kill him

height-s
Mat. 6:27 ⎱
Luke 12:25 ⎰ add a foot to his *h*.
Eph. 4:8. he ascended into the *h*.
Phil. 2:9. God raised him to the *h*.
Rev. 2:5. from what a *h*. you have fallen
14:20. to the height of the horses' bridles

heir-s
Acts 3:25. you are the *h*. of the prophets
Heb. 11:8. a land destined for himself and his *h*.

held
Mat. 12:5. it is not *h*. against them
13:57. a prophet will always be *h*. in honour
26:50. seized Jesus, and *h*. him fast
27:48. wine, and *h*. it to his lips
Mark 6:4. a prophet will always be *h*. in honour except in his home town
11:32. all *h*. that John was in fact a prophet
14:46. they seized him and *h*. him fast
15:36. on the end of a cane, and *h*. it to his lips
Luke 5:29. Levi *h*. a big reception
14:10. will see the respect in which you are *h*.
John 2:6. each *h*. from twenty to thirty gallons
19:29. fixed it on a javelin, and *h*. it up to his lips
Acts 2:44. all whose faith had drawn them together *h*. everything in common
4:32. everything was *h*. in common
5:34. *h*. in high regard by all the people
7:6. *h*. in slavery and oppression for four hundred years
7:41. the idol, and *h*. a feast in honour
9:31. the church . . . it *h*. on its way and grew in numbers
18:4. *h*. discussions in the synagogue
18:8. Crispus, who *h*. office in the synagogue
18:17. Sosthenes, who *h*. office in the synagogue
18:19. *h*. a discussion with the Jews
23:35. ordered him to be *h*. in custody
Rom. 5:14. death *h*. sway from Adam to Moses
Eph. 4:4. one hope *h*. out in God's call
Col. 1:17. all things are *h*. together in him
2 Tim. 2:20. the latter *h*. cheap
2:26. the devil's snare, in which they have been caught and *h*. at his will
Heb. 10:32. you met the challenge of great sufferings and *h*. firm
Rev. 8:6. the seven angels that *h*. the seven trumpets

helmsman
Jam. 3:4. whatever course the *h.* chooses

help-ed-ing
Mat. 8:5. a centurion came up to ask his *h.*
25:36. when I was ill you came to my *h.*
25:43. you did not come to my *h.*
Mark 1:31. *h.* her to her feet
1:40. knelt before him begging his *h.*
14:7. you can *h.* them whenever you like
Luke 4:38. they asked him to *h.* her
5:12. bowed to the ground and begged his *h.*
15:32. how could we *h.* celebrating this happy day
Acts 4:9. *h.* given to a sick man
9:41 *h.* her to her feet
10:2. gave generously to *h.* the Jewish people
14:27. all that God had *h.* them to do
15:4. reported all that God had *h.* them to do
20:35. it is our duty to *h.* the weak
Rom. 12:8. *h.* others in distress
16:2. business in which she may need your *h.*
1 Cor. 9:16. I cannot *h.* myself; it would be misery to me not to preach
10:23. does everything *h.* the building of the community
14:5. so *h.* to build up the community
14:17. it is no *h.* to the other man
2 Cor. 1:6. to *h.* us to bring you comfort
8:19. *h.* in this beneficent work
9:2. I know how eager you are to *h.*
Gal. 6:2. *h.* one another
Phil. 1:12. the work of the Gospel has been *h.* on
1:25. stand by you all to *h.* you forward
1 Thess. 2:2. by the *h.* of our God
2 Tim. 1:14. with the *h.* of the Holy Spirit
2:7. the Lord will *h.* you to full understanding
Tit. 3:13. do your utmost to *h.* Zenas
Heb. 2:18. he is able to *h.* those who are meeting their test
12:3. that will *h.* you not to lose heart
Jam. 1:27. go to the *h.* of orphans and widows
3 John 6. please *h.* them on their journey

helper
Eph. 6:21. trustworthy *h.* in the Lord's work
Col. 4:7. Tychicus, our dear brother and trustworthy *h.*

helpful
Eph. 4:29. only what is good and *h.* to the occasion

helpless
Mat. 9:36. without a shepherd, harassed and *h.*
Luke 19:48. found they were *h.*
21:25. nations will stand *h.*

hem-med-ming
Luke 8:45. Master, the crowds are *h.* you in
19:43. they will encircle you and *h.* you in
2 Cor. 4:8. hard-pressed on every side, we are never *h.* in

henchmen
John 19:6. the chief priests and their *h.*

herald-s
Mat. 11:10. here is my *h.*, whom I send
24:30. the sign that *h.* the Son of Man
Mark 1:2 ⎫
Luke 7:27 ⎬ here is my *h.* whom I send
1 Tim. 2:7. I was appointed *h.*
2 Tim. 1:11. I, by his appointment, am *h.*

hereafter
Rom. 8:17. to share his splendour *h.*

heritage
Acts 13:19. whose lands he gave them to be their *h.*
20:32. build you up and give you your *h.*
Eph. 1:11. we have been given our share in the *h.*
1:14. that Spirit is the pledge that we shall enter upon our *h.*
1:18. among his people in their *h.*
Col. 1:12. made you fit to share the *h.* of God's people
3:24. a Master who will give you your *h.*
Rev. 21:7. all this is the victor's *h.*

herself
Mark 5:28. said to *h.*, 'If I touch even his clothes
5:29. knew in *h.* that she was cured
Luke 1:36. Elizabeth has *h.* conceived a son
10:39. Mary, who seated *h.* at the Lord's feet
Acts 7:21. Pharoah's daughter *h.* adopted him
Rev. 12:6. the woman *h.* fled into the wilds

hesitate
Mat. 14:31. why did you *h*? How little faith you have
Luke 14:5. will he *h.* to haul it up on the Sabbath day
2 Pet. 1:12. I will not *h.* to remind you of this

hew-ed
Mat. 21:33 ⎫
Mark 12:1 ⎬ *h.* out a winepress

hide-den-ing

Luke 8:17. there is nothing *h*. that will not become public

1 Cor. 13:2. and know every *h*. truth

Eph. 1:9. he has made known to us his *h*. purpose

5:32. it is a great truth that is *h*. here

6:19. freely make known his *h*. purpose

Heb. 4:13. nothing in creation that can *h*. from him

11:38. *h*. in caves and holes

Rev. 3:18. clothes to put on to *h*. the shame

10:7. the *h*. purpose of God

high-er-est

Mat. 5:19. stand *h*. in the kingdom of Heaven

Mark 14:65. the *H*. Priest's men set upon him with blows

Luke 1:52. the humble have been lifted *h*.

4:38. in the grip of a *h*. fever

21:28. stand upright and hold your heads *h*.

22:24. who among them should rank *h*.

22:26. the *h*. among you must bear himself like the youngest

John 5:36. a testimony *h*. than John's

Acts 3:13. the *h*. honour to his servant Jesus

4:33. they were all held in *h*. esteem

5:34. held in *h*. regard by all the people

8:10. all of them, *h*. and low, listened eagerly

8:27. a *h*. official of the Kandake

19:25. our *h*. standard of living

25:23. accompanied by *h*.-ranking officers

Rom. 3:17. strangers to the *h*.-road of peace

1 Cor. 12:31. the *h*. gifts are those you should aim at

2 Cor. 8:18. whose reputation is *h*.

Gal. 2:6. men of *h*. reputation

Col. 3:2. let your thoughts dwell on that *h*. realm

1 Tim. 2:2. sovereigns and all in *h*. office . . . *h*. standards of morality

3:4. a man of the *h*. principles

3:8. deacons, likewise, must be men of *h*. principle

3:11. their wives, equally, must be women of *h*. principle

3:13. deacons with a good record of service may claim a *h*. standing

3:16. glorified in *h*. heaven

6:6. religion does yield *h*. dividends

Tit. 2:2. sober, *h*.-principled

2:3. set a *h*. standard

2:7. show integrity and *h*. principle

Heb. 3:6. fearless and keep our hope *h*.

1 Pet. 3:4. a gentle, quiet spirit, which is of *h*. value

Rev. 18:5. her sins are piled *h*. as heaven

highly

Luke 7:2. a servant whom he valued *h*.

Acts 5:13. people in general spoke *h*. of them

Rom. 14:5. regards one day more *h*. than another

1 Cor. 1:26. few are powerful or *h*. born

highway

John 1:23. make the Lord's *h*. straight

hill-s-side-s-country

Mat. 5:1, 14:23, 18:12, 24:16; Mark 3:13, 5:5, 11, 6:46, 13:14; Luke 9:28, 19:29, 21:21, 37; John 6:3; Acts 1:12; Heb. 11:38; Rev. 17:9

himself

Mat. 12:35. a good man produces good from the store of good within *h*.

14:23. he was there by *h*.

16:25. let *h*. be lost for my sake

22:31. have you never read what God *h*. said

Mark 6:45. he *h*. sent the people away

8:12. he sighed deeply to *h*.

8:35. if a man will let *h*. be lost for my sake

16:8. Jesus *h*. sent out by them

Luke 6:45. good from the store of good within *h*.

John 1:13. the offspring of God *h*.

2:25. he *h*. could tell what was in a man

6:6. Jesus *h*. knew what he meant to do

12:25. the man who loves *h*. is lost, but he who hates *h*. in this world will be kept safe

Acts 7:35. as ruler and liberator by God *h*.

17:25. he is *h*. the universal giver of life

20:28. he won for *h*. by his own blood

Rom. 1:19. God *h*. has disclosed it to them

8:26. the Spirit *h*. is pleading for us

13:14. let Christ Jesus *h*. be the armour that you wear

1 Cor. 3:11. I mean Jesus Christ *h*.

5:7. the sacrifice is offered—Christ *h*.

11:23. came to me from the Lord *h*.

2 Cor. 2:14. the fragrance of the knowledge of *h*.

5:5. God *h*. has shaped us for this very end

5:21. one with the goodness of God *h*.

8:19. we do honour to the Lord *h*.

Eph. 1:23. who *h*. receives the entire fullness of God

Col. 1:22. God has reconciled you to *h*., so that he may present you before *h*.

2:2. that secret is Christ *h*.

Heb. 11:8. a land destined for *h*. and
his heirs
1 John 2:2. he is *h*. the remedy for the
defilement of our sins
4:21. this command comes to us from
Christ *h*.
5:9. this threefold testimony is indeed
that of God *h*.

hinder-ed-ing
Phil. 1:12. the Gospel has been helped
on, rather than *h*.
1 Thess. 2:16. *h*. us from speaking to the
Gentiles

hindrance
Acts 28:31. teaching the facts about the
Lord Jesus Christ quite openly and
without *h*.

history
Acts 17:26. he fixed the epochs of their *h*.
Heb. 9:26. at the climax of *h*. to abolish
sin
Rev. 16:18. a violent earthquake, like
none before it in human *h*.

hoard
1 Tim. 6:18. *h*. a wealth of noble actions

hoist-ed
Acts 27:17. they had *h*. it aboard

hold-s-ing
Mat. 10:22 ⎰ the man who *h*. out to the
24:13 ⎱ end will be saved
24:44. *h*. yourselves ready
Mark 2:2. the space in front of the door
was not big enough to *h*. them
7:11. you *h*. that if a man says to his
father
13:13. the man who *h*. out to the end
Luke 8:15. the hearing of the word, *h*.
it fast
18:39. told him sharply to *h*. his
tongue
21:28. *h*. your heads high, because
your liberation is near
John 3:36 ⎰ has *h*. of eternal life
5:24 ⎱
5:31. if I testify on my own behalf,
that testimony does not *h*. good
5:32. I know that his testimony *h*.
20:31. *h*. the faith that Jesus is the
Christ
21:25. the whole world would not *h*.
the books that would be written
Acts 6:10. could not *h*. their own against
the inspired wisdom
7:60. Lord, do not *h*. this sin against
them
11:23. to *h*. fast to the Lord
13:43. to *h*. fast to the grace of God
19:9. continued to *h*. discussions daily
24:15. in reliance on God I *h*. the hope
Rom. 4:14. those who *h*. by the law

4:16. not only for those who *h*. by the
law
7:16. *h*. it to be admirable
11:20. by faith you *h*. your place
14:3. the man who eats must not *h*. in
contempt the man who does not
14:10. why do you *h*. your brother in
contempt
16:1. who *h*. office in the congregation
1 Cor. 14:22. those who *h*. the faith
15:2. *h*. fast the Gospel
2 Cor. 1:24. your *h*. on the faith is
secure enough
5:19. no longer *h*. men's misdeeds
against them
7:14. the same *h*. of the proud boast
we made
Gal. 2:12. he drew back and began to
h. aloof
Eph. 1:23. *h*. within it the fullness of him
Phil. 1:7. you *h*. me in such affection
3:12. hoping to take *h*. of that for
which Christ once took *h*. of me
3:13. not reckon myself to have got
h. of it yet
Col. 1:4. the faith you *h*. in Christ Jesus
1 Thess. 2:13. you who *h*. the faith
2 Thess. 3:6. *h*. aloof from every
Christian brother who falls into
idle habits
1 Tim. 6:15. God who in eternal felicity
alone *h*. sway
Heb. 6:19. that hope we *h*.
7:24. the priesthood which Jesus *h*. is
perpetual
1 Pet. 2:12. when he comes to *h*. assize
3:15. *h*. the Lord Christ in reverence
5:11. he *h*. dominion for ever and ever
5:12. our trusty brother as I *h*. him
Rev. 3:1. the One who *h*. the seven
spirits of God
8:3. another angel came and stood at
the altar, *h*. a golden censer
15:2. *h*. the harps which God had
given them
17:18. the great city that *h*. sway over
the kings of the earth

hole-s
Mat. 9:16. leaves a bigger *h*.
25:18. dug a *h*. in the ground
Mark 2:21. leaves a bigger *h*.
Luke 5:36. a *h*. in the new cloak
Acts 26:26. no *h*.-and-corner business
Eph. 4:27. leave no loop-*h*. for the devil
Heb. 11:38. hiding in caves and *h*. in
the ground

hollow
Col. 2:8. *h*. and delusive speculations

holy
Luke 10:21. Jesus exulted in the *H*. Spirit
John 6:69. we know that you are the
H. One of God

Acts 4:25. by the *H*. Spirit, through the mouth of David
13:34. blessings promised to David, *h*. and sure
Rom. 1:4. on the level of the spirit—the *H*. Spirit
6:19. making for a *h*. life
15:19. by the power of the *H*. Spirit
1 Cor. 12:13. that one *H*. Spirit was poured out
Eph. 5:18. let the *H*. Spirit fill you
1 Thess. 4:3. this is the will of God, that you should be *h*.
5:23. make you *h*. in every part
Heb. 9:2. this is called the *H*. Place
Rev. 16:5. thou *H*. One who art and wast

homage
Mat. 2:2. we have come to pay him *h*.
2:8. that I may go myself and pay him *h*.
2:11. bowed to the ground in *h*.
4:9. if you will only fall down and do me *h*.
4:10. you shall do *h*. to the Lord your God
Mark 15:19. paid mock *h*. to him
Luke 4:7. you have only to do *h*. to me
4:8. you shall do *h*. to the Lord your God
Rom. 11:4. who have not done *h*. to Baal
Heb. 1:6. let all the angels of God pay him *h*.
Rev. 11:13. the rest in terror did *h*. to the God of heaven
14:7. fear God and pay him *h*.
15:4. and do *h*. to thy name
16:9. refused to repent or do him *h*.
19:7. shout for joy and do him *h*.

home-s
Mat. 1:20. do not be afraid to take Mary *h*. with you
1:24. took Mary *h*. to be his wife
2:12. they returned *h*. another way
8:13. go *h*. now; because of your faith, so let it be
9:6. stand up, take your bed, and go *h*.
10:11. make your *h*. there until you leave
12:44. it says, 'I will go back to the *h*. I left
13:54. Jesus left that place, and came to his *h*. town
13:57. a prophet will always be held in honour, except in his *h*. town
20:14. take your pay and go *h*.
25:35. when I was a stranger you took me into your *h*.
25:38. a stranger and took you *h*.
25:43. when I was a stranger you gave me no *h*.
Mark 2:1. news went round that he was at *h*.

2:11. take your bed, and go *h*.
6:1. went to his *h*. town
6:4. except in his *h*. town
7:29. for saying that, you may go *h*. content
7:30. when she returned *h*., she found the child lying in bed
8:3. if I send them *h*. unfed
8:26. then Jesus sent him *h*.
10:29. no one who has given up *h*.
13:34. it is like a man away from *h*.
Luke 1:23. his period of duty was completed Zechariah returned *h*.
1:56. Mary stayed with her about three months and then returned *h*.
2:43. the festive season was over and they started for *h*.
4:23. do the same here in your own *h*. town
5:24. stand up, take your bed, and go *h*.
5:25. went *h*. praising God
8:39. go back *h*.,' he said, 'and tell them everything that God has done for you
9:61. let me first say good-bye to my people at *h*.
10:38. Martha made him welcome in her *h*.
11:24. I will go back to the *h*. I left
15:13. left *h*. for a distant country
15:27. your brother has come *h*.
16:4. there will be people to give me house and *h*.
16:9. you may be received into an eternal *h*.
18:14. went *h*. acquitted of his sins
18:29. no one who has given up *h*.
23:48. went *h*. beating their breasts
23:56. they went *h*. and prepared spices
24:12. went *h*. amazed at what had happened
John 3:13. the Son of Man whose *h*. is in heaven
4:16. go *h*., call your husband
4:50. return *h*.; your son will live
5:38. his word has found no *h*. in you
8:23. your *h*. is in this world, mine is not
11:1. his *h*. was at Bethany
11:20. Mary stayed at *h*.
16:32. scattered, each to his *h*., leaving me alone
Acts 8:28. to Jerusalem on a pilgrimage and was now on his way *h*.
18:3. he made his *h*. with them
20:20. I taught you, in public and in your *h*.
21:8. we went to the *h*. of Philip
1 Cor. 11:22. have you no *h*. of your own to eat and drink in
2 Cor. 5:8. rather leave our *h*. in the body

Eph. 5:8. live like men who are at *h*. in daylight
1 Tim. 5:14. preside over a *h*.
2 Tim. 4:2. proclaim the message, press it *h*.
Heb. 11:8. left *h*. without knowing where he was to go
13:14. here we have no permanent *h*.
2 Pet. 3:13. new heavens and a new earth, the *h*. of justice
Jude 6. abandoned their proper *h*.
Rev. 2:13. your city, the *h*. of Satan

homestead
Acts 1:20. let his *h*. fall desolate

homosexual
1 Cor. 6:9. guilty either of adultery or of *h*. perversion

honest-ly-y
Mat. 5:45. sends the rain on the *h*. and the dishonest
22:16. Master, you are an *h*. man, we know; you teach in all *h*.
23:28. outside you look like *h*. men
Mark 12:14. Master, you are an *h*. man, we know, and truckle to no man, whoever he may be; you teach in all *h*.
Luke 20:20. in the guise of *h*. men
20:21. teach in all *h*.
John 3:21. the *h*. man comes to the light
Gal. 4:16. your enemy by being *h*. with you
4:17. not with an *h*. envy
4:18. deserve an *h*. envy
Eph. 4:28. *h*. with his own hands
Tit. 2:10. strictly *h*. and trustworthy
2:12. a life of temperance, *h*.
3:14. engage in *h*. employment
Heb. 12:11. peaceful harvest of an *h*. life
2 Pet. 3:1. to rouse you to *h*. thought

honour-ed
Mat. 22:8. did not deserve the *h*.
23:6 ⎫ places of *h*. at feasts
Mark 12:39 ⎭
Luke 11:43. you love the seats of *h*. in synagogues
14:7. trying to secure the places of *h*.
14:8. do not sit down in the place of *h*.
20:46. places of *h*. at feasts
John 7:18. aims at *h*. for himself. But if a man aims at the honour of him who sent him
12:2. a supper was given in his *h*.
12:43. the *h*. which comes from God
Acts 3:13. the highest *h*. to his servant Jesus
7:41. a feast in *h*. of the thing
12:23. usurped the *h*. due to God
19:17. the name of the Lord Jesus gained in *h*.
Rom. 1:21. they have refused to *h*. him as God

3:7. all the greater *h*. because of my falsehood
4:20. strong in faith, gave *h*. to God
11:13. I give all honour to that ministry
1 Cor. 6:20. *h*. God in your body
10:31. do all for the *h*. of God
2 Cor. 8:19. we do *h*. to the Lord himself
8:23. an *h*. to Christ
9:13. many will give *h*. to God
Phil. 2:29. you should *h*. men like him
1 Thess. 2:6. we have never sought *h*. from men
Jam. 2:7. the *h*. name by which God has claimed you
1 Pet. 4:16. confess that name to the *h*. of God
Rev. 11:18. all who *h*. thy name
13:14. an image in *h*. of the beast

honourable
Rom. 12:17. such as all men count *h*.
2 Cor. 8:21. our aims are entirely *h*.
1 Tim. 3:1. to aspire to leadership is an *h*. ambition
2 Tim. 2:21. fit for any *h*. purpose
Tit. 3:1. ready for any *h*. form of work
3:8. engage in *h*. occupations, which are not ohly *h*. in themselves

hope-s-ing
Mat. 12:21. in him the nations shall place their *h*.
Luke 24:21. *h*. that he was the man to liberate Israel
John 5:45. Moses on whom you have set your *h*.
7:4. no one can *h*. to be in the public eye
Acts 27:12. *h*., if they could get so far, to winter at Phoenix
Rom. 1:13. in the *h*. of achieving something among you
15:12. on him the Gentiles shall set their *h*.
2 Cor. 1:10. he on whom our *h*. is fixed
Eph. 1:12. the first to set our *h*. on Christ
Phil. 2:19. I *h*. (under the Lord Jesus) to send Timothy to you
1 Tim. 4:10. we have set our *h*. on the living God
5:5. has all her *h*. set on God
6:17. not to fix their *h*. on so uncertain a thing as money
Tit. 1:1. faith and knowledge and *h*.
Heb. 10:23. the confession of our *h*.
1 Pet. 3:5. women who fixed their *h*. on him

horror
Mark 14:33. *h*. and dismay came over him
Rev. 18:10 ⎫ at a distance, for *h*. at her
18:15 ⎭ torment

horse-s
Rev. 9:19. the power of the *h*. lay in their mouths

Hosea
Rom. 9:25. it says in the Book of *H*.

hospitably
Acts 28:7. entertained us *h*.

hospitality
1 Tim. 5:10. given *h*.

host-s
Luke 7:39. his *h*. the Pharisee
  11:53. to ply him with a *h*. of questions
  14:9. the *h*. will come and say to you
  14:10. when your *h*. comes he will say
  14:12. then he said to his *h*.
Rom. 9:29. the Lord of *H*.
Jam. 5:4. the ears of the Lord of *H*.
Rev. 20:8. the *h*. of Gog and Magog

hot
Jam. 3:6. it keeps the wheel of our existence red-*h*.

hound
Mat. 23:34. *h*. from city to city

hour-s
Luke 1:10. the *h*. of the incense-offering
  12:56. you cannot interpret this fateful *h*.
  22:40. spared the *h*. of testing
John 12:31. the *h*. of judgement
2 Cor. 6:2. in the *h*. of my favour I gave heed to you . . . The *h*. of favour has now come
  11:25. for twenty-four *h*. I was adrift
2 Tim. 4:6. the *h*. of my departure
1 John 2:18. this is the last *h*. . . . this is indeed the last *h*.
Rev. 1:3. the *h*. of fulfilment is near
  12:10. the *h*. of victory for our God, the *h*. of his sovereignty
  22:10. the *h*. of fulfilment is near

house-s
Mat. 6:1. your Father's *h*. in heaven
  26:57. Jesus was led off under arrest to the *h*. of Caiaphas
Mark 14:17. he came to the *h*. with the Twelve
  14:53. led Jesus away to the High Priest's *h*.
Luke 2:7. no room for them to lodge in the *h*.
  2:49. I was bound to be in my Father's *h*.
  11:6. has turned up at my *h*.
  11:53. after he had left the *h*.
  15:20. he set out for his father's *h*.
Acts 7:48. the Most High does not live in *h*. made by men
  15:16. rebuild the fallen *h*. of David
2 Tim. 2:21. of use to the Master of the *h*.

Jam. 2:25. welcoming the messengers into her *h*.
Rev. 1:6. who made of us a royal *h*.
  5:10. thou hast made of them a royal *h*.

household
John 8:35. the slave has no permanent standing in the *h*.
Acts 7:10. the whole of the royal *h*.
1 Tim. 3:15. conduct themselves in God's *h*.
Heb. 3:2. Moses also was faithful in God's *h*.
  3:5. as a servitor in God's whole *h*.
  3:6. Christ is faithful as a son, set over his *h*. And we are that *h*. of his

householder
Mat. 24:43. if the *h*. had known at what time of night the burglar was coming
Mark 14:14. this message to the *h*.: 'The Master says
Luke 12:39. if the *h*. had known what time
  22:11. give this message to the *h*.

hubbub
Acts 21:34. could not get at the truth because of the *h*.

huge
Mark 8:1. a *h*. crowd had collected
  13:1. look, Master, what *h*. stones
  16:4. the stone, *h*. as it was
Jam. 3:5. a small member but it can make *h*. claims. What a *h*. stack of timber can be set ablaze
Rev. 16:21. *h*. hailstones, weighing perhaps a hundredweight

hug-ging
Acts 27:8. *h*. the coast
  27:13. *h*. the land

human
Mark 14:58. this temple, made with *h*. hands
John 1:13. not born of any *h*. stock, or by the fleshly desire of a human father
  5:34. not that I rely on *h*. testimony
Acts 5:38. of *h*. origin, it will collapse
  14:11. the gods have come down to us in *h*. form
  14:15. we are only *h*. beings
  17:29. shaped by *h*. craftsmanship
  19:26. gods made by *h*. hands are not gods at all
Rom 1:3. on the *h*. level he was born of David's stock
  2:9. for every *h*. being who is an evil-doer
  2:16. the secrets of *h*. hearts
  3:5. is it unjust of God (I speak of him in *h*. terms
  3:20. no *h*. being can be justified

Rom. 3:27. what room then is left for *h*. pride

5:12. death pervaded the whole *h*. race

6:19. words that suit your *h*. weakness

12:4. in a single *h*. body there are many limbs

1 Cor. 1:26. few of you are men of wisdom, by any *h*. standard

1:29. no place for *h*. pride in the presence of God

2:5. that your faith might be built not upon *h*. wisdom

2:13. not by our *h*. wisdom but by the Spirit

3:3. living on the purely *h*. level

3:4. are you not all too *h*.

4:3. by any *h*. court of judgement

9:8. do not suppose I rely on these *h*. analogies

2 Cor. 3:3. on the pages of the *h*. heart

5:1. a house not made by *h*. hands

10:4. weapons we wield are not merely *h*.

10:5. every *h*. thought

12:4. *h*. lips may not repeat them

Gal. 1:1. not by *h*. appointment or *h*. commission

1:11. the gospel you heard me preach is no *h*. invention

1:16. without consulting any *h*. being

Eph. 3:5. not disclosed to the *h*. race

4:22. lay aside that old *h*. nature

6:12. our fight is not against *h*. foes

Phil. 2:8. bearing the *h*. likeness, revealed in *h*. shape

4:12. the *h*. lot with all its ups and downs

Col. 1:24. in my poor *h*. flesh

2:22. merely *h*. injunctions

2 Thess. 2:3. wickedness will be revealed in *h*. form

Tit. 1:14. commandments of merely *h*. origin

Jam. 5:17. Elijah was a man with *h*. frailties

1 Pet. 2:13. every *h*. institution

2 Pet. 1:21. not through any *h*. whim that men prophesied

2:16. the dumb beast spoke with a *h*. voice

1 John 5:9. we accept *h*. testimony

Rev. 4:7. the third had a *h*. face

9:7. their faces were like *h*. faces

16:18. earthquake, like none before it in *h*. history

21:17. by *h*. measurements

humanity

1 Cor. 4:13. the dregs of *h*.

2 Cor. 4:16. our outward *h*. is in decay

Eph. 2:15. a single new *h*. in himself

Rev. 14:4. ransomed as the firstfruits of *h*. for God

humble-r

Mat. 11:29. I am gentle and *h*.-hearted

25:40. anything you did for one of my brothers here, however *h*.

25:45. anything you did not do for one of these, however *h*.

Luke 1:48. his servant, *h*. as she is

1:52. the *h*. have been lifted high

Rom. 1:9. the *h*. service of my spirit

12:16. go about with *h*. folk

1 Cor. 12:24. special honour to the *h*. parts

Eph. 4:2. be *h*. always and gentle

Phil. 3:21. the body belonging to our *h*. state

Heb. 5:7. because of his *h*. submission his prayer was heard

Jam. 1:9. the brother in *h*. circumstances

1 Pet. 3:8. kindly and *h*.-minded

humbly

1 Cor. 4:13. we *h*. make our appeal

2 Cor. 9:13. how *h*. you obey him

Phil. 2:3. *h*. reckon others better than yourselves

humiliate

2 Cor. 12:21. God may *h*. me in your presence

humiliation

1 Cor. 15:43. sown in *h*., it is raised in glory

hundredweight

Mat. 13:33 ⎱ half a *h*. of flour
Luke 13:21 ⎰

John 19:39. myrrh and aloes, more than half a *h*.

Rev. 16:21. hailstones, weighing perhaps a *h*.

hung

Luke 19:48. the people all *h*. upon his words

John 19:25. near the cross where Jesus *h*.

hunger

Luke 16:21. glad to satisfy his *h*. with the scraps

John 6:26. your *h*. was satisfied with the loaves

Rom. 8:35. persecution, *h*., nakedness

hungry

Acts 27:33. lived in suspense and gone *h*.

hunted

2 Cor. 4:9. *h*., we are never abandoned

hurl-ed

Mat. 21:21. *h*. into the sea

27:39. the passers-by *h*. abuse at him

Mark 11:23. *h*. into the sea

15:29. passers-by *h*. abuse at him

Luke 4:29. meaning to *h*. him over the edge

Rev. 8:7. this was *h*. upon the earth
8:8. a great blazing mountain was *h*.
18:21. a great milestone and *h*. it

hurry-ies-ied-ing
Mat. 28:8. they *h*. away from the tomb
Mark 6:33. *h*. from all the towns
1 Cor. 11:21. in such a *h*. to eat his own
Jam. 1:21. the malice that *h*. to excess

hurt
John 21:17. Peter was *h*. that he asked
him a third time
2 Cor. 7:10. the *h*. which is borne in the
world's way
7:11. you bore your *h*. in God's way
13:7. our prayer to God is that we
may not have to *h*. you
2 Pet. 2:12. suffering *h*. for the *h*. they
have inflicted

hurtling
Rev. 18:21. thus shall Babylon, the great
city, be sent *h*. down

husband
Mat. 19:10. if that is the position with
h. and wife
Luke 1:34. how can this be,' said Mary,
'when I have no husband
Rom. 7:4. have found another *h*. in him
1 Cor. 7:15. the Christian *h*. or wife is
under no compulsion.

hush
Mark 4:39. said to the sea, '*H*! Be still

hymn-s
Rom. 15:9. sing *h*. to thy name
1 Cor. 14:15. I will sing *h*. as I am
inspired to sing
14:26. each of you contributes a *h*.
Eph. 5:14. and so the *h*. says

I

ice
Rev. 4:6. a sea of glass, like a sheet of *i*.

idea-s
John 18:34. Jesus said, 'Is that your
own *i*.
Acts 5:38. if this *i*. of theirs
12:9. no *i*. that the angel's intervention
was real
17:20. you are introducing *i*. that
sound strange to us
23:5. I had no *i*. that he was High
Priest
Jam. 4:14. no *i*. what tomorrow will
bring
2 Pet. 2:13. their *i*. of pleasure
1 John 2:11. no *i*. where he is going

identical
Rom. 7:7. the law *i*. with sin

identify-ied
Acts 28:1. we *i*. the island as Malta
Rom. 7:4. *i*. with the body of Christ

idle-rs-ing
2 Thess. 3:6. who falls into *i*. habits
3:7. we were no *i*. among you
3:11. *i*. their time away
2 Pet. 2:3. judgement long decreed for
them has not been *i*.

idolatry
1 Cor. 8:7. so accustomed to *i*.

ignoramus
1 Tim. 6:4. I call him a pompous *i*.

ignorance
Heb. 9:7. people's sins of *i*.

ignorant
John 3:10. teacher of Israel *i*. of such
things
1 Thess. 4:5. pagans who are *i*. of God
2 Tim. 2:23. foolish and *i*. speculations
2 Pet. 3:16. the *i*. and unstable misinterpret
1 John 2:21. not because you are *i*. of the
truth

ignore
Rom. 10:3. they *i*. God's way of right-
eousness
Heb. 2:3. if we *i*. a deliverance so great

ill
Mat. 8:16. healed all who were *i*.
25:36. when I was *i*. you came to my
help
Mark 1:32. after sunset they brought to
him all who were *i*.
Luke 7:2. this servant was *i*. and near to
death
John 5:6. he had been *i*. a long time
1 Cor. 5:6. your self-satisfaction *i*. becomes you
also: Mat. 12:15, 14:35, 25:39, 43, 44;
Mark 1:30; John 11:1, 2, 3; Acts
5:16, 9:37; Phil. 2:26, 27; 2 Tim.
4:20; Jam. 5:14

illegal
Acts 16:21. customs which it is *i*. for us
Romans to adopt

ill-informed
Rom. 10:2. to their zeal for God I can
testify; but it is an *i*. zeal

illness-es
Mat. 4:23. curing whatever *i.*
   4:24. sufferers from every kind of *i.*
   8:17. he took away our *i.*
John 11:6. hearing of his *i.* Jesus waited
Gal. 4:13. it was bodily *i.* that originally led

ill-treat-ed-ing
Acts 7:24. saw one of them being *i.*
   7:26. why are you *i.* one another

ill-treatment
Jam. 5:10. patience under *i.*

illuminate
2 Pet. 1:19. the morning star rises to *i.* your minds

illumined
Eph. 1:18. that your inward eyes may be *i.*
   5:13. *i.*, and everything thus *i.* is all light

illusion
1 John 2:27. which is real and no *i.*

illustration
Gal. 3:15. let me give you an *i.*

image-s
Acts 7:43. *i.* which you had made
   17:29. not to suppose that the deity is like an *i.*

imagine-s-ing
Mat. 6:7. who *i.* that the more they say
Luke 13:2. do you *i.* that, because these Galileans
   13:4. do you *i.* they were more guilty
John 5:45. do not *i.* that I shall be your accuser
Acts 2:15. these men are not drunk, as you *i.*
   8:22. forgive you for *i.* such a thing
Rom. 2:3. do you *i.*—you who pass judgement on the guilty while committing the same crimes yourself—do you *i.*
1 Cor. 2:9. things beyond our *i.*
Gal. 6:3. if a man *i.* himself to be somebody

imitate
Mat. 6:8. do not *i.* them
2 Thess. 3:9. an example for you to *i.*
Heb. 6:12. *i.* those who, through faith and patience
3 John 11. do not *i.* bad examples

immature
Rom. 2:20. teach the *i.*

immeasurably
Rom. 5:20. grace *i.* exceeded it
Eph. 3:20. *i.* more than all we can ask

immediately
Mark 5:42. *i.* the girl got up
Luke 8:55. she stood up *i.*
   21:9. the end does not follow *i.*
Acts 16:33. *i.* afterwards he and his whole family were baptized

immense-ly
Acts 20:12. were *i.* comforted
Eph. 2:7. how *i.* are the resources of his grace.

imminent
Luke 21:36. through all these *i.* troubles

immoral
Luke 7:37. a woman who was living an *i.* life
Heb. 12:16. no *i.* person, no one worldly-minded

immorality
1 Cor. 5:1. sexual *i.* among you, *i.* such as even pagans do not tolerate
   7:2. because there is so much *i.*

immortal
Rom. 1:23. the splendour of *i.* God
1 Pet. 1:23. not of mortal parentage but of *i.*

immortality
1 Cor. 15:50. the perishable cannot possess *i.*
   15:54. when our mortality has been clothed with *i.*
Eph. 6:24. grace and *i.*

impart-ed-ing
1 Cor. 15:3. the facts which had been *i.* to me
2 Cor. 8:1. the grace of generosity which God has *i.*
   9:14. the grace which God has *i.* to you
Eph. 1:8. *i.* full wisdom and insight
1 John 4:13. he has *i.* his Spirit to us

impartiality
1 Tim. 5:21. act with strict *i.*

impartially
1 Pet. 1:17. the One who judges every man *i.*

impeach-ed
Acts 26:7. for this very hope I am *i.*, and *i.* by Jews

impediment
Mark 7:35. the *i.* was removed

impel-led
2 Pet. 1:21. *i.* by the Holy Spirit

impend-ing
Col. 3:6. God's dreadful judgement is *i.*

impenitence
Mat. 11:20. denounced them for their *i.*

imperial
Luke 1:52. torn *i.* powers from their thrones
Acts 25:21. for His *I.* Majesty's decision
25:25. appealed to His *I.* Majesty
Phil. 4:22. who belong to the *i.* establishment

imperishable
Mark 16:8. *i.* message of eternal salvation
1 Cor. 15:42. sown in the earth as a perishable thing is raised *i.*
15:53. this perishable being must be clothed with the *i.*
1 Pet. 3:4. with its *i.* ornament, a gentle, quiet spirit

impious
1 Tim. 1:9. the *i.* and sinful
1 Pet. 4:18. what will become of the *i.*

implacable
2 Tim. 3:3. *i.* in their hatreds

implanted
Jam. 4:5. the spirit which God *i.* in man

implement-s
Rom. 6:13. as *i.* for doing wrong . . . yield your bodies to him as *i.* for doing right

implore-d
Luke 8:28. I *i.* you, do not torment me
9:38. Master, look at my son, I *i.* you
Acts 21:12. *i.* Paul to abandon his visit
Rom. 12:1. I *i.* you by God's mercy
15:30. I *i.* you by our Lord Jesus Christ
16:17. I *i.* you, my friends
2 Cor. 5:20. we *i.* you, be reconciled to God

imply-ies-ied
1 Cor. 10:19. what do I *i.* by this
Eph. 4:9. ascended' *i.* that he also descended
Heb. 8:5. this is *i.* when Moses
12:27. the words 'once again'—and only once—*i.*

import
2 Pet. 2:1. they will *i.* disastrous heresies

importance
1 Cor. 4:18. certain persons who are filled with self-*i.*
Gal. 2:6. not that their *i.* matters to me
2 Tim. 3:4. swollen with self-*i.*

important
Mat. 23:19. which is the more *i.*
1 Cor. 4:7. who makes you, my friend, so *i.*

impose-d
Acts 15:19. *i.* no irksome restrictions
Rom. 13:5. an obligation *i.*

2 Thess. 2:10. the deception that sinfulness can *i.*
Rev. 2:24. on you I will *i.* no further burden

impossible
Mark 7:24. remain unrecognized, but this was *i.*
Acts 27:15. it was *i.* to keep head to wind
Rom. 9:6. *i.* that the word of God should have proved false
1 Cor. 11:20. *i.* for you to eat the Lord's Supper

impostor-s
Mat. 24:24. *i.* will come claiming to be messiahs
27:63. we recall how that *i.* said
Mark 13:22. *i.* will come claiming to be messiahs
Acts 13:10. you utter *i.*
2 Cor. 6:8. we are the *i.* who speak the truth

impotent
Heb. 7:18. the earlier rules are cancelled as *i.*

impress-ed
Luke 1:66. all who heard it were deeply *i.*
16:15. *i.* your fellow-men with your righteousness
Acts 13:12. deeply *i.* by what he learned about the Lord
1 Cor. 12:3. for this reason I must *i.* upon you

imprison-ed
Acts 26:10. *i.* many of God's people
1 Pet. 3:19. made his proclamation to the *i.* spirits

imprisonment
John 3:24. this was before John's *i.*
Acts 20:23. *i.* and hardships await me
23:29. meriting death or *i.*
26:31. nothing that deserves death or *i.*
Phil. 1:13. my *i.* in Christ's cause

improvement-s
Mark 5:26. there had been no *i.*
Acts 24:2. *i.* are being made

impulse-s
Gal. 6:1. do something wrong, my brothers, on a sudden *i.*
2 Tim. 2:22. turn from the wayward *i.*

impure
Rom. 14:14. nothing is *i.* in itself; only, if a man considers a particular thing *i.*, then to him it is *i.*

impurity
Rom. 6:19. *i.* and lawlessness
Gal. 5:19. fornication, *i.*

1 Thess. 4:7. God called us to holiness,
not to *i.*

imputation
Tit. 1:6. under no *i.* of loose living

inanimate
1 Cor. 14:7. *i.* things that produce sounds

inarticulate
Rom. 8:26. through our *i.* groans

inasmuch
Rom. 5:12. *i.* as all men have sinned

inaugurate-d
2 Cor. 3:7. it was *i.* with divine splendour
Heb. 9:18. not *i.* without blood

incapable
Mat. 19:12. some are *i.* of marriage
2 Tim. 3:7. *i.* of reaching a knowledge
of the truth

incense
2 Cor. 2:15. we are indeed the *i.* offered
by Christ to God
Heb. 9:4. here was a golden altar of *i.*
Rev. 5:8. golden bowls full of *i.*
18:13. *i.,* perfumes

incident
Mark 6:52. not understood the *i.* of the
loaves

incite-d
Mark 15:11. *i.* the crowd to ask him to
release Barabbas

include-ing
Luke 7:29. *i.* the tax-gatherers, praised
Acts 1:14. women, *i.* Mary
17:34. became believers, *i.* Dionysius
Rom. 16:2. a good friend to many, *i.*
myself
Phil. 1:1. live at Philippi, *i.* their bishops
and deacons
Col. 4:3. and *i.* a prayer for us
2 Tim. 1:15. deserted me, *i.* Phygelus
and Hermogenes

incompetent
1 Cor. 6:2. are you *i.* to deal with these
trifling cases

inconsistent
Jam. 2:4. do you not see that you are *i.*

inconvenient
2 Tim. 4:2. press it home on all occasions, convenient or *i.*

incorporate
Rom. 6:5. *i.* with him in a death like his
Eph. 1:1. believers *i.* in Christ Jesus
1:13. became *i.* in Christ
Phil. 1:1. *i.* in Christ Jesus
3:9. finding myself *i.* in him
Col. 1:2. brothers in the faith, *i.* in
Christ

increase-s-d
Acts 7:17. *i.* in numbers
2 Thess. 1:3. your faith *i.* mightily

incredulity
Mark 16:14. reproached them for their *i.*

inculcate
1 Tim. 4:3. *i.* abstinence from certain
foods

incur-red
Rom. 7:3. she will *i.* the charge of
adultery
Jude 4. the doom they have *i.*

indecency
Mark 7:22. fraud, *i.,* envy
Gal. 5:19. impurity, and *i.*
Eph. 5:3. *i.* of any kind
5:5. no one given to fornication or *i.*
Col. 3:5. fornication, *i.,* lust

indecently
Rom. 1:27. males behave *i.* with males

indeed
Mat. 8:3. *i.* I will; be clean again
11:9. yes *i.,* and far more than a
prophet
27:42. King of Israel, *i.*! Let him
come down now from the cross
Mark 1:41. *i.* I will; be clean again
Luke 1:66. *i.* the hand of the Lord was
upon him
5:13. *i.* I will; be clean again
12:51. do you suppose I came to
establish peace on earth? No *i.*
John 13:38. will you *i.* lay down your
life for me
14:13. *i.* anything you ask in my name
I will do
Acts 7:34. I have *i.* seen how my people
are oppressed in Egypt
13:27. *i.* they fulfilled them by con-
demning him
16:37. to smuggle us out privately?
No *i.*
17:27. *i.* he is not far from each one
of us

indefatigable
Acts 18:28. he was *i.* in confuting the
Jews

independently
Rom. 3:21. *i.* of law, God's justice has
been brought to light

indicate-d-ing
John 12:33. to *i.* the kind of death he
was to die
18:32. Jesus had *i.* the manner of his
death
21:19. to *i.* the manner of death
Acts 25:27. a prisoner without *i.* the
charges

indignant-ly
Mat. 21:16. they asked him *i.*
Mark 10:14. when Jesus saw this he was *i.*
   10:41. they were *i.* with James and John
John 7:23. why are you *i.* with me for giving health on the Sabbath
Heb. 3:10. I was *i.* with that generation
   3:17. was God *i.* for forty years

indignation
Mark 1:41. in warm *i.* Jesus stretched out his hand
2 Cor. 11:29. does my heart not blaze with *i.*

indignity
Acts 5:41. suffer *i.* for the sake of the Name

indispensable
1 Cor. 12:22. more frail than others are *i.*

individual-s-ly
Mat. 19:6. they are no longer two *i.*
Mark 10:8. no longer two *i.*
Rom. 12:5. form one body, serving *i.*
1 Cor. 12:11. to each *i.* at will
Eph. 5:33. it applies also *i.*
3 John 14. greet our friends *i.*

indoors
Mat. 9:28. when he had gone *i.* they came to him
   17:25. when he went *i.* Jesus forestalled him
Mark 7:17. left the people and gone *i.*
   9:28. Jesus went *i.*
   9:33. when he was *i.*, he asked them
   10:10. when they were *i.* again

induce-d-ing
Acts 5:37. he *i.* some people to revolt
   18:13. *i.* people to worship God
   20:30. to *i.* the disciples to break away

indulge-ing
2 Cor. 11:21. I can *i.* in it too
1 Tim. 3:8. not *i.* in double talk
2 Tim. 2:16. those who *i.* in it will stray further

indulgence-t
Mat. 23:25. by robbery and self-*i.*
Acts 24:4. I crave your *i.*
1 Tim. 5:6. given over to self-*i.*
2 Pet. 3:3. live self-*i.* lives

industry
Acts 19:25. living depends on this *i.*

indwelling
1 Cor. 6:19. a shrine of the *i.* Holy Spirit

ineffective
Gal. 3:17. its promises rendered *i.*

infamous
Luke 6:22. ban your very name as *i.*

infant
1 Cor. 3:1. as *i.* in Christ
Heb. 5:13. lives on milk, being an *i.*
1 Pet. 2:2. like the new-born *i.* you are

infantry
Acts 23:23. get ready two hundred *i.*
   23:31. the *i.* took Paul

infected
2 Pet. 1:4. lust has *i.* the world

infection
2 Tim. 2:17. the *i.* of their teaching

inferior
1 Cor. 15:9. *i.* to all other apostles

infirmity
Mat. 4:23. curing whatever illness or *i.*

inflate-d
1 Cor. 4:6. *i.* with pride

inflict-ed
2 Pet. 2:13. suffering hurt for the hurt they have *i.*
Rev. 16:9. the power to *i.* such plagues

influence
Rom. 1:12. the *i.* of your faith on me
1 Cor. 12:3. under the *i.* of the Spirit of God. And no one can say 'Jesus is Lord!' except under the *i.* of the Holy Spirit
2 Cor. 3:18. the *i.* of the Lord who is Spirit

influential
Acts 17:4. a good many *i.* women

inform-ed
Luke 1:4. the matters of which you have been *i.*
   7:18. John too was *i.* of all this
Acts 23:30. *i.* of an attempt to be made on the man's life
   24:22. Felix, who happened to be well *i.*
Rom. 10:2. it is an ill-*i.* zeal

information
John 11:57. who knew where he was should give information
Acts 21:21. given certain *i.* about you
   23:20. more precise *i.* about him
   23:22. had given him this *i.*
   24:1. laid an *i.* against Paul
   25:15. the Jews laid an *i.* against him

infringe-ing
1 Pet. 4:15. *i.* the rights of others

infuriate-d
Luke 4:28. the whole congregation were *i.*

ingratiate
Acts 25:9. Festus, anxious to *i.* himself

inhabit-ed
Acts 1:20. let there be none to *i.* it
Rom. 10:18. to the bounds of the *i.*
world

inhabitant-s
Acts 2:9. *i.* of Mesopotamia
26:20. the *i.* of Damascus
Rev. 3:10. test its *i.*
6:10. the *i.* of the earth
13:12. made the earth and its *i.* worship this first beast
13:14. it deluded the *i.* of the earth

inherent
Eph. 4:13. the unity *i.* in our faith

inherit
Heb. 1:14. those who are to *i.* salvation
Jam. 2:5. *i.* the kingdom he has promised

inheritance
Rom. 4:13. the world should be his *i.*
Gal. 4:30. the slave shall not share the *i.*
Heb. 11:39. did not enter upon the
promised *i.*
1 Pet. 3:9. a blessing is the *i.*

initiate-d
Phil. 4:12. *i.* into the human lot
1 John 2:20. you, no less than they, are
among the initiated

initiation
1 John 2:27. the *i.* which you received
from him stays with you; you need
no other teacher, but learn all you
need to know from his *i.*

initiative
2 Cor. 8:4. on their own initiative

injunction-s
Mat. 12:16. he gave strict *i.* that they
were not to make him known
1 Cor. 11:17. in giving you these *i.*
Col. 2:22. merely human *i.*
1 Thess. 2:11. by solemn *i.*

injure
1 Cor. 6:8. you actually *i.* and rob—
i. and rob your brothers

injury-ies
Luke 4:35. left him without doing him
any *i.*
1 Cor. 6:7. why not rather suffer *i.*
2 Cor. 2:5. any *i.* that has been done,
has not been done to me
1 Thess. 2:2. all the *i.* and outrage
Rev. 9:4. told to do no *i.* to the grass
9:19. with them too they dealt *i.*

injustice
Rom. 1:29. they are filled with every
kind of *i.*
3:5. if our *i.* serves to bring out God's
justice

3:8. to condemn such men as these is
surely no *i.*
9:14. is God to be charged with *i.*

inkling
Mark 8:17. have you no *i.* yet

inland
Acts 19:1. Paul travelled through the
i. regions

inmost
Rom. 5:5. God's love has flooded our
i. heart
7:22. in my *i.* self I delight in the law
of God
8:27. God who searches our *i.* being
1 Pet. 3:4. in the *i.* centre of your being

inner
Mat. 24:26. he is there in the *i.* room
John 4:14. an *i.* spring always welling up

innkeeper
Luke 10:35. gave them to the *i.*

innocence
2 Cor. 6:6. the *i.* of our behaviour

innocent
Mat. 10:16. *i.* as doves
12:7. you would not have condemned
the *i.*
23:35. all the *i.* blood spilt on the
ground, from *i.* Abel
27:19. have nothing to do with that
i. man
Luke 23:47. this man was *i.*
Rom. 16:18. seduce the minds of *i.*
people
1 Cor. 14:20. be as *i.* of evil as babes
2 Cor. 5:21. Christ was *i.* of sin
Col. 1:22. *i.* in his sight
Jam. 5:6. you have condemned the *i.*

innumerable
Jam. 5:20. cancelling *i.* sins
1 Pet. 4:8. love cancels *i.* sins

inquire-d
Luke 1:62. they *i.* of his father

inquiry
Mat. 2:8. a careful *i.* for the child
Acts 25:26. this preliminary *i.*

inscribe-d
Rom. 2:15. the law *i.* on their hearts
Rev. 17:8. *i.* in the roll of the living
21:12. on the gates were *i.* the names
21:27. *i.* in the Lamb's roll of the
living

inscription
Mat. 22:20. whose head is this, and
whose *i.*
27:37. over his head was placed the *i.*
Mark. 12:16. whose head is this, and
whose *i.*
15:26. the *i.* giving the charge

Luke 23:38. there was an *i*. above his head
John 19:19. Pilate wrote an *i*.
19:20. this *i*. was read by many . . . the *i*. was in Hebrew, Latin, and Greek
2 Tim. 2:19. this *i*.: 'The Lord knows his own

insensitive
2 Cor. 3:14. their minds had been made *i*.

inside
Mat. 23:25. you have filled *i*. by robbery
23:26. clean the *i*. of the cup
23:27. *i*. they are full of dead men's bones
23:28. *i*. you are brim-full of hypocrisy
Mark 7:21. from *i*., out of a man's heart
7:23. these evil things all come from *i*.
15:16. the soldiers took him *i*. the courtyard
Luke 1:21. he was staying so long *i*.
11:7. he replies from *i*., 'Do not bother me
11:39. *i*. you there is nothing but greed
11:40. make the *i*. too
24:2. the tomb, they went *i*.
Acts 5:23. we found no one *i*.
Rev. 4:8. eyes all over, *i*. and out
5:1. with writing *i*. and out
5:3. no one . . . able to open the scroll or to look *i*. it
5:4. or to look *i*. it
5:6. *i*. the circle of living creatures

insight
Eph. 1:8. imparting full wisdom and *i*.
Phil. 1:9. knowledge and *i*. of every kind
Col. 1:9. full *i*. into his will

insinuate
2 Tim. 3:6. *i*. themselves into private houses

insipid
Col. 4:6. gracious, and never *i*.

insist-ed-ing
Mark 3:12. he *i*. that they should not make him known
10:24. Jesus *i*., 'Children how hard it is to enter the kingdom of God
14:31. he *i*. and repeated: 'Even if I must die with you
Luke 23:5. they *i*.: 'His teaching is causing disaffection
23:23. they *i*. on their demand
John 18:26. *i*., 'Did I not see you with him in the garden
Acts 12:15. she *i*. that it was so
16:15. she *i*. on our going
20:21. I *i*. on repentance before God

25:24. *i*. that he had no right to remain alive
1 Cor. 11:16. if you *i*. on arguing
Gal. 2:14. how can you *i*. that Gentiles must live like Jews
Tit. 3:8. the points I should wish you to *i*. on

insistently
2 Cor. 8:4. they begged us most *i*.

insolent
Rom. 1:30. *i*., arrogant, and boastful

inspiration
Mat. 22:43. David by *i*. calls him 'Lord
1 Cor. 14:16. in the language of *i*.
14:32. control prophetic *i*.
Eph. 3:5. revealed by *i*.
1 Thess. 5:19. do not stifle *i*.

inspire-s-d-ing
Mark 12:36. *i*. by the Holy Spirit
Acts 6:10. the *i*. wisdom with which he spoke
11:28. *i*. to stand up and predict
Rom. 12:6. the gift of *i*. utterance
14:18. *i*. by the Holy Spirit
15:30. the love that the Spirit *i*.
1 Cor. 14:2. *i*., but he speaks mysteries
14:15. *i*. to pray, but I will also pray intelligently. I will sing hymns as I am *i*.
14:33. the God who *i*. them
14:37. if anyone claims to be *i*.
Phil. 2:13. *i*. both the will and the deed
2 Thess. 1:11. every act *i*. by faith
1 Tim. 4:1. doctrines *i*. by devils
2 Tim. 1:7. no craven spirit, but one to *i*. strength
2 Pet. 3:15. he wrote to you with his *i*. wisdom
1 John 4:1. many prophets falsely *i*.
4:4. he who *i*. you is greater than he who *i*. the godless
Rev. 19:10. those who bear testimony to Jesus are *i*.
22:6. the Lord God who *i*. the prophets

instance
Mark 6:17. at the *i*. of his brother Philip's wife
2 Cor. 8:5. offering them in the first *i*. to the Lord
Heb. 7:8. in the one *i*. tithes are received

instantly
Luke 8:47. how she had been *i*. cured
18:43. he recovered his sight *i*.
John 5:9. the man recovered *i*.
Acts 12:23. *i*. an angel of the Lord struck him
13:11. *i*. mist and darkness came over him
22:13. *i*. I recovered my sight

instead
Rom. 1:25. worship to created things *i.* of to the Creator
1 Cor. 6:1. to pagan law-courts *i.* of to the community of God's people

instinct-s
1 Cor. 7:36. his *i.* are too strong for him
Eph. 2:3. obeyed the promptings of our own *i.*
Jude 10. by *i.* like brute beasts

institute-d
Rom. 13:1. existing authorities are *i.* by him
Tit. 1:5. *i.* elders in each town

institution
Rom. 13:2. resisting a divine *i.*
1 Pet. 2:13. to every human *i.*

instruct-ed
Mark 6:8. *i.* them to take nothing for the journey
Luke 12:12. the Holy Spirit will *i.* you what to say
Acts 15:20. *i.* them by letter
23:30. *i.* his accusers
Col. 1:28. *i.* everyone in all the ways of wisdom
3:16. *i.* and admonish each other
1 Tim. 2:7. *i.* the nations in the true faith
6:17. *i.* those who are rich
Heb. 8:5. *i.* by God
11:22. *i.* them what to do with his bones

instruction-s
Mat. 10:5. Jesus sent out with the following *i.*
11:1. giving his twelve disciples their *i.*
21:1. two disciples with these *i.*
Mark 11:1 ⎱ two of his disciples with
14:13 ⎰ these *i.*
16:8. delivered all these *i.*
Luke 19:29. sent two of the disciples with these *i.*
22:8. sent Peter and John with these *i.*
Acts. 1:2. *i.* through the Holy Spirit
11:26. gave *i.* to large numbers
13:47. our *i.* from the Lord
15:24. without any *i.* from us
16:35. with *i.* to release the men
17:15. with *i.* for Silas and Timothy
22:24. *i.* to examine him by flogging
Rom. 15:4. written for our own *i.*
1 Cor. 7:25. I have no *i.* from the Lord
9:14. the Lord gave *i.*
14:6. or prophecy, or *i.*
14:26. a hymn, some *i.*
14:31. the whole congregation may receive *i.*
Gal. 6:6. under *i.* in the faith
Eph. 6:4. give them the *i.*

Col. 4:10. you have had *i.* about him
2 Thess. 3:14. if anyone disobeys our *i.*
1 Tim. 4:6. the sound *i.* which you have followed
Heb. 6:2. by *i.* about cleansing rites

instrument
Acts 9:15. this man is my chosen *i.*
Rom. 15:18. Christ's *i.* to bring the Gentiles
2 Tim. 4:17. his *i.* in making the full proclamation

insult-s-ing
Mat. 5:11. suffer *i.* and persecution
Luke 6:22. when they outlaw you and *i.* you
11:45. you are *i.* us too
22:65. they went on heaping *i.* upon him
Acts 23:4. would you *i.* God's High Priest
Jam. 2:6. you have *i.* the poor man
1 Pet. 4:14. if Christ's name is flung in your teeth as an *i.*
2 Pet. 2:10. not afraid to *i.* celestial beings
2:11. employ no *i.* in seeking judgement
Jude 8. *i.* celestial beings
9. to condemn him in *i.* words

insurrection-s
Luke 21:9. when you hear of wars and *i.*
23:25. put in prison for *i.*

integrity
Eph. 6:14. for coat of mail put on *i.*
2 Tim. 2:22. pursue justice, *i.*
Tit. 2:7. you must show *i.*
Jam. 2:22. the *i.* of his faith

intellect
1 Cor. 14:14. my *i.* lies fallow

intelligence
Luke 2:47. amazed at his *i.*
Rev. 13:18. anyone who has *i.*

intelligent-ly
Acts 13:7. Sergius Paulus, an intelligent man.
1 Cor. 14:15. I will also pray *i.* I will sing hymns as I am inspired to sing, but I will sing *i.*

intelligible
1 Cor. 14:19. rather speak five *i.* words

intemperate
2 Tim. 3:3. *i.* and fierce

intend-ed-ing
Mark 16:1. *i.* to go and anoint him
John 7:35. where does he *i.* to go
Acts 16:27. *i.* to kill himself
1 Cor. 9:15. nor do I *i.* to claim it in this letter
14:22. not *i.* as a sign for believers

2 Cor. 1:15. I had *i.* to come first of all
     to you
Gal. 3:16. the 'issue' *i.* is Christ

intense
Acts 26:7. worshipping with *i.* devotion

intention
Mat. 22:18. aware of their malicious *i.*
Acts 17:5. with the *i.* of bringing Paul
     24:7. our *i.* to try him under our law
2 Cor. 1:17. to Judaea. That was my *i.*
1 Tim. 2:8. lift up their hands with a
     pure *i.*
2 Tim. 1:3. worship with a pure *i.*
Tit. 1:5. my *i.* in leaving you behind in
     Crete

intently
Acts 1:10. gazing *i.* into the sky
     7:55. gazing *i.* up to heaven
     11:6. I looked *i.*

intercede-ing
Eph. 6:18. *i.* for all God's people

intercourse
Mat. 1:25. no *i.* with her until her son
     was born
Rom. 1:26. women have exchanged
     natural *i.* for unnatural

interest-s
Mat. 15:3. in the *i.* of your tradition
     25:27. I should have got it back with *i.*
Luke 19:23. I could have claimed it
     with *i.*
John 11:50. more to your *i.* that one
     man should die
     18:14. their *i.* if one man died
1 Cor. 10:24. not his own *i.*, but the
     other man's
2 Cor. 8:10. to do is in your own *i.*
Phil. 2:4. look to each other's *i.*
     2:20. a genine *i.* in your concerns
1 Tim. 4:15. your absorbing *i.*

interfere-s
3 John. 10. he *i.* with those who would
     do so

interloper-s
Gal. 2:4. *i.* who had stolen in to spy

intermediary
Gal. 3:19. there was an *i.*
     3:20. an *i.* is not needed for one
     party

interminable
1 Tim. 1:4. *i.* myths and genealogies

interpose-d
Luke 8:50. Jesus heard, and *i.*

interpret-ing
1 Cor. 2:13. *i.* spiritual truths
     12:10. the ability to *i.*
Rev. 17:9. the clue for those who can *i.*

interrogate-d
Acts 12:19. he *i.* the guards

interval-s
Acts 25:13. after an *i.* of some days
     King Agrippa
     27:28. sounding again after a short *i.*
1 Cor. 14:7. unless their notes mark
     definite *i.*

intervene-d
Luke 13:14. *i.* and said to the congrega-
     tion
John 7:50. *i.* 'Does our law,' he asked
     them
Acts 23:27. I *i.* with the troops
     24:7. the commandant *i.*

intervention
Acts 12:9. no idea that the angel's *i.* was
     real

interview
Gal. 2:2. at a private *i.* with the men of
     repute

intolerable
Luke 11:46. load men with *i.* burdens

intractable
Jam. 3:8. the tongue. It is an *i.* evil

intrigue-s
Gal. 5-20. party *i.* and jealousies

introduce-d-ing
Acts 9:27. *i.* him to the apostles
     17:20. you are *i.* ideas that sound
     strange to us
Heb. 7:19. a better hope is *i.*

introduction
1 Cor. 16:3. I will give letters of *i.*
2 Cor. 3:1. need letters of *i.* to you

intrude-d
Rom. 5:20. law *i.* into this process

invade
1 Thess. 4:6. wrong in this matter, or
     i. his rights

invalidated
Gal. 3:17. validated by God; it cannot
     be *i.*

invention
Gal. 1:11. is no human *i.*

invested
2 Pet. 1:17. *i.* with honour and glory

investigation
Acts 23:15. a closer *i.* of his case

inviolate
Heb. 13:4. the marriage-bond *i.*

invisible
Heb. 11:3. the visible came forth from
     the *i.*

invitation-s
Luke 14:10. when you receive an *i.*
    14:16. sent out many *i.*
Acts 7:14. Joseph sent an *i.* to his father

invite-s-d
Mat. 9:13. I did not come to *i.* virtuous
    people
    22:3. the guests he had *i.*
    22:8. the guests I *i.* did not deserve
    22:9. *i.* everyone you can find
    22:14. though many are *i.*
Mark 2:17. not come to *i.* virtuous
    people
Luke 5:32. to *i.* virtuous people
    7:36. one of the Pharisees *i.* him.
    11:37. a Pharisee *i.* him
    14:8. more distinguished than yourself
    has been *i.*
    14:12. do not *i.* your friends
    14:24. not one of those who were *i.*
Acts 28:14. were *i.* to stay a week
1 Cor. 10:27. if an unbeliever *i.* you
Rev. 19:9. *i.* to the wedding-supper of
    the Lamb

invocation
Acts 22:16. be baptized at once, with *i.*
    of his name

invoke-s
Acts 2:21. *i.* the name of the Lord shall
    be saved
    9:14. arrest all who *i.* thy name
    9:21. to destroy those who *i.* this
    name
Rom. 10:12. the need of all who *i.* him
    10:13. everyone who *i.* the name
    of the Lord
    10:14. *i.* one in whom they had no
    faith
1 Cor. 1:2. who *i.* the name of our Lord
    Jesus Christ
2 Tim. 2:22. all who *i.* the Lord
Jam. 3:9. to *i.* curses upon our fellow-
    men.

involve-s-ed
Mat. 5:32. he *i.* her in adultery
2 Tim. 2:4. not let himself be *i.* in
    civilian affairs

inward-ly
Mark 11:23. has no *i.* doubts
Rom. 8:23. groaning *i.* while we wait
1 Cor. 4:5. disclose men's *i.* motives
2 Cor. 5:12. in outward show and not in
    i. worth
Eph. 1:18. that your *i.* eyes may be
    illumined
1 Tim. 4:3. *i.* knowledge of the truth
Heb. 9:9. cannot give the worshipper *i.*
    perfection

irksome
Acts 15:19. impose no *i.* restrictions

irons
Acts 22:29. that he had put him in *i.*

irreligious
1 Tim. 1:9. *i.* and worldly

irreproachably
1 Tim. 6:14. obey your orders *i.*

irrevocable
Rom. 11:29. gifts of God and his calling
    are *i.*
Heb. 6:18. two *i.* acts in which God

Isaiah
Mat. 13:35. making good the prophecy
    of *I.*
Mark. 1:2. in the prophet *I.* it stands
    written

islanders
Acts 28:2. *i.* treated us with uncommon
    kindness
    28:4. the *i.*, seeing the snake

Israel
Luke 1:33. he will be king over *I.* for
    ever
    2:35. many in *I.* will stand or fall
Acts 3:23. extirpated from *I.*
    26:23. announce the dawn to *I.*
Rom. 11:11. to stir *I.* to emulation
Heb. 11:28. not touch the first-born of *I.*
2 Pet. 2:1. *I.* had false prophets
Jude 5. delivered the people of *I.* out of
    Egypt.

issue-s-ed
Mat. 24:45. *i.* their rations
Mark 12:20. died without *i.*
    12:21. he too died without *i.*
    12:22. died, all without *i.*
Luke 2:1. a decree was *i.*
    12:42. *i.* their rations
John 15:26. the Spirit of truth that *i.*
    from the Father
Acts 17:18. joined *i.* with him
    18:2. Claudius had *i.* an edict
    19:40. if the *i.* is raised
    23:6. the true *i.* in this trial is our hope
    of the resurrection
    23:23. *i.* these orders
    24:21. the true *i.* in my trial before
    you
    25:20. stand his trial there on these *i.*
Rom. 5:16. *i.* in a verdict of condem-
    nation, but the act of grace, fol-
    lowing upon so many misdeeds, *i.*
    in a verdict of acquittal
    5:18. the *i.* of one misdeed was con-
    demnation for all men, so the *i.* of
    one just act

Rom. 5:21. *i.* in eternal life
2 Cor. 9:11. such generosity will *i.* in
    thanksgiving
Gal. 3:16. to his 'issue'. It does not say
    '*i.*' in the plural, but in the singular,
    'and to your *i.*'; and the '*i.*' intended
    is Christ
    3:19. the '*i.*' to whom the promise was
    made
    3:29. you are the '*i.*' of Abraham
Phil. 1:19. the *i.* of it all will be my
    deliverance
1 Tim. 1:4. which *i.* in mere speculation
    5:21. never pre-judge the *i.*

itself
Mat. 12:45. more wicked than *i.*

Luke 14:34. if salt *i.* becomes tasteless
    16:15. sets *i.* up to be admired
Rom. 3:31. placing law *i.* on a firmer
    footing
    7:12. the law is in *i.* holy
    8:10. the spirit is life *i.*
    14:20. everything is pure in *i.*
2 Cor. 4:10. life may reveal *i.*
Eph. 4:24. shows *i.* in the just and devout
    life
Jam. 2:17. faith; if it does not lead to
    action, it is in *i.* a lifeless thing
    2:24. not by faith in *i.*
1 Pet. 1:7. that your faith may prove *i.*
    worthy
1 John 3:18. show *i.* in action

J

jail-ed
Mat. 5:25. you will be put in *j.*
    18:30. had him *j.* until he should pay
Luke 12:58. the constable put you in *j.*
Acts 5:21. sent to the *j.* to fetch the
    prisoners
    5:23. we found the *j.* securely locked
    16:26. the foundations of the *j.* were
    shaken

jailer
Acts 16:23. ordered the *j.* to keep them
    under close guard
    16:27. the *j.* woke up
    16:29. the *j.* called for lights
    16:36. the *j.* reported the message

jar
Mk. 14:13 ⎫
Luke 22:10 ⎭ carrying a *j.* of water
John. 2:6. six stone water-*j.*
    2:7. fill the *j.* with water
    4:28. the woman put down her water-*j.*
    19:29. a *j.* stood there full of sour wine
Heb. 9:4. a golden *j.* containing the
    manna

javelin
John 19:29. soaked a sponge with the
    wine, fixed it on a *j.*

jaws
2 Tim. 4:17. rescued out of the lion's *j.*

jealous-ies-y
Mat. 20:15. why be *j.* because I am kind
Luke 22:24. a *j.* dispute broke out
Acts 5:17. goaded into action by *j.*
    7:9. the patriarchs out of *j.* sold Joseph
    13:45. filled with *j.* resentment
    17:5. the Jews in their *j.*
Rom. 13:13. no quarrels or *j.*
1 Cor. 3:3. *j.* and strife among you

2 Cor. 12:20. I may find quarrelling
    and *j.*
Gal. 5:20. party intrigues, and *j.*
    5:26. *j.* of one another
Phil. 1:15. in a *j.* and quarrelsome spirit
1 Tim. 6:4. *j.*, quarrelling
Jam. 3:14. harbouring bitter *j.*
    3:16. *j.* and ambition
1 Pet. 2:1. away with all pretence and *j.*

jeer-s-ed
Mat. 27:29. they *j.* at him
Luke 23:35. their rulers *j.* at him
Heb. 11:36. had to face *j.* and flogging

Jerusalem
Acts 25:4. I shall be leavin g *J.* shortly
    25:6. eight or ten days at most in *J.*

jested
Mark 15:31. *j.* with one another

Jesus
Mat. 14:35. *J.* was recognized by the
    people
    27:16. a man of some notoriety, called
    J. Bar-Abbas
Mark 6:14. the fame of *J.* had spread
    15:11. to release Barabbas rather
    than *J.*
    16:19. the Lord *J.* was taken up into
    heaven
Acts 16:7. the Spirit of *J.* would not
    allow them
Heb. 3:3. *J.*, of whom I speak, has been
    deemed worthy
    Also the name *J.* is more frequently
    used than in the Authorized Ver-
    sion where it says 'he'

jettisoned
Acts 27:19. they *j.* the ship's gear

Jew-s
John 4:20. you *J.* say that the temple
  5:2. in the language of the *J.* is
  Bethesda
  19:4. said to the *J.*
  19:13. in the language of the *J.*
  19:17. in the *J.* language, 'Golgotha
Acts 2:14. addressed them: 'Fellow *J.*
  6:1. spoke the language of the *J.*
  9:29. the Greek-speaking *J.*
  10:37. all over the land of the *J.*
  21:24. you are a practising *J.*
Rom. 3:2. the *J.* were entrusted with the
  oracles of God
Gal. 2:7. the Gospel for *J.*
  2:8. an apostle to the *J.*
  2:9. while they went to the *J.*
Eph. 2:14. Gentiles and *J.*, he has made
  the two one
  3:6. joint heirs with the *J.*
1 Thess. 2:15. the *J.* who are heedless of
  God's will

jewel-s
Rev. 17:4. gold and *j.* and pearls
  18:12. *j.* and pearls
  18:16. gold and *j.* and pearls
  21:11. some priceless *j.*
  21:19. *j.* of every kind

jewellery
1 Pet. 3:3. or *j.*, or dress

Jewish
Mat. 2:4. lawyers of the *J.* people
  28:15. current in *J.* circles to this day
Acts 4:5. *J.* rulers, elders, and doctors
  10:2. gave generously to help the *J.*
  people
  10:45. men of *J.* birth
  11:2. those who were of *J.* birth
  18:15. your *J.* law, you may see to it
  yourselves
  21:40. addressed them in the *J.*
  language
  26:14. a voice saying to me in the
  J. language
Rom. 15:8. Christ became a servant of
  the *J.* people
  15:27. the *J.* Christians
1 Cor. 10:18. look at the *J.* people
Col. 4:11. of the *J.* Christians
Tit. 1:10. among *J.* converts

John
Mat. 3:15. *J.* then allowed him to come
  11:14. *J.* is the destined Elijah
  14:12. *J.* disciples came and took away
  the body
Mark. 6:27. with orders to bring *J.* head
  6:29. when *J.* disciples heard
John 5:35. *J.* was a lamp
  21:15, 16, 17. Simon son of *J.*, do you
  love me
Acts 8:17. Peter and *J.* laid their hands
  on them

join-s-ed
Mat. 20:4 ⎫
  20:7 ⎬ go and *j.* the others
Mark 3:13. they went and *j.* him
Luke 23:36. the soldiers *j.* in the mockery
John 6:17. Jesus had not yet *j.* them
  19:39. he was *j.* by Nicodemus
Acts 1:22. *j.* us as a witness
  10:2. his whole family *j.* in the worship
  of God
  16:22. the mob *j.* in the attack
  17:4. some of them were convinced
  and *j.* Paul
  17:18. philosophers *j.* issue with him
  17:34. some men *j.* him and became
  believers
  20:18. when they *j.* him, he spoke as
  follows
Rom. 8:16. the Spirit of God *j.* with
  our spirit
1 Cor. 16:11. send him happily on his
  way to *j.* me
2 Cor. 6:15. a believer *j.* hands with an
  unbeliever
  9:14. they *j.* in prayer on your behalf
1 Thess. 4:17. we who are left alive shall
  j. them
Tit. 3:12. make haste to *j.* me at
  Nicopolis
Jude 3. *j.* the struggle in defence of the
  faith

joint
Eph. 3:6. the Gentiles are *j.* heirs with
  the Jews
Heb. 12:13. the disabled limb will not
  be put out of *j.*

Jonathan
Acts 4:6. Caiaphas, *J.*, Alexander

Joseph
Mat. 2:14. so *J.* rose from sleep
  13:55. his brothers James, *J.*
  27:56. Mary the mother of James
  and *J.*
Acts 4:36. *J.*, surnamed by the apostles
  Barnabas

Joshua
Acts 7:45. the next generation, with *J.*
Heb. 4:8. if *J.* had given them rest

journey-s-ing
Mat. 20:17. Jesus was *j.* towards
  Jerusalem
Mark 6:7. one of his teaching *j.* round
  the villages
  7:31. on his return *j.* from Tyrian
  territory
  9:30. made a *j.* through Galilee
  10:17. as he was starting out on a *j.*
Luke 8:1. he went *j.* from town to town
  17:11. in the course of his *j.* to
  Jerusalem

joy-ful

Luke 19:12. a man of noble birth went on a long *j*.
24:28. he made as if to continue his *j*.
24:35. their account of the events of their *j*.
John 12:35. he who *j*. in the dark
Acts 9:27. Saul had seen the Lord on his *j*.
13:14. from Perga they continued their *j*.
15:30. they were sent off on their *j*.
15:40. he started on his *j*.
16:36. blessings on your *j*.
18:23. made a *j*. through the Galatian country
20:1. set out on his *j*. to Macedonia
21:5. we left and continued our *j*.
22:10. continue your *j*. to Damascus

joy-ful

Mark 4:16. the word, they accept it with *j*.
Luke 19:37. in their *j*. began to sing
John 20:20. when the disciples saw the Lord, they were filled with *j*.
Acts 2:26. my tongue spoke my *j*.
2:46. shared their meals with un-affected *j*.
Rom. 12:12. let hope keep you *j*.
12:15. with the *j*. be *j*.
1 Cor. 7:30. the *j*. as if they did not rejoice
2 Cor. 6:10. cause for *j*.
12:9. to find my *j*.
Gal. 4:27. break into a shout of *j*.
Phil. 3:1. I wish you *j*. in the Lord
4:4. I wish you all *j*. in the Lord. I will say it again: all *j*. be yours
4:10. it is a great *j*. to me
1 Thess. 5:16. be always *j*.
1 Pet. 1:6. cause for great *j*.
Rev. 19:7. exult and shout for *j*.

jubilant

Luke 10:17. the seventy-two came back *j*.
Jude 24. *j*. and above reproach

Judaism

Acts 6:5. a former convert to *J*.

Judaea

Luke 4:44. the Gospel in the synagogues of *J*.
23:5. among the people all through *J*.
John 7:1. he wished to avoid *J*.
11:54. Jesus no longer went about publicly in *J*.

judge-d-ing

Luke 20:35. *j*. worthy of a place in the other world
John 3:17. not to *j*. the world that God sent his Son
3:18. the unbeliever has already been *j*.
Acts 15:38. Paul *j*. that the man

1 Cor. 2:14. *j*. in the light of the Spirit
1 Tim. 1:12. I thank him for *j*. me worthy
Jam. 3:1. we who teach shall ourselves be *j*.

judgement

Mat. 7:1. pass no *j*., and you will not be judged
Mark 14:64. their *j*. was unanimous
Luke 6:37. pass no *j*.
21:23. terrible *j*. upon this people
John 3:18. does not come under *j*.
5:24. does not come up for *j*.
11:50. you do not use your *j*.
Acts 15:19. my *j*. therefore is that we should impose no irksome restrictions
Rom. 3:19. exposed to the *j*. of God
8:3. he has passed *j*. against sin
1 Cor. 3:13. the day of *j*. will expose it
11:29. eats and drinks *j*. on himself
11:34. you may not fall under *j*.
Eph. 2:3. lay under the dreadful *j*. of God
5:6. God's dreadful *j*.
Col. 3:6. God's dreadful *j*. is impending
1 Thess. 1:10. the terrors of *j*. to come
5:9. God has not destined us to the terrors of *j*.
2 Thess. 2:12. may all be brought to *j*.
1 Tim. 3:6. a *j*. contrived by the devil
Jam. 5:12. expose yourselves to *j*.
2 Pet. 2:11. no insults in seeking *j*.
1 John 4:18. the pains of *j*.
Rev. 18:20. in the *j*. against her

judicial

Rom. 5:16. the *j*. action

jugs

Mark 7:4. washing of cups and *j*.

jump

Acts 27:43. should *j*. overboard first

jurisdiction

Luke 20:20. the *j*. of the Governor
John 5:22. has given full *j*. to the Son
1 Cor. 6:4. entrust *j*. to outsiders

just-ly

Mat. 9:18. my daughter has *j*. died
Mark 7:13. other things that you do are *j*. like that
Luke 24:24. found things *j*. as the women had said
John 7:24. be *j*. in your judgements
18:27. *j*. then a cock crew
Acts 12:9. he thought it was *j*. a vision
17:31. he will have the world judged, and *j*. judged
Rom. 1:32. they know well enough the *j*. decree of God
3:10. there is no *j*. man, not one
4:6. the happiness of the man whom God 'counts' as *j*.

Rom. 5:7. even for a *j.* man one of us
would hardly die
5:18. the issue of one *j.* act is acquittal
Eph. 4:24. the *j.* and devout life
2 Thess. 1:6. it is surely *j.* that God
should balance the account
2 Tim. 4:8. the Lord, the all-*j.* Judge
1 Pet. 2:23. the One who judges *j.*
1 John 2:1. Jesus Christ, and he is *j.*
Rev. 15:4. thy *j.* dealings stand revealed
16:5. *j.* art thou in these thy judgements
16:7. true and *j.* are thy judgements
19:2. true and *j.* are his judgements
19:11. he is *j.* in judgement and *j.* in
war

justice
Mat. 6:33. God's kingdom and his *j.*
12:20. he leads *j.* on to victory
23:23. *j.,* mercy, and good faith
Luke 11:42. but have no care for *j.*
18:3. demanding *j.* against her
opponent
23:41. for us it is plain *j.*
Acts 24:10. for many years you have
administered *j.*
28:4. divine *j.* has not let him live
Rom. 3:5. if our injustice serves to bring
out God's *j.*
3:25. to demonstrate his *j.*
3:26. to demonstrate his *j.* now

4:6. any specific acts of *j.*
12:19. *j.* is mine, says the Lord
14:17. *j.,* peace, and joy
2 Cor. 7:11. your eagerness to see *j.* done
Eph. 5:9. all *j.* and truth
2 Thess. 1:5. the *j.* of God's judgement
1:8. he will do *j.* upon those who
refuse
1 Tim. 6:11. pursue *j.,* piety
2 Tim. 2:22. pursue *j.,* integrity, love
Heb. 1:8. the sceptre of *j.*
10:30. *j.* is mine: I will repay
11:33. they overthrew kingdoms,
established *j.*
Jam. 1:20. man's anger cannot promote
the *j.* of God
3:18. true *j.* is the harvest
2 Pet. 1:1. the *j.* of our God
3:13. new heavens and a new earth,
the home of *j.*

justification
Acts 19:40. charged with riot for this
day's work. There is no *j.* for it

justify-ied
Rom. 1:17. he shall gain life who is
j. through faith
8:10. life itself because you have
been *j.*
2 Cor. 7:14. to show my pride in you
has been *j.*
8:24. *j.* our pride in you; *j.* it to them

K

Kandake
Acts 8:27. *K.,* or Queen, of Ethiopia

Kedron
John 18:1. Jesus went out with his
disciples, and crossed the *K.* ravine

keen-ly
2 Cor. 8:8. by telling you how *k.* others
are
8:16. I thank God that he has made
Titus as *k.*
1 Tim. 6:4. morbidly *k.* on mere verbal
questions
Heb. 4:12. it cuts more *k.* than any
two-edged sword

keep-s-ing
Mat. 5:19. anyone who *k.* the Law
6:25. anxious thoughts about food
and drink to *k.* you alive
10:10. the worker earns his *k.*
18:8. than to *k.* two hands or two feet
18:9. than to *k.* both eyes and be
thrown into the fires of hell
24:42. *k.* awake, then; for you do not

know on what day your Lord is to
come
25:13. *k.* awake then; for you never
know the day or the hour
Mark 2:18. John's disciples and the
Pharisees were *k.* a fast
9:43. than to *k.* both hands and go
to hell
9:45. than to *k.* both your feet and be
thrown into hell
9:47. than to *k.* both eyes and be
thrown into hell
13:35⎱ *k.* awake
13:37⎰
14:37. were you not able to *k.* awake
for one hour
Luke 9:39. it *k.* on mauling him
9:62. and then *k.* looking back
12:22. food to *k.* you alive
17:3. *k.* watch on yourselves
18:1. *k.* on praying
19:40. if my disciples *k.* silence
21:34. *k.* a watch on yourselves
John 11:37. have done something to *k.*
Lazarus from dying

Acts 2:24. it could not be that death should *k.* him in its grip
5:38. *k.* clear of these men, I tell you
12:17. he signed to them to *k.* quiet
13:2. while they were *k.* a fast
20:28. *k.* watch over yourselves
20:35. we should *k.* in mind the words of the Lord Jesus
23:11. *k.* up your courage
24:16. *k.* at all times a clear conscience
27:25. so *k.* up your courage
Rom. 3:27. the *k.* of the law would not exclude it
3:28. success in *k.* the law
16:17. *k.* your eye on those who stir up quarrels
1 Cor. 1:8. he will *k.* you firm to the end
1:9. God *k.* faith
4:6. learn to '*k.* within the rules'
7:30. buyers must not count on *k.* what they buy
7:35. no wish to *k.* you on a tight rein
10:13. God *k.* faith
13:6. love *k.* no score of wrongs
16:2. put aside and *k.* by him a sum
2 Cor. 3:13. to *k.* the Israelites from gazing
Gal. 2:10. *k.* their poor in mind
3:2. did you receive the Spirit by *k.* the law
3:5. is it because you *k.* the law
3:21. righteousness would have come from *k.* the law
4:10. you *k.* special days
5:3. under obligation to *k.* the entire law
1 Thess. 4:11. let it be your ambition to *k.* calm
5:6. *k.* awake and sober
5:8. *k.* sober, armed with faith and love
5:23. *k.* you sound in spirit, soul, and body
1 Tim. 4:7. *k.* yourself in training for the practice of religion
4:16. *k.* close watch on yourself and your teaching
2 Tim. 1:13. *k.* before you an outline of the sound teaching
2:13. if we are faithless, he *k.* faith
3:5. *k.* clear of men like these
4:5. *k.* calm and sane at all times
4:18. *k.* me safe until his heavenly reign begins
Tit. 2:1. in *k.* with wholesome doctrine
Philem. 13. I should have liked to *k.* him with me
Heb. 2:13. I will *k.* my trust fixed on him
3:6. *k.* our hope high
3:14. if only we *k.* our original confidence
11:11. he who had promised would *k.* faith

12:13. *k.* your steps from wavering
13:4. marriage is honourable; let us all *k.* it so
Jam. 1:8. never can *k.* a steady course
2:16. good luck to you, *k.* yourselves warm
3:6. it *k.* the wheel of our existence red-hot
4:11. if you judge the law, you are not *k.* it
1 Pet. 3:16. *k.* your conscience clear
4:8. *k.* your love for one another
2 Pet. 1:13. I think it right to *k.* refreshing your memory.
1 John 2:24. *k.* in your hearts that which you heard
Jude 1. in the safe *k.* of Jesus Christ
Rev. 13:8. those whose names the Lamb that was slain *k.* in his roll of the living
20:13. Death and Hades gave up the dead in their *k.*

kept
Mat. 5:33. oaths sworn to the Lord must be kept
24:43. at what time of night the burglar was coming, he would have *k.* awake
26:63. Jesus *k.* silence
Mark 9:30. Jesus wished it to be *k.* secret
10:20. I have *k.* all these since I was a boy
14:61. he *k.* silence
Luke 13:16. who has been *k.* prisoner by Satan
18:13. but the other *k.* his distance
22:53. you *k.* your hands off me
Acts 2:46. they *k.* up their daily attendance at the temple
20:27. I have *k.* back nothing
Rom. 3:20. no human being can, be justified in the sight of God for having *k.* the law
5:13. in the absence of law no reckoning is *k.* of sin
2 Tim. 2:5. no athlete can win a prize unless he has *k.* the rules
Rev. 14:4. they have *k.* themselves chaste

key
Rev. 13:18. here is the *k.*; and anyone who has intelligence may work out the number of the beast

keystone
Acts 4:11. Jesus is the stone rejected by the builders which has become the *k.*

kidnapper-s
1 Tim. 1:9. perverts, *k.*, liars

kill-s-ed
Mat. 22:6. attacked them brutally, and *k.* them

Mat. 22:7. he sent troops to *k*. those murderers

Luke 11:49. some of these they will persecute and *k*.

13:4. eighteen people who were *k*. when the tower fell

18:33. they will flog him and *k*. him

Acts 2:23. you used heathen men to crucify and *k*. him

5:36. he was *k*. and his whole following was broken up

7:52. they *k*. those who foretold the coming

21:36. yelling, '*K*. him

22:20. I looked after the clothes of those who *k*. him

23:14. not to taste food until we have *k*. Paul

Rom. 7:11. through the commandment *k*. me

7:13. it was sin that *k*. me

2 Cor. 2:16. a deadly fume that *k*.

Eph. 2:16. the cross, on which he *k*. the enmity

2 Pet. 2:12. in the course of nature to be caught and *k*.

Rev. 2:13. Antipas, my faithful witness, was *k*.

9:15. to *k*. a third of mankind

11:13. seven thousand people were *k*. in the earthquake

19:21. the rest were *k*. by the sword

kind-s-ly

Mat. 4:24. sufferers from every *k*. of illness

5:11. every *k*. of calumny for my sake

9:35. curing every *k*. of ailment

10:1. and to cure every *k*. of ailment

20:15. why be jealous because I am *k*.

23:27. full of dead men's bones and all *k*. of filth

Mark 1:27. a new *k*. of teaching

3:10. sick people of all *k*. came crowding

4:19. all *k*. of evil desire

Luke 2:2. the first registration of its *k*.

12:15. be on your guard against greed of every *k*.

16:8. in dealing with their own *k*.

John 2:6. the *k*. used for Jewish rites of purification

5:16. works of this *k*. done on the Sabbath

12:33. to indicate the *k*. of death he was to die

Acts 7:49. what *k*. of house will you build for me

10:12. in it he saw creatures of every *k*.

10:33. it was *k*. of you to come

19:11. through Paul God worked miracles of an unusual *k*.

24:2. in all *k*. of ways

Rom. 1:30. they invent new *k*. of mischief

7:8. produced in me all *k*. of wrong desires

14:2. faith enough to eat all *k*. of food

15:14. knowledge of every *k*.

1 Cor. 12:28. ecstatic utterance of various *k*.

15:24. abolishing every *k*. of domination

15:35. in what *k*. of body

15:37. of wheat, or of some other *k*.

2 Cor. 8:7. knowledge, and zeal of every *k*.

Gal. 3:24. the law was a *k*. of tutor

5:19. the *k*. of behaviour that belongs to the lower nature

Eph. 4:31. bad feeling of every *k*.

5:3. fornication and indecency of any *k*.

Phil. 1:9. richer in knowledge and insight of every *k*.

3:4. for confidence of that *k*.

4:14. *k*. of you to share the burden of my troubles

Col. 1:10. active goodness of every *k*.

1 Thess. 1:5. that is the *k*. of men we were

3:6. you always think *k*. of us

5:22. avoid the bad of whatever *k*.

2 Tim. 2:24. *k*. towards all

3:6. led on by all *k*. of desires

3:17. equipped for good work of every *k*.

Tit. 2:5. temperate, chaste, and *k*.

3:3. slaves to passions and pleasures of every *k*.

Heb. 11:31. she had given the spies a *k*. welcome

Jam. 1:7. a man of that *k*. must not expect the Lord to give him anything

1:27. the *k*. of religion which is without stain or fault

3:16. disorder and evil of every *k*.

3:17. the *k*. deeds that are its fruit

1 Pet. 1:6. under trials of many *k*.

2:1. recrimination of every *k*.

2:18. not only when they are *k*. and considerate

3:8. brotherly affection, *k*. and humble-minded

5:9. going through the same *k*. of suffering

1 John 1:9. cleanse us from every *k*. of wrong

Rev. 11:1. a *k*. of measuring-rod

11:6. with every *k*. of plague

18:12. all *k*. of scented woods

21:8. liars of every *k*.

21:19. adorned with jewels of every *k*.

kindle-d

Acts 26:6. hope *k*. by God's promise

kindness
Luke 10:37. the one who showed him
   k.' Jesus said
Acts 9:36. who filled her days with acts
   of *k.*
14:17. in the *k.* he shows
Rom. 2:4. his wealth of *k.*, of tolerance,
   and of patience, without recognizing
   that God's *k.*
3:12. there is no one to show *k.*
11:22. the *k.* and the severity of God
   ... divine *k.* to you
Gal. 5:22. patience, *k.*, goodness
Philem. 14. that your *k.* may be a
   matter not of compulsion
Heb. 13:16. never forget to show *k.*
3 John 6. they have spoken of your *k.*

king-s
Mat. 2:22. succeeded his father Herod
   as *k.* of Judaea
Luke 1:33. David, and he will be *k.* over
   Israel
19:12. to be appointed *k.*
19:14. we do not want this man as
   our *k.*
19:15. back he came as *k.*
19:27. who did not want me for
   their *k.*
Rev. 16:16. they assembled the *k.* at
   the place

kinsmen
Heb. 7:5. to tithe the people, that is,
   their *k.*

kinswoman
Luke 1:36. your *k.* Elizabeth

Kish
Acts 13:21. Saul the son of *K.*

kneel
Eph. 3:14. I *k.* in prayer to the Father

knew
Mark 2:8. Jesus *k.* in his own mind
5:29. she *k.* in herself that she was
   cured
7:37. their astonishment *k.* no bounds
Luke 5:22. Jesus *k.* their thoughts
9:47. Jesus *k.* what was passing in
   their minds
Gal. 4:27. you who never *k.* a mother's
   pangs

knit
Eph. 4:16. bonded and *k.* together

know-s-ing-n
Mat. 5:3. how blest are those who *k.*
   that they are poor
8:9. I *k.*, for I am myself under orders
16:8. *k.* what was in their minds
21:27. they answered, 'We do not *k.*
27:8. the name 'Blood Acre', by
   which that field has been *k.*
28:15. this story became widely *k.*

Luke 7:8. I *k.*, for in my position I am
   myself under orders
8:2. *k.* as Mary of Magdala
11:44. graves over which men may
   walk without *k.* it
21:25. nations will stand helpless, not
   k. which way to turn
22:1. the Festival of Unleavened
   Bread, *k.* as Passover
John 1:18. no one has ever seen God;
   but God's only Son, he who is
   nearest to the Father's heart, he has
   made him *k.*
11:3. Sir, you should *k.* that your
   friend lies ill
16:13. he will make *k.* to you the
   things that are coming
16:14 } everything that he makes *k.*
16:15 } to you
17:6. I have made thy name *k.*
17:26. I made thy name *k.* to them,
   and will make it *k.*
Acts 2:22. made *k.* to you through
   miracles
Rom. 1:9. God *k.* how continually I
   make mention of you in my prayers
1 Cor. 9:27. I bruise my own body and
   make it *k.* its master
2 Cor. 2:11. we *k.* his wiles all too well
Gal. 1:18. to Jerusalem to get to *k.*
   Cephas
1 Tim. 1:4. cannot make *k.* God's plan
   for us
Tit. 2:2. let the older men *k.* that they
   should be sober
Heb. 5:13. anyone who lives on milk,
   being an infant, does not *k.* what
   is right
13:2. entertained angels without *k.* it
2 Pet. 3:1. recalling to you what you
   already *k.*
1 John 2:27. learn all you need to *k.*
   from his initiation
3:16. by this that we *k.* what love is
Rev. 1:1. made it *k.* by sending his angel

knowledge
Luke 1:4. to give you authentic *k.*
Acts 4:16. it is common *k.* in Jerusalem
   that a notable miracle
5:2. with the full *k.* of his wife he kept
   back part
2 Cor. 1:14. partial as your present *k.*
   of us is
Phil. 1:13. my imprisonment in Christ's
   cause has become common *k.*
1 Tim. 6:20. contradictions of so-called
   '*k.*
Tit. 1:1. faith and *k.* and hope—the faith
   of God's chosen people, *k.* of the
   truth

Korah
Jude 11. they have rebelled like *K.*

L

labour-ing
Mark. 6:48. *l.* at the oars against a head-
wind
John 16:21. a woman in *l.* is in pain
2 Cor. 2:5. not to *l.* the point
Rev. 12:2. in the anguish of her *l.* she
cried out

labourer
2 Tim. 2:15. as a *l.* who need not be
ashamed

lack-s-ed
Acts 15:21. Moses, after all, has never
l. spokesmen
17:25. not because he *l.* anything that
he accepts service
Rom. 11:20. they were lopped off for
l. of faith
1 Cor. 1:7. no single gift you *l.*
7:5. for *l.* of self-control, you may be
tempted
Gal. 2:13. the other Jewish Christians
showed the same *l.* of principle

laid
Mat. 8:4. the offering *l.* down by Moses
12:14. *l.* a plot to do away with him
21:7. *l.* their cloaks on them and
Jesus mounted
27:12. charges *l.* against him
Mark 1:44. the offering *l.* down by
Moses
8:23. *l.* his hands upon him
8:25. Jesus *l.* his hands on his eyes
10:16. *l.* his hands upon them, and
blessed them
12:19. Moses *l.* it down for us
Luke 2:35. thoughts of many will be *l.*
bare
5:14. the offering *l.* down by Moses
7:14. *l.* his hand on the bier
12:19. Man you have plenty of good
things *l.* by
20:28. Moses *l.* it down for us
John 8:5. in the Law Moses has *l.* down
Acts 9:17. *l.* his hands on him and said,
'Saul
22:10. told of all the tasks that are *l.*
upon you
25:14. Festus *l.* Paul's case before the
king
1 Cor. 14:24. the secrets of his heart are
l. bare
16:15. have *l.* themselves out to serve
2 Cor. 5:10. our lives *l.* open before the
tribunal of Christ
10:13. the limit God *l.* down for us

Gal. 2:2. I *l.* before them . . . the gospel
which I am accustomed to preach
Eph. 2:20. the foundation *l.* by the
apostles
2 Thess. 3:10. we *l.* down the rule
2 Tim. 2:19. God has *l.* a foundation
Jam. 2:8. the sovereign law *l.* down in
Scripture
2 Pet. 3:4. our fathers have been *l.* to
their rest
3:10. the earth with all that is in it
will be *l.* bare
Rev. 11:19. God's temple in heaven was
l. open   . .
18:17. alas that in one hour so much
wealth should be *l.* waste
18:19. in a single hour she should be
l. waste
20:9. *l.* siege to the camp of God's
people

lake
Mat. 4:18. casting a net into the *l.*
8:24. a great storm arose on the *l.*
8:32. rushed over the edge into the *l.*
13:1. Jesus went out and sat beside
the *l.*
14:25. walking over the *l.*
14:26. the disciples saw him walking
on the *l.*
17:27. cast a line in the *l.*
Mark 1:16. on the *l.* at work with a
casting-net
2:13. he went away to the *l.*-side
3:7. Jesus went away to the *l.*-side
4:1. he began to teach by the *l.*-side
. . . he had to get into a boat on the *l.*
4:35. let us cross over to the other
side of the *l.*
5:1. they came to the other side of
the *l.*
5:13. rushed over the edge into the *l.*
5:21. while he was by the *l.*-side
6:48. walking on the *l.*
6:49. they saw him walking on the *l.*
8:13. went off to the other side of
the *l.*

lamb-s
Mark 14:12. the Passover *l.* were being
slaughtered
Rev. 5:7. the *L.* went up and took the
scroll
6:3. the *L.* broke the second seal
8:1. the *L.* broke the seventh seal

lame
Mat. 18:8. enter into life maimed or *l.*

Luke 14:21. the crippled, the blind, and
    the *l*.
John 5:3. blind, *l*., and paralysed
Acts 14:8. a crippled man, *l*. from birth

lament-ing
Luke 8:52. weeping and *l*. for her
Rev. 1:7. all the peoples of the world
    shall *l*. in remorse

lamentation
Mat. 24:30. all the peoples of the world
    will make *l*.

lamp-stand
Mat. 5:15. when a lamp is lit, it is not
    put under the meal-tub, but on
    the *l*.
    5:16. you, like the *l*., must shed light
    among your fellows
    6:22. the *l*. of the body is the eye
Mark. 4:21. do you bring in the *l*. to put
    it under the meal-tub
Luke 8:16. nobody lights a *l*., and then
    covers it . . . he puts it on a *l*.
    11:33. no one lights a *l*. and puts it in
    a cellar, but rather on the *l*.
    11:34. the *l*. of your body is the eye
    11:36. as when a *l*. flashes its rays
    upon you
    12:35. with belts fastened and *l*. alight
    15:8. does she not light the *l*.
John 5:35. John was a *l*.
Acts 20:8. many *l*. in the upper room
Heb. 9:2. the first tent—in which was
    the *l*.
2 Pet. 1:19. a *l*. shining in a murky place
Rev. 1:12. seven standing *l*. of gold
    1:13. among the *l*. one like a son of
    man
    1:20. the seven *l*. of gold . . . the seven
    l. are the seven churches
    2:1. walks among the seven *l*. of gold
    2:5. remove your *l*. from its place
    11:4. the two *l*. that stand in the
    presence of the Lord
    18:23. no more shall the light of the
    l. be seen in you
    21:23. its *l*. was the Lamb
    22:5. nor will they need the light of *l*.

lance
John 19:34. stabbed his side with a *l*.

land-s-ed
Mat. 4:16. in the *l*. of death's dark
    shadow
    10:5. do not take the road to gentile *l*.
    14:13. came after him in crowds by *l*.
Mark 4:26. a man scatters seed on the *l*.
    6:33. came round by *l*., hurrying from
    all the towns
Luke 8:26. they *l*. in the country of the
    Gergesenes
    12:16. a rich man whose *l*. yielded
    heavy crops

    14:18. I have bought a piece of *l*.
    23:44. there came a darkness over the
    whole *l*.
Acts 1:18. buying a plot of *l*. with the
    price of his villainy
    10:37. happened lately all over the *l*.
    of the Jews
    27:3. we *l*. at Sidon
    27:13. hugging the *l*.
    27:27. the sailors felt that *l*. was
    getting nearer
    28:7. *l*. belonging to the chief magis-
    trate
Rom. 9:28. the Lord's sentence on the
    l. will be summary
2 Cor. 10:16. carry the Gospel to *l*. that
    lie beyond you
Eph. 2:19. no longer aliens in a foreign *l*.
    6:3. that you may live long in the *l*.
Heb. 11:8. a *l*. destined for himself and
    his heirs
Jam. 5:7. the precious crop his *l*. may
    yield
    5:17. no rain, not a drop fell on the *l*.
    5:18. the *l*. bore crops once more
1 Pet. 2:11. as aliens in a foreign *l*.
Rev. 7:1. no wind should blow on sea
    or *l*.
    7:2. power to ravage *l*. and sea
    7:3. do no damage to sea or *l*.
    10:2. his left on the *l*.
    10:5. the angel that I saw standing on
    the sea and the *l*.
    10:8. the angel that stands on the sea
    and the *l*.
    20:9. they marched over the breadth
    of the *l*.

landowner-s
Mat. 20:1. a *l*. who went out early
    21:33. a *l*. who planted a vineyard
Luke 15:15. attached himself to one of
    the local *l*.

landward
Acts 27:14. the 'North-easter' as they
    call it, tore down from the *l*. side

language-s
John 5:2. in the *l*. of the Jews is
    Bethesda
    8:43. why do you not understand my *l*.
    8:44. when he tells a lie he is speaking
    his own *l*.
    19:13. Gabbatha in the *l*. of the Jews
    19:17. in the Jews' *l*., 'Golgotha
Acts 1:19. in their own *l*. Akeldama,
    which means 'Blood Acre'
    2:8. each of us in his own native *l*.
    6:1. those who spoke the *l*. of the Jews
    21:40. he addressed them in the
    Jewish *l*.
    22:2. heard him speaking to them in
    their own *l*.

Acts 26:14. I heard a voice saying to me
in the Jewish *l.*
1 Cor. 1:17. without relying on the *l.* of
worldly wisdom
14:2
14:4 }the *l.* of ecstasy
14:6. I use ecstatic *l.*
14:14. I use such *l.* in my prayer
14:16. the *l.* of inspiration
14:19. in the *l.* of ecstasy
2 Cor. 1:18. the *l.* in which we address
you
Gal. 1:10. does my *l.* now sound as if I
were canvassing
Eph. 4:29. no bad *l.* must pass your lips
Heb. 11:14. those who use such *l.* show
plainly
Rev. 5:9. men of every tribe and *l.*
7:9. of all tribes, peoples, and *l.*
10:11. nations and *l.*
11:9. of every *l.* and nation
13:7. tribe and people, *l.* and nation
14:6. to every nation and tribe, *l.* and
people
17:15. peoples and populations,
nations and *l.*

lap
Luke 6:38. running over, will be poured
into your *l.*

lapis lazuli
Rev. 21:19. the first of the foundation-
stones being jasper, the second *l. l.*

large-r
Mat. 21:36. he sent other servants, this
time a *l.* number
27:60. rolled a *l.* stone against the
entrance
Mark 4:1. the crowd that gathered round
him was so *l.*
4:32. branches so *l.* that the birds can
settle
5:11. a *l.* herd of pigs
6:2. the *l.* congregation who heard
him were amazed
9:14. a *l.* crowd surrounding them
10:46. with his disciples and a *l.* crowd
12:41. rich people were giving *l.* sums
Luke 5:29. a *l.* party of tax-gatherers
6:17. a *l.* concourse of his disciples
8:4. people were now gathering in *l.*
numbers
8:32. a *l.* herd of pigs nearby
9:37. he was met by a *l.* crowd
Acts 10:27. found a *l.* gathering
11:24. *l.* numbers were won over to
the Lord
11:26. gave instruction to *l.* numbers
12:12. a *l.* company was at prayer
14:1. a *l.* body both of Jews and
Greeks became believers
16:16. *l.* profits to her owners by
telling fortunes

28:23. came in *l.* numbers as his
guests
Rom. 8:29. the eldest among a *l.* family
of brothers
Phil. 1:13. among the public at *l.*
Jam. 3:4. ships: *l.* they may be

lash-ings
Acts 22:25. tied him up for the *l.*, Paul
said
27:40. loosened the *l.* of the steering-
paddles

last-s-ed-ing
Mat. 5:26. till you have paid the *l.*
farthing
27:19. much troubled on his account
in my dreams *l.* night
27:50. Jesus again gave a loud cry, and
breathed his *l.*
Mark 15:33. darkness fell over the
whole land, which *l.* till three
Luke 1:25. at *l.* he has deigned to take
away my reproach
13:7. for the *l.* three years I have come
looking for fruit
23:44. a darkness over the whole land,
which *l.* until three
24:18. what has happened there in the
l. few days
John 6:27. the food that *l.*, the food of
eternal life
9:4. while daylight *l.* we must carry on
the work
15:16. bear fruit, fruit that shall *l.*
19:16. at *l.*, to satisfy them, he handed
Jesus over
Acts 20:11. much conversation, which
l. until dawn
Rom. 1:10. succeed at long *l.* in coming
to visit you
1 Cor. 7:29. the time we live in will not
l. long. While it *l.*
13:13. three things that *l.* for ever:
faith, hope, and love
2 Cor. 5:18. from first to *l.* this has been
the work of God
Eph. 4:13. so shall we all at *l.* attain to
the unity
Heb. 10:34. you possessed something
better and more *l.*
Rev. 8:13. the three *l.* angels must now
blow
21:3. now at *l.* God has his dwelling
among men

late-r-st-ly
Mat. 14:15. when it grew *l.* the disciples
came up to him
14:23. it grew *l.*, and he was there by
himself
20:3. *l.* he saw some more men standing idle
25:5. as the bridegroom was *l.* in coming they all dozed off to sleep

Mark 6:35. this is a lonely place and it is getting very *l.*
   6:47. it grew *l.* and the boat was already well out
   11:11. as it was now *l.*, he went out to Bethany
Luke 15:13. a few days *l.* the younger son
John 7:39. the Spirit which believers in him would receive *l.*
   20:19. *l.* that Sunday evening . . . Jesus came
Acts 10:37. what happened *l.* all over the land
   16:33. at that *l.* hour of the night he took them and washed their wounds
   17:21. hearing about the *l.* novelty

late-comers
Mat. 20:12. these *l.* have done only one hour's work

latter
2 Cor. 2:16. to the *l.* it is a deadly fume that kills
2 Tim. 2:20. the former are valued, the *l.* held cheap
Heb. 10:9. he thus annuls the former to establish the *l.*

laugh
Luke 14:29. all the onlookers will *l.* at him

lavish-ed-ly
Rom. 8:32. how can he fail to *l.* upon us all he has to give
2 Cor. 8:2. shown themselves *l.* open-handed
   8:7. equally *l.* in this generous service
   9:9. he has *l.* his gifts on the needy
Eph. 1:7. God's free grace *l.* upon us
1 Tim. 1:14. the grace of our Lord was *l.* upon me

law-s
Mat. 5:19. the least of the *L.* demands . . . anyone who keeps the *L.*
   8:19. a doctor of the *l.* came up
   12:38. some of the doctors of the *l.* and the Pharisees
   13:52. a teacher of the *l.*
   15:6. you have made God's *l.* null and void
   20:18. given up to the chief priests and the doctors of the *l.*
   21:15. the chief priests and doctors of the *l.* saw the wonderful things he did.
   23:2. the doctors of the *l.* and the Pharisees
Mark 1:22. unlike the doctors of the *l.*, he taught with a note of authority
   2:16. some doctors of the *l.* who were Pharisees
   3:22. the doctors of the *l.*, too

   7:1. a group of Pharisees, with some doctors of the *l.*
   8:31. rejected by the elders, chief priests, and doctors of the *l.*
   12:35. how can the teachers of the *l.* maintain that the Messiah is 'Son of David
John 7:22. Moses gave you the *l.* of circumcision
Acts 17:7. they all flout the Emperor's *l.*
2 Cor. 3:6. the written *l.* condemns to death
   3:7. the *l.*, then, engraved letter by letter upon stone
   3:15. every time the *L.* of Moses is read
Gal. 2:17. sinners against the *l.*
   2:18. a transgressor of the *l.*
Col. 2:14. pledged us to the decrees of the *l.*

lawless
Rom. 4:7. happy are they,' he says, 'whose *l.* deeds are forgiven
2 Pet. 2:7. the *l.* society in which he lived

lawlessness
Mat. 24:12. as *l.* spreads, men's love for one another will grow cold
Rom. 6:19. the service of impurity and *l.*
1 John 3:4. sin, in fact, is *l.*

lawyer-s
Mat. 2:4. *l.* of the Jewish people
   also Mat. 9:3, 15:1, 16:21, 23:13, 15, 23, 25, 27, 29; Mark 2:6, 7:5, 9:14, 11:27, 12:28, 32, 14:43, 15:1; Luke 5:21, 30, 6:7, 11:53, 19:47, 23:10

lay-s-ing
Mat. 2:9. above the place where the child *l.*
   19:7. did Moses *l.* it down that a man might divorce his wife
   19:13. children for him to *l.* his hands on them
   26:55. you did not *l.* hands on me
   28:4. the guards shook with fear and *l.* like the dead
Mark 7:32. with the request that he would *l.* his hand on him
   14:8. she has done what *l.* in her power
   14:49. you did not *l.* hands on me
Luke 24:13. Emmaus, which *l.* about seven miles from Jerusalem
John 10:11. the good shepherd *l.* down his life for the sheep
Acts 4:25. the peoples *l.* their plots in vain
   9:12. *l.* his hands on him
   11:3. Peter began by *l.* before them the facts
   15:10. *l.* on the shoulders of these converts a yoke

Acts 27:30. pretending they were going to *l.* out anchors

Rom. 2:5. *l.* up for yourself a store of retribution

6:4. by baptism we were buried with him, and *l.* dead

Eph. 2:3. *l.* under the dreadful judgement of God

4:22. *l.* aside that old human nature

Col. 3:8. *l.* aside all anger, passion

1 Tim. 1:18. this charge, son Timothy, I *l.* upon you

6:21. many who *l.* claim to it have shot far wide of the faith

2 Tim. 1:6. through the *l.* on of my hands

Heb. 3:17. whose bodies *l.* where they fell in the desert

12:2. Jesus who, for the sake of the joy that *l.* ahead

12:6. he *l.* the rod on every son

Rev. 4:10. *l.* their crowns before the throne

12:11. did not hold their lives too dear to *l.* them down

laymen
Acts 4:13. they were untrained *l.*

Lazarus
John 11:17. *L.* had already been four days in the tomb

11:37. have done something to keep *L.* from dying

lazy
Mat. 25:26. you *l.* rascal!' said the master

Tit. 1:12. Cretans were always liars, vicious brutes, *l.* gluttons

Heb. 6:12. we want you not to become *l.*

lead-s-ing
Mat. 5:29. if your right eye *l.* you astray

12:20. he *l.* justice on to victory

Mark 6:21. the *l.* men of Galilee

9:42. the man who *l.* astray one of these little ones

9:45. if it is your foot that *l.* you astray

10:32. Jesus *l.* the way

Luke 1:77. *l.* his people to salvation

14:1. the house of a *l.* Pharisee

19:42. the way that *l.* to peace

19:47. with the support of the *l.* citizens

John 7:12. he is *l.* the people astray

Acts 13:50. the *l.* men of the city

15:22. two *l.* men in the community

25:5. let your *l.* men come down with me

Rom. 1:5. in his name to *l.* to faith and obedience

1:28. *l.* them to break all rules

7:10. proved in my experience to *l.* to death

8:15. not a spirit of slavery *l.* you back into a life of fear

10:10. the faith that *l.* to righteousness is in the heart, and the confession that *l.* to salvation is upon the lips

12:8. if you are a leader, exert yourself to *l.*

16:17. *l.* others astray

1 Cor. 5:10. pagans who *l.* loose lives

5:11. so-called Christian who *l.* a loose life

2 Cor. 2:14. God, who continually *l.* us about

Eph. 4:26. do not let anger *l.* you into sin

1 Thess. 2:16. to *l.* them to salvation

2 Tim. 3:15. *l.* you to salvation through faith

Tit. 1:10. talk wildly and *l.* men's minds astray

Jam. 2:17. if it does not *l.* to action, it is in itself a lifeless thing

1 Pet. 4:7. you must *l.* an ordered and sober life

Jude 8. their dreams *l.* them to defile the body

leader
Mat. 2:6. a *l.* to be the shepherd of my people

Acts 5:31. as *l.* and saviour

25:2. the Jewish *l.* brought before him the case

28:17. the local Jewish *l.*

Rom. 12:8. if you are a *l.*, exert yourself

1 Thess. 5:12. your *l.* and counsellors

1 Tim. 3:2. our *l.*, therefore, or bishop, must be above reproach

5:17. elders who do well as *l.*

Heb. 2:10. the *l.* who delivers them

13:7. remember your *l.*

13:17. obey your *l.* and defer to them

13:24. greet all your *l.*

3 John 9. Diotrephes, their would-be *l.*

leadership
Acts 5:37. he induced some people to revolt under his *l.*

7:39. our forefathers would not accept his *l.*

1 Tim. 3:1. to aspire to *l.* is an honourable ambition

lean-ed
John 13:25. *l.* back close to Jesus and asked

leap-t
Luke 4:29. they *l.* up, threw him out of the town

learn-ed-ing
Mat. 5:21. you have *l.* that our forefathers were told

11:25. hiding these things from the *l.*

16:17. you did not *l.* that from mortal man

Luke 7:37. *l.* that Jesus was dining
  10:21. hiding these things from the *l.*
  23:7. *l.* that he belonged to Herod's
    jurisdiction
John 4:3. when Jesus *l.* this
  7:51. given him a hearing and *l.* the
    facts
  8:38. what you *l.* from your father
  17:8. I have taught them all that I *l.*
    from thee
  17:23. then the world will *l.* that thou
    didst send me
Acts 13:12. deeply impressed by what he
    l. about the Lord
  17:13. *l.* that the word of God had
    now been proclaimed
  23:34. *l.* that he was from Cilicia
Rom. 1:14. to *l.* and simple
1 Cor. 1:20. your man of *l.*
Col. 1:5. that hope of which you *l.*
1 Thess. 4:4. must *l.* to gain mastery
  over his body
2 Thess. 2:15. hold fast to the traditions
  which you have *l.*
Jam. 4:4. have you never *l.* that love of
  the world is enmity to God
1 John 2:27. *l.* all you need to know
  from his initiation

learner
Mat. 13:52. a teacher of the law has
  become a *l.*

least
Mat. 24:44. the Son of Man will come
  at the time you *l.* expect him
Luke 12:40. the Son of Man is coming
  at the time you *l.* expect him
1 Cor. 4:3. it does not matter to me in
  the *l.*
  14:20. at *l.* be grown-up in your
    thinking

leather
Mark 1:6. John . . . with a *l.* belt round
  his waist

leave-s-ing
Mat. 8:22. *l.* the dead to bury their dead
  8:34. begged him to *l.* the district
  9:16. *l.* a bigger hole
  10:11. make your home there until
    you *l.*
  10:14. as you *l.* that house
  10:29. without your Father's *l.* not one
    of them can fall to the ground
  12:14. the Pharisees, on *l.* the syna-
    gogue, laid a plot
  16:24. he must *l.* self behind
  28:10. they are to *l.* for Galilee
Mark 2:21. *l.* a bigger hole
  3:6. the Pharisees, on *l.* the synagogue,
    began plotting against him
  5:17. they begged Jesus to *l.* the dis-
    trict

  6:10. stay there until you *l.* those parts
  6:11. shake the dust off your feet as
    you *l.*
  6:33. many saw them *l.* and recognized
    them
  6:46. after taking *l.* of them, he went
    up the hill-side to pray
  8:34. a follower of mine must *l.* self
    behind
  10:1. on *l.* those parts
  15:45. he gave Joseph *l.* to take the
    dead body
Luke 4:42. they pressed him not to *l.*
    them
  5:8. go, Lord, *l.* me, sinner that I am
  8:32. he gave them *l.*
  8:38. begged *l.* to go with him
  9:5. when you *l.* their town shake the
    dust
  9:23. he must *l.* self behind
  9:60. *l.* the dead to bury their dead
  13:8. *l.* it, sir, this one year
  13:31. you should *l.* this place
  14:33. taking *l.* of all his possessions
  16:4. when I have to *l.*
  20:28. dies *l.* a wife but no child
  21:21. those who are in the city itself
    must *l.* it
  21:37. *l.* the city and spend the night
    on the hill called Olivet
  22:31. Satan has been given *l.* to sift all
    of you
John 5:14. now that you are well again,
    l. your sinful ways
  6:67. Jesus asked the Twelve, 'Do you
    also want to *l.* me
  7:3. you should *l.* this district and go
    into Judaea
  11:31. they saw her start up and *l.* the
    house
  11:48. if we *l.* him alone like this the
    whole populace will believe
  12:7. *l.* her alone,' said Jesus
  13:1. he must *l.* this world
  16:7. it is for your good that I am *l.*
    you
  19:23. four parts, one for each soldier,
    l. out the tunic.
Acts 1:4. he told them not to *l.* Jerusalem
  4:15. they ordered them to *l.* the court
  5:38. keep clear of these men, I tell
    you; *l.* them alone
  7:3. *l.* your country and your kinsfolk
  13:42. as they were *l.* the synagogue
    they were asked to come again
  18:2. an edict that all Jews should *l.*
    Rome
  25:4. I shall be *l.* Jerusalem shortly
  28:10. when we were *l.* they put on
    board provision for our needs
Rom. 12:19. *l.* a place for divine
    retribution
  13:8. *l.* no claim outstanding against
    you

1 Cor. 15:34. *l.* your sinful ways
2 Cor. 5:8. *l.* our home in the body and go to live with the Lord
   5:14. the love of Christ *l.* us no choice
   6:17. come away and *l.* them
   8:17. he is now *l.* to come to you
Eph. 4:22. *l.* your former way of life
   4:27. *l.* no loop-hole for the devil
1 Tim. 6:7. when we *l.* it we cannot take anything with us
2 Pet. 1:14. in this body. I know that very soon I must *l.* it
Rev. 3:12. in the temple of my God; he shall never *l.* it
   17:16. *l.* her desolate

lecture
Acts 19:9. in the *l.*-hall of Tyrannus

led
Mat. 13:57. this *l.* him to say
   17:1. *l.* them up a high mountain
Mark 15:1. they *l.* him away and handed him over to Pilate
Luke 4:5. the devil *l.* him up
John 2:11. *l.* his disciples to believe in him
   6:52. this *l.* to a fierce dispute among the Jews
Acts. 3:15. killed him who has *l.* the way to life
   7:4. God *l.* him to migrate to this land
   7:36. it was Moses who *l.* them out
Rom. 7:10. the commandment which should have *l.* to life
2 Cor. 7:9. the wound *l.* to a change of heart
Col. 2:15. *l.* them as captives in his triumphal procession
Heb. 3:16. whom Moses had *l.* out of Egypt
Rev. 12:9. that serpent of old that *l.* the whole world astray

ledge
Acts 20:9. Eutychus, who was sitting on the window-*l.*

lee
Acts 27:4. we sailed under the *l.* of Cyprus
   27:7. we began to sail under the *l.* of Crete
   27:16. under the *l.* of a small island called Cauda

left
Mat. 5:39. someone slaps you on the right cheek, turn and offer him your *l.*
   12:44. I will go back to the home I *l.*
   17:18. the devil *l.* him
   19:27. *l.* everything to become your followers
   19:29. anyone who has *l.* brothers or sisters

   25:15. then he *l.* the country
Mark 1:18. *l.* their nets and followed him
   6:20. the listening *l.* him greatly perplexed
   12:6. he had now only one *l.* to send
Luke 5:11. they *l.* everything and followed him
   15:13. *l.* home for a distant country
John 2:3. they have no wine *l.*
   6:12. collect the pieces *l.* over
   6:13. pieces *l.* uneaten of the five barley loaves
   19:18. with him two others, one on the right, one on the *l.*
Acts 9:31. the church . . . was *l.* in peace to build up its strength
   12:17. then he *l.* the house
   13:13. John, however, *l.* them
Rom. 11:4. I have *l.* myself seven thousand men
1 Cor. 4:8. you have come into your kingdom—and *l.* us out
2 Cor. 2:2. who is *l.* to cheer me up, except you
   4:9. struck down, we are not *l.* to die
1 Thess. 4:15. we who are *l.* alive until the Lord comes
   4:17. we who are *l.* alive shall join them
1 Tim. 5:13. speaking of things better *l.* unspoken
2 Tim. 4:16. they all *l.* me in the lurch
Heb. 11:8. *l.* home without knowing where he was to go
   11:15. if their hearts had been in the country they had *l.*
   11:27. by faith he *l.* Egypt
Rev. 3:2. put some strength into what is *l.*
   12:8. no foothold was *l.* them in heaven
   20:11. no place was *l.* for them

leg-s
Rev. 10:1. his *l.* were like pillars of fire
   19:16. on his *l.* there was written the name

legal
Rom. 10:5. of *l.* righteousness Moses writes
Gal. 3:18. if the inheritance is by *l.* right
   3:19. to make wrongdoing a *l.* offence
Phil. 3:6. in *l.* rectitude, faultless
   3:9. no righteousness of my own, no *l.* rectitude

legally
Acts 22:25. can you *l.* flog a man who is a Roman citizen
Heb. 8:6. the promises upon which it is *l.* secured

lend-ing

Luke 10:40. tell her to come and *l.* a hand

22:32. you must *l.* strength to your brothers

Tit. 1:14. instead of *l.* their ears to Jewish myths

length

Mat. 13:3. he spoke to them in parables, at some *l.*

Luke 23:9. he questioned him at some *l.*

Acts 12:10. walked the *l.* of one street; and the angel left him

28:23. he dealt at *l.* with the whole matter

2 Tim. 1:10. has now at *l.* been brought fully into view

leniency

2 Cor. 13:2. when I come this time, I will show no *l.*

lent

2 Tim. 4:17. the Lord stood by me and *l.* me strength

less

Mat. 2:16. all children in Bethlehem and its neighbourhood, of the age of two years or *l.*

Mark 12:44. she, with *l.* than enough, has given all

Luke 21:4. had more than enough, but she, with *l.* than enough

John 3:30. as he grows greater, I must grow *l.*

Acts 11:17. God gave them no *l.* a gift than he gave us

14:15. we are only human beings, no *l.* mortal than you

Rom. 11:15. nothing *l.* than life from the dead

14:6. he who abstains has the Lord in mind no *l.*

Gal. 2:17. we ourselves no *l.* than the Gentiles turn out to be sinners

Eph. 4:13. measured by nothing *l.* than the full stature of Christ

Col. 3:5. greed which is nothing *l.* than idolatry

1 Tim. 6:2. slaves must not respect them any *l.*

Heb. 5:3. sin-offerings for himself no *l.* than for the people

Jude 3. our salvation—which is yours no *l.* than ours

lesson-s

Mat. 24:32 ⎫
Mark 13:28 ⎭ learn a *l.* from the fig-tree

Luke 4:16. he stood up to read the *l.*

John 9:34. who are you to give us *l.*

2 Cor. 3:14. when the *l.* is read from the old covenant

Phil. 4:9. the *l.* I taught you

2 Pet. 2:6. an object-*l.* for godless men

let

Mat. 3:15. Jesus replied, '*L.* it be so for the present

9:29. as you have believed, so *l.* it be

14:18. *l.* me have them,' he replied

19:14. *l.* the children come to me

23:37. but you would not *l.* me

Mark. 1:34. he would not *l.* the devils speak

6:56. begged him to *l.* them simply touch the edge of his cloak

Luke 7:42. he *l.* them both off

7:43. I should think the one that was *l.* off most

8:32. the spirits begged him to *l.* them go into these pigs

20:16. and *l.* the vineyard to others

22:51. Jesus answered, '*L.* them have their way

John 13:8. I will never *l.* you wash my feet

Acts 13:35. thou wilt not *l.* thy loyal servant suffer corruption

24:24. he *l.* him talk to him about faith in Christ Jesus

28:4. divine justice has not *l.* him live

Rom. 5:2. *l.* us exult in the hope of the divine splendour

5:3. *l.* us even exult in our present sufferings

12:12. *l.* hope keep you joyful

1 Cor. 6:12. I for one will not *l.* anything make free with me

letter-s

Mat. 5:18. not a *l.*, not a stroke, will disappear from the Law

Acts 15:20. instruct them by *l.*

15:30. delivered the *l.*

23:33. delivered the *l.* to the Governor

Rom. 16:22. I Tertius, who took this *l.* down

1 Cor. 5:9. In my *l.* I wrote

9:15. nor do I intend to claim it in this *l.*

2 Cor. 1:13. nothing in our *l.* to you but what you can read for yourselves

2:3. this is precisely the point I made in my *l.*

2:4. that *l.* I sent you came out of great distress

3:2. you are all the *l.* we need, a *l.* written on our heart

3:3. a *l.* that has come from Christ

3:7. the law, then, engraved *l.* by *l.* upon stone

7:12. although I did send you that *l.*

13:10. my purpose in writing this *l.* before I come

Col. 4:16. when this *l.* is read among you

1 Thess. 5:27. have this *l.* read to the whole brotherhood

2 Thess. 2:15. learned from us by word or by *l.*

2 Thess. 3:14. our instructions given by *l.*
  3:17. this authenticates all my *l.*
2 Pet. 3:1. this is now my second *l.* to you
  3:16. his other *l.*, wherever he speaks of this subject
1 John 5:13. this *l.* is to assure you that you have eternal life
3 John 9. I sent a *l.* to the congregation
Rev. 13:18. the numerical value of its *l.*

level-led
Mat. 20:12. you have put them on a *l.* with us
Luke 3:5. every mountain and hill *l.*
  6:17. took his stand on *l.* ground
  6:40. will reach his teacher's *l.*
Rom. 1:3. on the human *l.* he was born of David's stock
  1:4. but on the *l.* of the spirit—the Holy Spirit
  7:5. while we lived on the *l.* of our lower nature
  8:5. live on the *l.* of our lower nature
  8:8. who live on such a *l.* cannot possibly please God
  8:9. you are on the spiritual *l.*
  8:12. we are not obliged to live on that *l.*
1 Cor. 3:3. you are living on the purely human *l.*
2 Cor. 11:12. their vaunted apostleship on the same *l.* as ours
Eph. 4:9. he also descended to the lowest *l.*
Phil. 3:16. the *l.* we have already reached

libellously
Rom. 3:8. some *l.* report me as saying

liberal
Acts 17:11. the Jews here were more *l.*-minded

liberate
Luke 24:21. hoping that he was the man to *l.* Israel
Heb. 2:15. *l.* those who, through fear of death

liberation
Luke 2:38. looking for the *l.* of Jerusalem
  21:28. your *l.* is near
Rom. 3:24. *l.* in the person of Christ Jesus
Eph. 4:30. the day of our final *l.*

liberator
Acts 7:35. commissioned as ruler and *l.*

liberty
1 Cor. 7:21. if a chance of *l.* should come, take it

licence
1 Cor. 14:34. they have no *l.* to speak
Gal. 5:13. do not turn your freedom into *l.*
1 Pet. 4:3. then you lived in *l.*

licentiousness
Jude 4. pervert the free favour of our God into *l.*

lie-s
Mat. 23:18. swears by the offering that *l.* on the altar
  23:20. the altar and by whatever *l.* on it
John 3:19. here *l.* the test
  11:3. Sir, you should know that your friend *l.* ill
  16:8. where wrong and right and judgement *l.*
  19:11. the deeper guilt *l.* with the man who handed me over to you
Acts 20:35. happiness *l.* more in giving than in receiving
Rom. 1:19. all that may be known of God by men *l.* plain before their eyes
  3:16. ruin and misery *l.* along their paths
1 Cor. 14:14. the Spirit in me prays, but my intellect *l.* fallow
2 Cor. 3:15. a veil *l.* over the minds of the hearers
  5:11. to God our lives *l.* open, as I hope they also *l.* open to you
  10:16. the Gospel to lands that *l.* beyond you
Eph. 1:7. therein *l.* the richness of God's free grace
Phil. 1:7. when I *l.* in prison
  1:17. fresh trouble for me as I *l.* in prison
Col. 2:3. in him *l.* hidden all God's treasures
  3:3. your life *l.* hidden with Christ in God
2 Thess. 2:9. powerful signs and miracles of the *L.*
Heb. 4:13. everything *l.* naked and exposed to the eyes of the One
Rev. 14:5. no *l.* was found in their lips

life
Mat. 11:5. the dead are raised to *l.*
  14:2. John has been raised to *l.*
  20:19. on the third day he will be raised to *l.* again
  22:16. you teach in all honesty the way of *l.*
Mark 6:14. John the Baptist has been raised to *l.*
  12:14. you teach in all honesty the way of *l.*
  12:23. at the resurrection, when they come back to *l.*
Luke 7:3. come and save his servant's *l.*
  7:22. the dead are raised to *l.*
  7:37. a woman who was living an immoral *l.*
  9:8. that one of the old prophets had come back to *l.*

Luke 9:19. one of the old prophets has come back to *l*.
12:19. take *l*. easy, eat, drink
12:20. this very night you must surrender your *l*.
15:24. this son of mine was dead and has come back to *l*.
15:32. your brother here was dead and has come back to *l*.
20:21. teach in all honesty the way of *l*.
21:19. by standing firm you will win true *l*. for yourselves
John 5:21. as the Father raises the dead and gives them *l*., so the Son gives *l*. to men
Acts 2:24. God raised him to *l*. again
2:42. to share the common *l*.
9:23. the Jews hatched a plot against his *l*.
10:40. raised him to *l*. on the third day
21:21. following our way of *l*.
23:30. an attempt to be made on the man's *l*.
26:8. why is it considered incredible among you that God should raise dead men to *l*.
Rom. 6:19. making for a holy *l*.
7:9. sin sprang to *l*. and I died
8:11. give new *l*. to your mortal bodies
8:15. a spirit of slavery leading you back into a *l*. of fear
14:9. Christ died and came to *l*. again
14:19 }
15:2 } build up the common *l*.
1 Cor. 1:9. share in the *l*. of his Son Jesus Christ
3:15. yet he will escape with his *l*.
4:17. the way of *l*. in Christ
5:11. any so-called Christian who leads a loose *l*.
7:17. order his *l*. according to the gift
7:28. those who marry will have pain and grief in this bodily *l*.
15:4. he was raised to *l*. on the third day
15:15. we bore witness that he raised Christ to *l*.
15:20. Christ was raised to *l*.
15:29. if the dead are not raised to *l*. at all
15:32. if the dead are never raised to *l*.
15:34. come back to a sober and upright *l*.
15:36. the seed you sow does not come to *l*. unless it has first died
15:45. the last Adam has become a *l*.-giving spirit
2 Cor. 1:23. I stake my *l*. upon it
4:14. he who raised the Lord Jesus to *l*.
13:5. are you living the *l*. of faith
Gal. 1:13. my manner of *l*.
Eph. 2:5. brought us to *l*. with Christ

4:22. leaving your former way of *l*.
4:24. the just and devout *l*.
Phil. 2:1. our common *l*. in Christ
2:5. your *l*. in Christ Jesus
2:17. if my *l*.-blood
3:14. God's call to the *l*. above
3:17. whose way of *l*. conforms
3:18. many whose way of *l*. makes them enemies
Col. 1:10. that your manner of *l*. may be worthy of the Lord
2:12. in baptism also you were raised to *l*.
3:1. were you not raised to *l*. with Christ
3:2. let your thoughts dwell on that higher realm, not on this earthly *l*.
1 Thess. 4:14. God will bring them to *l*. with Jesus
1 Tim. 6:13. God who gives *l*. to all things
2 Tim. 1:9. called us to a dedicated *l*.
Tit. 3:14. engage in honest employment to produce the necessities of *l*.
Heb. 4:12. the place where *l*. and spirit, joints and marrow, divide
5:7. in the days of his earthly *l*. he offered up prayers
10:39. we have the faith to make *l*. our own
11:5. by faith Enoch was carried away to another *l*.
11:22. Joseph, at the end of his *l*.
12:10. they disciplined us for this short *l*.
12:11. the peaceful harvest of an honest *l*.
13:7. the outcome of their *l*. and work
Jam. 4:12. One who is able to save *l*.
1 Pet. 3:18. in the spirit he was brought to *l*.
4:7. you must lead an ordered and sober *l*.
1 John 1:3. a common *l*., that life which we share with the Father
1:6. if we claim to be sharing in his *l*.
1:7. we share together a common *l*.
2 John 6. your rule of *l*.
3 John 3. you are true in your whole *l*.
Rev. 1:5. freed us from our sins with his *l*.'s blood

lifeless
Jam. 2:17. if it does not lead to action, it is in itself a *l*. thing
2:26. faith divorced from deeds is *l*.

lift-s-ed
Mat. 8:17. *l*. our diseases from us
21:21. be *l*. from your place and hurled into the sea
23:4. will not raise a finger to *l*. the load
Mark 11:23. be *l*. from your place and hurled into the sea

Luke 1:52. the humble have been *l.* high
10:34. he *l.* him on to his own beast
15:5. he *l.* it on to his shoulders
Acts 1:9. as they watched, he was *l.* up
2 Cor. 3:14. it is never *l.*, because only
in Christ is the old covenant
abrogated
Jam. 1:9. be proud that God *l.* him up
1 Pet. 5:6. he will *l.* you up in due time

ligaments
Col. 2:19. the whole body, with all its
joints and *l.*

light-s
Acts 23:23. two hundred *l.*-armed troops
Rom. 2:14. carry out its precepts by the
l. of nature
1 Cor. 2:14. judged in the *l.* of the Spirit
3:13. the work that each man does
will at last be brought to *l.*
Eph. 3:9. bringing to *l.* how this hidden
purpose
5:9. where *l.* is, there all goodness
springs up
Heb. 12:2. the cross, making *l.* of its
disgrace
12:10. according to their *l.*
Rev. 8:12. a third of the *l.* of the day
failed

lightly
Rom. 2:4. do you think *l.* of his wealth
of kindness
Heb. 12:5. do not think *l.* of the Lord's
discipline

like-d-ing
Mat. 7:12. treat others as you would *l.*
them to treat you
9:36. *l.* sheep without a shepherd
14:5. Herod would have *l.* to put him
to death
18:4. humble himself till he is *l.* this
child
20:15. do what I *l.* with my own money
23:6. they *l.* to have places of honour
23:28. outside you look *l.* honest men
27:17. which would you *l.* me to
release
Mark 2:12. never before', they said,
'have we seen the *l.*
6:20. he *l.* to listen to him
6:34. *l.* sheep without a shepherd
7:24. he would have *l.*
9:26. the boy looked *l.* a corpse
14:7. you can help them whenever
you *l.*
Luke 19:3. eager to see what Jesus
looked *l.*
20:46. a great *l.* for respectful greetings
21:34. the great Day closes upon you
suddenly *l.* a trap
John 12:21. Sir, we should *l.* to see
Jesus

18:39. would you *l.* me to release the
king of the Jews
Acts 2:2. a noise *l.* that of a strong
driving wind
7:51. *l.* fathers, *l.* sons
22:22. a scoundrel *l.* that is better
dead
25:22. I should rather *l.* to hear the
man myself
1 Cor. 13:12. *l.* God's knowledge of me
Eph. 5:1. as God's dear children, try to
be *l.* him
5:8. live *l.* men who are at home in
daylight
1 Thess. 4:5. not giving way to lust *l.* the
pagans
2 Tim. 3:5. keep clear of men *l.* these
Philem. 13. I should have *l.* to keep him
with me
Jam. 1:24. at once forgets what he
looked *l.*
2:19. the devils have faith *l.* that
1 Pet. 1:15. *l.* him, be holy in all your
behaviour
Rev. 2:24. what they *l.* to call the deep
secrets of Satan

likely
Mat. 6:7. imagine that the more they say
the more *l.* they are to be heard
John 7:31. is it *l.* that he will perform
more signs than this man

likeness
Rom. 8:29. they should be shaped to the
l. of his Son
1 Cor. 15:49. we have worn the *l.* of the
man made of dust, so we shall wear
the *l.* of the heavenly man
2 Cor. 3:18. we are transfigured into
his *l.*
Heb. 4:15. because of his *l.* to us, has
been tested
Jam. 3:9. our fellow-men who are made
in God's *l.*

likewise
2 Pet. 2:1. you *l.* will have false teachers

limb-s
Rom. 12:4. in a single human body
there are many *l.*
12:5. one body, serving individually
as *l.*
1 Cor. 6:15. your bodies are *l.* and
organs of Christ
12:12. Christ is like a single body
with its many *l.*
12:18. God appointed each *l.* and
organ to its own place
12:27. you are Christ's body, and each
of you a *l.*
Heb. 12:13. the disabled *l.* will not be
put out of joint

limit-s-ed
Acts 17:26. and the *l.* of their territory

1 Cor. 1:20. *l.*, all of them, to this
 passing age
 13:7. there is no *l.* to its faith, its hope
 15:58. work for the Lord always,
 work without *l.*
2 Cor. 8:3. going to the *l.* of their resources, as I can testify, and even
 beyond that *l.*
 10:13. the *l.* God laid down for us
 10:15. within the *l.* of our sphere
 12:15. spend myself to the *l.*
1 Tim. 4:8. the training of the body does
 bring *l.* benefit, but the benefits of
 religion are without *l.*

line
Mat. 17:27. go and cast a *l.* in the lake
Acts 19:27. our *l.* of business will be
 discredited
Rom. 4:1. Abraham, our ancestor in the
 natural *l.*
 9:7. through the *l.* of Isaac your
 posterity shall be traced
2 Tim. 2:8. Jesus Christ, risen from the
 dead, born of David's *l.*
Heb. 11:18. through the *l.* of Isaac your
 posterity shall be traced
Jude 19. these men draw a *l.* between
 spiritual and unspiritual persons

lineage
Heb. 7:3. he has no father, no mother,
 no *l.*

linen
John 11:44. his hands and feet swathed
 in *l.* bands

link-s
1 Cor. 6:16. anyone who *l.* himself
 with a harlot
 6:17. he who *l.* himself with Christ

lip-s
Mat. 12:36. a thoughtless word that
 comes from men's *l.*
 27:48. held it to his *l.* on the end of a
 cane
Mark 15:36. on the end of a cane, and
 held it to his *l.*
Luke 1:64. immediately his *l.* and tongue
 were freed
 1:70. by the *l.* of his holy prophets
 4:22. words of such grace should fall
 from his *l.*
 9:34. the words were still on his *l.*
 22:71. we have heard it ourselves from
 his own *l.*
John 4:41. what they heard from his
 own *l.*
 19:29. fixed it on a javelin, and held
 it up to his *l.*
Acts 15:7. that from my *l.* the Gentiles
 should hear
Rom. 10:8. it is upon your *l.* and in your
 heart

10:9. if on your *l.* is the confession
 10:10. the confession that leads to
 salvation is upon the *l.*
2 Cor. 12:4. words so secret that human
 l. may not repeat them.
Eph. 4:29. no bad language must pass
 your *l.*
2 Tim. 2:19. takes the Lord's name upon
 his *l.*
Heb. 2:3. first announced through the
 l. of the Lord himself
 4:7. speaking through the *l.* of David
Jude 16. big words come rolling from
 their *l.*
Rev. 14:5. no lie was found in their *l.*

listen-s-ed-ing
Mat. 10:14. if anyone will not receive
 you or *l.* to what you say
 13:13. *l.* without hearing or understanding
 15:10. *l.* to me, and understand this
 17:5. my Beloved, on whom my
 favour rests; *l.* to him
 18:15. if he *l.* to you, you have won
 your brother over
 18:16. if he will not *l.*
 18:17. if he refuses to *l.* to them,
 report the matter to the congregation; and if he will not *l.*
 21:33. *l.* to another parable
Mark. 4:3. *l.*! A sower went out to sow
 6:11. where they will not receive you
 or *l.* to you
 6:20. he liked to *l.* to him, although
 the *l.* left him greatly perplexed
 7:14. *l.* to me, all of you
 9:7. this is my Son, my Beloved; *l.* to
 him
 11:14. his disciples were *l.*
 12:28. one of the lawyers, who had
 been *l.*
 12:38. a great crowd and they *l.*
 eagerly
Luke 1:20. now *l.*: you will lose your
 powers of speech
 2:46. *l.* to them and putting questions
 5:2. to *l.* to the word of God
 8:18. take care, then, how you *l.*
 9:35. this is my Son, my Chosen;
 l. to him
 10:16. whoever *l.* to you *l.* to me
 10:39. stayed there *l.* to his words
 13:32. *l.*: today and tomorrow, I shall
 be casting out devils
 15:1. all crowding in to *l.* to him
 16:29. Moses and the prophets; let
 them *l.* to them
 16:31. if they do not *l.* to Moses and
 the prophets
 18:7. he *l.* patiently to them
 19:11. while they were *l.* to this
 21:38. people flocked to *l.* to him

John 3:29. the bridegroom's friend, who
  stands by and *l.* to him
  6:60. why *l.* to such words
  8:47. *l.* to the words of God. You are
  not God's children; that is why you
  do not *l.*
  9:31. God does not *l.* to sinners;
  he *l.* to anyone who is devout
  10:16. they too will *l.* to my voice
  10:20. why *l.* to him
  10:27. my own sheep *l.* to my voice
  18:37. all who are not deaf to truth
  l. to my voice
Acts 2:22. Men of Israel, *l.* to me
  3:22. you shall *l.* to everything he
  says to you
  3:23. anyone who refuses to *l.* to that
  prophet
  7:1. fathers of this nation, *l.* to me
  8:6. the crowds, to a man, *l.* eagerly
  8:10. all of them, high and low, *l.*
  eagerly to him
  8:11. they *l.* because they had for so
  long been carried away by his magic
  10:22. to *l.* to what you have to say
  10:44. the Holy Spirit came upon all
  who were *l.*
  13:16. you who worship our God, *l.*
  to me
  14:9. this man *l.* while Paul was
  speaking
  15:12. the whole company fell silent
  and *l.*
  15:13. my friends,' he said, '*l.* to me
  16:14. was *l.*, and the Lord opened
  her heart
  16:25. the other prisoners were *l.*
  18:8. a number of Corinthians *l.* and
  believed
  22:2. they *l.*
  23:21. do not *l.* to them
  26:29. all those also who are *l.*
1 Cor. 15:51. *l.*! I will unfold a mystery
Gal. 4:21. will you not *l.* to what the
  law says
1 Tim. 2:11. a woman must be a learner,
  l. quietly
2 Tim. 2:14. is the ruin of those who
  l.
Jam. 1:19. each of you must be quick
  to *l.*
  1:22. act on the message and do not
  merely *l.*
  1:23. a man who *l.* to the message
  2:5. *l.*, my friends
1 John 4:5. that is why the world *l.* to
  them
  4:6. a man who knows God *l.* to us
  5:14. if we make requests which
  accord with his will he *l.* to us
Rev. 1:3. happy those who *l.* to the
  words of this prophecy
  22:18. everyone who is *l.* to the words
  of prophecy

lit
Luke 22:55. they *l.* a fire in the middle of
  the courtyard
Acts 28:2. they *l.* a bonfire and made us
  all welcome

little
Mat. 13:5. rocky ground, where it had
  l. soil
Mark 4:5. it had *l.* soil, and it sprouted
  quickly
Luke 12:26. if, then, you cannot do even
  a very *l.* thing
  16:10. trusted in *l.* things can be
  trusted also in great; and the man
  who is dishonest in *l.* things
John 5:14. a *l.* later Jesus found him
  in the temple
  15:20. they will follow your teaching
  as *l.* as they have followed mine
Acts 26:29. much or *l.*,' said Paul
  27:7. a good many days we made *l.*
  headway
Philem. 11. once so *l.* use to you, but
  now useful indeed
1 Pet. 1:6. for a *l.* while, if need be,
  under trials
Rev. 17:10. he is only to last for a *l.* while

live-s-d-ing
Mat. 4:16. the people that *l.* in darkness
  21:32. John came to show you the
  right way to *l.*
  24:22. no *l.* thing could survive
  24:34. the present generation will *l.*
  to see it all
Mark 13:20. that time of troubles, no
  l. thing could survive
  13:30. the present generation will *l.*
  to see it
Luke 1 24. for five months she *l.* in
  seclusion
  1:79. to shine on those who *l.* in
  darkness
  1:80. he *l.* out in the wilds
  7:37. a woman who was *l.* an immoral
  life
  8:27. neither worn clothes nor *l.* in a
  house
  13:4. all the other people *l.* in
  Jerusalem
  17:33. whoever loses it will save it,
  and *l.*
  21:32. the present generation will *l.*
  to see it
John 4:18. the man with whom you are
  now *l.*
  12:1. Bethany where Lazarus *l.*
Acts 2:5. there were *l.* in Jerusalem
  devout Jews
  2:14. all you who *l.* in Jerusalem
  7:6. Abraham's descendants shall *l.*
  as aliens
  7:38. he received the *l.* utterances of
  God

Acts 7:48. the Most High does not *l.* in houses made by men
10:42. judge of the *l.* and the dead
11:26. the two of them *l.* in fellowship with the congregation
13:17. when they were still *l.* as aliens in Egypt
16:3. the Jews who *l.* in those parts
17:24. does not *l.* in shrines made by men
18:7. Titius Justus, who *l.* next door to the synagogue
19:25. our high standard of *l.*
27:24. the *l.* of all who are sailing with you
27:33. you have *l.* in suspense
27:34. something to eat; your *l.* depend on it
Rom. 3:4. though every man *l.* were a liar
4:17. the God who makes the dead *l.*
7:5. while we *l.* on the level of our lower nature
8:5. those who *l.* on the level of our lower nature
8:9. that is not how you *l.*
12:20. you will heap *l.* coals on his head
1 Cor. 3:3. you are *l.* on the purely human level
5:10. pagans who lead loose *l.*
7:15. God's call is a call to *l.* in peace
7:29. the time we *l.* in will not last long
9:6. are Barnabas and I alone bound to work for our *l.*
2 Cor. 5:8. go to *l.* with the Lord
5:10. have our *l.* laid open
5:11. to God our *l.* lie open
12:21. have not repented of their unclean *l.*
13:5. are you *l.* the life of faith
Gal. 4:27. the deserted wife shall have more children than she who *l.* with her husband
Eph. 2:3. we all *l.* our lives in sensuality
4:1. *l.* up to your calling
4:17. give up *l.* like pagans
5:2. *l.* in love as Christ loved you
5:8. *l.* like men who are at home in daylight
5:30. his body, of which we are *l.* parts
Col. 2:6. *l.* your *l.* in union with him
1 Thess. 2:9. we worked for a *l.* night and day
2:12. *l. l.* worthy of the God who calls you
4:1. the way we must *l.* to please God
5:13. *l.* at peace among yourselves
2 Thess. 3:8. we worked for a *l.* night and day
3:12. work quietly for their *l.*
2 Tim. 1:5. which, I am confident, *l.* in you also

1:13. *l.* by the faith and love
3:9. their successes will be short-*l.*
3:16. discipline in right *l.*
4:1. who is to judge men *l.* and dead
Tit. 1:6. under no imputation of loose *l.*
Heb. 5:13. anyone who *l.* on milk
6:19. an anchor for our *l.*
11:9. *l.* in tents, as did Isaac and Jacob
13:5. do not *l.* for money
Jam. 1:25. who *l.* in its company
1 Pet. 1:17. while you *l.* out your time on earth
2:12. see for themselves that you *l.* good *l.*
2:16. *l.* as free men
4:5. pass judgement on the *l.* and the dead
2 Pet. 2:7. the lawless society in which he *l.*
3:3. *l.* self-indulgent *l.*
3:11. what devout and dedicated *l.* you should *l.*
1 John 1:6. our words and our *l.* are a lie
2:6. to *l.* as Christ himself *l.*
3:17. if a man has enough to *l.* on
2 John 4. your children are *l.* by the truth
3 John 3. to hear that my children are *l.* by the truth
Jude 1. who *l.* in the love of God
Rev. 4:6, 8, 9. 5:6, 8, 11, 14. 6:1, 6. 7:11. 14:3. 19:4. *l.* creatures
18:13. chariots, slaves, and the *l.* of men

livers
1 Cor. 5:9. have nothing to do with loose *l.*

load-s-ed
Mat. 11:30. my *l.* is light
23:4. will not raise a finger to lift the *l.*
Luke 5:7. *l.* both boats
11:46. you *l.* men with intolerable burdens, and will not put a single finger to the *l.*
Gal. 6:2. help one another to carry these heavy *l.*

loaf
1 Cor. 10:17. there is one *l.*, we, many as we are, are one body; for it is one *l.* of which we all partake

loathe-ing
Rom. 12:9. *l.* evil

loathsome
Rev. 18:2. every foul and *l.* bird

loaves
Mat. 12:4. he went into the House of God and ate the consecrated *l.*
Mark 2:26. ate the consecrated *l.*
Luke 6:4. took the consecrated *l.* to eat

local
Luke 15:15. attached himself to one of the *l.* landowners
Acts 21:12. the *l.* people begged and implored Paul
28:17. he called together the *l.* Jewish leaders

locked
Luke 13:25. the master of the house has got up and *l.* the door
John 20:19. the disciples were together behind *l.* doors
20:26. although the doors were *l.*, Jesus came
Acts 5:23. we found the jail securely *l.*

lock-s
1 Cor. 11:14. flowing *l.* disgrace a man
11:15. her *l.* were given for covering

lodge-s-ing
Luke 2:7. no room for them to *l.* in the house
Acts 1:13. the room upstairs where they were *l.*
28:16. Paul was allowed to *l.* by himself
Rom. 7:17. sin that *l.* in me
7:18. nothing good *l.* in me
7:20. sin that has its *l.* in me
2 Thess. 3:8. *l.* from anyone without paying for it
1 Pet. 1:1. people who *l.* for a while in Pontus
2 Pet. 1:13. so long as I still *l.* in this body

lonely
Mat. 14:13. privately by boat to a *l.* place
14:15. this is a *l.* place, and the day has gone
15:33. where in this *l.* place can we find bread
Mark. 1:35. he went away to a *l.* spot
6:31. some *l.* place where you can rest quietly
6:32. by boat for a *l.* place
6:35. this is a *l.* place and it is getting very late
8:4. with bread in this *l.* place
Luke 4:42. made his way to a *l.* spot
5:16. withdraw to *l.* places for prayer
9:12. we are in a *l.* place here

long-ed-er-ing
Mat. 19:6. they are no *l.* two individuals
20:12. sweated the whole day *l.*
23:37. how often have I *l.* to gather your children
24:48. the master is a *l.* time coming

Mark 5:3. he could no *l.* be controlled
5:26. in spite of *l.* treatment by doctors
7:12. no *l.* permitted to do anything for his father
10:8. they are no *l.* two individuals
15:44. asked him whether it was *l.* since he died
Luke 1:75. in his presence, our whole life *l.*
13:16. prisoner by Satan for eighteen *l.* years
13:34. I *l.* to gather your children
14:32. *l.* before the enemy approaches
15:19. I am no *l.* fit to be called your son
15:20. a *l.* way off his father saw him
17:22. you will *l.* to see one of the days of the Son of Man
18:4. for a *l.* time he refused
19:12. a man of noble birth went on a *l.* journey
20:36. they are not subject to death any *l.*
22:15. I have *l.* to eat this Passover with you before my death
John 2:12. they did not stay there *l.*
4:42. it is no *l.* because of what you said
6:24. neither Jesus nor his disciples were any *l.* there
6:66. withdrew and no *l.* went about with him
7:33. Jesus said, 'For a little *l.* I shall be with you
11:54. Jesus no *l.* went about publicly
12:35. the light is among you still, but not for *l.*
13:33. for a little *l.* I am with you
14:30. I shall not talk much *l.* with you
15:15. I call you servants no *l.*
16:25. a time is coming when I shall no *l.* use figures
17:11. I am to stay no *l.* in the world
20:27. be unbelieving no *l.*
Acts 15:18. whose work it is, Made known *l.* ago
16:18. until Paul could bear it no *l.*
26:5. they have known me *l.* enough
28:6. a *l.* time without seeing anything extraordinary happen
Rom. 1:10. succeed at *l.* last in coming to visit you
3:7. should I any *l.* be condemned as a sinner
6:6. we may no *l.* be the slaves of sin
6:7. a dead man is no *l.* answerable for his sin
6:12. sin must no *l.* reign in your mortal body
6:13. no *l.* put its several parts at sin's disposal
6:14. sin shall no *l.* be your master,

because you are no *l.* under law

Rom. 7:17. it is no *l.* I who perform the action

7:20. no *l.* I who am the agent

8:4. no *l.* under the control of our lower nature

12:2. adapt yourselves no *l.* to the pattern of this present world

14:15. your conduct is no *l.* guided by love

15:23. I have been *l.* for many years to visit you

16:12. Persis who has toiled in his service so *l.*

16:25. that divine secret kept in silence for *l.* ages

1:Cor. 7:29. the time we live in will not last *l.*

2 Cor. 5:16. they do so now no *l.*

5:19. no *l.* holding men's misdeeds against them

7:7. he has told us how you *l.* for me

7:11. how your *l.* for me awoke

Eph. 3:9. it was hidden for *l.* ages in God

3:11. in accord with his age-*l.* purpose

Col. 1:26. the secret hidden for *l.* ages

2 Tim. 1:4. I *l.* to see you again

Tit. 1:2. eternal life that God, who cannot lie, promised *l.* ages ago

Philem. 16. no *l.* as a slave, but as more than a slave

Heb. 5:14. trained by *l.* use to discriminate

6:11. we *l.* for everyone of you to show the same eager concern

11:16. *l.* for a better country

1 Pet. 1:12. these are things that angels *l.* to see

4:4. no *l.* plunge with them into all this reckless dissipation

2 Pet. 3:5. there were heavens and earth *l.* ago

Jude 4. whom Scripture *l.* ago marked down for the doom

Rev. 9:6. they will *l.* to die

11:1. I was given a *l.* cane

17:8. once was alive, and is alive no *l.*

18:11. no one any *l.* buys their cargoes

18:14. the fruit you *l.* for

21:1. there was no *l.* any sea

21:16. was as wide as it was *l.*

look-ed-ing

Mat. 6:16. do not *l.* gloomy like the hypocrites

6:26. *l.* at the birds of the air

6:34. tomorrow will *l.* after itself

7:3. *l.* at the speck of sawdust in your brother's eye

10:11. *l.* for some worthy person in it

10:16. *l.*, I send you out like sheep among wolves

11:8. you must *l.* in palaces for that

11:19. *l.* at him! a glutton and a drinker

12:2. *l.*, your disciples are doing something which is forbidden on the Sabbath

13:13. they *l.* without seeing

13:14. you will *l.* and *l.*, but never see.

13:45. a merchant *l.* out for fine pearls

18:10. angels in heaven, who *l.* continually on the face of my heavenly Father

19:26. Jesus *l.* them in the face

21:46. *l.* on Jesus as a prophet

23:27. they *l.* well from outside

23:28. outside you *l.* like honest men

23:38. *l.*, *l.*! there is your temple

26:16. *l.* for a good opportunity to betray him

28:1. came to *l.* at the grave

28:5. you are *l.* for Jesus who was crucified

Mark 1:37. they are all *l.* for you

4:12. they may *l.* and *l.*, but see nothing

9:26. the boy *l.* like a corpse

10:21. Jesus *l.* straight at him

11:21. Rabbi, *l.*, the fig-tree which you cursed

12:12. *l.* for a way to arrest him

12:15. fetch me a silver piece, and let me *l.* at it

13:1. *l.*, Master, what huge stones

14:11. *l.* for a good opportunity to betray him

16:6. you are *l.* for Jesus of Nazareth

Luke 1:48. so tenderly has he *l.* upon his servant

2:44. only then did they begin *l.* for him

2:45. returned to Jerusalem to *l.* for him

6:41. why do you *l.* at the speck of sawdust

8:10. *l.* but see nothing

10:34. *l.* after him there

10:35. *l.* after him

13:6. he came *l.* for fruit

13:7 he said to the vine-dresser, '*L.* here

13:35. *l.*, *l.*! there is your temple

14:9 you will *l.* foolish as you begin to take the lowest place

14:18. I must go and *l.* over it

15:8. *l.* in every corner till she has found it

16:23. where he was in torment, he *l.* up

17:23. they will say to you, '*L.*! There!' and '*L.*! Here

18:9. *l.* down on everyone else

19:3. he was eager to see what Jesus *l.* like

Luke 20:17. he *l.* straight at them
  22:6. *l.* out for an opportunity to betray him
  23:35. the people stood *l.* on
  23:51. who *l.* forward to the kingdom of God
John 1:29. *l.*,' he said, 'there is the Lamb of God
  1:38. What are you *l.* for
  1:42. Jesus, who *l.* him in the face
  5:41. I do not *l.* to men for honour
  6:26. you have come *l.* for me
  7:1. the Jews were *l.* for a chance to kill him
  7:11. the Jews were *l.* for him
  7:34. you will *l.* for me, but you will not find me.
  8:21. you will *l.* for me
  11:56. they *l.* out for Jesus
  13:22. the disciples *l.* at one another in bewilderment
  17:1. Jesus *l.* up to heaven and said
  20:15. who is it you are *l.* for
Acts 1:11. why stand there *l.* up into the sky
  7:23. to *l.* into the conditions of his fellow-countrymen
  7:32. Moses was terrified and dared not *l.*
  7:56. *l.*,' he said, 'there is a rift in the sky
  10:11. *l.* like a great sheet of sail-cloth
  10:19. some men are here *l.* for you
  10:21. you are *l.* for me
  11:5. *l.* like a great sheet of sail-cloth
  11:6. I *l.* intently to make out what was in it
  11:25. went off to Tarsus to *l.* for Saul
  13:9. Paul, filled with the Holy Spirit, *l.* him in the face
  14:9. Paul *l.* him in the face
  15:6. a meeting to *l.* into this matter
  17:23. *l.* at the objects of your worship
  28:26. you will *l.* and *l.*, but never see
Rom. 10:20. I was found,' he says, 'by those who were not *l.* for me
Gal. 3:6. *l.* at Abraham: he put his faith in God
Philem. 13. to *l.* after me
Heb. 11:14. *l.* for a country of their own
1 Pet. 5:8. the devil, like a roaring lion, prowls round *l.* for someone to devour

loop-hole
Eph. 4:27. leave no *l.* for the devil

loose
Luke 8:29. each time he broke *l.*
1 Cor. 5:9. have nothing to do with *l.* livers
  5:10. pagans who lead *l.* lives
  5:11. any so-called Christian who leads a *l.* life

Tit. 1:6. under no imputation of *l.* living

lop-ped
Rom. 11:17. some of the branches have been *l.* off
  11:19. branches were *l.* off so that I might be grafted in
  11:20. they were *l.* off for lack of faith

lord
Mat. 20:25. rulers *l.* it over their subjects
Luke 1:49. the *L.*, the Mighty One
  7:19. he sent them to the *L.* with this message
  10:39. Mary, who seated herself at the *L.* feet
Acts 8:22. pray the *L.* to forgive you
  10:33. to hear all that the *L.* has ordered you to say
  15:40. commended by the brothers to the grace of the *L.*
  20:28. shepherds of the church of the *L.*
1 Cor. 10:9. not put the power of the *L.* to the test
Col. 3:22. out of reverence for the *L.*
2 Thess. 2:2. that the Day of the *L.* is already here
Jam. 3:9. sing the praises of our *L.*
Rev. 7:14. my *l.*, you know, not I
  11:4. in the presence of the *L.* of the earth
  16:14. God the sovereign *L.*

lose
Mat. 5:29 } *l.* one part of your body
     5:30 }
  24:10. many will *l.* their faith
Luke 1:20. you will *l.* your powers of speech
  16:17. one dot or stroke of the Law to *l.* its force
  18:1. they should keep on praying and never *l.* heart
Acts 27:22. I urge you not to *l.* heart
2 Cor. 4:1. we never *l.* heart
  4:16. no wonder we do not *l.* heart
  11:3. *l.* your single-hearted devotion to Christ
Eph. 3:13. not to *l.* heart over my sufferings
Col. 2:19. *l.* hold upon the Head
2 Thess. 2:2. do not suddenly *l.* your heads
Heb. 12:3. that will help you not to *l.* heart
  12:5. nor *l.* heart when he corrects you
2 Pet. 3:5. they *l.* sight of the fact
  3:8. one point, my friends, which you must not *l.* sight of
  3:17. do not *l.* your own safe foothold

loser-s
2 Cor. 7:9. you are no *l.* by what we did

loss

Luke 24:4. they stood utterly at a *l.*

Acts 27:10. it will mean grave *l.*, *l.* not only of ship

lost

Mat. 18:14. that one of these little ones should be *l.*

Mark 2:22. then wine and skins are both *l.*

Luke 5:26. they were all *l.* in amazement

21:18. not a hair of your head shall be *l.*

Acts 27:9. by now much time had been *l.*

27:34. not a hair of your heads will be *l.*

1 Cor. 15:18. it follows also that those who have died within Christ's fellowship are utterly *l.*

15:58. in the Lord your labour cannot be *l.*

Gal. 4:11. may prove to be labour *l.*

1 Thess. 2:17. you were *l.* to us—*l.* to sight, not to our hearts

3:5. my labour might be *l.*

1 Tim. 6:5. have *l.* grip of the truth

2 Tim. 3:8. they have *l.* the power to reason

Philem. 15. perhaps this is why you *l.* him for a time

Heb. 10:39. among those who shrink back and are *l.*

Jam. 1:11. what was lovely to look at is *l.* for ever

2 Pet. 2:15. abandoned the straight road and *l.* their way

3:9. it is not his will for any to be *l.*

Rev. 2:4. you have *l.* your early love

18:14. all the glitter and the glamour are *l.*

lot

Mat. 10:25. content to share his teacher's *l.*

2 Cor. 1:6. if distress be our *l.*, it is the price we pay for your consolation, for your salvation; if our *l.* be consolation

6:8. praise and blame, are alike our *l.*

Eph. 5:7. have no part or *l.* with them

Phil. 4:12. the human *l.* with all its ups and downs

1 Thess. 3:3 this is our appointed *l.*

Heb. 9:27. it is the *l.* of men to die once

1 Pet. 2:8. such was their appointed *l.*

Rev. 21:8. their *l.* will be the second death

loud-er-ly

Mat. 2:18. wailing and *l.* laments

27:23. they shouted all the *l.*, 'Crucify him

Mark 5:7. shouting *l.*, 'What do you want with me, Jesus

5:38. with *l.* crying and wailing

15:14. they shouted all the *l.,* 'Crucify him

Acts 20:37. there were *l.* cries of sorrow

25:24. *l.* insisting that he had no right to remain alive

Heb. 5:7. prayers and petitions, with *l.* cries

Jam. 5:4. wages you never paid to the men who mowed your fields are *l.* against you

Rev. 1:10. behind me I heard a *l.* voice

11:12. a *l.* voice was heard speaking

16:1. from the sanctuary I heard a *l.* voice

16:17. out of the sanctuary came a *l.* voice

21:3. a *l.* voice proclaiming from the throne

love-d

Luke 16:14. the Pharisees, who *l.* money

Rom. 14:15. your conduct is no longer guided by *l.*

1 Cor. 8:1. it is *l.* that builds

13:1. if I am without *l.*, I am a sounding gong

13:2. if I have no *l.*, I am nothing

13:3. if I have no *l.*, I am none the better

also verses 4, 6, 7, 8, 13

14:1. put *l.* first

16:14. let all you do be done in *l.*

Col. 3:14. to crown all, there must be *l.*

1 Thess. 2:8. with such yearning *l.*

3:6. good news of your faith and *l.*

4:10. practising this rule of *l.*

2 Thess. 1:3. the *l.* you have, each for all

1 Tim. 1:5. *l.* which springs from a clean heart

2:15. faith, *l.*, and holiness

4:12. *l.*, fidelity, and purity

2 Tim. 2:22. integrity, *l.*, and peace

3:10. patience, and spirit of *l.*

Tit. 2:2. sound in faith, in *l.*

Jam. 4:4. *l.* of the world is enmity to God

1 Pet. 4:8. keep your *l.* for one another at full strength, because *l.* cancels innumerable sins

5:14. greet one another with the kiss of *l.*

2 Pet. 1:7. brotherly kindness with *l.*

Jude 1. who live in the *l.* of God

12. a blot on your *l.*-feasts

Rev. 2:19. your *l.* and faithfulness

lovely

Jam. 1:11. what was *l.* to look at

lover-s

1 Tim. 3:3. no *l.* of money

Rev. 2:22. plunge her *l.* into terrible suffering

low

Mat. 8:2. a leper approached him, bowed *l.*

9:18. a president of the synagogue, who bowed *l.* before him

20:20. she bowed *l.* and begged a favour

Acts 8:10. high and *l.*, listened eagerly to him

17:5. some *l.* fellows

1 Cor. 1:28. he has chosen things *l.*

Phil. 4:12. I know what it is to be brought *l.*

lower-ed-ing

Mark 2:4. they *l.* the stretcher

Acts 9:25. *l.* him in a basket

10:11. being *l.* to the ground

11:5. *l.* from the sky till it reached me

27:17. they *l.* the mainsail

27:30. they had already *l.* the ship's boat

Rom. 7:5. we lived on the level of our *l.* nature

8:3. our *l.* nature robbed it of all potency

8:4. no longer under the control of our *l.* nature

8:5. live on the level of our *l.* nature

8:7. the outlook of the *l.* nature

8:12. our *l.* nature has no claim upon us.

1 Cor. 3:3. the purely human level of your *l.* nature

2 Cor. 11:7. *l.* myself to help in raising you

Gal. 5:13. do not turn your freedom into licence for your *l.* nature

5:16. you will not fulfil the desires of your *l.* nature

5:19. behaviour that belongs to the *l.* nature

5:24. crucified the *l.* nature with its passions

6:8. sows seed in the field of his *l.* nature

Col. 2:11. divested of the *l.* nature

lowest

Mat. 5:19. the *l.* place in the kingdom of heaven

loyal-ly

Acts 2:27. nor let thy *l.* servant suffer corruption

13:35. thou wilt not let thy *l.* servant suffer corruption

Phil. 4:3. my *l.* comrade

Heb. 10:33. while others stood *l.* by

Rev. 14:12. remaining *l.* to Jesus

loyalty

Rom. 1:30. they show no *l.* to parents

1 Tim. 5:4. show *l.* to the family

3 John 5. you show a fine *l.* in everything

luck

Jam. 2:16. good *l.* to you, keep yourselves warm

lunch

Luke 14:12. when you give a *l.* or dinner party

lurch

2 Tim. 4:16. they all left me in the *l.*

lure-s-d

Jam. 1:14. *l.* away by his own lust

2. Pet. 2:14. they *l.* the unstable to their ruin

Rev. 2:20. by her teaching *l.* my servants into fornication

lust-s

1 Cor. 6:13. it is not true that the body is for *l.*

Col. 3:5. indecency, *l.*, foul cravings

2 Pet. 2:10. punish those who follow their abominable *l.*

Jude 7. followed unnatural *l.*

lustre

Tit. 2:10. they will add *l.* to the doctrine of God

luxury

Luke 7:25. look in palaces for grand clothes and *l.*

Jam. 5:5. you have lived on earth in wanton *l.*

Rev. 18:9. wallowed in her *l.*

lying

Mat. 13:44. like treasure *l.* buried in a field

Mark 7:30. she found the child *l.* in bed

Luke 5:2. two boats *l.* at the water's edge

5:25. took up the bed he had been *l.* on

John 4:46. whose son was *l.* ill at Capernaum

1 Cor. 15:15. we turn out to be *l.* witnesses for God

lyre

1 Cor. 14:7. things that produce sounds —a flute, say, or a *l.*

M

machinations

Acts 20:19. through the *m.* of the Jews

mad

2 Cor. 11:23. I am *m.* to speak like this

made

Mat. 12:13. it was *m.* sound again like the other

13:25. sowed darnel among the wheat, and *m.* off

Mat. 13:35. kept secret since the world
was *m*.
19:5. be *m*. one with his wife
20:5. *m*. the same arrangement as
before
25:17. *m*. a profit of five bags, and the
man who had the two bags *m*. two
25:34. the kingdom that has been
ready for you since the world was *m*.
27:12. to the charges laid against him
. . . he *m*. no reply
Mark 1:45. *m*. the whole story public
10:5. he *m*. this rule for you
15:1. the chief priests, having *m*. their
plan
15:5. to Pilate's astonishment, Jesus
m. no further reply
Luke 2:42. when he was twelve, they *m*.
the pilgrimage as usual
3:18. he *m*. his appeal to the people
7:44. this woman has *m*. my feet wet
with her tears
10:38. Martha *m*. him welcome in her
home
12:20. you have *m*. your money—who
will get it
12:47. knew his master's wishes, yet
m. no attempt to carry them out
17:27. the flood came and *m*. an end
of them all
17:29. rained fire and sulphur from
heaven and *m*. an end of them all
John 1:18. he has *m*. him known
17:2. thou hast *m*. him sovereign
over all mankind
17:6. I have *m*. thy name known to
the men
17:26. I *m*. thy name known to them
Acts 2:22. *m*. known to you through
miracles
4:26. *m*. common cause Against the
Lord
5:4. what *m*. you think of doing this
7:19. he *m*. a crafty attack on our race
12:12. he *m*. for the house of Mary
13:17. he *m*. them into a nation
13:24. John *m*. ready for his coming
17:6. the men who have *m*. trouble
1 Cor. 15:28. the Son himself will also
be *m*. subordinate to God who *m*.
all things subject to him
Heb. 9:26. he would have had to suffer
many times since the world was *m*.
Rev. 13:8. his roll of the living, written
there since the world was *m*.
17:8. the roll of the living ever since
the world was *m*.

madman-men
Mat. 8:33. what had happened to the *m*.
Mark 5:15. the *m*. who had been
possessed
5:16 ⎫
Luke 8:36 ⎬ how the *m*. had been cured

magic
Acts 8:11. carried away by his *m*.
19:19. those who formerly practised *m*.

magical
Acts 8:9. swept the Samaritans off their
feet with his *m*. arts
19:18. confessed that they had been
using *m*. spells

magistrate-s
Acts 17:6. before the *m*., shouting
17:8. commotion in the mob, which
affected the *m*.
28:7. chief *m*. of the island

magnanimity
2 Cor. 10:1. the gentleness and *m*. of
Christ
Phil. 4:5. let your *m*. be manifest

magnates
Rev. 6:15. the kings of the earth, *m*. and
marshals

magnificence
Luke 16:19. feasted in great *m*. every
day
2 Cor. 12:7. the *m*. of such revelations
Phil. 4:19. the *m*. of his riches in Christ
Jesus

maid
Mat. 26:69. a serving-*m*. accosted him
John 18:17. the *m*. on duty at the door
Acts 12:13. a *m*. called Rhoda came to
answer it

mail
Eph. 6:14. for coat of *m*. put on integrity

main
Mat. 21:42. the *m*. corner-stone
22:9. go out to the *m*. thoroughfares
Mark 12:10. has become the *m*. corner-
stone
Luke 20:17. the *m*. corner-stone
Acts 16:19. to the city authorities in the
m. square
Heb. 8:1. now this is my *m*. point

mainsail
Acts 27:17. they lowered the *m*. and let
her drive

maintain-ed-ing
Mat. 22:23. *m*. that there is no resurrection
Mark 7:4. a traditional rule to *m*.
7:8. in order to *m*. the tradition of men
7:9. in order to *m*. your tradition
12:35. *m*. that the Messiah is 'Son of
David
Rom. 15:4. we may *m*. our hope with
fortitude
15:8. to *m*. the truth of God
1 Cor. 11:2. *m*. the tradition I handed
on to you

Gal. 2:5. the full truth of the Gospel should be *m*.
1 Tim. 5:21. I solemnly charge you, *m*. these rules
Rev. 12:17. *m*. their testimony to Jesus

maintenance
2 Thess. 3:9. not because we have not the right to *m*.

majesty
Luke 9:43. struck with awe at the *m*. of God
Acts 25:21. in custody for His Imperial *M*. decision
25:25. he himself appealed to His Imperial *M*.
26:8. your *M*. Why is it considered incredible
26:13. as I was on my way, Your *M*.

majority
Acts 27:12. the *m*. were in favour of putting out to sea

make-s-ing
Mat. 2:8. *m*. a careful inquiry for the child
5:24. *m*. your peace with your brother
6:1. not to *m*. a show of your religion
8:17. to *m*. good the prophecy of Isaiah
10:11. *m*. your home there until you leave
12:29. *m*. off with his goods
13:35. *m*. good the prophecy of Isaiah
16:21. Jesus began to *m*. it clear to his disciples
20:25. *m*. them feel the weight of authority
23:4. they *m*. up heavy packs
28:19. *m*. all nations my disciples
Mark 3:6. how they could *m*. away with him
3:27. *m*. off with his goods
9:22. often it has tried to *m*. an end of him
9:35. he must *m*. himself last of all
11:18. sought some means of *m*. away with him
13:8. nation will *m*. war upon nation
16:20. went out to *m*. their proclamation
Luke 1:22. he stood there *m*. signs to them
3:14. *m*. do with your pay
9:7. did not know what to *m*. of it
9:53. he was *m*. for Jerusalem
10:8. and they *m*. you welcome
10:10. they do not *m*. you welcome
14:23. *m*. them come in
19:47. were bent on *m*. an end of him
21:10. nation will *m*. war upon nation
21:14. *m*. up your minds not to prepare your defence beforehand

John 8:37. my teaching *m*. no headway with you
16:26. you will *m*. your request in my name
18:9. this was to *m*. good his words
Acts 5:28. trying to *m*. us responsible for that man's death
6:11. alleged that they had heard him *m*. blasphemous statements
7:26. tried to bring them to *m*. up their quarrel
24:10. I *m*. my defence with confidence
24:13. they cannot *m*. good the charges
24:23. *m*. themselves useful to him
Rom. 6:19. lawlessness, *m*. for moral anarchy, so now you must yield them to the service of righteousness, *m*. for a holy life
8:15. a Spirit that *m*. us sons
11:32. *m*. all mankind prisoners to disobedience
16:25. him who has power to *m*. your standing sure
Gal. 6:7. *m*. no mistake about this: God is not to be fooled
Heb. 10:39. we have the faith to *m*. life our own
11:1. faith . . . *m*. us certain of realities we do not see
12:2. endured the cross, *m*. light of its disgrace
Jam. 4:13. trading and *m*. money

Maker
1 Pet. 4:19. their *M*. will not fail them

malcontent-s
Jude 16. a set of grumblers and *m*.

male-s
Rom. 1:27. *m*. behave indecently with *m*.
Rev. 12:5. she gave birth to a *m*. child
12:13. the woman who had given birth to the *m*. child

malevolence
Rom. 1:29. rivalry, treachery, and *m*.

malice
Mark 7:22. ruthless greed, and *m*.
Jam. 1:21. the *m*. that hurries to excess

malicious
Mat. 22:18. Jesus was aware of their *m*. intention

malign
1 Pet. 2:12. they *m*. you as criminals
3:16. those who *m*. your Christian conduct

malignant
Rev. 16:2. foul *m*. sores appeared

malpractice-s
Phil. 3:2. beware of those dogs and their *m*.

maltreat-ed

Luke 18:32. he will be mocked, *m.*, and spat upon

Acts 14:5. to *m.* them and stone them

Heb. 13:3. those who are being *m.*

man

Mat. 5:39. do not set yourself against the *m.* who wrongs you

8:21. another *m.*, one of his disciples, said to him

John 9:35. have you faith in the Son of *M.*

9:36. the *m.* answered, 'Tell me who he is, sir

Rom. 5:14. Adam foreshadows the *M.* who was to come

manage-s-d-ing

Mat. 24:45. charged by his master to *m.*

Luke 12:42. as his steward, to *m.* his servants

Acts 14:18. barely *m.* to prevent the crowd

27:16. *m.* to get the ship's boat under control

2 Cor. 11:4. you *m.* to put up with that

1 Tim. 3:4. one who *m.* his own household well

3:12. good at *m.* his children

manager

Luke 16:2. you cannot be *m.* here any longer

manger

Luke 13:15. loose his ox or his donkey from the manger

manhood

Eph. 4:13. to mature *m.*, measured by nothing less than the full stature of Christ

manifest-ed

Phil. 4:5. let your magnanimity be *m.* to all

Col. 3:4. when Christ, who is our life, is *m.*, then you too will be *m.* with him

manifold

Heb. 2:4. by *m.* works of power

mankind

Luke 3:6. all *m.* shall see God's deliverance

John 17:2. thou hast made him sovereign over all *m.*

Acts 15:17. that they may seek the Lord —all the rest of *m.*

17:30. he commands *m.*, all men everywhere, to repent

Rom. 11:32. in making all *m.* prisoners to disobedience, God's purpose was to show mercy to all *m.*

1 Cor. 4:9. made us apostles the most abject of *m.*

2 Cor. 5:14. therefore all *m.* has died

1 Tim. 2:6. sacrificed himself to win freedom for all *m.*

Tit. 2:11. with healing for all *m.*

Rev. 9:10. power to plague *m.* for five months

9:15. to kill a third of *m.*

9:18. a third of *m.* was killed

9:20. the rest of *m.* who survived

manner-s

John 18:32. Jesus had indicated the *m.* of his death

21:19. he said this to indicate the *m.* of death

Acts 24:14. in that *m.* that I worship the God

Rom. 15:5. after the *m.* of Christ Jesus

Gal. 1:13. what my *m.* of life was

Col. 1:10. that your *m.* of life may be worthy

2 Tim. 3:16. for reformation of *m.*

3 John 6. in a *m.* worthy of the God we serve

mantle

Mat. 27:28. dressed him in a scarlet *m.*

27:31. they took off the *m.*

manure

Luke 13:8. while I dig round it and *m.* it

march-ed

Luke 14:31. what king will *m.* to battle

Rev. 20:9. they *m.* over the breadth of the land

marjoram

Heb. 9:19. with water, scarlet wool, and *m.*

mark-s-ed

Luke 22:21. *m.* this—my betrayer is here

24:49. *m.* this: I am sending upon you my Father's promised gift

John 20:25. the *m.* of the nails on his hands

Acts 2:14. *m.* this and give me a hearing

4:29. O Lord, *m.* their threats

13:48. *m.* out for eternal life

28:10. many *m.* of respect

Rom. 2:28. the external *m.* in the flesh

5:12. *m.* what follows

1 Cor. 7:18. with the *m.* of circumcision on him

14:7. unless their notes *m.* definite intervals

2 Cor. 7:14. bore the *m.* of truth

12:12. the *m.* of a true apostle were there

Gal. 5:2. *m.* my words

Eph. 4:30. *m.* for the day of our final liberation

2 Thess. 3:14. *m.* him well

1 Tim. 3:10. if there is no *m.* against them

Tit. 1:1. *m.* as such by faith and knowledge
  2:14. a pure people *m.* out for his own
1 Pet. 1:19. a lamb without *m.* or blemish
Jude 4. *m.* down for the doom they have incurred
Rev. 5:6. a Lamb with the *m.* of slaughter

market
Mark 6:56. they laid out the sick in the *m.*-places
John 2:16. you must not turn my Father's house into a *m.*
1 Cor. 10:25. you may eat anything sold in the meat-*m.*

marriage
Mat. 1:18. before their *m.* she found that she was with child by the Holy Spirit
  1:19. to have the *m.* contract set aside
  19:12. some are incapable of *m.* because they were born so, or were made so by men, there are others who have themselves renounced *m.*
Rom. 7:2. discharged from the obligations of the *m.*-law
1 Cor. 7:27. are you bound in *m*? Do not seek a dissolution. Has your *m.* been dissolved
1 Tim. 5:9. faithful in *m.* to one man

marry-ied
Mat. 22:28. they had all *m.* her
Mark 12:19. the next should *m.* the widow
  12:21. then the second *m.* her
  12:23. all seven had *m.* her
Luke 2:36. after she was first *m.*
  20:28. the next should *m.* the widow
  20:30. then the second *m.* her
  20:33. since all seven had *m.* her
Rom. 7:2. a *m.* woman is by law bound to her husband
1 Cor. 7:29. *m.* men should be as if they had no wives
1 Pet. 3:7. conduct your *m.* life with understanding

marshal-s
Rev. 6:15. the kings of the earth, magnates and *m.*

marvel-s
Acts 2:43. many *m.* and signs were brought about
2 Cor. 12:12. attended by signs, *m.*, and miracles

Mary
Mat. 1:24. took *M.* home to be his wife
John 11:29. when *M.* heard this she rose up quickly

masquerade-s-ing
2 Cor. 11:13. *m.* as apostles of Christ
  11:14. Satan himself *m.* as an angel
  11:15. to *m.* as agents of good

mass
Luke 13:17. the *m.* of the people were delighted
Acts 14:4. the *m.* of the townspeople were divided
Rom. 1:29. they are one *m.* of envy, murder

massacre
Mat. 2:16. gave orders for the *m.* of all children in Bethlehem

master-s-ed
Mat. 13:27. the farmer's men went to their *m.*
  18:25. his *m.* ordered him to be sold
  18:26. fell prostrate at his *m.* feet
  18:27. the *m.* was so moved with pity
  18:31. went to their *m.* and told him
  18:34. so angry was the *m.*
  21:3. our *M.* needs them
  24:45. charged by his *m.* to manage
  24:46. found at his task when his *m.* comes
  24:47. in charge of all his *m.* property
  24:48. the *m.* is a long time coming
  24:50. the *m.* will arrive
  25: 18, 19, 20, 21, 22, 23, 24, 26
Mark 5:4. no one was strong enough to *m.* him
  10:51. *M.*,' the blind man answered
  11:3. our *M.* needs it
Luke 2:29. *M.*, thou givest thy servant his discharge
  12:36. be like men who wait for their *m.* return
  14:23. the *m.* replied, 'Go out on to the highways
  16: 5, 6, 8.
  17:7. will the *m.* say, 'Come along at once and sit down
  19:31 ⎫
  19:34 ⎬ *M.* needs it
John 11:12. *M.*, if he has fallen asleep he will recover
  13:16. a servant is not greater than his *m.*
  15:15. a servant does not know what his *m.* is about
  15:20. a servant is not greater than his *m.*
Acts 16:30. *m.*, what must I do to be saved
Rom. 6:14. sin shall no longer be your *m.*
  6:16. if you put yourselves at the disposal of a *m.*, to obey him, you are slaves of the *m.*
1 Cor. 9:19. I am a free man and own no *m.*

1 Cor. 9:27. I bruise my own body and make it know its *m.*

Col. 3:24. there is a *M.* who will give you your heritage ... Christ is the *M.*

1 Pet. 3:6. Sarah, who obeyed Abraham and called him 'my *m.*

2 Pet. 2:1. disowning the very *M.* who bought them

2:14. past *m.* in mercenary greed

2:19. a man is the slave of whatever has *m.* him

2:20. are *m.* by them

1 John 2:13 ⎫
     2:14 ⎭ you have *m.* the evil one

Jude 4. disowning Jesus Christ, our only *M.*

mastery
1 Thess. 4:4. learn to gain *m.* over his body

1 John 4:4. the *m.* over these false prophets

match
Luke 5:36. the patch from the new will not *m.* the old

Rev. 18:7. to *m.* her voluptuous pomp

mate-s
2 Cor. 6:14. they are no fit *m.* for you

material
Rom. 15:27. duty to contribute to their *m.* needs

1 Cor. 9:11. expect from you a *m.* harvest

Gal. 3:3. do you now look to the *m.*

Heb. 9:1. a *m.* sanctuary

matricide-s
1 Tim. 1:9. parricides and *m.*

matter-s
Mat. 18:15. take the *m.* up with him

18:17. report the *m.* to the congregation

28:14. we will put *m.* right with him

Luke 1:4. authentic knowledge about the *m*

19:17. trustworthy in a very small *m.*

Acts 4:15. discussed the *m.* among themselves

6:3. appoint them to deal with these *m.*

23:29. controversial *m.* in their law

26:3. you are expert in all Jewish *m.*

26:26. the king is well versed in these *m.*

28:23. he dealt at length with the whole *m.*

Rom. 4:16. a *m.* of sheer grace

8:1. the conclusion of the *m.* is this

1 Cor. 4:3. it does not *m.* to me in the least

4:20. the kingdom of God is not a *m.* of talk

6:3. mere *m.* of business

7:19. what *m.* is to keep God's commands

14:27. if it is a *m.* of ecstatic utterance

2 Cor. 7:11. it made you take the *m.* seriously

8:10. my considered opinion on the *m.*

9:3. said about you in this *m.* should not prove to be an empty boast

11:10. I will preserve my pride in this *m.*

Gal. 2:6. not that their importance *m.* to me

3:12. law is not at all a *m.* of having faith

1 Tim. 3:13. speak openly on *m.* of the Christian faith

4:15. make these *m.* your business and your absorbing interest

Philem. 14. your kindness may be a *m.* not of compulsion

Heb. 9:10. a *m.* of food and drink

1 Pet. 1:12. the *m.* they treated of was not for their time but for yours

Rev. 2:14. I have a few *m.* to bring against you

mature
Eph. 4:13. to *m.* manhood

Phil. 3:15. those of us who are *m.*

Col. 1:28. as a *m.* member of Christ's body

maturity
Luke 8:14. bring nothing to *m.*

Heb. 6:2. let us advance towards *m.*

mauling
Luke 9:39. keeps on *m.* him

meal-s
Mat. 14:21. five thousand men shared in this *m.*

15:2. they do not wash their hands before *m.*

15:38. four thousand men shared in this *m.*

Mark 6:37. spend twenty pounds on bread to give them a *m.*

Luke 11:38. washing before the *m.*

14:1. a *m.* in the house of a leading Pharisee

17:8. wait on me while I have my *m.*

John 18:28. so that they could eat the Passover *m.*

Acts 2:46. shared their *m.* with unaffected joy

16:34. set out a *m.*, and rejoiced

1 Cor. 8:10. sitting down to a *m.* in a heathen temple

10:18. partake in the sacrificial *m.*

10:27. if an unbeliever invites you to a *m.*

11:33. when you meet for a *m.*, wait for one another

Gal. 2:12. he was taking his *m.* with gentile Christians

Heb. 12:16. he sold his birthright for a single *m.*

Rev. 6:6. three quarts of barley-*m.*

meal-tub

Mat. 5:15. a lamp is lit, it is not put under the *m.-t.*

Mark 4:21. to put it under the *m.-t.*

mean-s-t-ing

Mat. 1:23. a name which *m.* 'God is with us

15:15. tell us what that parable *m.*

17:13. he *m.* John the Baptist

18:25. he had no *m.* of paying

26:22. can you *m.* me, Lord

26:25. Rabbi,' he said 'can you *m.* me

26:58. *m.* to see the end of it all

26:70. I do not know what you *m.*

27:46. which *m.,* 'My God, my God, why hast thou forsaken me

27:57. Joseph by name, who was a man of *m.*

Mark 7:11. Corban' (*m.,* set apart for God

9:29. no *m.* of casting out this sort but prayer

11:18. sought some *m.* of making away with him

14:68. I do not understand what you *m.*

15:22. Golgotha, which *m.,* 'Place of a skull

Luke 1:29. wondered what this greeting might *m.*

2:50. they did not understand what he *m.*

4:29. *m.* to hurl him over the edge

8:9. his disciples asked him what this parable *m.*

8:11. this is what the parable *m.*

9:45. they were afraid to ask him what it *m.*

12:1. I *m.* their hypocrisy

14:14. they have no *m.* of repaying you

18:34. its *m.* was concealed from them

20:17. what does this text of Scripture *m.*

22:2. to devise some *m.* of doing away with him

22:4. ways and *m.* of putting Jesus into their power

24:19. what do you *m?'* he said

24:44. this is what I *m.* by saying

John 1:15. this is the man I *m.*

6:6. Jesus himself knew what he *m.* to do

6:15. Jesus, aware that they *m.* to come and seize him

6:46. I do not *m.* that anyone has seen the Father

6:71. one of you is a devil.' He *m.* Judas

7:36. what did he *m.* by saying, 'You will look for me

8:22. perhaps he will kill himself: is that what he *m.*

9:15. by what *m.* he had gained his sight

9:40. do you *m.* that we are blind

10:6. they did not understand what he *m.*

11:13. they thought that he *m.* natural sleep

12:34. what do you *m.* by saying that the Son of Man must be lifted up

13:24. ask who it is he *m.*

13:28. no one at the table understood what he *m.*

14:22. you *m.* to disclose yourself to us alone

16:17. what does he *m.* by this

16:18. we do not know what he *m.*

21:23. taken to *m.* that that disciple would not die

Acts 5:20. this new life and all it *m.*

9:36. Dorcas, *m.* a gazelle

11:18. this *m.* that God has granted life-giving repentance to the Gentiles

11:29. each according to his *m.*

12:4. *m.* to produce him in public

13:47. a *m.* of salvation to earth's farthest bounds

22:26. what do you *m.* to do

Rom. 2:4. God's kindness is *m.* to lead you to a change of heart

3:25. the *m.* of expiating sin by his sacrificial death, effective through faith. God *m.* by this to demonstrate his justice

3:31. does this *m.* that we are using faith to undermine law? By no *m.*

6:19. I *m.,* as you once yielded your bodies

7:13. this good thing was the death of me? By no *m.*

7:16. it *m.* that I agree with the law

8:27. God . . . knows what the Spirit *m.*

9:14. is God to be charged with injustice? By no *m.*

10:8. this *m.* the word of faith

11:11. did their failure *m.* complete downfall

11:12. if their falling-off *m.* the enrichment of the Gentiles

11:15. if their rejection has *m.* the reconcilation of the world, what will their acceptance *m.*

1 Cor. 1:12. what I *m.* is this: each of you is saying

7:29. what I *m.,* my friends, is this

10:16. a *m.* of sharing in the blood of Christ? When we break the bread, is it not a *m.* of sharing in the body of Christ

1 Cor. 14:5. unless indeed he can explain its *m*.

14:9. if your ecstatic utterance yields no precise *m*.

15:27. it clearly *m*. to exclude God

2 Cor. 5:19. what I *m*. is, that God was in Christ

8:11. give according to your *m*.

9:3. by that I *m*., I want you to be prepared

9:8. ample *m*. in yourselves to meet each and every situation

Gal. 4:9. *m*. and beggarly spirits

Phil. 1:17. *m*. to stir up fresh trouble for me

1 Thess. 1:6. *m*. grave suffering for you

Heb. 7:2. his name, in the first place, *m*. 'king of righteousness

7:12. a change of priesthood must *m*. a change of law

Jam. 4:5. do you suppose that Scripture has no *m*. when it says

2 Pet. 1:15. you will have *m*. of remembering

1 John 4:3. this is what is *m*. by 'Antichrist

Rev. 1:20. the secret *m*. of the seven stars

13:10. whoever is *m*. for prison, to prison he goes

17:5. a name with a secret *m*.

measure-d

Rom. 5:17. receive in far greater *m*. God's grace

15:29. a full *m*. of the blessing of Christ

1 Cor. 4:19. I shall take the *m*. of these self-important people

Gal. 3:19. it was a temporary *m*.

6:4. *m*. his achievement by comparing himself with himself

Eph. 1:20. they are *m*. by his strength

1 Thess. 2:16. making up the full *m*. of their guilt

1 Pet. 1:2. grace and peace to you in fullest *m*.

2 Pet. 1:2. grace and peace be yours in fullest *m*.

Jude 2. mercy, peace, and love be yours in fullest *m*.

meat

Acts 21:25. abstain from *m*. that has been offered to idols

Rom. 14:6. he who eats *m*. has the Lord in mind

14:21. it is a fine thing to abstain from eating *m*.

1 Cor. 10:25. you may eat anything sold in the *m*-market

meet-ing-ings

Mat. 2:4. he called a *m*. of the chief priests

2:7. called the astrologers to *m*. him in private

17:27. it will *m*. the tax for us both

18:25. ordered him to be sold to *m*. the debt

28:12. after *m*. with the elders

28:16. where Jesus had told them to *m*. him

Luke 13:33. a prophet to *m*. his death

15:20. he ran to *m*. him

John 11:47. convened a *m*. of the Council

Acts 15:6. the apostles and elders held a *m*.

17:2. Paul went to their *m*.

19:25. he called a *m*. of these men

1 Cor. 10:33. I always try to *m*. everyone half-way

11:17. your *m*. tend to do more harm than good

11:18 ⎱ when you *m*. as a congrega-
11:20 ⎰ tion

11:33. when you *m*. for a meal

11:34. in *m*. together you may not fall under judgement

14:26. when you *m*. for worship

14:28. better not address the *m*. at all

14:34. women should not address the *m*.

2 Cor. 2:6. the general *m*. has agreed

2:13. Titus was not there to *m*. me

7:3. come death, come life, we *m*. it together

7:15. *m*. him as you did in fear and trembling

8:14. your surplus *m*. their need

11:15. they will *m*. the end their deeds deserve

Phil. 1:28. *m*. your opponents without so much as a tremor

Col. 1:11. with ample power to *m*. whatever comes

4:6. study how best to talk with each person you *m*.

1 Tim. 5:5. regularly attends the *m*. for prayer

Philem. 21. confident that you will *m*. my wishes

Heb. 2:18. he is able to help those who are *m*. their test

10:25. not staying away from our *m*.

member-s

Mat. 10:4 ⎱ Simon, a *m*. of the Zealot
Mark 3:18 ⎰ party

15:43. a respected *m*. of the Council

Luke 12:52. five *m*. of a family will be divided

23:50. Joseph, a *m*. of the Council

John 3:1. Nicodemus, a *m*. of the Jewish Council

Acts 5:34. a *m*. of the Council rose to his feet

6:9. *m*. of the synagogue

Acts 9:41. he called the *m.* of the congregation
10:23. accompanied by some *m.* of the congregation
11:1. *m.* of the church in Judaea
12:1. King Herod attacked certain *m.* of the church
12:17. report this to James and the *m.* of the church
15:23. to encourage and strengthen the *m.*
17:6 ⎤
17:10 ⎬ *m.* of the congregation
17:14 ⎦
17:34. Dionysius, a *m.* of the Court of Areopagus
1 Cor. 11:19. which of your *m.* are sound
11:22. you shame its poorer *m.*
2 Cor. 2:17. in God's sight, as *m.* of Christ
Gal. 6:10. *m.* of the household of the faith
Eph. 2:19. *m.* of God's household
Col. 1:28. a mature *m.* of Christ's body
3:15. as *m.* of a single body
1 Tim. 5:8. especially for *m.* of his own household
Heb. 7:13. no *m.* of which has ever had anything to do with the altar

memorial
1 Cor. 11:24 ⎤
11:25 ⎦ do this as a *m.* of me

memory
Rom. 15:15. written to refresh your *m.*
2 Pet. 1:13. to keep refreshing your *m.*

mend
2 Cor. 13:11. *m.* your ways
1 Thess. 3:10. to *m.* your faith where it falls short

mention-ed
Rom. 9:32. the 'stumbling-stone' *m.* in Scripture
1 Cor. 11:17. *m.* a practice which I cannot commend
Eph. 5:3. must not be so much as *m.*
5:12. it would be shameful even to *m.*
2 Thess. 3:11. we *m.* this because we hear
2 Tim. 1:3. when I *m.* you in my prayers
Philem. 19. not to *m.* that you owe your very self to me

mercenary
2 Pet. 2:14. past masters in *m.* greed

mercy
Mark 5:19. what the Lord in his *m.* has done for you
Luke 1:55. he has not forgotten to show *m.* to Abraham

mere-ly
John 7:17. whether my teaching comes from him or is *m.* my own

7:18. anyone whose teaching is *m.* his own
10:33. you, a *m.* man, claim to be a god
Acts 25:19. *m.* had certain points of disagreement
Rom. 9:29. left us the *m.* germ of a nation
13:5. not *m.* by fear of retribution
1 Cor. 1:28. things low and contemptible, *m.* nothings
3:1. deal with you on the *m.* natural plane
3:3. you are still on the *m.* natural plane
3:21. never make *m.* men a cause for pride
6:3. how much more, *m.* matters of business
2 Cor. 10:4. the weapons we wield are not *m.* human
Eph. 6:6. do not offer *m.* the outward show
Phil. 2:4. not *m.* to your own
Col. 2:22. to follow *m.* human injunctions
3:22. not *m.* with an outward show of service
1 Thess. 1:5. not in *m.* words but in the power of the Holy Spirit
1 Tim. 1:4. issue in *m.* speculation
6:4. *m.* verbal questions
2 Tim. 2:14. stop disputing about *m.* words
Tit. 1:14. commandments of *m.* human origin
Jam. 1:22. act on the message and do not *m.* listen

merit-ing
Acts 23:29. no charge against him *m.* death
1 Tim. 1:15 ⎤ words that *m.* full accep-
4:9 ⎦ tance
2 Tim. 1:9 not for any *m.* of ours

merry
Rom. 15:10. Gentiles, make *m.* together with his own people

message
Mat. 4:17. Jesus began to proclaim the *m.*
10:7. as you go proclaim the *m.*
11:3. sent his own disciples to him with this *m.*
12:48. Jesus turned to the man who brought the *m.*
27:19. a *m.* came to him from his wife
Mark. 1:38. I have to proclaim my *m.*
2:2. while he was proclaiming the *m.*
3:31. sent in a *m.* asking him to come
4:33. with many such parables he would give them his *m.*

Mark 5:35. a *m*. came from the president's house
  5:36. Jesus, overhearing the *m*.
  14:14. give this *m*. to the householder
  16:7. give this *m*. to his disciples
  16:8. imperishable *m*. of eternal salvation
Luke 1:27. a *m*. for a girl betrothed to a man named Joseph
  7:6. the centurion sent friends with this *m*.
  7:19. sent them to the Lord with this *m*.
  8:49. from the president's house with the *m*.
  14:17. with a *m*. for his guests
  22:11. give this *m*. to the householder
John 11:3. the sisters sent a *m*. to him
  20:18. gave them his *m*.
Acts 4:4. heard the *m*. became believers
  10:44. all who were listening to the *m*.
  11:19. bringing the *m*. to Jews only
  13:15. sent this *m*. to them
  13:26. the *m*. of this salvation
  14:3. the *m*. of his grace
  14:25. when they had given the *m*. at Perga
  15:7. believe the *m*. of the Gospel
  16:6. delivering the *m*.
  16:36. the jailer reported the *m*. to Paul
  17:11. they received the *m*. with great eagerness
  20:20. I delivered the *m*. to you
Rom. 10:16. Lord, who has believed our *m*.
  10:17. faith is awakened by the *m*., and the *m*. that awakens it
  10:19. Israel failed to recognize the *m*.
2 Cor. 5:19. the *m*. of reconciliation
Gal. 3:2. believing the gospel *m*.
  3:5. faith in the gospel *m*.
Eph. 1:13. heard the *m*. of the truth
Col. 1:5. the *m*. of the true Gospel
  1:25. deliver his *m*. in full
  3:16. let the *m*. of Christ dwell among you
1 Thess. 1:6. the welcome you gave the *m*.
  2:13. we handed on God's *m*.
2 Tim. 4:2. proclaim the *m*.
Heb. 4:2. the *m*. they heard did no good
  13:7. who first spoke God's *m*. to you
Jam. 1:21. the *m*. planted in your hearts
  1:22. be sure that you act on the *m*.
  1:23. a man who listens to the *m*. but never acts upon it
2 Pet. 1:19. the *m*. of the prophets
1 John 2:7. the old command is the *m*.

messenger-s
Mat. 11:7. the *m*. were on their way back
  23:37. stones the *m*. sent to her
Luke 7:10. the *m*. returned to the house

  7:20. the *m*. made their way to Jesus
  11:49. send them prophets and *m*.
  13:34. stones the *m*. sent to her
John 5:33. your *m*. have been to John
  13:16. nor a *m*. than the one who sent him
  13:20. receives any *m*. of mine receives me
Acts 10:17. the *m*. of Cornelius
Rom. 10:15. the *m*. of good news

messiah-s
Mat. 1:16, 17, 18, 2:4, 16:16, 20, 22:42, 23:10, 24:5, 23, 24, 26:63, 68, 27:17, 22; Mark 8:29, 9:41, 12:35, 13:21, 22, 14:61, 15:32; Luke 2:11, 26, 3:15, 4:41, 9:20, 20:41, 22:67, 23:2, 39, 24:26, 46; John 1:20, 25, 3:28, 4:29, 7:26, 27, 31, 41, 42, 9:22, 10:24, 11:27, 12:34; Acts 2:31, 36, 38, 3:18, 20, 4:26, 27, 5:42, 8:5, 9:22, 17:3, 18:5, 28, 26:23; Rom. 9:5

met
Mat. 18:20. where two or three have *m*. together in my name
  27:1. *m*. in conference to plan the death of Jesus
Luke 7:12. he *m*. a funeral
John 1:43. he *m*. Philip
  1:45. we have *m*. the man spoken of by Moses
  18:2. Jesus had often *m*. there with his disciples
Acts 2:42. they *m*. constantly to hear the apostles teach
  10:33. we are all *m*. here before God
  16:40. they *m*. their fellow-Christians
Heb. 10:32. you *m*. the challenge of great sufferings

mete
Rev. 18:7. *m*. out grief and torment

method
Acts 19:14. seven sons of Sceva . . . were using this *m*.

mettle
Rev. 3:19. be on your *m*. therefore and repent

midday
Mat. 27:45 darkness . . . from *m*. until three in the afternoon
Mark. 15:33. at *m*. darkness fell over the whole land
Luke 23:44. about *m*. and there came a darkness
Acts 22:6. about *m*. a great light flashed from the sky

middle
Luke 5:19. into the *m*. of the company in front of Jesus

Luke 11:5. comes to him in the *m.* of the
   night
  12:38. the *m.* of the night or before
   dawn
Rev. 5:6. in the very *m.* of the throne
   . . . a Lamb

midge
Mat. 23:24. you strain off a *m.*

might
Luke 1:51. the deeds his own right arm
   has done disclose his *m.*
2 Thess. 1:9. the splendour of his *m.*
1 Tim. 6:16. to him be honour and *m.*
   for ever
2 Pet. 1:3. his own splendour and *m.*
  1:4. this *m.* and splendour he has
   given us
Jude 24. glory and majesty, *m.* and
   authority
Rev. 5:12. power and wealth, wisdom
   and *m.*
  5:13. praise and honour, glory and *m.*

mightily
2 Thess. 1:3. your faith increases *m.*
  1:11. *m.* bring to fulfilment every good
   purpose

mighty
Rom. 1:4. declared Son of God by a
   m. act
Rev. 5:2. a *m.* angel proclaiming in a
   loud voice
  18:8. *m.* is the Lord God

migrate
Acts 7:4. God led him to *m.* to this land

miles
Luke 24:13. which lay about seven *m.*
   from Jerusalem
John 6:19. when they had rowed about
   three or four *m.*
  11:18. Bethany was just under two *m.*
   from Jerusalem
Rev. 14:20. for two hundred *m.* around
   blood flowed

military
Acts 10:7. a *m.* orderly who was a
   religious man
  12:4. in prison under a *m.* guard

million-s
Mat. 18:24. whose debt ran into *m.*
Rev. 9:16. cavalry, whose count I heard,
   numbered two hundred *m.*

mind-s-ed-ing
Mat. 6:33. set your *m.* on God's kingdom
  12:25. he knew what was in their *m.*
  16:8. knowing what was in their *m.*
  21:30. afterwards he changed his *m.*
  21:32. you did not change your *m.* and
   believe him

Mark 2:8. Jesus knew in his own *m.*
  3:21. people were saying that he was
   out of his *m.*
  6:52. their *m.* were closed
  8:17. are your *m.* closed
Luke 1:51. the arrogant of heart and
   m. he has put to rout
  1:72. calling to *m.* his solemn covenant
  6:8. he knew what was in their *m.*
  9:47. Jesus knew what was passing in
   their *m.*
  11:17. he knew what was in their *m.*
  12:31. set your *m.* upon his kingdom
  15:15. to *m.* the pigs
  17:7. *m.* sheep
  21:14. make up your *m.* not to prepare
   your defence
  21:34. do not let your *m.* be dulled
  24:38. why do questionings arise in
   your *m.*
  24:45. he opened their *m.* to understand the scriptures
John 12:40. dulled their minds, lest they
   should see with their eyes, and
   perceive with their *m.*
  13:2. the devil had already put it into
   the *m.* of Judas
  14:26. call to *m.* all that I have told
   you
Acts 1:20. the text I have in *m.*,' Peter
   continued
  2:46. with one *m.* they kept up their
   daily attendance
  5:3. Satan so possessed your *m.*
  7:10. gave him a presence and powers
   of *m.*
  15:8. God, who can read men's *m.*
  15:24. unsettled your *m.*
  18:15. I have no *m.* to be a judge of
   these matters
  19:21. Paul made up his *m.* to visit
   Macedonia
  20:35. keep in *m.* the words of the
   Lord Jesus
Rom. 1:21. their misguided *m.*
  12:1. the worship offered by *m.* and
   heart
  14:6. he who respects the day has the
   Lord in *m.* in doing so, and he who
   eats meat has the Lord in *m.* . . . . he
   who abstains has the Lord in *m.*
  15:32. a happy frame of *m.*
  16:18. seduce the *m.* of innocent
   people
1 Cor. 7:33. he has a divided *m.*
2 Cor. 2:1. I made up my *m.* that my
   next visit
  2:13. I still found no relief of *m.*
  3:15. a veil lies over the *m.* of the
   hearers
  5:13. if we are in our right *m.*
  7:13. set his *m.* completely at rest
Gal. 1:7. unsettle your *m.* by trying to
   distort the gospel

Gal. 2:10. keep their poor in *m.*
Eph. 3:1. with this in *m.* I make my
   prayer
   3:14. with this in *m.*, then, I kneel in
   prayer
   4:18. their *m.* have grown hard as
   stone
Col. 2:8. do not let your *m.* be captured
   by hollow and delusive speculations
   4:2. with *m.* awake and thankful heart
1 Thess. 1:3. we call to *m.*, before our
   God and Father
2 Thess. 1:11. with this in *m.* we pray
   for you always
   2:10. did not open their *m.* to love of
   the truth
   3:11. *m.* everybody's business but
   their own
1 Tim. 2:15. with a sober *m.*
   4:1. give their *m.* to subversive
   doctrines
   6:3. will not give his *m.* to wholesome
   precepts
2 Tim. 2:22. invoke the Lord in single-
   ness of *m.*
Tit. 1:10. lead men's *m.* astray
   3:11. a man of that sort has a distorted *m.*
Heb. 10:3. sins are brought to *m.*
   11:40. with us in *m.*, God had made
   a better plan
Jam. 1:6. without a doubt in his *m.*
2 Pet. 1:19. the morning star rises to
   illuminate your *m.*
   3:15. bear in *m.* that our Lord's
   patience with us

mine
Mat. 10:42. because he is a disciple of *m.*
   15:5. anything of *m.* which might have
   been used for your benefit
   16:24. if anyone wishes to be a follower of *m.*
Mark 8:34. anyone who wishes to be a
   follower of *m.*
   8:38. if anyone is ashamed of me
   and *m.*
Luke 9:23. if anyone wishes to be a
   follower of *m.*
   9:26. whoever is ashamed of me
   and *m.*
   14:26. he cannot be a disciple of *m.*
   14:27. no one who does not carry his
   cross and come with me can be a
   disciple of *m.*
   14:33. none of you can be a disciple
   of *m.* without taking leave of all his
   possessions
   22:21. my betrayer is here, his hand
   with *m.* on the table
John 3:29. this joy, this perfect joy, is
   now *m.*
   8:23. your home is in this world, *m.*
   is not

   10:16. there are other sheep of *m.*
   12:30. this voice spoke for your sake,
   not *m.*
   15:20. they will follow your teaching
   as little as they have followed *m.*
   16:33. the victory is *m.*; I have conquered the world
Acts 22:28. Paul said, 'But it was *m.* by
   birth
Rom. 1:12. the influence of your faith
   on me as of *m.* on you
   7:15. not even acknowledge my own
   actions as *m.*
   9:26. you are no people of *m.*
1 Cor. 4:15. you are my offspring, and
   m. alone
   5:13. what business of *m.* is it to judge
   outsiders
Heb. 10:30. justice is *m.*: I will repay
Rev. 3:5. I will acknowledge him as *m.*

minister
Heb. 8:5. they *m.* in a sanctuary which
   is only a copy
Rev. 7:15. *m.* to him day and night

ministry
Acts 1:22. John's *m.* of baptism
Rom. 11:13. I give all honour to that *m.*

minor
Gal. 4:1. the heir is a *m.*, he is no better
   off than a slave

minority
Gal. 4:3. during our *m.* we were slaves
   to the elemental spirits

minstrels
Rev. 18:22. no more shall the sound of
   harpers and *m.*

miracle-s
Mat. 7:22. in your name perform
   many *m.*
   11:20. towns in which most of his *m.*
   had been performed
   11:21. if the *m.* that were performed
   in you
   11:23. if the *m.* had been performed in
   Sodom
   13:58. he did not work many *m.* there
Mark 6:2. how does he work such *m.*
   6:5. he could work no *m.* there
   16:17. faith will bring with it these *m.*
   16:20. confirmed their words by the
   m.
Luke 10:13. if the *m.* that were performed in you
Acts 7:36. working *m.* and signs in
   Egypt
   14:3. *m.* to be worked at their hands
1 Cor. 1:22. Jews call for *m.*
2 Cor. 12:12. signs, marvels, and *m.*
2 Thess. 2:9. *m.* of the Lie
Rev. 13:13. it worked great *m.*

miraculous
Mat. 13:54. these *m.* powers
14:2. these *m.* powers are at work in him
Mark 6:14. that is why these *m.* powers
Rom. 15:19. by the force of *m.* signs

mirror
1 Cor. 11:7. and the *m.* of his glory
13:12. puzzling reflections in a *m.*
2 Cor. 3:18. we all reflect as in a *m.*
Jam. 1:23. like one who looks in a *m.*

mischief
Rom. 1:29. injustice, *m.*, rapacity
1:30. they invent new kinds of *m.*

misdeed-s
Luke 3:19. and for his other *m.*
23:41. we are paying the price for our *m.*
Rom. 4:25. he was delivered to death for our *m.*
5:16. following upon so many *m.*
5:18. one *m.* was condemnation for all men
2 Cor. 5:19. no longer holding men's *m.* against them
1 Tim. 5:22. responsible for other people's *m.*

misdemeanour
Acts 18:14. crime or grave *m.*

miserable
Rom. 7:24. *m.* creature that I am
2 Cor. 2:3. be made *m.* by the very people
2 Tim. 3:6. get *m.* women into their clutches

misery
Rom. 2:9. *m.* for every human being who is an evil-doer
1 Cor. 9:16. would be *m.* to me not to preach
Heb. 11:37. in poverty, distress, and *m.*

misgiving
Acts 10:20. go with them without any *m.*

misguided
Rom. 1:21. their *m.* minds are plunged in darkness

misinterpret
2 Pet. 3:16. *m.* to their own ruin

mislead-s-led
Mat. 24:4. take care that no one *m.* you
24:5. many will be *m.* by them
24:11. many false prophets will arise, and will *m.* many
24:24. to *m.* even God's chosen
Mark 13:5. take care that no one *m.* you
13:6. many will be *m.* by them
13:22. to *m.* God's chosen
Luke 21:8. take care that you are not *m.*
John 7:47. have you too been *m.*

Jam. 1:22. that would be to *m.* yourselves
1 John 2:26. so much for those who would *m.* you
3:7. my children, do not be *m.*

miss-ed-ing
Luke 15:4. go after the *m.* one until he has found it
Phil. 2:26. he has been *m.* all of you
Heb. 4:1. found to have *m.* his chance

mission
Mark 6:7. sent them out in pairs on a *m.*
Acts 13:4. sent out on their *m.* by the Holy Spirit
Phil. 4:15. in the early days of my *m.*

missionary
Rom. 11:13. I am a *m.* to the Gentiles

mist
Jam. 4:14. your life, what is it? You are no more than a *m.*

mistake-n
Mat. 22:29. Jesus answered: 'You are *m.*
Mark 12:24. Jesus said to them, 'You are *m.*
12:27. you are greatly *m.*
Acts 6:2. a grave *m.* for us to neglect the word of God
1 Cor. 3:18. make no *m.* about this
6:9. make no *m.*: no fornicator
15:33. make no *m.*: 'Bad company is the ruin of a good character
Gal. 6:7. make no *m.* about this: God is not to be fooled

mix-ed
Mat. 13:33. *m.* with half a hundredweight of flour
27:34. a draught of wine *m.* with gall
Luke 13:1. whose blood Pilate had *m.* with their sacrifices
13:21. yeast which a woman took and *m.*
Phil. 1:17. present Christ from *m.* motives
Jude 23. pity must be *m.* with fear
Rev. 18:6. the strength of the potion she *m.*

mob-bed
Mark 15:15. Pilate, in his desire to satisfy the *m.*
Acts 16:22. the *m.* joined in the attack
17:5. they *m.* Jason's house
17:8. a great commotion in the *m.*
21:35. because of the violence of the *m.*
2 Cor. 6:5. flogged, imprisoned, *m.*

mock
Mark 15:19. paid *m.* homage to him
Heb. 6:6. making *m.* of his death

mockery
Rom. 5:5. such a hope is no *m.*

model
Phil. 3:17. you have us for a *m.*
1 Thess. 1:7. a *m.* for all believers

modesty
Jam. 3:13. with the *m.* that comes of wisdom
1 Pet. 3:15. make that defence with *m.*

modify
Gal. 4:20. then I could *m.* my tone

moment
Mat. 3:16. at that *m.* heaven opened
8:13. at that *m.* the boy recovered
9:22. from that *m.* she recovered
15:28. from that *m.* her daughter was restored
17:18. from that *m.* he was cured
26:16. from that *m.* he began to look for a good opportunity to betray him
26:51. at that *m.* one of those with Jesus reached for his sword
26:74. at that *m.* the cock crew
27:51. at that *m.* the curtain of the temple
Mark 1:10. at the *m.* when he came up out of the water
13:33. you do not know when the *m.* comes
Luke 2:38. coming up at that very *m.*, she returned thanks to God
10:21. at that *m.* Jesus exulted in the Holy Spirit
12:36. ready to let him in the *m.* he arrives
19:11. the reign of God might dawn at any *m.*
19:44. you did not recognize God's *m.* when it came
22:18. from this *m.* I shall drink from the fruit of the vine no more
22:53. this is your *m.*—the hour when darkness reigns
22:60. at that *m.*, while he was still speaking, a cock crew
24:33. without a *m.* delay they set out
John 4:27. at that *m.* his disciples returned
16:22. for the *m.* you are sad at heart
19:12. from that *m.* Pilate tried hard to release him
19:27. from that *m.* the disciple took her into his home
Acts 11:11. at that *m.* three men
28:6. they still expected that any *m.*
Rom. 13:11. remember how critical the *m.* is
2 Cor. 3:11. its *m.* of splendour
8:14. at the *m.* your surplus meets their need

Gal. 2:5. not for one *m.* did I yield to their dictation
Rev. 3:3. you will not know the *m.* of my coming
9:15. held ready for this *m.*
11:13. at that same *m.* there was a violent earthquake

monarchs
Mat. 17:25. from whom do earthly *m.* collect tax

money
Mat. 6:24. you cannot serve God and *M.*
20:15. do what I like with my own *m.*
26:9. and the *m.* given to the poor
27:5. he threw the *m.* down in the temple
27:6. taking up the *m.*, the chief priests argued: 'This cannot be put into the temple fund; it is blood-*m.*
27:10. gave the *m.* for the potter's field
Mark 14:5. sold for thirty pounds and the *m.* given to the poor
Luke 7:41. two men were in debt to a *m.*-lender
12:20. you have made your *m.*
15:30. after running through your *m.*
16:9. when *m.* is a thing of the past
16:13. you cannot serve God and *M.*
16:14. the Pharisees who loved *m.*
John 12:6. pilfer the *m.* put into the common purse
Acts 4:35. laid the *m.* at the feet of the apostles
5:2. kept back part of the purchase-*m.*
5:4. when it was turned into *m.*
20:33. I have not wanted anyone's *m.*
2 Cor. 12:14. it is you I want, not your *m.*
1 Tim. 3:3. and no lover of *m.*
3:8. nor to *m.*-grubbing
6:17. so uncertain a thing as *m.*
2 Tim. 3:2. men will love nothing but *m.*
Tit. 1:7. no drinker, no brawler, no *m.*-grubber
Heb. 13:5. do not live for *m.*
Jam. 4:13. trading and making *m.*
2 Pet. 2:3. in their greed for *m.*

mongers
Rom. 1:30. whisperers and scandal-*m.*

monster
Mat. 12:40. Jonah was in the sea-*m.* belly

monstrous
1 Cor. 15:8. this birth of mine was *m.*

monuments
Mat. 23:29. embellish the *m.* of the saints

moral-ly-ity
Acts 24:25. the discourse turned to questions of *m.*

Rom. 2:18. you are aware of *m*. distinctions
  6:19. making for *m*. anarchy
2 Cor. 10:2. charge us with *m*. weakness
Col. 2:13. *m*. uncircumcised
1 Tim. 1:7. teachers of the *m*. law
  2:2. high standards of *m*.

morbidly
1 Tim. 6:4. *m*. keen on mere verbal questions

more
Mat. 2:18. because they were no *m*.
  6:7. imagine that the *m*. they say the *m*. likely they are to be heard
  6:26. you are worth *m*. than the birds
Mark 14:39. once *m*. he went away and prayed
Acts 8:16. baptized into the name of the Lord Jesus, that and nothing *m*.
  19:20. spreading *m*. and *m*. widely
2 Cor. 4:15. grace of God is shared by *m*. and *m*.
Eph. 3:20. able to do immeasurably *m*. than all we can ask

morning
Mat. 14:25. between three and six in the *m*. he came to them
  27:62. the *m*. after that Friday
Mark 4:27. gets up in the *m*.
  6:48. somewhere between three and six in the *m*.
  15:25. the hour of the crucifixion was nine in the *m*.
  16:9. risen from the dead early on Sunday *m*.
Luke 1:78. the *m*. sun from heaven will rise upon us
John 6:22. next *m*. the crowd was standing on the opposite shore
  18:28. it was now early *m*.
  20:1. early on the Sunday *m*.
Acts 2:15. it is only nine in the *m*.
  12:18. when *m*. came, there was consternation
2 Pet. 1:19. the *m*. star rises

mortal-s
Mat. 16:17. you did not learn that from *m*. man
Acts 14:15. no less *m*. than you
Rom. 1:23. an image shaped like *m*. man
2 Cor. 1:10. from such *m*. peril God delivered us
Gal. 2:16. no *m*. man shall be justified
1 Pet. 1:23. not of *m*. parentage
  1:24. all *m*. are like grass
Rev. 13:3. the *m*. wound was healed
  13:12. whose *m*. wound had been healed

mortality
Rom. 8:21. the shackles of *m*.

mortification
Col. 2:18. self-*m*. and angel-worship
  2:23. its forced piety, its self-*m*.

Moses
Acts 7:36. it was *M*. who led them out
Rom. 2:11. outside the pale of the Law of *M*.
1 Cor. 9:20. as they are subject to the Law of *M*.
2 Tim. 3:9. like those opponents of *M*.

Most
Luke 1:32. he will bear the title 'Son of the *M*. High
  1:35. the power of the *M*. High will overshadow you
  6:35. you will be sons of the *M*. High
Heb. 9:3. the tent called the *M*. Holy Place

mother-s
Mat. 1:3. Their *m*. was Tamar
  1:5. his *m*. was Rahab
  1:6. his *m*. was Ruth
  11:11 }
Luke 7:28 } a *m*. son greater than John
John 2:4. your concern, *m*., is not mine
Acts 16:1. Timothy, the son of a Jewish Christian *m*.
Gal. 4:27. you who never knew a *m*. pangs
  4:31. our *m*. is the free woman
Tit. 2:4. to be loving wives and *m*.

motherhood
1 Tim. 2:15. she will be saved through *m*.

motion-ed-ing
Acts 19:33. *m*. for silence
  24:10. *m*. to Paul to speak

motive-s
1 Cor. 4:5. disclose men's inward *m*.
Phil. 1:17. present Christ from mixed *m*.
1 Thess. 2:3. never springs from error or base *m*.
Jam. 4:3. you pray from wrong *m*.
  4:8. see that your *m*. are pure

mount-s-ed-ing
Mat. 21:7. they laid their cloaks on them and Jesus *m*.
Mark 11:7. spread their cloaks on it, and he *m*.
Luke 19:35. their cloaks on the colt, for Jesus to *m*.
John 12:14. Jesus found a donkey and *m*. it
  12:15. *m*. on an ass's colt
Acts 9:23. as the days *m*. up, the Jews hatched a plot
  23:10. the dissension was *m*.
  23:24. provide also *m*. for Paul
1 Thess. 3:12. may the Lord make your love *m*.
Rev. 17:3. a woman *m*. on a scarlet beast

mourn-ed-ing-er
Luke 23:27. *m.* and lamented over him
John 16:20. you will weep and *m.*
Rom. 12:15. *m.* with the *m.*
1 Cor. 7:30. *m.* should be as if they had
    nothing to grieve them
Rev. 18:7. no *m.* for me, no widow's
    weeds
18:15 ⎫weeping and *m.*
18:19 ⎭
21:4. an end to death, and to *m.*

mouth
Mat. 12:37. out of your own *m.* you will
    be acquitted; out of your own *m.*
    you will be condemned
Mark 9:18. he foams at the *m.*
9:20. rolled about foaming at the *m.*
Luke 9:39. with foaming at the *m.*

move-d-ing
Mat. 17:20. *m.* from here to there!' and
    it will *m.*
20:34. Jesus was deeply *m.*
Mark 1:38. let us *m.* on to the country
    towns
Luke 9:33. as these were *m.* away from
    Jesus
10:7. do not *m.* from house to house
10:33. when he saw him was *m.* to pity
John 5:7. while I am *m.*, someone else is
    in the pool
5:29. shall hear his voice and *m.*
    forth
11:33. he sighed heavily and was
    deeply *m.*
20:1. she saw that the stone had been
    m. away
Acts 5:34. he *m.* that the men be put
    outside
9:28. *m.* about freely in Jerusalem
14:5. a *m.* was made by Gentiles and
    Jews
Rom. 8:14. *m.* by the Spirit of God
1 Cor. 8:6. towards whom we *m.*
2 Cor. 6:16. I will live and *m.* about
    among them
Phil. 1:16. *m.* by love for me
1:17. *m.* by personal rivalry
Tit. 1:9. able both to *m.* his hearers

movement
Acts 12:17. with a *m.* of the hand
19:23. the Christian *m.*
22:4. I began to persecute this *m.*
24:22. well informed about the
    Christian *m.*

mowed
Jam. 5:4. the men who *m.* your fields

mud
2 Pet. 2:22. the sow after a wash rolls
    in the *m.* again

multiply-ied
Rom. 5:20. to *m.* law-breaking. But
    where sin was thus *m.*

murder-s-ed
Mat. 5:21. do not commit *m.*; anyone
    who commits *m.*
21:35. thrashed one, *m.* another
21:39. out of the vineyard, and *m.* him
23:30. the *m.* of the prophets
23:35. Zechariah son of Berachiah,
    whom you *m.*
23:37. Jerusalem, the city that *m.* the
    prophets
Mark 10:19. the commandments: 'Do
    not *m.*
Luke 11:47. the prophets whom your
    fathers *m.*
11:48. they committed the *m.*
13:34. Jerusalem, the city that *m.* the
    prophets
18:20. do not *m.*; do not steal
Acts 8:1. Saul was among those who
    approved of his *m.*
9:24. so that they might *m.* him
9:29. they planned to *m.* him.
23:27. on the point of being *m.*
Jam. 2:11. thou shall not commit *m.*'.
    You may not be an adulterer, but
    if you commit *m.*
4:2. you are bent on *m.*
5:6. condemned the innocent and *m.*
    him
1 John 3:12. *m.* his brother. And why
    did he *m.* him

murderous
Acts 9:1. *m.* threats against the dis-
    ciples

murky
2 Pet. 1:19. a lamp shining in a *m.* place

music
Eph. 5:19. make *m.* in your hearts to the
    Lord

must
Mat. 5:16. you, like the lamp, *m.* shed
    light
5:18. all that *m.* happen has hap-
    pened
5:21 ⎫*m.* be brought to judgement
5:22 ⎭
5:31. *m.* give her a note of dismissal
9:38. you *m.* therefore beg the owner

mustard
Mat. 13:32. as a seed, *m.* is smaller than
    any other

muster-ed
Rev. 16:14. to *m.* all the kings of the
    world
19:19. their armies *m.* to do battle
20:8. to *m.* them for battle

mutilation
Phil. 3:2. beware of those who insist on *m.*

mutterings
John 7:32. these *m.* of the people about him

mutual
Rom. 12:10. warmth of *m.* affection
13:8. *m.* love
Gal. 5:15. all you can expect is *m.* destruction

muzzled
Heb. 11:33. they *m.* ravening lions

myriads
Heb. 12:22. before *m.* of angels
Jude 14. the Lord come with his *m.* of angels
Rev. 5:11. *m.* upon *m.* there were

myrrh
Luke 7:37. brought oil of *m.* in a small flask
7:38. anointing them with the *m.*
7:46. she has anointed my feet with *m.*

myself
Mat. 2:8. that I may go *m.* and pay him homage
Luke 9:9. as for John, I beheaded him *m.*
12:19, then say to *m.*
21:15. I *m.* will give you power of utterance
John 1:34. I saw it *m.*, and I have borne witness
Acts 9:16. I *m.* will show him all that he must go through
25:20. finding *m.* out of my depth in such discussions
Phil. 3:8. gaining Christ and finding *m.* incorporate in him
4:11. find resources in *m.*

myth-s
1 Tim. 1:4. interminable *m.* and genealogies
4:7. have nothing to do with those godless *m.*
Tit. 1:14. lending their ears to Jewish *m.*

mythology
2 Tim. 4:4. turn to *m.*

N

nail-ed
1 Cor. 1:23. yes, Christ *n.* to the cross
2:2. Christ *n.* to the cross
Gal. 5:15. fighting one another, tooth and *n.*

naked
1 Cor. 15:37. a *n.* grain, perhaps of wheat

name-s-d
Mat. 27:8. this explains the *n.* 'Blood Acre
Mark 3:16. to Simon he gave the *n.* Peter
3:17. he gave the *n.* Boanerges
5:8. in God's *n.* do not torment me
John 1:47. an Israelite worthy of the *n.*
9:7. the *n.* means 'sent'
Acts 1:19. they *n.* the property in their own language
1:23. two *n.* were put forward
9:11. a man from Tarsus *n.* Saul
11:26. the disciples first got the *n.* of Christians
Rom. 2:17. you may bear the *n.* of Jew
2 Cor. 5:20. in Christ's *n.*, we implore you
11:31. blessed be his *n.* for ever
Eph. 4:17. I urge it upon you in the Lord's *n.*
1 Thess. 4:2. orders we gave you, in the *n.* of the Lord Jesus

2 Thess. 3:12. we appeal to them in the *n.* of the Lord Jesus
3:17. signed with my *n.*, PAUL
Heb. 5:10. *n.* by God high priest
7:2. his *n.*, in the first place, means 'king of righteousness
1 Pet. 4:16. confess that *n.* to the honour of God
Rev. 12:9. whose *n.* is Satan, or the Devil
13:18. the number represents a man's *n.*
19:11. its rider's *n.* was Faithful
20:15. whose *n.* were not to be found in the roll of the living

namely
Eph. 1:10. *n.*, that the universe

nard
Mark 14:3. very costly perfume, oil of pure *n.*
John 12:3. a pound of very costly perfume, oil of pure *n.*

narrative
Luke 1:3. a connected *n.* for you

narrow
Mat. 7:13. enter by the *n.* gate
Luke 13:24 struggle to get in through the *n.* door

nation-s
Mat. 12:18. he will proclaim judgement among the *n*.
  12:21. in him the *n*. shall place their hope
  21:23. the chief priests and elders of the *n*.
  26:3. the elders of the *n*. met
  26:47. sent by the chief priests and the elders of the *n*.
  27:1. elders of the *n*.
Luke 2:31. in full view of all the *n*.
  22:66. the elders of the *n*.
Acts 5:21. the full senate of the Israelite *n*.
  7:2. fathers of this *n*., listen to me
  7:17. our *n*. in Egypt grew
  7:45. they dispossessed the *n*.
  9:15. to bring my name before the *n*.
  13:17. he made them into a *n*.
  13:31. his witnesses before our *n*.
Rom. 9:25. the unloved *n*. I will call My Beloved
  9:29. the mere germ of a *n*.
1 Cor. 14:21. I will speak to this *n*.
Col. 1:27. how rich and glorious it is among all *n*.
1 Tim. 2:7. to instruct the *n*. in the true faith
  3:16. proclaimed among the *n*.

national
Gal. 1:14. the practice of our *n*. religion

native
Acts 2:8. each of us in his own *n*. language
  11:20. *n*. of Cyprus and Cyrene
  14:11. in their *n*. Lycaonian
  18:2. Aquila, a *n*. of Pontus
  22:3. a *n*. of Tarsus in Cilicia
Rom. 11:21. if God did not spare the *n*. branches
  11:24. if you were cut from your *n*. wild olive and against all nature grafted into the cultivated olive, how much more readily will they, the natural olive-branches, be grafted into their *n*. stock

natural
John 11:13. they thought that he meant *n*. sleep
Rom. 4:1. Abraham, our ancestor in the *n*. line
  9:3. my *n*. kinsfolk
  9:5. in *n*. descent, sprang the Messiah
1 Cor. 3:1. on the merely *n*. plane
  3:3. you are still on the merely *n*. plane
Gal. 4:29. the *n*.-born son persecuted the spiritual son

nature
Acts 14:17. he has not left you without some clue to his *n*.

Rom. 7:5. the level of our lower *n*.
  7:18. in my unspiritual *n*.
  7:25. in my unspiritual *n*., a slave to the law of sin
  8:3. our lower *n*. robbed it of all potency
  8:4. the control of our lower *n*.
  8:5. the level of our lower *n*.
  8:7. the outlook of the lower *n*.
  8:12. our lower *n*. has no claim upon us
  9:8. not those born in the course of *n*.
  12:2. your whole *n*. thus transformed
1 Cor. 2:10. the depths of God's own *n*.
  3:3. human level of your lower *n*.
Gal. 4:23. the slave-woman's son was born in the course of *n*.
  5:13. licence for your lower *n*.
  5:16. the desires of your lower *n*.
  5:17. *n*. sets its desires against the Spirit
  5:19. behaviour that belongs to the lower *n*.
  5:24. crucified the lower *n*.
  6:8. sows seed in the field of his lower *n*.
Eph. 4:22. lay aside that old human *n*.
  4:24. the new *n*. of God's creating
Phil. 2:6. the divine *n*. was his from the first
  2:7. assuming the *n*. of a slave
Col. 2:11. divested of the lower *n*.
  3:9. you have discarded the old *n*.
  3:10. have put on the new *n*.

near-est
Mat. 24:6. the noise of battle *n*. at hand
  26:18. my appointed time is *n*.
John 1:18. God's only Son, he who is *n*. to the Father's heart
Rom. 13:12. day is *n*.
Heb. 10:25. you see the Day drawing *n*.
Jam. 5:3. an age that is *n*. its close
Rev. 1:3 ⎫
  22:10 ⎬ the hour of fulfilment is *n*.

nearing
Acts 13:25. John was *n*. the end of his course

necessary
Luke 10:42. one thing is *n*.
1 Cor. 11:19. dissensions are *n*.
Jude 3. urgently *n*. to write

necessity
2 Cor. 10:2. spare me, I beg you, the *n*. of such bravery

necks
Mat. 11:29. bend your *n*. to my yoke

need-s-y
Mat. 5:37. plain 'Yes' or 'No' is all you *n*. to say

Mat. 8:8. you *n.* only say the word
   10:19. the words you *n.* will be given you
   21:21. you *n.* only say to this mountain
Acts 4:34. they had never a *n.* person among them
   10:37. I *n.* not tell you what happened lately
   20:34. earned enough for the *n.*
   28:10. put on board provision for our *n.*
Rom. 10:12. rich enough for the *n.* of all
   12:13. contribute to the *n.* of God's people
   15:27. contribute to their material *n.*
1 Cor. 2:14. *n.* to be judged in the light of the Spirit
2 Cor. 8:14. your surplus meets their *n.*, but one day your *n.* may be met from their surplus
   9:9. he has lavished his gifts on the *n.*
   9:12. a contribution towards the *n.* of God's people
   9:13. contribution to their *n.*
   11:9. anything I *n.* was fully met
   12:9. my grace is all you *n.*
Gal. 3:20. an intermediary is not *n.* for one party
Phil. 2:25. to minister to my *n.*
   4:16. contributed to my *n.*
Jude 22. doubting souls who *n.* your pity

neglect-ing
Mat. 23:23. without *n.* the others
Mark 7:8. you *n.* the commandment of God
Luke 11:42. without *n.* the others
Acts 6:2. a grave mistake for us to *n.* the word of God

neighbour-s-ing
Mat. 11:1. preach in the *n.* towns
Luke 1:65. the *n.* were struck with awe
Rom. 13:8. he who loves his *n.*
Jam. 4:12. who are you to judge your *n.*
Jude 7. remember Sodom and Gomorrah and the *n.* towns

neighbourhood
Mat. 2:16. all children in Bethlehem and its *n.*
Mark 1:38. to the country towns in the *n.*
   3:8. the *n.* of Tyre and Sidon
Luke 7:17. Judaea and the whole *n.*
Acts 28:7. in the *n.* of that place

neither
Luke 12:27. they *n.* spin nor weave
1 Cor. 7:19. circumcision or uncircumcision is *n.* here nor there
Jam. 1:5. God is a generous giver who *n.* refuses nor reproaches

nervous
1 Cor. 2:3. I was then, *n.* and shaking with fear

never
Mat. 7:3. *n.* a thought for the great plank in your own
   11:11. *n.* has there appeared on earth a mother's son greater than John the Baptist
   16:18. the forces of death shall *n.* overpower it
   18:3. you will *n.* enter the kingdom of Heaven
   18:10. *n.* despise one of these little ones
Mark 9:25. come out of him and *n.* go back
   13:31. my words will *n.* pass away
   14:31. I will *n.* disown you
Luke 1:33. his reign shall *n.* end
   1:37. God's promises can *n.* fail
   3:17. burn the chaff on a fire that can *n.* go out
   6:46. calling me 'Lord, Lord'—and *n.* do what I tell you
   10:24. wished to see what you now see, yet *n.* saw it; to hear what you hear, yet *n.* heard it.
   18:1. keep on praying and *n.* lose heart
   21:33. my words will *n.* pass away
John 1:5. the darkness has *n.* quenched it
   5:17. my Father has *n.* yet ceased his work
   6:37. the man who comes to me I will *n.* turn away
Acts 4:17. *n.* again to speak to anyone in this name
Rom. 4:20. *n.* doubted God's promise
   8:3. what the law could *n.* do
2 Cor. 1:3. the God whose consolation *n.* fails us
   4:1. we never lose heart
   4:8. we are *n.* hemmed in; bewildered, we are *n.* at our wits' end
   4:9. hunted, we are *n.* abandoned to our fate
Heb. 13:1. *n.* cease to love your fellow-Christians
Jam. 5:4. the wages you *n.* paid

nevertheless
Rom. 9:30. Gentiles, who made no effort after righteousness, *n.* achieved it

new-s
Mat. 9:35. announcing the good *n.* of the Kingdom
   11:5. the poor are hearing the good *n.*
   24:6. the *n.* of battles far away
   24:8. the birth-pangs of the *n.* age begin

Mark 1:28. the *n.* spread rapidly
 2:1. the *n.* went round that he was at home
 5:14. carried the *n.* to the town
 5:20. spread the *n.* in the Ten Towns
 6:29. when John's disciples heard the *n.*
 13:7. the *n.* of battles far away
 13:8. the birth-pangs of the *n.* age begin
 16:10. carried the *n.* to his mourning and sorrowful followers
 16:13. took the *n.* to the others
 16:15. Good *N.* to the whole creation
Luke 1:19. bring you this good *n.*
 2:10. I have good *n.* for you
 3:18. announced the good *n.*
 4:18. announce good *n.* to the poor
 4:37. so the *n.* spread
 4:43. the good *n.* of the kingdom of God
 7:22. the poor are hearing the good *n.*
 8:1. proclaiming the good *n.*
 8:34. they carried the *n.* to the town
 8:39. spreading the *n.* of what Jesus had done
 9:6. everywhere they told the good *n.*
 16:16. there is the good *n.* of the kingdom
 20:1. telling them the good *n.*
John 4:51. his servants met him with the *n.*
 20:18. went to the disciples with her *n.*
Acts 5:20. tell them about this *n.* life
 5:42. the good *n.* of Jesus the Messiah
 8:12. believe Philip with his good *n.*
 8:25. bringing the good *n.* to many Samaritan villages
 8:35. told him the good *n.* of Jesus
 9:2. who followed the *n.* way
 9:42. the *n.* spread all over Joppa
 10:36. the good *n.* of peace through Jesus Christ
 11:1. *n.* came to the apostles
 11:20. the good *n.* of the Lord Jesus
 11:22. the *n.* reached the ears of the church
 13:32. give you the good *n.* that God
 14:7. continued to spread the good *n.*
 14:15. the good *n.* we bring tells you
 14:21. after bringing the good *n.* to that town
 15:3. the *n.* caused great rejoicing
 15:41. bringing *n.* strength to the congregations
 16:10. to bring them the good *n.*
 16:34. his *n.*-found faith in God
 18:23. bringing *n.* strength to all the converts
 18:26. expounded the *n.* way to him
 19:9. speaking evil of the *n.* way
 24:14. I am a follower of the *n.* way
 28:15. the Christians there had had *n.* of us

Rom. 1:30. they invent *n.* kinds of mischief
 8:11. *n.* life to your mortal bodies
 10:15. without someone to spread the *n.*? And how could anyone spread the *n.* without a commission to do so? And that is what Scripture affirms: 'How welcome are the feet of the messengers of good *n.*
 10:16. not all have responded to the good *n.*
 15:21. they who had no *n.* of him shall see
Gal. 1:23. preaching the good *n.* of the faith
Eph. 1:13. the good *n.* of your salvation
 2:17. proclaimed the good *n.*
 3:8. the good *n.* of the unfathomable riches of Christ
 4:23. *n.* in mind and spirit
 6:21. Tychicus will give you all the *n.*
Phil. 2:19. it will cheer me to hear *n.* of you
Col. 1:8. the *n.* of your God-given love
 4:9. they will tell you all the *n.*
1 Thess. 1:9. spread the *n.* of our visit
 2:9. we proclaimed before you the good *n.* of God
 3:6. good *n.* of your faith and love
Heb. 4:2. we have heard the good *n.*, as they did
 4:6. those who first heard the good *n.*
 7:15. if the *n.* priest who arises is one like Melchizedek
1 Pet. 1:3. gave us *n.* birth into a living hope

newly
1 Tim. 3:6. he must not be a convert *n.* baptized
Heb. 10:32. *n.* enlightened, you met the challenge

next
Mat. 2:7. Herod *n.* called the astrologers
 20:21. in your kingdom my two sons here may sit *n.* to you
Mark 12:19. the *n.* should marry the widow
Luke 13:9. if it bears *n.* season, well and good
 13:33. today and tomorrow and the *n.* day
 20:28. then the *n.* should marry the widow
Acts 1:5. baptized with the Holy Spirit, and within the *n.* few days
Heb. 7:2. *n.* he is king of Salem

night
Mat. 21:17. Bethany, where he spent the *n.*
 24:43. at what time of *n.* the burglar was coming

Mat. 27:19. much troubled on his
account in my dreams last *n.*
Luke 11:7. the door is shut for the *n.*
Acts 4:3. put in prison for the *n.*
    10:23. gave them a *n.* lodging

nightfall
John 6:16. at *n.* his disciples went down
to the sea

nine
Mark 15:25. the hour of the crucifixion
was *n.* in the morning
Acts 2:15. it is only *n.* in the morning
2 Cor. 11:24. given me the thirty-*n.*
strokes

noble-y
Phil. 4:8. all that is true, all that is *n.*
1 Tim. 6:12. confessed your faith *n.*
    before many witnesses
    6:13. Jesus Christ, who himself made
the same *n.* confession
    6:18. a wealth of *n.* actions

nobody
Mat. 8:4. be sure you tell *n.*
Mark 9:8. there was *n.* to be seen but
Jesus
    12:34. *n.* ventured to put any more
questions
Luke 1:61. *n.* in your family who has
that name
    8:16. *n.* lights a lamp and then covers
it
    8:43. *n.* had been able to cure her
    9:36. told *n.* anything of what they
had seen
2 Cor. 12:11. even if I am a *n.*
Heb. 5:4. *n.* arrogates the honour to
himself

nod-ded
John 13:24. Simon Peter *n.* to him

noise
Mat. 24:6 ⎫
Mark 13:7 ⎬ the *n.* of battle near at hand
Acts 2:2. a *n.* like that of a strong driv-
ing wind
Rev. 9:9. the sound of their wings was
like the *n.* of horses
    14:2 ⎫
    19:6 ⎬ like the *n.* of rushing water

none
John 4:48. will *n.* of you ever believe
without seeing signs
Acts 28:5. shook off the snake into the
fire and was *n.* the worse
1 Cor. 8:8. if we do not eat, we are *n.* the
worse, and if we eat, we are *n.* the
better
Tit. 2:8. wholesome speech to which *n.*
can take exception

nonsense
Luke 24:11. the story appeared to them
to be *n.*

noon
Mat. 20:5. at *n.* he went out again
John 4:6. it was about *n.*, and Jesus,
tired
    19:14. it was the eve of Passover,
about *n.*
Acts 10:9. about *n.* Peter went up on the
roof to pray

north
Acts 27:14. a fierce wind, the 'N.-easter'
as they call it

note-s-d
Mat. 5:31. must give her a *n.* of dismissal
    7:29. he taught with a *n.* of authority
    19:7. divorce his wife by *n.* of dis-
missal
Mark 1:22. he taught with a *n.* of
authority
    4:24. take *n.* of what you hear
    10:4. divorce his wife by *n.* of dis-
missal
    12:28. had *n.* how well he answered
Luke 4:32. what he said had the *n.* of
authority
    10:11. take *n.* of this
    23:55. they took *n.* of the tomb
John 4:9. Jews and Samaritans, it
should be *n.*
    4:53. the father *n.* that this was the
exact time
Acts 1:18. this Judas, be it *n.*
    4:13. *n.* that they were untrained lay-
men
1 Cor. 14:7. unless their *n.* mark definite
intervals
2 Pet. 1:20. but first *n.* this
    3:3. *n.* this first

notebook-s
2 Tim. 4:13. and the books, above all
my *n.*

nothing-s
Mat. 6:24. think *n.* of the second
    9:33. *n.* like this has ever been seen in
Israel
    14:21. to say *n.* of women and child-
ren
    20:6. all day with *n.* to do
    22:12. he had *n.* to say
    24:39. knew *n.* until the flood came
    25:42. when I was hungry you gave
me *n.* to eat, when thirsty *n.* to
drink
    25:44. and did *n.* for you
    28:5. you', he said, 'have *n.* to fear
Mark 2:25. he and his men were hungry
and had *n.* to eat
    3:4. they had *n.* to say

Mark 4:12. look and look, but see *n*.; they may hear and hear, but understand *n*.
14:51. *n*. on but a linen cloth
14:68. he denied it: 'I know *n*.
Luke 8:10. look but see *n*., hear but understand *n*.
9:13. five loaves and two fishes, *n*. more
11:39. *n*. but greed and wickedness
12:4. have *n*. more they can do
14:4. they said *n*.
16:13. think *n*. of the second
18:2. cared *n*. for God or man
18:4. true, I care *n*. for God or man
18:34. they understood *n*. of all this
23:14. found *n*. in him to support your charges
24:12. saw the wrappings and *n*. more
John 1:47. there is *n*. false in him
4:32. I have food to eat of which you know *n*.
5:44. care *n*. for the honour that comes from him
7:18. there is *n*. false in him
7:49. this rabble, which cares *n*. for the Law
10:1. *n*. but a thief or a robber
Acts 7:5. gave him *n*. in it to call his own
7:11. our ancestors could find *n*. to eat
7:18. king, who knew *n*. of Joseph
8:16. baptized into the name of the Lord Jesus, that and *n*. more
20:27. I have kept back *n*.
25:26. I have *n*. definite about him
Rom. 4:14. and the promise goes for *n*.
6:21. *n*. but what now makes you ashamed
7:18. I know that *n*. good lodges in me
8:38. I am convinced that there is *n*. in death or life
8:39. *n*. in all creation that can separate us
11:15. *n*. less than life from the dead
13:4. it is not for *n*. that they hold the power
1 Cor. 1:28. things low and contemptible, mere *n*.
2:2. I would think of *n*. but Jesus Christ
4:3. I have *n*. on my conscience
5:9. you must have *n*. to do with loose livers
5:11. have *n*. to do with any so-called Christian who leads a loose life
6:4. men who count for *n*. in our community
7:1. a good thing for a man to have *n*. to do with women
7:28. if, however, you do marry, there is *n*. wrong in it
7:30. mourners should be as if they had *n*. to grieve them

7:36. there is *n*. wrong in it; let them marry
13:7. there is *n*. love cannot face
14:10. *n*. is altogether soundless
15:17. if Christ was not raised, your faith has *n*. in it
15:34. there are some who know *n*. of God
2 Cor. 6:1. the grace of God; do not let it go for *n*.
11:10. *n*. shall stop me
11:14. there is *n*. surprising about that
Gal. 2:21. if righteousness comes by law, then Christ died for *n*.
6:15. circumcision is *n*.; uncircumcision is *n*.
Eph. 4:13. *n*. less than the full stature of Christ
4:17. pagans with their good-for-*n*. notions
4:19. stop at *n*. to satisfy their foul desires
Phil. 2:7. but made himself *n*.
1 Tim. 4:7. have *n*. to do with those godless myths
5:23. stop drinking *n*. but water
2 Tim. 2:23. have *n*. to do with foolish and ignorant speculations
3:2. men will love *n*. but money
Heb. 4:13. *n*. in creation that can hide from him
Jam. 2:14. say he has faith when he does *n*. to show it
2:16. does *n*. to supply their bodily needs
1 Pet. 1:4. is one that *n*. can destroy
2 Pet. 2:14. they have eyes for *n*. but women
1 John 4:8. the unloving know *n*. of God
3 John 9. their would-be leader, will have *n*. to do with us
Rev. 11:2. but have *n*. to do with the outer court of the temple
21:27. *n*. unclean shall enter

notice-d-ing
Mat. 9:11 ⎱ the Pharisees *n*. this
12:2 ⎰
22:5. but they took no *n*.
Mark 2:16. Pharisees *n*. him eating in this bad company
7:2. *n*. that some of his disciples were eating their food with 'defiled' hands
11:13. *n*. in the distance a fig-tree
Luke 5:2. he *n*. two boats lying at the water's edge
11:38. the Pharisee *n*. with surprise
14:7. when he *n*. how the guests
21:2. he *n*. a poor widow
22:58. a little later someone else *n*. him
John 9:27. but you took no *n*.

Acts 15:14. God took *n*. of the Gentiles
  17:23. I *n*. among other things an altar
  21:26. went into the temple to give *n*. of the date
  27:39. *n*. a bay with a sandy beach
  28:28. take *n*. that this salvation of God has been sent to the Gentiles

notion-s
Eph. 2:3. the promptings of our own instincts and *n*.
  4:17. pagans with their good-for-nothing *n*.

notoriety
Mat. 27:16. a man of some *n*., called Jesus Bar-Abbas

novelty
Acts 17:21. hearing about the latest *n*.

nowhere
Mat. 8:10. *n*., even in Israel, have I found such faith
Luke 7:9. *n*., even in Israel, have I found faith like this

noxious
Heb. 12:15. who forfeits the grace of God, no bitter, *n*. weed

nuisance
Luke 18:5. this widow is so great a *n*.

null
Mat. 15:6. you have made God's law *n*. and void
Mark 7:13. you make God's word *n*. and void
1 Cor. 15:14. if Christ was not raised, then our gospel is *n*. and void

nullify
Gal. 2:21. I will not *n*. the grace of God

number-s-ed
Mat. 10:31. you are worth more than any *n*. of sparrows
  21:36. other servants, this time a larger *n*.
  27:55. a *n*. of women were also present
Mark 3:7. great *n*. from Galilee
  6:44. who ate the loaves *n*. five thousand men
  8:9. the people *n*. about four thousand
  12:13. a *n*. of Pharisees and men of Herod's party
  15:40. a *n*. of women were also present
Luke 6:17. great *n*. of people from Jerusalem
  7:19. two of their *n*. he sent them to the Lord
  8:2. a *n*. of women who had been set free from evil spirits
  8:4. people were now gathering in large *n*.
  13:31. a *n*. of Pharisees came to him

  23:27. great *n*. of people followed
John 7:50. one of their *n*., Nicodemus
  12:9. a great *n*. of the Jews heard that he was there
  12:42. among those in authority a *n*. believed in him
Acts 2:41. three thousand were added to their *n*.
  2:47. day by day the Lord added to their *n*.
  5:13. no one from outside their *n*.
  5:14. *n*. of men and women were added
  6:3. seven men of good reputation from your *n*.
  7:17. our nation in Egypt grew and increased in *n*.
  9:31. it held on its way and grew in *n*.
  11:24. large *n*. were won over to the Lord
  11:26. gave instruction to large *n*.
  15:24. we have heard that some of our *n*.
  17:4. a great *n*. of godfearing Greeks
  17:12. became believers, and so did a fair *n*. of Greeks
  18:8. a *n*. of Corinthians listened and believed
  19:1. there he found a *n*. of converts
  28:23. came in large *n*. as his guests
1 Cor. 6:1. if one of your *n*. has a dispute with another
  11:30. a *n*. have died
Eph. 2:3. we too were of their *n*.
Col. 4:5. behave wisely towards those outside your own *n*.
1 Thess. 4:12. the respect of those outside your own *n*.
Jam. 5:19. if one of your *n*. should stray from the truth
Rev. 8:11. men in great *n*. died of the water
  11:1. and the *n*. of the worshippers

numbness
Rom. 11:8. God brought upon them a *n*. of spirit

numerical
Rev. 13:18. the *n*. value of its letters

numerous
Heb. 7:23. other priests are appointed in *n*. succession
  11:12. descendants *n*. as the stars

nurse-s-d-ing
Mat. 5:22. anyone who *n*. anger against his brother
Mark 6:19. Herodias *n*. a grudge against him
Acts 7:20. for three months he was *n*. in his father's house
Eph. 4:26. do not let sunset find you still *n*. it

O

oar-s
Mark 6:48. seeing them labouring at the *o.*

oath
Mat. 23:16 }
23:18 } he is bound by his *o.*
26:74. with an *o.*: 'I do not know the man
Mark 6:23. he swore an *o.* to her
14:71. broke out into curses, and with an *o.*
Acts 23:12. took an *o.* not to eat or drink
23:14. we have bound ourselves by a solemn *o.*

obdurate
Acts 19:9. some proved *o.* and would not believe

obedience
Mark 7:3. in *o.* to an old-established tradition
Luke 23:56. they rested in *o.* to the commandment
Gal. 3:10. those who rely on *o.* to the law
1 Tim. 3:4. wins *o.* from his children
1 Pet. 3:20. they had refused *o.* long ago

obedient
1 John 2:5. the man who is *o.* to his word

obey-s-ed
John 8:51 { if anyone *o.* my teaching he
52 { shall never know what it is to
{ die
8:55. I know him and *o.* his word
9:31. devout and *o.* his will
14:15. if you love me you will *o.* my commands
14:21. received my commands and *o.* them
17:6. they have *o.* thy command
Acts 4:19. for us to *o.* you rather than God
2 Cor. 9:13. how humbly you *o.* him
Eph. 2:2. you *o.* the commander of the spiritual powers of the air
2:3. *o.* the promptings of our own instincts
1 Tim. 6:14. I charge you to *o.* your orders
Heb. 11:8. by faith Abraham *o.* the call
1 John 5:2. when we love God and *o.* his commands

object-s-ed
Mat. 19:7. why then', they *o.*, 'did Moses

Acts 17:23. the *o.* of your worship
28:19. but the Jews *o.*
Rom. 9:22. *o.* of retribution due for destruction
9:23. *o.* of mercy
Gal. 6:12. their sole *o.* is to escape persecution
2 Thess. 2:4. every *o.* of men's worship
1 Tim. 1:5. the aim and *o.* of this command
Jam. 2:18. but someone may *o.*
2 Pet. 2:6. an *o.*-lesson for godless men

objector-s
Tit. 1:9. to confute *o.*

obligation-s
Rom. 1:14. under *o.* to Greek and non-Greek
7:2. the *o.* of the marriage-law
13:5. it is an *o.* imposed
13:7. discharge your *o.* to all men
15:27. they are under an *o.* to them
Gal. 5:3. under *o.* to keep the entire law

oblige-d
Rom. 8:12. we are not *o.* to live on that level
13:5. that is why you are *o.* to submit
2 Cor. 12:1. I am *o.* to boast

obscenity-ies
Rev. 17:4. a gold cup, full of *o.*
17:5. every *o.* on earth

obscure
2 Pet. 3:16. they contain some *o.* passages

observance
Acts 16:4. enjoined their *o.*
Col. 2:16. the *o.* of festival
1 Tim. 2:2. full *o.* of religion

observation
2 Cor. 11:32. King Aretas kept the city under *o.*

observe-d-ing
Mat. 2:2. we *o.* the rising of his star
22:11. he *o.* one man who was not dressed for a wedding
Luke 1:6. blamelessly *o.* all the commandments
23:55. *o.* how his body was laid
Acts 4:13. they *o.* the boldness of Peter and John
Rom. 11:22. *o.* the kindness and the severity of God
1 Cor. 5:8. we who *o.* the festival
Tit. 1:5. *o.* the tests I prescribed
Jam. 2:8. *o.* the sovereign law

observer-s
1 Pet. 3:2. *o.* the chaste and reverent behaviour of their wives
Rev. 3:3. the teaching you received; *o.* it
3:8. you have *o.* my commands

observer-s
Acts 22:12. Ananias, a devout *o.* of the law
Gal. 6:13. thoroughgoing *o.* of the law

obstacle
Rom. 14:13. no *o.* or stumbling-block be placed in a brother's way

obstinacy
Rom. 2:5. the rigid *o.* of your heart
Tit. 1:16. their detestable *o.* disqualifies them
3:3. in our folly and *o.*

obstinate
Mark 3:5. sorrow at their *o.* stupidity

obtain-ed-ing
Acts 23:16. *o.* entry, and reported it to Paul
23:20. on the pretext of *o.* more precise information
26:10. by authority *o.* from the chief priests
26:18. by trust in me, they may *o.* forgiveness
1 John 3:22. *o.* from him whatever we ask

obvious
1 Tim. 5:24. whose offences are so *o.*
5:25. good deeds are *o.*

occasion-s
Mark 3:1. on another *o.* when he went to synagogue
4:1. on another *o.* he began to teach
7:14. on another *o.* he called the people
8:1. another *o.* about this time when a huge crowd
Luke 10:25. on one *o.* a lawyer came forward
Acts 26:12. on one such *o.* I was travelling to Damascus
Rom. 14:16. an *o.* for slanderous talk
Eph. 4:29. only what is good and helpful to the *o.*
6:18. pray on every *o.* in the power of the Spirit
1 Tim. 1:16. the first *o.* for displaying all his patience
2 Tim. 4:2. the message, press it home on all *o.*

occupation-s
Tit. 3:8. engage in honourable *o.*

occur-red
Acts 7:23. it *o.* to him to look into the conditions
11:28. *o.* in the reign of Claudius

ocean
Rev. 17:1. the great whore, enthroned above the *o.*
17:15. the *o.* you saw, where the great whore sat, is an *o.* of peoples

odious
Tit. 3:3. we were *o.* ourselves

offence-s
Luke 23:22. I have not found him guilty of any capital *o.*
Acts 25:10. against the Jews I have committed no *o.*
Rom. 11:12. if their *o.* means the enrichment of the world
1 Cor. 13:5. not quick to take *o.*
2 Cor. 2:6. has met the *o.* well enough
Gal. 3:19. to make wrong doing a legal *o.*
1 Thess. 4:6. the Lord punishes all such *o.*
1 Tim. 5:24. whose *o.* are so obvious that they run before them into court, there are others whose *o.*
2 Pet. 2:16. was sharply rebuked for his *o.*

offend-ed
Rom. 11:11. because they *o.*, salvation has come to the Gentiles
2 Cor. 2:2. you, whom I have *o.*

offender
Rom. 13:4. retribution on the *o.*
2 Cor. 2:7. you must forgive the *o.*
7:12. not the *o.* or his victim

offer-s-ed-ing-ings
Mat. 2:11. *o.* him gifts
5:39. turn and *o.* him your left
7:9. *o.* his son a stone
23:18. swears by the *o.*
23:19. which is the more important, the *o.*
26:27. took a cup, and having *o.* thanks to God
27:34. they *o.* him a draught of wine
28:12. *o.* the soldiers a substantial bribe
Mark 14:23. having *o.* thanks to God
15:23. he was *o.* drugged wine
Luke 1:9. *o.* the incense
1:10. the hour of the incense-*o.*
6:39. he also *o.* them a parable
11:6. I have nothing to *o.* him
21:5. votive *o.*
24:30. he broke the bread, and *o.* it to them
24:42. they *o.* him a piece of fish
Acts 7:25. God was *o.* them deliverance
13:2. *o.* worship to the Lord
14:13. all the people were about to *o.* sacrifice
14:18. prevent the crowd from *o.* sacrifice

Rom. 1:9. God to whom I *o*. the humble service

1:25. *o*. reverence and worship to created things

12:1. *o*. your very selves to him: a living sacrifice, dedicated and fit for his acceptance, the worship *o*. by mind and heart

1 Cor. 5:8. the sacrifice is *o*.—Christ himself

9:12. rather than *o*. any hindrance to the gospel

9:13. eat the temple *o*.

10:20. the sacrifices the heathen *o*. are *o*. (in the words of Scripture) 'to demons

16:12. he will go when opportunity *o*.

2 Cor. 2:15. the incense *o*. by Christ to God

8:5. *o*. them in the first instance to the Lord

Gal. 6:10. as opportunity *o*., let us work for the good of all

Eph. 1:18. the wealth and glory of the share he *o*.

6:6. do not *o*. merely the outward show

Phil. 4:18. it is a fragrant *o*.

Col. 1:23. the hope *o*. in the gospel

1 Tim. 2:1. and thanksgivings be *o*. for all men

4:6. *o*. such advice as this

Heb. 11:4. his *o*. had God's approval

13:11. whose blood is brought as a sin-*o*.

Jam. 5:6. he *o*. no resistance

5:15. prayer *o*. in faith will save the sick

office

John 11:51. the High Priest in *o*. that year

Acts 1:25. this *o*. of ministry and apostle-ship

18:8. Crispus, who held *o*. in the synagogue

18:17. Sosthenes, who held *o*. in the synagogue

Rom. 16:1. Phoebe, a fellow-Christian who holds *o*. in the congregation

1 Tim. 2:2. for sovereigns and all in high *o*.

Heb. 7:23. prevented by death from continuing in *o*.

officer-s

Luke 22:4. Judas went to the chief priests and *o*.

22:52. the *o*. of the temple police

John 4:46. an *o*. in the royal service

4:49. the *o*. pleaded with him

Acts 16:35. the magistrates sent their *o*.

16:37. Paul said to the *o*.

16:38. the *o*. reported his words

21:31. a report reached the *o*.

24:22. Lysias the commanding *o*.

25:23. accompanied by high-ranking *o*.

2 Tim. 2:4. at his commanding *o*. disposal

official-s

Mark 6:21. gave a banquet to his chief *o*.

Acts 5:18. put them in *o*. custody

8:27. a eunuch, a high *o*.

13:15. the *o*. of the synagogue

offspring

John 1:13. the *o*. of God himself

Acts 3:25. in your *o*. all the families on earth shall find blessing

Rom. 9:7. Abraham's *o*.

1 Cor. 4:15. in Christ Jesus you are my *o*.

Rev. 12:17. to wage war on the rest of her *o*.

oil-s

Mat. 26:7. a small bottle of fragrant *o*.

26:12. she poured this *o*. on my body

Mark 14:3. very costly perfume, *o*. of pure nard. She broke it open and poured the *o*. over his head

16:1. bought aromatic *o*. intending to go and anoint him

Luke 7:37. had brought *o*. of myrrh

John 12:3. very costly perfume, *o*. of pure nard

ointment

Rev. 3:18. *o*. for your eyes

old-er

Mat. 15:2. break the *o*.-established tradition

Mark 5:42. she was twelve years *o*.

7:3. in obedience to an *o*.-established tradition

Luke 2:36. she was a very *o*. woman

8:42. an only daughter, about twelve years *o*.

2 Cor. 5:4. we do not want to have the *o*. body stripped off

Tit. 2:2. let the *o*. men know that they should be sober

2:3. the *o*. women, similarly

Heb. 1:10. earth's foundations laid of *o*.

1:11. like clothes they shall all grow *o*.

11:2. for their faith that the men of *o*. stand on record

1 Pet. 1:2. chosen of *o*. in the purpose of God

Rev. 21:4. the *o*. order has passed away

olive

Luke 16:6. a thousand gallons of *o*. oil

Rev. 6:6. spare the *o*. and the vine

Olivet

Luke 19:29. the hill called *O*.

21:37. spend the night on the hill called *O*.

once

Mat. 3:16. Jesus came up out of the water at *o.*

4:20. they left their nets at *o.*

4:22. at *o.* they left the boat

8:24. all at *o.* a great storm arose

13:21. he falls away at *o.*

14:27. at *o.* he spoke to them

20:34. at *o.* their sight came back

21:2. you will at *o.* find a donkey

21:3. he will let you take them at *o.*

21:19. the tree withered away at *o.*

22:4. come to the wedding at *o.*

25:16. went at *o.* and employed them in business

26:53. my Father, who would at *o.* send to my aid

Mark 1:30. they told him about her at *o.*

7:25. almost at *o.* a woman . . . came in, and fell at his feet

Eph. 2:13. you who *o.* were far off have been brought near

Tit. 3:10. a heretic should be warned *o.*, and *o.* again

One, one

Mat. 10:40. to receive me is to receive the *O.* who sent me

27:22. with *o.* voice they answered, 'Crucify him

27:25. with *o.* voice the people cried

Luke 1:49. the Lord, the Mighty *O.*

9:48. receives the *O.* who sent me

10:16. rejects the *O.* who sent me

John 1:34. this is God's Chosen *O.*

4:52. at *o.* in the afternoon the fever left him

6:69. you are the Holy *O.* of God

7:28. I was sent by the *O.* who truly is

13:10. you are clean, though not every *o.* of you

13:11. he added the words 'not every *o.* of you

13:20. he receives the *O.* who sent me

15:21. they do not know the *O.* who sent me

17:15. keep them from the evil *o.*

Heb. 4:13. the *O.* with whom we have to reckon

12:25. the *O.* who speaks from heaven

Jam. 2:11. the *O.* who said

1 Pet. 1:15. the *O.* who called you is holy

2:23. the *O.* who judges justly

2 Pet. 1:3. to know the *O.* who called us

Jude 24. the *O.* who can keep you from falling

Rev. 2:1. the *O.* who holds the seven stars

3:1. the *O.* who holds the seven spirits of God

3:7. these are the words of the holy *O.* the true *o.*

4:9. thanks to the *O.* who sits on the throne

4:10. the *O.* who sits on the throne

5:1 ⎫
5:7 ⎭ the *O.* who sat on the throne

6:16. the face of the *O.* who sits on the throne

16:5. thou Holy *O.* who art and wast

20:11. a great white throne, and the *O.* who sat upon it

oneself

Jam. 1:27. keep *o.* untarnished by the world

onlooker-s

Mat. 9:33. the *o.* said, 'Nothing like this

Luke 14:29. all the *o.* will laugh at him

only

Mat. 4:9. if you will *o.* fall down and do me homage

5:45. *o.* so can you be children of your heavenly Father

6:23. if then the *o.* light you have is darkness

7:21. those who do the will of my heavenly Father

19:11. *o.* those for whom God has appointed it

Mark 1:40. if *o.* you will,' said the man, 'you can cleanse me

12:29. the Lord your God is the *o.* Lord

Rom. 7:21. when I want to do the right, *o.* the wrong is within my reach

2 Cor. 11:2. as a chaste virgin to her true and *o.* husband

onwards

Acts 3:24. so said all the prophets, from Samuel *o.*

open-ed-ly

Mark 2:4. so they *o.* up the roof

4:22. unless it is to come into the *o.*

Luke 4:25. three years and six months the skies never *o.*

8:17. made known and brought into the *o.*

15:4. leave the ninety-nine in the *o.* pasture

23:2. they *o.* the case against him by saying

John 7:26. here he is, speaking *o.*

Acts 9:29. he spoke out boldly and *o.*

14:3. spoke boldly and *o.* in reliance on the Lord

19:18. *o.* confessed that they had been using magical spells

23:9. *o.* took sides and declared

24:2. Tertullus *o.* the case

24:21. this one *o.* assertion which I made

24:23. to keep Paul under *o.* arrest

Acts 25:11. it is not *o*. to anyone to hand
me over
27:5. then across the *o*. sea
28:31. teaching the facts about the
Lord Jesus Christ quite *o*.
2 Cor. 4:2. by declaring the truth *o*.
5:10. our lives laid *o*. before the
tribunal of Christ
5:11. to God our lives lie *o*., as I hope
they also lie *o*. to you
6:13. *o*. wide your hearts to us
8:2. lavishly *o*.-handed
11:25. for twenty-four hours I was
adrift on the *o*. sea
Gal. 3:1. Jesus Christ was *o*. displayed
upon his cross
Eph. 1:19. the resources of his power *o*.
to us
2 Thess. 2:10. they did not *o*. their
minds to love of the truth
1 Tim. 3:13. speak *o*. on matters of the
Christian faith
Tit. 1:3. *o*. declared himself
Heb. 4:1. the promise of entering his
rest remains *o*.
10:20. the new, living way which he
has *o*. for us
12:17. found no way *o*. for second
thoughts
Jam. 3:17. *o*. to reason
1 Pet. 1:12. it has been *o*. announced to
you

opening
Jam. 3:11. fresh and brackish water from
the same *o*.

operative
Heb. 9:17. a testament is *o*. only after a
death

opinion
Mat. 22:42. what is your *o*. about the
Messiah
26:66. what is your *o*.?' 'He is guilty
Mark 14:64. you have heard the blasphemy. What is your *o*.
1 Cor. 7:26. it is my *o*., then, that in a
time of stress
7:40. that is my *o*., and I believe that I
too have the Spirit of God
2 Cor. 8:10. here is my considered *o*.

opponent-s
Luke 12:58. going with your *o*. to court
13:17. all his *o*. were covered with
confusion
18:3. demanding justice against her *o*.
21:15. no *o*. will be able to resist
Phil. 1:28. meeting your *o*. without so
much as a tremor
1 Tim. 5:14. give no *o*. occasion for
slander
2 Tim. 3:9. like those *o*. of Moses
Tit. 2:8. they will shame any *o*.

opportunity-ies
Mark 6:21. Herodias found her *o*.
14:11. look for a good *o*. to betray him
Luke 20:20. they watched their *o*.
21:13. your *o*. to testify
Acts 25:16. given an *o*. of answering
Rom. 7:8. sin found its *o*.
7:11. sin found its *o*. in the commandment
1 Cor. 16:9. *o*. has opened for effective
work
16:12. he will go when *o*. offers
2 Cor. 8:22. many *o*. of testing
Eph. 5:16⎫
Col. 4:5⎬use the present *o*. to the full
1 Tim. 5:10. every *o*. of doing good

oppose-s-ed-ing
Luke 23:2. *o*. the payment of taxes
Acts 13:8. *o*. them, trying to turn the
Governor away
Gal. 2:11. I *o*. him to his face
2 Tim. 4:15. he violently *o*. everything I
said
Jam. 4:6. God *o*. the arrogant

opposite
Mat. 21:2. go to the village *o*.
27:61. sitting *o*. the grave
Mark 11:2. go to the village *o*.
12:41. standing *o*. the temple treasury
15:39. the centurion who was standing *o*. him
Luke 8:26. the country of the Gergesenes,
which is *o*. Galilee
19:30. go to the village *o*.
John 6:22. standing on the *o*. shore

opposition
1 Cor. 16:9. there is much *o*.
Heb. 12:3. *o*. from sinners

oppress-ed
Acts 7:34. how my people are *o*. in
Egypt
2 Cor. 5:4. *o*. because we do not want to
have the old body stripped off

oppression
Acts 7:6. *o*. for four hundred years

option
Acts 28:19. I had no *o*. but to appeal to
the Emperor

oracle
Rom. 11:4. what does the *o*. say
Heb. 12:25. the *o*. speaking on earth

oracular
Acts 16:16. possessed by an *o*. spirit
2 Thess. 2:2. some *o*. utterance
Heb. 12:19. the trumpet-blast and the
o. voice

ordain-ed
Acts 15:7. *o*. that from my lips
27:24. it is *o*. that you shall appear

Rom. 8:29. *o.* that they should be shaped
  to the likeness of his Son
1 Cor. 1:21. as God in his wisdom *o.*

ordeal
Luke 12:50. hampered I am until the *o.*
  is over
1 Pet. 4:12. do not be bewildered by the
  fiery *o.*
Rev. 3:10. the *o.* that is to fall upon the
  whole world
  7:14. the men who have passed
  through the great *o.*

order-s-ed-ing
Mat. 2:16. gave *o.* for the massacre of
  all children in Bethlehem
  8:9. I am myself under *o.*
  14:9. he *o.* the request to be granted
  15:35. he *o.* the people to sit down
  16:20. strict *o.* not to tell anyone that
  he was the Messiah
  18:25. his master *o.* him to be sold
  20:21. to give *o.* that in your kingdom
  my two sons
  27:58. asked for the body of Jesus;
  and Pilate gave *o.* that he should
  have it
  27:64. give *o.* for the grave to be made
  secure
Mark 1:27. when he gives *o.*, even the
  unclean spirits submit
  5:43. strict *o.* to let no one hear
  about it
  6:27. with *o.* to bring John's head
  6:39. he *o.* them to make the people
  sit down
  7:8. in *o.* to maintain the tradition of
  men
  8:6. he *o.* the people to sit down
  8:7. which he blessed and *o.* them to
  distribute
  13:34. he has *o.* the door-keeper to
  stay awake
Luke 4:10. give his angels *o.* to take
  care of you
  4:36. he gives *o.* to the unclean spirits
  5:14. Jesus then *o.* him not to tell anybody
  7:8. I am myself under *o.*
  8:25. he gives his *o.* to wind and waves
  8:29. *o.* the unclean spirit to come out
  of the man
  9:21. strict *o.* not to tell this to anyone
  14:22. your *o.* have been carried out
  15:29. I never once disobeyed your *o.*
  17:9. is he grateful to the servant for
  carrying out his *o.*
  17:10. when you have carried out all
  your *o.*
  18:40. Jesus stopped and *o.* the man to
  be brought
John 2:8. now draw some off', he *o.*
  11:57. given *o.* that anyone who knew
  where he was

Acts 4:15. *o.* them to leave the court
  4:18. *o.* them to refrain from all
  public speaking
  5:28. *o.* you', he said, 'to desist from
  teaching in that name
  5:40. *o.* them to give up speaking in
  the name of Jesus
  8:38. he *o.* the carriage to stop
  10:33. to hear all that the Lord has
  o. you to say
  10:48. he *o.* them to be baptized
  12:19. *o.* their execution
  16:22. *o.* them to be flogged
  16:23. *o.* the jailer to keep them
  under close guard
  16:24. in view of these *o.*
  21:33. *o.* him to be shackled with two
  chains
  21:34. *o.* him to be taken into barracks
  22:24. *o.* him to be brought into the
  barracks
  22:30. *o.* the chief priests and the
  entire Council to assemble
also 23:2, 3, 10, 22, 23, 31, 35; 24:23;
  25:6, 17, 21, 23; 27:43
1 Cor. 1:28. to overthrow the existing *o.*
  7:17. each one must *o.* his life
2 Cor. 4:15. it is for your sake that all
  things are *o.*
  5:17. the old *o.* has gone, and a new
  order has already begun
  8:8. this is not meant as an *o.*
  9:5. see that your promised bounty is
  in *o.*
Col. 1:16. the invisible *o.* of thrones
1 Thess. 4:2. you know what *o.* we gave
  you
  4:11. work with your hands as we
  o. you
2 Thess. 3:4. will continue to do what we
  o.
  3:6. these are our *o.* to you
  3:12. we give these *o.*
1 Tim. 4:11. pass on these *o.* and these
  teachings
  5:7. add these *o.* to the rest
  6:14. I charge you to obey your *o.*
  irreproachably
Heb. 1:2. through whom he created all
  o. of existence
1 Pet. 4:7. you must lead an *o.* and sober
  life
Rev. 21:4. for the old *o.* has passed
  away

orderly
Acts 10:7. a military *o.* who was a
  religious man

ordinance
Tit. 1:3. by *o.* of God our Saviour

ordinary
1 Cor. 12:23. a more than *o.* seemliness

2 Cor. 2:4. the more than *o*. love, that I
    have for you
Gal. 3:15. in *o*. life, when a man's will

ordination
1 Tim. 5:22. do not be over-hasty in
    laying on hands in *o*.

organ-s
Rom. 12:4. in a single human body there
    are many limbs and *o*.
    12:5. as limbs and *o*. to one another
1 Cor. 6:15. your bodies are limbs and
    o. of Christ
    12:12. Christ is like a single body with
    its many limbs and *o*.
    12:14. a body is not one single *o*.
    12:18. God appointed each limb and
    o.
    12:19. if the whole were one single
    o.
    12:20. there are many different *o*.
    12:22. those *o*. of the body
    12:25. all its *o*. might feel the same
    concern
    12:26. if one *o*. suffers
    12:27. each of you a limb or *o*.

orgies
Gal. 5:21. drinking bouts, *o*., and the
    like

origin-s
Mat. 15:18. what comes out of the
    mouth has its *o*. in the heart
Acts 5:38. is of human *o*., it will collapse
Col. 1:18. the church. He is its *o*.
Tit. 1:14. commandments of merely
    human *o*.

original-ly
Luke 1:2. handed down to us by the *o*.
    eyewitnesses
Acts 14:26. *o*. been commended to the
    grace of God
1 Cor. 11:8. man did not *o*. spring from
    woman
Gal. 4:13. illness that *o*. led to my bring-
    ing you the Gospel
Heb. 3:14. keep our *o*. confidence firm
    to the end

originate-d
John 7:22. not that it *o*. with Moses
1 Cor. 14:36. did the word of God *o*. with
    you

orphan-s
Jam. 1:27. to go to the help of *o*.

others
Mat. 7:12. treat *o*. as you would like
    them to treat you

otherwise
Mat. 5:25. *o*. he may hand you over to
    the judge
    13:15. *o*., their eyes might see

27:64. *o*. his disciples may come, steal
    the body
Mark 4:12. *o*. they might turn to God

ought
John 3:7. you *o*. not to be astonished
Heb. 6:1. we *o*. not to be laying over
    again the foundations of faith
Jam. 4:17. the man who knows the good
    he *o*. to do

ours
Jude 3. salvation—which is yours no
    less than *o*.

ourselves
Luke 9:13. unless perhaps we *o*. are to
    go and buy
Acts 10:47. received the Holy Spirit just
    as we did *o*.
1 Cor. 4:12. we wear *o*. out
    9:10. or is the reference clearly to *o*.
    15:30. we *o*.—why do we face these
    dangers
2 Cor. 5:3. we shall not find *o*. naked
    6:6. we recommend *o*. by the inno-
    cence of our behaviour
    6:10. poor *o*., we bring wealth to
    many
    10:16. never priding *o*. on work
    already done
Heb. 12:1. and what of *o*.

outcast
Rom. 9:3. *o*. from Christ myself for the
    sake of my brothers
1 Cor. 16:22. if anyone does not love
    the Lord, let him be *o*.
Gal. 1:8. he shall be held *o*.
    1:9. let him be *o*.

outcome
2 Cor. 4:17. their *o*. an eternal glory
Heb. 13:7. the *o*. of their life and work

outcry
Luke 23:18. a general *o*., 'Away with him
Acts 8:7. unclean spirits came out with
    a great *o*.
    22:24. what reason there was for such
    an *o*.
Jam. 5:4. the *o*. of the reapers

outdo
2 Cor. 11:23. I can *o*. them

outdone
1 Cor. 15:10. I have *o*. them all

outer
Acts 12:13. he knocked at the *o*. door
Rev. 11:2. the *o*. court of the temple

outlandish
Heb. 13:9. all sorts of *o*. teachings

outlaw-s
Luke 6:22. they *o*. you and insult you

Luke 22:37. he was counted among the *o.*

outline
2 Tim. 1:13. an *o.* of the sound teaching

outlook
Rom. 8:5. have their *o.* formed by it
8:6. on the level of the spirit have the spiritual *o.*
8:7. the *o.* of the lower nature is enmity with God
1 Cor. 13:11. my *o.*, and my thoughts were all childish

outrage-d
Rom. 14:15. if your brother is *o.* by what you eat
1 Thess. 2:2. *o.* which to your knowledge we had suffered
1 Tim. 1:13. persecution and *o.*

outrageously
Mark 12:4. beat about the head and treated *o.*
Luke 20:11. *o.* treated

outset
Mat. 18:24. at the *o.* there appeared before him a man

outshone
2 Cor. 3:10. it is *o.* by a splendour greater still

outside
Mat. 23:27. they look well from *o.*
23:28. *o.* you look like honest men
Mark 1:45. stayed *o.* in the open country
3:31. his mother and his brothers arrived, and remaining *o.*
3:32. *o.* asking for you
4:11. to those who are *o.* everything comes by way of parables
Luke 11:40. did not he who made the *o.* make the inside too
Acts 5:13. no one from *o.* their number venturing to join with them
12:14. Peter was standing *o.*
14:13. Jupiter, whose temple was just *o.* the city
Eph. 2:12. *o.* God's covenants
Col. 4:5. those *o.* your own number
1 Thess. 4:12. the respect of those *o.* your own number
1 Pet. 2:10. *o.* his mercy once, you have now received his mercy

outsiders
1 Cor. 5:12. what business of mine is it to judge *o.*
6:4. how can you entrust jurisdiction to *o.*

outspoken
Acts 13:46. Paul and Barnabas were *o.*

outstanding
Rom. 13:8. leave no claim *o.* against you
16:13. Rufus, an *o.* follower of the Lord

outstretched
Acts 13:17. brought them out of that country with arm *o.*

outstrip-ping
Gal. 1:14. I was *o.* many of my Jewish contemporaries

outward-ly
2 Cor. 5:12. all in *o.* show
Gal. 6:12. a fair *o.* and bodily show
6:13. that *o.* rite
Eph. 2:11. Gentiles as you are *o.* . . . only with reference to an *o.* rite
6:6. do not offer merely the *o.* show of service
Col. 3:22. not merely with an *o.* show of service
2 Tim. 3:5. the *o.* form of religion
Heb. 9:10. *o.* ordinances in force

outweigh-s-ed
2 Cor. 4:17. an eternal glory which *o.* them
Phil. 3:8. far *o.* by the gain of knowing Christ Jesus

overbearing
Tit. 1:7. he must not be *o.*

overboard
Acts 27:43. who could swim should jump *o.*

overcame
Luke 1:12. fear *o.* him

overcome
Mark 9:15. the whole crowd were *o.* with awe
Luke 9:1. authority to *o.* all the devils
Acts 20:9. completely *o.* by sleep

overflow-s-ing
Mat. 12:34 ⎱ the *o.* of the heart
Luke 6:45 ⎰
Rom. 15:13. you *o.* with hope
2 Cor. 1:5. as Christ's cup of suffering *o.*, and we suffer with him, so also through Christ our consolation *o.*
7:4. my cup is full of consolation, and *o.* with joy
9:12. *o.* in a flood of thanksgiving to God
Col. 2:7. let your hearts *o.* with thankfulness
1 Thess. 3:12. your love mount and *o.*

over-hasty
1 Tim. 5:22. do not be *o.* in laying on hands in ordination

overhaul-ing
Mat. 4:21 ⎫
Mark 1:19 ⎭ *o.* their nets

overhear-d-ing
Mark 2:17. Jesus *o.*
  5:36. Jesus, *o.* the message
John 7:32. the Pharisees *o.* these mutterings

overjoyed
Mat. 2:10. at the sight of the star they were *o.*
John 3:29. *o.* at hearing the bridegroom's voice
  8:56. Abraham was *o.* to see my day
Acts 12:14. she recognized Peter's voice and was so *o.*
  13:48. when the Gentiles heard this, they were *o.*

overlook-ed
Mat. 23:23. *o.* the weightier demands of the Law
Luke 12:6. not one of them is *o.* by God
Acts 6:1. their widows were being *o.*
  17:30. the times of ignorance, God has *o.* them
Rom. 3:25. he had *o.* the sins of the past

overmuch
2 Cor. 12:15. if I love you *o.*

overpower-s-ed
Mat. 16:18. the forces of death shall never *o.* it
Luke 11:22. someone stronger comes upon him and *o.* him
Acts 19:16. flew at them, *o.* them all

overshadow-ing
Heb. 9:5. *o.* the place of expiation

overstretch-ing
2 Cor. 10:14. not *o.* our commission

overtake-n
John 12:35. so that darkness may not *o.* you
1 Thess. 2:16. retribution has *o.* them
1 Tim. 5:24. whose offences have not yet *o.* them

overthrew
Acts 13:19. in the Canaanite country he *o.* seven nations
Heb. 11:33. through faith they *o.* kingdoms

overthrow-n
Rom. 11:3. they have *o.* thine altars
1 Cor. 1:28. to *o.* the existing order
Rev. 12:10. the accuser of our brothers is *o.*

overwhelm-ing
Rom. 8:37. *o.* victory is ours
2 Cor. 2:7. made so severe as to *o.* him

overwork-ed
2 Cor. 6:5. *o.*, sleepless, starving
  11:23. more *o.* than they

owe-d-ing
John 1:10. the world, though it *o.* its being to him
Acts 24:2. we *o.* it to you that we enjoy unbroken peace
2 Cor. 4:1. which we *o.* entirely to God's mercy
1 Tim. 5:4. repay what they *o.* to their parents
Heb. 7:16. *o.* his priesthood not to a system of earth-bound rules

own-ed
Mat. 11:2. sent his *o.* disciples to him
Mark 13:20. his *o.*, whom he has chosen
Luke 1:51. the deeds his *o.* right arm has done
Acts 4:37. a Cypriot, *o.* an estate
2 Cor. 6:10. penniless, we *o.* the world
1 Thess. 3:13. all those who are his *o.*
2 Thess. 1:10. glorified among his *o.*
Heb. 10:39. we have the faith to make life our *o.*
  11:14. looking for a country of their *o.*
2 Pet. 3:2. God's *o.* prophets

owner
Mat. 9:38. beg the *o.* to send labourers
  20:8. the *o.* of the vineyard
  20:13. the *o.* turned to one of them
  21:40. when the *o.* of the vineyard comes
Mark 12:9. what will the *o.* of the vineyard do
Luke 10:2. beg the *o.* to send labourers

ox
Rev. 4:7. the second like an *o.*

P

pack-s-ed
Mat. 10:10. no *p.* for the road
  22:10. the hall was *p.* with guests
  23:4. they make up heavy *p.*

Mark 6:8. no bread, no *p.*, no money in their belts
Luke 9:3. neither stick nor *p.*
  10:4. carry no purse or *p.*

Luke 12:1. many thousands had gathered, *p.* so close
22:35. barefoot without purse or *p.*
22:36. take it with him, and his *p.* too
Acts 21:15. we *p.* our baggage

paddle-s
Acts 27:40. the lashings of the steering-*p.*

pagan-s
Mat. 18:17. treat him as you would a *p.*
Acts 11:20. began to speak to *p.* as well
18:4. trying to convince both Jews and *p.*
19:10. Jews and *p.*, heard the word of the Lord
19:17. known to everybody in Ephesus, whether Jew or *p.*
20:21. with Jews and *p.* alike I insisted on repentance
1 Cor. 5:1. such as even *p.* do not tolerate
5:10. I was not, of course, referring to *p.*
6:1. *p.* law-courts
12:2. in the days when you were still *p.*
Eph. 4:17. give up living like *p.*
1 Thess. 4:5. *p.* who are ignorant of God
2 Tim. 4:17. the Gospel for the whole *p.* world to hear
1 Pet. 2:12. even *p.* can recognize as good
4:3. the things that men want to do in the *p.* world
3 John 7. they would accept nothing from *p.*

page-s
2 Cor. 3:3. on the *p.* of the human heart

paid
Mat. 20:9. were *p.* the full day's wage
20:10. *p.* the same amount as the others
22:19. the money in which the tax is *p.*
Mark. 15:19. *p.* mock homage to him
Luke 15:17. father's *p.* servants have more food than they can eat
15:19. treat me as one of your *p.* servants
Acts 5:8. were you *p.* such and such a price
7:16. the tomb which Abraham had bought and *p.* for
18:22. *p.* his respects to the church
27:11. the centurion *p.* more attention to the captain
Rom. 1:27. *p.* in their own persons the fitting wage
4:4. they are *p.* as debt
Phil. 4:18. I am *p.* in full
Heb. 12:9. we *p.* due respect to the earthly fathers
Jam. 5:4. the wages you never *p.*
1 Pet. 1:19. the price was *p.* in precious blood

Jude 7. they *p.* the penalty in eternal fire

pail-s
Mat. 13:48. collected the good fish into *p.*

pain-s
Mat. 4:24. every kind of illness, racked with *p.*
8:6. paralysed and racked with *p.*
John 16:21. in *p.* because her time has come
1 Cor. 7:28. *p.* and grief in this bodily life
2 Cor. 2:2. if I cause *p.* to you
2:4. I never meant to cause you *p.*
7:8. I saw that the letter had caused you *p.*
12:7. I was given a sharp *p.* in my body
Gal. 4:11. all the *p.* I spent on you
2 Tim. 1:17. took *p.* to search me out
Heb. 13:17. a happy task for them, and not *p.*
1 Pet. 2:19. the *p.* of undeserved suffering
1 John 4:18. fear brings with it the *p.* of judgement
Rev. 2:22. I will throw her on to a bed of *p.*

painful
2 Cor. 2:1. must not be another *p.* one
Heb. 12:11. at the time it seems *p.*

pair-s
Mat. 4:21. saw another *p.* of brothers
Mark 6:7. sent them out in *p.* on a mission
Luke 10:1. sent them on ahead in *p.*
1 Cor. 6:16. the *p.* shall become one flesh

palace-s
Mat. 11:8. you must look in *p.* for that
Luke 7:25. you must look in *p.* for grand clothes
Acts 23:35. his headquarters in Herod's *p.*

pale
Rom. 2:11. those who have sinned outside the *p.* of the Law of Moses will perish outside its *p.*
3:19. within the *p.* of the law

pall
Rev. 6:12. the sun turned black as a funeral *p.*

palpable
Heb. 12:18. the *p.*, blazing fire of Sinai

pander-s
1 John 2:16. all that *p.* to the appetites

pangs
Mat. 24:8 } the birth-*p.* of the new age
Mark 13:8 } begin

Acts 2:24. setting him free from the *p.* of death

Rom. 8:22. as if in the *p.* of childbirth

Gal. 4:27. you who never knew a mother's *p.*

1 Thess. 5:3. as the *p.* that come upon a woman with child

panic
Luke 21:9. do not fall into a *p.*

parable
Mark 4:30. by what *p.* shall we describe it

parade
Acts 23:23. *p.* three hours after sunset

paralysed
Mat. 4:24. *p.*, were all brought to him

Mark 2:3. a man was brought who was *p.*
2:4, 5, 9, 10 ⎱ *p.* man
Luke 5:18, 24 ⎰
John 5:3. blind, lame, and *p.*

Acts 8:7. many *p.* and crippled folk

paralysis
Acts 9:33. bed-ridden with *p.*

paralytic
Mat. 9:2. a *p.* lying on a bed
9:6. he now addressed the *p.*

parapet
Mat 4:5 ⎱ set him on the *p.* of the
Luke 4:9 ⎰ temple

parent-s
Luke 2:43. his *p.* did not know of this
2:48. his *p.* were astonished to see him

1 John 5:1. to love the *p.* means to love his child

parentage
1 Pet. 1:23. not of mortal *p.* but of immortal

parricide-s
1 Tim. 1:9. at *p.* and matricides

part-s-ed
Mat. 5:29 ⎱ better for you to lose one *p.*
5:30 ⎰ of your body
15:22. a Canaanite woman from those *p.*

Mark 6:10. stay there until you leave those *p.*
10:1. on leaving those *p.*
16:15. go forth to every *p.* of the world

Luke 1:8. to take *p.* in divine service
7:17. the story of what he had done ran through all *p.* of Judaea
24:27. which referred to himself in every *p.* of the scriptures

John 2:24. Jesus for his *p.* would not trust himself to them
14:27. peace is my *p.* gift to you
18:38. for my *p.*,' he said, 'I find no case against him

19:6. said Pilate; 'for my *p.* I find no case against him

Acts 1:1. in the first *p.* of my work Theophilus
15:39. the dispute was so sharp that they *p.* company
16:3. out of consideration for the Jews who lived in those *p.*
21:1. we had *p.* from them and set sail
27:44. some on *p.* of the ship

Rom. 1:13. as I have in other *p.* of the world
6:13. no longer put its several *p.* at sin's disposal
8:22. whole created universe groans in all its *p.*

1 Cor. 6:15. shall I then take from Christ his bodily *p.*

2 Cor. 5:4. our mortal *p.* may be absorbed into life immortal

Eph. 3:6. *p.* of the same body
4:25. all of us are the *p.* of one body
5:11. take no *p.* in the barren deeds of darkness
5:32. I for my *p.* refer it to Christ

Phil. 1:5, the *p.* you have taken in the work of the Gospel

Col. 3:5. put to death those *p.* of you which belong to the earth

1 Thess. 5:23. the God of peace, make you holy in every *p.*

2 Tim. 3:14. for your *p.*, stand by the truths you have learned

Tit. 2:1. for your own *p.*, what you say must be in keeping with wholesome doctrine

Philem. 12. I am sending a *p.* of myself

3 John 8. play our *p.* in spreading the truth

particular-ly
Acts 25:26. *p.* before you, King Agrippa
26:3. *p.* as you are expert in all Jewish matters

Rom. 14:14. if a man considers a *p.* thing impure, then to him it is impure

1 Cor. 12:7. the Spirit is manifested in one *p.* way
15:38. each seed with its own *p.* body

Phil. 4:22. *p.* those who belong to the imperial establishment

1 Tim. 5:17. in *p.* those who labour at preaching

Tit. 1:5. in *p.* should institute elders

partisan-s
Mark 3:6. the *p.* of Herod

partner-s
1 Cor. 7:15. the heathen *p.* wishes for a separation
7:36. if a man has a *p.* in celibacy
7:37. preserve his *p.* in her virginity

1 Cor. 7:38. he who marries his *p*. does well

10:20. become *p*. with demons

Gal. 2:9. accepted Barnabas and myself as *p*.

Phil. 4:15. the only congregation that were my *p*.

Heb. 3:14. we have become Christ's *p*.

party-ies

Mat. 10:4. Simon, a member of the Zealot *p*.

22:16. men of Herod's *p*.

Mark 3:18. Simon, a member of the Zealot *p*.

12:13. men of Herod's *p*. were sent

14:47. one of the *p*. drew his sword

Luke 2:44. thinking that he was with the *p*.

5:29. a large *p*. of tax-gatherers

12:36. their master's return from a wedding-*p*.

14:12. when you give a lunch or dinner *p*.

14:13. when you give a *p*.

14:16. a man was giving a big dinner *p*.

Acts 5:17. the Sadducean *p*.

6:1. the former *p*. complained

15:5. the Pharisaic *p*.

19:38. let the *p*. bring their charges

23:9. belonging to the Pharisaic *p*.

23:21. a *p*. more than forty strong

27:2. in our *p*. was Aristarchus.

Gal. 3:20. not needed for one *p*. acting alone

5:20. dissensions, *p*. intrigues

pass-es-ed-ing

Mat. 7:1. *p*. no judgement

9:27. as he *p*. on Jesus was followed by two blind men

15:17. goes in by the mouth *p*. into the stomach

19:24. a camel to *p*. through the eye of a needle

24:29. as soon as the distress of those days has *p*.

28:1. the Sabbath had *p*.

Mark 7:19. *p*. out into the drain

10:25. a camel to *p*. through the eye of a needle

Luke 6:37. *p*. no judgement

9:47. Jesus knew what was *p*. in their minds

22:58. about an hour *p*. and another spoke

John 1:36. Jesus *p*. by

4:4. he had to *p*. through Samaria

5:27. given the right to *p*. judgement

7:51. permit us to *p*. judgement on a man

8:15. I *p*. judgement on no man

Acts 7:7. I will *p*. judgement,' said God

7:30. after forty years had *p*.

7:38. the living utterances of God, to *p*. on to us

20:16. Paul had decided to *p*. by Ephesus

28:11. three months had *p*. when we set sail

Rom. 2:2. God's judgement is rightly *p*. upon all who commit such crimes

8:3. he has *p*. judgement against sin

14:4. who are you to *p*. judgement

1 Cor. 1:20 ⎱
2:6 ⎰ this *p*. age

3:18. by the standards of this *p*. age

2 Cor. 4:4. the god of this *p*. age

4:18. what is seen *p*. away

Eph. 4:29. no bad language must *p*. your lips

Phil. 4:9. the tradition I have *p*. on

Col. 2:20. *p*. beyond reach of the elemental spirits

1 Thess. 4:1. we *p*. on to you the tradition

1 Tim. 4:11. *p*. on these orders

6:15. that appearance God will bring to *p*.

2 Tim. 3:8. they cannot *p*. the tests of faith

Tit. 3:3. our days were *p*. in malice and envy

Heb. 1:11. they shall *p*. away, but thou endurest

2:18. he himself has *p*. through the test of suffering

11:5. without *p*. through death

11:13. *p*. travellers on earth

Jam. 1:12. having *p*. that test

1:17. no play of *p*. shadows

1 Pet. 1:7. gold *p*. through the assayer's fire

1 John 1:5. we heard from him and *p*. on to you

Rev. 7:14. the men who have *p*. through the great ordeal

11:15. the sovereignty of the world has *p*. to our Lord

passage-s

Mat. 4:14. the *p*. in the prophet Isaiah

Luke 4:17. he opened the scroll and found the *p*.

24:27. the *p*. which referred to himself

Acts 8:32. the *p*. he was reading was this

8:35. Philip began. Starting from this *p*.

13:35. this is borne out by another *p*.

16:10. getting a *p*. to Macedonia

21:7. we made the *p*. from Tyre

2 Cor. 3:17. the Lord of whom this *p*. speaks

Heb. 4:5. in the *p*. above we read

2 Pet. 3:16. they contain some obscure *p*.

passer-s

Mark 15:35. some of the *p*.-by, on hearing this

Acts 17:17. every day with casual
p.-by

passion-s
Mat. 2:16. he fell into a p.
Rom. 1:26. God has given them up to
shameful p.
7:5. the sinful p. evoked by the law
Gal. 5:24. the lower nature with its p.
and desires
Eph. 4:31. have done with spite and p.
Col. 3:8. lay aside all anger, p.
1 Tim. 5:11. their p. draw them away
from Christ
Tit. 3:3. we were slaves to p.

passionately
Phil. 1:20. I p. hope, I shall have no
cause to be ashamed

Passover
Mat. 26:30 ⎱ after singing the P. Hymn
Mark 14:26 ⎰
John 19:31, it was the eve of P.
Acts 12:4. meaning to produce him in
public after P.
20:6. after the P. season

past
Luke 16:9. when money is a thing of
the p.
2 Tim. 3:6. women burdened with a sinful p.
2 Pet. 2:14. p. masters in mercenary
greed

paste
John 9:6. he spat on the ground and
made a p.
9:11. the man called Jesus made a p.
9:14. Jesus made the p. and opened
his eyes
9:15. he spread a p. on my eyes

pasture
Luke 15:4. leave the ninety-nine in the
open p.

patch
Mat. 9:16. a p. of unshrunk cloth on to
an old coat; for then, the p. tears
away
Mark 2:21. a p. of unshrunk cloth on to
an old coat; if he does the p. tears
away
Luke 5:36. a piece from a new cloak to
p. an old one; if he does, . . . and
the p. from the new

path-s
Mat. 21:8. branches from the trees to
spread in his p.
28:9. suddenly Jesus was there in
their p.
Rom. 3:16. ruin and misery lie along
their p.
6:4. set our feet upon the new p. of
life

patience
Rom. 2:4. wealth of kindness, of
tolerance, and of p.
2 Cor. 6:6. our p. and kindliness
Gal. 5:22. love, joy, peace, p.
Col. 3:12. humility, gentleness, p.
1 Tim. 1:16. displaying all his p.
2 Tim. 4:2. the p. that the work of
teaching requires
2 Pet. 3:15. our Lord's p. with us

patient-ly
Mat. 9:33. the p. recovered his speech
Luke 18:7. he listens p.
Acts 18:14. given you Jews a p. hearing
Rom. 9:22. tolerated very p. those vessels
1 Cor. 13:4. love is p.
Eph. 4:2. gentle, and p. too
Heb. 5:2. he is able to bear p. with the
ignorant
1 Pet. 3:20. God waited p. in the days of
Noah
2 Pet. 3:9. he is very p. with you

patriarch-s
John 7:22. not that it originated with
Moses but with the p.
Rom. 9:5. theirs are the p.
11:28. they are his friends for the sake
of the p.
15:8. making good his promises to
the p.

patronize
1 Cor. 4:6. as you p. one and flout the
other

pattern
Acts 7:44. told Moses to make it after
the p.
Rom. 6:17. obedience to the p. of
teaching
12:2. the p. of this present world
1 Cor. 15:48. the man made of dust is
the p. of all men of dust
Jam. 5:10. a p. of patience under ill-
treatment

Paul
Acts 14:3. P. and Barnabas stayed on
17:5. the intention of bringing P. and
Silas before the town assembly

pauper
Luke 12:21. remains a p. in the sight of
God

pause
Rev. 4:8. without a p. they sang

pay-s-ing
Mat. 2:2. we have come to p. him
homage
2:8. that I may go myself and p. him
homage
15:8. this people p. me lip-service
17:27. take that and p. it in
20:2. p. them the usual day's wage

Mat. 20:4. I will *p*. you a fair wage
  20:8. call the labourers and give them their *p*.
  20:14. take your *p*. and go home
  22:17. permitted to *p*. taxes to the Roman Emperor
  22:21. *p*. Caesar what is due to Caesar, and *p*. God what is due to God
  23:3. *p*. attention to their words
Mark 7:6. this people *p*. me lip-service
  12:14. *p*. taxes to the Roman Emperor
  12:15. shall we *p*. or not
  12:17. *p*. Caesar what is due to Caesar, and *p*. God what is due to God
Luke 3:14. make do with your *p*.
  10:7. the worker earns his *p*.
  16:31. they will *p*. no heed even if someone should rise from the dead
  18:12. I *p*. tithes on all that I get
  20:21. you *p*. deference to no one
  20:22. *p*. taxes to the Roman Emperor
  20:25. *p*. Caesar what is due to Caesar, and *p*. God what is due to God
  22:5. undertook to *p*. him a sum of money
  23:41. we are *p*. the price for our misdeeds
John 4:36. the reaper is drawing his *p*.
  5:23. all should *p*. the same honour to the Son as to the Father
  12:47. hears my words and *p*. no regard to them
Acts 21:24. *p*. their expenses
Rom. 2:6. he will *p*. every man for what he has done
  6:23. sin *p*. a wage
  13:7. *p*. tax and toll
1 Cor. 3:8. his own *p*. for his own labour
  9:17. I should be earning my *p*.
  9:18. what is my *p*.
2 Cor. 1:6. the price we *p*. for your consolation
  12:14. preparing to *p*. you a third visit
Eph. 5:33. she *p*. her husband all respect
1 Thess. 5:15. see to it that no one *p*. back wrong for wrong
2 Thess. 3:8. board and lodging from anyone without *p*. for it
1 Tim. 5:18. the workman earns his *p*.
Heb. 1:6. let all the angels of God *p*. him homage
  2:1. we are bound to *p*. all the more heed
1 Pet. 3:7. *p*. honour to the woman's body
2 Pet. 2:15. who consented to take *p*. for doing wrong
Jude 11. Balaam's error for *p*.
Rev. 14:7. fear God and *p*. him homage
  18:6. *p*. her back in her own coin

payment-s
Luke 23:2. opposing the *p*. of taxes to Caesar
Phil. 4:15. my partners in *p*. and receipts

peace
Mat. 5:24. make your *p*. with your brother
  10:12. wish the house *p*. as you enter it
Acts 9:31. left in *p*. to build up its strength
  24:2. we owe it to you that we enjoy unbroken *p*.
Rom. 16:16 ⎱ greet one another with the
1 Cor.16:20 ⎰ kiss of *p*.

peal-s
Rev. 4:5. flashes of lightning and *p*. of thunder
  8:5. *p*. of thunder
  11:19. flashes of lightning and *p*. of thunder
  16:18, there followed flashes of lightning and *p*. of thunder

peculiar
Acts 25:19. their *p*. religion

peered
John 20:5. he *p*. in and saw the linen wrappings
  20:11. she *p*. into the tomb

penalty
Acts 25:11. I do not ask to escape the death *p*.
2 Cor. 2:6. the *p*. on which the general meeting has agreed
Heb. 10:29. severe a *p*. that man will deserve
Jude 7. paid the *p*. in eternal fire

pending
Gal. 3:19. *p*. the arrival of the 'issue'
  3:23. *p*. the revelation of faith

penniless
2 Cor. 6:10. *p*., we own the world

penny
Mat. 10:29. are not sparrows two a *p*.

people
Mat. 27:52. many of God's *p*. arose from sleep
Mark 2:17. I did not come to invite virtuous *p*.
Frequent use of the word 'people'

perceive
John 12:40. *p*. with their minds
Rom. 7:23. I *p*. that there is in my bodily members a different law
Eph. 3:4. *p*. that I understand the secret of Christ
Heb. 3:19. we *p*. that it was unbelief

Heb. 11:3. we *p*. that the universe was fashioned by the word of God

perception-s
Heb. 5:14. their *p*. are trained by long use

perdition
Mat. 7:13. the gate is wide that leads to *p*.
2 Cor. 2:15. those who are on the way to *p*.
4:3. those on the way to *p*.
2 Pet. 2:3. *p*. waits for them with un-sleeping eyes

perfect-ly
John 3:29. this *p*. joy, is now mine
Acts 23:1. with a *p*. clear conscience before God
24:5. we have found this man to be a *p*. pest
2 Cor. 7:4. I am *p*. frank with you
2 Thess. 3:4. we feel *p*. confidence about you
Heb. 7:28. the Son, made *p*. now for ever
1 Pet. 1:13. *p*. self-controlled

perform-ed-ing
Mat. 7:22. in your name *p*. many miracles
11:20. in which most of his miracles had been *p*.
11:21. if the miracles that were *p*. in you had been *p*. in Tyre and Sidon
11:23. if the miracles had been *p*. in Sodom which were *p*. in you
Luke 10:13. the miracles that were *p*. in you had been *p*. in Tyre and Sidon
23:8. hoping to see some miracle *p*. by him
John 2:23. saw the signs that he *p*.
3:2. no one could *p*. these signs of yours
4:54. the second sign which Jesus *p*.
6:2. the signs he *p*. in healing the sick
6:14. the sign Jesus had *p*.
7:31. *p*. more signs than this man
11:47. this man is *p*. many signs
12:18. heard of this sign that he had *p*.
12:37. the many signs which Jesus had *p*.
16:2. will suppose that he is *p*. a religious duty
20:30. signs that Jesus *p*. in the presence of his disciples
Acts 4:22. upon whom this miracle of healing had been *p*.
8:6. saw the miracles that he *p*.
Rom. 7:17. no longer I who *p*. the action
1 Cor. 3:5. each of us *p*. the task which the Lord allotted to him
9:13. those who *p*. the temple service
1 Tim. 5:10. evidence of good deeds *p*.
Heb. 10:11. *p*. his service daily

Rev. 13:14. the miracles it was allowed to *p*.

perfume-s
Mark 14:3. a small bottle of very costly *p*.
14:5. the *p*. might have been sold for thirty pounds
Luke 23:56. prepared spices and *p*.
John 12:3. Mary brought a pound of very costly *p*.
12:5. why was this *p*. not sold
Rev. 18:13. incense, *p*. and frankincense

perhaps
Luke 3:15. John, whether *p*. he was the Messiah
20:13. my own dear son; *p*. they will respect him

peril
2 Cor. 1:10. from such mortal *p*. God delivered us

period
Luke 1:23. when his *p*. of duty was completed
Acts 1:3. over a *p*. of forty days he appeared
6:1. during this *p*., when disciples were growing
11:27. during this *p*. some prophets came down
13:31. a *p*. of many days during which he appeared
21:26. when the *p*. of purification would end
21:27. before the *p*. of seven days
1 Pet. 1:20. in this last *p*. of time he was made manifest

perished
Acts 5:37. he too *p*. and his whole following was scattered

perishable
1 Cor. 15:42. sown in the earth as a *p*. thing
15:50. the *p*. cannot possess immor-tality
15:53. this *p*. being must be clothed with the imperishable
1 Pet. 1:18. no *p*. stuff, like gold or silver

perjury
Mat. 15:19. *p*., slander—these all pro-ceed from the heart

permanent
John 8:35. the slave has no *p*. standing
Heb. 13:14. here we have no *p*. home

permission
Mat. 19:8. Moses gave you *p*. to divorce your wives
John 19:38. Pilate gave the *p*.

Acts 21:39. I ask your *p*. to speak to the people
21:40. when *p*. had been given
26:1. *p*. to speak for yourself

permit-ted
Mat. 12:10. is it *p*. to heal on the Sabbath
12:12. *p*. to do good on the Sabbath
22:17. are we or are we not *p*. to pay taxes
Mark 3:4. *p*. to do good or to do evil
7:12. no longer *p*. to do anything for his father or mother
10:4. Moses *p*. a man to divorce his wife
12:14. *p*. to pay taxes to the Roman Emperor
Luke 6:9. is it *p*. to do good or to do evil
14:3. is it *p*. to cure people on the Sabbath
20:22. *p*. to pay taxes to the Roman Emperor
John 7:51. *p*. us to pass judgement on a man
2 Cor. 10:13. *p*. us to come as far as Corinth
1 Tim. 2:12. I do not *p*. a woman to be a teacher

perpetual
Heb. 7:24. the priesthood which Jesus holds is *p*.

perplexed
Mark 6:20. listening left him greatly *p*.
Acts 2:12. all amazed and *p*.

perseverance
Luke 8:15. by their *p*. yield a harvest

persevere-s
Gal. 3:10. cursed are all who do not *p*.
Col. 4:2. *p*. in prayer, with mind awake
1 Tim. 4:16. *p*. in them, keeping close watch on yourself
Rev. 2:26. who *p*. in doing my will to the end
22:11. let the good man *p*. in his goodness

persist
Rom. 6:1. shall we *p*. in sin
12:12. *p*. in prayer
Heb. 10:26. if we *p*. in sin after receiving

persistence
Luke 18:5. before she wears me out with her *p*.
Rom. 2:7. steady *p*. in well-doing

person-s
Mat. 10:11. look for some worthy *p*.
Luke 7:7. I did not presume to approach you in *p*.
14:8. some *p*. more distinguished than yourself

24:18. are you the only *p*. staying in Jerusalem not to know
Acts 4:34. they had never a needy *p*. among them
7:14. Jacob and all his relatives, seventy-five *p*.
10:47. these *p*., who have received the Holy Spirit
15:1. certain *p*. who had come down from Judaea
16:37. let them come in *p*. and escort us out
24:20. for these *p*. here present to say
Rom. 1:27. paid in their own *p*. the fitting wage
3:24. his act of liberation in the *p*. of Christ Jesus
7:1. a *p*. is subject to the law so long as he is alive
13:1. every *p*. must submit to the supreme authorities
1 Cor. 4:18. certain *p*. who are filled with self-importance
5:11. you should not even eat with any such *p*.
14:23. some uninstructed *p*.
16:3. *p*. approved by you
16:16. give their due position to such *p*.
2 Cor. 9:7. each *p*. should give as he has decided
13:2. I gave it in *p*.
Gal. 1:7. there are *p*. who unsettle your minds
3:28. you are all one *p*. in Christ Jesus
4:17. the *p*. I have referred to are envious of you
Phil. 1:20. the greatness of Christ will shine out clearly in my *p*.
Col 4:6. study how best to talk with each *p*.
1 Tim. 1:3. certain *p*. to give up teaching erroneous doctrines
Heb. 11:13. all these *p*. died in faith
1 Pet. 2:24. in his own *p*. he carried our sins to the gallows
3:20. in the ark a few *p*., eight in all
2 John 7. these are the *p*. described as the Antichrist
Jude 4. certain *p*. who have wormed their way in
19. spiritual and unspiritual *p*.
Rev. 3:4. a few *p*. in Sardis who have not polluted their clothing

personal
2 Cor. 12:20. *p*. rivalries, backbiting and gossip
Gal. 2:6. God does not recognize these *p*. distinctions
Phil. 1:17. moved by *p*. rivalry
2:3. rivalry and *p*. vanity

persuasion
Acts 19:8. using argument and *p*.

perturbed
Mat. 2:3. King Herod was greatly *p.*
Luke 24:38. he said, 'Why are you
   so *p.*
1 Pet. 3:14. have no fear of them: do
   not be *p.*

pervade-d
Rom. 5:12. death *p.* the whole human
   race

perverse
Mark 9:19. what an unbelieving and *p.*
   generation
1 Pet. 2:18. even when they are *p.*

perversion
Rom. 1:27. the fitting wage of such *p.*
1 Cor. 6:9. homosexual *p.*

pervert-s-ed
Acts 19:26. has *p.* crowds of people
1 Tim. 1:10. *p.,* kidnappers, liars
Jude 4. they *p.* the free favour of our
   God

pestilence
Rev. 6:8. to kill by sword and by famine,
   by *p.*
18:8. *p.,* bereavement, famine

petal-s
James 1:11. the flower withers, its *p.* fall

Peter
Mark 16:8. delivered all these instructions briefly to *P.*
John 1:42. you shall be called Cephas'
   (that is, *P.*
Acts 1:20. the text I have in mind', *P.*
   continued
8:17. *P.* and John laid their hands on
   them

petition-s
Luke 7:4. pressed their *p.* earnestly
Phil. 4:6. in prayer and *p.* with thanks-
   giving

Phoenician
Mark 7:26. she was a Gentile, a *P.* of
   Syria

physical-ly
1 Cor. 6:16. becomes *p.* one with her
Col. 2:11. circumcised, not in a *p.* sense

pick-ed
Mat. 7:16. can grapes be *p.* from briars
14:20. scraps left over, which they
   p. up
15:37. they *p.* up., were enough to fill
   seven baskets
16:9 ⎫ how many basketfuls you *p.*
16:10 ⎭ up
Mark 6:43. twelve great basketfuls of
   scraps were *p.* up
8:19. how many basketfuls of scraps
   did you *p.* up

Luke 6:44. you do not *p.* grapes from
   brambles
9:17. the scraps they left were *p.* up
17:31. must not come down to *p.* them
   up
John 8:59. they *p.* up stones to throw at
   him
10:31. the Jews *p.* up stones to stone
   him
Acts 20:9. was *p.* up for dead
2 Tim. 4:11. *p.* up Mark and bring him
   with you
Tit. 3:2. to slander no one, not to *p.*
   quarrels

picture
Mat. 13:45. another *p.* of the kingdom
   of Heaven
Mark. 4:30. how shall we *p.* the kingdom of God
1 Cor. 4:6. into this general *p.,* my
   friends

piece-s
Mat. 7:6. turn and tear you to *p.*
22:19. they handed him a silver *p.*
24:51. will cut him in *p.*
Mark 12:15. fetch me a silver *p.*
Luke 7:41. owed him five hundred
   silver *p.*
10:35. he produced two silver *p.*
12:46. will cut him in *p.*
20:18. on that stone will be dashed
   to *p.*
20:24. show me a silver *p.*
John 6:12. collect the *p.* left over
6:13. filled twelve baskets with the *p.*
   left
13:26. the man to whom I give this *p.*
   of bread
19:23. the tunic was seamless, woven
   in one *p.*
Acts 27:41. pounded to *p.* by the
   breakers
Rom. 4:4. if a man does a *p.* of work
2 Cor. 9:12. as a *p.* of willing service

piety
Col. 2:23. an air of wisdom, with its
   forced *p.*
1 Tim. 6:11. pursue justice, *p.,* fidelity
2 Tim. 3:2. no gratitude, no *p.*
2 Pet. 1:7. fortitude with *p., p.* with
   brotherly kindness

pig-s
Mat. 7:6. do not feed your pearls to *p.*
8:30. a large herd of *p.* was feeding
8:31. send us into that herd of *p.*
8:32. and went into the *p.*
Mark 5:11. *p.* feeding on the hill-side
5:12. send us among the *p.*
5:13. and went into the *p.*
5:16. what had happened to the *p.*
Luke 8:32. a large herd of *p.* near by,
   feeding on the hill; and the spirits

begged him to let them go into
these *p.*
Luke 8:33. and went into the *p.*
15:15. to his farm to mind the *p.*
15:16. with the pods that the *p.* were
eating

pigeons
Mat. 21:12. the dealers in *p.*
Mark 11:15. the seats of the dealers in *p.*
John 2:14. dealers in cattle, sheep, and *p.*
2:16. he turned on the dealers in *p.*

pile-d
Mat. 23:4. heavy packs and *p.* them on
men's shoulders
Jam. 5:3. you have *p.* up wealth
Rev. 18:5. her sins are *p.* high as heaven

pilfer
John 12:6. *p.* the money put into the
common purse
Tit. 2:10. not to *p.*, but to show themselves strictly honest

pilgrim-s
John 12:12. *p.* who had come to the
festival

pilgrimage
Luke 2:42. they made the *p.* as usual
Acts 8:27. he had been to Jerusalem on
a *p.*
24:11. I went up to Jerusalem on a *p.*

pillar
1 Cor. 10:1. our ancestors were all under
the *p.* of cloud

pinch
Luke 15:14. he began to feel the *p.*

pious
Phil. 3:6. in *p.* zeal, a persecutor of the
church

pit-s
2 Pet. 2:4. consigned them to the dark
p. of hell

pitch
Acts 26:11. my fury rose to such a *p.*

pitfall
1 Cor. 8:9. this liberty of yours does not
become a *p.* for the weak

pitiful
Rev. 3:17. though you do not know it,
you are the most *p.* wretch

pity-ied
Mat. 9:27. Son of David, have *p.* on us
9:36. the sight of the people moved
him to *p.*
15:22. Sir! have *p.* on me
17:15. have *p.*, sir, on my son
18:27. the master was so moved
with *p.*
20:30. have *p.* on us, Son of David

20:31. Sir, have *p.* on us, have *p.* on us
Mark 9:22. take *p.* upon us and help us
10:47. Son of David, Jesus, have *p.*
on me
10:48. Son of David, have *p.* on me
Luke 10:33. when he saw him was moved
to *p.*
16:24. Abraham, my father', he called
out, 'take *p.* on me
17:13. Jesus, Master, take *p.* on us
18:38. Jesus, Son of David, have *p.* on
me
18:39. Son of David, have *p.* on me
Rom. 1:31. without natural affection
and without *p.*
9:15. where I *p.*, I will *p.*
1 Cor. 15:19. we of all men are most to
be *p.*
Heb. 10:28. he is put to death without *p.*
Jude 22. some doubting souls who need
your *p.*
23. your *p.* must be mixed with fear

place-s-d-ing
Mat. 2:9. stopped above the *p.* where
the child lay
5:19. the lowest *p.* in the kingdom of
Heaven
6:6. your Father who is there in the
secret *p.*
6:18. your Father who is in the
secret *p.*
8:12. the *p.* of wailing and grinding of
teeth
12:21. in him the nations shall *p.* their
hope
13:50. the *p.* of wailing and grinding
of teeth
15:33. where in this lonely *p.* can we
find bread
22:13. the *p.* of wailing and grinding
of teeth
23:6. they like to have *p.* of honour
at feasts
24:51. find his *p.* among the hypocrites
25:30. the *p.* of wailing and grinding
of teeth
25:33. he will *p.* the sheep on his
right hand
27:29. a crown of thorns they *p.* it on
his head
27:37. over his head was *p.* the inscription
Mark. 2:4. opened up the roof over the
p. where Jesus was
6:1. he left that *p.* and went to his
home
6:11. at any *p.* where they will not
receive you
6:31. to some lonely *p.* where you can
rest
6:55. the sick on stretchers to any *p.*
where he was
7:24. then he left that *p.*

Mark 8:4. with bread in this lonely *p.*
11:23. says to this mountain, 'Be lifted from your *p.*
12:39. *p.* of honour at feasts
13:14. usurping a *p.* which is not his
14:60. the Hight Priest stood up in his *p.*
15:17. a crown of thorns, *p.* it on his head
Luke 5:16. withdraw to lonely *p.* for prayer
7:36. took his *p.* at table
7:38. she took her *p.* behind him
8:29. with the devil in charge made off to the solitary *p.*
13:31. you should leave this *p.*
14:7. trying to secure the *p.* of honour
14:8. do not sit down in the *p.* of honour
14:10. sit down in the lowest *p.*
20:35. worthy of a *p.* in the other world
20:46. *p.* of honour at feasts
22:14. he took his *p.* at table
23:19. a rising that had taken *p.* in the city
John 1:28. this took *p.* at Bethany
5:2. a *p.* with five colonnades
6:62. the Son of Man ascending to the *p.* where he was before
19:2. a crown of thorns and *p.* it on his head
20:25. put my finger into the *p.* where the nails were
Acts 1:17. had his *p.* in this ministry
1:26. assigned a *p.* among the twelve apostles
5:12. wonderful things took *p.*
5:20. go, take your *p.* in the temple
8:13. miracles that were taking *p.*
16:13. thought there would be a *p.* of prayer
16:16. on our way to the *p.* of prayer
26:18. a *p.* with those whom God has made his own
28:7. that *p.* there were lands belonging to the chief magistrate
Rom. 3:2. in the first *p.*, the Jews were entrusted with the oracles of God
3:31. *p.* law itself on a firmer footing
11:20. by faith you hold your *p.*
12:10. give pride of *p.* to one another
14:13. no obstacle or stumbling-block be *p.* in a brother's way
15:20. *p.* where the very name of Christ has not been heard
1 Cor. 1:29. there is no *p.* for human pride in the presence of God
4:11. we wander from *p.* to *p.*
12:18. each limb and organ to its own *p.*
12:28. in the first *p.* apostles, in the second *p.* prophets
14:34. keep their *p.* as the law directs

15:23. each in his own proper *p.*
2 Cor. 1:9. not to *p.* reliance on ourselves
7:2. do make a *p.* for us in your hearts
Gal. 4:12. put yourselves in my *p.*, my brothers
Eph. 5:4. these things are out of *p.*
Phil. 2:3. personal vanity should have no *p.*
1 Tim. 5:11. younger widows may not be *p.* on the roll
2 Tim. 2:18. saying that our resurrection has already taken *p.*
3:4. put pleasure in the *p.* of God
Heb. 4:12. the *p.* where life and spirit, joints and marrow, divide
9:2. this is called the Holy *P.*
9:3. called the Most Holy *P.*
Jam. 2:2. Your *p.* of worship
2 Pet. 2:17. the *p.* reserved for them
1 John 1:10. then his word has no *p.* in us
Jude 13. the *p.* for ever reserved for them
Rev. 13:10. the fortitude and faithfulness of God's people have their *p.*
14:12. the fortitude of God's people has its *p.*

plague-s
Luke 21:11. famines and *p.* in many places
Rev. 9:10. power to *p.* mankind
9:18. by these three *p.* that is, by the fire, the smoke, and the sulphur

plain-ly
Mat. 5:37. *p.* 'Yes' or 'No' is all you need to say
Mark 8:32. he spoke about it *p.*
Luke 23:41. for us it is *p.* justice
Acts 2:29. let me tell you *p.*
Rom. 1:19. all that may be known of God by men lies *p.*
1 Cor. 14:16. the *p.* man who is present
2 Cor. 3:3. it is *p.* that you are a letter that has come from Christ
Gal. 1:20. what I write is *p.* truth
Phil. 3:15. God will make *p.* to you
2 Cor. 7:12. help to make *p.* to you
Col. 4:4. pray that I may make the secret *p.*
1 Tim. 4:15. that your progress may be *p.* to all
Jam. 5:12. let it be *p.* 'Yes' or 'No'

plan-s-ned-ning
Mat. 22:15. a *p.* to trap him in his own words
27:1. met in conference to *p.* the death of Jesus
Mark 14:1. some cunning *p.* to seize him
15:1. the chief priests, having made their *p.*

Acts 2:23. by the deliberate will and *p.* of God
9:24. their *p.* became known to Saul
9:29. they *p.* to murder him
12:6. the very night before Herod had *p.*
23:20. the Jews have made a *p.* among themselves
25:3. they were *p.* an ambush to kill him
27:39. they *p.*, if possible, to run the ship ashore
27:43. prevented them from carrying out their *p.*
Rom. 1:13. I have often *p.* to come
2 Cor. 1:17. when I frame my *p.*
1 Tim. 1:4. cannot make known God's *p.* for us
Heb. 11:40. God had made a better *p.*

plane
1 Cor. 3:1. on the merely natural *p.*
3:3. you are still on the merely natural *p.*

plank-s
Mat. 7:3. never a thought for the great *p.* in your own
7:4. there is that *p.* in your own
7:5. take the *p.* out of your own eye
Luke 6:41. the great *p.* in your own
6:42. blind to the *p.* in your own? You hypocrite! First take the *p.* out of your own eye
Acts 27:44. some on *p.*

plant-ed
Mat. 13:32. bigger than any garden-*p.*
Mark 4:32. grows taller than any other *p.*
Jam. 1:21. accept the message *p.* in your hearts
Rev. 9:4. to do no injury to the grass or to any *p.*
10:2. his right foot he *p.* on the sea

plated
Heb. 9:4. ark of the covenant *p.* all over with gold

play-ed-ing
1 Cor. 14:7. how can you tell what tune is being *p.*
Gal. 2:13. *p.* false like the rest
Heb. 6:18. God could not possibly *p.* us false
Jam. 1:4. give fortitude full *p.*
1:17. no *p.* of passing shadows
3 John 8. *p.* our part in spreading the truth
Rev. 14:2. the sound of harpers *p.* on their harps

players
Mat. 9:23. saw the flute-*p.*
Rev. 18:22. flute-*p.* and trumpeters

plea
Acts 25:8. Paul's *p.* was

plead-s-ed-ing
Mark 5:23. *p.* with him
Luke 15:28. his father came out and *p.* with him
John 4:49. the officer *p.* with him
Acts 2:40. *p.* with them
Rom. 8:26. the Spirit himself is *p.* for us
8:27. he *p.* for God's own people
8:34. indeed *p.* our cause
11:2. Elijah *p.* with God against Israel
Heb. 7:25. always living to *p.* on their behalf
1 John 2:1. we have one to *p.* our cause with the Father

pleasant
Heb. 12:11. discipline, no doubt, is never *p.*

please-s-d-ing
Mark 14:11. they were greatly *p.*, and promised him money
Luke 14:17. *p.* come, everything is now ready
14:18, 19. *p.* accept my apologies
22:5. they were greatly *p.* and undertook to pay him a sum of money
23:8. when Herod saw Jesus he was greatly *p.*
Acts 7:20. he was a fine child, and *p.* to God
8:34. tell me, *p.*, who it is that the prophet is speaking about
9:38. *p.* come over to us without delay
1 Cor. 7:36. he may do as he *p.*
14:5. *p.* for you all to use the tongues of ecstasy, but better *p.*
Eph. 5:2. sacrifice whose fragrance is *p.* to God
Phil. 4:18. an acceptable sacrifice, *p.* to God
Jam. 2:3. *p.* take this seat
3 John 6. *p.* help them on their journey

pleasure-s
1 Cor. 16:17, it is a great *p.* to me
Gal. 1:15. in his good *p.* God, who had set me apart
Jam. 4:3. to spend what you get on your *p.*

pledge-d
2 Cor. 1:22. as a *p.* of what is to come
5:5. as a *p.* of it he has given us the Spirit
Eph. 1:14. that Spirit is the *p.*
Col. 2:14. the bond which *p.* us

plentiful-ly
John 3:23. water was *p.* in that region
Tit. 3:6. he sent down the Spirit upon us *p.*

plenty
Mat. 7:13. there is *p.* of room on the road
Luke 12:19. you have *p.* of good things laid by
John 6:10. there was *p.* of grass there
15:8. that you may bear fruit in *p.*
Acts 14:17. gives you food and good cheer in *p.*
Phil. 4:12. I know what it is to have *p.* . . . *p.* and want
Jam. 2:16. have *p.* to eat

plight-ed
Mat. 12:45. the man's *p.* is worse than before
Luke 11:26. in the end the man's *p.* is worse
Rom. 1:31. no fidelity to their *p.* word
2 Tim. 1:12. that is the reason for my present *p.*
2 Pet. 2:20. their *p.* in the end is worse than before

plot-ted-ting
Mat. 12:14. laid a *p.* to do away with him
Mark 3:6. began *p.* against him
John 4:5. near the *p.* of ground which Jacob gave
11:53. from that day on they *p.* his death
Acts 1:18. Judas, be it noted, after buying a *p.* of land
4:25. the peoples lay their *p.* in vain
9:23. the Jews hatched a *p.* against his life
20:3. a *p.* was laid against him by the Jews

ploughman
1 Cor. 9:10. in the sense that the *p.*

plucked
Acts 27:36. they all *p.* up courage

plunder
Luke 11:22. divides the *p.*

plunge-d
John 5:4. the first to *p.* in after this disturbance
16:6. you are *p.* into grief
16:20. you will be *p.* in grief
21:7. *p.* into the sea
Rom. 1:21. their misguided minds are *p.* in darkness
1 Tim. 6:9. harmful desires which *p.* men into ruin
1 Pet. 4:4. no longer *p.* with them into all this reckless dissipation
Jude 11. *p.* into Balaam's error for pay
Rev. 2:22. *p.* her lovers into terrible suffering
16:10. its kingdom was *p.* in darkness

plural
Gal. 3:16. it does not say 'issues' in the *p.*

ply
Luke 11:53. to *p.* him with a host of questions

pod-s
Luke 15:16. with the *p.* that the pigs were eating

point-s-ed-ing
Mat. 12:49. *p.* to the disciples, he said
24:1. *p.* to the temple buildings
Mark 7:4. many other *p.* on which they have a traditional rule
14:59. even on this *p.* their evidence did not agree
Luke 5:7. loaded both boats to the *p.* of sinking
19:43. encircle you and hem you in at every *p.*
21:24. fall at the sword's *p.*
John 5:39. their testimony *p.* to me
Acts 5:23. the jail securely locked at every *p.*
20:3. on the *p.* of embarking for Syria
22:3. trained in every *p.* of our ancestral law
23:27. was on the *p.* of being murdered
25:19. certain *p.* of disagreement with him
Rom. 14:1. without attempting to settle doubtful *p.*
14:5. on such a *p.* everyone should have reached conviction
2 Cor. 2:3. the *p.* I made in my letter
2:5. not to labour the *p.*
7:11. at every *p.* you have cleared yourselves
Phil. 3:15. any *p.* on which you think differently
1 Tim. 1:18. that prophetic utterance which first *p.* you out to me
2 Tim. 2:9. to the *p.* of being shut up like a common criminal
Tit. 3:8. the *p.* I should wish you to insist on
Philem. 8. make bold to *p.* out your duty
Heb. 8:1. this is my main *p.*
9:9. this is symbolic, *p.* to the present time
11:17. on the *p.* of offering his only son
12:4. to the *p.* of shedding your blood
12:17. although he strove, to the *p.* of tears
Jam. 2:18. another who *p.* to his deeds
1 Pet. 1:11. to which the spirit of Christ in them *p.*
2 Pet. 3:8. here is one *p.*, my friends, which you must not lose sight of

pointless
Tit. 3:9. they are unprofitable and *p.*

poison-ed
Mark 16:18. or drink any deadly *p.*
Acts 14:2. *p.* their minds against the Christians
Heb. 12:15. noxious weed growing up to *p.* the whole
Rev. 8:11. numbers died of the water because it had been *p.*

police
Luke 22:4 } officers of the temple *p.*
    22:52 }
John 7:32. sent temple *p.* to arrest him
  7:45. the temple *p.* came back to the chief priests
  18:3. *p.* provided by the chief priests
  18:12. the Jewish *p.*, now arrested Jesus
  18:18. the *p.* had made a charcoal fire
  18:22. one of the *p.* struck him on the face
Acts 5:22. the *p.* who went to the prison failed to find them
  5:26. the Controller went off with the *p.*

policy
Luke 23:51. upright man, who had dissented from their *p.*

pollute-s-d
1 Cor. 8:7. their conscience, being weak, is *p.*
Jam. 3:6. it *p.* our whole being
Rev. 3:4. who have not *p.* their clothing

pollution
1 Pet. 3:21. baptism is not the washing away of bodily *p.*

pomp
Rev. 18:7. her voluptuous *p.*

pompous
1 Tim. 6:4. I call him a *p.* ignoramus

ponder-ed
Luke 9:44. *p.* my words
1 Pet. 1:10. the theme which the prophets *p.*

poor-er
Mat. 7:17. a *p.* tree bad fruit
  7:18. or a *p.* tree good fruit
Luke 16:20. lay a *p.* man named Lazarus
  16:22. one day the *p.* man died
John 2:10. before serving the *p.* sort
1 Cor. 11:22. you shame its *p.* members
2 Cor. 7:5. no relief for this *p.* body of ours
Gal. 4:14. the state of my *p.* body
Col. 1:24. my *p.* human flesh

populace
John 11:48. the whole *p.* will believe in him
Acts 12:22. the *p.* shouted back
  17:5. from the dregs of the *p.*

popular
Mark 12:12. they were afraid of *p.* feeling
1 Tim. 3:1. there is a *p.* saying

population-s
Luke 8:37. whole *p.* of the Gergesene district
Acts 19:10. the whole *p.* of the province of Asia
Rev. 17:15. an ocean of peoples and *p.*

port-s
Acts 21:3. Cyprus, and leaving it on our *p.* beam
  27:2. bound for *p.* in the province of Asia

portent-s
Luke 21:11. in the sky terrors and great *p.*
  21:25. *p.* will appear in sun, moon, and stars
John 4:48. will none of you ever believe without seeing signs and *p.*
Acts 2:19. I will show *p.* in the sky
  2:22. made known to you through miracles, *p.*
Rev. 12:1. a great *p.* in heaven, a woman robed with the sun
  12:3. a second *p.* appeared in heaven
  15:1. astonishing *p.* in heaven

portion
Acts 2:17. I will pour out upon everyone a *p.* of my spirit
  2:18. with a *p.* of my spirit
Rom. 11:16. if the first *p.* of dough is consecrated
Eph. 4:7. his due *p.* of Christ's bounty
Heb. 7:2. Abraham gave him a tithe of everything as his *p.*

pose-d
Acts 13:6. a sorcerer, a Jew who *p.* as a prophet

position
Mat. 19:10. if that is the *p.* with husband and wife
Luke 7:8. in my *p.* I am myself under orders
Acts 21:22. what is the *p.*, then
1 Cor. 16:16. give their due *p.* to such persons
2 Cor. 10:15. we may attain a *p.* among you

possess-es-ed
Mat. 11:18. they say, 'He is *p.*
  25:34. enter and *p.* the kingdom
Mark 1:23. a man in the synagogue *p.* by an unclean spirit
  3:22. he is *p.* by Beelzebub
  3:30. they had declared that he was *p.*
  5:2. a man *p.* by an unclean spirit

Mark 7:25. whose young daughter was *p*.
  9:17. *p*. by a spirit which makes him speechless
Luke 1:17. *p*. by the spirit and power of Elijah
  4:33. a man in the synagogue *p*. by a devil
  7:33. you say, 'He is *p*.
  8:27. a man from the town who was *p*. by devils
  13:11. a woman there *p*. by a spirit
John 3:15. faith in him may in him *p*. eternal life
  6:40. puts his faith in him shall *p*. eternal life
  6:47. the believer *p*. eternal life
  6:54. eats my flesh and drinks my blood *p*. eternal life
  7:20. the crowd answered, 'You are *p*.
  8:48. you are a Samaritan, and that you are *p*.
  8:49. I am not *p*.,' said Jesus
  8:52. now we are certain that you are *p*.
  10:20. he is *p*.
  10:21. no one *p*. by an evil spirit could speak like this
  20:31. through this faith you may *p*. eternal life
Acts 5:3. Satan so *p*. your mind that you lied to the Holy Spirit
  19:13. on those *p*. by evil spirits
  21:9. daughters, who *p*. the gift of prophecy
Rom. 2:14. Gentiles who do not *p*. the law
  8:9. does not *p*. the Spirit of Christ, he is no Christian
  12:6. the gifts we *p*. differ
1 Cor. 1:5. you *p*. full knowledge
  2:16. we, however, *p*. the mind of Christ
  4:7. what do you *p*. that was not given you
  6:10. or swindlers, will *p*. the kingdom of God
  13:3. I may dole out all I *p*.
  15:50. flesh and blood can never *p*. the kingdom of God, and the perishable cannot *p*. immortality
2 Cor. 5:1. we *p*. a building which God has provided
2 Thess. 2:14. *p*. for your own the splendour of our Lord Jesus Christ
1 Tim. 4:14. do not neglect the spiritual endowment you *p*.
  6:16. he alone *p*. immortality
2 Pet. 1:8. gifts which, if you *p*. and foster them
1 John 5:12. he who *p*. the Son has life indeed; he who does not *p*. the Son of God has not that life
2 John 9. *p*. both the Father and the Son

possession-s
Mat. 5:5. have the earth for their *p*.
  19:21. sell your *p*., and give to the poor
Luke 8:30. many devils had taken *p*. of him
  11:21. his *p*. are safe
  12:33. sell your *p*. and give in charity
  14:33. taking leave of all his *p*.
  19:8. I give half my *p*. to charity
John 19:23. the soldiers, having crucified Jesus, took *p*. of his clothes
1 Cor. 6:9. the unjust will never come into *p*. of the kingdom
Heb. 10:34. you cheerfully accepted the seizure of your *p*.
  11:13. not yet in *p*. of the things promised
Jam. 5:1. you who have great *p*.
Jude 9. disputing the *p*. of Moses's body

possible
Mat. 26:42. My Father, if it is not *p*. for this cup to pass
Mark 9:22. if it is at all *p*. for you, take pity upon us
John 3:4. how is it *p*.,' said Nicodemus, 'for a man to be born when he is old
  3:9. Nicodemus replied, 'How is this *p*.
Rom. 1:20. no *p*. defence for their conduct
1 Cor. 9:19. to win over as many as *p*.
1 Thess. 5:13. in the highest *p*. esteem and affection

possibly
Luke 22:23. which of them it could *p*. be who was to do this thing
Acts 4:20. we cannot *p*. give up speaking
  11:17. how could I *p*. stand in God's way
Rom. 8:8. who live on such a level cannot *p*. please God
Heb. 6:18. God could not *p*. play us false
  9:17. it cannot *p*. have force while the testator is alive

post-s
Acts 5:23. the warders at their *p*. by the doors
  12:10. they passed the first guard-*p*.

posterity
Acts 8:33. who will be able to speak of his *p*.
  13:23. the man from whose *p*. God, as he promised
Rom. 4:13. not through law that Abraham, or his *p*.
  4:16. valid for all Abraham's *p*.
  4:18. thus shall your *p*. be
  9:7 ⎱ through the line of Isaac
Heb. 11:18 ⎰ your *p*.

pot-s
Rom. 9:20. can the *p*. speak to the potter
2 Cor. 4:7. we are no better than *p*. of
    earthenware

potency
Rom. 8:3. our lower nature robbed it of
    all *p*.

potent
2 Cor. 10:4. divinely *p*. to demolish
    strongholds

potentate-s
Eph. 6:12. *p*. of this dark world

potion
Rev. 18:6. the strength of the *p*. she
    mixed

potter
Rom. 9:20. can the pot speak to the *p*.

pounded
Acts 27:41. *p*. to pieces by the breakers

pound-s
Mat. 18:28. a fellow-servant who owed
    him a few *p*.
Mark 6:38. spend twenty *p*. on bread
    14:5. the perfume might have been
    sold for thirty *p*.
John 6:7. twenty *p*. would not buy
    enough bread
    12:5. why was this perfume not sold
    for thirty *p*.

pour-s-ed
Luke 6:38. will be *p*. into your lap
Acts 1:18. his entrails *p*. out
1 Cor. 12:13. that one Holy Spirit was
    p. out for all of us
2 Tim. 4:6. my life is being *p*. out on the
    altar
Jam. 2:7. *p*. contempt on the honoured
    name
2 Pet. 2:12 ⎫ *p*. abuse upon things
Jude 10   ⎭ they do not understand
Jude 18. men who *p*. scorn on religion
Rev. 11:5. fire *p*. from their mouths

poverty
Heb. 11:37. in *p*., distress, and misery

power-s
Mat. 9:28. do you believe that I have
    the *p*.
    13:21. he has no staying-*p*.
    13:54. these miraculous *p*.
    14:2. miraculous *p*. are at work in him
    17:22. the Son of Man is to be given
    up into the *p*. of men
    20:19. hand him over to the foreign *p*.
Mark 4:17. they have no staying-*p*.
    5:30. aware that *p*. had gone out of
    him
    6:14. these miraculous *p*. are at work
    in him

    9:31. the Son of Man is now to be
    given up into the *p*. of men
    9:39. a work of divine *p*. in my name
    10:33. hand him over to the foreign *p*.
    14:8. she has done what lay in her *p*.
Luke 1:20. you will lose your *p*. of
    speech
    1:52. torn imperial *p*. from their
    thrones
    1:69. a deliverer of victorious *p*.
    6:19. *p*. went out from him and cured
    them all
    8:46. I felt that *p*. had gone out from
    me
    9:44. the Son of Man is going to be
    given up into the *p*. of men
    18:32. he will be handed over to the
    foreign *p*.
    21:15. I myself will give you *p*. of
    utterance
    22:4. of putting Jesus into their *p*.
    24:7. into the *p*. of sinful men and be
    crucified
John 5:26. the Father has life-giving *p*.
    in himself
    9:3. that God's *p*. might be displayed
    10:32. many good deeds, done by my
    Father's *p*.
    12:38. to whom has the Lord's *p*. been
    revealed
    17:11. protect by the *p*. of thy name
    17:12. by the *p*. of thy name
Acts 2:4. the Spirit gave them *p*. of
    utterance
    7:10. gave him a presence and *p*. of
    mind
    11:21. the *p*. of the Lord was with
    them
    19:20. the word of the Lord showed
    its *p*.
    20:32. *p*. to build you up
Rom. 3:9. all under the *p*. of sin
    4:21. his *p*. to do what he had
    promised
    11:23. it is in God's *p*. to graft them
    in again
    13:4. they hold the *p*. of the sword
    14:4. his Master has *p*. to enable him
1 Cor. 2:6. its governing *p*.
    2:8. the *p*. that rule the world
    10:9. let us not put the *p*. of the Lord
    to the test
    10:13. will not allow you to be tested
    above your *p*.
    12:8. by the *p*. of the same Spirit
    12:10. and another miraculous *p*.
    12:28. help others or *p*. to guide them
    14:3. his words have *p*. to build
    15:56. sin gains its *p*. from the law
2 Cor. 9:8. in God's *p*. to provide you
    richly
    13:3. makes his *p*. felt among you
    13:8. we have no *p*. to act against the
    truth

Gal. 3:21. if a law had been given which had *p*. to bestow life

Eph. 1:17. spiritual *p*. of wisdom and vision

3:16. *p*. through his Spirit in your inner being

6:18. pray on every occasion in the *p*. of the Spirit

Phil. 3:21. by the very *p*. which enables him

4:13. strength for anything through him who gives me *p*.

Col. 1:29. the energy and *p*. of Christ at work in me

2:12. the active *p*. of God who raised him from the dead

2 Thess. 2:7. the secret *p*. of wickedness is at work

1 Tim. 6:5. let their reasoning *p*. become atrophied

2 Tim. 1:10. he has broken the *p*. of death

1:12. confident of his *p*. to keep

3:8. they have lost the *p*. to reason

3:15. the sacred writings which have *p*. to make you wise

Tit. 3:5. the renewing *p*. of the Holy Spirit

Heb. 2:4. by manifold works of *p*.

9:13. ashes of a heifer have *p*. to hallow

9:14. how much greater is the *p*. of the blood of Christ

11:19. God had *p*. even to raise from the dead

12:13. regain its former *p*.

1 Pet. 1:12. in the *p*. of the Holy Spirit

4:11. to him belong glory and *p*.

1 John 5:19. godless world lies in the *p*. of the evil one

Jude 20. pray in the *p*. of the Holy Spirit

Rev. 7:2. given the *p*. to ravage land and sea

16:14. devils, with *p*. to work miracles

powerful

Luke 24:19. a prophet *p*. in speech and action

Acts 7:22. a *p*. speaker and a man of action

8:13. he saw the *p*. signs and miracles that were taking place

18:24. *p*. in his use of the scriptures

1 Cor. 1:26. few are *p*. or highly born

4:10. we are weak; you are so *p*.

Heb. 6:18. to give *p*. encouragement to us

11:34. they grew *p*. in war

Jam. 5:16. a good man's prayer is *p*.

Rev. 6:15. the rich and the *p*.

powerless

Rom. 5:6. when we were still *p*., then Christ died for the wicked

practical-ly

Acts 19:26. in *p*. the whole of the province of Asia

Jam. 3:13. let his right conduct give *p*. proof

practice-s

Mat. 23:3. do not follow their *p*.

Mark 10:1. followed his usual *p*. and taught

Luke 2:41. the *p*. of his parents to go to Jerusalem

5:33. the *p*. of prayer

John 3:20. for fear their *p*. should be shown up

Acts 15:1. circumcised in accordance with Mosaic practice

17:2. following his usual *p*. Paul

25:16. it is not Roman *p*.

Rom. 1:32. they actually applaud such *p*.

1 Cor. 11:17. a *p*. which I cannot commend

2 Cor. 11:13. crooked in all their *p*.

Gal. 1:14. the *p*. of our national religion

Phil. 4:9. or saw me do, put into *p*.

1 Tim. 4:7. in training for the *p*. of religion

2 Pet. 2:2. adherents to their dissolute *p*.

Rev. 2:6. you hate the *p*. of the Nicolaitans

practise-d-ing

Mat. 23:23. it is these you should have *p*.

Luke 11:42. these you should have *p*.

Acts 19:19. those who formerly *p*. magic

21:24. you are a *p*. Jew

Rom. 12:13. *p*. hospitality

2 Cor. 4:2. we neither *p*. cunning nor distort

Gal. 1:13. when I was still a *p*. Jew

1 Thess. 4:10. *p*. this rule of love

Rev. 22:15. all who love and *p*. deceit

praise-s-d-ing

Mat. 5:16. give *p*. to your Father in heaven

9:8. *p*. God for granting such authority to men

15:31. they gave *p*. to the God of Israel

Mark 2:12. were astounded and *p*. God

Luke 1:68. *p*. to the God of Israel

2:28. he took him in his arms, *p*. God

4:15. all men sang his *p*.

5:25. went home *p*. God

5:26. all lost in amazement and *p*. God

7:16. awe fell upon them all and they *p*. God

7:29. including the tax-gatherers, *p*. God

13:13. she straightened up and began to *p*. God

17:15. finding himself cured, turned back *p*. God

Luke 17:18. to come back and give *p.* to God

18:43. followed Jesus, *p.* God

23:47. the centurion saw it all, and gave *p.* to God

Acts 11:18. they gave *p.* to God and said

21:20. when they heard this, they gave *p.* to God

Rom. 15:6. with one mind and one voice you may *p.*

15:9. I will *p.* thee among the Gentiles

1 Cor. 14:16. *p.* God in the language of inspiration

15:57. God be *p.*, he gives us the victory

2 Cor. 1:3. *p.* be to the God and Father

6:8. *p.* and blame, are alike our lot

Gal. 1:24. they *p.* God for me

Eph. 1:3. *p.* be to the God and Father

Jam. 3:9. to sing the *p.* of our Lord

3:10. out of the same mouth come *p.* and curses

5:13. he should sing *p.*

1 Pet. 1:3. *p.* be to the God and Father

Rev. 5:12. honour and glory and *p.*

5:13. *p.* and honour

7:12. *p.* and glory and wisdom

pray-ed

Acts 27:29. *p.* for daylight to come

Rom. 9:3. I could even *p.* to be outcast from Christ

Eph. 1:17. I *p.* that the God of our Lord Jesus Christ

1:18. I *p.* that your inward eyes may be illumined

Col. 1:10. we *p.* that you may bear fruit

4:4. *p.* that I may make the secret plain

1 Thess. 4:1. *p.* of you, by our fellowship with the Lord Jesus

Jam. 4:2. you do not get what you want, because you do not *p.* for it

4:3. you *p.* from wrong motives

3 John 2. I *p.* that you may enjoy good health

prayer-s

1 Cor. 14:17. your *p.* of thanksgiving

2 Cor. 13:9. my whole *p.* is

Eph. 3:1. I make my *p.*

3:14. I kneel in *p.* to the Father

1 Tim. 2:3. such *p.* is right, and approved by God

Philem. 6. my *p.* is

Heb. 13:19. all the more earnestly I ask for your *p.*

preach-ed-ing

Acts 18:5. Paul devoted himself entirely to *p.*

18:9. go on with your *p.*

Rom. 1:9. *p.* the gospel of his Son

15:16. the *p.* of the gospel of God

1 Cor. 4:15. through the *p.* of the Gospel

Col. 4:3. that God may give us an opening for *p.*

I Tim. 5:17. those who labour at *p.*

6:3. this is what you are to teach and *p.*

Rev. 1:9. because I had *p.* God's word

precept-s

Rom. 2:14. carry out its *p.* by the light of nature

2:26. keeps the *p.* of the law

2:29. not by written *p.* but by the Spirit

1 Tim. 4:6. bred in the *p.* of our faith

6:3. will not give his mind to wholesome *p.*

precincts

Mat. 21:12. buying and selling in the temple *p.*

John 10:23. Jesus was walking in the temple *p.*

precise-ly

Acts 23:20. more *p.* information about him

1 Cor. 14:9. utterance yields no *p.* meaning

2 Cor. 2:3. *p.* the point I made in my letter

predestine-d

1 Pet. 1:20. *p.* before the foundation of the world

predict-ed

Acts 3:24. they all *p.* this present time

11:28. *p.* a severe and world-wide famine

prediction-s

2 Pet. 3:2. the *p.* made by God's own prophets

Jude 17. the *p.* made by the apostles

pre-eminence

Acts 19:27. brought down from her divine *p.*

prefer-red-ring

John 3:19. men *p.* darkness to light

2 Cor. 12:9. *p.* to find my joy and pride

Heb. 11:25. *p.* to suffer hardship with the people of God

prefigured

1 Pet. 3:21. this water *p.* the water of baptism

pregnant

Luke 2:6. she was *p.*, and while they were there

Rev. 12:2. she was *p.*, and in the anguish of her labour

pre-judge

1 Tim. 5:21. never *p.* the issue

preliminary
Acts 25:26. this *p*. enquiry

premature
1 Cor. 4:5. pass no *p*. judgement

preparations
Luke 22:12. make the *p*. there

prepare-s-d-ing
Mat. 22:2. a king who *p*. a feast
26:12. her way of *p*. me for burial
26:19. *p*. for Passover
Mark 14:16. so they *p*. for Passover
Luke 17:8. *p*. my supper
21:14. not to *p*. your defence beforehand
22:13. so they *p*. for Passover
John 12:7. the day when she *p*. for my
burial
Acts 10:47. is anyone *p*. to withhold the
water for baptism
2 Cor. 9:3. I want you to be *p*.
10:6. we are *p*. to punish all rebellion
12:14. *p*. to pay you a third visit
Heb. 9:2. a tent was *p*.

prescribe-s-d
Luke 2:23. as *p*. in the law of the Lord
2:39. done everything *p*. in the law of
the Lord
Tit. 1:5. observe the tests I *p*.
Heb. 8:4. who offer the gifts which the
Law *p*.
9:9. the offerings and sacrifices there *p*.
10:8. the Law *p*. them

presence
Mat. 17:2 ⎱ in their *p*. he was trans-
Mark 9:2 ⎰ figured
13:9. to testify in their *p*.
Luke 1:75. in his *p*., our whole life long
9:18. praying alone in the *p*. of his
disciples
19:27. slaughter them in my *p*.
21:36. to stand in the *p*. of the Son of
Man
23:14. examined him in your *p*.
John 8:38. what I saw in my Father's *p*.
12:37. signs which Jesus had performed in their *p*.
17:5. glorify me in thine own *p*.
Acts 2:25. the *p*. of the Lord would be
with me always
2:28. thou wilt fill me with gladness
by thy *p*.
7:10. he also gave him a *p*.
Rom. 9:4. theirs is the splendour of the
divine *p*.
1 Cor. 8:8. food will not bring us into
God's *p*.
2 Cor. 4:14. and bring us to his *p*.
7:14. proud boast we made in the *p*.
of Titus
12:21. God may humiliate me in
your *p*.

1 Tim. 6:13. now in the *p*. of God
2 Tim. 2:2. in the *p*. of many witnesses
Heb. 9:2. the table with the bread of
the *P*.
2 Pet. 1:17. from the sublime *P*. a voice
Rev. 3:5. in the *p*. of my Father and his
angels
8:2. the seven angels that stand in the
p. of God
9:13. the golden altar that stood in
the *p*. of God
11:4. that stand in the *p*. of the Lord
of the earth
13:12. the first beast in its *p*.
13:14. allowed to perform in the
p. of the beast
15:4. all nations shall come and worship in thy *p*.
19:20. worked miracles in its *p*.
20:11. from his *p*. earth and heaven
vanished away

present-s
Mat. 3:15. let it be so for the *p*.
24:34. the *p*. generation will live to
see it all
27:55. a number of women were
also *p*.
Mark 13:30. the *p*. generation will live
to see it
14:4. some of those *p*. said to one
another
15:40. a number of women were
also *p*.
Luke 21:32. the *p*. generation will live
to see it
John 8:29. he who sent me is *p*. with me
12:17. the people who were *p*. when he
called Lazarus
Acts 3:24. they all predicted this *p*. time
24:20. it is for these persons here *p*.
to say
24:25. that will do for the *p*.
Rom. 3:26. demonstrate his justice now
in the *p*.
5:3. exult in our *p*. sufferings
8:22. up to the *p*., we know, the whole
created universe groans
12:2. adapt yourselves no longer to
the pattern of this *p*. world
1 Cor. 14:16. the plain man who is *p*.
16:12. he was quite determined not to
go at *p*.
2 Cor. 1:14. partial as your *p*. knowledge
of us is
5:2. in this *p*. body we do indeed
groan
Gal. 2:20. my *p*. bodily life is lived by
faith
Eph. 2:2. the evil ways of this *p*. age
5:16. use the *p*. opportunity to the full
Phil. 1:17. *p*. Christ from mixed motives
Col. 2:5. the firm front which your faith
in Christ *p*.

Col. 4:5. use the *p*. opportunity to the full

2 Thess. 2:7. secret only for the *p*.

2 Tim. 1:12. that is the reason for my *p*. plight

Heb. 1:6. when he *p*. the first-born to the world

2 Pet. 3:7. the *p*. heavens and earth

Rev. 11:10. make merry, and exchange *p*.

presented

Acts 6:6. these they *p*. to the apostles

12:20. *p*. themselves at his court

presently

Mark 12:42. *p*. there came a poor widow

preserve-d

1 Cor. 7:37. to *p*. his partner in her virginity

2 Cor. 11:10. I will *p*. my pride in this matter

2 Pet. 2:5. whom he *p*. with seven others

preside

1 Tim. 5:14. *p*. over a home

president

Mat. 9:18. there came a *p*. of the synagogue

9:23. Jesus arrived at the *p*.'s house

Mark 5:22. the *p*. of one of the synagogues

5:35. a message came from the *p*.'s house

5:36. said to the *p*. of the synagogue

5:38. they came to the *p*.'s house

Luke 8:41. he was *p*. of the synagogue

8:49. a man came from the *p*.'s house

13:14. but the *p*. of the synagogue, indignant

press-ed-ing

Mat. 27:32. *p*. him into service to carry his cross

Mark 5:24. a great crowd which *p*. upon him

5:31. you see the crowd *p*. upon you

15:21. they *p*. him into service to carry his cross

Luke 4:42. they *p*. him not to leave them

7:4. approached Jesus and *p*. their petition

23:10. *p*. the case against him

24:29. they *p*. him: 'Stay with us

John 4:40. they *p*. him to stay with them

8:7. they continued to *p*. their question

Acts 2:40. he *p*. his case and pleaded with them

25:3. *p*. for him to be brought up to Jerusalem

2 Cor. 4:8. hard-*p*. on every side

Phil. 3:12. not yet reached perfection, but I *p*. on

2 Tim. 4:2. *p*. it home on all occasions

Rev. 2:9. hard *p*. you are, and poor

presume

Mat. 3:9. do not *p*. to say to yourselves

Luke 7:7. I did not *p*. to approach you in person

Jude 9. he did not *p*. to condemn him

pretence

1 Pet. 2:1. away with all *p*. and jealousy

pretending

Acts 27:30. *p*. they were going to lay out anchors

pretext

Luke 20:20. as a *p*. for handing him over to the authority

Acts 23:15. on the *p*. of a closer investigation

23:20. on the *p*. of obtaining more precise information

prevail-s

Mat. 5:6. hunger and thirst to see right *p*.

Eph. 4:18. ignorance *p*. among them

prevent-ed

Acts 8:36. What is there to *p*. my being baptized

14:18. to *p*. the crowd from offering sacrifice

16:6. *p*. by the Holy Spirit

24:23. not to *p*. any of his friends

27:43. *p*. them from carrying out their plan

Rom. 15:22. I have been *p*. all this time

Heb. 3:19. it was unbelief which *p*. their entering

7:23. *p*. by death from continuing in office

previously

Acts 21:29. had *p*. seen Trophimus the Ephesian with him

Rom. 9:29. as also he said *p*., 'If the Lord of Hosts

price

Luke 23:41. we are paying the *p*. for our misdeeds

Acts 1:18. buying a plot of land with the *p*. of his villainy

5:8. paid such and such a *p*. for the land?' 'Yes,' she said, 'that was the *p*.

2 Cor. 1:6. the *p*. we pay for your consolation

1 Pet. 1:19. the *p*. was paid in precious blood

2 Pet. 1:4. his promises, great beyond all *p*.

priceless

Rev. 21:11. it had the radiance of some *p*. jewel

pride-ing

Rom. 2:23. while you take *p*. in the law

Rom. 3:27. what room then is left for human *p.*
4:2. then he has a ground for *p.*
11:20. put away your *p.*
12:10. give *p.* of place to one another
15:17. I have ground for *p.* in the service of God
1 Cor. 1:29. no place for human *p.* in the presence of God
3:21. never make mere men a cause for *p.*
4:6. may not be inflated with *p.*
15:31. I swear it by my *p.* in you
2 Cor. 5:12. whose *p.* is all in outward show
7:4. I have great *p.* in you
7:14. my *p.* in you has been justified
9:2. eager you are to help; I speak of it with *p.*
10:16. never *p.* ourselves on work already done
11:10. I will preserve my *p.* in this matter
12:9. *p.* in the very things that are my weakness
Phil. 1:26. your *p.* in me may be unbounded
2:16. my *p.* on the Day of Christ
3:3. whose *p.* is in Christ Jesus
1 Thess. 2:19. what hope or joy or crown of *p.* is there for us
2 Thess. 2:4. he rises in his *p.* against every god
Jam. 1:10. the wealthy brother must find his *p.* in being brought low

priest-s
Mat. 28:12. the chief *p.* offered the soldiers a substantial bribe
Mark 14:65. the High *P.*s' men set upon him with blows
Heb. 2:11. a consecrating *p.*
13:10. the *p.* of the sacred tent

priesthood
Heb. 7:16. owing his *p.* not to a system of earth-bound rules

priestly
Rom. 15:16. my *p.* service is the preaching of the gospel

primacy
Col. 1:15. his is the *p.* over all created things

prime
Rev. 3:14. the *p.* source of all God's creation

prince-s
Mat. 14:1. reports about Jesus reached the ears of *P.* Herod
Luke 3:1. Herod was *p.* of Galilee
3:19. *P.* Herod
9:7. *P.* Herod heard of all that was happening

11:15. Beelzebub *p.* of devils
Acts 13:1. the court of *P.* Herod
Rev. 18:23. the merchant *p.* of the world

principle-d
Mat. 1:19. being a man of *p.*
Rom. 3:27. on what *p.*
7:21. I discover this *p.*
Gal. 2:13. showed the same lack of *p.*
6:16. take this *p.* for their guide
1 Tim. 3:8. men of high *p.*
3:11. women of high *p.*
Tit. 2:2. they should be sober, high-*p.*
2:7. you must show integrity and high *p.*

prison
Acts 4:3. put in *p.* for the night
Phil. 1:7. when I lie in *p.*
1:17. fresh trouble for me as I lie in *p.*
Col. 4:3. that indeed is why I am now in *p.*
4:18. remember I am in *p.*
Philem. 10. whose father I have become in this *p.*
13. here in *p.* for the Gospel
Heb. 11:36. even fetters and *p.* bars
13:3. remember those in prison
Rev. 13:10. whoever is meant for *p.*, to *p.* he goes

prisoner-s
Luke 4:18. to proclaim release for *p.*
13:16. kept *p.* by Satan for eighteen long years
John 18:39. I release one *p.* for you at Passover
Acts 5:21. to the jail to fetch the *p.*
16:22. tore off the *p.*s' clothes
16:26. the *p.* found their fetters unfastened
22:5. bring the Christians there to Jerusalem as *p.*
24:2. when the *p.* was called
Rom. 7:23. making me a *p.* under the law
11:32. making all mankind *p.* to disobedience
Gal. 3:22. *p.* in subjection to sin
3:23. we were close *p.* in the custody of law
2 Tim. 1:16. he was not ashamed to visit a *p.*
Heb. 10:34. you shared the sufferings of the *p.*
Rev. 19:20. the beast was taken *p.*

private-ly
Mat. 14:13. Jesus withdrew *p.*
17:19. the disciples came to Jesus and asked him *p.*
Mark 4:34. *p.* to his disciples he explained everything
Acts 2:46. breaking bread in *p.* houses

Acts 5:42. teaching in the temple and in
   p. houses
2 Tim. 3:6. insinuate themselves into *p*.
   houses

privilege
Rom. 1:5. the *p*. of a commission in his
   name
2 Cor. 11:16. give me the *p*. of a fool
Eph. 3:8. the *p*. of proclaiming to the
   Gentiles
Phil. 1:7. you all share in the *p*. that is
   mine
   1:29. the *p*. not only of believing in
   Christ
2 Pet. 1:1. enjoy equal *p*. with ourselves

prize
2 Tim. 2:5. no athlete can win a *p*. unless
   he has kept the rules
   4:8. and now the *p*. awaits me
Jam. 1:12. for his *p*. the gift of life

proceed-s-ed
Mat. 15:19. these all *p*. from the heart
   25:19. *p*. to settle accounts
Acts 4:34. brought the *p*. of the sale
   5:18. *p*. to arrest the apostles
   23:23. to *p*. to Caesarea
Rom. 15:28. delivered the *p*. under my
   own seal.

process
Rom. 5:20. law intruded into this *p*.

procession
2 Cor. 2:14. captives in Christ's triumphal *p*.
Col. 2:15. captives in his triumphal *p*.

proclaim-s-ed-ing
Mat. 4:17. Jesus began to *p*. the
   message
   10:7. as you go *p*. the message
   12:18. *p*. judgement among the
   nations
   24:14. this gospel of the Kingdom will
   be *p*.
   26:13. in all the world this gospel
   is *p*.
Mark 1:4. in the wilderness *p*. a baptism
   1:14. Jesus came into Galilee *p*. the
   Gospel
   1:38. I have to *p*. my message there
   2:2. while he was *p*. the message
   3:14. send out to *p*. the Gospel
   13:10. before the end the Gospel must
   be *p*.
   14:9. wherever in all the world the
   Gospel is *p*.
   16:15. *p*. the Good News to the whole
   creation
Luke 1:70. age after age he *p*.
   3:3. *p*. a baptism in token of repentance

   4:18. to *p*. release for prisoners
   4:19. *p*. the year of the Lord's favour
   4:44. he *p*. the Gospel
   8:1. *p*. the good news of the kingdom
   9:2. sent them to *p*. the kingdom of
   God
   24:47. the forgiveness of sins is to
   be *p*.
John 6:15. seize him to *p*. him king
Acts 4:2. *p*. the resurrection
   8:5. *p*. the Messiah
   9:20. *p*. Jesus publicly
   10:37. the baptism *p*. by John
   10:42. to *p*. him to the people
   13:24. made ready for his coming by
   p. baptism
   13:38. forgiveness of sins is now
   being *p*.
   13:40. the doom *p*. by the prophets
   15:36. towns where we *p*. the word
   17:3. this Jesus,' he said, 'whom I am
   p. to you
   17:13. the word of God had now
   been *p*.
   17:23. this is what I now *p*.
   19:13. Jesus whom Paul *p*.
   20:25. I have gone about among you
   p. the Kingdom
   28:31. *p*. the kingdom of God
Rom. 2:21. you *p*., 'Do not steal
   10:8. the word of faith which we *p*.
1 Cor. 1:17. to *p*. the Gospel
   1:23. we *p*. Christ
   2:4. the gospel I *p*.
   9:23. to bear my part in *p*. it.
   11:26. You *p*. the death of the Lord
   15:11. this is what we all *p*.
   15:12. if this is what we *p*.
2 Cor. 1:19. Christ Jesus, *p*. among you
   by us
   4:5 it is not ourselves that we *p*.; we *p*.
   Christ Jesus as Lord
   11:4. *p*. another Jesus, not the Jesus
   whom we *p*.
Gal. 1:16. *p*. him among the Gentiles
Eph. 2:17. *p*. the good news
   3:8. *p*. to the Gentiles
Phil. 1:15. *p*. Christ in a jealous and
   quarrelsome spirit
   1:16. others *p*. him in true goodwill
Heb. 2:12. I will *p*. thy name to my
   brothers
1 Pet. 2:9. to *p*. the triumphs of him
Col. 1:23. the gospel which has been *p*.
   1:28. he it is whom we *p*.
1 Thess. 2:9. we *p*. before you the good
   news of God
1 Tim. 3:16. *p*. among the nations
2 Tim. 4:2. *p*. the message, press it home
Rev. 12:10. I heard a voice in heaven *p*.
   14:6. an eternal gospel to *p*.
   18:2. in a mighty voice he *p*.
   21:3. I heard a loud voice *p*.

proclamation
Mark 1:7. his *p*. ran: 'After me comes one
16:20. to make their *p*. everywhere
Rom. 9:27. Isaiah makes this *p*. about Israel
16:25. the *p*. of Jesus Christ
2 Tim. 2:15. in your *p*. of the truth
4:17. making the full *p*. of the Gospel
Tit. 1:3. the *p*. which was entrusted to me
1 Pet. 3:19. made his *p*. to the imprisoned spirits

proconsul-s
Acts 18:12. when Gallio was *p*. of Achaia
19:38. there are such people as *p*.

produce-s-ed-ing
Mat. 3:10. every tree that fails to *p*. good fruit
12:35. a good man *p*. good from the store of good within himself; and an evil man from evil within *p*. evil
13:52. *p*. from his store both the new and the old
21:34. to collect the *p*. due to him
24:24. they will *p*. great signs and wonders
25:20. *p*. the five he had made
Mark 4:28. the ground *p*. a crop by itself
12:2. to collect from them his share of the *p*.
13:22. they will *p*. signs and wonders
Luke 3:9. fails to *p*. good fruit is cut down
6:43. no such thing as a good tree *p*. worthless fruit, nor yet a worthless tree *p*. good fruit
6:45. a good man *p*. good . . . and an evil man from evil within *p*. evil
10:35. next day he *p*. two silver pieces
12:17. I have not the space to store my *p*.
16:2. *p*. your accounts
20:10. his share of the *p*.
Acts 6:13. they *p* false witnesses
12:4. meaning to *p*. him in public after Passover
Rom. 7:8. *p*. in me all kinds of wrong desires
1 Cor. 9:10. in the hope of getting some of the *p*.
14:7. inanimate things that *p*. sounds
2 Cor. 3:1. to *p*. our credentials
1 Tim. 5:10. *p*. evidence of good deeds performed
Tit. 3:14. to *p*. the necessities of life

profane-d
Acts 10:14. I have never eaten anything *p*.

10:15. not for you to call *p*. what God counts clean
10:28. God has shown me clearly that I must not call any man *p*.
11:8. nothing *p*. or unclean has ever entered my mouth
11:9. it is not for you to call *p*.
21:28. *p*. this holy place
Heb. 10:29. *p*. the blood of the covenant

proffer
Phil. 2:16. *p*. the word of life

profit
Mat. 25:16. made a *p*. of five bags
Luke 19:15. to see what *p*. each had made
Acts 16:16. brought large *p*. to her owners
Phil. 4:17. all I care for is the *p*. accruing to you

progress
1 Tim. 4:15. so that your *p*. may be plain to all
2 Tim. 3:13. charlatans will make *p*. from bad to worse

prolong
Gal. 2:6. did not *p*. the consultation

prominent
Acts 25:23. *p*. citizens

promise-s-d
Luke 1:37. God's *p*. can never fail
1:45. faith that the Lord's *p*. would be fulfilled
1:54. firm in his *p*. to our forefathers
1:70. so he *p*.: age after age he proclaimed
2:29. now thy *p*. is fulfilled
Acts 13:34. the blessings *p*. to David
Rom. 4:17. this *p*., then, was valid before God
2 Cor. 9:5. to see that your *p*. bounty is in order
Rev. 10:7. as he *p*. to his servants the prophets

promote
Jam. 1:20. a man's anger cannot *p*. the justice of God

prompt-ed-ings-ly
Mat. 5:25. come to terms with him *p*.
14:8. *p*. by her mother
Eph. 2:3. obeyed the *p*. of our own instincts

promulgated
Gal. 3:19. *p*. through angels

pronounce-s-d
John 20:23. if you *p*. them unforgiven
Rom. 8:33. it is God who *p*. acquittal
2 Cor. 1:20. he is the Yes *p*. upon God's promises
Gal. 3:16. the promises were *p*. to Abraham

Heb. 8:13. he has *p*. the first one old
Rev. 18:8. the Lord God who has *p*. her
doom

pronouncement
2 Thess. 2:2. some oracular utterance,
or *p*.

proof-s
Acts 9:22. cogent *p*. that Jesus was the
Messiah
Rom. 5:4. *p*. that we have stood the
test, and this *p*. is the ground of
hope
5:8. God's own *p*. of his love towards
us
2 Cor. 9:13. through the *p*. which this
affords
Phil. 2:16. *p*. that I did not run my
race in vain
1 Tim. 2:6. *p*. of the divine purpose
Jam. 3:13. let his right conduct give
practical *p*. of it
1 John 4:13. here is the *p*. that we dwell
in him
Rev. 2:2. put to the *p*. those who claim
to be apostles

propaganda
Acts 19:26. this fellow Paul with his *p*.

propagandist
Acts 17:18. a *p*. for foreign deities

proper-ly
Mat. 21:43. a nation that yields the
p. fruit
24:45. issue their rations at the *p*. time
Mark 4:6. as it had no *p*. root it withered
away
Luke 1:20. at their *p*. time my words will
be proved true
12:42. issue their rations at the *p*. time
Acts 19:36. your *p*. course is to keep
quiet
1 Cor. 7:36. feels that he is not behaving
p. towards her
15:23. each in his own *p*. place
2 Cor. 10:13. no attempt to boast beyond
our *p*. sphere
10:15. work beyond our *p*. sphere
Gal. 6:5. everyone has his own *p*. burden
2 Thess. 2:6. revealed only at the *p*. time
Jude 6. abandoned their *p*. home

property
Mat. 24:47. in charge of all his master's
p.
Mark 12:7. let us kill him, and the *p*.
will be ours
12:40. men who eat up the *p*. of
widows
Luke 12:13. to divide the family *p*. with
me
12:44. put in charge of all his
master's *p*.

15:12. Father, give me my share of
the *p*.
16:1. this man was squandering the *p*.
20:14. so that the *p*. may come to us
20:47. these are the men who eat up
the *p*. of widows
Acts 1:19. named the *p*. in their own
language Akeldama
2:45. they would sell their *p*. and
possessions
4:34. all who had *p*. in land or houses
5:1. Ananias, with his wife Sapphira,
who sold a *p*.

prophecy-ies
Mat. 2:5. referred him to the *p*. which
reads
8:17. to make good the *p*. of Isaiah
12:17. in fulfilment of Isaiah's *p*.
13:35. thus making good the *p*. of
Isaiah
21:4. in fulfilment of the *p*. which
says
Luke 3:4. in the book of the *p*. of Isaiah
Acts 1:16. the *p*. in Scripture was bound
to come true

prophets
1 John 4:4. you have the mastery over
these false *p*.

proportion
Rom. 5:15. out of all *p*. to Adam's
wrongdoing
1 Cor. 16:2. a sum in *p*. to his gains

proposal
Acts 6:5. this *p*. proved acceptable

propose
Luke 23:16. I therefore *p*. to let him off
with a flogging
Gal. 4:9. why do you *p*. to enter their
service
1 Thess. 2:18. we did *p*. to come to
Thessalonica

propound
Acts 17:19. may we know what this new
doctrine is that you *p*.

prosecute
Acts 25:5. if there is anything wrong, let
them *p*. him

prostitutes
Mat. 21:31. *p*. are entering the kingdom
of God ahead of you
21:32. but the tax-gatherers and *p*.
did
Heb. 11:31. by faith the *p*. Rahab
escaped the doom
Jam. 2:25. the same is true of the *p*.
Rahab

prostrate
Mat. 18:26. the man fell *p*. at his
master's feet

Mat. 28:9. clasped his feet, falling *p*.
   before him
   28:17. when they saw him, they fell
   p. before him

protect-ed
John 17:11. Holy Father, *p*. by the power
   of thy name
   17:12. I *p*. by the power of thy name

protection
Heb. 6:18. claimed his *p*. by grasping the
   hope
1 Pet. 1:5. under the *p*. of his power

protest-ed
John 8:57. the Jews *p*., 'You are not yet
   fifty years old
Acts 13:51. shook the dust off their feet
   in *p*.

proud
Luke 16:3. too *p*. to beg
Rom. 2:17. are *p*. of your God
1 Cor. 1:31. if a man is *p*., let him be *p*.
   of the Lord
   5:2. and you can still be *p*. of yourselves
   15:31. I am *p*. of you
2 Cor. 1:12. one thing we are *p*. of
   1:14. you have as much reason to be
   p. of us
   5:12. a chance to show yourselves *p*.
   of us
   7:14. the *p*. boast we made in the
   presence of Titus
   10:5. all that rears its *p*. head against
   the knowledge of God
1 Tim. 6:17. rich in this world's goods
   not to be *p*.
Jam. 1:9. may well be *p*. that God lifts
   him up

prove-s-d
Mat. 3:8. *p*. your repentance by the fruit
   it bears
   11:19. God's wisdom is *p*. right by its
   results
   13:22. it *p*. barren
   17:20. nothing will *p*. impossible for
   you
   25:21 ⎱ you have *p*. trustworthy in a
   25:23 ⎰ small way
Mark 4:19. choke the word, and it *p*.
   barren
Luke 1:20. my words will be *p*. true
   3:8. *p*. your repentance by the fruit it
   bears
   7:35. God's wisdom is *p*. right
   7:47. her great love *p*. that her many
   sins have been forgiven
   16:11. if, then, you have not *p*. trustworthy
   16:12. if you have *p*. untrustworthy
John 8:46. which of you can *p*. me in the
   wrong

Acts 6:5. this proposal *p*. acceptable
   19:9. some *p*. obdurate
   26:20. *p*. their repentance by deeds
Rom. 7:10. *p*. in my experience to lead
   to death
   9:6. impossible that the word of God
   should have *p*. false
   11:31. they have *p*. disobedient
   16:10. well *p*. in Christ's service
2 Cor. 4:7. this *p*. that such transcendent
   power does not come from us
   7:14. that also has *p*. true
   9:3. should not *p*. to be an empty
   boast
   12:16. I did not *p*. a burden to you
Gal. 4:6. to *p*. that you are sons
   4:11. may *p*. to be labour lost
2 Thess. 1:5. *p*. you worthy of the kingdom of God
1 Tim. 4:6. you will *p*. a good servant of
   Christ Jesus
Jam. 2:18. *p*. to me that this faith you
   speak of is real . . . by my deeds I
   will *p*. to you my faith
   2:22. the integrity of his faith was
   fully *p*.
1 Pet. 1:7. that your faith may *p*. itself
   worthy
2 Pet. 2:22. for them the proverb has *p*.
   true
1 John 2:18. which *p*. to us that this is
   indeed the last hour
Jude 10. things they do understand, by
   instinct like brute beasts, *p*. their
   undoing

provide-s-d-ing
Mark 8:4. how can anyone *p*. all these
   people with bread
Luke 7:44. you *p*. no water for my feet
   8:3. these women *p*. for them out of
   their own resources
   10:8. eat the food *p*. for you
   11:8. if he will not *p*. for him out of
   friendship
   11:48. you *p*. the tombs
John 18:3. police *p*. by the chief priests
Acts 7:46. asked to be allowed to *p*. a
   dwelling-place for the God of Jacob
   19:24. *p*. a great deal of employment
Rom. 2:25. circumcision has value, *p*.
   you keep the law
1 Cor. 7:39. *p*. the marriage is within the
   Lord's fellowship
   10:13. he will at the same time *p*. a
   way out
2 Cor. 5:1. a building which God has *p*.
   8:12. *p*. there is an eager desire to give
   9:8. it is in God's power to *p*. you
   richly
   9:10. he who *p*. seed for sowing and
   bread for food will *p*. the seed
Eph. 5:29. he *p*. and cares for it

Eph. 6:11. put on all the armour which
God *p.*
1 Tim. 1:8. the law is an excellent thing,
p. we treat it as law
2:6. *p.*, at the fitting time, proof of the
divine purpose
Heb. 6:16. the oath *p.* a confirmation
10:1. *p.* for the same sacrifices year
after year
1 Pet. 2:16. to *p.* a screen for wrongdoing

province
p. of Asia. Acts 16:6, 19:10, 22,
26, 20:16, 18, 21:27, 24:18, 27:2;
2 Cor. 1:8; 2 Tim. 1:15; Rev. 1:4
Acts 19:31. some of the dignitaries of
the *p.*
23:34. asked him what *p.* he was from
24:2. for the good of this *p.*
24:10. administered justice in this *p.*

provision-s
Luke 9:13. go and buy *p.* for all this
company
Acts 28:10. put on board *p.* for our needs
2 Cor. 9:1. the *p.* of aid for God's people
12:14. parents should make *p.* for
their children
1 Tim. 5:8. if anyone does not make *p.*
for his relations

provoke-d
John 10:39. this *p.* them to one more
attempt to seize him
Acts 15:10. *p.* God by laying on the
shoulders of these converts

prowls
1 Pet. 5:8. the devil, like a roaring lion,
p. round

prudent
Mat. 25:2. five of them were foolish, and
five *p.*
25:8. the foolish said to the *p.*

public-ly
Mark 1:45. made the whole story *p.*
6:12. called *p.* for repentance
Luke 1:80. until the day when he
appeared *p.*
8:17. nothing hidden that will not
become *p.*
20:26. their attempt to catch him out
in *p.* failed
John 7:4. no one can hope to be in the
p. eye if he works in seclusion
7:10. he went up himself, not *p.*
11:54. Jesus no longer went about *p.*
Acts 4:18. ordered them to refrain from
all *p.* speaking
9:20. proclaiming Jesus *p.*
12:4. meaning to produce him in *p.*
after Passover
16:37. they gave us a *p.* flogging
19:19. books and burnt them *p.*
Phil. 1:13. among the *p.* at large

Col. 2:15. he made a *p.* spectacle of them
1 Tim. 3:7. a good reputation with the
non-Christian *p.*
4:13. the *p.* reading of the scriptures
5:20. those who commit sins you must
expose *p.*
Heb. 10:33. tormented to make a *p.* show

pull-ed-ing
Mat. 13:29. you might *p.* up the wheat
26:61. I can *p.* down the temple of God
27:40 } you would *p.* the temple
Mark 15:29 } down, would you
Acts 3:7. by the right hand and *p.* him
up
23:10. *p.* him out of the crowd
Gal. 2:18. a system which I have *p.* down
Tit. 1:13. *p.* them up sharply
Jude 12. dead twice over and *p.* up by
the roots
2 Cor. 10:8. not *p.* you down
13:10. for building up and not for
p. down

punish-es
2 Cor. 10:6. we are prepared to *p.* all
rebellion
1 Thess. 4:6. the Lord *p.* all such offences
2 Pet. 2:10. he will *p.* those who follow
their abominable lusts

punishment
Mat. 24:9 handed over for *p.*
Rom. 13:2. the *p.* they will receive
13:4. they are God's agents of *p.*

pupil
Mat. 10:24. a *p.* does not rank above his
teacher
10:25. the *p.* should be content to
share his teacher's lot
Luke 6:40. a *p.* is not superior to his
teacher
Acts 22:3. as a *p.* of Gamaliel I was
thoroughly trained

purchase-d
Acts 5:2. kept back part of the *p.*-money
Rom. 7:14. the *p.* slave of sin
Gal. 4:5. to *p.* freedom for the subjects
of the law
Rev. 5:9. didst *p.* for God men of every
tribe

pure-ly
Mark 14:3 } oil of *p.* nard
John 12:3 }
1 Cor. 3:3. you are living on the *p.*
human level
1 Tim. 2:8. lift up their hands with a *p.*
intention
1 Pet. 2:2. you must crave for *p.* milk
(spiritual milk, I mean)

purify-ing
1 Cor. 6:11. you have been through the
p. waters

purporting
2 Thess. 2:2. some letter *p.* to come from us

purpose-s
Luke 2:3. for this *p.* everyone made his way to his own town
　7:30. rejected God's *p.* for themselves
John 14:2. I am going there on *p.* to prepare a place for you
Acts 9:21. for the sole *p.* of arresting them
　13:22. who will carry out all my *p.*
　13:36. served the *p.* of God
　14:1. spoke to such *p.* that a large body
　20:27. disclosed to you the whole *p.* of God
Rom. 11:32. God's *p.* was to show mercy
1 Cor. 2:7. his secret *p.* framed from the very beginning
　7:37. if a man is steadfast in his *p.*
　12:7. for some useful *p.*
2 Cor. 5:15. his *p.* in dying for all
　9:3. my *p.* in sending these friends
　13:10. my *p.* in writing this letter
Gal. 3:14. the *p.* of it all was that the blessing
Eph. 2:16. this was his *p.*, to reconcile the two
　3:9. how this hidden *p.* was to be put into effect
　6:19. make known his hidden *p.*
Phil. 1:22. may serve some good *p.*
　2:13. for his own chosen *p.*
2 Thess. 1:11. bring to fulfilment every good *p.*
1 Tim. 1:16. I was mercifully dealt with for this very *p.*
　2:6. proof of the divine *p.*
2 Tim. 2:21. fit for any honourable *p.*
Heb. 4:12. it sifts the *p.* and thoughts of the heart
　6:17. how unchanging was his *p.*
Jam. 1:18. of his set *p.*, by declaring the truth
1 Peter 1:2. chosen of old in the *p.* of God
1 John 2:1. my *p.* is that you should not commit sin
Rev. 10:7. the hidden *p.* of God will have been fulfilled
　17:13. they have but a single *p.* among them
　17:17. God has put it into their heads to carry out his *p.*

purse-s
Luke 12:33. *p.* that do not wear out
John 12:6. pilfer the money put into the common *p.*
　13:29. Judas was in charge of the common *p.*

pursue
Rom. 2:7. to those who *p.* glory, honour

　14:19. *p.* the things that make for peace
1 Tim. 6:11. *p.* justice, piety
2 Tim. 2:22. *p.* justice, integrity
1 Pet. 3:11. seek peace and *p.* it.

pursuit-s
Luke 17:23. do not go running off in *p.*
Rom. 8:13. put to death all the base *p.* of the body
Rev. 12:13. he went in *p.* of the woman

pushed
John 6:17. *p.* off to cross the water
Acts 7:27. the man who was at fault *p.* him away
　19:33. Alexander, whom the Jews had *p.* to the front

put-s-ting
Mat. 2:4. *p.* before them the question
　4:6. he will *p.* his angels in charge of you
　4:7. you are not to *p.* the Lord your God to the test
　16:21. to be *p.* to death and to be raised again
　20:12. you have *p.* them on a level with us
　21:33. planted a vineyard: he *p.* a wall round it
　24:47. *p.* in charge of all his master's property
　25:14. *p.* his capital in their hands
　25:21. I will now *p.* you in charge of something big
　27:2. they then *p.* him in chains
　27:20. and to have Jesus *p.* to death
　28:14. if this should reach the Governor's ears, we will *p.* matters right with him
Mark 6:5. *p.* his hands on a few sick people
　9:36. *p.* his arm round him
　14:64. that he was guilty and should be *p.* to death
Luke 1:51. the arrogant of heart and mind he has *p.* to rout
　2:46. listening to them and *p.* questions
　4:6. it has been *p.* in my hands
　5:3. to *p.* out a little way from the shore
　5:4. *p.* out into deep water
　9:22. to be *p.* to death and to be raised again
　10:25. a lawyer came forward to *p.* this test question
　11:46. will not *p.* a single finger to the load
　19:20. I kept it *p.* away in a handkerchief
　21:2. he noticed a poor widow *p.* in two tiny coins
　22:4. ways and means of *p.* Jesus into their power

John 3:18. the man who *p.* his faith in him
  3:36. he who *p.* his faith in the Son
  5:24. *p.* his trust in him
  6:40. *p.* his faith in him shall possess eternal life
  7:25. is not this the man they want to *p.* to death
  8:30. many *p.* their faith in him
  9:36. tell me who he is, sir, that I should *p.* my faith in him
  11:45. *p.* their faith in him
  12:11. going over to Jesus and *p.* their faith in him
  20:27. reach your hand here and *p.* it into my side
Acts 5:9. conspire to *p.* the Spirit of the Lord to the test
  5:33. they wanted to *p.* them to death
  10:39. he was *p.* to death by hanging on a gibbet
  11:17. when we *p.* our trust in the Lord Jesus Christ
  16:31. *p.* your trust in the Lord Jesus

  19:4. he told the people to *p.* their trust
  22:4. *p.* them in chains
Rom. 4:3. Abraham *p.* his faith in God
  8:13. *p.* to death all the base pursuits of the body
1 Cor. 16:2. every Sunday each of you is to *p.* aside and keep by him a sum
2 Cor. 11:20. *p.* on airs, and hits you in the face, you *p.* up with it
  13:5. *p.* yourselves to the test
Gal. 3:6. Abraham: he *p.* his faith in God
Eph. 3:9. this hidden purpose was to be *p.* into effect

puzzle-ing
Acts 10:17. Peter was still *p.* over the meaning of the vision
1 Cor. 13:12. we see only *p.* reflections in a mirror

Pyrrhus
Acts 20:4. accompanied by Sopater son of *P.*

Q

qualification
2 Cor. 5:6. such *q.* as we have comes from God

qualify-ied
2 Cor. 3:5. no question of our being *q.* in ourselves
  3:6. it is he who has *q.* us to dispense his new covenant

quantity
Rev. 8:3. he was given a great *q.* of incense

quarrel-s-ling
Acts 7:26. tried to bring them to make up their *q.*
Rom. 13:13. no *q.* or jealousies
  16:17. keep your eye on those who stir up *q.*
1 Cor. 1:11. that there are *q.* among you
2 Cor. 7:5. trouble at every turn, *q.* all round
  12:20. I fear I may find *q.*
Gal. 5:20. *q.*, a contentious temper
1 Tim. 3:3. of a forbearing disposition, avoiding *q.*
  6:4. jealous, *q.*, slander
2 Tim. 2:23. you know they breed *q.*
Tit. 3:2. to slander no one, not to pick *q.*
  3:9. *q.*, and controversies
Jam. 4:1. what causes conflicts and *q.*
  4:2. so you *q.* and fight

quarrelsome
Phil. 1:15. some, indeed, proclaim Christ in a jealous and *q.* spirit
1 Tim. 2:8. excluding angry or *q.* thoughts
2 Tim. 2:24. the servant of the Lord must not be *q.*

quart-s
Rev. 6:6. a whole day's wage for a *q.* of flour . . . three *q.* of barley-meal

quarter
Rev. 6:8. to him was given power over a *q.* of the earth

quenched
John 1:5. the darkness has never *q.* it

question-s-ed-ings
Mat. 2:4. put before them the *q.*
  15:1. approached by a group of Pharisees and lawyers from Jerusalem, with the *q.*
  17:10. the disciples put a *q.* to him
  21:23. the chief priests and elders of the nation came to him with the *q.*
  21:24. Jesus replied, 'I have a *q.* to ask too
  22:23. their *q.* was this
Mark 4:10. *q.* him about the parables
  12:13. sent to trap him with a *q.*
  12:15. saw how crafty their *q.* was

Acts 24:25. the discourse turned to *q.*
of morals
also Mat. 9:14; Mark 7:17, 9:11, 10:2,
10:10, 12:18, 13:3, 14:60, 61, 15:4;
Luke 6:9, 10:25, 11:53, 18:18, 20:3,
21, 27, 22:68, 24:38; John 8:6, 7,
9:2, 17, 19, 16:19, 30, 18:19, 21,
21:20; Acts 4:9, 11:2, 18:14, 19:39;
Rom. 3:5; 1 Cor. 7:25, 10:29,
15:36; 2 Cor. 3:5, 8:13, 14, 23;
Gal. 3:2; Col. 3:11; 1 Tim. 3:16

quibbler
Jam. 2:20. can you not see, you *q.*
quibble-s
1 Tim. 6:4. keen on mere verbal questions and *q.*

quick-ly
Mat. 13:5. it sprouted *q.*
Mark 4:5. it had little soil, and it
sprouted *q.*
Luke 15:22. *q.*! fetch a robe, my best one
16:6. make it five hundred; and be *q.*
19:5. Zacchaeus, be *q.* and come down
1 Cor. 13:5. not *q.* to take offence
Gal. 1:6. turning so *q.* away from him
Jam. 1:19. you must be *q.* to listen

quiet-ed-ly
Mat. 1:19. have the marriage contract
set aside *q.*
20:31. told them to be *q.*
Mark 6:31. to some lonely place where
you can rest *q.*
10:48. be *q.*,' they said; but he
shouted all the more

Acts 12:17. he signed to them to keep *q.*
19:35. the town clerk, however, *q.*
the crowd
21:40. as soon as *q.* was restored, he
addressed them
22:2. they listened the more *q.*
1 Tim. 2:11. a woman must be a learner,
listening *q.*
2:12. she should be *q.*
Jam. 1:21. *q.* accept the message

Quirinius
Luke 2:2. it took place when *Q.* was
governor

quite
Luke 13:11. *q.* unable to stand up
straight
Acts 3:17. I know *q.* well that you acted
in ignorance
18:17. all this left Gallio *q.* unconcerned
22:30. to be *q.* sure what charge the
Jews were bringing
28:31. teaching the facts about the
Lord Jesus Christ *q.* openly
Rom. 3:28. justified by faith *q.* apart
from success in keeping the law
1 Cor. 12:22 ⎫
1 Tim. 6:2 ⎭ *q.* the contrary

quote-d-ing
Luke 4:23. no doubt you will *q.* the
proverb to me
Acts 17:2. *q.* texts of Scripture
Heb. 4:7. he uses the words already *q.*

R

Rabbi-uni
Mat. 26:25. *R.*,' he said, 'can you mean
me
26:49. he said, 'Hail, *R.*!', and kissed
him
Mark 5:35. why trouble the *R.* further
9:5. *R.*, ' he said, 'how good it is that
we are here
11:21. *R.*, look, the fig-tree which you
cursed
14:45. said to Jesus, '*R.*,' and kissed
him
Luke 8:49. trouble the *R.* no further
John 4:31. *R.*, have something to eat
9:2. *R.*, who sinned, this man or his
parents
11:8. *R.*', his disciples said
20:16. *R.*!' (which is Hebrew for 'My
Master

rabble
John 7:49. this *r.*, which cares nothing
for the Law

Acts 17:5. roused the *r.*, and had the
city in an uproar
17:13. to stir up trouble and rouse
the *r.*

race
Acts 7:19. he made a crafty attack on
our *r.*
10:28. associate with a man of
another *r.*
17:26. he created every *r.* of men of
one stock
20:24. I only want to finish the *r.*
Rom. 5:12. death pervaded the whole
human *r.*
11:14. to stir emulation in the men of
my own *r.*
Gal. 2:2. the *r.* I had run, and was
running
Eph. 3:5. this was not disclosed to the
human *r.*
Phil. 2:16. proof that I did not run my
r. in vain

Phil. 3:5. Israelite by *r.*
1 Tim. 6:12. run the great *r.* of faith
2 Tim. 4:7. I have run the great *r.*
1 Pet. 2:9. you are a chosen *r.*

rack-ed-ing
Mat. 4:24. every kind of illness, *r.* with
    pain
    8:6. paralysed and *r.* with pain
Mark 9:26. after crying aloud and *r.* him
    fiercely

radiance
2 Thess. 2:8. annihilate by the *r.* of his
    coming
Rev. 21:11. it had the *r.* of some price-
    less jewel

rag-s
1 Cor. 4:11. we go hungry and thirsty
    and in *r.*
Jam. 2:15. suppose a brother or a sister
    is in *r.*

rage-d-ing
Acts 27:20. a great storm was *r.*
Gal. 5:20. envy, fits of *r.*
Rev. 11:18. the nations *r.*

rain
Luke 12:54. it is going to *r.*', and *r.* it
    does
Jude 12. clouds carried away by the
    wind without giving *r.*

raise-d-ing
Mat. 17:8. when they *r.* their eyes they
    saw no one
    21:9. others that came behind *r.* the
    shout
    23:4. will not *r.* a finger to lift the load
Mark 9:27. Jesus took his hand and
    r. him to his feet
Luke 18:13. would not even *r.* his eyes
    to heaven
John 2:20. are you going to *r.* it again
    in three days
    6:5. *r.* his eyes and seeing a large
    crowd
    11:43. he *r.* his voice in a great cry:
    'Lazarus, come forth
Acts 2:14. *r.* his voice, and addressed
    them
    4:24. they *r.* their voices as one man
    10:26. Peter *r.* him to his feet
    11:2. those who were of Jewish birth
    r. the question with him
    17:32. when they heard about the *r.*
    of the dead, some scoffed
    19:39. some further question to *r.*
    19:40. if the issue is *r.*
Rom. 6:13. as dead men *r.* to life
    15:26. *r.* a common fund for the
    benefit of the poor
Cor. 10:25 } without *r.* questions of
    10:27 } conscience

2 Cor. 11:7. lowering myself to help in *r.*
    you
Phil. 2:9. God *r.* him to the heights
Heb. 1:4. *r.* as far above the angels
    7:26. such a high priest . . . *r.* high
    above the heavens
Rev. 10:5. *r.* his right hand to heaven

ran
Mat. 18:24. whose debt *r.* into millions
    26:56. the disciples all deserted him
    and *r.* away
Mark 1:7. his proclamation *r.*
    14:50. all deserted him and *r.* away
    14:52. *r.* away naked
    16:8. *r.* away from the tomb
Luke 7:17. the story of what he had done
    r. through all parts
    23:38. an inscription above his head
    which *r.*
Acts 19:16. they *r.* out of the house
    stripped
2 Cor. 11:9. if I *r.* short I sponged on no
    one

rang
1 Thess. 1:8. the word of the Lord *r.* out

range-d
Luke 1:54. he has *r.* himself at the side
    of Israel

rank-s-ing
Mat. 10:24. a pupil does not *r.* above
    his teacher
Luke 22:24. who among them should
    r. highest
John 1:15. he comes after me, but takes
    r. before me
    1:30. after me a man is coming who
    takes *r.* before me
Acts 5:14. added to their *r.* as believers
    16:12. Philippi, a city of the first *r.*
    25:23. accompanied by high-*r.* officers

ransack ing
Mat. 12:29. tied the strong man up
    before *r.* the house
Mark 3:27. then he can *r.* the house

ransom-ed
Rev. 14:3. from the whole world had
    been *r.*
    14:4. *r.* as the firstfruits of humanity

rapacity
Rom. 1:29. mischief, *r.*, and malice

rapid-ly
Mark 1:28. the news spread *r.*
Acts 6:7. the number of disciples in
    Jerusalem went on increasing *r.*

rascal
Mat. 25:26. you lazy *r.*!' said the master
Luke 19:22. you *r.*!' he replied

rather

Mat. 3:14. I need *r.* to be baptized by you

John 12:44. he believes in him who sent me *r.* than in me

Acts 4:19. to obey you *r.* than God

25:22. I should *r.* like to hear the man myself

1 Cor. 9:15. I had *r.* die

2 Cor. 5:4. *r.* our desire is to have the new body put on

5:12. we are *r.* giving you a chance

ration-s

Mat. 24:45 ⎱ issue their *r.* at the proper
Luke 12:42 ⎰ time

rational

Rom. 7:25. subject to God's law as a *r.* being

ravage

Rev. 7:2. the power to *r.* land and sea

rave-ing

John 10:20. he is possessed, he is *r.*

Acts 26:24. Paul, you are *r.*

ravening

Heb. 11:33. they muzzled *r.* lions

ravine

Luke 3:5. every *r.* shall be filled in

John 18:1. crossed the Kedron *r.*

raw

Acts 5:33 ⎱ this touched them on the *r.*
    7:54 ⎰

ray-s

Luke 11:36. as when a lamp flashes its *r.* upon you

reach-ed-ing

Mat. 4:24. his fame *r.* the whole of Syria

8:28. he *r.* the other side, in the country of the Gadarenes

14:1. reports about Jesus *r.* the ears of Prince Herod

14:31. Jesus at once *r.* out and caught hold of him

21:1. they *r.* Bethany

26:51. one of those with Jesus *r.* for his sword and drew it

Mark 11:1. they *r.* Bethphage and Bethany

14:32. they *r.* a place called Gethsemane

14:45. when he *r.* the spot, he stepped forward at once

14:49. I was within your *r.* as I taught in the temple

Luke 6:40. will *r.* his teacher's level

9:42. before the boy could *r.* him the devil dashed him

13:32. on the third day I *r.* my goal

16:26. no one from our side who wants to *r.* you can cross it

23:33. when they *r.* the place called The Skull

24:28. they had *r.* the village

John 4:1. a report now *r.* the Pharisees

6:21. immediately the boat *r.* the land

11:30. Jesus had not yet *r.* the village

20:4. *r.* the tomb first

20:8. the disciple who had *r.* the tomb first

Acts 4:4. the number of men now *r.* about five thousand

9:26. when he *r.* Jerusalem he tried to join the body of disciples

11:5. lowered from the sky till it *r.* me

11:22. the news *r.* the ears of the church

12:10. *r.* the iron gate

15:4. when they *r.* Jerusalem they were welcomed by the church

16:8. *r.* the coast at Troas

18:19. when they *r.* Ephesus

19:21. when things had *r.* this stage

20:6. in five days *r.* them at Troas

21:7. and *r.* Ptolemais

21:17. we *r.* Jerusalem, where the brotherhood welcomed us

21:35. when Paul *r.* the steps, he had to be carried

27:7. we were hard put to it to *r.* Cnidus

28:13. we *r.* Puteoli in two days

28:25. without *r.* any agreement

Rom. 7:21. only the wrong is within my *r.*

14:5. *r.* conviction in his own mind

2 Cor. 5:14. *r.* the conclusion that one man died for all

Phil. 3:12. not yet *r.* perfection, but I press on

3:16. conduct be consistent with the level we have already *r.*

Col. 2:20. pass beyond *r.* of the elemental spirits of the world

1 Thess. 1:8. your faith in God has *r.* men's ears

1 Tim. 6:10. in *r.* for it have wandered from the faith

2 Tim. 3:7. incapable of *r.* a knowledge of the truth

Heb. 11:40. should they *r.* their perfection

Jam. 5:4. the outcry of the reapers has *r.* the ears of the Lord of Hosts

2 Pet. 1:12. the truth that has already *r.* you

Rev. 12:14. out of *r.* of the serpent

read-s

Mat. 2:5. the prophecy which *r.*

9:4. Jesus *r.* their thoughts

Mark 15:25. the charge against him *r.*

John 19:19. it *r*.,'Jesus of Nazareth King of the Jews

Acts 15:8. God, who can *r*. men's minds

Rom. 3:4. we *r*. in Scripture

    12:19. there is a text which *r*.

    1:Cor. 9:9. in the Law of Moses we *r*.

    14:21. we *r*. in the Law

Gal. 3:11. because we *r*., 'he shall gain life

    3:12. we *r*., 'he who does this shall gain life

Heb. 4:5. in the passage above we *r*.

readily

Rom. 11:24. how much more *r*. will they, the natural olive-branches

Heb. 12:9. submit even more *r*. to our spiritual Father

readiness

Mark 14:15. a large room upstairs, set out in *r*.

ready

Mat. 3:12. his shovel is *r*. in his hand

    25:34. the kingdom that has been *r*. for you

    25:41. the eternal fire that is *r*. for the devil

    26:38. my heart is *r*. to break with grief

Mark. 3:9. he told his disciples to have a boat *r*. for him

    14:34. my heart is *r*. to break with grief

Luke 2:31. the deliverance which thou hast made *r*.

    3:17. his shovel is *r*. in his hand

    12:35. be *r*. for action

    12:36. *r*. to let him in the moment he arrives

    19:8. I am *r*. to repay him four times over

John 5:35. you were *r*. to exult in his light

    6:21. then they were *r*. to take him aboard

Acts 13:24. John made *r*. for his coming

1 Cor. 3:2. solid food, for which you were not yet *r*.

    3:3. you are still not *r*. for it

2 Cor. 7:15. how *r*. you all were to do what he asked

    12:5. about such a man as that I am *r*. to boast

Heb. 11:16. he has a city *r*. for them

Rev. 9:15. they had been held *r*. for this moment

    21:2. made *r*. like a bride

real

Luke 7:39. if this fellow were a *r*. prophet

    16:11. the wealth that is *r*.

John 1:9. the *r*. light which enlightens every man

    4:23. *r*. worshippers will worship the Father

    6:32. my Father gives you the *r*. bread

    6:55. my flesh is *r*. food; my blood is *r*. drink

    15:1. I am the *r*. vine

Acts 12:9. no idea that the angel's intervention was *r*.

1 Cor. 8:4. a false god has no existence in the *r*. world

Heb. 8:2. a ministrant in the *r*. sanctuary

Jam. 2:18. prove to me that this faith you speak of is *r*.

1 John 2:8. the *r*. light already shines

    2:27. his initiation, which is *r*.

    5:20. to know him who is *r*.; indeed we are in him who is *r*.

reality

Col. 2:17. the solid *r*. is Christ's

2 Tim. 3:5. but are a standing denial of its *r*.

Heb. 9:24. sanctuary made by men's hands which is only a symbol of the *r*.

realize-d

Luke 1:22. they *r*. that he had had a vision

Acts 12:12. when he *r*. how things stood

    22:29. when he *r*. that Paul was a Roman citizen

Heb. 6:11. until your hope is finally *r*.

really

John 7:4. if you *r*. are doing such things as these

Acts 9:26. they did not believe that he was *r*. a convert

1 Cor. 4:7. if then you *r*. received it all as a gift

Gal. 4:17. what they *r*. want is to bar the door to you

1 John 2:19. from our company, but never *r*. belonged to us

realm-s

John 1:11. he entered his own *r*.

Rom. 8:38. in the *r*. of spirits

Eph. 1:3. every spiritual blessing in the heavenly *r*.

    1:20. at his right hand in the heavenly *r*.

    2:6. enthroned us with him in the heavenly *r*.

    3:10. authorities in the *r*. of heaven

Col. 1:12. God's people in the *r*. of light

    3:1. aspire to the *r*. above

    3:2. let your thoughts dwell on that higher *r*.

1 John 3:14. the man who does not love is still in the *r*. of death

    3:19. know that we belong to the *r*. of truth

reap-ed-ing
Phil. 1:11. *r.* the full harvest of righteousness
Jam. 3:18. the harvest *r.* by peacemakers
1 Pet. 1:9. you *r.* the harvest of your faith

rear-s
2 Cor. 10:5. all that *r.* its proud head against the knowledge of God

reason-ing
Mat. 19:5 ⎫ for this *r.* a man shall leave
Mark 10:7 ⎭ his father and mother
  12:24. you are mistaken, and surely this is the *r.*
Luke 1:35. for that *r.* the holy child to be born will be called 'Son of God
  14:20. just got married and for that *r.* I cannot come
John 1:31. the very *r.* why I came
  15:19. for that *r.* the world hates you
  15:25. they hated me without *r.*
Acts 10:29. what was your *r.* for sending
  22:24. what *r.* there was for such an outcry
  24:26. for this *r.* he sent for him very often
Rom. 1:20. to the eye of *r.*
  1:28. he has given them up to their own depraved *r.*
  7:23. the law that my *r.* approves
1 Cor. 4:14. to bring you to *r.*
  12:3. for this *r.* I must impress upon you
2 Cor. 1:14. you have as much *r.* to be proud of us, as we of you
1 Tim. 6:5. let their *r.* powers become atrophied
2 Tim. 1:12. that is the *r.* for my present plight
  3:8. they have lost the power to *r.*
Tit. 1:13. all the more *r.* why you should pull them up sharply
  1:15. tainted alike in *r.* and conscience
Jam. 3:17. open to *r.*
1 John 3:1. the *r.* why the godless world does not recognise us
  5:14. we can approach God with confidence for this *r.*

reassure-s
1 Thess. 3:7. your faith *r.* us about you

rebel-s-led
Mark 15:7. Barabbas was then in custody with the *r.*
Rom. 13:2. anyone who *r.* against authority
Eph. 2:2. God's *r.* subjects
  5:6. judgement is coming upon his *r.* subjects
Heb. 3:16. those who heard and *r.*
Jude 11. they have *r.* like Korah

rebellion
Mark 3:26. if Satan is in *r.* against himself
2 Cor. 10:6. we are prepared to punish all *r.*
2 Thess. 2:3. the final *r.* against God
Heb. 3:8. those days of *r.*
  3:15. do not grow stubborn as in those days of *r.*

rebellious
Luke 1:17. to convert the *r.* to the ways of the righteous

rebirth
Tit. 3:5. he saved us through the water of *r.*

rebuild
Mat. 26:61. I can pull down the temple of God, and *r.* it in three days
Acts 15:16. *r.* the fallen house of David

rebuke-d
Luke 3:19. he was *r.* by him over the affair of his brother's wife

recalcitrant
Rom. 10:21. an unruly and *r.* people

recall-s-ed-ing
Mat. 27:63. we *r.* how that imposter said
Mark 11:21. Peter, *r.* what had happened
Luke 24:8. then they *r.* his words
John 2:17. his disciples *r.* the words of Scripture
  2:22 after his resurrection his disciples *r.* what he had said
Acts 11:16. then I *r.* what the Lord had said
2 Cor. 7:15. he *r.* how ready you all were to do what he asked
2 Pet. 3:1. I have been *r.* to you what you already know
2 John 5. I am *r.* the one we have had before us

receipt-s
Phil. 4:15. my partners in payments and *r.*
  4:18. I give you my *r.* for everything

receive-s-d-ing
Mat. 7:7. ask, and you will *r.*
Mark 4:18. *r.* the seed among thistles
  4:24. is the measure you will *r.*
  4:33. as they were able to *r.* it
  12:38. *r.* respectful greetings
  16:16. those who believe it and *r.* baptism
Luke 12:10. speaks a word against the Son of Man will *r.* forgiveness
  14:10. when you *r.* an invitation
  16:1. he *r.* complaints that this man
John 10:17. I lay down my life, to *r.* it back
  13:27. as soon as Judas had *r.* it.

John 14:21. has *r.* my commands and obeys them
Acts 1:25. to *r.* this office of ministry
4:12. by which we may *r.* salvation
Rom. 1:12. to *r.* encouragement myself
2:18. you *r.* instruction from the law
2:29. *r.* his commendation not from men but from God
11:30. now have *r.* mercy in the time of their disobedience
11:31. so now, when you *r.* mercy, they have proved disobedient, but only in order that they too may *r.* mercy
11:35. to *r.* a gift in return
16:17. contrary to the teaching you *r.*
1 Cor. 4:5. to *r.* from God such praise as he deserves
7:22. who as a slave *r.* the call to be a Christian is the Lord's freed man, and, equally, the free man who *r.* the call
7:24. the condition in which he *r.* his call
10:2. they all *r.* baptism
14:30. *r.* a revelation
14:31. that the whole congregation may *r.* instruction
15:29. those who *r.* baptism on behalf of the dead
2 Cor. 1:4. the consolation we ourselves *r.* from God
1:9. we had *r.* a death-sentence
Gal. 5:2. if you *r.* circumcision
5:3. every man who *r.* circumcision
6:13. even those who do *r.* circumcision
Eph. 1:13. *r.* the seal of the promised Holy Spirit
1:23. *r.* the entire fullness of God
Col. 1:9. *r.* from him all wisdom
2:19. from the Head that the whole body, with all its joints and ligaments, *r.* its supplies
Heb. 4:16. where we may *r.* mercy
1 Pet. 2:10. you have now *r.* his mercy
3:22. after *r.* the submission of angelic
4:6. they *r.* the sentence common to men
Rev. 7:4. those who had *r.* the seal
9:4. those men who had not *r.* the seal
13:3. one of its heads appeared to have *r.* a death-blow

recently
Acts 18:2. he had *r.* arrived from Italy

reception
Luke 5:29. Levi held a big *r.*

recite-d
Heb. 9:19. Moses had *r.* all the commandments

reckless
Luke 15:13. squandered it in *r.* living

1 Pet. 4:4. all this *r.* dissipation
2 Pet. 2:10. *r.* and headstrong

reckon-ed-ing
Acts 19:19. the total value was *r.* up
Rom. 5:13. in the absence of law no *r.* is kept of sin
9:8. *r.* as Abraham's descendants
2 Cor. 10:2. I *r.* I could put on as bold a face as you please
10:11. people who talk in that way should *r.* with this
Phil. 2:3. *r.* others better than yourselves
3:13. I do not *r.* myself to have got hold of it yet
1 Tim. 5:17. *r.* worthy of a double stipend
Heb. 4:13. the One wi h whom we have to *r.*
11:19. he *r.* that God had power even to raise from the dead

recline-d-ing
John 13:23. *r.* close beside Jesus
13:25. that disciple, as he *r.*, leaned back

recognition
1 Cor. 16:18. such men deserve *r.*

recognize-d-ing
Mat. 7:16. *r.* them by the fruits they bear
7:20. why I say you will *r.* them by their fruits
14:35. Jesus was *r.* by the people
17:12. they failed to *r.* him
Mark 6:33. saw them leave and *r.* them
6:54. when they came ashore, he was immediately *r.*
10:42. the *r.* rulers lord it over their subjects
Luke 4:24. no prophet is *r.* in his own country
19:44. you did not *r.* God's moment when it came
24:31. their eyes were opened, and they *r.* him
24:35. told how he had been *r.* by them
John 1:10. the world, though it owed its being to him, did not *r.* him
10:5. they do not *r.* the voice of strangers
10:38. *r.* and know that the Father is in me
20:14. saw Jesus standing there, but did not *r.* him
Acts 3:10. they *r.* him as the man who used to sit begging
4:13. *r.* them as former companions of Jesus
7:13. Joseph was *r.* by his brothers
12:14. she *r.* Peter's voice
13:27. their rulers did not *r.* him
19:34. they *r.* that he was a Jew

Acts 27:39. they could not *r.* the land
Rom. 2:4. without *r.* that God's kindness
  10:19. that Israel failed to *r.* the message
1 Cor. 14:37. let him *r.* that what I write has the Lord's authority
  14:38. if he does not *r.* this, he himself should not be *r.*
2 Cor. 13:5. surely you *r.* that Jesus Christ is among you
Gal. 2:6. God does not *r.* these personal distinctions
  2:9. *r.,* then, the favour thus bestowed upon me
Col. 1:6. the graciousness of God and *r.* it
1 Tim. 1:9. *r.* that it is not aimed at good citizens
2 Tim. 3:9. *r.* by everyone for the fools they are
Tit. 3:11. *r.* that a man of that sort has a distorted mind
1 Pet. 2:12. behaviour be such as even pagans can *r.* as good
1 John 2:29. *r.* that every man who does right
  3:1. the godless world does not *r.* us
  4:2. how we may *r.* the Spirit of God

recommend-s
2 Cor. 4:2. by declaring the truth openly do we *r.* ourselves
  5:12. not another attempt to *r.* ourselves
  6:4. to *r.* ourselves in all circumstances
  6:6. *r.* ourselves by the innocence of our behaviour
  10:18. not the man who *r.* himself, but the man whom the Lord *r.*

recompense
Rev. 11:18. *r.* to thy servants the prophets
  22:12. bringing my *r.* with me

reconcile-d
Luke 1:17. to *r.* father and child
Col. 1:22. God has *r.* you to himself

reconciliation
Rom. 5:11. we have now been granted *r.*
  11:15. the *r.* of the world

record-ed
John 20:30. which are not *r.* in this book
  20:31. *r.* in order that you may hold the faith
  21:25. if it were all to be *r.* in detail
1 Cor. 10:11. *r.* for our benefit as a warning
Phil. 2:22. Timothy's *r.* is known to you
1 Tim. 3:13. deacons with a good *r.* of service

Heb. 11:2. for their faith that the men of old stand on *r.*
1 Pet. 1:17. impartially on the *r.* of his deeds
Rev. 14:13. the *r.* of their deeds
  20:12. the dead were judged upon the *r.* of their deeds
  20:13. each man on the *r.* of his deeds

recount-ed
Luke 2:17. they *r.* what they had been told about this child

recover-ed
Mat. 8:13. at that moment the boy *r.*
  9:22. from that moment she *r.*
  9:33. the patient *r.* his speech
  11:5. the blind *r.* their sight
Mark. 10:52. at once he *r.* his sight
Luke 7:22. how the blind *r.* their sight
  18:43. he *r.* his sight instantly
John 5:4. *r.* from whatever disease
  5:6. do you want to *r.*
  5:9. the man *r.* instantly
  11:12. if he has fallen asleep he will *r.*
Acts 9:17. that you may *r.* your sight
  22:13. Saul, my brother, *r.* your sight.' Instantly I *r.* my sight

recovery
Acts 3:19. the Lord may grant you a time of *r.*

recrimination
1 Pet. 2:1. jealousy and *r.*

recruited
Acts 17:5. the Jews in their jealousy *r.* some low fellows

rectitude
Phil. 3:6. in legal *r.,* faultless
  3:9. no righteousness of my own, no legal *r.*

recurrent
Acts 28:8. suffering from *r.* bouts of fever

red
1 Cor. 10:1. all of them passed through the *R.* Sea
Jam. 3:6. it keeps the wheel of our existence *r.*-hot
Rev. 6:12. the moon all *r.* as blood
  9:17. they wore breastplates, fiery *r.*

redeem-ed
Eph. 1:14. when God has *r.* what is his own

redound
Eph. 1:6. might *r.* to his praise

redress
Acts 8:33. he has been humiliated and has no *r.*

re-embark-ed
Mark 8:13. with that he left them, *r.*

refer-s-red-ring
Mat. 2:5. *r.* him to the prophecy which reads
21:45. saw that he was *r.* to them
Luke 23:15. he has *r.* him back to us
24:27. the passages which *r.* to himself
1 Cor. 5:10. I was not, of course, *r.* to pagans
9:10. of course it *r.* to us
Gal. 4:17. the persons I have *r.* to
Eph. 5:32. I for my part *r.* it to Christ
Heb. 4:3. believers, who enter the rest *r.* to

reference
1 Cor. 9:10 .is the *r.* clearly to ourselves
Eph. 2:11. only with *r.* to an outward rite
Heb. 7:14. Moses made no *r.* in speaking of priests

refine-d
Rev. 1:15. like burnished brass *r.* in a furnace
3:18. gold *r.* in the fire

reflect-s-ing
1 Cor. 11:7. woman *r.* the glory of man
2 Cor. 3:18. we all *r.* as in a mirror the splendour of the Lord
10:7. *r.* that we belong to Christ
2 Tim. 2:7. *r.* on what I say, for the Lord will help you
Heb. 13:7. *r.* upon the outcome of their life and work

reflection-s
1 Cor. 13:12. now we see only puzzling *r.*

reformation
2 Tim. 3:16. *r.* of manners

refractory
2 Tim. 2:25. when discipline is needed for the *r.*

refrain
Mat. 19:10. it is better to *r.* from marriage
Acts 4:18. ordered them to *r.* from all public speaking
2 Cor. 12:6. I *r.*, because I should not like anyone

refresh-ing
Rom. 15:15. I have written to *r.* your memory
2 Pet. 1:13. I think it right to keep *r.* your memory

refuge
Mat. 10:23. persecuted in one town, take *r.* in another

refugee-s
Heb. 11:38. they were *r.* in deserts and on the hills

refusal
John 16:9. by their *r.* to believe in me

refuse-s-d-ing
Mat. 2:18. *r.* all consolation
18:17. if he *r.* to listen to them
18:30. but he *r.*, and had him jailed
27:14. he still *r.* to answer one word
Mark 6:26. he could not bring himself to *r.* her
Luke 7:30. the Pharisees and lawyers, who *r.* his baptism
15:28. he was angry and *r.* to go in
18:4. for a long time he *r.*
John 5:40. you *r.* to come to me for that life
19:10. do you *r.* to speak to me
Acts 3:23. anyone who *r.* to listen to that prophet
Rom. 1:21. they have *r.* to honour him as God
2:8. who *r.* obedience to the truth
1 Cor. 2:14. a man who is unspiritual *r.* what belongs to the Spirit of God
Gal. 5:1. *r.* to be tied to the yoke of slavery
2 Thess. 1:8. those who *r.* to acknowledge God
Heb. 3:18. those who had *r.* to believe
Jam. 1:5. who neither *r.* nor reproaches anyone
1 Pet. 3:20. they had *r.* obedience long ago
4:17. those who *r.* to obey the gospel of God
1 John 4:6. he who does not belong to God *r.* us a hearing
5:10. *r.* to accept God's own witness to his Son
3 John 10. *r.* to receive our friends
Rev. 2:21. she *r.* to repent of her fornication
11:9. gaze upon their corpses and *r.* them burial
16:9. they *r.* to repent or do him homage

refute-ing
Mat. 12:27 ⎱ they themselves will *r.* you
Luke 11:19 ⎰
21:15. no opponent will be able to resist or *r.*
2 Tim. 3:16. teaching the truth and *r.* error

regain-ed
Acts 9:18. scales fell from his eyes, and he *r.* his sight
Heb. 12:13. *r.* its former powers

regard-s-ed-ing
Mat. 14:9 ⎱ out of *r.* for his oath
Mark 6:26 ⎰
John 12:47. hears my words and pays no *r.* to them

Acts 5:34. held in high *r.* by all the people

Rom. 6:11. *r.* yourselves as dead to sin
12:16. have equal *r.* for one another
14:5. this man *r.* one day more highly than another, while that man *r.* all days alike

1 Cor. 4:1. we must be *r.* as Christ's underlings
10:24. *r.*, not his own interests
10:33. *r.* not my own good
11:10. out of *r.* for the angels
12:23. which we *r.* as less honourable

2 Cor. 8:7. the loving *r.* you have for us

Heb. 2:6. that thou hast *r.* to him

region-s

Mat. 2:22. he withdrew to the *r.* of Galilee
15:21. withdraw to the *r.* of Tyre and Sidon
15:29. leaving that *r.* Jesus took the road
19:1. came into the *r.* of Judaea

Mark 10:1. came into the *r.* of Judaea and Transjordan

John 3:23. water was plentiful in that *r.*
11:54. left that *r.* for the country

Acts 19:1. Paul travelled through the inland *r.*

register-ed

Luke 2:4. to be *r.* at the city of David

registration

Luke 2:1. a general *r.*
2:2. this was the first *r.* of its kind

regret

2 Cor. 7:8. if I did wound you by the letter I sent, I do not now *r.* it
7:10. a change of heart too salutary to *r.*

regular-ly

Luke 4:16 on the Sabbath day as he *r.* did

Acts 10:2. was *r.* in his prayers to God

1 Tim. 5:5. *r.* attends the meetings for prayer

regulation-s

Eph. 2:15. the law with its rules and *r.*

reign-s-ed-ing

Mat. 2:1. during the *r.* of Herod

Luke 19:11. the *r.* of God might dawn at any moment
22:53. the hour when darkness *r.*

Acts 11:28. occurred in the *r.* of Claudius
13:21. who *r.* for forty years

2 Tim. 4:1. by his coming appearance and his *r.*
4:18. until his heavenly *r.* begins

Jam. 2:1. our Lord Jesus Christ, who *r.* in glory

Rev. 13:5. given the right to *r.* for forty-two months
17:10. five have already fallen one is now *r.*
17:12. ten kings who have not yet begun to *r.*

rein

1 Cor. 7:35. I have no wish to keep you on a tight *r.*

reject-s-ed

Luke 2:34. this child is destined to be a sign which men *r.*
10:16. whoever *r.* you *r.* me. And whoever *r.* me *r.* the One who sent me

John 3:11. you all *r.* our testimony

Acts 4:11. this Jesus is the stone *r.* by the builders
7:35. this Moses, whom they had *r.*
13:46. you *r.* it and thus condemn yourselves

Rom. 11:1. has God *r.* his people
11:2 God has not *r.* the people

1 Cor. 9:27. after preaching to others I should find myself *r.*

1 Tim. 4:4. nothing is to be *r.* when it is taken with thanksgiving

1 Pet. 2:4. the stone *r.* by men
2:7. the stone which the builders *r.*

rejection

Rom. 11:15. if their *r.* has meant the reconciliation of the world

rejoice-d-ing

Acts 11:23. saw the divine grace at work, he *r.*
15:3. the news caused great *r.*

Col. 2:5. *r.* to see your orderly array

1 Thess. 1:6. you *r.* in the Holy Spirit
3:9. making us *r.* before our God

rejoin-ed

Mark. 6:30. the apostles now *r.* Jesus

Luke 11:28. he *r.*, 'No, happy are those who hear the word of God and keep it
11:46. Jesus *r.*: 'Yes, you lawyers

Acts 17:15. instructions for Silas and Timothy to *r.* him
22:28. the commandant *r.*

relation-s

Luke 2:44. looking for him among their friends and *r.*
14:12. your brothers or other *r.*
21:16. your *r.* and friends

John 18:26. a *r.* of the man whose ear Peter had cut off

Rom. 1:27. giving up natural *r.* with women

Gal. 5:4. your *r.* with Christ

1 Tim. 5:8. does not make provision for his *r.*

relative-s
Luke 1:58. *r*. heard what great favour the Lord had shown her
Acts 7:14. hid father Jacob and all his *r*.
10:24. called together his *r*.

release-d
Mat. 27:20. to ask for the *r*. of Barabbas
Luke 4:18. to proclaim *r*. for prisoners
Acts 3:14. Pilate had decided to *r*. him. You begged as a favour the *r*. of a murderer
16:35. with instructions to *r*. the men
16:36. the magistrates have sent word that you are to be *r*.
22:30. he *r*. him and ordered the chief priests
28:18. to *r*. me because there was no capital charge
Eph. 1:7. in Christ our *r*. is secured
Col. 1:14. his dear Son, in whom our *r*. is secured
Heb. 11:35. tortured to death, disdaining *r*.
13:23. our friend Timothy has been *r*.
Rev. 9:14. *r*. the four angels held bound

reliance
Acts 14:3. in *r*. on the Lord
24:15. in *r*. on God I hold the hope
2 Cor. 1:9. not to place *r*. on ourselves
3:4. it is in full *r*. upon God

relief
Mat. 11:28. I will give you *r*.
11:29. your souls will find *r*.
2 Cor. 2:13. I still found no *r*. of mind
7:5. no *r*. for this poor body of ours
2 Thess. 1:7. *r*. to you who are troubled

relieve-d-ing
1 Cor. 16:18. they have *r*. my mind
2 Cor. 8:13. *r*. others at the cost of hardship
Phil. 2:28. to *r*. my sorrow
2 Tim. 1:16. he has often *r*. me in my troubles
Philem. 20. *r*. my anxiety

religion
Mat. 6:1. not to make a show of your *r*.
Acts 10:28. a Jew is forbidden by his *r*.
14:22. to be true to their *r*.
17:22. in everything that concerns *r*.
25:19. their peculiar *r*.
1 Tim. 2:2. in full observance of *r*.
3:16. is the mystery of our *r*.
4:7. the practice of *r*.
4:8. the benefits of *r*. are without limit
6:5. think *r*. should yield dividends
6:6. *r*. does yield high dividends
2 Tim. 3:5. the outward form of *r*.
Tit. 1:1. the truth as our *r*. has it
Heb. 3:1. the *r*. we profess
4:14. hold fast to the *r*. we profess

2 Pet. 1:3. life and true *r*.
3:3. there will come men who scoff at *r*.
Jude 4. they are the enemies of *r*.
18. men who pour scorn on *r*.

religious
John 16:2. suppose that he is performing a *r*. duty
Acts 10:2. he was a *r*. man
10:7. a military orderly who was a *r*. man
10:22. Cornelius,' they replied, 'a good and *r*. man
1 Tim. 2:10. as befits women who claim to be *r*.
6:3. good *r*. teaching

reluctance
2 Cor. 9:7. there should be no *r*.

rely-ied-ing
Luke 11:22. armour on which the man had *r*.
John 5:34. not that I *r*. on human testimony
5:36. I *r*. on a testimony higher than John's
Rom. 2:17. you *r*. upon the law
4:12. do not *r*. upon their circumcision alone
1 Cor. 1:17. without *r*. on the language of worldly wisdom
9:8. do not suppose I *r*. on these human analogies
Gal. 3:10. those who *r*. on obedience to the law
2 Pet. 1:16. not on tales artfully spun that we *r*.

remade
Rom. 12:2. let your minds be *r*.

remain-s-ed-ing
Mark 1:13. he *r*. for forty days tempted by Satan
1:35. *r*. there in prayer
3:31. *r*. outside sent in a message
7:24. he would have liked to *r*. unrecognized
14:54. there he *r*., sitting among the attendants
Luke 1:20. lose your powers of speech, and *r*. silent
12:21. *r*. a pauper in the sight of God
John 12:24. a grain of wheat *r*. a solitary grain
12:46. no one who has faith in me should *r*. in darkness
15:4. only if it *r*. united with the vine; no more can you bear fruit, unless you *r*. united with me
20:23. unforgiven they *r*.
Acts 7:16. their *r*. were later removed
25:24. insisting that he had no right to *r*. alive

Acts 28:24. others *r*. sceptical
Rom. 11:22. if only you *r*. within its scope
1 Cor. 7:20. *r*. in the condition in which he was called
7:24. *r*. before God in the condition
16:8. I shall *r*. at Ephesus
Gal. 1:22. *r*. unknown by sight
1 Thess. 3:1. decided to *r*. alone at Athens
4:13. we want you not to *r*. in ignorance
2 Thess. 1:4. your faith *r*. so steadfast
Heb. 4:1. the promise of entering his rest *r*.
7:3. *r*. a priest for all time
7:24. he *r*. for ever
9:8. the way into the sanctuary *r*. unrevealed
Jam. 1:12. *r*. steadfast under trial
Rev. 14:12. *r*. loyal to Jesus

remand-ed

Acts 25:21. Paul appealed to be *r*. in custody

remarkable

Acts 5:12. many *r*. and wonderful things

remedy

1 John 2:2. he is himself the *r*. for the defilement of our sins
4:10. sending his Son as the *r*.

remember-est-ed-ing

Mat. 24:42. *r*., if the householder had known at what time
Mark 14:72. Peter *r*. how Jesus had said
Luke 12:39. *r*., if the householder had known
Acts 27:34. *r*., not a hair of your heads will be lost
Rom. 11:18. *r*. that it is not you who sustain the root
13:11. *r*. how critical the moment is
2 Cor. 9:6. *r*.; sparse sowing, sparse reaping
Gal. 5:9. a little leaven', *r*., 'leavens all the dough
Eph. 6:9. *r*. you both have the same Master
2 Tim. 1:4. I *r*. the tears you shed
3:14. *r*. from whom you learned them
3:15. *r*. that from early childhood
Heb. 2:6. what is man, that thou *r*. him
12:18. *r*. where you stand
13:2. *r*. to show hospitality
Jam. 5:10. the prophets who spoke in the name of the Lord; *r*.
1 Pet. 4:1. *r*. that Christ endured bodily suffering
5:9. *r*. that your brother Christians
Jude 6. *r*. too the angels
7. *r*. Sodom and Gomorrah
Rev. 22:7. *r*., I am coming soon

remind-ed-ing

John 5:34. I *r*. you of it for your own salvation
1 Cor. 15:1. I must *r*. you of the gospel
2 Tim. 1:5. I am *r*. of the sincerity of your faith
1:6. I now *r*. you to stir into flame
2:14. go on *r*. people of this
Tit. 3:1. *r*. them to be submissive to the government
2 Pet. 1:12. I will not hesitate to *r*. you of this
Jude 5. let me *r*. you how the Lord

remit-ted

Mat. 18:27. let the man go and *r*. the debt
18:32. I *r*. the whole of your debt
Luke 23:7. Herod's jurisdiction he *r*. the case to him

remorse

Mat. 27:3. he was seized with *r*.
Rev. 1:7. all the peoples of the world shall lament in *r*.

removal

Heb. 12:27. the shaking of these created things means their *r*.

remove-d

Mark 7:35. the impediment was *r*.
John 11:41. so they *r*. the stone
19:38. asked to be allowed to *r*. the body of Jesus
20:15. if it is you, sir, who *r*. him
Acts 1:9. a cloud *r*. him from their sight
7:16. their remains were later *r*. to Shechem
23:27. I intervened with the troops and *r*. him
Rom. 11:26. he shall *r*. wickedness from Jacob
1 Cor. 7:18. let him not *r*. them
2 Cor. 3:16. the veil is *r*.
Heb. 10:4. sins can never be *r*. by the blood of bulls
10:11. sacrifices, which can never *r*. sins

render-ed

Rom. 1:21. to *r*. him thanks
Gal. 3:17. its promises *r*. ineffective
Phil. 2:30. risking his life to *r*. me the service
2 Tim. 1:18. the many services he *r*. at Ephesus
Heb. 6:10. you *r*. service to his people
13:17. men who must *r*. an account

renounce-d

Mat. 19:12. *r*. marriage for the sake of the kingdom of Heaven
Acts 26:11. to make them *r*. their faith
Tit. 2:12. *r*. godless ways

repaid
Mat. 19:29. will be *r.* many times over
Luke 6:34. you expect to be *r.*, what credit is that to you? Even sinners lend to each other if they are to be *r.* in full
14:12. so you will be *r.*
14:14. but you will be *r.*
18:30. *r.* many times over in this age
Eph. 6:8. will be *r.* him by the Lord

repay-ing
Luke 12:48. the more he will be required to *r.*
14:14. they have no means of *r.* you
19:8. I am ready to *r.* him four times over
1 Tim. 5:4. to *r.* what they owe to their parents
Heb. 10:30. justice is mine: I will *r.*
1 Pet. 3:9. do not *r.* wrong with wrong
Rev. 18:6. *r.* her twice over for her deeds

repeat-ed
Mat. 10:27. you must *r.* in broad daylight
19:24. I *r.*, it is easier for a camel
Mark 14:31. *r.*: 'Even if I must die with you
Luke 13:27. he will *r.*, 'I tell you, I do not know where you come from
John 20:21. Jesus *r.*, 'Peace be with you
Acts 4:21. the court *r.* the caution
26:11. I tried by *r.* punishment
2 Cor. 5:8. we are confident, I *r.*
12:4. so secret that human lips may not *r.* them
13:2. I *r.* the warning I gave before
Gal. 1:9. I now *r.* what I have said before
Phil. 3:1. to *r.* what I have written to you before
Col. 3:3. I *r.*, you died

replant-ed
Luke 17:6. be rooted up and *r.* in the sea

replied, reply
Frequently used in the Gospels and elsewhere

report-s-ed
Mat. 2:8. when you have found him, *r.* to me
14:1. *r.* about Jesus reached the ears of Prince Herod
18:17. *r.* the matter to the congregation
28:11. *r.* to the chief priests everything that had happened
Mark 6:30. *r.* to him all that they had done
6:55. any place where he was *r.* to be
15:45. when he heard the centurion's *r.*
Luke 4:14. *r.* about him spread

14:21. he *r.* this to his master
24:9. they *r.* all this to the Eleven
John 4:1. a *r.* now reached the Pharisees
8:26. I *r.* to the world
11:46. to the Pharisees and *r.* what he had done
Acts 5:22. *r.*, 'We found the jail securely locked
5:25. the *r.*, 'Look! the men you put in prison
12:17. *r.* this to James
14:27 ⎱ *r.* all that God had helped
15:4 ⎰ them to do
16:36. the jailer *r.* the message to Paul
16:38. the officers *r.* his words
21:31. a *r.* reached the officer
22:26. *r.* it to the commandant
23:16. *r.* it to Paul
23:17. he has something to *r.*
23:19. what is it you have to *r.*
25:26. I may have something to *r.*
28:21. any *r.* or gossip to your discredit

represent-s
Mat. 13:22. *r.* the man who hears the word
Luke 8:14. that which fell among thistles *r.*
8:15. the seed in good soil *r.*
Gal. 4:25. *r.* the Jerusalem of today
Jam. 3:6. it *r.* among our members
Rev. 13:18. the number *r.* a man's name
17:10. they *r.* also seven kings

representative-s
Acts 15:22. choose *r.* and send them
15:25. our chosen *r.*
2 Cor. 2:10. as the *r.* of Christ
Heb. 5:1. their *r.* before God

reprimand
Luke 19:39. Master, *r.* your disciples

reproach-es-ed
Mark 16:14. *r.* them for their incredulity
1 Cor. 1:8. without *r.* on the Day of our Lord Jesus
Phil. 2:15. show yourselves guileless and above *r.*
1 Tim. 3:2. bishop, must be above *r.*
5:7. that the widows may be above *r.*
Jam. 1:5. who neither refuses nor *r.* anyone
2 Pet. 3:14. above *r.* in his sight
Jude 24. jubilant and above *r.*

reprove
Rev. 3:19. all whom I love I *r.* and discipline

repudiate-d
Luke 17:25. be *r.* by this generation
Acts 3:13. *r.* in Pilate's court
3:14. *r.* the one who was holy and righteous

reputation

John 12:43. valued their *r.* with men
Acts 6:3. look out seven men of good *r.*
2 Cor. 8:18. whose *r.* is high
Gal. 2:6. as for the men of high *r.*
1 Tim. 3:7. a good *r.* with the non-Christian public

repute-d

Luke 1:36. she who is *r.* barren is now in her sixth month
Gal. 2:9. those *r.* pillars of our society

request-s-ed

Mat. 14:9. he ordered the *r.* to be granted
18:19. agree on earth about any *r.* you have to make, that *r.* will be granted
Mark 6:25. hastened back at once to the king with her *r.*
7:32. with the *r.* that he would lay his hand on him
15:6. release one prisoner at the people's *r.*
Luke 7:3. the *r.* that he would come and save his servant's life
11:8. the *r.* will make him get up and give him all he needs
John 16:26. you will make your *r.* in my name
19:31. *r.* Pilate to have the legs broken
Acts 9:38. sent two men to him with the urgent *r.*
16:39. *r.* them to go away from the city
23:20. will *r.* you to bring Paul down to the Council
1 Cor. 16:15. I have a *r.* to make of you
2 Cor. 8:17. Titus not only welcomed our *r.*
Jam. 4:3. your *r.* are not granted because you pray from wrong motives
1 John 5:14. if we make *r.* which accord with his will
5:15. we know that our *r.* are heard
2 John 5. I have a *r.* to make of you

require-s-d

Mat. 3:15. we do well to conform in this way with all that God *r.*
9:13
12:7 } I *r.* mercy, not sacrifice
22:16
Mark 12:14 } the way of life that God *r.*
Luke 20:21
John 6:29. this is the work that God *r.*
Acts 2:45. as the need of each *r.*
2 Tim. 4:2. the patience that the work of teaching *r.*
Heb. 9:23. *r.* better sacrifices to cleanse them

requite-d

Col. 3:25. dishonesty will be *r.*
Rev. 22:12. to *r.* everyone according to his deeds

rescue-d-ing

Mat. 27:43. let God *r.* him, if he wants him
Luke 1:74. to *r.* us from enemy hands
Acts 7:10. *r.* him from all his troubles
7:34. I have come down to *r.* them
12:11. *r.* me from Herod's clutches
26:17. I will *r.* you from this people
Rom. 7:24. who is there to *r.* me out of this body
Gal. 1:4. *r.* us out of this present age
Col. 1:13. *r.* us from the domain of darkness
2 Thess. 3:2. *r.* from wrong-headed and wicked men
2 Tim. 3:11. the Lord *r.* me out of them all
4:17. I was *r.* out of the lion's jaws
4:18. the Lord will *r.* me from every attempt to do me harm
Jam. 5:20. *r.* his soul from death
2 Pet. 2:7. he *r.* Lot, who was a good man
2:9. the Lord is well able to *r.* the godly
Rev. 12:16. the earth came to her *r.*

resentment

Acts 13:45. they were filled with jealous *r.*
Eph. 6:4. must not goad your children to *r.*

reserve-d

Mark 14:14. the room *r.* for me to eat the Passover
John 1:20. he confessed without *r.* and avowed

reside

Acts 12:19. to *r.* for a time at Caesarea
1 Pet. 3:3. your beauty should *r.*, not in outward adornment

resist-ed

Gal. 4:14. you *r.* any temptation to show scorn

resolute-ly

Luke 9:51. he set his face *r.* towards Jerusalem
Acts 11:23. hold fast to the Lord with *r.* hearts
Heb. 11:27. he was *r.*, as one who saw the invisible God

resolution

Acts 21:13. why are you trying to weaken my *r.*
2 Tim. 3:10. my manner of life, my *r.*
Heb. 12:1. run with *r.* the race

resolve-d
Mat. 1:20. he had *r*. on this
John 12:10. *r*. to do away with Lazarus
Acts 15:22. *r*. to choose representatives
  15:25. we have *r*. unanimously
Rom. 15:26. have *r*. to raise a common
  fund
  15:27. *r*. to do so, and indeed they
  are under an obligation
1 Cor. 2:2. I *r*. that while I was with you
  I would think of nothing but Jesus
  Christ

resort-ed
Acts 18:6. they opposed him and *r*. to
  abuse

resource-s
Luke 8:3. provided for them out of their
  own *r*.
2 Cor. 8:3. going to the limit of their *r*.
Eph. 1:19. how vast the *r*. of his power
  2:7. how immense are the *r*. of his
  grace
Phil. 4:11. I have learned to find *r*. in
  myself
1 Tim. 6:6. the man whose *r*. are within
  him

respect-s-ed-ing
Mat. 15:6. out of *r*. for your tradition
        21:37 ⎫
Mark 12:6 ⎬ they will *r*. my son
  15:43. a *r*. member of the Council
Luke 14:10. see the *r*. in which you are
  held
  20:13. perhaps they will *r*. him
Acts 18:22. paid his *r*. to the church
  19:27. the great goddess Diana will
  cease to command *r*.
  28:10. they honoured us with many
  marks of *r*.
Rom. 13:7. reverence and *r*., to those to
  whom they are due
  14:6. he who *r*. the day has the Lord
  in mind
2 Cor. 12:11. in no *r*. did I fall short
Eph. 5:33. she pays her husband all *r*.
1 Thess. 4:12. the *r*. of those outside
  your own number
1 Tim. 6:1. their own masters worthy of
  all *r*.
2 Tim. 3:2. with no *r*. for parents
Tit. 2:5. *r*. the authority of their own
  husbands
  2:9. tell slaves to *r*. their masters'
  authority
Heb. 12:9. we paid due *r*. to the earthly
  fathers
1 Pet. 3:15. make that defence with
  modesty and *r*.

respectful-ly
Mat. 23:7. greeted *r*. in the street
Mark 12:38. receiving *r*. greetings
Luke 20:46. a great liking for *r*. greetings

respite
Rev. 14:11. no *r*. day or night for those
  who worship the beast

resplendent
Acts 2:20. before that great, *r*. day, the
  day of the Lord, shall come
Phil. 3:21. a form like that of his own *r*.
  body

respond-ed
Acts 16:14. the Lord opened her heart
  to *r*.
Rom. 10:16. not all have *r*. to the good
  news

response
Phil. 3:9. given by God in *r*. to faith

responsibility
2 Cor. 11:28. the *r*. that weighs on me
  every day

responsible
Acts 5:28. to make us *r*. for that man's
  death
1 Tim. 5:22. *r*. for other people's misdeeds

rest-s-ing
Mat. 3:17. my beloved on whom my
  favour *r*.
  6:33. all the *r*. will come to you
  12:18. my Beloved, on whom my
  favour *r*.
  15:16. are you still as dull as the *r*.
  17:5. on whom my favour *r*.; listen to
  him
Mark 1:11. on thee my favour *r*.
  7:18. are you as dull as the *r*.
Luke 2:14. men on whom his favour *r*.
  3:22. on thee my favour *r*.
  12:31. all the *r*. will come to you as
  well
  18:11. I am not like the *r*. of men
  24:33. the *r*. of the company had
  assembled
John 1:32. like a dove and *r*. upon him
  1:33. *r*. upon him
  1:39. spent the *r*. of the day with him
  3:36. God's wrath *r*. upon him
  14:1 ⎫
  14:27 ⎬ set your troubled hearts at *r*.
  20:24. was not with the *r*.
  21:8. the *r*. of them
Acts 2:3. dispersed among them and *r*.
  on each one
  15:17. all the *r*. of mankind
  23:32. the cavalry to escort him the
  r. of the way
  26:30. and the *r*. of the company
Rom. 11:6. if it is by grace, then it does
  not *r*. on deeds done
  15:32. enjoy a time of *r*. with you
1 Cor. 9:5. like the *r*. of the apostles
  11:32. from being condemned with the
  r. of the world

1 Cor. 14:29. the *r*. exercise their judgement

2 Cor. 1:17. it should *r*. with me to say 'yes

3:8. greater splendour *r*. upon the divine dispensation

7:13. set his mind completely at *r*.

Gal. 2:13. played false like the *r*.

Eph. 2:3. we, like the *r*., lay under the dreadful judgement

2:22. built with all the *r*. into a spiritual dwelling

1 Thess. 4:13. you should not grieve like the *r*. of men

5:6. we must not sleep like the *r*.

1 Tim. 5·7. add these orders to the *r*.

Heb. 11:26. the stigma that *r*. on God's Anointed

2 Pet. 1:17. my Beloved, on whom my favour *r*.

2:14. eyes never at *r*. from sin

3:4. our fathers have been laid to their *r*.

Rev. 11:13. the *r*. in terror did homage to the God of heaven

12:17. wage war on the *r*. of her offspring

19:21. the *r*. were killed by the sword

restoration

Luke 2:25. waited for the *r*. of Israel

Acts 3:21. until the time of universal *r*.

restore-ed-ing

Mat. 5:13. how is its saltness to be *r*.

9:30. their sight was *r*.

12:22. Jesus cured him, *r*. both speech and sight

15:28. from that moment her daughter was *r*.

15:31. sight *r*. to the blind

Acts 9:12. laying his hands on him to *r*. his sight

21:40. as soon as quiet was *r*.

Heb. 9:13. *r*. their external purity

1 Pet. 5:10. *r*., establish, and strengthen

restrain-ing

2 Thess. 2:6. now be aware of the *r*. hand

1 Pet. 3:10. must *r*. his tongue from evil

Restrainer

2 Thess. 2:7. until the *R*. disappears

restrictions

Acts 15:19. no irksome *r*. on those of the Gentiles

result-s

Mat. 11:19. God's wisdom is proved right by its *r*.

Acts 19:10. this went on for two years, with the *r*. that

25:26. as a *r*. of this preliminary enquiry

Rom. 6:16. serve sin, with death as its *r*.; or obedience, with righteousness as its *r*.

15:19. as a *r*. I have completed the preaching

1 Cor. 11:20. the *r*. is that when you meet

2 Cor. 7:11. see what its *r*. have been

resurrection

Mark 12:26. now about the *r*. of the dead

John 2:22. after his *r*. his disciples recalled

21:14. the third time that Jesus appeared to his disciples after his *r*.

retaliate

1 Pet. 3:9. *r*. with blessing

retinue

Acts 13:7. he was in the *r*. of the Governor

retort-ed

Luke 15:28. his father came out and pleaded with him; but he *r*.

John 7:47. the Pharisees *r*., 'Have you too been misled

7:52. are you a Galilean too?' they *r*.

8:39. they *r*., 'Abraham is our father

9:27. I have told you already,' he *r*.

9:34. who are you to give us lessons,' they *r*.

Acts 23:3. Paul *r*., 'God will strike you

1 Pet. 2:23. when he was abused he did not *r*. with abuse

retribution

Mat. 3:7 ⎫ to escape from the com-
Luke 3:7 ⎭ ing *r*.

21:22. this is the time of *r*.

Rom. 1:18. we see divine *r*. revealed

2:5. a store of *r*. for the day of *r*.

2:8. the fury of *r*.

3:5. to bring *r*. upon us

4:15. law can bring only *r*.

5:9. saved through him from final *r*.

9:22. his *r*. at work and to make his power known, tolerated very patiently those vessels which were objects of *r*.

11:9. stumbling-block and *r*.

12:19. leave a place for divine *r*.

13:4. *r*. on the offender

13:5. not merely by fear of *r*.

1 Thess. 2:16. *r*. has overtaken them

2 Tim. 4:14. *r*. will fall upon him from the Lord

Heb: 2:2. disobedience met with due *r*.

Rev. 11:18. thy day of *r*. has come

19:15. the wrath and *r*. of God

return-ed

Mat. 17:14. they *r*. to the crowd

19:4. he asked in *r*.

25:19. a long time afterwards their master *r*.

25:27. on my *r*. I should have got it back with interest

Mat. 27:3. *r.* the thirty silver pieces to the chief priests

Mark 2:1. he *r.* to Capernaum

5:21. Jesus had *r.* by boat

7:30. she *r.* home

7:31. on his *r.* journey from Tyrian territory

Luke 1:23. Zechariah *r.* home

2:38. she *r.* thanks to God

2:45. they *r.* to Jerusalem to look for him

6:35. lend without expecting any *r.*

6:38. will be dealt to you in *r.*

8:55. her spirit *r.*

24:23. *r.* with a story that they had seen a vision of angels

John 4:27. his disciples *r.*, and were astonished

4:50. Jesus said, '*R.* home,; your son will live

9:7. when he *r.* he could see

Acts 9:19. he took food and his strength *r.*

15:33. to *r.* to those who had sent them

22:17. after my *r.* to Jerusalem, I was praying

Rom. 11:35. to receive a gift in *r.*

2 Cor. 1:16. leaving Macedonia, to *r.* to you

Col. 1:18. the first to *r.* from the dead

4:16. you in *r.* read the one from Laodicea

1 Thess. 3:8. what thanks can we *r.* to God for you

reveal-ed-ing

John 1:31. that he might be *r.* to Israel

2:11. the signs by which Jesus *r.* his glory

8:38. I am *r.* in words what I saw in my Father's presence; and you are *r.* in action

Rom. 2:5. God's just judgement will be *r.*

8:19. expectation for God's sons to be *r.*

1 Cor. 1:7. our Lord Jesus Christ to *r.* himself

2 Cor. 2:14. uses us to *r.* and spread abroad

4:10. in this body also life may *r.* itself

4:11. so that the life of Jesus also may be *r.*

Gal. 2:2. it had been *r.* by God that I should do so

Phil. 2:8. *r.* in human shape

1 Pet. 1:7 ⎰
     1:13 ⎱ when Jesus Christ is *r.*

Rev. 15:4. thy just dealings stand *r.*

revel-ling

Rom. 13:13. no *r.* or drunkenness

2 Pet. 2:13. they *r.* in their own deceptions

revelation

Luke 2:32. a light that will be a *r.* to the heathen

John 8:31. if you dwell within the *r.* I have brought

8:43. my *r.* is beyond your grasp

1 Cor. 14:30. receives a *r.*, let the first speaker stop

2 Cor. 4:6. to give the light of *r.*—the *r.* of the glory of God

Gal. 3:23. pending the *r.* of faith

revenge

Rom. 12:19. do not seek *r.*

revere

Acts 13:26. others among you who *r.* our God

Rev. 15:4. who shall not *r.* thee, Lord

reverence

Acts 10:25. bowed to the ground in deep *r.*

Rom. 1:25. offered *r.* and worship to created things

3:18. *r.* for God does not enter their thoughts

13:7. pay tax and toll, *r.* and respect

Eph. 5:21. *r.* for Christ

Col. 3:22. out of *r.* for the Lord

1 Pet. 2:17. *r.* to God, honour to the sovereign

3:15. hold the Lord Christ in *r.* in your hearts

Jude 12. they eat and drink without *r.*

reverent

Tit. 2:3. older women, similarly, should be *r.*

1 Pet. 3:2. chaste and *r.* behaviour

revert

Acts 13:34. never again to *r.* to corruption

revile-ing

Rev. 13:6. *r.* his name and his heavenly dwelling

revolt

Acts 5:37. he induced some people to *r.*

21:38. the Egyptian who started a *r.*

reward

Eph. 2:9. not a *r.* for work done

Rev. 2:23. I will *r.* each one of you according to his deeds

rich-es-er

Mat. 5:12. you have a *r.* reward in heaven

19:21. then you will have *r.* in heaven

Mark 10:21. and you will have *r.* in heaven

Luke 6:23. assuredly you have a *r.* reward

Luke 6:35. and you will have a *r.* reward
18:22. *r.* in heaven
John 12:24. it bears a *r.* harvest
2 Cor. 3:9. how much *r.* in splendour
8:7. you are so *r.* in everything
9:10. you will always be *r.* enough to be generous
Phil. 1:9. that your love may grow ever *r.* and *r.*
Jam. 3:17. *r.* in mercy

richly
2 Cor. 9:8. to provide you *r.* with every good gift

richness
2 Cor. 9:14. the *r.* of the grace

rid
Luke 13:12. you are *r.* of your trouble
Acts 19:12. they were *r.* of their diseases
2 Cor. 12:8. three times I begged the Lord to *r.* me of it

ride-s-den-ing
Mat. 21:5. *r.* on an ass, *r.* on the foal
Mark 11:2 ⎱ a colt which no one has
Luke 19:30 ⎰ yet *r.*
Acts 23:24. provide also mounts for Paul so that he may *r.*
Rev. 17:7. the woman and of the beast she *r.*

rider-s
Rev. 6:2. its *r.* held a bow
6:4. to its *r.* was given power
6:5. its *r.* held in his hand a pair of scales
6:8. its *r*'s name was Death
9:17. horses and their *r.* in my vision
19:11. its *r*'s name was Faithful
19:18. the flesh of horses and their *r.*
19:19. the *R.* and his army
19:21. the sword which went out of the *R.*'s mouth

ridicule
Luke 23:11. Herod and his troops treated him with contempt and *r.*

rift
Acts 7:56. there is a *r.* in the sky
10:11. he saw a *r.* in the sky

right-s-ed-ing
Mat. 5:6. hunger and thirst to see *r.* prevail
5:10. persecution for the cause of *r.*
8:24. waves were breaking *r.* over the boat
9:6. the Son of Man has the *r.* on earth to forgive sins
11:19. God's wisdom is proved *r.* by its results
12:4. neither he nor his men had a *r.* to eat them
14:4. you have no *r.* to her
15:7. Isaiah was *r.*

15:26. it is not *r.* to take the children's bread
17:11. Elijah will come and set everything *r.*
21:32. John came to show you the *r.* way to live
28:14. we will put matters *r.* with him
Mark 2:10. the *r.* on earth to forgive sins
6:18. you have no *r.* to your brother's wife
7:6. Isaiah was *r.* when he prophesied
9:12. Elijah does come first to set everything *r.*
12:32. you are *r.* in saying that God is one
14:54. *r.* into the High Priest's courtyard
Luke 1:51. the deeds his own *r.* arm has done
5:24. the Son of Man has the *r.* on earth to forgive sins
7:35. God's wisdom is proved *r.*
18:5. I will see her *r.* before she wears me out
John 1:12. the *r.* to become children of God
4:17. you are *r.*', said Jesus
5:27. the *r.* to pass judgement
5:29. who have done *r.* will rise to life
7:6, 8. the *r.* time for me has not yet come, but any time is *r.* for you
8:48. are we not *r.* in saying that you are a Samaritan
10:18. I have the *r.* to lay it down, and I have the *r.* to receive it back again
14:30. he has no *r.* over me
16:8. show where wrong and *r.* and judgement lie
16:10. he will convince them that *r.* is on my side
19:18. with him two others, one on the *r.*, one on the left
Acts 15:29. you will be doing *r.*
25:24. insisting that he had no *r.* to remain alive
Rom. 1:17 ⎱ God's way of *r.* wrong
3:21 ⎰
6:13. yield your bodies to him as implements for doing *r.*
7:21. when I want to do *r.*
13:3. continue to do *r.*
1 Cor. 5:10. to avoid them you would have to get *r.* out of the world
9:4. have I no *r.* to eat and drink
9:5. have I no *r.* to take a Christian wife
9:12. if you allow others these *r.* . . . . but I have availed myself of no such *r.*
9:15. I have never taken advantage of any such *r.*

1 Cor. 9:18. waiving the *r.* which my preaching gives me
2 Cor. 13:7. we want you to do what is *r.*
13:9. that all may be put *r.* with you
Gal. 3:18. if the inheritance is by legal *r.*
6:1. set him *r.* again very gently
Eph. 6:19. that I may be granted the *r.* words
Phil. 1:7. only *r.* that I should feel like this about you
1 Thess. 4:6. invade his *r.*
2 Thess. 1:3. it is *r.* that we should thank him
3:9. not because we have not the *r.* to maintenance
3:13. never tire of doing *r.*
1 Tim. 2:3. such prayer is *r.*
3:13. the *r.* to speak openly on matters of the Christian faith
2 Tim. 3:16. discipline in *r.* living
Tit. 1:8. *r.*-minded, temperate
Heb. 5:13. an infant, does not know what is *r.*
13:18. our one desire is always to do what is *r.*
Jam. 3:13. let his *r.* conduct give practical proof of it
1 Pet. 2:14. the commendation of those who do *r.*
4:15. nor for infringing the *r.* of others
2 Pet. 2:21. how much better never to have known the *r.* way
1 John 2:29. every man who does *r.* is his child
3:7. the man who does *r.*
3:10. no one who does not do *r.* is God's child
3:12. his own actions were wrong, and his brother's were *r.*
Rev. 2:7. the *r.* to eat from the tree of life
5:5. won the *r.* to open the scroll
6:8. the *r.* to kill by sword and by famine
10:5. raised his *r.* hand to heaven
13:5. the *r.* to reign for forty-two months

righteous
Luke 1:17. to the ways of the *r.*
15:7. ninety-nine *r.* people
Acts 3:14. the one who was holy and *r.*
7:52. the coming of the *R.* One
22:14. to see the *R.* One
Heb. 10:38. by faith my *r.* servant shall find life

righteousness
Luke 16:15. impress your fellow-men with your *r.*

rightful
Rev. 12:10. his Christ comes to his *r.* rule

rightly
John 13:13. you call me 'Master' and 'Lord', and *r.* so
Rom. 2:2. God's judgement is *r.* passed upon all

rigid
Mark 9:18. grinds his teeth, and goes *r.*
Rom. 2:5. the *r.* obstinacy of your heart

ring
Acts 14:20. the converts formed a *r.* round him

riot-ing
Mat. 26:5. there may be *r.* among the people
27:24. a *r.* was starting
Mark 14:2. we should have *r.* among the people
Acts 19:40. charged with riot for this day's work
1 Pet. 4:3. drunkenness, *r.*

rioters
Acts 21:32. came down on the *r.*

ripe
Mark 4:29. as soon as the crop is *r.*
John 4:35. already white, *r.*, for harvest
1 Cor. 2:6. words of wisdom to those who are *r.* for it
Eph. 1:10. to be put into effect when the time was *r.*
Col. 4:12. that you may stand fast, *r.* in conviction

rise-s-ing
Mat. 1:24. *r.* from sleep Joseph did as the angel
2:2. we observed the *r.* of his star
2:9. the star which they had seen at its *r.*
2:13 ⎱ *r.* up, take the child
2:20 ⎰
Mark 15:7. committed murder in the *r.*
Luke 1:78. the morning sun from heaven will *r.*
14:14. the day when good men *r.* from the dead
23:19. a *r.* that had taken place
John 5:29. those who have done right will *r.* to life; those who have done wrong will *r.* to hear their doom
Acts 19:23. the Christian movement gave *r.* to a serious disturbance
Eph. 5:14. awake, sleeper, *r.* from the dead
2 Thess. 2:4. he *r.* in his pride against every god
1 Tim. 6:4. which give *r.* to jealousy
2 Pet. 1:19. the morning star *r.* to illuminate your minds
Rev. 7:2. another angel *r.* out of the east
14:11. the smoke of their torment will *r.* for ever and ever

risk-ed-ing

Acts 5:39. you *r.* finding yourselves at war with God
  19:40. run the *r.* of being charged with riot
Rom. 16:4. they *r.* their necks to save my life
Phil. 2:30. *r.* his life to render me the service

risky

Acts 27:9. *r.* to go on with the voyage

rite-s

John 2:6. Jewish *r.* of purification
Rom. 4:11. the symbolic *r.* of circumcision
Gal. 6:13. submitted to that outward *r.*
Eph. 2:11. only with reference to an outward *r.*
Heb. 6:2. cleansing *r.*
  9:10. various *r.*

ritual

Acts 21:24 ⎱ the *r.* of purification
  21:26 ⎰

ritually

Acts 24:18. found me in the temple *r.* purified

rivalry-ies

Rom. 1:29. murder, *r.*, treachery
2 Cor. 12:20. personal *r.*
Gal. 5:26. challenging one another to *r.*
Phil. 1:17. moved by personal *r.*
  2:3. *r.* and personal vanity

river-s

Mat. 3:6. baptized by him in the *R.* Jordan
Luke 6:48. the *r.* burst upon that house
  6:49. the *r.* burst upon it, the house collapsed
2 Cor. 11:26. I have met dangers from *r.*
Rev. 12:16. swallowed the *r.* which the dragon spewed

road

Mat. 4:15. the *r.* by the sea
  7:13. there is plenty of room on the *r.*
  7:14. the *r.* is narrow
  10:5. do not take the *r.* to gentile lands
  10:10. no pack for the *r.*
  15:29. Jesus took the *r.* by the Sea of Galilee
  21:8. carpeted the *r.* with their cloaks
Mark 10:32. on the *r.*, going up to Jerusalem
  10:52. followed him on the *r.*
  11:8. people carpeted the *r.* with their cloaks
Luke 10:4. exchange no greetings on the *r.*
  10:31. a priest was going down by the same *r.*

19:36. they carpeted the *r.* with them
  24:32. our hearts on fire as he talked with us on the *r.*
Acts 8:26. go south to the *r.* that leads down from Jerusalem to Gaza.' (This is the desert *r.*
  8:36. as they were going along the *r.*, they came to some water
  9:3. on the *r.* and nearing Damascus
  20:13. he was going to travel by *r.*
  21:15. took the *r.* up to Jerusalem
  22:6. I was on the *r.* and nearing Damascus
Rom. 3:17. strangers to the high-*r.* of peace
2 Cor. 11:26. I have been constantly on the *r.*
2 Pet. 2:15. abandoned the straight *r.*

roadside

Mat. 20:30. at the *r.* sat two blind men
  21:19. seeing a fig-tree at the *r.*
Mark. 10:46. a blind beggar, was seated at the *r.*
Luke 18:35. a blind man sat at the *r.*

roar-s

Rev. 14:2. the deep *r.* of thunder
  19:1. like the *r.* of a vast throng
  19:6. and deep *r.* of thunder

rob-bed

John 10:18. no one has *r.* me of it
  16:22. no one shall *r.* you of your joy
Rom. 2:22. do you *r.* their shrines
  8:3. our lower nature *r.* it of all potency
1 Cor. 6:7. why not rather let yourself be *r.*
  6:8. you actually injure and *r.*—injure and *r.* your brothers
Rev. 3:11. let no one *r.* you of your crown

robbers

Mat. 21:13. you are making it a *r.* cave
Mark 11:17. you have made it a *r.* cave
Luke 10:30. to Jericho when he fell in with *r.*
  10:36. the man who fell into the hands of the *r.*
  19:46. you have made it a *r.* cave

robbery-ies

Mat. 23:25. cup and dish, which you have filled inside by *r.*
Rev. 9:21. their fornication, or their *r.*

robe-s-d

Mat. 23:5. wear deep fringes on their *r.*
  26:65. the High Priest tore his *r.*
Mark 12:38. walk up and down in long *r.*
  14:63. the High Priest tore his *r.* and said
  16:5. wearing a white *r.*

Acts 10:30. a man in shining *r.*

12:21. attired in his royal *r.*

Rev. 1:13. like a son of man, *r.* down to his feet

3:5. who is victorious shall thus be *r.* all in white

4:4. twenty-four elders, *r.* in white

12:1. a woman *r.* with the sun

15:6. *r.* in fine linen, clean and shining

19:13. *r.* in a garment drenched in blood

19:16. on his *r.* and on his leg there was written

22:14. happy are those who wash their *r.* clean

robust

Rom. 15:1. those of us who have a *r.* conscience

rock-ed

Luke 23:53. laid it in a tomb cut out of the *r.*

John 1:42. you shall be called Cephas' (that is, Peter, the *R.*)

Acts 4:31. the building where they were assembled *r.*

rocky

Mat. 13:5. some seed fell on *r.* ground

13:20. the seed sown on *r.* ground

Mark. 4:5. on *r.* ground, where it had little soil

4:16. receive the seed on *r.* ground

rod

Heb. 12:6. he lays the *r.* on every son whom he acknowledges

Rev. 21:15. the angel who spoke with me carried a gold measuring-*r.*

21:16. it measured by his *r.* twelve thousand furlongs

rode

Rev. 6:2. he *r.* forth, conquering and to conquer

rogues

Eph. 4:14. crafty *r.*

roll-s-ed-ing

Mark 9:20. *r.* about foaming at the mouth

Luke 4:20. he *r.* up the scroll

John 20:7. *r.* together in a place by itself

1 Tim. 5:9. a widow should not be put on the *r.* under sixty years of age

5:11. younger widows may not be placed on the *r.*

2 Pet 2:22. the sow after a wash *r.* in the mud

Jude 16. big words come *r.* from their lips

Rev. 3:5. his name I will never strike off the *r.* of the living

13:8. keeps in his *r.* of the living

17:8. inscribed in the *r.* of the living

20:12. another book was opened, the *r.* of the living

20:15. whose names were not to be found in the *r.* of the living

21:27. inscribed in the Lamb's *r.* of the living

Roman

Mat. 22:17. to pay taxes to the *R.* Emperor

27:2. to hand him over to Pilate, the *R.* Governor

Mark 12:14. to pay taxes to the *R.* Emperor

Luke 2:1. a general registration throughout the *R.* world

20:22. pay taxes to the *R.* Emperor

Acts 16:12. a *R.* colony

roof

Mat. 10:36. find his enemies under his own *r.*

24:17 ⎫ if a man is on the *r.*
Mark 13:15 ⎭

Luke 5:19. they went up on to the *r.* and let him down

17:31. the man who is on the *r.* and his belongings in the house

Acts 10:9. Peter went up on the *r.* to pray

room

Mat. 6:6. when you pray, go into a *r.* by yourself

7:13. there is plenty of *r.* on the road

9:25. he went into the *r.* and took the girl by the hand

24:26. he is there in the inner *r.*", do not believe it

Mark 14:14. where is the *r.* reserved for me

Luke 22:11. where is the *r.* in which I may eat the Passover

John 20:26. a week later his disciples were again in the *r.*

Acts 9:37. washed her body and laid it in a *r.* upstairs

9:39. they took him upstairs to the *r.*

10:3. an angel of God, who came into his *r.*

20:8. there were many lamps in the upper *r.*

Rom. 3:27. what *r.* then is left for human pride

Philem. 22. have a *r.* ready for me

1 John 4:18. there is no *r.* for fear in love

roost-s

Mat. 8:20. foxes have their holes, the birds their *r.*

13:32. big enough for the birds to come and *r.*

Luke 9:58. foxes have their holes, the birds their *r.*

Luke 13:19. the birds came to *r*. among
its branches

root-s-ed
John 8:44. is not *r*. in the truth
1 Cor. 5:2. should have been *r*. out of
your company
5:13. *r*. out the evil-doer from your
community
Eph. 3:18. with deep *r*. and firm
foundations, may you be strong

rose
Mat. 7:25. ⎫ the floods *r*.
        7:27 ⎭
13:6. ⎱ when the sun *r*. the young
Mark 4:6 ⎰ corn was scorched
John 18:40. the clamour *r*.: 'Not him;
we want Barabbas
Acts 26:11. my fury *r*. to such a pitch
Rom. 1:4. a mighty act in that he *r*. from
the dead

rostrum
Acts 12:21. seated on the *r*., Herod
harangued them

rotted
Jam. 5:2. your riches have *r*.

rough-ly
Mat. 3:4. John's clothing was a *r*. coat
of camel's hair
14:24. a head-wind and a *r*. sea
Mark 1:6. John was dressed in a *r*. coat
of camel's hair
John 6:18. a strong wind was blowing
and the sea grew *r*.
Acts 28:2. the *r*. islanders treated us
with uncommon kindness
1 Cor. 4:11. we are *r*. handled

round-ed-ing
Mat. 4:23. he went *r*. the whole of
Galilee, teaching
5:1. his disciples had gathered *r*. him
9:26. this story became the talk of all
the country *r*.
9:35. Jesus went *r*. all the towns and
villages
13:2. many people gathered *r*. him
18:3. turn *r*. and become like children
20:31. the people *r*. on them
27:27. collected the whole company *r*.
him
Mark 2:1. the news went *r*. that he was
at home
6:33. and came *r*. by land
9:36. put his arm *r*. him
10:1. a crowd gathered *r*.
10:16. put his arms *r*. them
10:48. many of the people *r*. on him
Luke 2:7. she wrapped him *r*
11:29. the crowds swarming *r*. him

15:20. ran to meet him, flung his arms
r. him
John 6:14. the word went *r*.
13:4. taking a towel, tied it *r*. him
Acts 16:18. *r*. on the spirit he said
17:23. I was going *r*. looking at the
objects of your worship
2 Cor. 7:5. trouble at every turn,
quarrels all *r*. us
1 Pet. 5:8. prowls *r*. looking for someone
to devour

rouse-d
Mark 4:38. they *r*. him and said, 'Master
Luke 8:24. *r*. him, crying, 'Master,
Master
Acts 17:5. *r*. the rabble, and had the city
in an uproar
17:13. to stir up trouble and *r*. the
rabble
19:28. they were *r*. to fury and shouted
Rom. 10:19. a foolish nation to *r*. your
anger
2 Pet. 3:1. to *r*. you to honest thought

rout
Luke 1:51. the arrogant of heart and
mind he has put to *r*.
Heb. 7:1. Abraham returning from the
r. of the kings
11:34. they put foreign armies to *r*.

route
Jam. 2:25. sending them away by a
different *r*.

rows
Mark 6:40. they sat down in *r*., a hundred
r. of fifty each

royal
John 4:46. an officer in the *r*. service was
there
Acts 7:10. chief administrator for Egypt
and the whole of the *r*. household
12:20. they won over Blastus the *r*.
chamberlain
Rev. 1:6. who made of us a *r*. house
5:10. thou hast made of them a *r*.
house
17:12. share with the beast the exercise of *r*. authority

rudder
Jam. 3:4. they can be directed by a tiny
r.

rude
1 Cor. 13:4. nor *r*.

rudiments
Heb. 6:1. stop discussing the *r*. of
Christianity

ruffled
Jam. 1:6. like a heaving sea *r.* by the
wind

rugged
Acts 27:29. fearing that we might be cast
ashore on a *r.* coast
ruin-ed-ing
Mat. 12:25. every kingdom divided
against itself goes to *r.*
Luke 5:37. the wine will be wasted, and
the skins *r.*
11:17. every kingdom divided against
itself goes to *r.*
Rom. 3:16. *r.* and misery lie along their
paths
14:20. do not *r.* the work of God for
the sake of food
1 Cor. 1:18. sheer folly to those on their
way to *r.*
15:33. bad company is the *r.* of a good
character
2 Cor. 7:2. we have wronged no one, *r.*
no one
2 Thess. 1:9. suffer the punishment of
eternal *r.*
1 Tim. 6:9. plunge men into *r.*
2 Tim. 2:14. is the *r.* of those who listen
Tit. 1:11. *r.* whole families by teaching
things they should not
2 Pet. 2:14. lure the unstable to their *r.*
3:16. misinterpret to their own *r.*
Rev. 16:19. the cities of the world fell in
r.

rule-s-ing
Mat. 22:17. give us your *r.* on this
Mark 7:4. a traditional *r.* to maintain
10:5. he made this *r.* for you
Luke 18:18. a man of the *r.* class put this
question to him
Rom. 1:28. to break all *r.* of conduct
13:9. are all summed up in the one *r.*
1 Cor. 2:8. the powers that *r.* the world
4:6. learn to 'keep within the *r.*
7:10. to the married I give this *r.*
11:9. I made it a *r.*
Eph. 2:15. he annulled the law with its
r.
1 Thess. 4:8. anyone therefore who flouts
these *r.*
4:10. practising this *r.* of love
2 Thess. 3:10. we laid down the *r.*
1 Tim. 5:21. maintain these *r.*, and never
pre-judge the issue
2 Tim. 2:5. no athlete can win a prize
unless he has kept the *r.*
Heb. 7:16. not to a system of earth-
bound *r.*
7:18. the earlier *r.* are cancelled
2 John 6. to be your *r.* of life
Rev. 12:10. Christ comes to his rightful
r.

13:2. the dragon conferred upon it his
power and *r.*

ruler-s
Mat. 2:6. the *r.* of Judah
20:25. *r.* lord it over their subjects
Mark 10:42. recognized *r.*
2 Cor. 6:18. the Lord, the *R.* of all being
Eph. 3:10. the *r.* and authorities in the
realms of heaven
Rev. 1:5. *r.* of the kings of the earth

run-s-ning
Mat. 6:32 ⎰ things for the heathen to
Luke 12:30 ⎱ *r.* after
15:30. after *r.* through your money
17:23. do not go *r.* off in pursuit
21:24. until their day has *r.* its course
John 10:5. a stranger; they will *r.* away
from him
10:12. abandons the sheep and *r.* away
10:13. the man *r.* away because he is a
hireling
Acts 2:1. while the day of Pentecost was
r. its course
16:11. made a straight *r.* to Samo-
thrace
19:40. *r.* the risk of being charged
21:1. a straight *r.* and came to Cos
27:15. we had to give way and *r.*
before it
27:17. afraid of *r.* on to the shallows
27:39. to *r.* the ship ashore
Rom. 9:9. the promise *r.*
1 Tim. 6:12. *r.* the great race of faith
2 Tim. 4:7. I have *r.* the great race
Heb. 2:6. a solemn assurance which *r.*
Jam. 4:7. stand up to the devil and he
will turn and *r.*

rush-ed-ing
Mat. 8:32. the whole herd *r.* over the
edge
Mark 5:13 ⎰ *r.* over the edge into the
Luke 8:33 ⎱ lake
Acts 7:57 they made one *r.* at him
14:14. *r.* into the crowd
16:29. the jailer called for lights, *r.* in
2 Pet. 3:10. the heavens will disappear
with a great *r.* sound
Rev. 1:15. his voice was like the sound
of *r.* waters
9:9. chariots *r.* to battle
14:2. a sound from heaven like the
noise of *r.* water
19:6. like the noise of *r.* water

ruthless
Mark 7:22. *r.* greed, and malice
Eph. 5:3. *r.* greed, must not be so much
as mentioned
Col. 3:5. the *r.* greed which is nothing
less than idolatry

S

sabbath
John 7:21. once only have I done work on the *S.*
19:42. it was the eve of the Jewish *S.*
Heb. 4:9. a *s.* rest still awaits the people of God

sacred
Mark 16:8. the *s.* and imperishable message
Rom. 1:2. this gospel God announced beforehand in *s.* scriptures
2 Tim. 3:15. you have been familiar with the *s.* writings
Heb. 13:10. the priests of the *s.* tent
2 Pet. 1:18. we were with him on the *s.* mountain
2:21. abandon the *s.* commandments
Jude 20. fortify yourselves in your most *s.* faith

sacrifice-s-d
Acts 24:17. to offer *s.*
Rom. 8:3. as a *s.* for sin
15:16. offer the Gentiles to him as an acceptable *s.*
1 Cor. 9:13. claim their share of the *s.*
Gal. 1:4. who *s.* himself for our sins
2:20. who loved me and *s.* himself for me
1 Tim. 2:6. *s.* himself to win freedom for all mankind
Tit. 2:14. he it is who *s.* himself for us
Heb. 9:12. the blood of his *s.* is his own blood
Rev. 12:11. by the *s.* of the Lamb they have conquered

sacrificial
Rom. 3:25. his *s.* death
5:9. Christ's *s.* death
1 Cor. 10:18. partake in the *s.* meal

sacrilege
Acts 19:37. have committed no *s.*

sad-ly
John 16:22. for the moment you are *s.* at heart
Phil. 2:26. he has been missing all of you *s.*

safe-ly
Mark 8:35. lost for my sake and for the Gospel, that man is *s.*
Luke 9:24. let himself be lost for my sake, that man is *s.*
11:21. on guard over his castle his possessions are *s.*

21:36. to pass *s.* through all these imminent troubles
John 10:9. who comes into the fold through me shall be *s.*
12:25. kept *s.* for eternal life
17:12. kept them *s.*
Acts 25:4. Paul is in *s.* custody
27:31. you can none of you come off *s.*
27:43. wanted to bring Paul *s.* through
27:44. all came *s.* to land
1 Tim. 6:20. keep *s.* that which has been entrusted to you
2. Tim. 1:12. his power to keep *s.*
4:18. keep me *s.* until his heavenly reign begins
Heb. 6:19. an anchor *s.* and sure
2 Pet. 3:17. do not lose your own *s.* foothold
1 John 5:18. it is the Son of God who keeps him *s.*
Jude. 1. in the *s.* keeping of Jesus Christ

safety
Mat. 16:25. whoever cares for his own *s.* is lost
Luke 8:29. for *s.* sake, they would secure him with chains
9:24. whoever cares for his own *s.* is lost
Acts 28:1. made our way to *s.*
1 Pet. 3:20. eight in all, were brought to *s.* through the water
3:21. baptism through which you are now brought to *s.*

safeguard
Phil. 3:1. a *s.* for you

sages
Mat. 23:34. I send you therefore prophets, *s.*, and teachers

sail-ed
Acts 10:11. like a great sheet of *s.*-cloth
11:5. looked like a great sheet of *s.*-cloth
16:11. so we *s.* from Troas
21:1. parted from them and set *s.*
27:21. you should have taken my advice, gentlemen, not to *s.* from Crete
28:11. we set *s.* in a ship which had wintered in the island
28:13. we *s.* round and arrived at Rhegium

sailors
Acts 27:27. the *s.* felt that land was getting nearer
27:30. the *s.* tried to abandon ship

saints
Mat. 13:17. *s.*, I tell you, desired to see what you now see
23:29. embellish the monuments of the *s.*

sake
Mark 2:27. the Sabbath was made for the *s.* of man
12:40. say long prayers for appearance' *s.*
Luke 8:29. for safety's *s.*, they would secure him with chains
20:47. they say long prayers for appearance' *s.*
John 11:42. I spoke for the *s.* of the people standing round
Acts 5:41. worthy to suffer indignity for the *s.* of the Name
28:20. for the *s.* of the hope of Israel that I am in chains
Rom. 9:3. outcast from Christ myself for the *s.* of my brothers
14:20. do not ruin the work of God for the *s.* of food
1 Cor. 11:9. man was not created for woman's *s.*, but woman for the *s.* of man
2 Cor. 5:15. for their *s.* died and was raised to life
5:21. for our *s.* God made him one with the sinfulness of men
Gal. 3:13. becoming for our *s.* an accursed thing
Eph. 4:1. a prisoner for the Lord's *s.*
Phil. 1:24. for your *s.* there is greater need for me to stay on in the body
3:8. my Lord, for whose *s.* I did in fact lose everything
2 Tim. 1:8. your share of suffering for the *s.* of the Gospel,
Heb. 1:14. for the *s.* of those who are to inherit salvation
12:2. for the *s.* of the joy that lay ahead of him
1 Pet. 1:20. made manifest for your *s.*
Rev. 20:4. beheaded for the *s.* of God's word

sale
Acts. 4:34. brought the proceeds of the *s.*
8:20. thinking God's gift is for *s.*

saltness
Mat. 5:13. how is its *s.* to be restored

salutary
2 Cor. 7:10. a change of heart too *s.* to regret

salutations
Luke 11:43. *s.* in the market-places

salvation
Mark 16:8. imperishable message of eternal *s.*
16:16. believe it and receive baptism will find *s.*
John 5:34. I remind you of it for your own *s.*
Acts 11:14. bring *s.* to you and all your household
Rom. 10:1. my prayer to God is for their *s.*
10:9. the faith that God raised him from the dead, then you will find *s.*
1 Cor. 1:18. us who are on the way to *s.*
7:16. as a wife you may be your husband's *s.*; as a husband you may be your wife's *s.*
15:2. which is now bringing you *s.*
2 Cor. 2:15. on the way to *s.*
1 Thess. 2:16. the Gentiles to lead them to *s.*
2 Thess. 2:10. love of the truth, so as to find *s.*
1 Tim. 2:4. whose will it is that all men should find *s.*
4:16. the *s.* of yourself and your hearers
2 Tim. 1:9. it is he who brought us *s.*
Jam. 1:21. message planted in your hearts, which can bring you *s.*
1 Pet. 3:21. *s.* through the resurrection of Jesus Christ

Samaritans
John 4:22. you *S.* worship without knowing what you worship

same
Mat. 1:19. at the *s.* time wanting to save her from exposure
5.12. in the *s.* way they persecuted the prophets
12:40. in the *s.* way the Son of Man will be three days
Luke 3:11. anyone who has food must do the *s.*
Acts. 1:11. come in the *s.* way as you have seen him go

sanctuary
Mat. 23:16. swears by the *s.*, that is nothing; but if he swears by the gold in the *s.*
23:35. you murdered between the *s.* and the altar
Luke 1:9. priestly custom, to enter the *s.* of the Lord
1:22. had a vision in the *s.*
11:51. perished between the altar and the *s.*
Acts 19:27. the *s.* of the great goddess Diana

Acts 21:28. attacking our people, our law, and this *s.*
Heb. 8:5. a *s.* which is only a copy
9:8. the way into the *s.* remains unrevealed
9:12. entered the *s.* once and for all
9:24. not that *s.* made by men's hands
9:25. the high priest enters the *s.*
10:19. enter boldly into the *s.*
Rev. 15:5. the *s.* of the heavenly Tent of Testimony
15:8. the *s.* was filled with smoke
16:1. from the *s.* I heard a loud voice
16:17. out of the *s.* came a loud voice

sandy
Acts 27:39. they noticed a bay with a *s.* beach

sane
2 Tim. 4:5. keep calm and *s.* at all times
Tit. 1:13. that they may come to a *s.* belief

sang
Luke 4:15. all men *s.* his praises
Rev. 4:8. by day and by night without a pause they *s.*

Sanhedrin
Acts 5:21. they summoned the '*S.*'

sank
Luke 18:23. at these words his heart *s.*

sap
Rom. 11:17. share the same root and *s.* as the olive

sat
Luke 13:26. we *s.* at table with you
John 8:7. he *s.* up straight and said
8:10. Jesus again *s.* up and said

satins
Mat. 11:8 ⎫ a man dressed in silks and
Luke 7:25 ⎭ *s.*

satisfaction
1 Cor. 5:6. your self-*s.* ill becomes you
9:18. the *s.* of preaching the Gospel without expense

satisfy-ied-ing
Mat. 5:6. they shall be *s.*
Mark 7:27. let the children be *s.*
15:15. Pilate, in his desire to *s.* the mob
Luke 1:53. the hungry he has *s.* with good things
6:21. your hunger shall be *s.*
16:21. glad to *s.* his hunger with the scraps
John 6:26. your hunger was *s.* with the loaves you ate
19:16. to *s.* them, he handed Jesus over to be crucified

Rom. 13:8. he who loves his neighbour has *s.* every claim of the law
13:14. give no more thought to *s.* the bodily appetites
Eph. 4:19. stop at nothing to *s.* their foul desires
3 John 10. not *s.* with that, he refuses to receive our friends

Saturday
Acts 20:7. on the *S.* night, in our assembly for the breaking of bread

Saul
Acts 9:27. described to them how *S.* had seen the Lord
9:28. *S.* now stayed with them

savage-ly
Mat. 7:15. underneath they are *s.* wolves
Acts 20:29. *s.* wolves will come in among you
Gal. 1:13. how *s.* I persecuted the church

save-d-ing
Mat. 1:19. wanting to *s.* her from exposure
6:13. *s.* us from the evil one
Mark 3:9. to *s.* him from being crushed by the crowd
5:23. to cure her and *s.* her life
Luke 1:68. *s.* them and set them free
7:3. come and *s.* his servant's life
John 18:36. fighting to *s.* me from arrest by the Jews
Rom. 1:16. it is the *s.* power of God
10:11. everyone who has faith in him will be *s.* from shame
15:31. that I may be *s.* from unbelievers
16:4. they risked their necks to *s.* my life
1 Cor. 11:32. to *s.* us from being condemned with the rest of the world
2 Cor. 12:7. this was to *s.* me from being unduly elated
Col. 2:4. to *s.* you from being talked into error

Saviour
Mat. 1:21. you shall give him the name Jesus (*S.*)

saw
Mat. 17:3. they *s.* Moses and Elijah apear
21:45. they *s.* that he was referring to them
27:53. entered the Holy City, where many *s.* them
Mark 12:12. they *s.* that the parable was aimed at them
12:15. he *s.* how crafty their question was
Luke 20:23. he *s.* through their trick

John 1:14. we *s.* his glory

Heb. 11:33. *s.* God's promises fulfilled

Jude 14. I *s.* the Lord come with his myriads of angels

sawdust

Mat. 7:3 ⎱ the speck of *s.* in your
Luke 6:41 ⎰ brother's eye

say-ing

Mat. 7:20. that is why I *s.* you will recognize them by their fruits

Acts 28:22. all we know about this sect is that no one has a good word to *s.* for it

1 Cor. 5:6 ⎱
  15:32 ⎰ the *s.*

scales

Rev. 6:5. its rider held in his hand a pair of *s.*

scandal

Rom. 1:30. whisperers and *s.*-mongers

1 Tim. 3:7. so that he may not be exposed to *s.*

  3:11. women of high principle, who will not talk *s.*

2 Tim. 3:3. *s.*-mongers, intemperate and fierce

Tit. 2:3. not *s.*-mongers or slaves to strong drink

scarce

Mat. 9:37 ⎱ the crop is heavy, but
Luke 10:2 ⎰ labourers are *s.*

scares

2 Cor. 10:9. you must not think of me as one who *s.* you

scarves

Acts 19:12. *s.* which had been in contact with his skin

scatter-s-ed-ing

Mat. 25:24. you gather where you have not *s.*

  25:26. gather where I have not *s.*

Mark 4:26. a man *s.* seed on the land

John 2:15. *s.* their coins

Acts 5:37. his whole following was *s.*

scene

Mark 11:11. into the temple, where he looked at the whole *s.*

Acts 14:19. Jews from Antioch and Iconium came on the *s.*

2 Thess. 2:7. until the Restrainer disappears from the *s.*

scented

Rev. 18:12. all kinds of *s.* woods

sceptical

Acts 28:24. others remained *s.*

scheme-s

Mat. 26:4. a *s.* to have Jesus arrested by some trick

2 Cor. 8:11. be as eager to complete the *s.*

Eph. 4:14. crafty rogues and their deceitful *s.*

school

Tit. 2:4. *s.* the younger women to be loving wives

Heb. 5:8. he learned obedience in the *s.* of suffering

scion

Rev. 22:16. I am the root and *s.* of David

scoff-ed

Luke 16:14. heard all this and *s.* at him

Acts 17:32. heard about the raising of the dead, some *s.*

2 Pet. 3:3. there will come men who *s.* at religion

scoffers

Acts 13:41. see this, you *s.*, wonder, and begone

scold-ed

Mat. 19:13 ⎱ the disciples *s.* them for it
Mark 10:13 ⎰

Luke 18:15. they *s.* them for it

scope

Rom. 11:22. divine kindness to you, if only you remain within its *s.*

  15:23. I have no further *s.* in these parts

scorching

Jam. 1:11. once the sun is up with its *s.* heat

Rev. 7:16. the sun shall not beat on them nor any *s.* heat

score

1 Cor. 13:6. love keeps no *s.* of wrongs

scorn

Gal. 4:14. you resisted any temptation to show *s.*

Jude 18. men who pour *s.* on religion

scoundrel

Mat. 18:32. you *s.*!' he said to him

Acts 22:22. down with him! A *s.* like that is better dead

scoured

Mark 6:55. the people *s.* that whole country-side

scourge-d

2 Cor. 11:23. *s.* more severely, more often imprisoned

scraps

Mat. 14:20. the *s.* left over, which they picked up

  15:27. the dogs eat the *s.*

  15:37. all ate to their hearts' content; and the *s.* left over

Mark 6:43. twelve great basketfuls of *s.*

Mark 7:28. the dogs under the table eat the children's *s*.
8:8. seven baskets were filled with the *s*.
8:19. how many basketfuls of *s*.
Luke 9:17. the *s*. they left were picked up
16:21. glad to satisfy his hunger with the *s*.

scream
Luke 9:39. a spirit seizes him, gives a sudden *s*.

screen
1 Pet. 2:16. to provide a *s*. for wrong-doing

scriptural
Rom. 3:10. this has *s*. warrant

scripture-s
(the word *S*. is constantly used in referring to the Old Testament)

scroll
Luke 4:17. was handed the *s*. of the prophet Isaiah. He opened the *s*.
4:20. he rolled up the *s*.
Heb. 10:7. as it is written of me in the *s*.
Rev. 1:11. write down what you see on a *s*.
also Rev. 5:1–5, 7, 9. 10:2, 8, 9, 10

scruples
Rom. 15:1. the tender *s*. of weaker men
Heb. 13:9. not from *s*. about what we eat

scrupulous
Acts 17:22. concerns religion you are uncommonly *s*.

scrutiny
1 Tim. 3:10. bishops, they must first undergo a *s*.

scum
1 Cor. 4:13. we are treated as the *s*. of the earth

sea
Mat. 12:40. Jonah was in the *s*.-monster's belly
Acts 27:2. put out to *s*.
27:12. putting out to *s*.
27:27. drifting in the *S*. of Adria
2 Cor. 11:25. I was adrift on the open *s*.

seaboard
Luke 6:17. from the *s*. of Tyre and Sidon

sealed
1 Cor. 11:25. this cup is the new covenant *s*. by my blood
Phil. 1:28. sure sign to them that their doom is *s*.

search-es-ed-ing
Mat. 2:13. Herod is going to *s*. for the child
18:12. go in *s*. of the one that strayed
Mark 1:36. Simon and his companions *s*. him out
Luke 2:48. your father and I have been *s*. for you
2:49. what made you *s*.
4:42. the people went in *s*. of him
24:5. why *s*. among the dead for one who lives
John 6:24. made for Capernaum in *s*. of Jesus
Acts 12:19. Herod made close *s*., but failed to find him
1 Cor. 14:24. something that *s*. his conscience
2 Tim. 1:17. took pains to *s*. me out
Heb. 11:6. rewards those who *s*. for him

sea-shore
Rev. 13:1. he took his stand on the *s*.

season-s
Mat. 21:34. when the vintage *s*. approached
27:15. at the festival *s*. it was the Governor's custom
Mark 11:13. it was not the *s*. for figs
15:6. at the festival *s*. the Governor used to
Luke 2:43. when the festive *s*. was over
13:9. if it bears next *s*., well and good
Acts 20:6. after the Passover *s*.
Gal. 4:10. you keep special days and months and *s*.
Jude 12. trees that in *s*. bear no fruit

seat
Luke 14:9. give this man your *s*.
2 Thess. 2:4. takes his *s*. in the temple of God
Heb. 8:1. taken his *s*. at the right hand

seclusion
Luke 1:24. for five months she lived in *s*.
John 7:4. no one can hope to be in the public eye if he works in *s*.

second
Mat. 6:24. love the *s*., or he will be devoted to the first and think nothing of the *s*.
10:10. no *s*. coat, no shoes
21:31. which of these two did as his father wished?' 'The *s*.,' they said
Mark 6:9. might wear sandals, but not a *s*. coat
Luke 9:3. nor are you each to have a *s*. coat

Luke 14:19. the *s*. said, 'I have bought five yoke of oxen
16:13. love the *s*., or he will be devoted to the first and think nothing of the *s*.
20:11. sent a *s*. servant
John 9:24. for the *s*. time they summoned the man
19:32. and to the *s*., and broke their legs
Acts 11:9. a voice from heaven answered a *s*. time
20:15. on the *s*. day we made Samos
Heb. 12:17. no way open for *s*. thoughts
Rev. 12:3. a *s*. portent appeared in heaven
14:8. another angel, a *s*., followed

secret-s
Mat. 13:11. the *s*. of the kingdom of Heaven
Mark 4:11. the *s*. of the kingdom of God
9:30. Jesus wished it to be kept *s*.
Luke 2:35. the *s*. thoughts of many will be laid bare
8:10. the *s*. of the kingdom of God
20:20. sent *s*. agents in the guise of honest men
1 Cor. 2:7. his *s*. purpose framed from the very beginning
4:1. as stewards of the *s*. of God
2 Cor. 12:4. heard words so *s*.
Eph. 3:3. his *s*. was made known to me
3:4. I understand the *s*. of Christ
Col. 1:26. the *s*. hidden for long ages
1:27. the *s*. is this: Christ in you
2:2. grasp God's *s*. That *s*. is Christ himself
4:3. to tell the *s*. of Christ
4:4. pray that I may make the *s*. plain
2 Thess. 2:7. the *s*. power of wickedness is at work, *s*. only for the present
Rev. 1:20. the *s*. meaning of the seven stars
2:24. the deep *s*. of Satan
17:5. on her forehead was a name with a *s*. meaning
17:7. I will tell you the *s*. of the woman

sect
Luke 5:30. the Pharisees and the lawyers of their *s*.
Acts 24:14. I am a follower of the new way (the *s*.

section
Acts 23:6. one *s*. of them were Sadducees

secure-d-ly
Mat. 27:64. for the grave to be made *s*.
27:65. make it *s*. as best you can
27:66. they went and made the grave *s*.
Luke 8:29. they would *s*. him with chains

14:7. the guests were trying to *s*. the places of honour
John 18:12. arrested Jesus and *s*. him
Acts 5:23. we found the jail *s*. locked
12:4. having *s*. him, he put him in prison
12:6. *s*. by two chains
16:24. *s*. their feet in the stocks
2 Cor. 1:24. your hold on the faith is *s*. enough
Eph. 1:7. in Christ our release is *s*.
Col. 1:14. his dear Son, in whom our release is *s*.
Heb. 8:6. the promises upon which it is legally *s*.
9:12. *s*. an eternal deliverance

security
1 Thess. 5:3. while they are talking of peace and *s*.

seduce-d
Rom. 7:11. sin found its opportunity in the commandment, *s*. me
16:18. *s*. the minds of innocent people
2 Cor. 11:3. the serpent in his cunning *s*. Eve
2 Pet. 3:17. unprincipled men *s*. you with their errors
Rev. 20:3. *s*. the nations no more
20:8. he will come out to *s*. the nations

seducer
Rev. 20:10. the Devil, their *s*.

see-s-n
Mat. 5:6. hunger and thirst to *s*. right prevail
6:16. that other people may *s*. that they are fasting
6:18. that men may not *s*. that you are fasting
13 26. the darnel could be *s*.
15:23. *s*. how she comes shouting after us.
24:34. the present generation will live to *s*. it
Mark 3:6. *s*. how they could make away with him
7:18. do you not *s*. that nothing that goes from outside
13:30. the present generation will live to *s*. it
Luke 16:15. God *s*. through you
21:32. the present generation will live to *s*. it
John 8:59. Jesus was not to be *s*.
12:17. told what they had *s*. and heard

seed-s
Mat. 13:5, 7, 8; Mark 4:3, 5, 7, 8, 16, 18, 20; Luke 8:6, 8, 13, 15
1 Cor. 3:6. I planted the *s*.
15:36. the *s*. you sow does not come to life

Gal. 6:8. sows *s*. in the field of his lower nature

Jam. 3:18. *s*. sown in a spirit of peace

seek-s-ing

Rom. 12:19. do not *s*. revenge

Gal. 5:4. you *s*. to be justified by way of law

1 Thess. 2:4. we *s*. only the favour of God

2 Pet. 2:11. employ no insults in *s*. judgement

Rev. 11:5. if anyone *s*. to do them harm . . . thus shall the man die who *s*. to do them harm

seem-s-ed

Luke 24:41. it *s*. too good to be true

Acts 9:18. it *s*. that scales fell from his eyes

Rom. 4:18. when hope *s*. hopeless

1 Cor. 4:9. it *s*. to me God has made us apostles the most abject of mankind

2 Cor. 13:7. even if we should *s*. to be discredited

Rev. 4:6. what *s*. a sea of glass

8:1. silence in heaven for what *s*. half an hour

15:2. I saw what *s*. a sea of glass

seemliness

1 Cor. 12:23. a more than ordinary *s*.

seemly

1 Cor. 7:35. of what is *s*.

12:23. our *s*. parts need no adorning

seize-s-d-ing

Mat. 11:12. violent men are *s*. it

14:30. he was *s*. with fear

22:6. the others *s*. the servants

26:48. the one I kiss is your man; *s*. him

26:50. *s*. Jesus, and held him fast

27:3. he was *s*. with remorse

Mark 9:10. they *s*. upon those words

12:8. they *s*. him and killed him

14:1. some cunning plan to *s*. him

14:44. *s*. him and get him safely away

14:46. then they *s*. him and held him fast

14:51. they tried to *s*. him; but he slipped out of the linen cloth

Luke 8:29. many a time it had *s*. him

9:39. from time to time a spirit *s*. him

20:20. to *s*. upon some word of his

22:52. who had come to *s*. him

23:26. they *s*. upon a man called Simon

John 6:15. *s*. him to proclaim him king

7:30. they tried to *s*. him, but no one laid a hand on him

7:44. some were for *s*. him

10:39. one more attempt to *s*. him

Acts 6:12. set upon him and *s*. him

8:3. *s*. men and women, and sending them to prison

16:19. they *s*. Paul and Silas

19:29. they *s*. Paul's travelling-companions

20:10. *s*. him in his arms

21:27. stirred up the whole crowd, and *s*. him

21:30. they *s*. Paul and dragged him out of the temple

23:27. this man was *s*. by the Jews

26:21. the Jews *s*. me in the temple

2 Cor. 11:12. those who would *s*. any chance

Rev. 20:2. he *s*. the dragon

seizure

Heb. 10:34. cheerfully accepted the *s*. of your possessions

selected

Rom. 11:5. *s*. by the grace of God

11:7. the *s*. few have achieved it

self

Mat. 16:24. a follower of mine, he must leave *s*. behind

16:25. he will find his true *s*.

16:26. at the cost of his true *s*. . . . buy that *s*. back

Mark 8:34. must leave *s*. behind

8:36. at the cost of his true *s*.

8:37. what can he give to buy that *s*. back

Luke 9:23. he must leave *s*. behind

9:25. at the cost of his true *s*.

John 5:43. if another comes *s*.-accredited

Acts 24:25. *s*.-control, and the coming judgement

Rom. 3:19. no one may have anything to say in *s*.-defence

6:6. for the destruction of the sinful *s*.

7:22. in my inmost *s*. I delight in the law of God

1 Cor. 4:18. filled with *s*.-importance

4:19. take the measure of these *s*.-important people

5:6. your *s*.-satisfaction ill becomes you

7:5. for lack of *s*.-control

Gal. 5:22. gentleness, and *s*.-control

Col. 2:18. *s*.-mortification and angel-worship

2:23. its forced piety, its *s*.-mortification

1 Tim. 5:6. a widow given over to *s*.-indulgence

2 Tim. 1:7. love, and *s*.-discipline

3:4. swollen with *s*.-importance

Tit. 1:8. devout, and *s*.-controlled

3:11. stands *s*.-condemned in his sin

1 Pet. 1:13. perfectly *s*.-controlled

2 Pet. 1:6. knowledge with *s*.-control, *s*.-control with fortitude

2 Pet. 3:3. live s.-indulgent lives
1 John 1:8. if we claim to be sinless, we are s.-deceived

selfish
Rom. 2:8. governed by s. ambition
1 Cor. 13:5. never s., not quick to take offence
Gal. 5:20. s. ambitions, dissensions
Jam. 3:14. s. ambition in your hearts

selves
Rom. 12:1. offer your very s. to him
1 Thess. 2:8. not only the gospel of God but our very s.

send-s-ing
Mat. 8:31. s. us into that herd of pigs
　10:21 ⎫
Mark 13:12 ⎬ s. them to their death
Acts 8:3. s. them to prison
　14:17. he s. you rain from heaven
2 Thess. 1:6. God should balance the account by s. trouble

sense-s
Mat. 7:24. the s. to build his house on rock
Luke 15:17. then he came to his s.
Acts 2:43. a s. of awe was everywhere
　25:27. there is no s., it seems to me
Rom. 4:6. in the same s. David speaks
1 Cor. 8:2. knows nothing yet, in the true s. of knowing
　8:7. eat this food with a s. of its heathen consecration
　9:10. in the s. that the ploughman should plough
　10:15. I speak to you as men of s.
　12:25. no s. of division in the body
　15:45. it is in this s. that Scripture says
2 Cor. 9:7. no s. of compulsion; God loves a cheerful giver
Col. 2:11. you were circumcised, not in a physical s.
1 Tim. 5:3. widows who are such in the full s.
　5:5. a widow, however, in the full s.
　5:16. widows in the full s. of the term
2 Tim. 2:26. come to their s. and escape from the devil's snare
Heb. 10:2. no longer have any s. of sin
　11:19. from the dead, he did, in a s., receive him back
1 John 2:8. new in the s. that the darkness is passing

senseless
1 Cor. 15:35. in what kind of body? A s. question

sensible-y
Mat. 24:45. the s. man charged by his master
Mark 12:34. when Jesus saw how s. he answered
Luke 12:42. the trusty and s. man

1 Cor. 4:10. you are such s. Christians
Eph. 5:15. like s. men, not like simpletons

sensual
2 Pet. 2:18. s. lusts and debauchery

sensuality
2 Cor. 12:21. their fornication and s.
Eph. 2:3. we all lived our lives in s.
Col. 2:23. of no use at all in combating s.
Jude 23. clothing that is contaminated with s.

sent
Mark 1:12. the Spirit s. him away into the wilderness
　16:8. Jesus himself s. out by them from east to west
Luke 14:4. cured him, and s. him away
　14:16. s. out many invitations
　19:15. s. for the servants
John 3:2. we know that you are a teacher sent by God
Acts 13:7. who had s. for Barnabas and Saul
　15:3. they were s. on their way by the congregation
　15:33. to return to those who had s. them
Tit. 3:6. he s. down the Spirit upon us
Rev. 16:14. they were s. out to muster all the kings of the world

sentence-d
Mat. 26:59. allegation against Jesus on which a death-s. could be based
Mark 12:40. they will receive the severest s.
　14:55. evidence against Jesus to warrant a death-s.
Luke 20:47. they will receive the severest s.
　23:40. you are under the same s. as he
　24:20. handed him over to be s. to death
Acts 13:28. failed to find grounds for the s. of death
Rom. 9:28. the Lord's s. on the land will be summary
1 Pet. 4:6. they received the s. common to men

sentry-ies
Acts 12:6. s. kept guard over the prison

separate-ly
Mat. 13:49. they will s. the wicked from the good
　19:6 ⎫ what God has joined to-
Mark 10:9 ⎭ gether, man must not s.
1 Cor. 7:10. a wife must not s. herself from her husband
　12:11. these gifts are the work of one and the same Spirit, distributing them s.

Eph. 2:12. you were at that time *s.* from Christ

separation
1 Cor. 7:15. the heathen partner wishes for a *s.*

serious-ly
Acts 19:23. the Christian movement gave rise to a *s.* disturbance

2 Cor. 1:8. how *s.* was the trouble that came upon us

7:11. it made you take the matter *s.*

servant-s
Mat. 20:26 }
Mark 10:43 } must be your *s.*

Luke 1:2. original eyewitnesses and *s.* of the Gospel

1:38. here am I,' said Mary; 'I am the Lord's *s.*

1:48. so tenderly has he looked upon his *s.*

12:42. appoint as his steward, to manage his *s.*

15:27. the *s.* told him, 'Your brother has come home

John 2:7. Jesus said to the *s.* 'Fill the jars with water

Acts 2:27. nor let thy loyal *s.* suffer corruption

3:13. has given the highest honour to his *s.* Jesus

3:26. when God raised up his *S.*

4:27. against thy holy *s.* Jesus

4:30. through the name of thy holy *s.* Jesus

13:35. thou wilt not let thy loyal *s.* suffer corruption

26:16. to appoint you my *s.* and witness

Rom. 9:12. the elder shall be *s.* to the younger

14:18. he who thus shows himself a *s.* of Christ

15:8. Christ became a *s.* of the Jewish people

16:18. such people are *s.* not of Christ our Lord

2 Cor. 6:4. as God's *s.*, we try to recommend ourselves

11:23. are they *s.* of Christ

Gal. 5:13. be *s.* to one another in love

Col. 1:25. I became its *s.* by virtue of the task assigned to me

1 Thess. 1:9. *s.* of the living and true God

1 Tim. 4:6. a good *s.* of Christ Jesus

6:2. they must be all the better *s.*

Heb. 10:38. by faith my righteous *s.* shall find life

serve-s-ed-ing
Mat. 18:23. to settle accounts with the men who *s.*

20:28. he did not come to be *s.*, but to *s.*

26:69. a *s.*-maid accosted him

Mark 8:6. they *s.* it out to the people

10:45. the Son of Man did not come to be *s.* but to *s.*

14:66. one of the High Priest's *s.*-maids

Luke 22:56. a *s.*-maid who saw him sitting in the firelight

John 2:10. everyone *s.* the best wine first, and waits until the guests have drunk freely before *s.* the poorer sort

Rom. 3:5. if our injustice *s.* to bring out God's justice

6:16. whether you *s.* sin, with death as its result

12:5. *s.* individually as limbs

1 Cor. 9:7. did you ever hear of a man *s.* in the army at his own expense

16:15. have laid themselves out to *s.* God's people

2 Cor. 8:19. show our own eagerness to *s.*

11:8. accepting support from them to *s.* you

Eph. 6:5. single-mindedly, as *s.* Christ

Phil. 1:22. what if my living on in the body may *s.* some good purpose

1 Tim. 3:10. if there is no mark against them, they may *s.*

Heb. 1:14. ministrant spirits, sent out to *s.*

3 John 6. in a manner worthy of the God we *s.*

Rev. 1:6. to *s.* as the priests of his God and Father

5:10. to *s.* our God as priests

22:2. the leaves of the trees *s.* for the healing of the nations

service-s
Mat. 15:8. this people pays me lip-*s.*

27:32. pressed him into *s.* to carry his cross

Mark 7:6. this people pays me lip-*s.*

15:21. they pressed him into *s.* to carry his cross

Luke 1:8. he was there to take part in divine *s.*

3:14. soldiers on *s.* also asked him, 'And what of us

John 4:46. an officer in the royal *s.* was there

Acts 17:25. he accepts *s.* at men's hands

22:3. I have always been ardent in God's *s.*

24:18. ritually purified and engaged in this *s.*

Rom. 1:1. set apart for the *s.* of the Gospel

1:9. the humble *s.* of my spirit

6:19. the *s.* of impurity and lawlessness, making for moral anarchy, so now you must yield them to the *s.* of righteousness

Rom. 6:22. bound to the s. of God
13:6. the authorities are in God's s.
15:16. my priestly s. is the preaching
of the gospel
15:17. I have ground for pride in the
s. of God
16:10. well proved in Christ's s.
16:12. who toil in the Lord's s., and
dear Persis who has toiled in his
s.
1 Cor. 7:22. a slave in the s. of Christ
9:13. those who perform the temple s.
12:5. there are varieties of s.
2 Cor. 5:18. he has enlisted us in this s.
of reconciliation
6:3. that our s. may not be brought
into discredit
8:4. this generous s. to their fellow-
Christians
8:7. show yourselves equally lavish in
this generous s.
8:18. for his s. to the Gospel
13:4. by the power of God live with
him in your s.
Gal. 4:9. propose to enter their s. all
over again
Eph. 4:12. to equip God's people for
work in his s.
6:6. outward show of s.
Phil. 2:22. in the s. of the Gospel
Col. 3:24. as a reward for your s.
4:17. in the Lord's s.
1 Thess. 3:2. in the s. of the gospel of
Christ
1 Tim. 1:12. appointing me to his s.
3:13. with a good record of s.
2 Tim. 1:18. the many s. he rendered
2:4. a soldier on active s.
2:9. in whose s. I am exposed to hardships
Heb. 6:10. you rendered s. to his people
9:14. fit us for the s. of the living God
9:21. the vessels of divine s.
10:11. performing his s. daily
1 Pet. 1:2. hallowed to his s. by the
Spirit
2:16. slaves in God's s.
4:10. use it in s. to one another
4:11. do you give s.
Rev. 6:11. all their brothers in Christ's s.

servitor
Heb. 3:5. a s. in God's whole household

servitude
Heb. 2:15. all their lifetime been in s.

set-s-ting
Mat. 1:19. the marriage contract s. aside
quietly
2:9. they set out at the king's bidding
5:19. s. aside even the least of the
Law's demands
5:39. do not s. yourself against the
man who wrongs you

6:33. s. your mind on God's kingdom
15:5. s. apart for God
17:11. Elijah will come and s. everything right
21:25. this s. them arguing among
themselves
Mark 3:21. they s. out to take charge of
him
6:12. they s. out and called publicly
for repentance
7:11. Corban' (meaning, set apart for
God
9:12. Elijah does come first to s.
everything right
14:15. a large room upstairs, s. out
in readiness
14:65. the High Priest's men s. upon
him with blows
Luke 1:39. about this time Mary s. out
1:68. saved them and s. them free
5:18. s. him down in front of Jesus
8:2. women who had been s. free from
evil spirits
12:14. who s. me over you to judge
12:31. s. your mind upon his kingdom
12:49. I have come to s. fire to the
earth
15:18. I will s. off and go to my father
15:.20 so he s. out for his father's
house
16:15. s. itself up to be admired by
men
21:12. they will s. upon you and
persecute you
22:10. as soon as you s. foot in the
city
22:12. a large room upstairs all s. out
John 5:45. Moses on whom you have s.
your hope
8:36. if then the Son s. you free
10:35. Scripture cannot be s. aside
Acts 1:7. which the Father has s. within
his own control
2:24. s. him free from the pangs of
death
Rom. 1:1. s. apart for the service of the
Gospel
2 Cor. 7:13. you have all helped to s.
his mind completely at rest
Gal. 5:1. Christ s. us free, to be free men
5:17. that nature s. its desires against
the Spirit
Eph. 1:12. s. our hope on Christ
Phil. 1:18. Christ is s. forth, and for that
I rejoice
1 Thess. 1:6. the example s. by us
1 Tim. 4:10. we have s. our hope on the
living God
2 Tim. 4:8. all who have s. their hearts
on his coming appearance
Tit. 2:14. to s. us free from all wickedness
Heb. 1:9. thy God has s. thee above thy
fellows
Jam. 1:18. of his s. purpose

1 Pet. 5:5. God *s.* his face against the arrogant

1 John 2:15. do not *s.* your hearts on the godless world

settle-d

Mat. 2:23. he *s.* in a town called Nazareth

4:13. *s.* at Capernaum on the sea of Galilee

12:45. they all come in and *s.* down

18:23. a king who decided to *s.* accounts

25:19. proceeded to *s.* accounts

Mark 4:32. the birds can *s.* in its shade

Luke 11:26. they all come in and *s.* down

12:58. *s.* with him while you are still on the way

Acts 7:2. before he had *s.* in Harran

7:4. and *s.* in Harran

7:29. Moses fled the country and *s.* in Midianite territory

18:11. he *s.* down for eighteen months

Rom. 14:1. without attempting to *s.* doubtful points

Heb. 11:9. by faith he *s.* as an alien in the land

seven

Luke 24:13. about *s.* miles from Jerusalem

2 Pet. 2:5. whom he preserved with *s.* others

Rev. 6:1. the Lamb broke the first of the *s.* seals

seventy

Acts 7:14. *s.*-five persons altogether

23:23. together with *s.* cavalry men

27:37. on board two hundred and *s.*-six of us

severed

Gal. 5:4. Your relation with Christ is completely *s.*

several

Mark 15:41. *s.* others who had come up to Jerusalem

Acts 21:10. when we had been there *s.* days

24:17. after an absence of *s.* years

25:14. they spent *s.* days there

Rom. 6:13. you must no longer put its *s.* parts at sin's disposal

severe-ly

Luke 12:47. will be flogged *s.*

12:48. did not know them and earned a beating will be flogged less *s.*

15:14. a *s.* famine fell upon that country

Acts 11:28. predict a *s.* and world-wide famine

16:23. after giving them a *s.* beating

2 Cor. 2:7. must not be made so *s.* as to overwhelm him

11:23. scourged more *s.*

Heb. 10:29. much more *s.* a penalty that man will deserve

Rev. 16:21. that plague was so *s.*

severest

Mark 12:40 ⎱ they will receive the *s.*
Luke 20:47 ⎰ sentence

severity

Col. 2:23. its *s.* to the body

sews

Mat. 9:16 ⎱ *s.* a patch of unshrunk
Mark 2:21 ⎰ cloth

sexual

1 Cor. 5:1. hear reports of *s.* immorality

shabby

Jam. 2:2. the other a poor man in *s.* clothes

shackle-d-s

Acts 21:33. ordered him to be *s.* with two chains

Rom. 8:21. freed from the *s.* of mortality

shade

Mark 4:32. the birds can settle in its *s.*

shadow

Mark. 9:7. a cloud appeared, casting its *s.* over them

Luke 9:34. a cloud which cast a *s.* over them

shaft

Rev. 9:1. the key of the *s.* of the abyss

9:2. he opened the *s.* of the abyss; and from the *s.* smoke rose like smoke from a great furnace, and the sun and the air were darkened by the smoke from the *s.*

shake-n-ing

Mat. 14:26. they were so *s.* that they cried out

Acts 2:25. so that I may not be *s.*

1 Cor. 2:3. as I was then, nervous and *s.* with fear

1 Thess. 3:3. under all these hardships, not to be *s.*

Heb. 12:12. stiffen your drooping arms and *s.* knees

shallow-s

Acts 27:17. the *s.* of Syrtis

Eph. 5:6. let no one deceive you with *s.* arguments

sham

2 Cor. 11:13. such men are *s.*-apostles

Gal. 2:4. a concession to certain *s.*-Christians

shame

Luke 10:11. dust of your town that clings to our feet we wipe off to your *s.*

Rom. 9:33. he who has faith in him will
not be put to *s.*
10:11. everyone who has faith in him
will be saved from *s.*
1 Cor. 1:27. to *s.* the wise, God has
chosen what the world counts folly,
and to *s.* what is strong, God has
chosen what the world counts
weakness
11:4. brings *s.* on his head
11:5. a woman, on the contrary, brings
s. on her head
2 Cor. 4:2. the deeds that men hide for
very *s.*
1 Pet. 2:6. the man who has faith in it
will not be put to *s.*

shameful
Rom. 1:26. God has given them up to
s. passions

shamelessness
Luke 11:8. the very *s.* of the request will
make him get up.

shape-d
Acts 17:29. *s.* by human craftsmanship
Rom. 1:23. an image *s.* like mortal man
2:20. the very *s.* of knowledge and
truth
8:29. *s.* to the likeness of his Son
2 Cor. 5:5. God himself has *s.* us for
this very end
Gal. 4:19. until you take the *s.* of Christ
Phil. 2:8. revealed in human *s.*
1 Pet. 1:14. do not let your characters
be *s.* any longer by the desires

share-s-d-ing
Mat. 10:25. the pupil should be content
to *s.* his teacher's lot, the servant to
s. his master's
14:21. five thousand men *s.* in this
meal
15:38. four thousand men *s.* in this
meal
20:23. you shall indeed *s.* my cup
21:41. who will let him have his *s.* of
the crop
25:21 ⎱ come and *s.* your master's
25:23 ⎰ delight
Mark 12:2. to collect from them his *s.*
Luke 3:11. the man with two shirts
must *s.*
10:7. stay in that one house, *s.* their
food
15:12. Father, give me my *s.* of the
property
15:13. turned the whole of his *s.* into
cash
20:10. his *s.* of the produce
20:36. they *s.* in the resurrection
22:17. take this and *s.* it among yourselves
John 18:18. Peter too was standing with
them, *s.* the warmth

19:24. they *s.* my garments among
them
Acts 2:42. to *s.* the common life
2:46. *s.* their meals with unaffected
joy
15:38. had not gone on to *s.* in their
work
Rom. 8:17. if we *s.* his sufferings now
in order to *s.* his splendour hereafter
11:17. to *s.* the same root and sap as
the olive
15:27. the Jewish Christians *s.* their
spiritual treasures
1 Cor. 1:9. to *s.* in the life of his Son
Jesus Christ
9:13. claim their *s.* of the sacrifice
10:16. *s.* in the blood of Christ . . .
s. in the body of Christ
11:28. eating his *s.* of the bread
2 Cor. 1:4. to *s.* with them the consolation
4:15. the abounding grace of God is
s. by more and more
6:1. *s.* in God's work
8:4. allowed to *s.* in this generous
service
11:29. do I not *s.* his weakness
13:4. we who *s.* his weakness
Gal. 3:9. who *s.* the blessing with faithful Abraham
4:30. the son of the slave shall not *s.*
the inheritance
6:6. he should give his teacher a *s.*
Eph. 1:11. given our *s.* in the heritage
1:18. glory of the *s.* he offers you
4:28. something to *s.* with the needy
5:5. has any *s.* in the kingdom of
Christ
Phil. 1:7. you all *s.* in the privilege
2:1. any *s.* of the Spirit
2:17. I *s.* my gladness with you
2:18. let us *s.* our joy
3:10. to *s.* his sufferings
4:3. *s.* my struggles in the cause of
the Gospel
4:14. to *s.* the burden of my troubles
Col. 1:12. fit to *s.* the heritage
1 Tim. 6:18. ready to give away and to *s.*
2 Tim. 1:8. take your *s.* of suffering
2:3. take your *s.* of hardship
Tit. 1:4. in the faith which we *s.*
Heb. 2:14. the children of a family *s.* the
same flesh and blood; and so he
too *s.* ours
3:1. who *s.* a heavenly calling
6:4. a *s.* in the Holy Spirit
6:7. receiving its *s.* of blessing
10:34. you *s.* the sufferings of the
prisoners
12:8. the discipline in which all sons
s.
12:10. so that we may *s.* his holiness
13:16. *s.* what you have with others

1 Pet. 3:7. you *s.* together in the grace of God

4:13. a *s.* in Christ's sufferings

2 Pet. 1:1. *s.* our faith

1:4. come to *s.* in the very being of God

1 John 1:3. so that you and we together may *s.* in a common life, that life which we *s.* with the Father

1:6. if we claim to be *s.* in his life

1:7. then we *s.* together a common life

Jude 11. they *s.* his doom

Rev. 1:9. who *s.* with you in the suffering

17:12. for one hour are to *s.* with the beast

17:14. his victory will be *s.* by his followers

18:4. *s.* in her plagues

20:6. the man who *s.* in this first resurrection

22:19. his *s.* in the tree of life

sharer-s

1 Cor. 10:18. *s.* in the altar

Eph. 3:6. *s.* together in the promise

sharp-ly

Luke 18:39. told him *s.* to hold his tongue

23:40. the other answered *s.*, 'Have you no fear of God

1 Cor. 11:18. you fall into *s.* divided groups

2 Cor. 12:7. I was given a *s.* pain in my body

2 Pet. 2:16. was *s.* rebuked

shed-ding

Mat. 5:16. must *s.* light among your fellows

2 Cor. 2:4. how many tears I *s.* as I wrote it

12:21. I may have tears to *s.* over many

Eph. 1:7. forgiven through the *s.* of his blood

2:13. brought near through the *s.* of Christ's blood

Col. 1:20. making peace through the *s.* of his blood

2 Tim. 1:4. I remember the tears you *s.*

Heb. 12:4. to the point of *s.* your blood

sheep

Luke 17:7. a servant ploughing or minding *s.*

sheepfold

John 10:7. I am the door of the *s.*

sheer

Mat. 13:44. for *s.* joy went and sold

Rom. 4:16. that it might be a matter of *s.* grace

1 Cor. 1:18. this doctrine of the cross is

s. folly to those on their way to ruin

Phil. 3:8. I count everything *s.* loss

1:Pet. 5:2. not for gain but out of *s.* devotion

2 Pet. 2:3. trade on your credulity with *s.* fabrications

sheet

Mat. 27:59. Joseph took the body, wrapped it in a clean linen *s.*

Mark 15:46. Joseph bought a linen *s.*, took him down from the cross, and wrapped him in the *s.*

Luke 23:53. he wrapped it in a linen *s.*

Rev. 4:6. a sea of glass, like a *s.* of ice

shelter-s

Mat. 17:4. I will make three *s.* here

Mark 9:5 ⎱
Luke 9:33 ⎰ shall we make three *s.*

shepherd-s

Mat. 2:6. to be the *s.* of my people Israel

Acts 20:28. as *s.* of the church of the Lord

1 Pet. 5:2. tend that flock of God whose *s.* you are

Jude 12. they are *s.* who take care only of themselves

Rev. 7:17. the Lamb who is at the heart of the throne will be their *s.*

shift

Luke 6:48. the river burst upon that house, but could not *s.* it

shine-ing

Luke 1:79. to *s.* on those who live in darkness

Acts 10:30. a man in *s.* robes stood before me

Eph. 5:14. Christ will *s.* upon you

Phil. 1:20. the greatness of Christ will *s.* out clearly

Rev. 15:6. they were robed in fine linen, clean and *s.*

19:8. she has been given fine linen, clean and *s.*

19:14. clothed in fine linen, clean and *s.*

ship-s

Luke 8:23. they began to *s.* water

Acts 27:16. managed to get the *s.* boat under control

shirt-s

Mat. 5:40. if a man wants to sue you for your *s.*

Luke 3:11. the man with two *s.* must share with him who has none

6:29. let him have your *s.* as well

Acts 9:39. the *s.* and coats that Dorcas used to make

shock-ed-ing

John 6:61. does this *s.* you

1 Cor. 14:35. a *s*. thing that a woman should address the congregation
2 Pet. 2:7. a good man, *s*. by the dissolute habits

shoes
Acts 12:8. do up your belt and put your shoes on
Eph. 6:15. let the *s*. on your feet be the gospel of peace

shone
Matt. 28:3. his face *s*. like lightning
John 17:10. through them has my glory *s*.
Rev. 10:1. his face *s*. like the sun
21:11. it *s*. with the glory of God

shook
Gal. 2:9. *s*. hands upon it

shoot-s
Mat. 24:32 ⎫ when its tender *s*. appear
Mark 13:28 ⎭
John 21:6. *s*. the net to starboard

shop
Mat. 25:9. go to the *s*. and buy some for yourselves

shore
Mat. 8:18. Jesus gave word to cross to the other *s*.
14:24. some furlongs from the *s*.
Mark 1:16. Jesus was walking by the *s*.
5:21. returned by boat to the other *s*.
Luke 5:3. asked him to put out a little way from the *s*.
John 6:1. Jesus withdrew to the farther *s*.
6:22. the crowd was standing on the opposite *s*.

short-ly
Mat. 19:20. where do I still fall *s*.
26:73. *s*. afterwards the bystanders came
Mark 9:24. help me where faith falls *s*.
Luke 22:35. were you ever *s*. of anything
Acts 27:28. sounding again after a *s*. interval
27:33. *s*. before daybreak Paul urged them all to take some food
1 Cor. 14:39. in *s*., my friends, be eager to prophesy
2 Cor. 4:17. our troubles are slight and *s*.-lived
8:15. the man who got little did not go *s*.
11:5. have I in any way come *s*.
11:9. if I ran *s*. I sponged on no one
12:11. in no respect did I fall *s*.
1 Thess. 3:10. to mend your faith where it falls *s*.
1 Tim. 1:6. through falling *s*. of these

5:10. in *s*., whether she has taken every opportunity of doing good
2 Tim. 3:9. their successes will be *s*.-lived
Tit. 1:7. he must not be overbearing or *s*.-tempered
3:13. see that they are not *s*. of anything
Heb. 2:7. for a *s*. while lower than the angels
2:9. for a *s*. while was made lower than the angels
8:13. growing old and ageing will *s*. disappear
11:32. time is too *s*. for me to tell
12:10. they disciplined us for this *s*. life
13:22. it is after all a *s*. letter
Jam. 1:4. a balanced character that will fall *s*. in nothing
1:5. if any of you falls *s*. in wisdom
2 Pet. 1:9. the man who lacks them is *s*.-sighted
Rev. 20:3. after that he must be let loose for a *s*. while

shot
Mat. 13:7 ⎫ thistles *s*. up, and choked
Mark 4:7 ⎭ the corn
1 Tim. 6:21. many who lay claim to it have *s*. far wide of the faith
2 Tim. 2:18. they have *s*. wide of the truth
Rev. 8:10. a great star *s*. from the sky
15:2. a sea of glass *s*. with fire

shoulder-s
Acts 12:7. he tapped Peter on the *s*.
15:10. laying on the *s*. of these converts a yoke

shout-ed-ing
Mat. 8:29. you son of God', they *s*.
10:27. what you hear whispered you must *s*.
11:16. in the market-place and *s*. at each other
12:19. he will not strive, he will not *s*.
15:23. see how she comes *s*. after us
20:30. they *s*., 'Have pity on us
20:31. they *s*. all the more
21:9. the others that came behind raised the *s*.
21:15. heard the boys in the temple *s*.
27:23. they *s*. all the louder, 'Crucify him
Mark 5:7. *s*. loudly, 'What do you want with me, Jesus
10:47. he began to *s*., 'Son of David, Jesus
10:48. he *s*. all the more
11:9. *s*., 'Hosanna! Blessings on him who comes
15:13. they *s*. back, 'Crucify him
15:14. they *s*. all the louder
Luke 4:41. *s*., 'You are the Son of God

Luke 7:32. *s.* at each other
    8:28. fell at his feet *s.*
    9:38. there was a *s.* from a man in the crowd
    12:3. will be *s.* from the house-tops
    18:38. he *s.* out, 'Jesus, Son of David
    19:40. the stones will *s.* aloud
    23:21. they *s.* back, 'Crucify him
    23:23. *s.* that Jesus should be crucified
John 12:13. *s.*, 'Hosanna
    19:12. the Jews kept *s.*, 'If you let this man go
    19:15. they *s.*, 'Away with him
Acts 7:57. they gave a great *s.* and stopped their ears
    14:11. they *s.*, in their native Lycaonian
    14:14. *s.*, 'Men, what is this that you are doing
    16:17. she followed Paul and the rest of us, *s.*
    16:28. Paul *s.*, 'Do yourself no harm
    17:6. *s.*, 'The men who have made trouble
    19:28. *s.*, 'Great is Diana of the Ephesians
    19:32. some were *s.*
    19:34. for about two hours they kept on *s.*
    21:28. *s.*, 'Men of Israel, help, help
    21:34. some in the crowd *s.* one thing
    22:22. now they began *s.*, 'Down with him
    26:24. Festus *s.* at the top of his voice
Gal. 4:27. break into a *s.* of joy
Eph. 4:31. all angry *s.* and cursing
Rev. 7:10. they *s.* together
    10:3. he gave a great *s.*, like the roar of a lion; and when he *s.*
    11:15. voices were heard in heaven *s.*
    14:18. he *s.* to the one with the sharp sickle
    19:1. they were *s.*: 'Alleluia
    19:3. then once more they *s.*
    19:7. exult and *s.* for joy

shovel
Mat. 3:12 ⎱ his *s.* is ready in his hand
Luke 3:17 ⎰

show-ing-ed-n
Mat. 5:7. how blest are those who *s.* mercy; mercy shall be *s.* to them
    5:20. unless you *s.* yourselves far better men than the Pharisees
    6:1. be careful not to make a *s.* of your religion
    12:38. master, we should like you to *s.* us a sign
    18:33. were you not bound to *s.* your fellow-servant the same pity as I *s.* to you
    21:32. John came to *s.* you the right way to live
    23:5. whatever they do is done for *s.*

Mark 1:45. until Jesus could no longer *s.* himself
Luke 1:55. he has not forgotten to *s.* mercy to Abraham
    7:16. God has *s.* his care for his people
    7:47. where little has been forgiven, little love is *s.*
    8:50. only *s.* faith and she will be well again
    18:1. to *s.* that they should keep on praying
    19:17. you have *s.* yourself trustworthy
John 3:20. for fear their practices should be *s.* up
    13:1. now he was to *s.* the full extent of his love
    14:31. the world must be *s.* that I love the Father
    16:8. *s.* where wrong and right and judgement lie
    16:10. *s.* that I go to the Father
    16:11. *s.* that the Prince of this world stands condemned
    20:9. the scriptures, which *s.* that he must rise
Acts 2:28. thou hast *s.* me the ways of life
    9:41. *s.* her to them alive
    14:17. in the kindness he *s.*
    15:8. God, who can read men's minds, *s.* his approval
    17:3. to *s.* that the Messiah had to suffer
    19:20. the word of the Lord *s.* its power
Rom. 1:30. they *s.* no loyalty to parents
    3:12. there is no one to *s.* kindness
    3:26. *s.* that he is both himself just and justifies
    8:25. in waiting for it, we *s.* our endurance
    9:15. where I *s.* mercy, I will *s.* mercy
    9:18. *s.* mercy as he chooses
    10:20. clearly *s.* to those who never asked about me
    11:32. God's purpose was to *s.* mercy to all mankind
    14:18. who thus *s.* himself a servant of Christ
1 Cor. 4:2. stewards are expected to *s.* themselves trustworthy
    11:19. to *s.* which of your members are sound
2 Cor. 1:11. the gracious favour God has *s.* towards us
    5:12. to *s.* yourselves proud of us; then you will have something to say to those whose pride is all in outward *s.*
    7:14. to *s.* my pride in you
    8:2. *s.* themselves lavishly open-handed

2 Cor. 8:7. should *s.* yourselves equally
    lavish
    8:19. *s.* our own eagerness to serve
    9:4. the confidence we have *s.*
    10:11. my actions will *s.* the same man
    as my letters *s.*
    11:30. things that *s.* up my weakness
Gal. 2:13. Jewish Christians *s.* the same
    lack of principle
    2:18. I *s.* myself up as a transgressor
    4:14. any temptation to *s.* scorn
Eph. 4:24. *s.* itself in the just and devout
    life
    5:11. *s.* them up for what they are
    5:13. when once the light has *s.* it up
    6:6. merely the outward *s.* of service
Phil. 2:15. *s.* yourselves guileless
Col. 3:22. not merely with an outward
    s. of service
1 Thess. 1:3. your faith has *s.* itself in
    action
2 Thess. 2:16. God our Father, who has
    s. us such love
1 Tim. 5:10. *s.* whether she has had the
    care of children
2 Tim. 2:25. *s.* them the truth
Heb. 10:33. tormented to make a public
    s.
    11:14. *s.* plainly that they are looking
    for a country
    13:2. remember to *s.* hospitality
    13:16. never forget to *s.* kindness
Jam. 2:1. you must never *s.* snobbery
    2:9. if you *s.* snobbery, you are com-
    mitting a sin
    2:14. to say he has faith when he does
    nothing to *s.* it
1 Pet. 3:6. if you do good and *s.* no fear
1 John 3:18. *s.* itself in action
    4:10. the love he *s.* to us in sending
    his Son
3 John 5. you *s.* a fine loyalty in every-
    thing

shrieked
Mark 1:23. he *s.*: 'What do you
    want with us
Luke 4:33. he *s.* at the top of his voice

shrine-s
Acts 7:43. the *s.* of Moloch
    17:24. does not live in *s.* made by men
Rom. 2:22. do you rob their *s.*
1 Cor. 6:19. your body is a *s.* of the
    indwelling Holy Spirit

shrink-s
Heb. 2:11. the Son does not *s.* from
    calling men his brothers
    10:38. if a man *s.* back, I take no
    pleasure in him
    10:39. we are not among those who
    s. back

shudder
Heb. 12:21. Moses said, 'I *s.* with fear

shun
1 Cor. 6:18. *s.* fornication
    10:14. *s.* idolatry
1 Tim. 6:11. *s.* all this, and pursue
    justice, piety

shut
2 Tim. 2:9. to the point of being *s* up
    like a common criminal; but the
    word of God is not *s.* up

sick-ly
Mark 3:10. *s.* people of all kinds came
    crowding in
Luke 5:17. the power of God was with
    him to heal the *s.*
    9:6. they told the good news and
    healed the *s.*
John 5:3. there lay a crowd of *s.* people
    6:2. the signs he performed in healing
    the *s.*
Acts 4:9. help given to a *s.* man
    28:9. the other *s.* people on the island
    came
Rev. 6:8. another horse, *s.* pale

side-s-ing
Mat. 24:31. the farthest bounds of
    heaven on every *s.*
Luke 1:54. he has ranged himself at the
    s. of Israel
    9:47. he took a child by the hand and
    stood him at his *s.*
    9:50. he who is not against you is on
    your *s.*
    16:26. no one from our *s.* who wants
    to reach you can cross it, and none
    may pass from your *s.* to us
    24:4. two men in dazzling garments
    were at their *s.*
John 3:26. a man with you on the other
    s. of the Jordan
    6:3. Jesus went up the hill-*s.*
    9:16. they took different *s.*
    16:10. he will convince them that
    right is on my *s.*
    20:4. they were running *s.* by *s.*
Acts 14:4. some *s.* with the Jews
    23:9. openly took *s.* and declared
    27:14. tore down from the landward
    s.
Rom. 2:15. their own thoughts argue
    the case on either *s.*
    8:31. if God is on our *s.*, who is
    against us
2 Cor. 7:7. how eager to take my *s.*
Phil. 2:22. at my *s.* in the service of the
    Gospel

siege
Luke 19:43. your enemies will set up
    s.-works
Rev. 20:9. laid *s.* to the camp of God's
    people

sift-s

Heb. 4:12. *s.* the purposes and thoughts of the heart

sighed

John 11:33. he *s.* heavily
11:38 Jesus again *s.* deeply

sight-ed

Mat. 2:10. at the *s.* of the star they were overjoyed
7:23. out of my *s.*, you and your wicked ways
8:18. at the *s.* of the crowds
9:8. the people were filled with awe at the *s.*
9:30. their *s.* was restored
9:36. the *s.* of the people moved him to pity
12:22. Jesus cured him, restoring both speech and *s.*
15:31. *s.* restored to the blind
20:33. Sir', they answered, 'we want our *s.*
20:34. at once their *s.* came back
21:20. the disciples were amazed at the *s.*
25:41. go from my *s.* to the eternal fire
28:4. at the *s.* of him the guards shook with fear
Mark 8:24. the man's *s.* began to come back
Luke 1:12. at this *s.* Zechariah was startled
7:21. on many blind people he bestowed *s.*
12:21. remains a pauper in the *s.* of God
13:27. out of my *s.*, all of you
19:41. in *s.* of the city, he wept over it
19:42. it is hidden from your *s.*
John 9:39. to give *s.*
11:32. she caught *s.* of him
16:10. I go to the Father when I pass from your *s.*
21:21. when he caught *s.* of him, Peter asked
Acts 8:27. he caught *s.* of an Ethiopian
21:3. we came in *s.* of Cyprus
Rom. 14:22. apply it to yourself in the *s.* of God
1 Cor. 3:19. the wisdom of this world is folly in God's *s.*
2 Cor. 12:19. we are speaking in God's *s.*
Gal. 1:22. unknown by *s.* to Christ's congregations
Eph. 1:4. to be without blemish in his *s.*
1 Thess. 2:17. lost to *s.*, not to our hearts
Jam. 1:27. without stain or fault in the *s.* of God
1 Pet. 2:4. precious in the *s.* of God

2:20. your fortitude is a fine thing in the *s.* of God
2 Pet. 1:9. the man who lacks them is short-*s.*
2:8. every *s.*, every sound, of their evil courses
3:5. lose *s.* of the fact that there were heavens
3:8. one point, my friends, which you must not lose *s.* of
3:14. above reproach in his *s.*
1 John 3:19. convince ourselves in his *s.*

sightless

John 9:39. to give sight to the *s.*

sign-s-ed

Luke 1:22. he stood there making *s.* to them
John 2:11. the first of the *s.* by which Jesus revealed his glory
2:23. gave their allegiance to him when they saw the *s.*
3:2. these *s.* of yours unless God were with him
4:54. the second *s.* which Jesus performed
6:2. the *s.* he performed in healing the sick
6:14. the *s.* Jesus had performed
6:26. not because you saw *s.*
7:31. is it likely that he will perform more *s.*
9:16. how could such *s.* come from a sinful man
10:41. John gave us no miraculous *s.*
11:47. this man is performing many *s.*
12:18. they had heard of this *s.*
12:37. in spite of the many *s.*
Acts 6:8. great miracles and *s.* among the people
12:17. he *s.* to them to keep quiet
15:12. the *s.* and miracles that God had worked
27:20. there was no *s.* of either sun or stars
1 Cor. 11:10. woman's duty to have a *s.* of authority
Phil 1:28. a sure *s.* to them that their doom is sealed, but a *s.* of your salvation
2 Thess. 3:17. *s.* with my name, PAUL
1 Tim. 4:2. conscience is branded with the devil's *s.*

signal-led

Mat. 24:3. what will be the *s.* for your coming
Mark 14:44. the traitor had agreed with them upon a *s.*
Luke 5:7. *s.* to their partners in the other boat

signature

Philem. 19. here is my *s.*, PAUL

signify-ies
Rev. 19:8. the fine linen *s*. the righteous deeds

silence-d
Mat. 26:63. but Jesus kept *s*.
Mark 14:61. he kept *s*.
Luke 9:36. the disciples kept *s*.
19:40. if my disciples keep *s*. the stones will shout aloud
Acts 9:22. *s*. the Jews of Damascus
11:18. their doubts were *s*.
18:9. go on with your preaching and do not be *s*.
19:33. motioning for *s*., attempted to make a defence
Rom. 16:25. that divine secret kept in *s*. for long ages

silent
Mark 1:25. be *s*.,' he said, 'and come out of him
9:34. they were *s*., because on the way they had been discussing
Luke 1:20. lose your powers of speech, and remain *s*.
4:35. be *s*.,' he said, 'and come out of him
20:26. astonished by his reply, they fell *s*.

silk-s
Mat. 11:8 ⎫ a man dressed in *s*. and
Luke 7:25 ⎭ satins

silver
Mat. 17:27. you will find a *s*. coin
22:19. they handed him a *s*. piece
Mark 12:15. fetch me a *s*. piece
Luke 7:41. one owed him five hundred *s*. pieces
10:35. next day he produced two *s*. pieces
20:24. show me a *s*. piece

similarly
Acts 14:1. at Iconium *s*. they went into the Jewish synagogue
Rom. 11:9. *s*. David says
1 Tim. 5:25. *s*., good deeds are obvious
Tit. 2:3. the older women, *s*., should be reverent in their bearing
2:6. urge the younger men, *s*., to be temperate

simple-y
Mat. 11:25. revealing them to the *s*.
14:36. *s*. to touch the edge of his cloak
Mark 6:56. let them *s*. touch the edge of his cloak
Luke 10:21. revealing them to the *s*.
Rom. 1:14. to learned and *s*.
4:5. he *s*. puts his faith in him who acquits the guilty
14:13. make this *s*. judgement
1 Cor. 3:5. we are *s*. God's agents

7:35. I am thinking *s*. of your own good
9:17. I am *s*. discharging a trust
2 Cor. 11:15. a *s*. thing for his agents to masquerade

simpleton-s
Rom. 16:19. experts in goodness but *s*. in evil
Eph. 5:15. like sensible men, not like *s*.

sin-s
Mat. 18:15. if your brother commits a *s*.
Mark 3:29. he is guilty of eternal *s*.
Luke 18:14. went home acquitted of his *s*.
Acts 8:23. the fetters of *s*.
1 Cor. 13:6. does not gloat over other men's *s*.
1 Tim. 2:14. the woman who, yielding to deception, fell into *s*.
3:6. for fear the *s*. of conceit
Heb. 9:7. for the people's *s*. of ignorance
9:15. deliverance from *s*. committed
Jam. 5:16. confess your *s*. to one another

Sinai
Heb. 12:18. the palpable, blazing fire of *S*.

sincere
John 7:18. aims at the honour of him who sent him he is *s*.
2 Cor. 6:6. by gifts of the Holy Spirit, by *s*. love
Jam. 3:17. it is straightforward and *s*.
1 Pet. 1:22. feel *s*. affection

sincerity
Rom. 12:9. love in all *s*.
Phil. 1:18. in pretence or in *s*., Christ is set forth
2 Tim. 1:5. the *s*. of your faith
Heb. 10:22. let us make our approach in *s*.

sinful
Mat. 26:45 ⎫ the Son of Man is be-
Mark 14:41 ⎭ trayed to *s*. men
John 5:14. leave your *s*. ways
9:16. how could such signs come from a *s*. man
Rom. 6:6. for the destruction of the *s*. self
7:5. the *s*. passions evoked by the law
7:13. sin became more *s*.
1 Cor. 15:34. leave your *s*. ways
1 Tim. 1:9. the impious and *s*.
2 Tim. 3:6. women burdened with a *s*. past
1 Pet. 4:18. what will become of the impious and *s*.

sinfulness
2 Cor. 5:21. God made him one with the *s*. of men

2 Thess. 2:10. all the deception that *s.* can impose

   2:12. make *s.* their deliberate choice

sing-ing

Mat. 26:30 ⎱ after *s.* the Passover
Mark 14:26 ⎰ Hymn

Luke 2:13. the heavenly host, *s.* the praises of God

   19:37. began to *s.* aloud the praises of God

Jam. 3:9. we use it to *s.* the praises of our Lord

single-d

Luke 11:46. will not put a *s.* finger to the load

   13:15. is there a *s.* one of you who does not loose his ox

John 1:3. no *s.* thing was created without him

   7:48. is there a *s.* one of our rulers who has believed in him

Acts 2:22. Jesus of Nazareth, a man *s.* out by God

   19:34. a *s.* cry arose from them all

   27:22. not a *s.* life will be lost

Rom. 5:17. death established its reign, through a *s.* sinner

   12:4. in a *s.* human body there are many limbs

1 Cor. 1:7. there is indeed no *s.* gift you lack

   6:5. can it be that there is not a *s.* wise man

   12:12. Christ is like a *s.* body with its many limbs

   12:14. a body is not one *s.* organ

   12:19. if the whole were one *s.* organ

2 Cor. 11:3. your *s.*-hearted devotion to Christ

Gal. 5:14. the whole law can be summed up in a *s.* commandment

Eph. 2:15. create out of the two a *s.* new humanity

   2:16. to reconcile the two in a *s.* body

   5:31. the two shall become a *s.* body

   6:5. *s.*-mindedly, as serving Christ

Col. 3:15. called as members of a *s.* body

Heb. 12:16. he sold his birthright for a *s.* meal

Jam. 2:10. the whole law apart from one *s.* point

Rev. 17:13. they have but a *s.* purpose among them

   18:8. her plagues shall strike her in a *s.* day

   18:10. in a *s.* hour your doom has struck

   18:19. alas that in a *s.* hour she should be laid waste

   21:21. each gate being made from a *s.* pearl

single-mindedness

Col. 3:22. with *s.*, out of reverence for the Lord

singleness

2 Tim. 2:22. invoke the Lord in *s.* of mind

singular

Gal. 3:16. it does not say 'issues' in the plural, but in the *s.*

sinking

Mat. 8:25. save us, Lord; we are *s.*

Mark 4:38. master, we are *s.*

Luke 8:24. Master, Master, we are *s.*

Eph. 4:22. old human nature which, deluded by its lusts, is *s.* towards death

sinless

1 John 1:8. if we claim to be *s.*, we are self-deceived

sinner

Rom. 5:17. death established its reign, through a single *s.*

Jam. 4:17. the man who knows the good he ought to do and does not do it is a *s.*

1 John 3:9. he cannot be a *s.*, because he is God's child

   5:18. we know that no child of God is a *s.*

sir

Jesus is frequently addressed as '*s.*'

sister

Philem. 2. Apphia our *s.*

sit-ting

Mark 4:36. the boat where he had been *s.*

Acts 11:3. *s.* at table with them

Jam. 4:11. the law, you are not keeping it but *s.* in judgement upon it

2 Pet. 2:13. they *s.* with you at table

situation

2 Cor. 9:8. means in yourselves to meet each and every *s.*

six

Mat. 14:25. between three and *s.* in the morning

Mark 6:48. somewhere between three and *s.* in the morning

Acts 27:37. on board two hundred and seventy-*s.* of us

sixty

1 Tim. 5:9. a widow should not be put on the roll under *s.* years of age

Rev. 11:3. all through those twelve hundred and *s.* days

   12:6. to be sustained for twelve hundred and *s.* days

Rev. 13:18. the numerical value of its letters is six hundred and s.-six

skilled
1 Cor. 3:10. a s. master-builder who by God's grace laid the foundation

skin-s
Mat. 9:17. no more do you put new wine into old wine-s.; if you do, the s. burst, and then the wine runs out and the s. are spoilt. No, you put new wine into fresh s.
Mark 2:22. no one puts new wine into old wine-s.; if he does, the wine will burst the s., and then wine and s. are both lost. Fresh s. for new wine
Luke 5:37. nor does anyone put new wine into old wine-s.; if he does, the new wine will burst the s., the wine will be wasted
5:38. and the s. ruined. Fresh s. for new wine
Acts 19:12. scarves which had been in contact with his s.

skirt-s-ed
Acts 16:8. s. Mysia and reached the coast
18:6. he shook out the s. of his cloak

skull
Luke 23:33. they reached the place called The S.

sky-ies
Mat. 11:23. Capernaum, will you be exalted to the s.
24:29. the stars will fall from the s.
Mark 13:25. the stars will come falling from the s.
Luke 4:25. for three years and six months the s. never opened
10:15. Capernaum, will you be exalted to the s.
10:18. Satan fell, like lightning, out of the s.
21:11. in the s. terrors and great portents
Acts 1:10. as they were gazing intently into the s.
1:11. why stand there looking up into the s.
2:2. suddenly there came from the s. a noise
2:19. I will show portents in the s. above
7:56. there is a rift in the s.
9:3. suddenly a light flashed from the s.
10:11. he saw a rift in the s.
10:16. the thing was taken up again into the s.
11:5. lowered from the s.
11:10. all drawn up again into the s.
22:6. a great light flashed from the s.

26:13. I saw a light from the s.
Rev. 6:13. the stars in the s. fell to the earth
6:14. the s. vanished
8:10. a great star shot from the s.
11:6. have the power to shut up the s.
12:4. he swept down a third of the stars in the s.
16:21. huge hailstones . . . fell on men from the s.

slacken
Gal. 6:9. if we do not s. our efforts

slander-s-ed
Mat. 12:31. no s., is beyond forgiveness for men, except s. spoken against the Spirit
15:19. perjury, s.
Mark 3:28. no s., is beyond forgiveness for men
3:29. whoever s. the Holy Spirit can never be forgiven
7:22. envy, s., arrogance
Luke 12:10. for him who s. the Holy Spirit
1 Cor. 4:13. they s. us
1 Tim. 5:14. give no opponent occasion for s.
6:4. jealousy, quarrelling, s.
Tit. 3:2. to s. no one
Rev. 2:9. s. by those who claim to be Jews

slanderer-s
1 Cor. 5:11. idolatrous, a s., a drunkard
6:10. or s. or swindlers

slanderous
Rom. 14:16. a good thing must not become an occasion for s. talk

slaps
Mat. 5:39. if someone s. you on the right cheek

slaughter-ed
Mat. 22:4. I have had my bullocks and fatted beast s.
Mark 14:12. the Passover lambs were being s.
Luke 19:27. s. them in m. presence
22:7. the Passover victim had to be s.
Rev. 5:6. a Lamb with the marks of s. upon him
6:4. make men s. one another
6:9. s. for Gods word

slave-s-d
Mat. 6:24. no servant can be s. to two masters
20:27. whoever would be first must be the willing s. of all
Mark 10:44. whoever wants to be first must be the willing s. of all
Luke 15:29. I have s. for you all these years

Luke 16:13. no servant can be the *s.* of two masters

John 8:34. everyone who commits sin is a *s.*

8:35. the *s.* has no permanent standing

Acts 2:18. I will endue even my *s.*, both men and women, with a portion of my spirit

7:7. the nation whose *s.* they are

16:16. a *s.*-girl who was possessed by an oracular spirit

Rom. 6:6. may no longer be the *s.* of sin

6:16. you are *s.* of the master whom you obey

6:17. who once were *s.* of sin

6:18. have become *s.* of righteousness

6:20. when you were *s.* of sin

7:14. the purchased *s.* of sin

7:25. a *s.* to the law of sin

1 Cor. 7:21. were you a *s.* when you were called

7:22. the man who as a *s.* received the call to be a Christian is the Lord's freedman, and, equally, the free man who received the call is a *s.* in the service of Christ

7:23. do not become *s.* of men

12:13. whether *s.* or free men

Gal. 3:28. *s.* and freeman, male and female

4:1. he is no better off than a *s.*

4:3. we were *s.* to the elemental spirits

4:7. you are therefore no longer a *s.* but a son

4:8. the *s.* of beings which in their nature are no gods

4:22. Abraham had two sons, one by his *s.*

4:23. the *s.*-woman's son was born in the course of nature

4:30. drive out the *s.*-woman and her son

4:31. we are no *s.*-woman's children

Eph. 6:5. *s.*, obey your earthly masters

6:6. *s.* of Christ

6:8. whatever good each man may do, *s.* or free

Phil. 2:7. assuming the nature of a *s.*

Col. 3:11. freeman, *s.*

3:22. *s.*, give entire obedience to your earthly masters

3:24. Christ is the Master whose *s.* you must be

4:1. masters, be just and fair to your *s.*

1 Tim. 6:2. the *s.* must not respect them any less

Tit. 2:3. *s.* to strong drink

2:9. tell *s.* to respect their masters' authority

3:3. *s.* to passions and pleasures

Philem. 16. no longer as a *s.*, but as more than a *s.*

1 Pet. 2:16. as *s.* in God's service

2 Pet. 2:19. *s.* of corruption; for a man is the *s.* of whatever has mastered him

Rev. 6:15. all men, *s.* or free, hid themselves

13:16. *s.* and free, to be branded with a mark

19:18. the flesh of all men, *s.* and free

slavery

John 8:33. we have never been in *s.* to any man

Acts 7:6. held in *s.* and oppression for four hundred years

7:9. sold Joseph into *s.*

Rom. 8:15. the Spirit you have received is not a spirit of *s.*

Gal. 4:24. the one bearing children into *s.*

4:25. she and her children are in *s.*

5:1. refuse to be tied to the yoke of *s.*

1 Tim. 6:1. all who wear the yoke of *s.*

sleep

Mat. 2:14. Joseph rose from *s.*

2 Cor. 11:27. I have often gone without *s.*

sleepless

2 Cor. 6:5. overworked, *s.*, starving

slight

1 Cor. 16:10. no one must *s.* him

2 Cor. 4:17. our troubles are *s.*

1 Tim. 4:12. let no one *s.* you because you are young

Tit. 2:15. speak with authority: let no one *s.* you

slipped

Mark 14:52. he *s.* out of the linen cloth

John 5:13. the place was crowded and Jesus had *s.* away

Acts 27:40. they *s.* the anchors and let them go

slow

2 Pet. 3:9. it is not that the Lord is *s.*

slung

Acts 10:11. it was *s.* by the four corners

11:5. *s.* by the four corners and lowered

small-er

Mat. 7:14. the gate that leads to life is *s.*

13:32. as a seed, mustard is *s.* than any other

15:34. there are a few *s.* fishes

25:21, 23. you have proved trustworthy in a *s.* way

26:7. a woman came to him with a *s.* bottle of fragrant oil

Mark 4:31. the mustard-seed, which is *s.* than any seed

14:3. carrying a *s.* bottle of very costly perfume

Luke 7:37. brought oil of myrrh in a *s.* flask

19:17. trustworthy in a very *s.* matter

Acts 27:16. we ran under the lee of a *s.* island

Heb. 8:11. all of them shall know me, from *s.* to great

Jam. 3:5. it is a *s.* member but it can make huge claims

smart

2 Cor. 7:9. you bore the *s.* as God would have you bear it

1 Pet. 1:6. great joy, even though now you *s.* for a little while

smashing

Rev. 2:27. *s.* them to bits like earthenware

smeared

John 9:11. Jesus made a paste and *s.* my eyes with it

smooth

Rom. 16:18. *s.* and specious words

smouldering

Mat. 12:20. nor snuff out the *s.* wick

smuggle

Acts 16:37. are they now to *s.* us out privately

snake-s

Mat. 7:10. or a *s.* when he asks for fish

23:33. you *s.*, you vipers' brood

Mark 16:18. if they handle *s.* or drink any deadly poison

Luke 10:19. power to tread underfoot *s.*

11:11. offer his son a *s.* when he asks for fish

Acts 28:4. seeing the *s.* hanging on to his hand

28:5. shook off the *s.* into the fire

Rev. 9:19. their tails were like *s.*

snap-ped

Mat. 12:20. he will not *s.* off the broken reed

Mark 5:4. he had *s.* his chains

snares

Luke 11:54. laying *s.* to catch him

snatch-ed

John 10:28. no one shall *s.* them from my care

10:29. no one can *s.* them out of the Father's care

Acts 8:39. the Spirit *s.* Philip away

Phil. 2:6. he did not think to *s.* at equality with God

Jude 22. *s.* them from the flames

Rev. 12:5. her child was *s.* up to God

sneers

Mat. 5:22. if he *s.* at him he will have to answer for it

snobbery

Jam. 2:1. you must never show *s.*

2:9. if you show *s.*, you are committing a sin

snuff

Mat. 12:20. nor *s.* out the smouldering wick

soaked

Mat. 27:48. fetched a sponge, which he *s.* in sour wine

Mark 15:36. running with a sponge, *s.* in sour wine

John 19:29. so they *s.* a sponge with the wine

sober

1 Cor. 15:34. come back to a *s.* and upright life

society

Gal. 2:9. reputed pillars of our *s.*

2 Pet. 2:7. shocked by the dissolute habits of the lawless *s.*

soil

Mat. 13:5. fell on rocky ground, where it had little *s.*

13:8. some of the seed fell into good *s.*

13:23. but the seed that fell into good *s.*

Mark 4:5. seed fell on rocky ground, where it had little *s.*

4:8. some of the seed fell into good *s.*

4:20. who receive the seed in good *s.*

Luke 6:49. built his house on the *s.* without foundations

8:8. some of the seed fell into good *s.*

8:15. seed in good *s.* represents

13:7. why should it go on using up the *s.*

soldier-s

Mark 6:27. sent a *s.* of the guard with orders to bring John's head

John 18:3. so Judas took a detachment of *s.*

Rom. 13:12. put on our armour as *s.* of the light

sole

Acts 9:21. for the *s.* purpose of arresting them

Gal. 6:12. their *s.* object is to escape persecution

solemn-ly

Luke 1:72. calling to mind his *s.* covenant

Acts 23:14. we have bound ourselves by a *s.* oath

1 Thess. 2:11. appealing to you by encouragement, as well as by *s.* injunctions

1 Tim. 5:21. I *s.* charge you, maintain these rules

Heb. 2:6. there is somewhere a *s.* assurance

solemnity
John 19:31. that Sabbath was a day of great *s.*

solid
1 Cor. 3:2. I gave you milk to drink, instead of *s.* food
Col. 2:17. the *s.* reality is Christ's
Heb. 5:12. you need milk instead of *s.* food
  5:14. grown men can take *s.* food

solitary
Luke 8:29. made off to the *s.* places
John 12:24. a grain of wheat remains a *s.* grain

some
Mat. 6:2, 3. when you do *s.* act of charity
  13:3. he spoke to them in parables, at *s.* length
  26:4. to have Jesus arrested by *s.* trick
  26:59. tried to find *s.* allegation against Jesus
Luke 23:9. he questioned him at *s.* length
Acts 14:17. he has not left you without *s.* clue to his nature
2 John 4. *s.* of your children are living by the truth

somebody
Gal. 6:3. if a man imagines himself to be *s.*

somehow
Rom. 1:10. *s.* or other, succeed at long last in coming to visit you

someone
Mat. 5:25. if *s.* sues you, come to terms
  5:39. if *s.* slaps you on the right cheek
  12:47. *s.* said, 'Your mother and your brothers are here
Luke 8:46. *s.* did touch me
  11:22. when *s.* stronger comes upon him
  13:23. *s.* asked him, 'Sir, are only a few to be saved
  14:8. you are asked by *s.* to a wedding feast
  16:30. if *s.* from the dead visits them
  16:31. even if *s.* should rise from the dead
  22:58. a little later *s.* else noticed him
John 1:33. when you see the Spirit coming down upon *s.*
  4:33. can *s.* have brought him food
  5:7. *s.* else is in the pool before me
  9:9. it is *s.* like him
Acts 25:19. *s.* called Jesus, a dead man whom Paul alleged to be alive

Rom. 10:14. how hear without *s.* to spread the news
  14:4. pass judgement on *s.* else's servant
1 Cor. 3:10. *s.* else is putting up the building
  14:27. *s.* must interpret
  14:30. if *s.* else, sitting in his place receives a revelation
2 Cor. 11:4. if *s.* comes who proclaims another Jesus
Heb. 5:12. *s.* to teach you the A.B.C. of God's oracles
Jam. 2:18. *s.* may object
1 Pet. 5:8. looking for *s.* to devour

something
Mat. 12:2. *s.* which is forbidden on the Sabbath
  12:6. there is *s.* greater than the temple here
  14:16. give them *s.* to eat yourselves
  19:11. *s.* which not everyone can accept
  20:10. they expected *s.* extra
  25:21 ⎫
  25:23 ⎭ put you in charge of *s.* big
Mark 4:24. with *s.* more besides
  6:36. to buy themselves *s.* to eat
  6:37. give them *s.* to eat yourselves
Luke 8:55. he told them to give her *s.* to eat
  9:13. give them *s.* to eat yourselves
  24:16. *s.* held their eyes from seeing who it was
John 4:31. Rabbi, have *s.* to eat
  5:14. you may suffer *s.* worse
  11:37. have done *s.* to keep Lazarus from dying
Acts 10:10. he grew hungry and wanted *s.* to eat
  21:37. may I say *s.* to you
  25:26. I may have *s.* to report
  27:34. I beg you to have *s.* to eat
Rom. 1:13. the hope of achieving *s.* among you
  8:25. if we hope for *s.* we do not yet see
  11:13. I have *s.* to say to you Gentiles
1 Cor. 7:36. *s.* must be done
  14:6. contains *s.* by way of revelation
  14:24. *s.* that searches his conscience
  14:35. if there is *s.* they want to know
2 Cor. 2:7. *s.* very different is called for now
  5:12. *s.* to say to those whose pride
Gal. 6:1. if a man should do *s.* wrong
Eph. 4:28. *s.* to share with the needy
Heb. 8:3. this one too must have *s.* to offer
Jam. 4:2. you want *s.* which you cannot have
1 Pet. 4:12. as though it were *s.* extra-ordinary

somewhat
Rom. 15:15. written *s.* boldly at times

somewhere
Mark 6:48. *s.* between three and six
    in the morning
Heb. 2:6. *s.* a solemn assurance which
    runs
    4:4. does not Scripture *s.* speak thus

son-s
Mat. 5:9. God shall call them his *s.*
    11:11. a mother's *s.* greater than John
    the Baptist
    16:17. Jesus said: 'Simon *s.* of Jonah
    23:31. the *s.* of the men who killed
    the prophets
    24:36. not even the *S.*; only the Father
    27:56. the mother of the *s.* of Zebedee
Luke 6:16. Judas *s.* of James
    6:35. you will be *s.* of the Most High
    7:28. not a mother's *s.* greater than
    John
    20:36. they are *s.* of God
John 1:14. such glory as befits the
    Father's only *S.*
    4:12. drank from it himself, he and his
    s.
Acts 7:51. like fathers, like *s.*
    13:10. you *s.* of the devil
Rom. 8:15. a Spirit that makes us *s.*
    8:23. we wait for God to make us his
    s.
    9:4. they were made God's *s.*
    9:26. they shall be called *S.* of the
    living God
Gal. 3:7. the men of faith who are
    Abraham's *s.*
    3:26. through faith you are all *s.* of
    God
    4:23. the slave-woman's *s.* was born
    in the course of nature
    4:29. the natural-born *s.* persecuted
    the spiritual *s.*
Eph. 1:5. to be accepted as his *s.* through
    Jesus Christ
2 Tim. 3:10. you, my *s.*, have followed,
    step by step my teaching
Heb. 1:3. the *S.* who is the effulgence of
    God's splendour
    2:11. the *S.* does not shrink from
    calling men his brothers
    2:16. it is not angels, mark you, that
    he takes to himself, but the *s.* of
    Abraham
1 John 5:18. it is the *S.* of God who
    keeps him safe

soon-er
Mat. 18:28. no *s.* had the man gone out
    24:29. as *s.* as the distress of those
    days has passed
Mark 1:28. he was *s.* spoken of all over
    the district

4:15. no *s.* have they heard it than
    Satan comes
4:16. as *s.* as they hear the word, they
    accept it
4:29. as *s.* as the crop is ripe
6:45. as *s.* as it was over he made his
    disciples embark
9:15. as *s.* as they saw Jesus the whole
    crowd were overcome with awe
9:20. as *s.* as the spirit saw him
Luke 5:11. as *s.* as they had brought the
    boats to land
    6:49. as *s.* as the river burst upon it
    18:8. he will vindicate them *s.* enough
    21:30. as *s.* as it buds, you can see for
    yourselves that summer is near
John 11:32. as *s.* as she caught sight of
    him she fell at his feet
    13:27. as *s.* as Judas had received it
    Satan entered him
Acts 4:23. as *s.* as they were discharged
    9:20. *s.* he was proclaiming Jesus
    publicly
    21:40. as *s.* as quiet was restored, he
    addressed them
Rom. 16:20. the God of peace will *s.*
    crush Satan
2 Cor. 3:11. that which was *s.* to fade
Col. 2:22. all of them things that must
    perish as *s.* as they are used
Heb. 10:37. for '*s.*, very *s.*' (in the
    words of Scripture
Rev. 2:16. I shall come to you *s.* and
    make war upon them
    3:11. I am coming *s.*
    22:7. remember, I am coming *s.*
    22:12, 20. yes, I am coming *s.*

sop
Acts 25:11. to hand me over as a *s.* to
    them

sophistry-ies
2 Cor. 10:5. we demolish *s.*

sorcery
Gal. 5:19. idolatry and *s.*
1 Pet. 4:15. murder, theft, or *s.*

sordid
Tit. 1:11. and all for *s.* gain
Jam. 1:21. away then with all that is *s.*

sorrow
Mark 3:5. looking round at them with
    anger and *s.*
Acts 20:19. amid the *s.* and trials that
    came upon me
    20:37. there were loud cries of *s.*

sorrowful
Mat. 5:4. how blest are the *s.*
Mark 16:10. his mourning and *s.*
    followers
Jam. 4:9. be *s.*, mourn and weep

sorry

Mat. 15:32 } I feel s. for all these
Mark 8:2 } people
Luke 17:4. comes back to you seven times saying, 'I am s.
2 Cor. 7:7. how s. you are, and how eager to take my side

sort

Mat. 8:27. what s. of man is this
Mark 9:29. there is no means of casting out this s. but prayer
Luke 7:39. what s. of woman she is, a sinner
John 2:10. before serving the poorer s.
Acts 24:2. in all s. of places, improvements are being made
1 Cor. 1:26. what s. of people you are, whom God has called
9:22. I have become everything in turn to men of every s.
Eph. 5:27. with no stain or wrinkle or anything of the s.
Tit. 3:11. a man of that s. has a distorted mind
Heb. 13:9. all s. of outlandish teachings
2 Pet. 3:11. what s. of people you ought to be
Rev. 18:12. every s. of thing made of costly woods

sought

Acts 28:23. s. to convince them about Jesus
Rom. 11:7. what Israel s., Israel has not achieved
Gal. 1:10. if I still s. men's favour, I should be no servant of Christ

soul-s

Heb. 13:9. our s. should gain their strength from the grace of God
1 Pet. 2:2. you may thrive upon it to your s. health
Jude 22. there are some doubting s. who need your pity

sound-s-ed-ly

Mat. 6:22. if your eyes are s., you will have light
12:13. it was made s. again like the other
17:6. at the s. of the voice the disciples fell on their faces
21:16. children and babes at the breast s. aloud thy praise
Luke 6:48. because it had been s. built
11:34. when your eyes are s., you have light
20:21. we know that what you speak and teach is s.
John 12:28. a voice s. from heaven
Acts 2:6. at this s. the crowd gathered
17:20. introducing ideas that s. strange to us
26:20. s. the call to repent

1 Cor. 11:19. to show which of your members are s.
14:10. how many different kinds of s. there are
14:11. if I do not know the meaning of the s.
Gal. 1:10. s. as if I were canvassing
1 Thess. 4:16. at the s. of the archangel's voice
5:23. keep you s. in spirit, soul, and body
1 Tim. 4:6. the s. instruction which you have followed
Heb. 3:13. while that word 'Today' still s. in your ears
2 Pet. 2:8. every s., of their evil courses tortured that good man's heart
3:10. the heavens will disappear with a great rushing s.
Rev. 1:10. I heard a loud voice, like the s. of a trumpet
6:6. I heard what s. like a voice
14:2. I heard a s. from heaven like the noise of rushing water and the deep roar of thunder; it was the s. of harpers
19:1. I heard what s. like the roar of a vast throng
19:6. again I heard what s. like a vast crowd

soundless

1 Cor. 14:10. nothing is altogether s.

sour

Mat. 27:48. a sponge, which he soaked in s. wine
Mark 15:36. a sponge, soaked in s. wine
Luke 23:36. offering him their s. wine
John 19:29. a jar stood there full of s. wine
Rev. 10:9. it will turn your stomach s.
10:10. my stomach turned s.

source

Mark 5:29. the s. of her haemorrhages dried up
John 2:9. not knowing its s.
8:42. God is the s. of my being
14:10. I am not myself the s. of the words I speak
Rom. 11:36. S., Guide, and Goal of all that is
15:5. God, the s. of all fortitude
1 Cor. 11:12. God is the s. of all
Gal. 5:25. if the Spirit is the s. of our life
Heb. 5:9. the s. of eternal salvation
Rev. 3:14. the prime s. of all God's creation

sovereign-s

Mat. 12:8. the Son of Man is s. over the Sabbath
Mark 2:28 } the Son of Man is s. even
Luke 6:5 } over the Sabbath

John 17:2. thou hast made him s. over all mankind

Acts 4:24. S. Lord, maker of heaven and earth

25:26. to put in writing for our S.

1 Tim. 2:2. for s. and all in high office

Jam. 2:8. the s. law laid down in Scripture

1 Pet. 2:13. whether to the s. as supreme

2:17. honour to the s.

Rev. 1:8 ⎫ the s. Lord of all
  4:8 ⎭

6:10. how long, s. Lord, holy and true

11:17. we give thee thanks, O Lord God, s. over all

15:3. O Lord God, s. over all

16:7. yes, Lord God, s. over all

16:14. God the s. Lord

19:6. the Lord our God, s. over all

19:15. retribution of God the s. Lord

21:22. its temple was the s. Lord God

sovereignty-ies

Acts 1:6. establish once again the s. of Israel

Eph. 1:21. any title of s.

Col. 1:16. thrones, s.

Rev. 1:9. the suffering and the s.

11:15. the s. of the world has passed to our Lord

12:10. the hour of his s.

17:17. conferring their s. upon the beast

sow-ed

Luke 13:19. a mustard-seed which a man took and s.

sown

Mat. 13:20. the seed s. on rocky ground

13:22. the seed s. among thistles

Luke 8:13. the seed s. on rock

space

Mark 2:2. the s. in front of the door was not big enough

Luke 12:17. I have not the s. to store my produce

spare-d

Mat. 13:12 ⎫ till he has enough and to
  25:29 ⎭ s.

26:41. stay awake, and pray that you may be s. the test

Mark 14:38. stay awake, all of you; and pray that you may be s. the test

Luke 22:40. pray that you may be s. the hour of testing

22:46. pray that you may be s. the test

2 Cor. 9:8. enough and to s. for every good cause

10:2. s. me, I beg you, the necessity of such bravery

13:10. to s. myself, when I come

Eph. 4:3. s. no effort to make fast with bonds of peace

Phil. 2:27. to s. me sorrow upon sorrow

Rev. 6:6. s. the olive and the vine

spark

Jam. 3:5. set ablaze by the tinest s.

sparkling

Rev. 22:1. the river of the water of life, s. like crystal

sparse

2 Cor. 9:6. s. sowing, s. reaping

spate

Rev. 12:15. after the woman to sweep her away with its s.

speak-s-ing-est

Mat. 11:7. Jesus began to s. to the people about John

Mark 1:27. he s. with authority

Luke 7:40. s. on Master

John 3:33. to attest that God s. true

6:50. I am s. of the bread that comes down from heaven

8:25. why should I s. to you at all

8:45. but I s. the truth

9:24. s. the truth before God

9:37. it is he who is s. to you

10:21. no one possessed by an evil spirit could s. like this

Acts 2:22. I s. of Jesus of Nazareth

2:32. the Jesus we s. of has been raised by God

7:35. s. through the angel who appeared

8:33 to s. of his posterity

10:4 your prayers and acts of charity have gone up to heaven to s. for you

12:22. it is a god s., not a man

13:42. asked to come again and s. on these subjects

15:13. when they had finished s.

20:2. often s. words of encouragement

24:14. the 'sect' they s. of

Rom. 3:4. when thou s. thou shalt be vindicated

9:1. I am s. the truth as a Christian

2 Cor. 3:17. the Lord of whom this passage s.

6:8. we are the imposters who s. the truth

Phil. 1:20. but shall s. so boldly

Col. 3:17. whether you s. or act

1 Tim. 3:13. the right to s. openly on matters of the Christian faith

Heb. 3:3. Jesus, of whom I s.

3:5. bear witness to the words that God would s.

4:7. s. through the lips of David

7:11. what further need would there have been to s. of another priest

1 Pet. 2:7. great worth of which it s.

1 John 4:10. the love I *s*. of is not our love for God

Rev. 4:1. the voice that I had first heard *s*.

speaker
Acts 7:22. a powerful *s*.
1 Cor. 14:30. let the first *s*. stop
2 Cor. 10:10. as a *s*. he is beneath contempt
11:6. I may be no *s*., but knowledge I have

special-ly
Mat. 13:46. fine pearls found one of very *s*. value
Luke 12:41. Lord, do you intend this parable *s*. for us
1 Cor. 12:23. treated with *s*. honour
12:24. giving *s*. honour to the humbler parts
Gal. 4:10. you keep *s*. days and months
Col. 4:17. this *s*. word to Archippus
Jam. 2:3. pay *s*. attention to the well-dressed man

specific
Rom. 4:6. apart from any *s*. acts of justice

specious
Rom. 16:18. with smooth and *s*. words
Col. 2:4. talked into error by *s*. arguments
1 Tim. 4:2. the *s*. falsehoods of men

speck
Mat. 7:3. the *s*. of sawdust in your brother's eye
7:4. let me take the *s*. out of your eye
7:5. to take the *s*. out of your brother's
Luke 6:41. the *s*. of sawdust in your brother's eye
6:42. let me take the *s*. out of your eye . . . see clearly to take the *s*.

spectacle
Mat. 11:7 ⎱ what was the *s*. that drew
Luke 7:24 ⎰ you to the wilderness
23:48. the crowd who had assembled for the *s*.
Col. 2:15. he made a public *s*. of them

spectators
Mark 5:16 ⎱ the *s*. told them how the
Luke 8:36 ⎰ madman had been cured

speculation-s
Col. 2:8. hollow and delusive *s*.
1 Tim. 1:4. myths and genealogies, which issue in mere *s*.
2 Tim. 2:23. have nothing to do with foolish and ignorant *s*.
Tit. 3:9. steer clear of foolish *s*.

speech
Mat. 9:33. the patient recovered his *s*.

12:22. Jesus cured him, restoring both *s*. and sight

Luke 1:20. you will lose your powers of *s*.
24:19. Jesus of Nazareth', they replied, 'a prophet powerful in *s*.
John 3:31. belongs to the earth and uses earthly *s*.
16:25. till now I have been using figures of *s*.
16:29. this is no figure of *s*.
Rom. 12:8. one who has the gift of stirring *s*.
1 Cor. 12:8. one man, through the Spirit, has the gift of wise *s*.
13:11. when I was a child, my *s*., my outlook
14:5. the prophet is worth more than the man of ecstatic *s*.
2 Cor. 8:7. you are so rich in everything—in faith, *s*.
1 Tim. 4:12. an example to believers in *s*.

speechless
Mark 9:17. possessed by a spirit which makes him *s*.

speed
Luke 2:16. they went with all *s*. and found their way to Mary and Joseph

spell-s
Acts 19:18. confessed that they had been using magical *s*.
1 Thess. 2:17. for a short *s*. you were lost to us

spellbound
Mark 11:18. the whole crowd was *s*. by his teaching

spend-ing
Mark 6:37. are we to go and *s*. twenty pounds on bread
Luke 21:37. *s*. the night on the hill called Olivet
Acts 15:33. after *s*. some time there
25:6. after *s*. eight or ten days at most in Jerusalem
1 Cor. 16:7. I hope to *s*. some time with you, if the Lord permits
Tit. 3:12. where I have determined to *s*. the winter
Jam. 4:3. to *s*. what you get on your pleasures
4:13. *s*. a year there trading

spent
Mat. 21:17. Bethany, where he *s*. the night
Luke 6:12. *s*. the night in prayer to God
24:53. *s*. all their time in the temple
John 1:39. *s*. the rest of the day with him
Acts 20:3. when he had *s*. three months there

Acts 20:6. Troas, where we *s.* a week
 21:7. *s.* one day with them
 25:14. they *s.* several days there
 28:12. at Syracuse and *s.* three days
  there
Gal. 4:11. all the pains I *s.* on you

spew-ed
Rev. 12:15. the serpent *s.* a flood of
 water after the woman
 12:16. the river which the dragon *s.*
  from his mouth

sphere
Rom. 5:2. enter the *s.* of God's grace
2 Cor. 10:13. our proper *s.*; and our *s.* is
 10:15. work beyond our proper *s.*
  Our hope is rather that, as your
  faith grows, we may attain a position among you greater than ever
  before, but still within the limits
  of our *s.*
 10:16. work already done in another
  man's *s.*

spice
Rev. 18:13. cinnamon and *s.*

spiked
1 Tim. 6:10. *s.* themselves on many
 thorny griefs

spilt
Mat. 23:35. the innocent blood *s.* on
 the ground

spirit-s
Mat. 5:5. how blest are those of a
 gentle *s.*
 12:31. slander spoken against the *S.*
Mark 5:12. the *s.* begged him
 7:26. begged him to drive the *s.* out
  of her daughter
 7:29. the unclean *s.* has gone out of
  your daughter
 7:30. the *s.* had left her
Luke 8:32. the *s.* begged him to let them
  go
John 10.21. possessed by an evil *s.* . . . .
 could an evil *s.*
 19:30. he bowed his head and gave
  up his *s.*
Acts 4:25. by the Holy *S.* through the
 mouth of David
 6:3. men full of the *S.* and of wisdom
 8:16. until then the *S.* had not come
  upon any of them
Rom. 8:38. in the realm of *s.*
1 Cor. 2:13. to those who have the *S.*,
 we speak of these gifts of God in
 words found for us not by our
 human wisdom but by the *S.*
 3:1. people who have the *S.*
 12:1. about gifts of the *S.*
 14:1. there are other gifts of the *S.*
 14:12. eager for gifts of the *S.*

Gal. 4:3. the elemental *s.* of the universe
 4:9. the mean and beggarly *s.* of the
  elements
Eph. 1:14. that *S.* is the pledge
Phil. 1:15. proclaim Christ in a jealous
 and quarrelsome *s.*
 4:23. the grace of our Lord Jesus
  Christ be with your *s.*
Col. 2:8. the elemental *s.* of the world
 2:20. beyond reach of the elemental
  s. of the world
2 Tim. 3:10. my faith, patience, and *s.* of
 love
Tit. 3:6. he sent down the *S.* upon us
 plentifully
Jam. 3:18. seeds sown in a *s.* of peace
1 John 5:7. three witnesses, the *S.*, the
 water, and the blood

The third Person of the Trinity is spoken
 of as the Holy *S.*

spiritual-ly
Acts 18:25. full of *s.* fervour
Rom. 8:9. you are on the *s.* level
1 Cor. 2:4. it carried conviction by *s.*
 power
 6:17. he who links himself with Christ
  is one with him, *s.*
2 Cor. 3:6. not in a written document,
 but in a *s.* bond
Gal. 3:3. you started with the *s.*
 4:29. the natural-born son persecuted
  the *s.* son
Eph. 1:17. the *s.* powers of wisdom and
 vision
 2:2. the commander of the *s.* powers
  of the air
 2:22. a *s.* dwelling for God
Phil. 3:3. we whose worship is *s.*
1 Tim. 4:14. do not neglect the *s.*
 endowment
Heb. 6:5. the *s.* energies of the age to
 come
 9:14. a *s.* and eternal sacrifice
 12:9. submit even more readily to our
  s. Father
1 Pet. 2:2. you must crave for pure
 milk (*s.* milk
Jude 19. these men draw a line between
 s. and unspiritual persons

spit
Rev. 3:16. I will *s.* you out of my mouth

spite
Mat. 27:18. it was out of *s.* that they had
 brought Jesus before him
Mark 5:26. in *s.* of long treatment by
 doctors
 15:10. he knew it was out of *s.* that
  they had brought Jesus
John 12:37. in *s.* of the many signs
 which Jesus had performed

Rom. 8:37. yet, in *s*. of all, overwhelm-
    ing victory is ours
Eph. 4:31. have done with *s*. and passion

spiteful
3 John 10. he lays baseless and *s*.
    charges against us

splendour-s
Mat. 6:29. Solomon in all his *s*.
    19:28. the Son of Man is seated on his
        throne in heavenly *s*.
Luke 2:9. the *s*. of the Lord shone round
    them
    12:27. even Solomon in all his *s*.
Rom. 1:23. the *s*. of immortal God
    3:23. deprived of the divine *s*.
    5:2. the divine *s*. that is to be ours
    6:4. raised from the dead in the *s*. of
        the Father
    8:17. in order to share his *s*. here-
        after
    8:18. bear no comparison with the *s*.
    8:21. the liberty and *s*. of the children
        of God
    8:30. whom he justified he has also
        given his *s*.
    9:4. the *s*. of the divine presence
    9:23. the full wealth of his *s*.
1 Cor. 15:40. the *s*. of the heavenly
    bodies is one thing, the *s*. of the
    earthly, another
    15:41. the sun has a *s*. of its own, the
        moon another *s*.
2 Cor. 3:7. inaugurated with divine *s*.
    That *s*., though it was soon to fade
    3:8. greater *s*. rest upon the divine
        dispensation
    3:9. if *s*. accompanied the dispensa-
        tion under which we are con-
        demned, how much richer in *s*.
    3:10. the *s*. that once was is now no
        s. at all; it is outshone by a *s*. greater
    3:11. soon to fade had its moment of
        s., how much greater is the *s*.
    3:13. from gazing on that fading *s*.
    3:18. as in a mirror the *s*. of the Lord;
        thus we are transfigured into his
        likeness, from *s*. to *s*.
2 Thess. 1:9. the *s*. of his might
    2:14. the *s*. of our Lord Jesus Christ
Tit. 2:13. the *s*. of our great God
Heb. 1:3. the Son who is the effulgence
    of God's *s*.
1 Pet. 1:11. the *s*. to follow
    1:24. their *s*. like the flower of the
        field
    5:1. the *s*. that is to be revealed
2 Pet. 1:3. the One who called us by his
    own *s*.
    1:4. through this might and *s*.
Rev. 18:1. the earth was lit up with his
    s.
    21:24. the kings of the earth shall
        bring into it all their *s*.

21:26. the wealth and *s*. of the nations

split
Mat. 27:51. the rocks *s*. and the graves
    opened
Luke 5:6. their nets began to *s*.
John 7:43. thus he caused a *s*. among
    the people
    10:19. these words once again caused
        a *s*.
Rev. 16:19. the great city was *s*. in three

spoil-t
Mat. 6:20. no moth and no rust to *s*. it
    9:17. the wine runs out and the skins
        are *s*.
1 Pet. 1:4. nothing can destroy or *s*.

spoke-n
Mat. 11:20. he *s*. of the towns
    11:25. Jesus *s*. these words: 'I thank
        thee, Father
    12:31. slander *s*. against the Spirit
    17:18. Jesus then *s*. sternly to the boy
Mark 1.11. a voice *s*. from heaven
    1:28. he was soon *s*. of all over the
        district
Luke 1:38. I am the Lord's servant; as
    you have *s*., so be it
    1:60. his mother *s*. up and said
John 1:45. the man *s*. of by Moses
Acts 2:26. my tongue *s*. my joy
    2:30. clear therefore that he *s*. as a
        prophet
    5:13. people in general *s*. highly of
        them
    6:1. disagreement between those of
        them who *s*. Greek and those who
        s. the language of the Jews
    16:2. he was well *s*. of by the Christ-
        ians
    16:40. *s*. words of encouragement to
        them
    20:18. when they joined him, he *s*. as
        follows
    22:12. well *s*. of by all the Jews
    28:23. he *s*. urgently of the kingdom of
        God
1 Cor. 2:4. the word I *s*., the gospel I
    proclaimed
2 Cor. 6:11. men of Corinth, we have *s*.
    very frankly to you
Heb. 11:20. *s*. of things to come
    11:22. *s*. of the departure of Israel
        from Egypt
3 John 6. *s*. of your kindness before the
    congregation
Rev. 10:3. the seven thunders *s*.
    17:17. until all that God has *s*. is
        fulfilled

spokes-man-men
Acts 14:12. because he was the *s*.
    15:21. Moses, after all, has never
        lacked *s*.

sponged
2 Cor. 11:9. if I ran short I *s.* on no one
  12:13. I never *s.* upon you
  12:14. I am not going to *s.* upon you

sports
1 Cor. 9:24. at the *s.* all the runners run
  the race

spot
Mark 1:35. a lonely *s.* and remained
  there in prayer
  14:45. when he reached the *s.*, he
  stepped forward
Luke 4:42. made his way to a lonely *s.*

sprang
Mark 10:50. *s.* up, and came to Jesus
Acts 3:8. he *s.* up, stood on his feet, and
  started to walk
  14:10. he *s.* up and started to walk
  27:13. a southerly breeze *s.* up
  28:13. a south wind *s.* up
Rom. 7:9. when the commandment
  came, sin *s.* to life
  9:5. from them, in natural descent, *s.*
  the Messiah

spread-s-ing
Mat. 24:12. as lawlessness *s.*, men's love
  for one another will grow cold
Mark 1:45. made the whole story public;
  he *s.* it far and wide
  5:20. the man went off and *s.* the news
  11:7. *s.* their cloaks on it
Luke 4:14. reports about him *s.*
  4:37. so the news *s.*
  5:15. the talk about him *s.*
  8:39. *s.* the news of what Jesus had
  done for him
  23:5. has *s.* as far as this city
John 9:6. he *s.* it on the man's eyes
Acts 6:7. the word of God now *s.* more
  and more
  9:42. the news *s.* all over Joppa
  12:24. the word of God continued to
  grow and *s.*
  13:49. the word of the Lord *s.* far and
  wide
  14:7. they continued to *s.* the good
  news
  19:20. the word of the Lord showed
  its power, *s.* more and more
  21:28. this is the fellow who *s.* his
  doctrine all over the world
Rom. 9:17. to *s.* my fame over all the
  world
  10:15. how hear without someone to
  s. the news? And how could anyone *s.* the news without a commission
  11:28. in the *s.* of the Gospel
  16:19. the fame of your obedience has
  s.
2 Cor. 2:14. *s.* abroad the fragrance of
  the knowledge of himself

1 Thess. 1:9. they themselves *s.* the news
  of our visit
2 Tim. 2:17. the infection of their
  teaching will *s.*
  4:5. work to *s.* the Gospel
3 John 8. play our part in *s.* the truth

spring-s
Mark 4:32. it *s.* up and grows taller than
  any other plant
John 4:6. the *s.* called Jacob's well
1 Cor. 11:8. man did not originally *s.*
  from woman
Eph. 5:9. where light is, there all goodness *s.* up
Col. 1:5. both *s.* from the hope stored
  up for you
1 Thess. 2:3. the appeal we make never
  s. from error
1 Tim. 1:5. the love which *s.* from a clean
  heart
Jam. 4:1. *s.* from the aggressiveness of
  your bodily desires
  5:7. until the winter and *s.* rains have
  fallen
2 Pet. 2:17. these men are *s.* that give no
  water
1 John 2:16. *s.* not from the Father but
  from the godless world
Rev. 7:17. the *s.* of the water of life
  8:10. it fell on a third of the rivers
  and *s.*
  14:7. who made heaven and earth,
  the sea and the water-*s.*
  16:4. poured his bowl on the rivers
  and *s.*
  21:6. the water-*s.* of life

sprout-s-ed
Mat. 13:5. it *s.* quickly because it had
  no depth of earth
  13:26. the corn *s.*
Mark 4:5. it *s.* quickly
  4:27. the seed *s.* and grows

sprung
Heb. 7:14. our Lord is *s.* from Judah

spun
2 Pet. 1:16. it was not on tales artfully
  s. that we relied

spurn-ing
1 Tim. 1:19. through *s.* conscience that
  certain persons made shipwreck

squad-s
Acts 12:4. a military guard, four *s.* of
  four men each

squadrons
Rev. 9:16. their *s.* of cavalry

squall
Mark 4:37. a heavy *s.* came on
Luke 8:23. a heavy *s.* struck the lake

squander-ed-ing
Luke 15:13. he *s*. it in reckless living
16:1. this man was *s*. the property

square
Acts 16:19. dragged them to the city authorities in the main *s*.
17:17. also in the city *s*. every day
Gal. 2:14. I saw that their conduct did not *s*. with the truth

stabbed
John 19:34. one of the soldiers *s*. his side

stack
Jam. 3:5. what a huge *s*. of timber can be set ablaze

staff
Mat. 24:45. charged by his master to manage his household *s*.
Heb. 9:4. Aaron's *s*. which once budded

stage
Acts 19:21. when things had reached this *s*.

stain
Eph. 5:27. present the church to himself all glorious, with no *s*.
Jam. 1:27. without *s*. or fault in the sight of God

stake
2 Cor. 1:23. I *s*. my life upon it

stamp
Heb. 1:3. the *s*. of God's very being

stand-s-ing
Mat. 5:14. a town that *s*. on a hill
5:19. will *s*. high in the kingdom of Heaven
9:5. or to say, '*S*. up and walk
9:6. *s*. up, take your bed, and go home
11:23. Sodom would be *s*. to this day
13:20. the seed sown on rocky ground *s*. for the man
13:38. the good seed *s*. for the children of the Kingdom
17:7. touched them, and said, '*S*. up
26:31. for it *s*. written
Mark 1:2. in the prophet Isaiah it *s*. written
2:9. *s*. up, take your bed, and walk
2:11. I say to you, *s*. up
10:49. *s*. up; he is calling you
12:41. he was *s*. opposite the temple treasury
14:27. it *s*. written
Luke 2:35. many in Israel will *s*. or fall because of him
5:23. *s*. up and walk
5:24. *s*. up, take your bed
6:17. took his *s*. on level ground
8:13. the seed sown on rock *s*. for those

13:11. quite unable to *s*. up straight
17:19. *s*. up and go on your way
19:44. not leave you one stone *s*. on another
21:19. by *s*. firm you will win true life
21:22. all that *s*. written is to be fulfilled
21:25. on earth nations will *s*. helpless
21:28. *s*. upright and hold your heads high
23:12. a *s*. feud between them
John 8:3. making her *s*. out in the middle
8:35. the slave has no permanent *s*. in the household
16:11. the Prince of this world *s*. condemned
20:23. if you forgive any man's sins, they *s*. forgiven
Acts 7:42. as it *s*. written in the book of the prophets
11:17. how could I possibly *s*. in God's way
13:33. it *s*. written, in the second Psalm
13:50. stirred up feeling among the women of *s*.
17:12. women of *s*. as well as men
25:9. *s*. trial on these charges
25:20. *s*. his trial there on these issues
26:22. to this very day I *s*. and testify
Rom. 11:8. exactly as it *s*. written
11:28. God's choice *s*.
12:12. in trouble *s*. firm
16:2. *s*. by her in any business
16:25. to him who has power to make your *s*. sure
1 Cor. 3:14. if a man's building *s*., he will be rewarded
15:58. *s*. firm and immovable
2 Cor. 9:9. his benevolence *s*. fast for ever
Gal. 4:24. the two women *s*. for two covenants
Phil. 1:25. *s*. by you all to help you forward
1 Thess. 2:19. when we *s*. before our Lord Jesus
3:2. *s*. firm for the faith
3:13. so that you may *s*. before our God
1 Tim. 3:13. may claim a high *s*.
5:12. *s*. condemned for breaking their troth
2 Tim. 3:5. are a *s*. denial of its reality
3:14. *s*. by the truths you have learned
4:3. the time will come when they will not *s*. wholesome teaching
Tit. 3:11. *s*. self-condemned in his sin
Heb. 2:9. in tasting death he should *s*. for us all
11:2. for their faith that the men of old *s*. on record
12:18. remember where you *s*.
12:22. you *s*. before Mount Zion

Jam. 2:9. you *s*. convicted by that law
4:7. *s*. up to the devil
1 Pet. 1:17. you must *s*. in awe of him
2:6. it *s*. written
4:5. him who *s*. ready to pass judgement
5:9. *s*. up to him, firm in faith
1 John 2:17. he who does God's will *s*.
for evermore
2 John 9. does not *s*. by the doctrine of
the Christ, is without God; he who
s. by that doctrine
Rev. 1:12. seven *s*. lamps of gold
2:7. the tree of life that *s*. in the Garden
of God
7:15. they *s*. before the throne of God
13:1. he took his *s*. on the sea-shore
15:4. thy just dealings *s*. revealed

standard-s
John 8:15. you judge by worldly *s*.
Acts 19:25. our high *s*. of living
1 Cor. 1:26. by any human *s*.
3:18. wise, I mean, by the *s*. of this
passing age
6:7. you already fall below your *s*.
2 Cor. 5:16. worldly *s*. have ceased to
count
10:12. their own *s*. of comparison
1 Tim. 2:2. high *s*. of morality
Tit. 2:3. they must set a high *s*.
Jam. 2:4. judge by false *s*.

stars
Phil. 2:15. shine like *s*. in a dark world

starboard
John 21:6. shoot the net to *s*.

stare-d
Luke 22:56. saw him sitting in the firelight *s*. at him
Acts 3:12. why *s*. at us as if we had made
this man walk
10:4. Cornelius!' He *s*. at him in terror

start-s-ed-ing
Mat. 20:9. *s*. work an hour before sunset
27:24. a riot was *s*.
28:11. the women had *s*. on their way
Mark. 10:17. as he was *s*. out on a
journey
Luke 2:43. they *s*. for home
14:30. *s*. to build and could not finish
23:5. it *s*. from Galilee
23:30. they will *s*. saying to the
mountains
John 4:50. believed what Jesus said and
s. for home
11:31. they saw her *s*. up and leave the
house
21:3. they *s*. and got into the boat
Acts 3:8. stood on his feet, and *s*. to
walk

8:26. the angel of the Lord said to
Philip, '*S*. out
8:35. Philip began. *S*. from this
passage
10:37. all over the land of the Jews
s. from Galilee
13:50. a persecution was *s*. against
Paul
14:10. he sprang up and *s*. to walk
15:40. he *s*. on his journey
21:38. the Egyptian who *s*. a revolt
22:5. *s*. out to bring the Christians
there
28:2. cold and had *s*. to rain
Rom. 1:17. a way that *s*. from faith
Gal. 2:18. if I *s*. building up again a
system
3:3. you *s*. with the spiritual
Phil. 1:6. the One who *s*. the good work
in you
1 Tim. 1:3. I was *s*. for Macedonia
1 Pet. 4:17. if it is *s*. with you, how will
it end
Heb. 12:2. Jesus, on whom faith depends
from *s*. to finish

startle-d
Luke 1:12. at this sight Zechariah was *s*.
24:37. *s*. and terrified, they thought
they were seeing a ghost

starving
Luke 15:17. here am I, *s*. to death
2 Cor. 6:5. overworked, sleepless, *s*.

state-d
Mat. 25:31. he will sit in *s*. on his throne
Mark 10:37. grant us the right to sit in
s. with you
Luke 2:24. to make the offering as *s*.
in the law
12:11. when you are brought before
synagogues and *s*. authorities
John 18:23. if I spoke amiss, *s*. it in
evidence
Acts 23:30. instructed his accusers to
s. their case
24:9. alleging that the facts were as
he *s*.
24:19. they who ought to have been
in court to *s*. it
25:23. Agrippa and Bernice came in
full *s*.
Rom. 2:27. he may be uncircumcised in
his natural *s*.
1 Cor. 15:17. you are still in your old
s. of sin
Gal. 4:14. scorn or disgust at the *s*. of
my poor body
Phil. 3:21. the body belonging to our
humble *s*.

statement
Mark 14:56. their *s*. did not tally
Acts 6:11. blasphemous *s*. against Moses
24:4. a brief *s*. of our case

stationed
Rev. 7:1. four angels *s*. at the four
* corners of the earth

status
Gal. 4:5. that we might attain the *s*. of
sons
1 Tim. 5:3. the *s*. of widow is to be
granted only to widows who are
such in the full sense

statutory
Acts 19:39. it will be dealt with in the
s. assembly

staunch
Acts 21:20. all of them *s*. upholders of
the Law

stay-s-ed-ing
Mat. 2:13. *s*. there until I tell you
2:15. there he *s*. till Herod's death
13:21. as it strikes no root in him he
has no *s*.-power
26:38. and *s*. awake with me
26:40. could none of you *s*. awake
with me
26:41. *s*. awake, and pray that you
may be spared the test
Mark 1:45. but *s*. outside in the open
country
4:17. they have no *s*.-power
6:10. *s*. there until you leave those
parts
7:24. he found a house to *s*. in
13:34. ordered the door-keeper to *s*.
awake
14:34. stop here and *s*. awake
14:38. *s*. awake, all of you
Luke 1:21. surprised that he was *s*. so
long inside
1:56. Mary *s*. with her about three
months
2:43. the boy Jesus *s*. behind in
Jerusalem
8:27. but *s*. among the tombs
9:4. when you are admitted to a house,
s. there
10:7. *s*. in that one house, sharing
their food
10:39. Mary, who seated herself at the
Lord's feet and *s*. there
19:5. I must come and *s*. with you
today
24:18. are you the only person *s*. in
Jerusalem not to know
24:29. *s*. with us, for evening draws
on
24:49. *s*. here in this city until you are
armed with the power from above
John 1:38. Rabbi' (which means a
teacher), 'where are you *s*.
1:39. saw where he was *s*.
2:12. but they did not *s*. there long
3:22. *s*. there with them, and baptized

4:40. they pressed him to *s*. with them;
and he *s*. there two days
7:9. he *s*. behind in Galilee
10:40. there he *s*.
11:20. while Mary *s*. at home
11:54. Ephraim, where he *s*. with his
disciples
18:28. the Jews themselves *s*. outside
Acts 9:19. he *s*. some time with the
disciples in Damascus
9:28. Saul now *s*. with them
9:43. Peter *s*. on in Joppa
10:48. they asked him to *s*. on with
them
11:11. arrived at the house where I
was *s*.
14:3. Paul and Barnabas *s*. on
14:28. they *s*. for some time with the
disciples
15:35. Paul and Barnabas *s*. on at
Antioch
16:12. here we *s*. for some days
16:15. I beg you to come and *s*. in
my house
17:14. Silas and Timothy both *s*.
behind
18:18. Paul *s*. on for some time
18:20. he was asked to *s*. longer
21:4. *s*. there a week
21:8. *s*. with him
21:15. at the end of our *s*. we packed
our baggage
27:31. unless these men *s*. on board
28:14. were invited to *s*. a week with
them
28:30. he *s*. there two full years at his
own expense
1 Cor. 7:8. it is a good thing if they *s*.
as I am
16:6. I may *s*. with you, perhaps even
for the whole winter
Gal. 1:18. Cephas. I *s*. with him for a
fortnight
Phil. 1:24. need for me to *s*. on in the
body
1:25. I shall *s*., and stand by you all
2 Thess. 3:10. during our *s*. with you
1 Tim. 1:3. I urged you to *s*. on at
Ephesus
2 Tim. 4:20. Erastus *s*. behind at Corinth
Heb. 10:25. not *s*. away from our
meetings
1 John 2:19. they would have *s*. with us
2:27. the initiation which you received
from him *s*. with you
Rev. 16:15. happy the man who *s*. awake

steadfast
2 Cor. 6:4. our *s*. endurance
2 Thess. 1:4. your faith remains so *s*.
Jam. 1:12. happy the man who remains *s*.

steadfastness
2 Thess. 3:5. the *s*. of Christ

steadily
Acts 5:42. they went *s*. on with their teaching
2 Cor. 3:7. the Israelites could not gaze *s*. at him

steady
Rom. 2:7. *s*. persistence in well-doing
Jam. 1:8. never can keep a *s*. course

steer-ing
Acts 27:40. loosened the lashings of the *s*.-paddles
Tit. 3:9. *s*. clear of foolish speculations

stench
John 11:39. by now there will be a *s*.

step-s-ped-ping
Mat. 14:29. Peter *s*. down from the boat
26:49. *s*. forward at once, he said, 'Hail, Rabbi
Mark 5:2. as he *s*. ashore, a man possessed
5:18. as he was *s*. into the boat
14:45. he *s*. forward at once and said to Jesus
Luke 7:14. he *s*. forward and laid his hand on the bier
8:27. as he *s*. ashore he was met by a man
Acts 21:33. the commandant *s*. forward, arrested him
21:35. When Paul reached the *s*.
21:40. Paul stood on the *s*.
2 Tim. 3:10. have followed, *s*. by *s*., my teaching
Heb. 12:13. keep your *s*. from wavering
2 Pet. 2:15. they have followed in the *s*. of Balaam

Stephen
Acts 7:55. but *S*., filled with the Holy Spirit

stern-ly
Mat. 9:30. Jesus said to them *s*., 'See that no one hears about this
17:18. Jesus then spoke *s*. to the boy
Mark 1:43. he dismissed him with this *s*. warning
4:38. he was in the *s*. asleep
Acts 8:20. said Peter *s*., 'may you come to a bad end
27:41. the *s*. was being pounded to pieces by the breakers

steward
John 2:8. take it to the *s*. of the feast
2:9. the *s*. tasted the water now turned into wine

stick
Mat. 10:10. no shoes, no *s*.
Mark 6:8. to take nothing for the journey beyond a *s*.
Luke 9:3. neither *s*. nor pack

stiffen
Heb. 12:12. *s*. your drooping arms

stifle-ing
Rom. 1:18. in their wickedness they are *s*. the truth
1 Thess. 5:19. do not *s*. inspiration

stigma
Heb. 11:26. the *s*. that rests on God's Anointed
13:13. bearing the *s*. that he bore

still
Mat. 19:20. where do I *s*. fall short
24:6. the end is *s*. to come
26:45. *s*. sleeping? *S*. taking your ease
Mark 13:7. the end is *s*. to come
14:41. *s*. sleeping? *S*. taking your ease
Luke 9:34. the words were *s*. on his lips

stimulate
1 Cor. 14:3. they *s*. and they encourage

sting
Rev. 9:5. with torment like a scorpion's *s*.

stipend
1 Tim. 5:17. reckoned worthy of a double *s*.

stir-red-ring
Luke 1:41. heard Mary's greeting, the baby *s*. in her womb
4:22. there was a general *s*. of admiration
John 5:4. an angel came down into the pool and *s*. up the water
John 5:16. that *s*. the Jews to persecute Jesus
Rom. 10:19. use a nation that is no nation to *s*. your envy
11:11. to *s*. Israel to emulation
11:14. I try to *s*. emulation in the men of my own race
12:8. one who has the gift of *s*. speech should use it to *s*. his hearers
16:17. keep your eye on those who *s*. up quarrels
Phil. 1:17. meaning to *s*. up fresh trouble for me
2:1. our common life in Christ yields anything to *s*. the heart

stock
John 1:13. not born of any human *s*.
Acts 17:26. he created every race of men of one *s*.
Rom. 1:3. he was born of David's *s*.
11:1. an Israelite myself, of the *s*. of Abraham
11:24. be grafted into their native *s*.
Heb. 2:11. a consecrating priest and those whom he consecrates are all of one *s*.

stolen
Gal. 2:4. interlopers who had *s.* in to spy

stomach
Mat. 15:17. whatever goes in by the mouth passes into the *s.*
Mark 7:19. does not enter into his heart but into his *s.*
John 6:60. this is more than we can *s.*
Rev. 10:9. it will turn your *s.* sour
10:10. my *s.* turned sour

stone-s
Eph. 4:18. their minds have grown hard as *s.*
Rev. 21:14. the city wall had twelve foundation-*s.*

stood
Mat. 8:26. he *s.* up and rebuked the wind
Mark 4:39. he *s.* up, rebuked the wind
9:27. raised him to his feet, and he *s.* up
14:57. some *s.* up and gave this false evidence
Luke 1:22. he *s.* there making signs to them
2:9. there *s.* before them an angel of the Lord
8:55. she *s.* up immediately
9:47. he took a child by the hand and *s.* him at his side
22:28. have *s.* firmly by me in my times of trial
24:5. they were terrified, and *s.* with eyes cast down
John 19:29. a jar *s.* there full of sour wine
Acts 4:35. distributed to any who *s.* in need
5:27. *s.* them before the Council
9:34. immediately he *s.* up
12:7. all at once an angel of the Lord *s.* there
12:12. when he realized how things *s.*
22:30. took Paul down and *s.* him before them
Rom. 5:4. endurance brings proof that we have *s.* the test
1 Cor. 10:7. *s.* up to play
2 Cor. 2:9. I wrote, I may say, to see how you *s.* the test
Eph. 2:14. the enmity which *s.* like a dividing wall between them
Col. 2:14. it *s.* against us, but he has set it aside
Heb. 10:33. *s.* loyally by those who were so treated
Jam. 5:11. we count those happy who *s.* firm.' You have all heard how Job *s.* firm
1 Pet. 1:7. faith which has *s.* the test
Rev. 3:10. you have kept my command and *s.* fast

4:2. there in heaven *s.* a throne
9:13. the golden altar that *s.* in the presence of God
22:2. on either side of the river *s.* a tree of life

stop-ped
Mat. 2:9. it *s.* above the place where the child lay
19:14. do not try to *s.* them
20:32. Jesus *s.* and called the men
23:13. when others are entering, you *s.* them
26:38. *s.* here, and stay awake with me
Mark 9:38. as he was not one of us, we tried to *s.* him
9:39. Jesus said, 'Do not *s.* him
10:14. let the children come to me; do not try to *s.* them
10:49: Jesus *s.* and said, 'Call him
14:34. *s.* here, and stay awake
Luke 8:44. at once her haemorrhage *s.*
9:49. as he is not one of us we tried to *s.* him
9:50. Jesus said to him, 'Do not *s.* him
11:52. those who were on their way in, you *s.*
18:16. let the little ones come to me; do not try to *s.* them
18:40. Jesus *s.* and ordered the man to be brought
John 6:43. Jesus answered, '*S.* murmuring
Acts 4:17. to *s.* this from spreading further
8:38. he ordered the carriage to *s.*
13:10. will you never *s.* falsifying the straight ways of the Lord
20:10. *s.* this commotion
21:32. they *s.* beating Paul
1 Cor. 14:30. let the first speaker *s.*
Eph. 4:19. *s.* at nothing to satisfy their foul desires
Col. 3:9. *s.* lying to one another
1 Tim. 5:23. *s.* drinking nothing but water
2 Tim. 2:14. *s.* disputing about mere words
4:4. they will *s.* their ears to the truth
Heb. 6:1. *s.* discussing the rudiments of Christianity
2 Pet. 2:16. put a *s.* to the prophet's madness

store
Mat. 6:19. do not *s.* up for yourselves treasure on earth
6:20. *s.* up treasure in heaven
6:26. they do not sow and reap and *s.* in barns
12:35. produces good from the *s.* of good within himself

Mat. 13:52. produce from his *s.* both the new and the old

Luke 6:45. a good man produces good from the *s.* of good within himself

12:17. I have not the space to *s.* my produce

John 1:16. out of his full *s.* we have all received grace upon grace

Acts 20:24. I set no *s.* by life

Rom. 2:5. a *s.* of retribution for the day of retribution

8:18. the splendour, as yet unrevealed, which is in *s.* for us

Col. 1:5. the hope *s.* up for you in heaven

1 Pet. 1:11. the sufferings in *s.* for Christ

storehouses

Luke 12:18. I will pull down my *s.* and build them bigger

storm

Mat. 8:24. a great *s.* arose on the lake

Luke 8:24. the *s.* subsided and all was calm

Acts 27:20. a great *s.* was raging

2 Pet. 2:17. mists driven by a *s.*

Rev. 11:19. an earthquake, and a *s.* of hail

story-ies

Mat. 1:18. the *s.* of the birth of the Messiah

8:33. made for the town, where they told the whole *s.*

9:26. this *s.* became the talk of all the country round

18:31. to their master and told him the whole *s.*

28:15. this *s.* became widely known

Mark 1:45. made the whole *s.* public

12:26. the *s.* of the burning bush

Luke 1:65. the whole *s.* became common talk

7:17. the *s.* of what he had done

20:37. shown by Moses himself in the *s.* of the burning bush

24:11. the *s.* appeared to them to be nonsense

24:23. a *s.* that they had seen a vision of angels

Acts 10:8. told them the whole *s.*, and sent them to Joppa

15:3. the full *s.* of the conversion of the Gentiles

21:24. nothing in the *s.* they were told about you

Rom. 1:8. they are telling the *s.* of your faith

11:2. what Scripture says in the *s.* of Elijah

Heb. 11:32. the *s.* of Gideon, Barak, Samson

stout

Jam. 5:8. you too must be patient and *s.*-hearted

stove

Mat. 6:30. there today, and tomorrow is thrown on the *s.*

Luke 12:28. growing in the field today, and tomorrow is thrown on the *s.*

straight

Mark 1:29. they went *s.* to the house of Simon and Andrew

10:21. Jesus looked *s.* at him

Luke 1:39. Mary set out and went *s.* to a town

2:15. we must go *s.* to Bethlehem

4:30. he walked *s.* through them all

13:11. quite unable to stand up *s.*

20:17. he looked *s.* at them

22:61. the Lord turned and looked *s.* at Peter

John 8:7. he sat up *s.* and said

Acts 13:10. falsifying the *s.* ways of the Lord

14:10. stand up *s.* on your feet

2 Tim. 2:15. driving a *s.* furrow, in your proclamation of the truth

2 Pet. 2:15. they have abandoned the *s.* road

straightforward

Jam. 3:17. it is *s.* and sincere

straits

2 Cor. 6:4. in hardships and dire *s.*

strange

1 Cor. 14:21. I will speak to this nation through men of *s.* tongues

14:22. *s.* tongues' are not intended as a sign

14:23. *s.* tongues' of ecstasy

stranger-s

Mark 10:17. as he was starting out on a journey, a *s.* ran up

John 17:14. the world hates them because they are *s.*

17:16. they are *s.* in the world, as I am

21:18. a *s.* will bind you fast

Rom. 3:17. *s.* to the high-road of peace

Eph. 4:18. *s.* to the life that is in God

2:Tim. 3:3. *s.* to all goodness

1 John 1:8. *s.* to the truth

2:4. a liar and a *s.* to the truth

2:15. a *s.* to the Father's love

straw

1 Cor. 3:12. wood, hay, and *s.*

stray-s-ed-ing

Mat. 18:12. if one of them *s.*, does he not leave the other ninety-nine on the hill-side and go in search of the one that *s.*

18:13. the ninety-nine that never *s.*

2 Tim. 2:16. *s.* further and further into
  godless courses
Jam. 5:19. if one of your number should
  s. from the truth
1 Pet. 2:25. you were *s.* like sheep

streams
John 7:38. *s.* of living water shall flow
  out from within him

street-s
Mat. 22:10. the servants went out into
  the *s.*
  23:7. to be greeted respectfully in the *s.*
Mark 11:4. the colt tethered to a door
  outside in the *s.*
  12:38. receiving respectful greetings in
  the *s.*
Luke 20:46. a great liking for respectful
  greetings in the *s.*

strength
Mat. 14:30. when he saw the *s.* of the
  gale
Luke 21:36. praying at all times for *s.*
  22:32. you must lend *s.* to your
  brothers
Acts 9:31. was left in peace to build up
  its *s.*
  15:41. bringing new *s.* to the congregations
Rom. 11:12. how much more their
  coming to full *s.*
  11:25. until the Gentiles have been
  admitted in full *s.*
1 Cor. 1:25. divine weakness stronger
  than man's *s.*
2 Cor. 1:6. *s.* to face with fortitude
Eph. 1:20. they are measured by his *s.*
  6:10. find your *s.* in the Lord
2 Tim. 1:7. to inspire *s.*
  1:8. in the *s.* that comes from God
  2:1. take *s.* from the grace of God
Heb. 11:34. their weakness was turned
  to *s.*
  13:9. our souls should gain their *s.*
  from the grace of God
1 Pet. 1:22. love one another whole-
  heartedly with all your *s.*
  4:8. keep your love for one another
  at full *s.*
  4:11. in the *s.* which God supplies
2 Pet. 2:11. angels, for all their superior
  s.
Rev. 12:8. they had not the *s.* to win
  18:6. the *s.* of the potion she mixed

strengthen-ed
Acts 3:16. the name of Jesus, by
  awakening faith, has *s.* this man
  15:32. said much to encourage and *s.*

strenuous-ly
Col. 1:29. to this end I am toiling *s.*
  2:1. how *s.* are my exertions for you

stress
1 Cor. 7:26. in a time of *s.* like the
  present

stretch-ed
Mat.   8:3 ⎫
Mark 1:41 ⎬ Jesus *s.* out his hand,
Luke 5:13 ⎭ touched him
Rev. 4:6. in front of it *s.* what seemed a
  sea of glass
  14:15. *s.* out your sickle and reap
  14:18. *s.* out your sickle, and gather
  in

stretcher-s
Mark 2:4. lowered the *s.* on which the
  paralysed man was lying
  2:12. took his *s.* at once, and went out
  6:55. brought the sick on *s.* to any
  place where he was
John 5:9. the man recovered instantly,
  took up his *s.*
Acts 5:15. laid there on beds and *s.*

strewn
1 Cor. 10:5. the desert was *s.* with their
  corpses

strict-ly
Mat. 12:16. he gave *s.* injunctions that
  they were not to make him known
  16:20. *s.* orders not to tell anyone
  that he was the Messiah
  18:15. take the matter up with him,
  s. between yourselves
Mark 5:43. gave them *s.* orders to let
  no one hear about it
  8:30. *s.* orders not to tell anyone about
  him
Luke 9:21. *s.* orders not to tell this to
  anyone
1 Cor. 9:25. every athlete goes into *s.*
  training
1 Tim. 5:21. act with *s.* impartiality
Tit. 2:10. to show themselves *s.* honest

strict-est
Acts 26:5. I belonged to the *s.* group in
  our religion

strictness
Jam. 3:1. shall ourselves be judged with
  greater *s.*

strike-s-ing
Mat. 4:6. *s.* your foot against a stone
  13:21. it *s.* no root in him
  26:31. I will *s.* the shepherd down
Mark 4:17. it *s.* no root in them
  14:27. I will *s.* the shepherd down
Luke 4:11. for fear you should *s.* your
  foot against a stone
John 18:23. if I spoke well, why *s.* me
Acts 7:24. *s.* down the Egyptian
  13:11. the hand of the Lord *s.*
  23:2. ordered his attendants to *s.* him
  on the mouth

Acts 23:3. God will *s.* you
Rev. 2:23. her children I will *s.* dead
  3:5. his name I will never *s.* off the
    roll of the living
  11:6. to *s.* the earth at will with every
    kind of plague
  18:8. her plagues shall *s.* her in a
    single day

strip-s-ped
Mark 15:20. they *s.* him of the purple
John 19:40. with the spices, in *s.* of
  linen cloth
  21:7. he wrapped his coat about him
    (for he had *s.*
Acts 19:16. they ran out of the house *s.*
  and battered
2 Cor. 5:4. we do not want to have the
  old body *s.* off
1 Pet. 1:13. be like men *s.* for action
Rev. 17:16. they will *s.* her naked

stroke-s
Mat. 5:18. not a letter, not a *s.*, will disappear from the Law
Luke 16:17. than for one dot or *s.* of
  the Law to lose its force
2 Cor. 11:24. the Jews have given me
  the thirty-nine *s.*

strolling
Acts 19:13. some *s.* Jewish exorcists

strong-er-ly
Mat. 15:31. the crippled *s.*, the lame
  walking
Mark 5:4. no one was *s.* enough to
  master him
Luke 16:3. I am not *s.* enough to dig
  22:59. another spoke more *s.* still
John 6:18. by now a *s.* wind was blowing
Acts 2:2. a noise like that of a *s.* driving
  wind
  3:7. at once his feet and ankles grew *s.*
  16:5. the congregations grew *s.* in
    faith
Rom. 1:11. some spiritual gift to make
  you *s.*
1 Cor. 1:27. to shame what is *s.*
  7:36. if, that is, his instincts are too
    s. for him
  9:12. have not we a *s.* claim
  13:2. I may have faith *s.* enough to
    move mountains
  16:12. I urged him *s.* to go to Corinth
Eph. 3:18. may you be *s.* to grasp
Phil. 3:4. I could make a *s.* case for
  myself
1 Thess. 1:5. in the power of the Holy
  Spirit, and with *s.* conviction
Tit. 2:3. not scandal-mongers or slaves
  to *s.* drink
Jam. 3:4. when driven by *s.* gales they
  can be directed
  4:6. the grace he gives is *s.*
1 John 5:9. surely divine testimony is *s.*

strove
Heb. 12:17. he *s.*, to the point of tears

struck
Mat. 26:67. said, as they *s.* him,
  'Now, Messiah
Mark 14:47. *s.* at the High Priest's
  servant
  14:65. blindfolded him, and *s.* him
Luke 1:65. all the neighbours were *s.*
  with awe
  2:9. they were terror-*s.*
  8:23. a heavy squall *s.* the lake
  9:43. they were all *s.* with awe at the
    majesty of God
  22:50. one of them *s.* at the High
    Priest's servant
John 18:10. *s.* at the High Priest's
  servant
  19:3. *s.* him on the face
Acts 7:11. famine *s.* the whole of Egypt
  12:23. an angel of the Lord *s.* him
    down
2 Cor. 4:9. *s.* down, we are not left to die
Rev. 8:12. a third part of the sun was
  s.
  18:10. in a single hour your doom
    has *s.*

struggle-s-d
Luke 13:24. *s.* to get in through the
  narrow door
Acts 27:8. *s.* on to a place called Fair
  Havens
  27:16. with a *s.* managed to get the
    ship's boat
Phil. 4:3. shared my *s.* in the cause of the
  Gospel
1 Thess. 2:2. a hard *s.* it was
1 Tim. 4:10. we labour and *s.*
Heb. 12:4. in your *s.* against sin
Jude 3. to join the *s.* in defence of the
  faith

stubborn
Acts 7:51. how *s.* you are, heathen still
  at heart
Rom. 9:18. makes men *s.* as he chooses
Heb. 3:8. do not grow *s.* as in those days
  of rebellion
  3:13. so that no one of you is made *s.*
    by the wiles of sin
  3:15. do not grow *s.* as in those days
  4:7. today if you hear his voice, do
    not grow *s.*

study-ing
John 5:39. you *s.* the scriptures dili-
  gently
  7:52. *s.* the scriptures and you will find
Acts 17:11. *s.* the scriptures every day
  26:24. too much *s.* is driving you mad
Col. 4:6. *s.* how best to talk with each
  person
1 Tim. 1:4. *s.* those interminable myths

stuff
1 Pet. 1:18. it was no perishable *s.*, like gold or silver, that bought your freedom

stumble-ing
Mat. 11:6. happy is the man who does not find me a *s.*-block
16:23. you are a *s.*-block to me
18:6. a cause of *s.* to one of these little ones
18:7. alas for the world that such causes of *s.* arise
Luke 7:23. happy is the man who does not find me a *s.*-block
17:1. causes of *s.* are bound to arise
17:2. cause one of these little ones to *s.*
2 Cor. 11:29. if anyone is made to *s.*
Gal. 5:11. my preaching of the cross is a *s.*-block no more

stupid
Rom. 2:20. to train the *s.*
Gal. 3:1. you *s.* Galatians
3:3. can it be that you are so *s.*
Eph. 5:4. no coarse, *s.*, or flippant talk

stupidity
Mark 3:5. sorrow at their obstinate *s.*
1 Pet. 2:15. put ignorance and *s.* to silence

styles
1 Tim. 2:9. not with elaborate hair-*s.*

subdue-d
Jam. 3:7. can be *s.* and have been *s.* by mankind
3:8. no man can *s.* the tongue

subject-s-ed
Mat. 11:12. the kingdom of Heaven has been *s.* to violence
20:25 ⎱ rulers lord it over their *s.*
Mark 10:42 ⎰
Luke 20:36. they are not *s.* to death any longer
22:25. kings lord it over their *s.*
Acts 13:42. speak on these *s.* next Sabbath
17:32. we will hear you on this *s.* some other time
Rom. 6:17. teaching to which you were made *s.*
7:1. a person is *s.* to the law so long as he is alive
7:25. I myself, *s.* to God's law
1 Cor. 2:15. *s.* to judgement
9:20. as they are *s.* to the Law of Moses, I put myself under that law to win them although I am not myself *s.* to it
Gal. 4:5. freedom for the *s.* of the law
Eph. 2:2. the spirit now at work among God's rebel *s.*

substance
5:6. judgement is coming upon his rebel *s.*
5:21. be *s.* to one another
5:22. wives, be *s.* to your husbands
Phil. 3:21. power which enables him to make all things *s.* to himself
Col. 2:10. the universe is *s.* to him as Head
3:18. wives, be *s.* to your husbands
1 Tim. 1:7. the *s.* about which they are so dogmatic
2 Pet. 3:16. wherever he speaks of this *s.*

subjection
1 Cor. 15:27. he has put all things in *s.* under his feet
Gal. 3:22. the whole world to be prisoners in *s.* to sin
Eph. 1:22. he put everything in *s.* beneath his feet

sublime
2 Pet. 1:17. from the *s.* Presence a voice

submission
1 Tim. 2:11. listening quietly and with due *s.*
Heb. 5:7. his humble *s.*
1 Pet. 2:18. accept the authority of your masters with all due *s.*
3:5. by *s.* to their husbands
3:22. after receiving the *s.* of angelic authorities

submissive
Tit. 3:1. *s.* to the government
Jam. 4:7. be *s.* then to God

submit-ted
Mark 1:27. even the unclean spirits *s.*
Luke 10:17. even the devils *s.* to us
10:20. rejoice over is not that the spirits *s.* to you
Rom. 13:1. every person must *s.* to the supreme authorities
13:5. you are obliged to *s.*
1 Cor. 4:12. they persecute us, and we *s.* to it
Gal. 6:13. to boast of your having *s.* to that outward rite
Heb. 12:3. *s.* to such opposition from sinners
12:9. *s.* even more readily to our spiritual Father

subordinate-s
1 Cor. 15:27. God who *s.* them
15:28. the Son himself will also be made *s.* to God
1 Pet. 5:5. you younger men must be *s.* to your elders

subsided
Luke 8:24. the storm *s.*

substance
Acts 25:11. if there is no *s.* in the charges

substantial
Mat. 28:12. offered the soldiers a *s*. bribe

subtle
1 Cor. 1:20. your *s*. debater
2:4. did not sway you with *s*. arguments

subversion
Luke 23:14. you brought this man before me on a charge of *s*.

subversive
1 Tim. 4:1. *s*. doctrines inspired by devils

subverting
Luke 23:2. we found this man *s*. our nation

succeed-ed
Mat. 2:22. Archelaus had *s*. his father
Acts 24:27. Felix was *s*. by Porcius Festus
Rom. 1:10. *s*. at long last in coming to visit you
Jam. 5:19. another *s*. in bringing him back

success-es
Rom. 1:13. planned to come, though so far without *s*.
3:28. quite apart from *s*. in keeping the law
2 Tim. 3:9. their *s*. will be short-lived

succession
Heb. 5:6. thou art a priest for ever, in the *s*. of Melchizedek
5:10. high priest in the *s*. of Melchizedek
6:20. a high priest for ever in the *s* of Melchizedek
7:11. in the *s*. of Melchizedek, instead of the *s*. of Aaron
7:17. a priest for ever, in the *s*. of Melchizedek
7:23. other priests are appointed in numerous *s*.

successive
Heb. 11:30. encircled on seven *s*. days

sudden-ly
Mat. 5:23. you *s*. remember that your brother has a grievance
17:5. a bright cloud *s*. overshadowed them
21:20. how is it,' they asked, 'that the tree has withered so *s*.
28:2. *s*. there was a violent earthquake
28:9. *s*. Jesus was there in their path
Mark 14:43. *s*., while he was still speaking, Judas
Luke 2:9. *s*. there stood before them an angel

9:30. *s*. there were two men talking with him
21:34. the great Day closes upon you *s*.
24:4. all of a *s*. two men in dazzling garments were at their side
Acts 5:10. *s*. she dropped dead at his feet
10:30. *s*. a man in shining robes stood before me
Gal. 6:1. do something wrong, my brothers, on a *s*. impulse
2 Thess. 2:2. do not *s*. lose your heads

sue-s-d
Mat. 5:25. if someone *s*. you
Acts 12:20. *s*. for peace

suffer-ed-ing-ings
Mat. 5:10. *s*. persecution for the cause of right
5:11. when you *s*. insults
9:20. *s*. from haemorrhages for twelve years
15:4. the man who curses his father or mother must *s*. death
28:14. put matters right with him and see that you do not *s*.
Mark 1:34. he healed many who *s*. from various diseases
5:25. a woman who had *s*. from haemorrhages
7:10. who curses his father or mother must *s*. death
Luke 4:40. friends *s*. from one disease or another
8:43. a woman who had *s*. from haemorrhages
14:2. a man *s*. from dropsy
John 4:14. will never *s*. thirst any more
5:14. or you may *s*. something worse
Acts 2:31. his flesh never *s*. corruption
13:36. gathered to his fathers, and *s*. corruption
13:37. did not *s*. corruption
28:8. *s*. from recurrent bouts of fever
Rom. 5:3. exult in our present *s*., because we know that *s*. trains us to endure
2 Cor. 6:9. disciplined by *s*.
11:27. I have *s*. from cold
Eph. 3:13. my *s*. for you
1 Thess. 1:6. meant grave *s*. for you
2 Thess. 1:9. they will *s*. the punishment of eternal ruin
2 Tim. 1:8. your share of *s*. for the sake of the Gospel
3:11. persecutions and *s*.
Heb. 10:32. the challenge of great *s*.
10:34. you shared the *s*. of the prisoners
1 Pet. 5:9. going through the same kinds of *s*.
2 Pet. 2:12. *s*. hurt for the hurt they have inflicted
Rev. 1:9. who share with you in the *s*.
2:22. plunge her lovers into terrible *s*.

sufferer-s
Mat. 4:24. *s.* from every kind of illness
  15:30. and many other *s.*
Luke 7:21. he cured many *s.*

sufficient
2 Cor. 2:3. I had *s.* confidence in you

suggest-ed
John 18:34. have others *s.* it to you
1 John 5:16. I do not *s.* that he should
  pray about that

suit
Rom. 6:19. to use words that *s.* your
  human weakness
Col. 3:12. the garments that *s.* God's
  chosen people

sulphur
Luke 17:29. it rained fire and *s.*
Rev. 9:17. *s.*-yellow; the horses had
  heads like lions' heads, and out of
  their mouths came fire, smoke,
  and *s.*
  9:18. the fire, the smoke, and the *s.*
  20:10. flung into the lake of fire and *s.*

sulphurous
Rev. 14:10. tormented in *s.* flames
  19:20. the lake of fire with its *s.*
  flames
  21:8. the lake that burns with *s.*
  flames

sum-s-med
Mat. 26:9. it could have been sold for a
  good *s.*
Mark 12:41. many rich people were
  giving large *s.*
Luke 22:5. undertook to pay him a *s.*
  of money
Acts 15:13. James *s.* up
Rom. 13:9. all *s.* up in the one rule
  13:10. the whole law is *s.* up in love
1 Cor. 14:26. to *s.* up, my friends
  16:2. a *s.* in proportion to his gains
Gal. 5:14. the whole law can be *s.* up
1 Pet. 3:8. to *s.* up: be one in thought
  and feeling

summary
Rom, 9:28. the Lord's sentence on the
  land will be *s.*

summon-s-ed-ing
Mat. 22:3. to *s.* the guests he had invited
Mark 6:7. he *s.* the Twelve and sent
  them out
  13:9. *s.* to appear before governors
Luke 7:19. *s.* two of their number
  16:5. he *s.* his master's debtors
John 9:18. until they had *s.* his parents
  9:24. *s.* the man who had been blind
  18:33. Pilate then . . . . *s.* Jesus
Acts 5:21. they *s.* the 'Sanhedrin
  10:7. *s.* two of his servants
  20:17. *s.* the elders of the congregation

Rom. 4:17. *s.* things that are not yet in
  existence

sun
Mat. 20:12. the whole day long in the
  blazing *s.*
Luke 1:78. the morning *s.* from heaven

Sunday
Mat. 28:1. it was about daybreak on *S.*
Mark 16:2. very early on the *S.* morning
  16:9. early on *S.* morning
Luke 24:1. on the *S.* morning very early
John 20:1. early on the *S.* morning
  20:19. late that *S.* evening
1 Cor. 16:2. every *S.* each of you is to
  put aside

sunlight
Acts 13:11. for a time you shall not see
  the *s.*

sunrise
Mark 16:2. just after *s.*, they came to the
  tomb

sunset
Mat. 20:6. an hour before *s.* he went out
  20:9. started work an hour before *s.*
Mark 1:32. after *s.* they brought to him
  all who were ill
Luke 4:40. at *s.* all who had friends
  suffering
Acts 23:23. parade three hours after *s.*
Eph. 4:26. do not let *s.* find you still
  nursing it

superficially
John 7:24. do not judge *s.*

superhuman
Rom. 8:38. in the realm of spirits or *s.*
  powers
Eph. 6:12. the *s.* forces of evil

superintendent
Luke 19:2. he was *s.* of taxes

superior
Luke 6:40. a pupil is not *s.* to his teacher
Rom. 11:18. do not make yourself *s.* to
  the branches
Heb. 1:4. the title he has inherited is *s.*
  to theirs
  7:22. how far *s.* must the covenant
  also be
  8:6. the ministry which has fallen to
  Jesus is as far *s.*
2 Pet. 2:11. angels, for all their *s.*
  strength

superlative
2 Cor. 11:5. have I in any way come
  short of those *s.* apostles
  12:11. in no respect did I fall short of
  these *s.* apostles

supernatural
1 Cor. 10:3. they all ate the same *s.* food

1 Cor. 10:4. all drank the same *s.* drink; I mean, they all drank from the *s.* rock

supersede-s
Heb. 7:28. the oath which *s.* the Law

supper
Mat. 26:17. prepare for your Passover *s.*
26:21. during *s.* he said
26:26. during *s.* Jesus took bread
Mark 14:12. prepare for your Passover *s.*
14:18. as they sat at *s.* Jesus said
14:22. during *s.* he took bread
Luke 17:8. rather say, 'Prepare my *s.*
22:8. go and prepare for our Passover *s.*

supplement
2 Pet. 1:5. *s.* your faith with virtue

supply-ies
Acts 12:20. drew its *s.* from the king's territory
Col. 2:19. the whole body, with all its joints and ligaments, receives its *s.*
Jam. 2:16. does nothing to *s.* their bodily needs
1 Pet. 4:11. the strength which God *s.*

support-ed
Mat. 4:6 } they will *s.* you in their
Luke 4:11 } arms
19:47. the *s.* of the leading citizens
23:14. nothing in him to *s.* your charges
Acts 18:27. the brotherhood gave him their *s.*
24:9. the Jews *s.* the attack
Rom. 15:24. to be sent there with your *s.*
2 Cor. 11:8. accepting *s.* from them to serve you
Gal. 1:10. canvassing for men's *s.*? Whose *s.* do I want but God's alone
Phil. 1:19. the Spirit of Jesus Christ is given me for *s.*
1 Tim. 5:10. or *s.* those in distress
5:16. if a Christian man or woman has widows in the family, he must *s.* them himself; the congregation must be relieved of the burden, so that it may be free to *s.*
5:19. *s.* by two or three witnesses
2 Tim. 4:16. no one came into court to *s.* me
3 John 8. we are bound to *s.* such men

suppose-d-ing
Mat. 5:17. do not *s.* that I have come to abolish the Law
12:11. *s.* you had one sheep
26:53. do you *s.* that I cannot appeal to my Father
Luke 11:5. *s.* one of you has a friend who comes to him
17:7. *s.* one of you has a servant ploughing
John 5:39. *s.* that in having them you have eternal life
11:31. they *s.* that she was going to the tomb
13:29. some *s.* that, as Judas was in charge
16:2. will *s.* that he is performing a religious duty
Acts 17:29. ought not to *s.* that the deity is like an image
Rom. 3:29. do you *s.* God is the God of the Jews alone
9:32. but (as they *s.*) on deeds
1 Cor. 9:8. do not *s.* I rely on these human analogies
9:9. do you *s.* God's concern is with oxen
12:15. *s.* the foot should say
12:16. *s.* the ear were to say
14:6. *s.*, my friends, that when I come to you
14:16. *s.* you are praising God
Jam. 2:3. *s.* you pay special attention to the well-dressed man
2:15. *s.* a brother or a sister is in rags
4:5. do you *s.* that Scripture has no meaning
2 Pet. 3:9. the Lord is slow in fulfilling his promise, as some *s.*

supreme-ly
Acts 16:17. these men are servants of the *S.* God
Rom. 9:5. God, *s.* above all
13:1. must submit to the *s.* authorities
Eph. 1:22. appointed him as *s.* head to the church
Col. 1:18. to be in all things alone *s.*
Jam. 1:2. count yourselves *s.* happy

sure-ly
Mat. 5:46. *s.* the tax-gatherers do as much as that
6:25. *s.* life is more than food
11:8. *s.* you must look in palaces for that
12:12. *s.* a man is worth far more than a sheep
20:15. *s.* I am free to do what I like with my own money
Mark 4:21. *s.* it is brought to be set on the lamp-stand
12:24. mistaken, and *s.* this is the reason
14:19. one by one they said to him, 'Not I, *s.*
Luke 1:18. how can I be *s.* of this
1:50. his mercy *s.* from generation to generation
7:25. *s.* you must look in palaces for grand clothes

Luke 16:4. to make *s*. that, when I have to leave

18:9. those who were *s*. of their own goodness

21:20. then you may be *s*. that her destruction is near

21:31. you may be *s*. that the kingdom of God is near

John 6:14. *s*. this must be the prophet

6:42. *s*. this is Jesus son of Joseph

Rom. 3:8. condemn such men as these is *s*. no injustice

9:21. *s*. the potter can do what he likes with the clay

16:25. power to make your standing *s*.

1 Cor. 1:13. *s*. Christ has not been divided

10:12. if you feel *s*. that you are standing firm, beware

Jam. 1:22. be *s*. that you act on the message

2:22. *s*. you can see that faith was at work

1 Pet. 2:3. *s*. you have tasted that the Lord is good

1 John 2:3. here is the test by which we can make *s*. that we know him

2:5. the test by which we can make *s*. that we are in him

3:24. we can make *s*. that he dwells within us

5:9. *s*. divine testimony is stronger

surface

Acts 17:26. to inhabit the whole earth's *s*.

surge

Luke 21:25. the roar and *s*. of the sea

surpass-ed

2 Cor. 8:5. their giving *s*. our expectations

surplus

2 Cor. 8:14. your *s*. meets their need, but one day your need may be met from their *s*.

surprise-d-ing

Mat. 22:22. this answer took them by *s*.

Mark 15:44. Pilate was *s*. to hear that he was already dead

Luke 1:21. *s*. that he was staying so long inside

4:22. *s*. that words of such grace should fall from his lips

11:38. *s*. that he had not begun by washing

Acts 3:12. why be *s*. at this

2 Cor. 11:14. there is nothing *s*. about that

1 John 3:13. do not be *s*. if the world hates you

surrender-ed

Mat. 20:28 ⎫
Mark 10:45 ⎬ *s*. his life as a ransom

Luke 12:20. this very night you must *s*. your life

Rom. 8:32. did not spare his own Son, but *s*. him

2 Cor. 4:11. we are being *s*. into the hands of death

10:5. thought to *s*. in obedience to Christ

surround-ed-ing

Mat. 8:18. at the sight of the crowds *s*. him

Mark 9:14. they saw a large crowd *s*. them

Luke 2:46. sitting in the temple *s*. by the teachers

Acts 14:6. cities of Lystra and Derbe and the *s*. country

survive-d

Mat. 24:22 ⎫
Mark 13:20 ⎬ no living thing could *s*.

Acts 7:19. expose their children so that they should not *s*.

Rev. 9:20. the rest of mankind who *s*. these plagues

suspense

John 10:24. how long must you keep us in *s*.

Acts 27:33. you have lived in *s*.

suspicions

1 Tim. 6:4. slander, base *s*.

sustain-s-ed

Rom. 11:18. remember that it is not you who *s*. the root: the root *s*. you

1 Cor. 10:13. a way out, by enabling you to *s*. it

Heb. 1:3. *s*. the universe by his word of power

Rev. 12:6. to be *s*. for twelve hundred and sixty days

12:14. for three years and a half she was to be *s*.

swallowed

Rev. 10:10. when I *s*. it my stomach turned sour

swamped

Mark 4:37. broke over the boat until it was all but *s*.

swarming

Luke 11:29. with the crowds *s*. round him

swathed

John 11:44. his hands and feet *s*. in linen bands

sway

Rom. 5:14. death held *s*. from Adam to Moses

1 Cor. 2:4. did not *s.* you with subtle arguments

1 Tim. 6:15. God who in eternal felicity alone holds *s.*

Rev. 17:18. the great city that holds *s.*

swear

1 Cor. 15:31. I *s.* it by my pride in you

sweat-ed

Mat. 20:12. *s.* the whole day long in the blazing sun

sweep

John 11:48. *s.* away our temple and our nation

Rev. 12:15. to *s.* her away with its spate

swell

2 Cor. 9:10. *s.* the harvest of your benevolence

swept

Mat. 11:7. a reed-bed *s.* by the wind

24:39. the flood came and *s.* them all away

Luke 7:24. a reed-bed *s.* by the wind

Acts 8:9. *s.* the Samaritans off their feet

1 Cor. 12:2. you were *s.* off to those dumb heathen gods

Heb. 13:9. do not be *s.* off your course

Rev. 12:4. with his tail he *s.* down a third of the stars

swerved

Rom. 3:12. all have *s.* aside

swift

2 Thess. 3:1. the word of the Lord may have everywhere the *s.* and glorious course

swim

Jam. 3:7. crawl on the ground or *s.* in the sea

swindler-s

1 Cor. 5:10. grabbers and *s.*

5:11. a drunkard, or a *s.*

6:10. slanderers or *s.*

swollen

2 Tim. 3:4. *s.* with self-importance

sworn

Mat. 5:33. oaths *s.* to the Lord must be kept

Acts 23:21. they have *s.* not to eat or drink

Heb. 7:20. an oath was *s.*

7:21. no oath *s.* when those others were made priests; but for this priest an oath was *s.*, as Scripture says of him; 'The Lord has *s.*

symbol

Acts 19:35. that *s.* of her which fell from heaven

1 Cor. 10:6. these events happened as *s.*

Heb. 9:24. sanctuary made by men's hands which is only a *s.*

symbolic

Rom. 4:11. the *s.* rite of circumcision

1 Cor. 10:11. these things that happened to them were *s.*

Heb. 9:9. all this is *s.*, pointing to the present time

sympathize

Heb. 4:15. ours is not a high priest unable to *s.*

synagogue

Mat. 9:18. there came a president of the *s.*

12:14. the Pharisees, on leaving the *s*, laid a plot

Mark 3:6. the Pharisees, on leaving the *s.*

John 9:34. they expelled him from the *s.*

Syria

Mark 7:26. a Phoenician of *S.* by nationality

Syrtis

Acts 27:17. the shallows of *S.*

system

Gal. 2:18. a *s.* which I have pulled down

Heb. 7:16. not to a *s.* of earth-bound rules

T

Tabernae

Acts 28:15. Appii Forum and Tres *T.*

table-s

Mat. 1:1. a *t.* of the descent of Jesus Christ

9:10. Jesus was at *t.* in the house

22:11. the king came in to see the company at *t.*

26:7. as he sat at *t.* she began to pour it

Mark 2:15. when Jesus was at *t.* in his house

14:3. as he sat at *t.*, a woman came in

16:14. while the Eleven were at *t.* he appeared

Luke 7:36. took his place at *t.*

Luke 12:37. he will buckle his belt, seat them at *t.*
  13:26. we sat at *t.* with you
  22:14. he took his place at *t.*
  22:27. the one who sits at *t.* or the servant who waits on him? Surely the one who sits at *t.*
  24:30. when he had sat down with them at *t.*
John 2:14. the money-changers seated at their *t.*
  13:4. rose from *t.*, laid aside his garments
Acts 11:3. and sitting at *t.* with them
2 Pet. 2:13. at *t.* they are an ugly blot on your company

tablet-s
Luke 1:63. he asked for a writing-*t.*
2 Cor. 3:3. not on stone *t.* but on the pages of the human heart
Heb. 9:4. and the *t.* of the covenant

tackle
Acts 27:17. they made use of *t.* and undergirded the ship

tainted
Tit. 1:15. nothing is pure to the *t.* minds of disbelievers, *t.* alike in reason and conscience

take-s-n-ing
Mat. 3:11. I am not fit to *t.* off his shoes
  7:4. let me *t.* the speck out of your eye
  7:5. *t.* the speck out of your brother's
  9:2. *t.* heart, my son
  10:23. persecuted in one town, *t.* refuge in another
  14:27. *t.* heart! It is I
  18:15. *t.* the matter up with him
  21:26. they all *t.* John for a prophet
  23:30. we should never have *t.* part with them
  24:16. must *t.* to the hills
Mark 3:21. they set out to *t.* charge of him
  6:6. he was *t.* aback by their want of faith
  6:50. *t.* heart! It is I
  10:49. *t.* heart; stand up; he is calling you
  13:14. must *t.* to the hills
  16:19. the Lord Jesus was *t.* up into heaven
Luke 1:8. to *t.* part in divine service
  4:10. give his angels orders to *t.* care of you
  6:42. let me *t.* the speck out of your eye . . . First *t.* the plank . . . see clearly to *t.* the speck
  8:30. many devils had *t.* possession of him
  8:34. *t.* to their heels

  10:11. only *t.* note of this
  12:3. you may *t.* it, then
  22:31. Simon, Simon, *t.* heed
John 1:15. *t.* rank before me
  7:21. you are all *t.* aback
  11:28. went to call her sister Mary, and *t.* her aside
  21:23. *t.* to mean that that disciple would not die
Acts 5:20. *t.* your place in the temple
  8:13. miracles that were *t.* place
  21:34. to be *t.* into barracks
  26:28. you think it will not *t.* much to win me over
Rom. 2:8. *t.* the wrong for their guide
  2:23. you *t.* pride in the law
  11:25. a deep truth here, my brothers, of which I want you to *t.* account
1 Cor. 4:6. *t.* our case as an example
  7:21. if a chance of liberty should come, *t.* it
  13:5. not quick to *t.* offence
Gal. 2:12. he was *t.* his meals with gentile Christians
  4:19. until you *t.* the shape of Christ
  5:10. confident that you will not *t.* the wrong view
Eph. 5:11. *t.* no part in the barren deeds of darkness
Phil. 1:5. the part you have *t.* in the work
  3:12. hoping to *t.* hold of that for which Christ once took hold of me
2 Thess. 2:4. even *t.* his seat in the temple of God
1 Tim. 4:4. when it is *t.* with thanksgiving
2 Tim. 1:8. *t.* your share of suffering
  2:1. *t.* strength from the grace of God
  2:3. *t.* your share of hardship
  2:19. *t.* the Lord's name upon his lips
Heb. 8:1. *t.* his seat at the right hand of the throne of Majesty
  9:7. he must *t.* with him the blood which he offers
  11:5. God had *t.* him. For it is the testimony of Scripture that before he was *t.* he had pleased God
  13:6. we can *t.* courage and say
2 Pet. 2:15. consented to *t.* pay for doing wrong
  3:5. in *t.* this view they lose sight of the fact
  3:17. *t.* care, then, not to let these unprincipled men seduce you
Jude 12. shepherds who *t.* care only of themselves
Rev. 14:13. they *t.* with them the record of their deeds
  18:4. lest you *t.* part in her sins

tale-s
Col. 1:24. the full *t.* of Christ's afflictions

2 Pet. 1:16. not on *t*. artfully spun that we relied

talk-ed-ing
Mat. 9:3. this is blasphemous *t*.
9:26. this story became the *t*. of all the country round
9:31. they *t*. about him all over the country-side
16:8. why do you *t*. about bringing no bread
Mark 2:7. why does the fellow *t*. like that
8:17. why do you *t*. about having no bread
16:19. after *t*. with them the Lord Jesus was taken up
Luke 1:65. the whole story became common *t*.
2:38. she *t*. about the child to all
4:37. he was the *t*. of the whole district
5:15. the *t*. about him spread all the more
5:21. who is this fellow with his blasphemous *t*.
7:15. the dead man sat up and began to *t*.
9:9. who is this I hear such *t*. about
18:34. they did not grasp what he was *t*. about
20:14. they *t*. it over together
21:5. some people were *t*. about the temple
22:60. man, I do not know what you are *t*. about
24:15. they *t*. and discussed it
24:36. as they were *t*. about all this, there he was
John 3:12. if you disbelieve me when I *t*. to you about things on earth, how are you to believe if I should *t*. about the things of heaven
7:13. no one *t*. about him openly
Acts 2:4. began to *t*. in other tongues
2:6. each one heard the apostles *t*. in his own language
9:29. *t*. and debating
15:24. have disturbed you with their *t*.
16:13. *t*. to the women who had gathered
17:21. *t*. or hearing about the latest novelty
20:9. Paul went on *t*.
24:24. let him *t*. to him about faith in Christ Jesus
24:26. sent for him very often and *t*. with him
28:20. why I have asked to see you and *t*. to you
Rom. 14:16. must not become an occasion for slanderous *t*.

1 Cor. 4:19. the kingdom of God is not a matter of *t*.
14:2. he is *t*. with God
14:3. he is *t*. to men
14:9. you will be *t*. into the air
2 Cor. 10:11. people who *t*. in that way
Col. 2:4. *t*. into error by specious arguments
3:8. cursing, filthy *t*.—have done with them
4:6. study how best to *t*. with each person
1 Thess. 5:3. while they are *t*. of peace
1 Tim. 3:8. not indulging in double *t*.
3:11. who will not *t*. scandal
1 John 3:18. love must not be a matter of words or *t*.

tall-er
Mark 4:32. grows *t*. than any other plant

tally
Mark 14:56. their statements did not *t*.
Rev. 6:11. until the *t*. should be complete

tap-ped
Acts 12:7. he *t*. Peter on the shoulder

Tarsian
Acts 21:39. I am a Jew, a *T*. from Cilicia

task-s
Mat. 24:46. found at his *t*. when his master comes
Luke 10:40. Martha was distracted by her many *t*.
12:43. happy that servant who is found at his *t*.
John 18:37. my *t*. is to bear witness to the truth
Acts 12:25. Barnabas and Saul, their *t*. fulfilled
14:26. the *t*. which they had now completed
20:24. complete the *t*. which the Lord Jesus assigned to me
22:10. told of all the *t*. that are laid upon you
1 Cor. 3:5. the *t*. which the Lord allotted to him
16:16. everyone who labours hard at our common *t*.
Eph. 6:13. to complete every *t*.
Col. 1:25. the *t*. assigned to me by God
2:16. take you to *t*. about what you eat
1 Tim. 1:12. made me equal to the *t*.
Heb. 3:5. his *t*. was to bear witness
13:17. let it be a happy *t*. for them

taste
Acts 8:23. *t*. the bitter fruit and wear the fetters of sin

Acts 23:14. not to *t.* food until we have killed Paul

Rev. 10:9. in your mouth it will *t.* sweet as honey

10:10. in my mouth it did *t.* sweet as honey

tasteless

Mat. 5:13. if salt becomes *t.*, how is its saltness to be restored

Luke 14:34. if salt itself becomes *t.*

taught

Mark 12:38. he said as he *t.* them

John 17:8. I have *t.* them all that I learned from thee

18:19. questioned Jesus about his disciples and about what he *t.*

Acts 1:3. *t.* them about the kingdom of God

Phil. 4:9. the lessons I *t.* you

Col. 1:7. you were *t.* this by Epaphras

2 Tim. 3:7. always wanting to be *t.*

Tit. 3:14. people must be *t.* to engage in honest employment

taunt-ed

Mat. 27:44. the bandits who were crucified with him *t.* him

Mark 15:32. those who were crucified with him *t.* him

Luke 23:39. one of the criminals who hung there with him *t.* him

tax-es

Mat. 17:25. from whom do earthly monarchs collect *t.*

17:27. it will meet the *t.* for us both

22:17. pay *t.* to the Roman Emperor

22:19. show me the money in which the *t.* is paid

Mark 12:14. are we or are we not permitted to pay *t.*

Luke 19:2. he was superintendent of *t.*

20:22. pay *t.* to the Roman Emperor

23:2. opposing the payment of *t.*

Rom. 13:6. that is also why you pay *t.*

13:7. pay *t.* and toll

tax-gatherer-s

Mat. 5:46. the *t.* do as much as that

9:10. many bad characters—*t.* and others

9:11. why is it that your master eats with *t.*

10:3. Matthew the *t.*

11:19. a friend of *t.* and sinners

18:17. treat him as you would a pagan or a *t.*

21:31. *t.* and prostitutes are entering the kingdom of God

21:32. you did not believe him, but the *t.* and prostitutes did

Mark 2:15. *t.* and others—were seated with him

2:16. he eats with *t.* and sinners

Luke 3:12. came to be baptized were *t.*

5:27. he saw a *t.*, Levi

5:29. a large party of *t.*

5:30. *t.* and sinners

7:29. all the people, including the *t.*, praised God

7:34. a friend of *t.* and sinners

15:1. the *t.* and other bad characters

18:10. one a Pharisee and the other a *t.*

18:11. or, for that matter, like this *t.*

teach-es-ing-ings

Mat. 7:28. the people were astounded at his *t.*

13:34. *t.* to the crowds, Jesus spoke in parables

16:12. but against their *t.*

22:33. were astounded at his *t.*

Mark 1:22. the people were astounded at his *t.*

1:27. a new kind of *t.*

11:18. the whole crowd was spellbound by his *t.*

Luke 4:32. they were astounded at his *t.*

John 7:16. the *t.* that I give is not my own; it is the *t.* of him who sent me

7:17. shall know whether my *t.* comes from him

7:18. anyone whose *t.* is merely his own

8:37. my *t.* makes no headway with you

8:51 $\}$ if anyone obeys my *t.*
8:52

12:34. our Law *t.* us that the Messiah continues

15:20. they will follow your *t.* as little as they have followed mine

Acts 2:42. they met constantly to hear the apostles *t.*

Rom. 6:17. obedience to the pattern of *t.*

16:17. contrary to the *t.* you received

1 Cor. 7:17. that is what I *t.* in all our congregations

2 Cor. 1:9. to *t.* us not to place reliance on ourselves

Eph. 4:14. whirled about by every fresh gust of *t.*

Col. 2:8. traditions of man-made *t.*

2:22. merely human injunctions and *t.*

1 Tim. 1:10. whose behaviour flouts the wholesome *t.*

4:13. to exhortation, and to *t.*

4:16. keeping close watch on yourself and your *t.*

5:17. labour at preaching and *t.*

6:1. the Christian *t.* are not brought into disrepute

2 Tim. 1:13. an outline of the sound *t.*

2:17. the infection of their *t.* will spread

2 Tim. 3:10. have followed, step by step, my *t*.

3:16. every inspired scripture has its use for *t*.

4:2. all the patience that the work of *t*. requires

Tit. 1:9. move his hearers with wholesome *t*.

2:7. in your *t*., you must show integrity

Heb. 13:9. all sorts of outlandish *t*.

Jam. 3:1. we who *t*. shall ourselves be judged

1 John 4:5. they are of that world, and so therefore is their *t*.

Rev. 2:14. the *t*. of Balaam

2:23. this will *t*. all the churches that I am the searcher

2:24. others in Thyatira, who do not accept this *t*.

3:3. remember the *t*. you received

teacher-s

Mat. 7:29. unlike their own *t*.

10:24. a pupil does not rank above his *t*.

10:25. content to share his *t*. lot

13:52. when, therefore, a *t*. of the law has become a learner

17:10. why then do our *t*. say that Elijah must come first

23:10. nor must you be called '*t*.'; you have one *T*.

23:34. I send you therefore prophets, sages, and *t*.

Mark 9:11. why do our *t*. say that Elijah must be the first to come

12:35. how can the *t*. of the law maintain

Luke 2:46. sitting in the temple surrounded by the *t*.

5:17. Pharisees and *t*. of the law were sitting round

6:40. a pupil is not superior to his *t*.; but everyone, when his training is complete, will reach his *t*. level

John 1:38. Rabbi' (which means a *t*.)

3:10. this famous *t*. of Israel

Acts 5:34. Gamaliel, a *t*. of the law

Jam. 3:1. not many of you should become *t*.

team

1 Cor. 3:8. they work as a *t*.

tear-s

Mat. 5:29. if your right eye leads you astray, *t*. it out

7:6. turn and *t*. you to pieces

9:16. then the patch *t*. away from the coat

18:9. if it is your eye that is your undoing, *t*. it out

Mark 2:21. the patch *t*. away from it

9:47. if it is your eye, *t*. it out

14:72. he burst into *t*.

Luke 5:36. no one *t*. a piece from a new cloak

John 19:24. we must not *t*. this

Acts 9:39. all the widows came and stood round him in *t*.

21:13. why all these *t*.

2 Cor. 12:21. that I may have *t*. to shed

Phil. 3:18. tell you with *t*. in my eyes

Rev. 5:4. I was in *t*. because no one was found

teeth

1 Pet. 4:14. if Christ's name is flung in your *t*. as an insult

temper-s-ed

2 Cor. 12:20. angry *t*. and personal rivalries

Gal. 5:20. a contentious *t*., envy

Tit. 1:7. not be overbearing or short-*t*.

1 Pet. 4:1. arm yourselves with a *t*. of mind like his

temperance

Tit. 2:12. live a life of *t*.

temperate

1 Tim. 3:2. sober, *t*., courteous

Tit. 2:5. *t*., chaste, and kind

2:6. *t*. in all things

temple

Mat. 17:24. collectors of the *t*.-tax came up to Peter and asked, 'Does your master not pay *t*.-tax

23:38. there is your *t*., forsaken by God

27:6. this cannot be put into the *t*. fund

Mark 12:41. standing opposite the *t*. treasury, watching

Luke 13:35. there is your *t*., forsaken by God

21:1. the chest of the *t*. treasury

22:4. went to the chief priests and officers of the *t*. police

John 4:20. the *t*. where God should be worshipped

7:32. sent *t*. police to arrest him

7:45. the *t*. police came back

11:48. sweep away our *t*. and our nation

Acts 14:13. Jupiter, whose *t*. was just outside the city

19:35. *t*.-warden of the great Diana

Rom. 9:4. the law, the *t*. worship

1 Pet. 2:5. as living stones, into a spiritual *t*.

temporary

1 Cor. 7:5. when you agree upon a *t*. abstinence

Gal. 3:19. it was a *t*. measure

temptation

Rev. 2:14. to put *t*. in the way of the Israelites

Ten
Mat. 4:25. from Galilee and the *T.* Towns
Mark 5:20. spread the news in the *T.* Towns
  7:31. through the territory of the *T.* Towns

tenant-s
Mat. 21:34. he sent his servants to the *t.*
  21:38. the *t.* said to one another
  21:40. how do you think he will deal with those *t.*
  21:41. hand the vineyard over to other *t.*
Mark 12:2. he sent a servant to the *t.*
  12:7. the *t.* said to one another
  12:9. put the *t.* to death
Luke 20:10. he sent a servant to the *t.*
  20:14. when the *t.* saw him they talked it over
  20:16. put these *t.* to death

tend
John 21:16. then *t.* my sheep
1 Cor. 9:7. *t.* a flock without using its milk
  11:17. your meetings *t.* to do more harm than good
1 Pet. 5:2. *t.* that flock of God whose shepherds you are

tender-ly
Luke 1:48. so *t.* has he looked upon his servant
Rom. 15:1. the *t.* scruples of weaker men

tent-s
Acts 7:44. the *T.* of the Testimony in the desert
Heb. 8:2. the *t.* pitched by the Lord
  8:5. Moses, about to erect the *t.*
  9:2. a *t.* was prepared—the first *t.*
  9:3. the *t.* called the Most Holy Place
  9:6. the priests are always entering the first *t.*
  9:8. so long as the earlier *t.* still stands
  9:11. the *t.* of his priesthood
  9:21. he also sprinkled the *t.* and all the vessels
  11:9. living in *t.*, as did Isaac and Jacob
  13:10. priests of the sacred *t.*
Rev. 15:5. the sanctuary of the heavenly *T.* of Testimony

Terah
Luke 3:34. Abraham, son of *T.*

term-s
Mat. 5:25. come to *t.* with him promptly
Luke 14:32. sends envoys, and asks for *t.*
Acts 7:6. God spoke in these *t.*
Rom. 3:5. God (I speak of him in human *t.*

2 Cor. 1:24. the *t.* of your faith
Gal. 3:11. no one is ever justified before God in *t.* of law
  4:4. when the *t.* was completed, God sent his own Son
1 Thess. 2:4. on those *t.* we speak
1 Tim. 5:16. widows in the full sense of the *t.*
Heb. 8:9. they did not abide by the *t.* of that covenant

terrible
Luke 21:23. a *t.* judgement upon this people
Heb. 10:31. it is a *t.* thing to fall into the hands of the living God
Rev. 2:22. plunge her lovers into *t.* suffering

terrify-ied-ing
Mark 6:50. they all saw him and were *t.*
  9:6. he did not know what to say; they were so *t.*
Luke 24:5. two men in dazzling garments were at their side. They were *t.*
John 6:19. they were *t.*, but he called out
Acts 7:32. Moses was *t.* and dared not look
Heb. 10:27. a *t.* expectation of judgement

territory
Mat. 16:13. he came to the *t.* of Caesarea Philippi
Mark 7:24. into the *t.* of Tyre
  7:31. Tyrian *t.*
Luke 4:26. Sarepta in the *t.* of Sidon
Acts 7:29. settled in Midianite *t.*
  12:20. drew its supplies from the king's *t.*
  17:26. the limits of their *t.*

terror-s
Mat. 14:26. they cried out in *t.*
  17:6. the disciples fell on their faces in *t.*
Mark 16:8. ran away from the tomb, beside themselves with *t.*
Luke 2:9. they were *t.*-struck, but the angel said
  21:11. in the sky *t.* and great portents
  21:26. *t.* at the thought of all that is coming
Acts 10:4. Cornelius!' He stared at him in *t.*
1 Thess. 1:10. Jesus our deliverer from the *t.* of judgement
  5:9. God has not destined us to the *t.* of judgement
Rev. 11:11. to the *t.* of all who saw it
  11:13. the rest in *t.* did homage to the God of heaven

terrorists
Acts 21:38. led a force of four thousand *t.*

test-s-ed-ing

Mat. 4:7. not to put the Lord your God to the *t.*
6:13. do not bring us to the *t.*
16:1. to *t.* him they asked him
19:3. Pharisees came and *t.* him by asking
22:35. one of their number *t.* him with this question
26:41. pray that you may be spared the *t.*

Mark 8:11. to *t.* him they asked him for a sign
10:2. this was to *t.* him
14:38. pray that you may be spared the *t.*

Luke 4:12. you are not to *t.* the Lord your God
8:13. in the time of *t.* they desert
10:25. a lawyer came forward to put this *t.* question to him
11:4. do not bring us to the *t.*
11:16. by way of a *t.*, demanded of him a sign
22:40. pray that you may be spared the hour of *t.*
22:46. pray that you may be spared the *t.*

John 3:19. here lies the *t.*
6:6. this he said to *t.* him
8:6. they put the question as a *t.*

Acts 5:9. why did you both conspire to put the Spirit of the Lord to the *t.*

Rom. 5:4. proof that we have stood the *t.*

1 Cor. 3:13. the fire will *t.* the worth of each man's work
10:9. let us not put the power of the Lord to the *t.*
10:13. he will not allow you to be *t.* above your powers
11:28. a man must *t.* himself before eating

2 Cor. 2:9. to see how you stood the *t.*
8:8. I am putting your love to the *t.*
8:22. many opportunities of *t.*
13:5. put yourselves to the *t.* . . . prove unequal to the *t.*

1 Thess. 2:4. God, who is continually *t.* our hearts
5:21. bring them all to the *t.*

2 Tim. 3:8. they cannot pass the *t.* of faith

Tit. 1:5. observe the *t.* I prescribed

Heb. 2:18. he himself has passed through the *t.* of suffering, he is able to help those who are meeting their *t.*
3:8. that time of *t.* in the desert
3:9. your forefathers tried me and *t.* me
4:15. has been *t.* every way, only without sin
11:17. Abraham, when the *t.* came

Jam. 1:3. such *t.* of your faith breeds fortitude
1:12. having passed that *t.* he will receive

1 Pet. 1:7. faith which has stood the *t.*

1 John 2:3. the *t.* by which we can make sure we know him
2:5. the *t.* by which we can make sure that we are in him
4:1. *t.* the spirits

Rev. 2:10. the Devil will throw some of you into prison, to put you to the *t.*
3:10. *t.* its inhabitants

testament

Gal. 3:15. when a man's will and *t.* has been duly executed
3:17. a *t.*, or covenant

testify-ied-ing

Mat. 10:18. to *t.* before them and the heathen

Mark 13:9. to *t.* in their presence

Luke 11:48. so *t.* that you approve of the deeds your fathers did
21:13. this will be your opportunity to *t.*

John 1:7. he came as a witness to *t.* to the light
1:32. John *t.* further
3:28. you yourselves can *t.* that I said
5:31. if I *t.* on my own behalf
5:36. enough to *t.* that the Father has sent me

Acts 10:43. it is to him that all the prophets *t.*
22:15. *t.* to what you have seen and heard
26:16. to *t.* both to what you have seen
26:22. *t.* to great and small alike

Rom. 8:16. *t.* that we are God's children
10:2. to their zeal for God I can *t.*

2 Cor. 8:3. to the limit of their resources, as I can *t.*

testimonial

3 John 12. Demetrius gets a good *t.*

testimony

Mat. 24:14. as a *t.* to all nations

John 1:15. here is John's *t.* to him
1:19. this is the *t.* which John gave
3:11. yet you all reject our *t.*
4:39. because of the woman's *t.*
5:31. that *t.* does not hold good
5:32. I know that his *t.* holds
5:33. you have his *t.* to the truth
5:34. not that I rely on human *t.*
5:36. I rely on a *t.* higher than John's
5:37. this *t.* to me was given by the Father
5:39. their *t.* points to me
8:13. your *t.* is not valid
8:14. my *t.* is valid

Acts 7:44. the Tent of the *T.*
8:25. after giving their *t.*
20:24. bearing my *t.* to the gospel
1 Tim. 6:13. gave his *t.* to it before
    Pontius Pilate
Heb. 2:4. God added his *t.* by signs
7:17. here is the *t.*
10:15. we have also the *t.* of the Holy
    Spirit
1 Pet. 5:12. my *t.* that this is the true
    grace of God
1 John 1:2. we have seen it and bear our
    t.
5:9. we accept human *t.*, but surely
    divine *t.* is stronger, and this three-
    fold *t.*
5:10. believes in the Son of God has
    this *t.* in his own heart
3 John 12. I add my *t.*, and you know
    that my *t.* is true
Rev. 17:6. those who had borne their
    t. to Jesus
20:4. their *t.* to Jesus
22:16. with this *t.* for the churches
22:20. he who gives this *t.* speaks

tethered
Mat. 21:2. find a donkey *t.*
Mark 11:2. find *t.* there a colt
11:4. found the colt *t.* to a door
Luke 19:30. *t.* there a colt which no one
    has yet ridden

text-s
Mat. 9:13. go and learn what that *t.*
    means
12:7. if you had known what that *t.*
    means
21:16. have you never read that *t.*
Mark 12:10. can it be that you have
    never read this *t.*
Luke 4:21. this *t.* has come true
20:17. then what does this *t.* of
    Scripture mean
John 12:14. in accordance with the *t.* of
    Scripture
13:18. there is a *t.* of Scripture to be
    fulfilled
15:25. this *t.* in their Law had to come
    true
19:24. thus the *t.* of Scripture came
    true
19:36. in fulfilment of the *t.* of
    Scripture
19:37. and another *t.* says
Acts 1:20. the *t.* I have in mind
17:2. quoting *t.* of Scripture
Rom. 9:13. accords with the *t.* of
    Scripture
11:26. in agreement with the *t.* of
    Scripture
12:19. there is a *t.* which reads
12:20. but there is another *t.*
Heb. 12:5. you have forgotten the *t.* of
    Scripture

thank-s
Rom. 13:2. have themselves to *t.* for the
    punishment
2 Cor. 9:13. *t.* him for your liberal
    contribution
Heb. 12:28. let us therefore give *t.* to
    God

thankfully
Acts 13:48. *t.* acclaimed the word of the
    Lord
Col. 3:16. sing *t.* in your hearts to God

theme-s
Mat. 3:2. his *t.* was: 'Repent
2 Tim. 2:8. this is the *t.* of my gospel
Tit. 2:15. these, then, are your *t.*
Heb. 2:5. the world to come, which is
    our *t.*
1 Pet. 1:10. this salvation was the *t.*
1 John 1:1. our *t.* is the word of life

Thessalonica
1 Thess. 1:5. that is the kind of men we
    were at *T.*
1:8. from *T.* the word of the Lord rang
    out
2:18. we did propose to come to *T.*
3:6. Timothy has just arrived from *T.*

thief
Rom. 2:21. are you yourself a *t.*
Eph. 4:28. the *t.* must give up stealing

thing-s
Mat. 24:22. no living *t.* could survive
24:24. if such a *t.* were possible
24:37. as *t.* were in Noah's days
26:10. it is a fine *t.* she has done for
    me
Mark 13:8. with these *t.* the birth-pangs
    of the new age begin
13:20. no living *t.* could survive
14:6. it is a fine *t.* she has done for me
Luke 6:43. no such *t.* as a good tree
    producing worthless fruit
16:9. when money is a *t.* of the past
16:10. the man who can be trusted in
    little *t.* . . . . dishonest in little *t.* is
    dishonest also in great *t.*
17:28. as *t.* were in Lot's days
19:37. the praises of God for all the *t.*
    they had seen
John 7:3. may see the great *t.* you are
    doing
Acts 2:11. the great *t.* God has done
7:41. the *t.* their hands had made
8:22. pray the Lord to forgive you
    for imagining such a *t.*
10:11. a *t.* coming down that looked
    like a great sheet
11:5. a *t.* was coming down
Rom. 1:25. worship to created *t.*
1 Cor. 15:42. sown in the earth as a
    perishable *t.*

Gal. 3:13. becoming for our sake an
  accursed *t.*
Eph. 5:4. these *t.* are out of place
Col. 1:15. his is the primacy over all
  created *t.*
1 Tim. 1:8. the law is an excellent *t.*
Jam. 2:17. it is in itself a lifeless *t.*
1 Pet. 2:20. fortitude is a fine *t.* in the
  sight of God
  4:2. not for the *t.* that men desire
1 John 5:15. the *t.* we ask for are ours
  5:16. there is such a *t.* as deadly sin
Rev. 16:3. every living *t.* in the sea died

think-s-ing
Mat. 6:24. *t.* nothing of the second
  16:23. you *t.* as men *t.*, not as God *t.*
Mark 2:8. Jesus knew in his own mind
  that this was what they were *t.*
  8:33. you *t.* as men *t.*, not as God *t.*
Luke 1:24. she lived in seclusion, *t.*
  2:44. *t.* that he was with the party
  8:18. forfeit even what he *t.* he has
  12:24. *t.* of the ravens
  14:28. *t.* of building a tower
John 20:15. *t.* it was the gardener
Acts 5:4. what made you *t.* of doing this
  thing
  14:19. dragged him out of the city,
  t. him dead
  26:28. you *t.* it will not take much to
  win me
Rom. 1:21. their *t.* has ended in futility
  12:16. do not keep *t.* how wise you
  are
1 Cor. 1:26. *t.* what sort of people you
  are
  2:2. I would *t.* of nothing but Jesus
  Christ
  7:35. I am *t.* simply of your own good
  14:20. be grown up in your *t.*
2 Cor. 11:2. *t.* to present you as a chaste
  virgin
Phil. 1:3. I thank my God whenever I
  t. of you
  2:2. *t.* and feeling alike
  3:15. keep to this way of *t.*
1 Thess. 3:6. you always *t.* kindly of us
1 Tim. 6:5. they *t.* religion should yield
  dividends
Heb. 3:1. *t.* of the Apostle and High
  Priest of the religion we profess
  12:3. *t.* of him who submitted to such
  opposition
  12:5. do not *t.* lightly of the Lord's
  discipline
Jam. 1:26. a man may *t.* he is religious
2 Pet. 3:11. *t.* what sort of people you
  ought to be

third
Mat. 21:35. stoned a *t.*
Luke 19:20. the *t.* came and said, 'Here
  is your pound

thirty
Mark 14:5. the perfume might have been
  sold for *t.* pounds
John 2:6. each held from twenty to *t.*
  gallons
  12:5. why was this perfume not sold
  for *t.* pounds
2 Cor. 11:24. five times the Jews have
  given me the *t.*-nine strokes

thistle-s
Mat. 13:7. some seed fell among *t.*; and
  the *t.* shot up
  13:22. the seed sown among *t.*
  represents
Mark 4:7. some seed fell among *t.*; but
  the *t.* shot up
  4:18. others again receive the seed
  among *t.*
Luke 6:44. you do not gather figs from
  t.
  8:7. the *t.* grew up with it and choked
  it
  8:14. that which fell among *t.* represents
Heb. 6:8. if it bears thorns and *t.*, it is
  worthless

thorny
1 Tim. 6:10. spiked themselves on many
  t. griefs

thoroughfare-s
Mat. 22:9. go out to the main *t.*
Mark 11:16. not allow anyone to use the
  temple court as a *t.*

thoroughgoing
Gal. 6:13. *t.* observers of the law

thoroughly
Acts 22:3. *t.* trained in every point of our
  ancestral law
Phil. 4:12. *t.* initiated into the human lot
1 Thess. 4:1. already following it, but
  we beg you to do so yet more *t.*

thought-s
Mat. 7:3. with never a *t.* for the great
  plank in your own
  18:23. the kingdom of Heaven, therefore, should be *t.* of in this way
Mark 2:6. lawyers sitting there and they
  t.
  2:8. why do you harbour *t.* like these
  6:49. they *t.* it was as a ghost
Luke 3:23. the son, as people *t.*, of
  Joseph
  6:41. never a *t.* for the great plank in
  your own
  21:26. the *t.* of all that is coming upon
  the world
  24:37. they *t.* they were seeing a ghost
Acts 7:25. he *t.* his fellow-countrymen
  would understand
  16:13. where we *t.* there would be a
  place of prayer

Acts 27:13. they *t*. that their purpose
    27:42. the soldiers *t*. they had better
      kill the prisoners
Rom. 3:18. reverence for God does not
      enter their *t*.
    13:14. give no more *t*. to satisfying the
      bodily appetites
1 Cor. 1:10. be firmly joined in unity of
      mind and *t*.
Phil. 4:7. will keep guard over your
      hearts and your *t*.
    4:8. fill all your *t*. with these things
Col. 3:2. let your *t*. dwell on that higher
      realm
1 Tim. 2:8. excluding angry or quarrel-
      some *t*.
Heb. 12:17. he found no way open for
      second *t*.
1 Pet. 2:19. because God is in his *t*.
    3:8. be one in *t*. and feeling
2 Pet. 3:1. to rouse you to honest *t*.
Rev. 2:23. I am the searcher of men's
      hearts and *t*.

thoughtless
Mat. 12:36. a *t*. word that comes from
      men's lips

thousand-s
Luke 12:1. a crowd of many *t*. had
      gathered
    16:6. a *t*. gallons of olive oil
    16:7. a *t*. bushels of wheat

thrash-ed
Mat. 21:35. took his servants and *t*. one
Mark 12:3. they took him, *t*. him
Luke 20:10. the tenants *t*. him
    20:11. he also was *t*., outrageously
      treated

threaten-ed
Mat. 2:20. the men who *t*. the child's
      life are dead

three
Mat. 14:25. between *t*. and six in the
      morning he came to them
    20:3. going out *t*. hours later
    20:5. at noon he went out again, and
      at *t*. in the afternoon
    26:34 ⎱
    26:75 ⎰ you will disown me *t*. times
    27:45. from midday until *t*. in the
      afternoon
    27:46. about *t*. Jesus cried aloud
Mark 6:48. between *t*. and six in the
      morning
    15:33. which lasted till *t*. in the after-
      noon
    15:34. at *t*. Jesus cried aloud
Luke 23:44. a darkness over the whole
      land, which lasted until *t*.
John 6:19. they had rowed about *t*. or
      four miles
Acts 3:1. at *t*. in the afternoon

    10:3. about *t*. in the afternoon he
      had a vision
Rev. 12:14. for *t*. years and a half she
      was to be sustained

threefold
1 John 5:9. this *t*. testimony is indeed
      that of God himself

thresh-ing-er
Mat. 3:12. he will winnow his *t*.-floor
Luke 3:17. to winnow his *t*.-floor
1 Cor. 9:9. ⎱
1 Tim. 5:18 ⎰ a *t*. ox shall not be muzzled
1 Cor. 9:10. the ploughman should
      plough, and the *t*. *t*.

threw
Mat. 13:48. *t*. the worthless away
    27:5. he *t*. the money down in the
      temple
Mark 1:26. the unclean spirit *t*. the man
      into convulsions
    5:22. *t*. himself down at his feet
    9:20. it *t*. the boy into convulsions
    10:50. he *t*. off his cloak, sprang up
    14:35. *t*. himself on the ground, and
      prayed
Luke 4:29. *t*. him out of the town
    17:16. he *t*. himself down at Jesus's
      feet
    19:35. they *t*. their cloaks on the colt
Acts 16:29. *t*. himself down before Paul
    16:37. they *t*. us into prison
    20:10. Paul went down, *t*. himself
      upon him
Rev. 8:5. *t*. it down upon the earth
    14:19. *t*. them into the great wine-
      press
    18:19. they *t*. dust on their heads
    20:3. he *t*. him into the abyss

thrill
Luke 1:14. your heart will *t*. with joy

thrive
1 Pet. 2:2. you may *t*. upon it to your
      souls' health

throne-s
Luke 1:52. torn imperial powers from
      their *t*.
    23:42. remember me when you come
      to your *t*.
Acts 7:18. another king, who knew
      nothing of Joseph, ascended the *t*.
Rev. 2:13. the place where Satan has his
      t.
    11:16. twenty-four elders, seated on
      their *t*.
    16:10. poured his bowl on the *t*. of the
      beast
    18:7. I am a queen on my *t*.
    20:12. standing before the *t*.
    21:3. I heard a loud voice pro-
      claiming from the *t*.

throng
Rev. 7:9. saw a vast *t*.
  19:1. the roar of a vast *t*. in heaven

through
Mat. 1:22. the Lord declared *t*. the prophet
  2:15. what the Lord had declared *t*. the prophet
  2:17. the words spoken *t*. Jeremiah
  2:23. the words spoken *t*. the prophets
  18:7. woe betide the man *t*. whom they come
Mark 2:4. when they had broken *t*. they lowered the stretcher
Luke 16:15. God sees *t*. you
  20:23. he saw *t*. their trick
John 1:3. *t*. him all things came to be
  10:9. anyone who comes into the fold *t*. me shall be safe
1 Cor. 8:6. Jesus Christ, *t*. whom all things came to be
  11:12. *t*. woman that man now comes to be
Heb. 4:14. a great high priest who has passed *t*. the heavens
Rev. 7:14. the men who have passed *t*. the great ordeal

throughout
Mat. 24:14. proclaimed *t*. the earth
Luke 2:1. a general registration *t*. the Roman world
2 Cor. 1:1. dedicated to him *t*. the whole of Achaia
1 Thess. 4:10. all your fellow-Christians *t*. Macedonia
1 Tim. 3:16. believed in *t*. the world
Jam. 1:1. the Twelve Tribes dispersed *t*. the world

throw-s-ing
Mat. 4:6. if you are the Son of God,' he said, '*t*. yourself down
  13:50. *t*. them into the blazing furnace
  15:26   } *t*. it to the dogs
Mark 7:27 }
  9:22. by *t*. him into the fire
  14:58. I will *t*. down this temple
Luke 4:9. *t*. yourself down
  8:41. *t*. himself down at Jesus's feet
  9:39. *t*. him into convulsions
  22:41. withdrew from them about a stone's *t*.
John 8:7. that one of you who is faultless shall *t*. the first stone
  8:59. they picked up stones to *t*. at him
Rom. 13:12. let us therefore *t*. off the deeds of darkness
Eph. 4:25. *t*. off falsehood
Heb. 10:35. do not then *t*. away your confidence
  12:1. we must *t*. off every encumbrance

Rev. 2:10. the Devil will *t*. some of you into prison
  2:22. I will *t*. her on to a bed of pain

thrown
Mat. 3:10. is cut down and *t*. on the fire
  5:13. good for nothing but to be *t*. away
  5:29. than for the whole of it to be *t*. into hell
  6:30. tomorrow is *t*. on the stove
  13:42. these will be *t*. into the blazing furnace
  14:3. *t*. him into prison
  18:8. be *t*. into the eternal fire
  18:9. be *t*. into the fires of hell
Mark 9:42. to be *t*. into the sea
  9:45 }
  9:47 } be *t*. into hell
Luke 3:9. cut down and *t*. on the fire
  12:28. tomorrow is *t*. on the stove
  13:28. and yourselves *t*. out
  14:35. it can only be *t*. away
  17:2. better for him to be *t*. into the sea
John 15:6. *t*. away like a withered branch. The withered branches are heaped together, *t*. on the fire
Acts 14:27. *t*. open the gates of faith to the Gentiles
Rev. 12:9. the great dragon was *t*. down, that serpent of old that led the whole world astray, whose name is Satan, or the Devil-*t*. down to the earth
  12:13. the dragon found that he had been *t*. down
  15:5. the heavenly Tent of Testimony was *t*. open
  19:20. were *t*. alive into the lake of fire

thwarted
1 Thess. 2:18. Satan *t*. us

tickle
2 Tim. 4:3. teachers to *t*. their ears

tidy
Mat. 12:44. house unoccupied, swept clean, and *t*.
Luke 11:25. house swept clean, and *t*.

tie-d
Mat. 12:29. unless he has first *t*. the strong man up
  13:30. *t*. it in bundles for burning
Mark 3:27. unless he has first *t*. the strong man up
John 13:4. taking a towel, *t*. it round him
Acts 22:25. when they *t*. him up for the lash
Gal. 5:1. refuse to be *t*. to the yoke of slavery again

tight

1 Cor. 7:35. I have no wish to keep you on a *t.* rein

timber

Jam. 3:5. a huge stack of *t.* can be set ablaze

time-s

Mat. 1:19. at the same *t.* wanting to save her

3:1. about that *t.* John the Baptist appeared

7:4. all the *t.* there is that plank in your own

9:15. the *t.* will come when the bridegroom will be taken away from them; that will be the *t.* for them to fast

10:19. when the *t.* comes, the words you need will be given

13:39. the harvest is the end of *t.*

13:40. at the end of *t.* the Son of Man will send out his angels

13:49. that is how it will be at the end of *t.*

19:29. will be repaid many *t.* over

21:36. sent other servants, this *t.* a larger number

23:30. if we had been alive in our fathers' *t.*

23:39. until the *t.* when you say

24:6. the *t.* is coming when you will hear the noise of battle

24:21. it will be a *t.* of great distress

24:22. if that *t.* of troubles were not cut short

24:43. at what *t.* of night the burglar was coming

24:44. the Son of Man will come at the *t.* you least expect him

24:45. issue their rations at the proper *t.*

24:48. the master is a long *t.* coming

24:50. at a *t.* he does not know

26:34 }
26:75 } you will disown me three *t.*

28:20. I am with you always, to the end of *t.*

Mark 2:20. the *t.* will come when the bridegroom will be taken away

2:26. in the *t.* of Abiathar the High Priest

13:11. when the *t.* comes say whatever is given you

13:20. he has cut short the *t.*

Luke 1:20. at their proper *t.* my words will be proved true

2:6. the *t.* came for her child to be born

2:21. the *t.* came to circumcise him

2:25. at that *t.* in Jerusalem a man called Simeon

4:2. all that *t.* he had nothing to eat

4:13. the devil departed, biding his *t.*

4:25. in Elijah's *t.*

5:16. from *t.* to *t.* he would withdraw to lonely places for prayer

5:35. a *t.* will come: the bridegroom will be taken away

6:24. you have had your *t.* of happiness

8:29. many a *t.* it had seized him

9:39. from *t.* to *t.* a spirit seizes him

12:12. when the *t.* comes the Holy Spirit will instruct you what to say

12:40. the Son of Man is coming at the *t.* you least expect him

12:45. the master is a long *t.* coming

12:46. at a *t.* he does not know

18:4. for a long *t.* he refused

21:6. the *t.* will come when not one stone of them will be left

21:36. praying at all *t.* for strength

22:28. stood firmly by me in my *t.* of trial

24:53. spent all their *t.* in the temple

John 4:53. this was the exact *t.* when Jesus had said

5:25. a *t.* is coming

5:28. the *t.* is coming when all who are in the grave

5:35. for a *t.* you were ready to exult in his light

9:32. it is unheard of since *t.* began

12:16. at the *t.* his disciples did not understand

19:3. *t.* after *t.* they came up to him

Acts 3:24. they all predicted this present *t.*

5:37. at the *t.* of the census

11:9. a voice from heaven answered a second *t.*

13:20. the *t.* of the prophet Samuel

17:32. we will hear you on this subject some other *t.*

24:4. not to take up too much of your *t.*

24:16. train myself to keep at all *t.* a clear conscience

Gal. 6:9. we shall in due *t.* reap our harvest

Eph. 2:1. *t.* was when you were dead in your sins

1 Thess. 2:16. all this *t.* they have been making up the full measure of their guilt

2 Thess. 3:11. idling their *t.* away

2 Tim. 4:5. keep calm and sane at all *t.*

Philem. 15. you lost him for a *t.*

Heb. 6:7. rain that falls upon it from *t.* to *t.*

7:3. he remains a priest for all *t.*

9:26. if that were so, he would have had to suffer many *t.*

10:11. offering *t.* after *t.* the same sacrifices

10:12. Christ offered for all *t.* one sacrifice

Heb. 10:14. perfected for all *t.* those who are thus consecrated

1 Pet. 1:12. the matter they treated of was not for their *t.*

2 Pet. 1:15. remembering these things at all *t.*

Jude 25. before all *t.*, now, and for evermore

Rev. 2:21. I have given her *t.* to repent

11:6. during the *t.* of their prophesying

timely
Heb. 4:16. find *t.* help

Timothy
Phil. 2:22. *T.* record is known to you

2:23. *T.*, then, I hope to send

tiny-iest
Mark 12:42. dropped in two *t.* coins

Luke 21:2. a poor widow putting in two *t.* coins

Jam. 3:4. can be directed by a *t.* rudder

3:5. set ablaze by the *t.* spark

tipple-ing
1 Pet. 4:3. drunkenness, riot, and *t.*

tiptoe
Luke 3:15. the people were on the *t.* of expectation

tire-d
John 4:6. Jesus, *t.* after his journey

Gal. 6:9. let us never *t.* of doing good

2 Thess. 3:13. never *t.* of doing right

tireless-ly
Col. 4:13. he works *t.* for you

Heb. 13:17. *t.* in their concern for you

tithe-s-d
Heb. 7:2. Abraham gave him a *t.* of everything

7:4. a *t.* of the finest of the spoil

7:6. Melchizedek, though he does not trace his descent from them, has *t.* Abraham

7:9. Levi, who receives *t.*, has himself been *t.*

Titius
Acts 18:7. a worshipper of God named *T.* Justus

title
Luke 1:32. he will bear the *t.* 'Son of the Most High

Eph. 1:21. any *t.* of sovereignty that can be named

Heb. 1:4. the *t.* he has inherited is superior

today
Mat. 6:11. give us *t.* our daily bread

Luke 2:11. *t.* in the city of David

4:21. *t.*,' he said', 'in your very hearing this text has come true

Acts 23:1. live *t.*, with a perfectly clear conscience

24:21. before you *t.* is the resurrection of the dead

26:2. make my defence *t.*

26:6. I stand in the dock *t.*

2 Cor. 5:1. the earthly frame that houses us *t.*

Gal. 4:25. represents the Jerusalem of *t.*

4:29. persecuted the spiritual son, so it is *t.*

Jude 8. so too with these men *t.*

together
Mat. 17:22. they were going about *t.* in Galilee

26:4. they conferred *t.* on a scheme

28:12. meeting with the elders and conferring *t.*

Mark 12:42. two tiny coins, *t.* worth a farthing

Luke 20:14. they talked it over *t.*

John 15:6. the withered branches are heaped *t.*

20:19. the disciples were *t.* behind locked doors

Acts 1:14. all these were constantly at prayer *t.*

2:1. all *t.* in one place

4:1. the chief priests came upon them, *t.* with the Controller of the Temple

6:2. called the whole body of disciples *t.*

14:5. a move was made by Gentiles and Jews *t.*

18:3. they carried on business *t.*

28:3. Paul had got *t.* an armful of sticks

Rom. 15:10. make merry *t.* with his own people

1 Cor. 12:12. many as they are, *t.* make up one body

12:26. if one organ suffers, they all suffer *t.* If one flourishes, they all rejoice *t.*

2 Cor. 1:1. *t.* with all who are dedicated

7:3. we meet it *t.*

Eph. 3:6. sharers *t.* in the promise

Phil. 4:2. to agree *t.* in the Lord's fellowship

Col. 1:17. all things are held *t.* in him

3:14. love, to bind all *t.*

1 John 1:3. that you and we *t.* may share in a common life

1:7. then we share *t.* a common life

Rev. 7:10. they shouted *t.*

17:16. they *t.* with the beast

toil-ed-ing
John 4:38. a crop for which you have not *t.* Others *t.* and you have come in for the harvest of their *t.*

Rom. 16:6. Mary, who *t.* hard for you

16:12. Tryphaena and Tryphosa, who

t. in the Lord's service and dear Persis who has *t.*

2 Cor. 11:27. I have *t.* and drudged

Col. 1:29. I am *t.* strenuously

1 Thess. 2:9. we *t.* and drudged

2 Thess. 3:8. we *t.* and drudged, we worked for a living

Rev. 2:2. I know all your ways, your *t.*

token

Mark 1:4 ⎫
Luke 3:3 ⎬ baptism in *t.* of repentance

Acts 13:24. baptism as a *t.* of repentance

19:4. was a baptism in *t.* of repentance

told

Mat. 5:21. our forefathers were *t.*

14:19. he *t.* the people to sit down on the grass

28:16. where Jesus had *t.* them to meet him

Mark 5:43. *t.* them to give her something to eat

16:11. when they were *t.* that he was alive

Luke 9:6. everywhere they *t.* the good news

John 12:17. *t.* what they had seen and heard

Acts 8:35. he *t.* him the good news of Jesus

10:8. *t.* them the whole story

Eph. 4:21. were you not *t.* of him

tolerance

Rom. 2:4. his wealth of kindness, of *t.*

tolerant

2 Tim. 2:24. a good teacher, *t.*, and gentle

tolerate-d

Rom. 9:22. *t.* very patiently those vessels

1 Cor. 5:1. such as even pagans do not *t.*

Rev. 2:20. you *t.* that Jezebel

toll

Mat. 17:25. collect tax or *t.*

Rom. 13:7. pay tax and *t.*

2 Cor. 11:8. I took *t.* of other congregations

tomb-s

Mat. 28:8. they hurried away from the *t.* in awe

Mark 15:46. a *t.* cut out of the rock

16:2. after sunrise, they came to the *t.*

16:3. the entrance to the *t.*

16:5. they went into the *t.*

16:8. ran away from the *t.*

Luke 11:47. you build the *t.* of the prophets

11:48. you provide the *t.*

23:53. laid it in a *t.* cut out of the rock

23:55. they took note of the *t.*

24:1. very early they came to the *t.*

24:2. the stone had been rolled away from the *t.*

24:9. returning from the *t.*, they reported

24:22. they went early to the *t.*

24:24. some of our people went to the *t.*

John 11:17. Lazarus had already been four days in the *t.*

11:31. they supposed that she was going to the *t.*

11:38. then he went over to the *t.*

12:17. he called Lazarus out of the *t.*

19:41. in the garden a new *t.*

19:42. the *t.* was near at hand

20:1. Mary of Magdala came to the *t.*

20:2. they have taken the Lord out of his *t.*

20:3. made their way to the *t.*

20:4. outran Peter and reached the *t.* first

20:6. he went into the *t.*

20:8. who had reached the *t.* first went in

20:11. Mary stood at the *t.* outside, weeping. As she wept, she peered into the *t.*

Acts 2:29. his *t.* is here to this very day

7:16. the *t.* which Abraham had bought

13:29. took him down from the gibbet and laid him in a *t.*

tone

Gal. 4:20. then I could modify my *t.*

tongue

Luke 18:39. told him sharply to hold his *t.*

tonight

Luke 22:34. Peter, the cock will not crow *t.*

22:61. *t.* before the cock crows

took

Mat. 8:15. so he *t.* her by the hand

12:1. Jesus *t.* a walk on the Sabbath

14:7. he *t.* an oath to give her anything

22:5. but they *t.* no notice

22:22. this answer *t.* them by surprise

Mark 5:14. the men in charge of them *t.* to their heels

12:3. they *t.* him, thrashed him

16:13. *t.* the news to the others

Luke 2:2. it *t.* place when Quirinius was governor

4:9. the devil *t.* him to Jerusalem

4:29. *t.* him to the brow of the hill

7:40. Jesus *t.* him up and said

Luke 23:55. they *t*. note of the tomb
John 9:16. so they *t*. different sides
9:27. but you *t*. no notice
13:26. he *t*. it out and gave it to Judas
18:3. Judas *t*. a detachment of soldiers
Acts 5:12. many remarkable and wonderful things *t*. place
5:40. they *t*. his advice
15:14. God *t*. notice of the Gentiles
23:9. openly *t*. sides and declared
28:7. he *t*. us in and entertained us
Rom. 16:22. I Tertius, who *t*. this letter down
Phil. 3:12. for which Christ once *t*. hold of me
2 Tim. 1:17. *t*. pains to search me out
Heb. 11:7. Noah, divinely warned about the unseen future, *t*. good heed
Rev. 13:1. he *t*. his stand on the seashore

tooth
Gal. 5:15. if you go on fighting one another, *t*. and nail

top
Luke 4:33. he shrieked at the *t*. of his voice
Acts 21:28. on *t*. of all this he has brought Greeks into the temple
26:24. Festus shouted at the *t*. of his voice

torch-es
Rev. 4:5. before the throne were seven flaming *t*.
8:10. a great star shot from the sky, flaming like a *t*.

tore
Mat. 26:65 ⎱ the High Priest *t*. his robes
Mark 14:63 ⎰
Acts 14:14. they *t*. their clothes
16:22. *t*. off the prisoners' clothes
27:14. a fierce wind, the 'Northeaster' as they call it, *t*. down

torment-ed
Mat. 15:22. my daughter is *t*. by a devil
Heb. 10:33. some of you were abused and *t*.

torn
Mat. 27:51. the curtain of the temple was *t*. in two
Mark 1:10. the heavens *t*. open and the Spirit, like a dove
15:38. the curtain of the temple was *t*. in two
Luke 1:52. he has *t*. imperial powers from their thrones
23:45. the curtain of the temple was *t*. in two
John 21:11. the net was not *t*.
Acts 23:10. afraid that Paul would be *t*. in pieces

Gal. 4:15. you would have *t*. out your very eyes
Phil. 1:23. I am *t*. two ways

torture-d
Mat. 18:34. he condemned the man to *t*.
2 Pet. 2:8. their evil courses *t*. that good man's heart

toss
John 19:24. we must not tear this; let us *t*. for it

total
Acts 19:19. the *t*. value was reckoned up
2 Pet. 2:6. condemned them to *t*. destruction

touch-ed
Luke 1:15. he shall never *t*. wine
24:39. it is I myself. *T*. me and see
Acts 5:33 ⎱ this *t*. them on the raw
7:54 ⎰
17:27. to seek God, and, it might be, *t*. and find him

tour-ed
Acts 8:40. *t*. the country, preaching
9:32. Peter was making a general *t*.

tow-ing
John 21:8. *t*. the net full of fish

toward-s
Mat. 14:29. walked over the water *t*. Jesus
20:17. Jesus was journeying *t*. Jerusalem
Mark 6:33. from all the towns *t*. the place
6:48. he came *t*. them, walking on the lake
Luke 1:50. *t*. those who fear him
9:51. set his face resolutely *t*. Jerusalem
John 1:29. he saw Jesus coming *t*. him
1:36. John looked *t*. him and said
4:30. made their way *t*. him
6:5. seeing a large crowd coming *t*. him
Acts 3:11. running in astonishment *t*. them
19:31. who were friendly *t*. him
2 Cor. 1:11. the gracious favour God has shown *t*. us
9:12. a contribution *t*. the needs of God's people
Eph. 1:15. the love you bear *t*. all God's people
4:22. deluded by its lusts, is sinking *t*. death
Phil. 2:5. your bearing *t*. one another
Col. 1:4. the love you bear *t*. all God's people
1 Thess. 2:10. our behaviour *t*. you
2 Thess. 3:5. may the Lord direct your hearts *t*. God's love
2 Tim. 2:24. kindly *t*. all

Tit. 3:2. a consistently gentle disposition
t. all men
Heb. 6:2. let us advance *t.* maturity
Jam. 4:5. turns *t.* envious desires
1 Pet. 1:22. sincere affection *t.* your
brother Christians
3:12. the Lord's eyes are turned *t.*
the righteous
5:5. humility *t.* each other

town-s, (the word town frequently used)
Mat. 2:23. he settled in a *t.* called
Nazareth
4:25. from Galilee and the Ten *T.*
5:14. a *t.* that stands on a hill
9:1. came to his own *t.*
13:54. came to his home *t.*
Mark 5:20. spread the news in the Ten
T.
6:1. went to his home *t.*
7:31. through the territory of the Ten
T.
Luke 4:23. do the same here in your
own home *t.*

townspeople
Luke 7:12. many of the *t.* were there
with her
Acts 14:4. the mass of the *t.* were
divided

trace-d
Luke 11:36. with no *t.* of darkness
Rom. 9:7. your posterity shall be *t.*
Heb. 7:6. he does not *t.* his descent from
them
11:18. of Isaac your posterity shall be
t.

trade-s-ing
Luke 19:13. *t.* with this while I am away
Acts 18:3. because he was of the same *t.*
19:25. these men and the workers in
allied *t.*
Jam. 4:13. *t.* and making money
2 Pet. 2:3. they will *t.* on your credulity
Rev. 18:22. no more shall craftsmen of
any *t.* be found in you

trader-s
Luke 19:45. began driving out the *t.*
Rev. 18:15. the *t.* in all these wares
18:23. your *t.* were once the merchant
princes

tradition-s
Luke 1:2. following the *t.* handed down
to us
1 Cor. 11:2. the *t.* I handed on to you
11:23. the *t.* which I handed on to you
Phil. 4:9. the *t.* I have passed on
1 Thess. 4:1. the *t.* of the way we must
live to please God

traditional
Mark 7:4. they have a *t.* rule to maintain

train-s-ed-ing
Luke 6:40. when his *t.* is complete, will
reach his teacher's level
Acts 7:22. Moses was *t.* in all the wisdom
of the Egyptians
22:3. *t.* in every point of our ancestral
law
24:16. *t.* myself to keep at all times a
clear conscience
Rom. 2:20. to *t.* the stupid
5:3. suffering *t.* us to endure
1 Cor. 9:25. every athlete goes into
strict *t.*
Eph. 4:8. with captives in his *t.*
1 Tim. 4:7. keep yourself in *t.* for the
practice of religion
4:8. the *t.* of the body
Heb. 5:14. their perceptions are *t.* by
long use
12:11. for those who have been *t.* by it

traitor
Mat. 26:46. the *t.* is upon us
26:48. the *t.* gave them this sign
27:3. Judas the *t.*
Mark 14:44. the *t.* had agreed with them
upon a signal
John 18:5. there stood Judas the *t.* with
them

trample-d
Luke 8:5. some seed fell along the footpath, where it was *t.* on
21:24. Jerusalem will be *t.* down by
foreigners
Heb. 10:29. who has *t.* under foot the
Son of God
Rev. 11:2. they will *t.* the Holy City
underfoot

tranquil
1 Tim. 2:2. that we may lead a *t.* and
quiet life

transcendent
2 Cor. 4:7. such *t.* power does not come
from us

transfigure-d
2 Cor. 3:18. we are *t.* into his likeness
Phil. 3:21. he will *t.* the body

transient
Heb. 11:25. the *t.* pleasures of sin

Transjordan
Mat. 4:25. Judaea, and from *T.*
Mark 3:8. Idumaea and *T.*
10:1. he came into the regions of
Judaea and *T.*

translate-d
Acts 13:8. Elymas the sorcerer (so his
name may be *t.*

translucent
Rev. 21:21. streets of the city were of
pure gold, like *t.* glass

transport-ed
1 Pet. 1:8. *t.* with a joy too great for words

trap-s
Mat. 22:15. a plan to *t.* him in his own words
Mark 12:13. were sent to *t.* him with a question
Luke 21:34. so that the great Day closes upon you suddenly like a *t.*
1 Cor. 3:19. he *t.* the wise in their own cunning

travel-s-ed-ing
Mat. 23:15. you *t.* over sea and land to win one convert
Luke 9:6. *t.* from village to village
  10:4. carry no purse or pack, and *t.* barefoot
  17:11. he was *t.* through the borderlands
Acts 9:7. who were *t.* with him stood speechless
  15:3. *t.* through Phoenicia and Samaria
  15:30. *t.* down to Antioch
  15:41. *t.* through Syria and Cilicia
  16:6. they *t.* through the Phrygian and Galatian region
  17:1. they now *t.* by way of Amphipolis
  19:1. Paul *t.* through the inland regions
  20:2. he *t.* through those parts of the country
  20:13. he was going to *t.* by road
  26:12. I was *t.* to Damascus
  26:13. my *t.*-companions
Rom. 15:24. see you as I *t.* through
1 Cor. 10:4. the supernatural rock that accompanied their *t.*
  16:5. I am *t.* by way of Macedonia
Tit. 3:13. help Zenas the lawyer and Apollos on their *t.*

traveller-s
Heb. 11:13. passing *t.* on earth

treachery
Rom. 1:29. rivalry, *t.*, and malevolence
  3:13. they use their tongues for *t.*

treasure-s-d
Luke 2:19. Mary *t.* up all these things
  2:51. his mother *t.* up all these things in her heart
Rom. 9:21. two vessels, one to be *t.*
  15:27. shared their spiritual *t.* with the Gentiles
Eph. 3:16. out of the *t.* of his glory
1 Tim. 6:19. to give away and to share, and so acquire a *t.*
2 Tim. 1:14. guard the *t.* put into our charge

treasurer
Rom. 16:23. Erastus, *t.* of this city

treat-s-ed-ing
Mat. 7:12. *t.* others as you would like them to *t.* you
  18:17. *t.* him as you would a pagan
Mark 9:12. to be *t.* with contempt
  12:4. *t.* outrageously
Luke 2:48. why have you *t.* us like this
  6:23. the same way did their fathers *t.* the prophets
  6:26. *t.* the false prophets
  6:28. pray for those who *t.* you spitefully
  6:31. *t.* others as you would like them to *t.* you
  15:19. *t.* me as one of your paid servants
  20:11. outrageously *t.*
  23:11. Herod and his troops *t.* him with contempt
John 15:21. it is on my account that they will *t.* you thus
Acts 28:2. the rough islanders *t.* us with uncommon kindness
Rom. 8:36. we have been *t.* like sheep for slaughter
  11:28. they are *t.* as God's enemies
1 Cor. 4:13. we are *t.* as the scum of the earth
  12:23. are *t.* with special honour
2 Cor. 12:13. *t.* worse than the other congregations
Eph. 5:29. that is how Christ *t.* the church
1 Thess. 2:14. you have been *t.* by your countrymen as they are *t.* by the Jews
2 Thess. 3:15. I do not mean *t.* him as an enemy
1 Tim. 1:8. provided we *t.* it as law
  5:1. *t.* the younger men as brothers
Heb. 10:33. others stood loyally by those who were so *t.*
  12:7. God is *t.* you as sons
Jam. 5:11. how the Lord *t.* him in the end
1 Pet. 1:12. the matter they *t.* of

treatment
Mark 5:26. in spite of long *t.* by doctors
Jam. 5:10. a pattern of patience under ill-*t.*

tree
Mark 11:14. he said to the *t.*, 'May no one ever again eat fruit from you
Rev. 22:19. his share in the *t.* of life

tremor
Phil. 1:28. without so much as a *t.*

Tres
Acts 28:15. Appii Forum and *T.* Tabernae

trial-s

Mat. 12:41 ⎱ the Judgement when this
12:42 ⎰ generation is on *t.*
Luke 11:31 ⎱ when the men of this
11:32 ⎰ generation are on *t.*
22:28. stood firmly by me in my times
of *t.*
Acts 3:13. Jesus, whom you committed
for *t.*
20:19. the sorrows and *t.* that came
upon me
23:6. the true issue in this *t.*
24:21. the true issue in my *t.*
25:9. stand *t.* on these charges before
me
25:20. stand his *t.* there on these
issues
Rom. 3:4. win the verdict when thou art
on *t.*
1 Cor. 10:13. faced no *t.* beyond what
man can bear
Jam. 1:2. to face *t.* of many kinds
1:12. the man who remains steadfast
under *t.*
1 Pet. 1:6. under *t.* of many kinds
2 Pet. 2:9. rescue the godly out of *t.*

tribe-s

Rev. 5:9. purchase for God men of
every *t.*
7:9. from every nation, of all *t.*
11:9. men from every people and *t.*
13:7. authority over every *t.* and
people
14:6. an eternal gospel to proclaim to
those on earth, to every nation and
t.

tribunal

John 5:45. your accuser at God's *t.*
19:13. took his seat on the *t.*
Acts 25:10. I am now standing before
the Emperor's *t.*
Rom. 14:10. we shall all stand before
God's *t.*
2 Cor. 5:10. our lives laid open before
the *t.* of Christ

tribute

Heb. 13:15. the *t.* of lips which acknowledge his name

trick-ed

Mat. 2:16. Herod saw how the astrologers had *t.* him
26:4. to have Jesus arrested by some
t.
Luke 20:23. he saw through their *t.*
2 Cor. 12:16. unscrupulous enough, you
say, to use a *t.* to catch you

tried

Mat. 3:14. John *t.* to dissuade him
26:59. *t.* to find some allegation
against Jesus

Mark 9:22. often it has *t.* to make an
end of him
9:38. as he was not one of us, we *t.* to
stop him
14:51. they *t.* to seize him
14:55. *t.* to find some evidence against
Jesus
Luke 5:18. they *t.* to bring him in and
set him down in front of Jesus
9:49. we *t.* to stop him
20:11. he *t.* again and sent a second
servant
20:12. he *t.* once more with a third
John 7:30. at this they *t.* to seize him
19:12. Pilate *t.* hard to release him
Acts 7:26. *t.* to bring them to make up
their quarrel
9:26. *t.* to join the body of disciples
19:13. *t.* their hand at using the name
of the Lord Jesus
25:10. the Emperor's tribunal, and
that is where I must be *t.*
26:11. I *t.* by repeated punishment to
make them renounce their faith
26:21. seized me in the temple and *t.*
to do away with me
27:30. the sailors *t.* to abandon ship
Gal. 1:13. persecuted the church of
God, and *t.* to destroy it
1:23. the faith which once he *t.* to
destroy
Heb. 3:9. your forefathers *t.* me
1 Pet. 1:11. they *t.* to find out what was
the time

tries

3 John 10. *t.* to expel them from the
congregation

trifling

1 Cor. 6:2. are you incompetent to deal
with these *t.* cases

trip

Rom. 9:32. a stumbling-stone and a
rock to *t.* them up
1 Pet. 2:7. a stone to *t.* over

triumph-s

Jam. 2:13. mercy *t.* over judgement
1 Pet. 2:9. the *t.* of him who has called
you out of darkness

triumphal

2 Cor. 2:14. captives in Christ's *t.*
procession

triumphant

1 Pet. 4:13. your joy will be *t.*

troops

Mat. 22:7. he sent *t.* to kill those
murderers
Luke 23:11. Herod and his *t.* treated
him with contempt
John 18:12. the *t.* with their commander
Acts 21:32. saw the commandant and

his *t.*, they stopped beating Paul

Acts 23:10. he ordered the *t.* to go down

23:23. two hundred light-armed *t.*

23:27. I intervened with the *t.*

troth

1 Tim. 5:12. condemned for breaking their *t.* with him

trouble-s-ed

Mat. 6:34. each day has *t.* enough of its own

13:21. when there is *t.* or persecution

24:22. if that time of *t.* were not cut short

27:19. I was much *t.* on his account in my dreams

Mark 4:17. when there is *t.* or persecution

5:29. knew in herself that she was cured of her *t.*

5:34. go in peace, free for ever from this *t.*

13:20. if the Lord had not cut short that time of *t.*

Luke 6:18. those who were *t.* with unclean spirits were cured

13:12. you are rid of your *t.*

21:36. strength to pass safely through all these imminent *t.*

John 16:33. in the world you will have *t.*

Acts 7:10. rescued him from all his *t.*

17:6. the men who have made *t.*

17:13. to stir up *t.*

19:33. some of the crowd explained the *t.* to Alexander

Rom. 12:12. in *t.* stand firm

1 Cor. 7:21. were you a slave when you were called? Do not let that *t.* you

2 Cor. 4:17. our *t.* are slight and short-lived

7:4. in all our many *t.* my cup is full of consolation

7:11. cleared yourselves of blame in this *t.*

8:2. the *t.* they have been through

Phil. 1:17. meaning to stir up fresh *t.* for me

3:1. to repeat what I have written to you before is no *t.* to me

4:14. kind of you to share the burden of my *t.*

2 Thess. 1:4. all the *t.* you endure

2 Tim. 1:16. he has often relieved me in my *t.*

3:1. the final age of this world is to be a time of *t.*

Jam. 5:9. do not blame your *t.* on one another

5:13. is anyone among you in *t.*

truckle-ing

Mat. 22:16. you teach in all honesty the

way of life that God requires, *t.* to no man

Mark 12:14. Master, you are an honest man, we know, and *t.* to no man

true

Mat. 16:25. let himself be lost for my sake, he will find his *t.* self

16:26. winning the whole world, at the cost of his *t.* self

Mark 8:36. gain by winning the whole world at the cost of his *t.* self

Luke 1:20. my words will be proved *t.*

4:21. in your very hearing this text has come *t.*

9:25. at the cost of his *t.* self

18:4. *t.*, I care nothing for God or man

18:31. written by the prophets will come *t.* for the Son of Man

21:19. standing firm you will win *t.* life

24:34. it is *t.*: the Lord has risen

24:41. it seemed too good to be *t.*

John 15:25. this text in their Law had to come *t.*

19:24. thus the text of Scripture came *t.*

Acts 1:16. the prophecy in Scripture was bound to come *t.*

10:34. how *t.* it is that God has no favourites

12:11. Peter came to himself. 'Now I know it is *t.*

14:22. encouraging them to be *t.* to their religion

22:3. I am a *t.*-born Jew

23:6. the *t.* issue in this trial is our hope of the resurrection

24:21. the *t.* issue in my trial before you

Rom. 1:25. the *t.* God for a false one

2:28. the *t.* Jew is not he who is such in externals, neither is the *t.* circumcision the external

2:29. the *t.* Jew is he who is such inwardly, and the *t.* circumcision is of the heart

3:30. if it be *t.* that God is one

6:16. this is *t.* whether you serve sin

7:13. sin exposed its *t.* character

9:7. nor, because they are Abraham's offspring, are they all his *t.* children

1 Cor. 3:18. he must become a fool to gain *t.* wisdom

6:13. food is for the belly and the belly for food,' you say. *T.* . . . it is not *t.* that the body is for lust

8:2. he knows nothing yet, in the *t.* sense of knowing

12:10. distinguish *t.* spirits from false

15:54. then the saying of Scripture will come *t.*

2 Cor. 11:2. as a chaste virgin to her *t.*
and only husband
11:8. it is *t.* that I took toll of other
congregations
11:31. knows that what I say is *t.*
12:12. the marks of a *t.* apostle were
there
13:4. *t.*, he died on the cross in weakness
Phil. 1:10. the gift of *t.* discrimination
1:15. others proclaim him in *t.* goodwill
Col. 2:23. *t.*, it has an air of wisdom
1 Tim. 1:2. his *t.*-born son in the faith
2:7. to instruct the nations in the *t.*
faith
Tit. 1:4. to Titus, my *t.*-born son in the
faith
1:9. he must adhere to the *t.* doctrine
Heb. 10:1. no *t.* image, of the good
things which were to come
12:8. no *t.* sons
12:10. for our *t.* welfare
Jam. 2:25. the same is *t.* of the prostitute
Rahab
3:18. *t.* justice is the harvest reaped by
peacemakers
2 Pet. 1:3. everything that makes for life
and *t.* religion
2:1. Israel had false prophets as well
as *t.*
Rev. 22:11. the dedicated man be *t.* to
his dedication

truly
John 7:28. I was sent by the One who *t.*
is
17:3. to know thee who alone art *t.*
God
Rom. 9:6. not all descendants of Israel
are *t.* Israel
1 John 2:19. not all in our company *t.*
belong to it
Rev. 3:18. gold refined in the fire, to
make you *t.* rich

trumpet-s
Mat. 6:2. do not announce it with a
flourish of *t.*
Rev. 8:7. the first blew his *t.*
8:8. the second angel blew his *t.*
8:10. the third angel blew his *t.*
8:12. the fourth angel blew his *t.*
9:1. then the fifth angel blew his *t.*
9:13. the sixth angel then blew his *t.*
10:7. when the time comes for the
seventh angel to sound his *t.*
11:15. then the seventh angel blew his
t.

trust-s-ed-ing
Luke 16:10. the man who can be *t.* in
little things can be *t.* also in great
John 2:24. Jesus for his part would not
t. himself to them

5:24. puts his *t.* in him who sent me
12:36. while you have the light, *t.* to
the light
14:1. *t.* in God always; *t.* also in me
19:35. an eyewitness, whose evidence
is to be *t.*
Acts 10:43. everyone who *t.* in him
receives forgiveness of sins
11:17. put our *t.* in the Lord Jesus
Christ
16:31. put your *t.* in the Lord Jesus
19:4. put their *t.* in one who was to
come
20:21. *t.* in our Lord Jesus
26:18. by *t.* in me, they may obtain
forgiveness of sins
27:25. I *t.* in God that it will turn out
as I have been told
1 Cor. 7:25. one who by God's mercy is
fit to be *t.*
9:17. I am simply discharging a *t.*
Eph. 1:19. the resources of his power
open to us who *t.* in him
2:8. you are saved, through *t.* him
3:12. the confidence born of *t.* in him
Col. 1:7. a *t.* worker for Christ
1 Thess. 5:24. he who calls you is to be
t.
2 Thess. 3:3. the Lord is to be *t.*
1 Tim. 1:12. judging me worthy of this *t.*
1:15 ⎫
4:9 ⎬ here are words you may *t.*
2 Tim. 1:12. I know who it is in whom I
have *t.*
2:2. into the charge of men you can *t.*
2:11. here are words you may *t.*
Tit. 3:8. these are words you may *t.*
Heb. 10:23. the Giver of the promise
may be *t.*
1 Pet. 1:8. *t.* in him now without seeing
him
1:21. through him you have come to
t. in God
1 John 1:9. may be *t.* to forgive our sins
4:1. do not *t.* any and every spirit

trustee-s
Gal. 4:2. under guardians and *t.*

trustworthy
Mat. 25:21, 23. you have proved *t.* in a
small way
Luke 16:11. if, then, you have not
proved *t.*
19:17. you have shown yourself *t.*
1 Cor. 4:2. stewards are expected to
show themselves *t.*
4:17. a most *t.* Christian
Eph. 6:21. *t.* helper in the Lord's work
Col. 4:7. our dear brother and *t.* helper
4:9. our *t.* and dear brother
1 Tim. 3:11. sober and *t.* in every way
Tit. 2:10. strictly honest and *t.*
Rev. 21:5 ⎫
22:6 ⎬ these words are *t.* and true

trusty
Mat. 24:45. who is the *t.* servant
25:21 ⎰ well done, my good and *t.*
25:23 ⎱ servant
Luke 12:42. who is the *t.* and sensible man
1 Pet. 5:12. Silvanus, our *t.* brother

truth-s
John 1:51. in *t.*, in very *t.* I tell you all
3:5. Jesus answered, 'In *t.* I tell you
4:18. you told me the *t.* there
4:42. this is in *t.* the Saviour of the world
6:32. the *t.* is, not that Moses gave you the bread
8:49. the *t.* is that I am honouring my Father
8:55. in *t.* I know him and obey his word
9:24. speak the *t.* before God
Acts 7:51. heathen still at heart and deaf to the *t.*
20:30. distort the *t.* to induce the disciples to break away
21:34. he could not get at the *t.* because of the hubbub
23:11. you have affirmed the *t.* about me
24:8. you can ascertain from him the *t.*
Rom. 11:7. the rest were made blind to the *t.*
11:25. there is a deep *t.* here
1 Cor. 1:6. the evidence for the *t.* of Christ
2:1. I declared the attested *t.* of God
2:13. we are interpreting spiritual *t.*
9:21. I am not in *t.* outside God's law
11:18. I believe there is some *t.* in it
13:2. I may have the gift of prophecy, and know every hidden *t.*
15:20. the *t.* is, Christ was raised to life
2 Cor. 6:6. our grasp of *t.*
11:6. we have made known to you the full *t.*
Gal. 1:20. what I write is plain *t.*
Eph. 4:24. the just and devout life called for by the *t.*
5:32. it is a great *t.* that is hidden here
Phil. 1:7. to vouch for the *t.* of the Gospel
1 Tim. 3:9. a firm hold on the deep *t.* of our faith
2 Tim. 3:14. stand by the *t.* you have learned
3:16. teaching the *t.*
Tit. 3:15. those who are our friends in *t.*

try-ing
Mat. 19:14. let the children come to me; do not *t.* to stop them
22:18. why are you *t.* to catch me out

Mark 10:14. let the children come to me; do not *t.* to stop them
12:15. why are you *t.* to catch me out
14:1. *t.* to devise some cunning plan to seize him
Luke 6:19. the crowd was *t.* to touch him
13:24. many will *t.* to enter and not be able
14:7. the guests were *t.* to secure the places of honour
14:19. I am on my way to *t.* them out
18:16. let the little ones come to me; do not *t.* to stop them
22:2. *t.* to devise some means of doing away with him
John 18:31. *t.* him by your own law
Acts 5:28. you are *t.* to make us responsible for that man's death
9:21. *t.* to destroy those who invoke this name
13:8. *t.* to turn the Governor away from the Faith
17:18. what can this charlatan be *t.* to say
18:4. *t.* to convince both Jews and pagans
21:13. why are you *t.* to weaken my resolution
Rom. 10:3. ignore God's way of righteousness, and *t.* to set up their own
11:14. I *t.* to stir emulation in the men of my own race
1 Cor. 10:33. I always *t.* to meet everyone half-way
Gal. 1:7. *t.* to distort the gospel of Christ
6:12. *t.* to force circumcision upon you
Eph. 5:1. as God's dear children, *t.* to be like him
5:17. *t.* to understand what the will of the Lord is
Col. 2:18. *t.* to enter into some vision of their own
2 Tim. 2:15. *t.* hard to show yourself worthy
2 Pet. 1:5. *t.* your hardest to supplement your faith with virtue

tune
1 Cor. 14:7. how can you tell what *t.* is being played

tunic
John 19:23. one for each soldier, leaving out the *t.* The *t.* was seamless

turbulent
Luke 8:24. rebuked the wind and the *t.* waters

turmoil
John 12:27. my soul is in *t.*
Acts 21:30. the whole city was in a *t.*

turn-s-ed-ing

Mat. 5:36. you cannot *t.* one hair of it white or black
9:25. when everyone had been *t.* out
10:21. children will *t.* against their parents
12:13. *t.* to the man he said
12:48. Jesus *t.* to the man who brought the message
13:15. they might *t.* again, and I would heal them
15:32. they might *t.* faint on the way
18:3. *t.* round and become like children
20:10. the *t.* of the men who had come first
20:13. the owner *t.* to one of them
20:22. Jesus *t.* to the brothers and said
22:13. *t.* him out into the dark
22:41. *t.* to the assembled Pharisees
Mark 2:10. he *t.* to the paralysed man
3:3. he *t.* to them
4:12. they might *t.* to God and be forgiven
5:40. after *t.* all the others out
8:3. they will *t.* faint on the way
13:12. children will *t.* against their parents
14:5. they *t.* upon her with fury
Luke 1:3. so I in my *t.*, your Excellency
1:8. when it was the *t.* of his division
1:68. he has *t.* to his people
5:24. he *t.* to the paralysed man
6:16. Judas Iscariot who *t.* traitor
6:20. *t.* to his disciples he began to speak
11:6. a friend of mine on a journey has *t.* up at my house
14:5. he *t.* to them and said
15:13. the younger son *t.* the whole of his share into cash
15:30. now that this son of yours *t.* up
19:24. *t.* to his attendants he said
21:25. not knowing which way to *t.*
22:52. *t.* to the chief priests
John 2:9. the water now *t.* into wine
2:16. he *t.* on the dealers in pigeons
4:46. where he had *t.* the water into wine
6:37. the man who comes to me I will never *t.* away
8:31. *t.* to the Jews who had believed him
12:40. *t.* to me to heal them
13:6. when it was Simon Peter's *t.*
13:18. he who eats bread with me has *t.* against me
Acts 3:19. repent then and *t.* to God
5:4. when it was *t.* into money
5:8. Peter *t.* to her and said
21:21. to *t.* their backs on Moses
24:25. the discourse *t.* to questions of morals

25:9. *t.* to Paul and asked
27:25. I trust in God that it will *t.* out as I have been told
28:27. they might *t.* again, and I would heal them
Rom. 1:27. their men in *t.*, giving up natural relations
1 Cor. 9:22. I have become everything in *t.* to men of every sort
15:15. we *t.* out to be lying witnesses for God
2 Cor. 1:4. so that we in *t.* may be able to comfort others
7:5. trouble at every *t.*
Gal. 1:6. *t.* so quickly away from him
2:17. we ourselves no less than the Gentiles *t.* out to be sinners
5:13. do not *t.* your freedom into licence
Phil. 2:2. the same love for one another, the same *t.* of mind
1 Thess. 1:6. you, in your *t.*, followed the example
3:4. bound to suffer hardship; and so it has *t.* out
1 Tim. 6:20. *t.* a deaf ear to empty and worldly chatter
2 Tim. 2:22. *t.* from the wayward impulses of youth
Jam. 4:5. the spirit which God implanted in man *t.* towards envious desires
4:7. stand up to the devil and he will *t.* and run
5:13. in trouble? He should *t.* to prayer
1 Pet. 2:25. now you have *t.* towards the Shepherd
3:11. must *t.* from wrong
3:12. the Lord's eyes are *t.* towards the righteous
1 John 3:16. we in our *t.* are bound to lay down our lives for our brothers
4:11. we in *t.* are bound to love one another
Rev. 6:12. the sun *t.* black as a funeral pall
7:13. one of the elders *t.* to me
8:8. a third of the sea was *t.* to blood
8:11. a third of the water *t.* to wormwood
10:9. it will *t.* your stomach sour
10:10. my stomach *t.* sour
16:3. on the sea, and it *t.* to blood
16:4. springs, and they *t.* to blood

turquoise
Rev. 21:20. the eleventh *t.*

tutor-s
1 Cor. 4:15. you may have ten thousand *t.* in Christ
Gal. 3:24. the law was a kind of *t.*
3:25. the *t.* charge is at an end

twelve
Mark 3:16. so he appointed the *T.*
Acts 1:26. assigned a place among the
   t. apostles
Rev. 11:3. all through those *t.* hundred
   and sixty days
   12:6. to be sustained for *t.* hundred and
   sixty days

twenty
Mark 6:37. spend *t.* pounds on bread
John 2:6. each held from *t.* to thirty
   gallons
   6:7. *t.* pounds would not buy enough
   bread
2 Cor. 11:25. for *t.*-four hours I was
   adrift on the open sea

twice
Mat. 23:15. make him *t.* as fit for hell as
   you are
Phil. 4:16. you contributed to my needs,
   not once but *t.* over
Rev. 18:6. repay her *t.* over for her
   deeds

twin
John 11:16. Thomas, called 'the *T.*
   20:24. one of the Twelve, Thomas,
   that is 'the *T.*
   21:2. Thomas 'the *T.*

two
Mat. 5:41. go with him *t.*
   19:5. the *t.* shall become one flesh
   19:6. they are no longer *t.* individuals
   25:32. he will separate men into *t.*
   groups
   27:21. which of the *t.* do you wish me
   to release
   27:51. the curtain of the temple was
   torn in *t.*
Mark 10:8. the *t.* shall become one flesh.
   It follows that they are no longer
   t. individuals
   15:38. the curtain of the temple was
   torn in *t.*
Luke 10:17. the seventy-*t.* came back
   jubilant

   19:32. the *t.* went on their errand
   23:45. the curtain of the temple was
   torn in *t.*
John 11:18. Bethany was just under *t.*
   miles from Jerusalem
   12:22. the *t.* of them went to tell Jesus
Acts 7:26. he came upon *t.* of them
   fighting
   11:26. the *t.* of them lived in fellowship with the congregation there
   13:4. so these *t.*, sent out on their
   mission by the Holy Spirit
   15:2. these *t.* and some others from
   Antioch
   15:22. they chose *t.* leading men in
   the community
   28:13. we reached Puteoli in *t.* days
Rom. 9:21. free to make out of the
   same lump *t.* vessels
Eph. 2:14. he has made the *t.* one
   2:15. to create out of the *t.* a single
   new humanity
   2:16. to reconcile the *t.* in a single
   body
Heb. 11:37. they were sawn in *t.*
Jam. 2:2. *t.* visitors may enter your
   place of worship
Rev. 11:6. these *t.* have the power to
   shut up the sky
   14:20. for *t.* hundred miles around
   blood flowed
   19:20. the *t.* of them were thrown alive
   into the lake of fire

twopence
Luke 12:6. are not sparrows five for *t.*

typical
1 Tim. 1:16. *t.* of all who were in future
   to have faith
   6:5. *t.* of men who have let their
   reasoning powers become atrophied

tyrannize-s-ing
2 Cor. 11:20. if a man *t.* over you
1 Pet. 5:3. not *t.* over those who are
   allotted to your care

U

ugly
2 Pet. 2:13. they are an *u.* blot on your
   company

unable
Luke 13:11. quite *u.* to stand up straight
Acts 19:40. we shall be *u.* to give any
   explanation of this uproar
   25:7. grave charges, which they were
   u. to prove

Heb. 4:15. ours is not a high priest *u.* to
   sympathize

unaffected
Acts 2:46. shared their meals with *u.* joy

unanimous-ly
Mark 14:64. their judgement was *u.*:
   that he was guilty

Acts 15:25. resolved *u.* to send to you our chosen representatives

unapproachable
1 Tim. 6:16. dwelling in *u.* light

unashamed
1 John 2:28. *u.* before him at his coming

unaware
Acts 5:7. his wife came in, *u.* of what had happened
26:26. *u.* of any of these facts
Rom. 7:1. you cannot be *u.*, my friends

unbelief
Jude 5. destroyed those who were guilty of *u.*

unbeliever-s
John 3:18. the *u.* has already been judged
Rom. 15:31. that I may be saved from *u.*
1 Cor. 10:27. if an *u.* invites you to a meal
14:22. strange tongues' are not intended as a sign for believers, but for *u.*, whereas prophecy is designed not for *u.*
2 Cor. 6:15. or a believer join hands with an *u.*
1 Tim. 5:8. is worse than an *u.*
Heb. 11:31. Rahab escaped the doom of the *u.*

unbelieving
Mat. 17:17⎫
Mark 9:19 ⎬ what an *u.* and perverse
Luke 9:41 ⎭ generation
John 20:27. be *u.* no longer, but believe
2 Cor. 4:4. their *u.* minds are so blinded

unblemished
2 Pet. 3:14. *u.* and above reproach

unbounded
Phil. 1:26. your pride in me may be *u.*

unbroken
Acts 24:2. we owe it to you that we enjoy *u.* peace

unceasing-ly
Mark 5:5. *u.*, night and day, he would cry aloud among the tombs
Rom. 9:2. in my heart there is great grief and *u.* sorrow

unchanging
Heb. 6:17. how *u.* was his purpose

unchastity
Mat. 5:32⎫
19:9 ⎬ any cause other than *u.*

unclean
Mark 7:29. the *u.* spirit has gone out of your daughter
9:25. he rebuked the *u.* spirit

Rev. 21:27. nothing *u.* shall enter

uncommon-ly
Acts 17:22. in everything that concerns religion you are *u.* scrupulous
28:2. the rough islanders treated us with *u.* kindness

unconcerned
Acts 18:17. all this left Gallio quite *u.*

unconverted
Acts 14:2. the *u.* Jews stirred up the Gentiles

unconvinced
Luke 24:41. they were still *u.*

uncovered
Mat. 10:26⎫ nothing covered up that
Luke 12:2 ⎭ will not be *u.*

under
Mat. 10:36. a man will find his enemies *u.* his own roof
22:44. until I put your enemies *u.* your feet
26:57. Jesus was led off *u.* arrest
Luke 1:79. who live in darkness, *u.* the cloud of death
2:51. continued to be *u.* their authority
8:17. nothing *u.* cover that will not be made known
23:40. you are *u.* the same sentence as he
John 3:18. the man who puts his faith in him does not come *u.* judgement
Acts 4:28. *u.* thy hand and by thy decree, were foreordained
12:5. Peter was kept in prison *u.* constant watch
20:22. *u.* the constraint of the Spirit
24:23. to keep Paul *u.* open arrest
Phil. 2:19. I hope (*u.* the Lord Jesus) to send Timothy
2:24. I am confident, *u.* the Lord
1 Thess. 3:3. *u.* all these hardships, not to be shaken
2 Thess. 1:4. faith remains so steadfast *u.* all your persecutions
1 Tim. 4:14. given you, *u.* the guidance of prophecy
2 Tim. 3:10. my fortitude *u.* persecutions
Jam. 1:12. happy the man who remains steadfast *u.* trial
1:13. no one *u.* trial or temptation should say
1 Pet. 1:5. *u.* the protection of his power
1:6. *u.* trials of many kinds
2 Pet. 2:9. reserve the wicked *u.* punishment

underfoot
Luke 10:19. power to tread *u.* snakes

undergo
Mark 8:31. the Son of Man had to *u.* great sufferings

Luke 9:22. the Son of Man has to *u.* great sufferings
12:50. I have a baptism to *u.*
1 Tim. 3:10. they must first *u.* a scrutiny

underling-s
1 Cor. 4:1. we must be regarded as Christ's *u.*

undermine
Rom. 3:31. does this mean that we are using faith to *u.* law

underneath
Mat. 7:15. *u.* they are savage wolves

understand-ing
Mat. 20:22. you do not *u.* what you are asking
Mark 4:13. you do not *u.* this parable? How then are you to *u.* any parable
10:38. you do not *u.* what you are asking
John 13:7. you do not *u.* now what I am doing
13:12. do you *u.*,' he asked, 'what I have done for you
Acts 8:31. how can I *u.* unless someone will give me the clue
13:27. or *u.* the words of the prophets
13:38. you must *u.*, my brothers
1 Cor. 10:1. you should *u.*, my brothers
11:3. I wish you to *u.*
2 Cor. 1:13. you can read for yourselves, and *u.* too
1:14. you will I hope come to *u.* fully
5:16. even if once they counted in our *u.* of Christ
Philem. 6. deepen the *u.* of all the blessings
Heb. 8:10. I will set my laws in their *u.*
10:16. write them on their *u.*
1 Pet. 3:7. conduct your married life with *u.*
4:4. you no longer plunge with them into all this reckless dissipation, they cannot *u.* it
Jude 10. pour abuse upon things they do not *u.*; the things they do *u.*, by instinct

understood
Mark 6:52. they had not *u.* the incident of the loaves
John 13:28. no one at the table *u.* what he meant
20:9. until then they had not *u.* the scriptures

undertake-n
Luke 1:1. many writers have *u.* to draw up an account
2 Cor. 8:10. the work you did and in your willingness to *u.* it
Philem. 19. I *u.* to repay

undertook
Luke 22:5. *u.* to pay him a sum of money

undeserved
1 Pet. 2:19. the pain of *u.* suffering because God is in his thoughts

undiluted
Rev. 14:10. poured *u.* into the cup of his vengeance

undoing
Mat. 5:30. if your right hand is your *u.*, cut it off
18:8. if your hand or your foot is your *u.*, cut it off
18:9. if it is your eye that is your *u.*, tear it out
Mark 9:43. if your hand is your *u.*, cut it off
1 John 3:8. for the very purpose of *u.* the devil's work
Jude 10. the things they do understand, by instinct like brute beasts, prove their *u.*

unduly
2 Cor. 12:7. to keep me from being *u.* elated by the magnificence of such revelations, I was given a sharp pain in my body which came as Satan's messenger to bruise me; this was to save me from being *u.* elated

uneaten
John 6:13. the pieces left *u.* of the five barley loaves

unequal
2 Cor. 13:5. unless of course you prove *u.* to the test
13:6. I hope you will come to see that we are not *u.* to it

unexpected
2 Pet. 3:10. it will come, *u.* as a thief

unfading
1 Pet. 5:4. the *u.* garland of glory

unfailing
2 Thess. 2:16. given us such *u.* encouragement

unfair
Mat. 20:13. I am not being *u.* to you
2 Cor. 12:13. how *u.* of me

unfaithful
Rom. 3:3. what if some of them were *u.*
Jam. 4:4. you false, *u.* creatures

unfasten
Mark 1:7 } I am not fit to *u.* his shoes
Luke 3:16 }
John 1:27. I am not good enough to *u.* his shoes

Acts 13:25. whose shoes I am not fit to *u*.

16:26. the prisoners found their fetters *u*.

unfathomable
Eph. 3:8. the *u*. riches of Christ

unfed
Mat. 15:32. I do not want to send them away *u*.
Mark 8:3. if I send them home *u*.

unflagging
Rom. 12:11. with *u*. energy

unfold
1 Cor. 15:51. I will *u*. a mystery

unforgiven
John 20:23. if you pronounce them *u*., *u*. they remain

ungrateful
Luke 6:35. he himself is kind to the *u*.

unheard
John 9:32. to open the eyes of a man born blind—it is *u*. of

unimpeachable
Tit. 1:6. a man of *u*. character
1:7. a bishop must be a man of *u*. character

uninstructed
1 Cor. 14:23. some *u*. persons

union
Rom. 6:3. baptized into *u*. with Christ Jesus
6:11. alive to God, in *u*. with Christ Jesus
6:23. his gift is eternal life, in *u*. with Christ Jesus
1 Cor. 5:1. even pagans do not tolerate: the *u*. of a man with his father's wife
Gal. 3:26. in *u*. with Christ Jesus
3:27. baptized into *u*. with him
5:6. if we are in *u*. with Christ Jesus
Eph. 2:6. in *u*. with Christ Jesus he raised us up
2:13. in *u*. with Christ Jesus you who once were far off
Col. 2:6. live your lives in *u*. with him
Philem. 6. the blessings that our *u*. with Christ brings

unite-d
John 15:4. *u*. with the vine; no more can you bear fruit, unless you remain *u*. with me
Acts 4:32. body of believers was *u*. in heart and soul
Rom. 8:1. *u*. with Christ Jesus
12:5. *u*. with Christ, form one body
2 Cor. 5:17. *u*. to Christ, there is a new world

6:14. do not *u*. yourselves with un-believers
Gal. 5:10. *u*. with you in the Lord

unity
1 Cor. 1:10. joined in *u*. of mind and thought
Eph. 1:10. brought into a *u*. in Christ
Phil. 2:2. a common care for *u*.
Col. 2:2. in the *u*. of love

universal
Acts 3:21. until the time of *u*. restoration
17:25. the *u*. giver of life

universe
Rom. 8:19. the created *u*. waits
8:21. the *u*. itself is to be freed from the shackles of mortality
8:22. the whole created *u*. groans
8:38. the forces of the *u*.
1 Cor. 4:9. a spectacle to the whole *u*.
Gal. 4:3. the elemental spirits of the *u*.
Eph. 1:10. the *u*., all in heaven and on earth
3:9. God the creator of the *u*.
4:10. that he might fill the *u*.
Col. 1:16. the whole *u*. has been created through him
1:20. reconcile the whole *u*. to him-self
2:10. every power and authority in the *u*.
Heb. 1:2. heir to the whole *u*.
1:3. sustains the *u*. by his word
11:3. the *u*. was fashioned by the word of God

unjust
Rom. 3:5. is it unjust of God
3:6. if God were *u*., how could he judge the world
1 Cor. 6:9. the *u*. will never come into possession of the kingdom of God
Heb. 6:10. God would not be so *u*. as to forget

unless
Mat. 5:20. *u*. you show yourselves far better men

unlike
Mat. 7:29. *u*. their own teachers he taught
Mark 1:22. *u*. the doctors of the law, he taught

unloved
Rom. 9:25. the *u*. nation I will call My Beloved

unloving
1 John 4:8. the *u*. know nothing of God

unmarked
Luke 11:44. you are like *u*. graves

unmarried
Acts 21:9. he had four *u*. daughters

unmerited
Eph. 3:7. God's gift, bestowed *u.* on me

unnatural
Rom. 1:26. exchanged natural inter-
    course for *u.*
Jude 7. followed *u.* lusts

unoccupied
Mat. 12:44. it returns and finds the
    house *u.*

unprincipled
2 Pet. 3:17. not to let these *u.* men seduce
    you

unproductive
Tit. 3:14. they must not be *u.*

unquenchable
Mark 9:43. go to hell and the *u.* fire

unrecognized
Mark 7:24. he would have liked to
    remain *u.*

unrevealed
Rom. 8:18. the splendour, as yet *u.*
Heb. 9:8. the way into the sanctuary
    remains *u.*

unrewarded
Mat. 10:42 ⎱ that man will assuredly
Mark 9:41 ⎰ not go *u.*

unrolled
Rev. 10:2. in his hand he held a little
    scroll *u.*

unruly
Rom. 10:21. *u.* and recalcitrant
1 Tim. 1:9. lawless and *u.*

unscrupulous
2 Cor. 12:16. I was *u.* enough, you say,
    to use a trick

unseemly
1 Cor. 12:23. our *u.* parts

unseen
2 Cor. 4:18. on the things that are *u.*: for
    what is seen passes away; what is *u.*
    is eternal
Heb. 11:7. Noah, divinely warned about
    the *u.* future

unsettle-d-ing
Acts 15:24. disturbed you with their
    talk and *u.* your minds
Gal. 1:7. persons who *u.* your minds
    5:10. the man who is *u.* your minds

unshakable
Heb. 12:28. the kingdom we are given
    is *u.*

unshrunk
Mat. 9:16 ⎱ a patch of *u.* cloth on to an
Mark 2:21 ⎰ old coat

unsightly
Mat. 6:16. the hypocrites: they make
    their faces *u.*

unsleeping
2 Pet. 2:3. perdition waits for them
    with *u.* eyes

unspiritual
Rom. 7:14. I am *u.*, the purchased slave
    of sin
    7:18. nothing good lodges in me—in
    my *u.* nature
    7:25. in my *u.* nature, a slave to the
    law of sin
1 Cor. 2:14. a man who is *u.* refuses
    what belongs to the Spirit
Jude 19. *u.* persons, although they are
    themselves wholly *u.*

unspoken
1 Tim. 5:13. speaking of things better
    left *u.*

unsuitable
Acts 27:12. the harbour was *u.* for
    wintering

unswerving
Heb. 10:23. *u.* in the confession of our
    hope

untarnished
Jam. 1:27. keep oneself *u.* by the world

unteachable
Mat. 19:8 ⎱ because you were so *u.*
Mark 10:5 ⎰

unthinkable
Luke 13:33. *u.* for a prophet to meet his
    death anywhere but in Jerusalem

untie
Mat. 21:2. *u.* them, and bring them to me
Mark 11:2 ⎱ *u.* it and bring it here
Luke 19:30 ⎰

untouched
Jam. 1:13. God is *u.* by evil

untraceable
Rom. 11:33. how *u.* his ways

untrained
John 7:15. how is it', they said, 'that this
    u. man has such learning
Acts 4:13. noted that they were *u.* lay-
    men

untrustworthy
Luke 16:12. proved *u.* with what belongs
    to another

untying
Mark 11:4. they were *u.* it
    11:5. what are you doing, *u.* that
    colt
Luke 19:31. if anyone asks why you are
    u. it

unused

Luke 19:33. while they were *u.* the colt, its owners asked, 'Why are you *u.* that colt

unused

Mat. 27:60. laid it in his own *u.* tomb

unusual

Acts 19:11. God worked miracles of an *u.* kind

upbringing

Eph. 6:4. a Christian *u.*

upheld

Acts 9:31. *u.* by the Holy Spirit

upholders

Acts 21:20. staunch *u.* of the Law

uplands

Luke 1:39. a town in the *u.* of Judah
1:65. in the *u.* of Judaea the whole story became common talk

uplifted

Luke 24:50. blessed them with *u.* hands

upright

Luke 1:6. both of them were *u.*
2:25. this man was *u.* and devout
21:28. stand *u.* and hold your heads high
23:50. a member of the Council, a good, *u.* man
Acts 26:16. rise to your feet and stand *u.*
1 Cor. 15:34. come back to a sober and *u.* life

uprightness

Luke 1:75. with a holy worship, with *u.* of heart

uproar

Acts 23:9. a great *u.* broke out

ups

Phil. 4:12. the human lot with all its *u.* and downs

upset-ting

Mat. 21:12 ⎫
Mark 11:15 ⎬ he *u.* the tables of the
John 2:15 ⎭ money-changers
2 Tim. 2:18. are *u.* people's faith

upshot

2 Cor. 8:6. the *u.* is that we have asked Titus

upstairs

Mark 14:15 ⎫ he will show you a large
Luke 22:12 ⎭ room *u.*
Acts 1:13. the room *u.* where they were lodging
9:37. they washed her body and laid it in a room *u.*
9:39. they took him *u.* to the room
20:11. he then went *u.*, broke bread and ate

upwards

John 11:41. Jesus looked *u.* and said

urge-d-ing

Mat. 15:23. his disciples came and *u.* him
John 4:31. the disciples were *u.* him
Acts 13:43. *u.* them to hold fast to the grace of God
19:31. *u.* him not to venture into the theatre
21:4. *u.* Paul to abandon his visit
27:22. I *u.* you not to lose heart
27:33. Paul *u.* them all to take some food
1 Cor. 16:12. I *u.* him strongly to go to Corinth
2 Cor. 2:8. I *u.* you therefore to assure him of your love
6:1. we *u.* this appeal upon you
Gal. 2:4. that course was *u.* only as a concession
Eph. 4:17. I *u.* it upon you in the Lord's name
1 Thess. 5:14. we would *u.* you, brothers, to admonish the careless
1 Tim. 1:3. I *u.* you to stay on at Ephesus
2:1. I *u.* that petitions, prayers
Tit. 2:6. *u.* the younger men
2:15. these, then, are your themes; *u.* them

urgent-ly

Luke 22:44. in anguish of spirit he prayed the more *u.*
Acts 9:38. sent two men to him with the *u.* request
28:23. he spoke *u.* of the kingdom of God
Jude 3. *u.* necessary to write at once

use-s-d-ing

Mat. 15:5. which might have been *u.* for your benefit
26:44. prayed the third time, *u.* the same words as before
27:7. they *u.* it to buy the Potter's Field
27:30. *u.* the cane to beat him about the head
Mark 7:11. might have been *u.* for your benefit
11:16. he would not allow anyone to *u.* the temple court as a thoroughfare
15:6. the Governor *u.* to release one prisoner
Luke 13:7. why should it go on *u.* up the soil
14:34. what will you *u.* to season it
16:9. *u.* your worldly wealth to win friends
22:49. Lord, shall we *u.* our swords
John 2:6. the kind *u.* for Jewish rites
3:31. *u.* earthly speech
4:9. do not *u.* vessels in common

John 9:8. the man who *u.* to sit and beg
  11:50. you do not *u.* your judgement
  16:25. I have been *u.* figures of speech
  19:41. a new tomb, not yet *u.* for burial
Acts 2:23. you *u.* heathen men to crucify and kill him
  3:2. a cripple from birth *u.* to be carried there
  5:12. they *u.* to meet by common consent in Solomon's Cloister
  5:26. without *u.* force for fear of being stoned
  18:24. powerful in his *u.* of the scriptures
  19:8. *u.* argument and persuasion
  19:13. exorcists tried their hand at *u.* the name of the Lord Jesus
  19:14. were *u.* this method
  19:18. confessed that they had been *u.* magical spells
Rom. 3:31. does this mean that we are *u.* faith to undermine law
  6:19. to *u.* words that suit your human weakness
  7:13. it *u.* a good thing to bring about my death
  9:21. the other for common *u.*
  10:19. I will *u.* a nation that is no nation
  12:8. one who has the gift of stirring speech should *u.* it
1 Cor. 5:8. must not *u.* the old leaven
  9:7. tending a flock without *u.* its milk
  14:2. *u.* the language of ecstasy
  14:5. to *u.* the tongues of ecstasy
  14:6. that when I come to you I *u.* ecstatic language
  14:14. if I *u.* such language in my prayer
  14:23. all are *u.* the 'strange tongues' of ecstasy
2 Cor. 2:14. *u.* us to reveal and spread abroad
  12:16. to *u.* a trick to catch you
  12:17. *u.* by me to defraud you
Gal. 5:8. persuasion he *u.*, it did not come from God
Eph. 5:16. *u.* the present opportunity to the full
  6:9. give up *u.* threats
Col. 2:23. of no *u.* at all in combating sensuality
  4:5. *u.* the present opportunity to the full
1 Tim. 1:7. without understanding either the words they *u.*
2 Tim. 3:16. inspired scripture has its *u.* for teaching
Tit. 2:8. *u.* wholesome speech
Philem. 11. Onesimus, once so little *u.* to you
Heb. 4:7. he *u.* the words already quoted

  11:14. those who *u.* such language show plainly
Jam. 2:14. what *u.* is it for a man to say he has faith
  3:9. we *u.* it to sing the praises of our Lord . . . we *u.* it to invoke curses
  5:12. do not *u.* oaths
1 Pet. 4:10. *u.* it in service to one another
Rev. 21:17. by human measurements, which the angel was *u.*

useful
Acts 24:23. making themselves *u.* to him
1 Cor. 12:7. for some *u.* purpose
2 Tim. 4:11. I find him a *u.* assistant
Tit. 3:8. *u.* to their fellow-men
Philem. 11. now *u.* indeed, both to you and to me
Heb. 6:7. yields a *u.* crop to those for whom it is cultivated

useless
Mat. 25:30. fling the *u.* servant out into the dark
Mark 5:3. even chains were *u.*
Luke 14:35. it is *u.* either on the land or on the dung-heap
Heb. 7:18. cancelled as impotent and *u.*
2 Pet. 1:8. *u.* or barren in the knowledge of our Lord

usual
Mat. 20:2. to pay them the *u.* day's wage
  20:13. you agreed on the *u.* wage for the day
Mark 10:1. he followed his *u.* practice and taught them
  15:8. the crowd appeared asking for the *u.* favour
Luke 2:42. they made the pilgrimage as *u.*
  22:39. made his way as *u.* to the Mount of Olives
Acts 17:2. following his *u.* practice Paul went to their meetings

usurp-ed-ing
Mark 13:14. when you see 'the abomination of desolation' *u.* a place
Acts 12:23. because he had *u.* the honour due to God

utensils
2 Tim. 2:20. there are not only *u.* of gold and silver

utmost
Phil. 4:7. the peace of God, which is beyond our *u.* understanding
Col. 3:16. admonish each other with the *u.* wisdom
Tit. 3:13. do your *u.* to help Zenas
2 Pet. 3:14. do your *u.* to be found at peace with him

utter-s-ed-ing

Mat. 4:4. he lives on every word that God *u.*

12:34. the words that the mouth *u.*

Luke 1:67. and *u.* this prophecy

6:45. the words that the mouth *u.*

John 3:34. he whom God sent *u.* the words of God

Acts 1:16. the Holy Spirit, through the mouth of David, *u.*

13:10. you *u.* imposter

19:37. *u.* no blasphemy against our goddess

1 Cor. 8:11. this 'knowledge' of yours is *u.* disaster to the weak

14:24. but if all are *u.* prophecies

1 Pet. 2:23. when he suffered he *u.* no threats

4:11. speak as if you *u.* oracles of God

2 Pet. 2:18. they *u.* big, empty words

Rev. 10:11. once again you must *u.* prophecies

12:11. by the testimony which they *u.*

utterance-s

Mat. 27:9. the prophetic *u.* of Jeremiah

Luke 21:15. I myself will give you power of *u.*

John 12:38. Isaiah's *u.* had to be fulfilled

Acts 3:18. the *u.* of all the prophets

7:38. he received the living *u.* of God

Rom. 12:6. the gift of inspired *u.*

1 Cor. 12:10. the gift of ecstatic *u.*

12:28. ecstatic *u.* of various kinds

14:9. if your ecstatic *u.* yields no precise meaning

14:13. the man who falls into ecstatic *u.*

14:18. more gifted in ecstatic *u.* than any of you

14:26. an ecstatic *u.*, or the interpretation of such an *u.*

14:27. if it is a matter of ecstatic *u.*

14:39. do not forbid ecstatic *u.*

1 Thess. 5:20. do not despise prophetic *u.*

2 Thess. 2:2. some oracular *u.*

1 Tim. 1:18. following that prophetic *u.*

utterly

Luke 24:4. while they stood *u.* at a loss

1 Cor. 15:18. it follows also that those who have died within Christ's fellowship are *u.* lost

V

vain

1 Cor. 7:9. burn with *v.* desire

valiant

1 Cor. 16:13. be *v.* and strong

valid

John 8:13. your testimony is not *v.*

8:14. my testimony is *v.*

8:16. my judgement is *v.*

8:17. the testimony of two witnesses is *v.*

Rom. 4:16. that it might be *v.* for all Abraham's posterity

4:17. this promise, then, was *v.* before God

validated

Gal. 3:17. had already been *v.* by God

valley

Mat. 3:5. the whole Jordan *v.*

Luke 3:3. he went all over the Jordan *v.*

value-d

Mat. 13:46. found one of very special *v.*

Luke 7:2. a servant whom he *v.* highly

John 12:43. they *v.* their reputation with men

Acts 19:19. the total *v.* was reckoned up

Rom. 2:25. circumcision has *v.*

3:1. what is the *v.* of circumcision

2 Tim. 2:20. the former are *v.*

2:21. those which are *v.* and dedicated

1 Pet. 3:4. a gentle, quiet spirit, which is of high *v.* in the sight of God

Rev. 13:18. the numerical *v.* of its letters is six hundred and sixty-six

vanish-es-ed

1 Cor. 13:10. the partial *v.* when wholeness comes

Rev. 6:14. the sky *v.*, as a scroll is rolled up

16:20. every island *v.*

20:11. earth and heaven *v.* away

21:1. the first heaven and the first earth had *v.*

vanity

Phil. 2:3. personal *v.* should have no place among you

variance

Gal. 1:8. preach a gospel at *v.* with the gospel we preached

1:9. a gospel at *v.* with the gospel which you received

variety-ies

1 Cor. 12:4. there are *v.* of gifts, but the same Spirit

1 Cor. 12:5. there are *v.* of service, but the same Lord

various
Mark 1:34. many who suffered from *v.* diseases
Acts 15:36. in the *v.* towns where we proclaimed the word
1 Cor. 12:24. God has combined the *v.* parts of the body
12:28. ecstatic utterance of *v.* kinds
Heb. 9:10. *v.* rites of cleansing

vary-ied
Eph. 3:10. the wisdom of God in all its *v.* forms
Heb. 1:1. he spoke in fragmentary and *v.* fashion
1 Pet. 4:10. the grace of God in its *v.* forms

vast-ly
Rom. 5:15. its effect is *v.* exceeded by the grace of God
Eph. 1:19. how *v.* the resources of his power
Rev. 7:9. I looked and saw a *v.* throng
19:1. like the roar of a *v.* throng
19:6. what sounded like a *v.* crowd

vaunt-ed
2 Cor. 11:12. their *v.* apostleship

vegetables
Rom. 14:2. a weaker man eats only *v.*

veil-ed
1 Cor. 11:6. if a woman is not to wear a *v.* she might as well have her hair cut off; but if it is a disgrace for her to be cropped and shaved, then she should wear a *v.*
2 Cor. 3:18. for us there is no *v.* over the face
4:3. if indeed our gospel be found *v.*

vengeance
Rev. 6:16. from the *v.* of the Lamb
6:17. the great day of their *v.* has come
14:10. poured undiluted into the cup of his *v.*
16:19. the fierce wine of his *v.*

venom
Rom. 3:13. adders' *v.* is on their lips
Jam. 3:8. it is an intractable evil, charged with deadly *v.*

venture-d-ing
Mark 12:34. after that nobody *v.* to put any more questions
Luke 20:40. no further question that they *v.* to put to him
Acts 5:13. no one from outside their number *v.* to join with them
19:31. urged him not to *v.* into the theatre

Rom. 15:18. I will *v.* to speak of those things alone

verbal
1 Tim. 6:4. morbidly keen on mere *v.* questions

verdict
John 5:30. I judge as I am bidden, and my *v.* is just
Rom. 3:4. win the *v.* when thou art on trial
5:16. issued in a *v.* of condemnation, but the act of grace, following upon so many misdeeds, issued in a *v.* of acquittal

versed
Acts 26:26. the king is well *v.* in these matters

very
Luke 1:15. from his *v.* birth he will be filled with the Holy Spirit
4:21. in your *v.* hearing this text has come true
Acts 22:14. to hear his *v.* voice
Rom. 8:3. within that *v.* nature
2 Pet. 1:4. share in the *v.* being of God

vessel-s
John 4:9. do not use *v.* in common
Acts 27:6. an Alexandrian *v.*
Rom. 9:24. such *v.* are we, whom he has called

vest-ed
Luke 22:29. I *v.* in you the kingship which my Father *v.* in me

vice
Rom. 13:13. no debauchery or *v.*
Eph. 4:19. they have abandoned themselves to *v.*

vicious
Tit. 1:12. Cretans were always liars, *v.* brutes

victim-s
Luke 4:18. to let the broken *v.* go free
22:7. the Passover *v.* had to be slaughtered
John 19:32. the soldiers accordingly came to the first of his fellow-*v.*
Acts 7:24. avenged the *v.* by striking down the Egyptian
7:42. did you bring me *v.* and offerings
Rom. 8:20. it was made the *v.* of frustration
2 Cor. 7:12. it was not the offender or his *v.* that most concerned me

victor
1 John 5:4. every child of God is *v.* over the godless world
5:5. who is *v.* over the world
Rev. 21:7. all this is the *v.* heritage

victorious
Luke 1:69. a deliverer of *v.* power
Rev. 2:7. to him who is *v.* I will give the
  right
  2:11. he who is *v.* cannot be harmed
  by the second death
  2:17. to him who is *v.* I will give some
  of the hidden manna
  2:26. to him who is *v.*, to him who
  perseveres in doing my will
  3:5. he who is *v.* shall thus be robed
  all in white
  3:12. he who is *v.*—I will make him a
  pillar
  3:21. to him who is *v.* I will grant a
  place on my throne, as I myself
  was *v.*

victory
John 16:33. the *v.* is mine
Rom. 8:37. overwhelming *v.* is ours
Rev. 7:10. *v.* to our God who sits on the
  throne
  12:10. this is the hour of *v.* for our
  God
  17:14. his *v.* will be shared by his
  followers
  19:1. *v.* and glory and power belong
  to our God

view-s
Mat. 27:24. washed his hands in full *v.*
  of the people
Luke 2:31. the deliverance which thou
  hast made ready in full *v.* of all the
  nations
Acts 16:24. in *v.* of these orders, he put
  them in the inner prison
  18:17. gave him a beating in full *v.*
  of the bench
  28:22. like to hear from you what your
  v. are
Gal. 5:10. confident that you will not
  take the wrong *v.*
2 Tim. 1:10. brought fully into *v.* by the
  appearance on earth of our Saviour
  2:10. with this end in *v.*, that they too
  may attain the glorious and eternal
  salvation
2 Pet. 1:5. with all this in *v.*
  3:5. taking this *v.* they lose sight of the
  fact
Rev. 11:12. they went up to heaven in a
  cloud, in full *v.* of their enemies

vigorously
Luke 23:10. pressed the case against him
  v.

vile
Rev. 21:8. the *v.*, murderers, fornicators

vileness
Rom. 1:24. the *v.* of their own desires

vilify
1 Pet. 4:4. they cannot understand it,
  and they *v.* you

village-s
Mat. 10:11. when you come to any town
  or *v.*
Mark 8:23. led him away out of the *v.*
  8:26. do not tell anyone in the *v.*
  8:27. set out for the *v.* of Caesarea
  Philippi
Luke 5:17. people had come from every
  v. of Galilee
  9:6. travelled from *v.* to *v.*
  9:12. then they can go into the *v.*
John 7:42. David's *v.* of Bethlehem
  11:1. Bethany, the *v.* of Mary and her
  sister Martha
  11:30. Jesus had not yet reached the
  v.

villagers
Luke 9:53. the *v.* would not have him

villainy
Acts 1:18. after buying a plot of land
  with the price of his *v.*

vindicate-d
Luke 10:29. he wanted to *v.* himself
  18:7. will not God *v.* his chosen
  18:8. he will *v.* them soon enough
Rom. 3:4. when thou speakest thou
  shalt be *v.*
2 Cor. 7:11. take the matter seriously
  and *v.* yourselves
  13:7. not concerned to be *v.* ourselves
1 Tim. 3:16. *v.* in the spirit
Rev. 6:10. *v.* us and avenge our blood
  18:20. he has *v.* your cause

vine
Rev. 6:6. spare the olive and the *v.*

vine-growers
Mat. 21:33 ⎤
Mark 12:1 ⎬ let it out to *v.*-growers
Luke 20:9 ⎦

vintage
Mat. 21:34. when the *v.* season ap-
  proached
Mark 12:2. when the *v.* season came

violence
Acts 19:16. handled them with such *v.*

violent-ly
Mat. 8:28. so *v.* that no one dared pass
  that way
  28:2. suddenly there was a *v.* earthquake
Acts 8:1. *v.* persecution for the church in
  Jerusalem
  13:45. contradicted what Paul and
  Barnabas said, with *v.* abuse
  16:26. a *v.* earthquake that the
  foundations of the jail were shaken

2 Tim. 4:15. he *v.* opposed everything I said
Rev. 6:12. there was a *v.* earthquake
  11:13. there was a *v.* earthquake, and a tenth of the city fell
  16:18. a *v.* earthquake, like none before it in human history, so *v.* it was

virtue-s
Rom. 3:30. in *v.* of their faith
  12:3. in *v.* of the gift that God in his grace has given me
  15:15. in *v.* of the gift I have from God
Col. 1:25. by *v.* of the task assigned to me
1 Pet. 3:14. if you should suffer for your *v.*

virtuous
Mat. 9:13 ⎱ I did not come to invite *v.*
Mark 2:17 ⎰ people
Luke 5:32. I have not come to invite *v.* people

visible
Rom. 1:20. his invisible attributes, that is to say his everlasting power and deity, have been *v.*
Heb. 11:3. the *v.* came forth from the invisible
1 John 1:2. this life was made *v.*; we have seen it and bear our testimony; we here declare to you the eternal life which dwelt with the Father and was made *v.* to us

vision
Eph. 1:17. spiritual powers of wisdom and *v.*
Col. 2:18. and try to enter into some *v.* of their own

visit-s-ed-ing
Mat. 25:36. when in prison you *v.* me
  25:39. when did we see you ill or in prison, and come to *v.* you
Luke 1:43. who am I, that the mother of my Lord should *v.* me
  10:1. he was going to *v.* himself
  16:30. if someone from the dead *v.* them, they will repent
John 4:46. once again he *v.* Cana-in-Galilee
  7:50. the man who had once *v.* Jesus
  11:45. the Jews who had come to *v.* Mary
  19:39. the man who had first *v.* Jesus by night
Acts 7:12. this was their first *v.*
  7:13. on the second *v.* Joseph was recognized
  9:32. he went down to *v.* God's people at Lydda
  10:28. a Jew is forbidden by his religion to *v.* or associate with a man of another race

11:3. you have been *v.* men who are uncircumcised
19:21. Paul made up his mind to *v.* Macedonia
21:4. urged Paul to abandon his *v.* to Jerusalem
21:12. implored Paul to abandon his *v.*
21:18. Paul paid a *v.* to James
25:13. on a courtesy *v.* to Festus
28:8. Paul *v.* him
Rom. 1:10. succeed at long last in coming to *v.* you
  15:23. longing for many years to *v.* you
1 Cor. 16:7. I do not want this to be a flying *v.*
2 Cor. 1:15. give you the benefit of a double *v.*
  1:16. I meant to *v.* you on my way to Macedonia
  2:1. my next *v.* to you
  8:6. asked Titus, who began it all, to *v.* you
  12:14. to pay you a third *v.*
  12:18. I begged Titus to *v.* you
  13:1. this will be my third *v.* to you
  13:2. I gave it in person on my second *v.*
1 Thess. 1:9. spread the news of our *v.* to you
  2:1. our *v.* to you was not fruitless
2 Tim. 1:16. he was not ashamed to *v.* a prisoner
2 John 12. I hope to *v.* you

visitor-s
Acts 2:10. *v.* from Rome
1 Cor. 14:24. the *v.*, when he enters, hears from everyone something
Jam. 2:2. two *v.* may enter your place of worship

vital
2 Cor. 2:16. a *v.* fragrance that brings life

voice
Mat. 17:6. at the sound of the *v.* the disciples fell on their faces
  27:22. with one *v.* they answered, 'Crucify him
  27:25. with one *v.* the people cried
Acts 3:24. with one *v.* they all predicted
  9:5. the *v.* answered, 'I am Jesus, whom you are persecuting
  9:10. he heard the *v.* of the Lord
  9:27. seen the Lord on his journey, and heard his *v.*
Rom. 10:18. their *v.* has sounded all over the earth
  15:6. with one mind and one *v.* you may praise
Heb. 12:25. do not refuse to hear the *v.* that speaks

Rev. 6:1. say in a *v*. like thunder

void
Mat. 15:6. you have made God's law
    null and *v*.
Mark 7:13. you make God's word null
    and *v*.
1 Cor. 15:14. if Christ was not raised,
    then our gospel is null and *v*.

voluptuous
Rev. 18:7. grief and torment to match
    her *v*. pomp

vote
Acts 26:10. my *v*. was cast against them

votive
Luke 21:5. the fine stones and *v*. offer-
    ings

vouch-ed
John 19:35. this is *v*. for by an eye-
    witness
Phil. 1:7. to *v*. for the truth of the Gospel

vow-ed
Heb. 3:11. I *v*. in my anger
    3:18. to whom did he *v*. that they
    should not enter his rest
    4:3. as I *v*. in my anger
    6:14. I *v*. that I will bless you
    abundantly

voyage
Acts 21:3. we continued our *v*. to
    Syria
    27:9. it was risky to go on with the *v*.

voyager-s
Rev. 18:17. all the sea-captains and *v*.

vulture-s
Mat. 24:28. wherever the corpse is,
    there the *v*. will gather
Luke 17:37. where the corpse is, there
    the *v*. will gather

Col. 4:13. I can *v*. for him, that he
    works tirelessly

W

wage-s-d
Mat. 20:2. to pay them the usual day's
    w.
    20:4. I will pay you a fair *w*.
    20:9. were paid the full day's *w*.
    20:13. you agreed on the usual *w*. for
    the day
Rom. 1:27. the fitting *w*. of such
    perversion
    4:4. his *w*. are not 'counted' as a
    favour
Jam. 5:4. the *w*. you never paid to the
    men
Rev. 6:6. a whole day's *w*. for a quart of
    flour, a whole day's *w*. for three
    quarts of barley-meal
    11:7. the beast that comes up from the
    abyss will *w*. war
    12:7. Michael and his angels *w*. war
    12:17. to *w*. war on the rest of her off-
    spring
    13:7. allowed to *w*. war on God's
    people
    17:14. they will *w*. war upon the
    Lamb

wail-ed-ing
Mat. 2:18. *w*. and loud laments
    8:12. the place of *w*. and grinding of
    teeth
    11:17. we wept and *w*., and you
    would not mourn
    22:13. the place of *w*. and grinding of
    teeth
    24:51. where there is *w*. and grinding
    of teeth

    25:30. the place of *w*. and grinding of
    teeth
Luke 7:32. we wept and *w*., and you
    would not mourn
    13:28. there will be *w*. and grinding of
    teeth
Jam. 5:1. weep and *w*. over the miserable
    fate
Rev. 18:9. will weep and *w*. over her

waist
Mat. 3:4 ⎱
Mark 1:6 ⎰ a leather belt round his *w*.

wait-s-ed-ing
Mat. 4:11. angels appeared and *w*. on
    him
    8:15. she got up and *w*. on him
    27:55. followed Jesus from Galilee
    and *w*. on him
Mark 1:13. among the wild beasts; and
    the angels *w*. on him
    1:31. the fever left her and she *w*.
    upon them
    15:41. followed him and *w*. on him
Luke 4:39. she got up at once and *w*. on
    them
    12:37. seat them at table, and come
    and *w*. on them
    17:8. *w*. on me while I have my meal
    22:27. the servant who *w*. on him
John 2:10. *w*. until the guests have
    drunk freely
    11:6. after hearing of his illness Jesus
    w. for two days

John 21:22, 23. if it should be my will
that he *w*. until I come
Acts 6:2. neglect the word of God in
order to *w*. at table
20:5. *w*. for us at Troas
28:6. *w*. a long time without seeing
anything
Rom. 8:24. *w*. for what he already sees
1 Cor. 4:5. *w*. until the Lord comes
7:35. *w*. upon the Lord without
distraction
11:33. when you meet for a meal, *w*.
for one another
16:11. I am *w*. for him
Heb. 6:15. Abraham, after patient *w*.
10:13. he *w*. henceforth until his
enemies
2 Pet. 2:3. perdition *w*. for them with
unsleeping eyes

waive-ing
1 Cor. 9:18. *w*. the rights which my
preaching gives

wake
Rev. 3:2. *w*. up
3:3. if you do not *w*. up, I shall come
upon you like a thief

wakeful
Mark 13:33. be *w*. You do not know
when the moment comes

walk-s-ed
Mat. 10:38. take up his cross and *w*. in
my footsteps
12:1. Jesus took a *w*. on the Sabbath
through the cornfields
Mark 12:38. who love to *w*. up and down
in long robes
Luke 4:30. he *w*. straight through them
all
23:26. made him *w*. behind Jesus
carrying it
24:15. Jesus himself came up and *w*.
along with them
Acts 10:12. whatever *w*. or crawls or
flies
12:10. *w*. the length of one street

wall-s
Mat. 21:33. he put a *w*. round it, hewed
out a winepress
Mark 12:1. planted a vineyard and put
a *w*. round it
Luke 19:44. bring you to the ground,
you and your children within your
w.

wallow-ed
Rev. 18:9. *w*. in her luxury
22:11. and the filthy-minded *w*. in his
filth

wander-s-ed
Mat. 12:43 ⎫ it *w*. over the deserts seek-
Luke 11:24 ⎭ ing a resting-place

John 8:12. no follower of mine shall *w*.
in the dark
1 Cor. 4:11. we *w*. from place to place
1 Tim. 6:10. have *w*. from the faith

want-s-ed-ing
Mat. 1:19. *w*. to save her from exposure
5:40. if a man *w*. to sue you for your
shirt
5:42. do not turn your back on a man
who *w*. to borrow
8:29. you son of God', they shouted,
'what do you *w*. with us
9:28. do you believe that I have the
power to do what you *w*.
12:46. they stood outside, *w*. to speak
to him
12:47. they *w*. to speak to you
13:58. such was their *w*. of faith
15:32. I do not *w*. to send them away
unfed
17:27. we do not *w*. to cause difficulty
for these people
20:21. I *w*. you', she said, 'to give
orders that in your kingdom
20:27. whoever *w*. to be great must be
your servant
20:32. what do you *w*. me to do for
you
21:46. they *w*. to arrest him
27:43. let God rescue him, if he *w*. him
Mark 1:24. *w*. do you want with us,
Jesus of Nazareth
3:13. called the men he *w*.
5:7. what do you *w*. with me, Jesus
6:6. he was taken aback by their *w*. of
faith
6:25. I *w*. you to give me . . . the head
of John the Baptist
9:35. if anyone *w*. to be first, he must
make himself last of all
10:36. what is it you *w*. me to do
10:43. whoever *w*. to be great must be
your servant
10:44. whoever *w*. to be first must be
the willing slave
10:51. what do you *w*. me to do for
you
Luke 4:34. what do you *w*. with us
5:39. no one after drinking old wine
w. new
8:20. they *w*. to see you
8:28. what do you *w*. with me, Jesus
10:29. he *w*. to vindicate himself
11:7. I cannot get up and give you
what you *w*.
14:23. I *w*. my house to be full
16:26. no one from our side who *w*.
to reach you can cross it
18:41. what do you *w*. me to do for
you
19:14. we do not *w*. this man as our
king

Luke 19:27. who did not *w.* me for their king
20:19. the lawyers and chief priests *w.* to lay hands on him
23:8. he had long been *w.* to see him
John 4:23. such are the worshippers whom the Father *w.*
4:27. none of them said, 'What do you *w.*
5:6. do you *w.* to recover
6:11. they had as much as they *w.*
6:67. do you also *w.* to leave me
7:20. who *w.* to kill you
7:25. is not this the man they *w.* to put to death
9:27. why do you *w.* to hear it again
11:8. the Jews there were *w.* to stone you
16:19. Jesus knew that they were *w.* to question him
18:4 ⎫
18:7 ⎬ who is it you *w.*
18:8. if I am the man you *w.*
18:40. we *w.* Barabbas
Acts 5:33. they *w.* to put them to death
10:10. *w.* something to eat
13:7. *w.* to hear the word of God
15:37. Barnabas *w.* to take John Mark
16:3. Paul *w.* to have him in his company
19:30. Paul *w.* to appear before the assembly
20:24. I only *w.* to finish the race
20:33. I have not *w.* anyone's money
27:38. when they had eaten as much as they *w.*
27:43. the centurion *w.* to bring Paul safely through
Rom. 1:11. I *w.* to bring you some spiritual gift
1:12. I *w.* to be among you to receive encouragement
7:19. the good which I *w.* to do, I fail to do
15:20. I do not *w.* to build on another man's foundation
1 Cor. 7:32. I *w.* you to be free from anxious care
14:35. if there is something they *w.* to know
16:7. I do not *w.* this to be a flying visit
2 Cor. 2:4. I *w.* you rather to know the love
5:4. we do not *w.* to have the old body stripped off
7:3. I do not *w.* to blame you
8:11. I *w.* you to go on and finish it
8:20. we *w.* to guard against any criticism
9:3. I *w.* you to be prepared
12:14. it is you I *w.*, not your money
13:7. we *w.* you to do what is right

Gal. 1:10. whose support do I *w.* but God's alone
2:4. these men *w.* to bring us into bondage
4:17. what they really *w.* is to bar the door
5:6. circumcision makes no difference at all, nor does the *w.* of it
6:12. those who *w.* to make a fair outward and bodily show
6:13. *w.* you to be circumcised in order to boast
Eph. 6:21. you will *w.* to know about my affairs
Phil. 1:12. I *w.* you to understand
4:12. fullness and hunger, plenty and *w.*
4:19. God will supply all your *w.*
Col. 2:1. I *w.* you to know how strenuous are my exertions
1 Thess. 4:12. and at the same time may never be in *w.*
1 Tim. 6:9. those who *w.* to be rich
2 Tim. 3:7. who are always *w.* to be taught
3:12. all who *w.* to live a godly life
Heb. 6:12. we *w.* you not to become lazy
12:17. he *w.* afterwards to claim the blessing
Jam. 4:2. you *w.* something which you cannot have, and so you are bent on murder; you are envious, and cannot attain your ambition, and so you quarrel and fight. You do not get what you *w.*

war
Mat. 24:7 ⎫
Mark 13:8 ⎬ nation will make *w.* upon
Luke 21:10 ⎭ nation
Acts 5:39. you risk finding yourselves at *w.* with God
Heb. 11:34. they grew powerful in *w.*
Rev. 2:16. make *w.* upon them with the sword

warden
Acts 19:35. temple-*w.* of the great Diana

warders
Acts 5:23. the *w.* at their posts by the doors

wares
Rev. 18:15. the traders in all these *w.*

warm-s-ed-ing
Mark 1:41. in *w.* indignation Jesus stretched out his hand
10:21. Jesus looked straight at him; his heart *w.* to him
14:54. *w.* himself at the fire
2 Cor. 7:15. his heart *w.* all the more to you

warmth
Rom. 12:10. *w.* of mutual affection
Phil. 2:1. any *w.* of affection

warn-ed-ing
Mark 1:43. dismissed him with this stern *w.*
6:11. shake the dust off your feet as you leave, as a *w.* to them
8:15. he began to *w.* them
Luke 9:5. shake the dust off your feet as a *w.*
12:5. I will *w.* you whom to fear
16:28. where I have five brothers, to *w.* them
John 16:4. you may remember my *w.*
Acts 14:22. they *w.* them that to enter the kingdom of God
21:4. they, *w.* by the Spirit, urged Paul to abandon his visit
1 Cor. 10:6. to *w.* us not to set our desires on evil things
10:11. for our benefit as a *w.*
2 Cor. 13:2. I repeat the *w.* I gave before
Gal. 5:21. I *w.* you, as I *w.* you before
1 Thess. 3:4. we *w.* you that we were bound to suffer hardship
Tit. 3:10. a heretic should be *w.* once
Jude 18. this was the *w.* they gave you
Rev. 22:18. I give this *w.* to everyone who is listening

warp-ed
Phil. 2:15. children of God in a *w.* and crooked generation

warrant
Mark 14:55. tried to find some evidence against Jesus to *w.* a death-sentence
Rom. 3:10. this has scriptural *w.*

wary
Mat. 10:16. be *w.* as serpents

wash-ing
Mat. 15:20. to eat without first *w.* his hands, that, cannot defile him
Mark 7:2. defiled hands—in other words, without *w.* them
1 Pet. 3:21. baptism is not the *w.* away of bodily pollution
Rev. 22:14. happy are those who *w.* their robes clean

waste-d
Luke 5:37. the wine will be *w.*
Rev. 18:17. so much wealth should be laid *w.*
18:19. alas that in a single hour she should be laid *w.*

watch-ed-ing
Mat. 27:55. a number of women were also present, *w.* from a distance
Mark 12:41. *w.* as people dropped their money into the chest

15:40. women were also present, *w.* from a distance
15:47. were *w.* and saw where he was laid
Luke 2:25. *w.* and waited for the restoration of Israel
10:18. I *w.* how Satan fell, like lightning
17:3. keep *w.* on yourselves
21:34. keep a *w.* on yourselves
23:49. stood with them and *w.* it all
Acts 1:9. as they *w.*, he was lifted up
12:5. Peter was kept in prison under constant *w.*
20:28. keep *w.* over yourselves
Phil. 3:17. *w.* those whose way of life conforms
1 Tim. 4:16. keeping close *w.* on yourself and your teaching
Heb. 9:28. salvation to those who are *w.* for him
1 John 5:21. be on the *w.* against false gods
Rev. 6:1. I *w.* as the Lamb broke the first of the seven seals
6:12. I *w.* as he broke the sixth seal

watch-tower
Mat. 21:33 ⎫
Mark 12:1 ⎬ built a *w.*-tower
       ⎭

water-s
Mark 4:1. the whole crowd on the beach right down to the *w.* edge
6:47. the boat was already well out on the *w.*
Luke 5:2. two boats lying at the *w.* edge
5:4. put out into deep *w.*
John 6:17. to cross the *w.* to Capernaum
1 Cor. 6:11. the purifying *w.*
Tit. 3:5. he saved us through the *w.* of rebirth
1 Pet. 3:21. this *w.* prefigured the *w.* of baptism

wave-s-ing
Luke 8:25. wind and *w.*, and they obey him
12:55. there will be a heat-*w.*
Acts 22:23. yelling and *w.* their cloaks
Eph. 4:14. tossed by the *w.* and whirled about

waver-ing
Heb. 12:13. keep your steps from *w.*

way-s
Mat. 3:15. we do well to conform in this *w.*
5:12. in the same *w.* they persecuted the prophets
7:23. out of my sight, you and your wicked *w.*
12:40. in the same *w.* the Son of Man will be three days and three nights

Mat. 17:12. in the same *w*. the Son of Man is to suffer

18:23. the kingdom of Heaven, therefore, should be thought of in this *w*.

19:21. if you wish to go the whole *w*., go, sell your possessions

21:18. on his *w*. to the city he felt hungry

25:21, 23. you have proved trustworthy in a small *w*.

26:12. it was her *w*. of preparing me for burial

26:24. the Son of Man is going the *w*. appointed for him

27:9. in this *w*. fulfilment was given to the prophetic utterance of Jeremiah

27:44. taunted him in the same *w*.

28:16. the eleven disciples made their *w*. to Galilee

Mark 4:11. everything comes by *w*. of parables

7:31. he went by *w*. of Sidon to the sea of Galilee

10:43. that is not the *w*. with you

11:28. who gave you authority to act in this *w*.

14:21. the Son of Man is going the *w*. appointed for him

Luke 1:17. to convert the rebellious to the *w*. of the righteous

2:3. everyone made his *w*. to his own town

2:16. found their *w*. to Mary and Joseph

3:18. in this and many other *w*. he made his appeal

5:3. asked him to put out a little *w*. from the shore

6:23. in just the same *w*. did their fathers treat the prophets

8:4. as they made their *w*. to him

8:42. while Jesus was on his *w*. he could hardly breathe for the crowds

10:35. I will repay you on my *w*. back

11:16. by *w*. of a test, demanded of him a sign

11:52. those who were on their *w*. in, you stopped

13:27. you and your wicked *w*.

13:31. you should leave this place and go on your *w*.

13:33. I must be on my *w*. today

16:16. everyone forces his *w*. in

19:42. the *w*. that leads to peace

21:31. in the same *w*. when you see all this happening

22:22. the Son of Man is going his appointed *w*.

22:51. let them have their *w*.

23:24. Pilate decided that they should have their *w*.

John 4:15. nor have to come all this *w*. to draw

4:30. made their *w*. towards him

5:14. now that you are well again, leave your sinful *w*.

7:7. it hates me for exposing the wickedness of its *w*.

11:20. she heard that Jesus was on his *w*.

12:35. go on your *w*. while you have the light

17:11. I am on my *w*. to thee

18:3. made his *w*. to the garden

18:22. is that the *w*. to answer the High Priest

21:13. and the fish in the same *w*.

Acts 1:11. will come in the same *w*. as you have seen him go

3:15. killed him who has led the *w*. to life

3:26. by turning every one of you from your wicked *w*.

8:25. bringing the good news to many Samaritan villages on the *w*.

8:27. was on his *w*. when he caught sight of an Ethiopian

9:31. it held on its *w*. and grew in numbers

10:9. on their *w*. and approaching the city

10:17. asking the *w*. to Simon's house

11:17. how could I possibly stand in God's *w*.

13:15. say to the people by *w*. of exhortation

18:13. worship God in *w*. that are against the law

19:20. in such *w*. the word of the Lord showed its power

21:21. following our *w*. of life

24:2. in all kinds of *w*. and in all sorts of places, improvements are being made

Rom. 1:17. God's *w*. of righting wrong, a *w*. that starts from faith

3:21. God's *w*. of righting wrong

5:21. sin established its reign by *w*. of death

7:6. to serve God in a new *w*., the *w*. of the spirit, in contrast to the old *w*., the *w*. of a written code

8:27. pleads for God's own people in God's own *w*.

10:3. they ignore God's *w*. of righteousness

12:3. think your *w*. to a sober estimate

1 Cor. 1:18. those on their *w*. to ruin, but to us who are on the *w*. to salvation

7:26. time of stress like the present this is the best *w*. for a man to live

9:12. I put up with all that comes my *w*.

10:33. I always try to meet everyone half-*w*.

1 Cor. 15:34. leave your sinful *w*.
2 Cor. 2:15. those who are on the *w*. to
salvation, and for those who are on
the *w*. to perdition
4:3. people who find it so are those on
the *w*. to perdition
7:10. the wound which is borne in
God's *w*. brings a change of heart
too salutary to regret; but the
hurt which is borne in the world's
w. brings death
7:11. you bore your hurt in God's *w*.
10:11. people who talk in that *w*.
11:5. have I in any *w*. come short
13:11. mend your *w*.
Gal. 5:4. you seek to be justified by *w*.
of law
5:12. better go the whole *w*. and make
eunuchs of themselves
5:21. those who behave in such *w*.
will never inherit the kingdom of
God
6:2. in this *w*. you will fulfil the law of
Christ
Eph. 2:2. the evil *w*. of this present age
4:22. leaving your former *w*. of life
5:18. do not give *w*. to drunkenness
Phil. 1:23. I am torn two *w*.
3:15. let us then keep to this *w*. of
thinking
3:17. watch those whose *w*. of life
conforms to it
3:18. many whose *w*. of life makes
them enemies
Col. 1:6. in the same *w*. it is coming to
men the whole world over
1:24. this is my *w*. of helping
1:28. we instruct everyone in all the
w. of wisdom
2:11. this is Christ's *w*. of circumcision
3:7. these are the *w*. you yourselves
followed
3:20. pleasing to God and is the
Christian *w*.
1 Thess. 4:1. the *w*. we must live to
please God
4:5. not giving *w*. to lust like the
pagans
2 Thess. 2:3. let no one deceive you in
any *w*.
1 Tim. 3:11. trustworthy in every *w*.
Tit. 2:10. in all such *w*. they will add
lustre to the doctrine
2:12. to renounce godless *w*.
Heb. 2:17. made like these brothers of
his in every *w*.
4:15. tested every *w*., only without
sin
6:1 ⎫
9:14 ⎬ the deadness of our former *w*.
12:17. he found no *w*. open for second
thoughts
1 Pet. 1:18. the empty folly of your
traditional *w*.

Jude 4. persons who have wormed their
w. in
Rev. 2:2. I know all your *w*.
2:14. put temptation in the *w*. of the
Israelites
2:19 ⎫
3:1, 8, 15 ⎬ I know all your *w*.
21:27. nor anyone whose *w*. are false
or foul

wayward
2 Tim. 2:22. turn from the *w*. impulses of
youth

weak
Mat. 17:20. your faith is too *w*.
2 Cor. 10:3. *w*. men we may be

weaken
Acts 21:13. why are you trying to *w*. my
resolution

weakness-es
Rom. 6:19. words that suit your human
w.
8:26. the Spirit comes to the aid of
our *w*.
2 Cor. 10:2. those who charge us with
moral *w*.
11:30. I will boast of the things that
show up my *w*.
12:5. I will not boast on my own
account, except of my *w*.
Heb. 4:15. not a high priest unable to
sympathize with our *w*.
5:2. he too is beset by *w*.

wealth-y
Mat. 6:21. where your *w*. is, there will
your heart be also
13:22. the false glamour of *w*.
19:22. he was a man of great *w*.
Mark 4:19. the false glamour of *w*.
10:22. he was a man of great *w*.
10:23. how hard it will be for the
w. to enter the kingdom
Luke 8:14. choked by cares and *w*.
12:15. his *w*. does not give him life
12:21. the man who amasses *w*. for
himself
12:33. never-failing *w*. in heaven
12:34. where your *w*. is, there will
your heart be also
16:9. use your worldly *w*. to win
friends
16:11. not proved trustworthy with
the *w*. of this world, who will trust
you with the *w*. that is real
18:24. how hard it is for the *w*. to
enter the kingdom
Rom. 2:4. do you think lightly of his *w*.
of kindness
9:23. the full *w*. of his splendour
11:33. O depth of *w*., wisdom

1 Cor. 7:31. those who use the world's
w.
2 Cor. 6:10. poor ourselves, we bring w.
to many
Eph. 1:18. the w. and glory of the share
he offers
Col. 2:2. the full w. of conviction
1 Tim. 6:18. a w. of noble actions
Heb. 11:26. greater w. than the treasures
of Egypt
Jam. 1:10. the w. brother must find his
pride in being brought low
5:3. you have piled up w.
Rev. 5:12. to receive all power and w.
18:3. grown rich on her bloated w.
18:15. who gained their w. from her
18:17. in one hour so much w. should
be laid waste
18:19. all who had ships at sea grew
rich on her w.
21:26. the w. and splendour of the
nations

weapons
2 Cor. 6:7. we wield the w. of righteousness

wear-s-ing
Mat. 6:31. what shall we w.
23:5. w. deep fringes on their robes
Mark 6:9. they might w. sandals
16:5. a youth sitting on the right-
hand side, w. a white robe
Luke 12:33. purses that do not w. out
18:5. before she w. me out with her
persistence
John 18:10. Peter drew the sword he was
w.
Acts 8:23. w. the fetters of sin
Rom. 13:14. let Christ Jesus himself be
the armour that you w.
1 Cor. 4:12. we w. ourselves out working with our own hands
11:6. if a woman is not to w. a veil . . .
then she should w. a veil
15:49. so we shall w. the likeness of
the heavenly man
1 Tim. 6:1. all who w. the yoke of
slavery
Rev. 4:4. robed in white and w. crowns
of gold

weather
Acts 27:18. we were making very heavy
w.

weave
Luke 12:27. think of the lilies: they
neither spin nor w.

wedding
Mat. 22:2. a feast for his son's w.
22:4. come to the w. at once
22:9. invite everyone you can find to
the w.

25:10. those who were ready went in
with him to the w.
John 2:1. there was a w. at Cana-in-
Galilee
Rev. 19:7. the w.-day of the Lamb has
come
19:9. the w.-supper of the Lamb

weed-s
Heb. 12:15. no bitter, noxious w. growing up
Rev. 18:7. no mourning for me, no
widow's w.

week
John 20:26. a w. later his disciples were
again in the room
Acts 20:6. Troas, where we spent a w.
21:4. and stayed there a w.
28:14. fellow-Christians and were
invited to stay a w.

weep
Rev. 18:9. will w. and wail over her

weigh-s-ed-ing
Mat. 26:15. they w. him out thirty
silver pieces
Acts 27:13. w. anchor
2 Cor. 11:28. the responsibility that w.
on me every day

weight
Mat. 20:25 ⎱ great men make them feel
Mark 10:42 ⎰ the w. of authority
1 Cor. 1:17. that the fact of Christ on
his cross might have its full w.
1 Thess. 2:6. as Christ's own envoys we
might have made our w. felt

welcome-s-ed-ing
Mark 4:20. they hear the word and w.
it
9:15. they ran forward to w. him
Luke 8:40. when Jesus returned, the
people w. him
9:11. he w. them
10:8. when you come into a town and
they make you w.
10:10. when you enter a town and they
do not make you w.
10:38. Martha made him w. in her
home
15:2. w. sinners and eats with them
19:6. he climbed down as fast as he
could and w. him gladly
John 4:45. the Galileans gave him a w.
5:43. you have no w. for me; if another
comes self-accredited you will w.
him
Acts 15:4. they reached Jerusalem they
were w.
18:27. wrote to the congregation
there to make him w.
21:17. the brotherhood w. us gladly
24:3. we w. this, sir, most gratefully

Acts 28:2. they lit a bonfire and made us all *w.*
28:30. with a *w.* for all who came to him
Rom. 10:15. how *w.* are the feet of the messengers
16:2. a *w.* worthy of God's people
2 Cor. 8:17. Titus not only *w.* our request
Gal. 4:14. you *w.* me as if I were an angel of God, as you might have *w.* Christ Jesus himself
Phil. 2:29. *w.* him then in the fellowship of the Lord
Col. 4:10. if he comes, make him *w.*
1 Thess. 1:6. the *w.* you gave the message
Philem. 17. *w.* him as you would *w.* me
Heb. 11:31. she had given the spies a kindly *w.*
Jam. 2:25. *w.* the messengers into her house
2 John 10. who does not bring this doctrine, do not *w.* him

welfare
Heb. 12:10. he does so for our true *w.*

well
Luke 14:5. it falls into a *w.*
John 5:14. now that you are *w.* again
Acts 3:16. this faith has made him completely *w.*
4:10. this man stands here before you fit and *w.*
22:12. Ananias . . . *w.* spoken of by all the Jews

well-doer
Rom. 2:10. for every *w.-d.* there will be glory

well-dressed
Jam. 2:2. a *w.-d.* man with gold rings
2:3. special attention to the *w.-d.* man

well-fed
Luke 6:25. alas for you who are *w.-f.* now

went
Mat. 21:10. the whole city *w.* wild with excitement
Mark 6:20. Herod *w.* in awe of John
6:34. his heart *w.* out to them
Luke 15:20. his heart *w.* out to him

wept
Mat. 11:17. we *w.* and wailed, and you would not mourn
Acts 20:31. how I *w.* over you

west
Mark 16:8. Jesus himself sent out by them from east to *w.* the sacred and imperishable message

wet-ted
Luke 7:38. his feet were *w.* with her tears
7:44. this woman has made my feet *w.* with her tears

whatever
Mat. 4:23. curing *w.* illness or infirmity
7:2. *w.* measure you deal out to others
23:5. *w.* they do is done for show
23:20. by the altar and by *w.* lies on it
Luke 6:38. *w.* measure you deal out to others
John 11:49. High Priest that year, said, 'You know nothing *w.*
Acts 10:12. *w.* walks or crawls or flies
27:33. you have eaten nothing *w.*
Gal. 5:8. *w.* persuasion he used, it did not come from God
Col. 1:11. ample power to meet *w.* comes
1 Thess. 5:18. give thanks *w.* happens
5:22. avoid the bad of *w.* kind
2 Thess. 2:3. let no one deceive you in any way *w.*
1 Pet. 4:10. *w.* gift each of you may have received
2 Pet. 2:19. a man is the slave of *w.* has mastered him

wheel
Jam. 3:6. it keeps the *w.* of our existence red-hot

whenever
1 Cor. 11:25. *w.* you drink it, do this as a memorial of me
2 Cor. 3:16. *w.* he turns to the Lord the veil is removed
Phil. 1:3. I thank my God *w.* I think of you
Jam. 1:2. *w.* you have to face trials
1 Pet. 3:15. *w.* you are called to account for the hope

whereas
Mat. 5:19. *w.* anyone who keeps the law
John 16:7. *w.* if I go, I will send him to you
Rom. 9:31. *w.* Israel made great efforts after a law of righteousness
11:23. *w.* they, if they do not continue faithless
1 Cor. 7:14. your children would not belong to God, *w.* in fact they do
11:7. *w.* woman reflects the glory of man
12:24. *w.* our seemly parts need no adorning
14:22. *w.* prophecy is designed not for unbelievers
15:45. *w.* the last Adam has become a life-giving spirit

2 Tim. 3:13. *w.* wicked men and charlatans will make progress from bad to worse

Heb. 11:29. *w.* the Egyptians, when they attempted the crossing, were drowned

whereupon

Acts 28:9. *w.* the other sick people on the island came

wherever

Luke 21:35. that day will come on all men, *w.* they are

2 Cor. 4:10. *w.* we go we carry death with us in our body

5:9. *w.* we are, here or there, to be acceptable to him

whether

Mark 8:23. asked *w.* he could see anything

Rom. 14:4. *w.* he stands or falls is his own Master's business

1 Cor. 3:8. *w.* they plant or water, they work as a team

2 Thess. 2:2. *w.* at some oracular utterance

1 Tim. 5:10. *w.* she has had the care of children, or given hospitality, or washed the feet of God's people, or supported those in distress—in short, *w.* she has taken every opportunity

Jam. 3:14. consider *w.* your claims are not false

whim

2 Pet. 1:21. not through any human *w.* that men prophesied

whip

John 2:15. Jesus made a *w.* of cords

whirl-ed

Eph. 4:14. *w.* about by every fresh gust of teaching

whirlwind

Heb. 12:18. darkness, gloom, and *w.*

whisper-ed-ing

Mat. 10:27. what you hear *w.*

Luke 12:3. what you have *w.* behind closed doors

John 7:12. much *w.* about him in the crowds

whisperers

Rom. 1:30. *w.* and scandal-mongers

Whitsuntide

1 Cor. 16:8. I shall remain at Ephesus until *W.*

whoever

Mat. 10:41. whoever receives a prophet as a prophet will be given a prophet's reward, and *w.* receives a good man

22:16. truckling to no man, *w.* he may be

Mark 3:29. *w.* slanders the Holy Spirit can never be forgiven

12:14. and truckle to no man, *w.* he may be

Luke 10:16. *w.* listens to you listens to me; *w.* rejects you rejects me. And *w.* rejects me rejects the One who sent me

22:36. *w.* has a purse had better take it with him

John 6:35. *w.* comes to me shall never be hungry, and *w.* believes in me shall never be thirsty

6:56. *w.* eats my flesh

6:58. *w.* eats this bread

7:17. *w.* has the will to do the will of God

7:38. *w.* believes in me, let him drink

12:26. *w.* serves me will be honoured by my Father

Gal. 6:16. *w.* they are who take this principle for their guide

1 Pet. 3:10. *w.* loves life

1 John 2:6. *w.* claims to be dwelling in him

Rev. 13:10. *w.* is meant for prison, to prison he goes. *W.* takes the sword to kill

14:9. *w.* worships the beast

whole

Mat. 2:3. perturbed when he heard this; and so was the *w.* of Jerusalem

3:5. the *w.* Jordan valley

4:23. he went round the *w.* of Galilee

4:24. his fame reached the *w.* of Syria

8:33. they told the *w.* story

18:31. told him the *w.* story

18:32. I remitted the *w.* of your debt

19:21. if you wish to go the *w.* way

20:12. who have sweated the *w.* day

26:59. the *w.* Council tried to find some allegation against Jesus

27:45. darkness fell over the *w.* land

Mark 1:5. the *w.* Judaean country-side

1:33. the *w.* town was there

1:45. made the *w.* story public

9:15. the *w.* crowd were overcome with awe

11:11. he looked at the *w.* scene

14:55. the *w.* Council tried to find some evidence against Jesus

16:15. proclaim the Good News to the *w.* creation

Luke 1:3. the *w.* course of these events

1:65. the *w.* story became common talk

1:75. to worship him . . . our *w.* life long

2:10. great joy coming to the *w.* people

Luke 4:14. reports about him spread through the *w.* countryside

4:25. famine lay hard over the *w.* country

4:28. the *w.* congregation were infuriated

4:37. he was the talk of the *w.* district

7:17. and the *w.* neighbourhood

John 11:48. the *w.* populace will believe in him

18:14. if one man died for the *w.* people

21:25. the *w.* world would not hold the books

Acts 4:32. the *w.* body of believers

5:11. a great awe fell upon the *w.* church

5:36. his *w.* following was broken up

5:37. his *w.* following was scattered

6:2. the *w.* body of disciples

10:2. his *w.* family joined in the worship of God

10:8. told them the *w.* story

10:22. religious man, acknowledged as such by the *w.* Jewish nation

13:24. baptism as a token of repentance to the *w.* people of Israel

17:26. to inhabit the *w.* earth's surface

19:9. speaking evil of the new way before the *w.* congregation

19:10. the *w.* population . . . heard the word of the Lord

19:26. the *w.* of the province of Asia

20:27. the *w.* purpose of God

22:5. the *w.* Council of Elders

25:24. the *w.* body of the Jews

28:23. he dealt at length with the *w.* matter

Rom. 3:19. the *w.* world may be exposed to the judgement of God

6:17. yielded *w.*-hearted obedience

8:23. Set our *w.* body free

11:16. the first portion of dough is consecrated, so is the *w.* lump

12:2. your *w.* nature thus transformed

13:10. the *w.* law is summed up in love

1 Cor. 4:9. a spectacle to the *w.* universe

13:12. my knowledge now is partial; then it will be *w.*

14:31. that the *w.* congregation may receive instruction

2 Cor. 1:1. dedicated to him throughout the *w.* of Achaia

13:9. my *w.* prayer is that all may be put right

Gal. 3:22. the *w.* world to be prisoners

4:1. even though the *w.* estate is his

5:12. go the *w.* way and make eunuchs of themselves

5:14. the *w.* law can be summed up

6:16. the *w.* Israel of God

Phil. 2:29. in the fellowship of the Lord with *w.*-hearted delight

Col. 1:6. coming to men the *w.* world over

1:16. the *w.* universe has been created through him

1:23. the *w.* creation under heaven

3:14. love, to bind all together and complete the *w.*

3:23. whatever you are doing, put your *w.* heart into it

1 Thess. 5:27. have this letter read to the *w.* brotherhood

2 Tim. 4:17. the *w.* pagan world

Heb. 1:2. heir to the *w.* universe

3:5. a servitor in God's *w.* household

10:6 ⎫
10:8 ⎭ *w.*-offerings and sin-offerings

11:7. he put the *w.* world in the wrong

12:15. noxious weed growing up to poison the *w.*

1 Pet. 1:22. love one another *w.*-heartedly

2 Pet. 3:11. the *w.* universe is to break up

3 John 3. you are true in your *w.* life

Rev. 3:10. the ordeal that is to fall upon the *w.* world

6:6. a *w.* day's wage for a quart of flour, a *w.* day's wage

11:10. a torment to the *w.* earth

13:3. the *w.* world went after the beast

14:3. who alone from the *w.* world had been ransomed

wholeness

1 Cor. 13:10. the partial vanishes when *w.* comes

wholesome

1 Tim. 1:10. whose behaviour flouts the *w.* teaching

2 Tim. 4:3. they will not stand *w.* teaching

Tit. 1:9. to move his hearers with *w.* teaching

2:1. what you say must be in keeping with *w.* doctrine

2:8. use *w.* speech

wholly

Eph. 6:18. give yourselves *w.* to prayer

Col. 4:12. *w.* devoted to doing God's will

2 Tim. 2:4. *w.* at his commanding officer's disposal

Jude 19. they are themselves *w.* unspiritual

whore-s

Rev. 17:5. Babylon the great, the mother of *w.*

whose

John 3:13. the Son of Man *w.* home is in heaven
Acts 2:44. all *w.* faith had drawn them together
Gal. 2:8. God *w.* action made Peter an apostle to the Jews
Eph. 5:2. sacrifice *w.* fragrance is pleasing to God
Col. 3:24. Christ is the Master *w.* slaves you must be

wick

Mat. 12:20. nor snuff out the smouldering *w.*

wicked

Mat. 7:23. you and your *w.* ways
12:39. it is a *w.*, godless generation
15:19. *w.* thoughts, murder
Mark 8:38. this *w.* and godless age
Luke 6:35. he himself is kind to the ungrateful and *w.*
11:29. this is a *w.* generation
13:27. you and your *w.* ways
Acts 3:26. by turning every one of you from your *w.* ways
24:15. there is to be a resurrection of good and *w.*
Rom. 5:6. Christ died for the *w.*
2 Thess. 2:9. the coming of that *w.* man is the work of Satan
2 Tim. 3:13. *w.* men and charlatans will make progress from bad to worse
Heb. 3:12. the *w.*, faithless heart of a deserter
8:12. I will be merciful to their *w.* deeds
10:17. their sins and *w.* deeds I will remember no more
2 Pet. 2:9. reserve the *w.* under punishment
2 John 11. an accomplice in his *w.* deeds

wickedness

John 7:7. it hates me for exposing the *w.* of its ways
Rom. 1:18. the godless *w.* of men. In their *w.*
11:26. he shall remove *w.* from Jacob
2 Cor. 6:14. what has righteousness to do with *w.*
Gal. 1:4. this present age of *w.*
Eph. 2:1. dead in your sins and *w.*
2 Thess. 2:3. when *w.* will be revealed in human form
2:7. the secret power of *w.*
2 Tim. 2:19. who takes the Lord's name upon his lips must forsake *w.*
Tit. 2:14. to set us free from all *w.*
Jam. 3:6. the world with all its *w.*

wide-ly

Mat. 28:15. this story became *w.* known
Mark 1:45. he spread it far and *w.*
John 1:51. you shall see heaven *w.* open

Acts 6:7. the word of God now spread more and more *w.*
11:28. a severe and world-*w.* famine
13:49. the word of the Lord spread far and *w.*
16:27. the prison doors *w.* open
19:20. spreading more and more *w.*
2 Cor. 6:11. we have opened our heart *w.* to you
6:13. open *w.* your hearts to us
1 Tim. 6:21. have shot far *w.* of the faith
2 Tim. 2:18. they have shot *w.* of the truth
Rev. 19:11. I saw heaven *w.* open
21:16. was as *w.* as it was long

widow-s

Mat. 22:24. his brother shall marry the *w.*
Mark 12:19⎱ the next should marry the
Luke 20:28⎰ *w.*
1 Tim. 5:6. a *w.* given over to self-indulgence
5:7. that the *w.* may be above reproach
5:14. that young *w.* shall marry again
5:15. *w.* who have taken the wrong turning

wield-ed

2 Cor. 6:7. we *w.* the weapons of righteousness
10:4. the weapons we *w.* are not merely human
Rev. 13:12. it *w.* all the authority of the first beast

wife

Mat. 10:35. a young *w.* against her mother-in-law
19:7. a man might divorce his *w.* by note of dismissal
Mark 10:4. Moses permitted a man to divorce his *w.*
Luke 12:53. mother against son's *w.* and son's *w.* against her mother-in-law
1 Cor. 7:15. the Christian husband or *w.* is under no compulsion
Gal. 4:22. the other by his free-born *w.*
4:27. the deserted *w.* shall have more children

wild-s

Mat. 21:10. the whole city went *w.* with excitement
Luke 1:80. he lived out in the *w.*
Acts 21:38. led a force of four thousand terrorists out into the *w.*
1 Cor. 15:32. I 'fought *w.* beasts'
Tit. 1:10. they talk *w.*
Rev. 6:8. by pestilence and *w.* beasts
12:6. the woman herself fled into the *w.*
17:3. in the Spirit he carried me away into the *w.*

wilderness
Mat. 24:26. he is there in the *w*.
1 Tim. 1:6. gone astray into a *w*. of words

wile-s
2 Cor. 2:11. we know his *w*. all too well
Heb. 3:13. the *w*. of sin

will
Mark 9:13. they have worked their *w*. upon him
John 10:18. I am laying it down of my own free *w*.
Acts 2:23. by the deliberate *w*. and plan of God
Rom. 7:19. the wrong which is against my *w*.
7:20. if what I do is against my *w*.
Gal. 3:15. a man's *w*. and testament

willing-ly
Mat. 20:27. the *w*. slave of all
Mark 6:19. would *w*. have killed him
10:44. whoever wants to be first must be the *w*. slave of all
14:38. the spirit is *w*., but the flesh is weak
Acts 25:20. I asked if he was *w*. to go to Jerusalem
1 Cor. 7:12. she is *w*. to live with him, he must not divorce her
7:13. a heathen husband *w*. to live with her
2 Cor. 9:12. as a piece of *w*. service

willingness
2 Cor. 8:10. the work you did and in your *w*. to undertake it

win-s-ning
Mat. 6:2. to *w*. admiration from men
16:26. what will a man gain by *w*. the whole world
23:15. you travel over sea and land to *w*. one convert
Mark 8:36. gain by *w*. the whole world
10:17. what must I do to *w*. eternal life
Luke 9:25. gain by *w*. the whole world
16:9. use your worldly wealth to *w*. friends
18:18. Master, what must I do to *w*. eternal life
21:19. by standing firm you will *w*. true life
John 4:1. Jesus is *w*. and baptizing more disciples than John
Acts 26:28. you think it will not take much to *w*. me
Rom. 3:4. *w*. the verdict when thou art on trial
1 Cor. 9:19. to *w*. over as many as possible
9:20. I became like a Jew, to *w*. Jews . . . I put myself under that law to *w*. them

9:21. to *w*. Gentiles, who are outside the Law
9:22. to the weak I became weak, to *w*. the weak
9:24. only one *w*. the prize. Like them, run to *w*.
Phil. 3:14. I press towards the goal to *w*. the prize
1 Tim. 2:6. sacrificed himself to *w*. freedom for all mankind
3:4. *w*. obedience from his children
2 Tim. 2:5. no athlete can *w*. a prize unless he has kept the rules
Heb. 10:36. *w*. what he has promised
11:35. to *w*. a better resurrection
Rev. 12:8. they had not the strength to *w*.

wind-s
Acts 14:6. they got *w*. of it and made their escape
Heb. 1:7. he who makes his angels *w*.

wine
Mat. 27:34. they offered him a draught of *w*.
27:48. a sponge, which he soaked in sour *w*.
Mark 15:36. running with a sponge, soaked in sour *w*.
Luke 23:36. offering him their sour *w*.
John 19:29. a jar stood there full of sour *w*.; so they soaked a sponge with the *w*.
19:30. having received the *w*.

winepress
Mark 12:1. hewed out a *w*.

winnow
Mat. 3:12. he will *w*. his threshing-floor
Luke 3:17. to *w*. his threshing-floor

winter
Jam. 5:7. until the *w*. and spring rains

wipe-d
Acts 3:19. so that your sins may be *w*. out

wisdom
Rom. 1:22. they boast of their *w*.
1 Cor. 1:25. divine folly is wiser than the *w*. of man
1:26. few of you are men of *w*.
3:18. he must become a fool to gain true *w*.

wise
1 Cor. 12:8. the gift of *w*. speech

wish-es-ed-ing
Mat. 10:12. *w*. the house peace as you enter it
15:28. what faith you have! Be it as you *w*.
16:24. if anyone *w*. to be a follower of mine

Mat. 19:17. if you *w.* to enter into life
Mark 8:34. anyone who *w.* to be a follower of mine
9:30. Jesus *w.* it to be kept secret
Luke 10:24. prophets and kings *w.* to see what you now see
12:49. how I *w.* it were already kindled
John 7:1. he *w.* to avoid Judaea
Acts 7:39. they *w.* themselves back in Egypt
15:33. with the good *w.* of the brethren
22:30. *w.* to be quite sure what charge the Jews were bringing
23:28. I *w.* to ascertain the charge
24:27. *w.* to curry favour with the Jews
Phil. 3:1. I *w.* you joy in the Lord
4:4. I *w.* you all joy in the Lord
Philem. 21. confident that you will meet my *w.*

wit-s

2 Cor. 4:8. we are never at our *w.* end
Gal. 4:20. I am at my *w.* end about you
Eph. 4:18. their *w.* are beclouded

withdrawn

Acts 26:31. after they had *w.*

withdrew

Mat. 2:22. he *w.* to the region of Galilee
4:12. Jesus *w.* to Galilee
14:13. Jesus *w.* privately by boat to a lonely place
15:21. *w.* to the region of Tyre and Sidon
Luke 9:10. *w.* privately to a town called Bethsaida
John 6:1. Jesus *w.* to the farther shore
6:15. *w.* again to the hills by himself
6:66. many of his disciples *w.*
10:40. Jesus *w.* again across the Jordan
Acts 19:9. *w.* his converts
22:29. who were about to examine him *w.* hastily

wither-ed

Mark 11:20. the fig-tree had *w.* from the roots
1 Pet. 1:4. nothing can destroy or spoil or *w.*

withhold

Acts 10:47. *w.* the water for baptism

within

Mat. 12:35. the store of good *w.* himself
Mark 14:49. I was *w.* your reach as I taught in the temple
Luke 6:45. the store of good *w.* himself
John 7:38. living water shall flow out from *w.* him

8:31. dwell *w.* the revelation I have brought
17:13. my joy *w.* them in full measure
Acts 1:7. which the Father has set *w.* his own control
3:25. you are *w.* the covenant
Rom. 3:19. those who are *w.* the pale of the law
7:21. only the wrong is *w.* my reach
8:3. sin *w.* that very nature
8:9. if only God's Spirit dwells *w.* you
8:10. if Christ is dwelling *w.* you
8:11. if the Spirit of him who raised Jesus from the dead dwells *w.* you
11:22. divine kindness to you, if only you remain *w.* its scope
1 Cor. 2:11. the man's own spirit *w.* him
4:6. learn to 'keep *w.* the rules
2 Cor. 5:4. enclosed *w.* this earthly frame
10:15. *w.* the limits of our sphere
Eph. 1:23. holds *w.* it the fullness of him
1 Tim. 6:6. the man whose resources are *w.* him

without

Mat. 10:8. you received *w.* cost; give *w.* charge
Luke 22:6. *w.* collecting a crowd
23:9. *w.* getting any reply
John 1:20. he confessed *w.* reserve
6:64. Jesus knew all along who were *w.* faith
Acts 15:24. *w.* any instructions from us
1 Tim. 4:8. the benefits of religion are *w.* limit
Heb. 11:5. carried away to another life *w.* passing through death
Jam. 1:27. the kind of religion which is *w.* stain
1 John 2:23. to deny the Son is to be *w.* the Father
Rev. 4:8. *w.* a pause they sang

witness-es

John 1:34. I saw it myself, and I have borne *w.*
3:32. bears *w.* to what he has seen and heard, yet no one accepts his *w.*
3:33. to accept his *w.* is to attest that God speaks true
8:13. you are *w.* in your own cause
8:14. even though I do bear *w.* about myself
15:26. he will bear *w.* to me
Acts 22:20. when the blood of Stephen thy *w.* was shed
2 Cor. 1:23. I appeal to God to *w.*
Heb. 3:5. bear *w.* to the words that God would speak
1 John 5:7. there are three *w.*, the Spirit, the water, and the blood
5:11. the *w.* is this
Rev. 1:2. has borne *w.* to the word of God
2:13. Antipas, my faithful *w.*

wives
Tit. 2:4. the younger women to be loving *w*.

woke
Acts 12:7. he tapped Peter on the shoulder and *w*. him

woman-en
Mat. 5:32. marries a *w*. so divorced
15:25. the *w*. came and fell at his feet
22:30. at the resurrection men and *w*. do not marry
24:19. alas for *w*. with child in those days
28:11. the *w*. had started on their way
Mark 12:25. men and *w*. do not marry
13:17. alas for *w*. with child in those days
Luke 2:36. she was a very old *w*.
15:30. running through your money with his *w*.
16:18. a *w*. divorced from her husband
20:34. the men and *w*. of this world marry
21:23. alas for *w*. who are with child in those days
John 8:5. Moses has laid down that such *w*. are to be stoned
11:2. the *w*. who anointed the Lord with ointment
18:16. spoke to the *w*. at the door
Acts 2:18. my slaves, both men and *w*.
Gal. 4:24. the two *w*. stand for two covenants
4:26. the heavenly Jerusalem is the free *w*.
4:27. O barren *w*. who never bore child
Eph. 5:23. the man is the head of the *w*.
5:24. the church is subject to Christ, so must *w*. be to their husbands
5:33. the *w*. must see to it that she pays her husband all respect
1 Tim. 2:15. if only *w*. continue in faith
3:11. must be *w*. of high principle
4:7. godless myths, fit only for old *w*.
1 Pet. 3:1. you *w*. must accept the authority of your husbands
3:7. pay honour to the *w*. body
2 Pet. 2:14. they have eyes for nothing but *w*.

won
Mat. 18:15. you have *w*. your brother
23:15. when you have *w*. him
Acts 11:24. large numbers were *w*. over to the Lord
12:20. they *w*. over Blastus the royal chamberlain
14:19. and *w*. over the crowds
20:28. which he *w*. for himself by his own blood
28:24. some were *w*. over by his arguments

1 Cor. 15:54. victory is *w*.
Rev. 5:5. has *w*. the right to open the scroll
15:2. *w*. the victory over the beast

wonder-ed-ing
Mark 16:3. *w*. among themselves who would roll away the stone
Luke 1:29. *w*. what this greeting might mean
2:33. full of *w*. at what was being said about him
3:15. all *w*. about John
John 5:20. will show greater yet, to fill you with *w*.
5:28. do not *w*. at this
Acts 4:13. they began to *w*.
5:24. were *w*. what could have become of them
2 Cor. 4:16. no *w*. we do not lose heart

wonderful-ly
Mat. 21:42 ⎫
Mark 12:11 ⎬ it is *w*. in our eyes
Luke 1:49. so *w*. has he dealt with me
13:17. all the *w*. things he was doing

wood
Luke 23:31. done when the *w*. is green

word-s
Mat. 2:17. the *w*. spoken through Jeremiah
2:23. the *w*. spoken through the prophets
7:24, 26. hears these *w*. of mine
8:18. Jesus gave *w*. to cross to the other shore
10:19. the *w*. you need will be given you
11:25. Jesus spoke these *w*.
12:23. the *w*. went round
12:34. how can your *w*. be good when you yourselves are evil? For the *w*. that the mouth utters
14:35. sent out *w*. to all the country round
22:15. to trap him in his own *w*.
23:1. addressed the people and his disciples in these *w*.
23:3. pay attention to their *w*.
26:25. Jesus replied, 'The *w*. are yours
26:26. with the *w*.: 'Take this and eat
26:27. with the *w*.: 'Drink from it, all of you
26:64. the *w*. are yours
26:65. at these *w*. the High Priest tore his robes
27:11. the *w*. are yours', said Jesus
28:10. go and take *w*. to my brothers
Mark 3:32. *w*. was brought to him
7:2. 'defiled' hands—in other *w*., without washing them
7:6. prophesied about you hypocrites in these *w*.

Mark 9:10. they seized upon those *w*.
  10:22. at these *w*. his face fell
  14:22. with the *w*.: 'Take this; this is my body
  15:2. he replied, 'The *w*. are yours
Luke 4:28. at these *w*. the whole congregation were infuriated
  6:45. the *w*. that the mouth utters
  9:34. the *w*. were still on his lips
  9:44. ponder my *w*.
  10:5. let your first *w*. be, 'Peace to this house
  11:54. to catch him with his own *w*.
  18:23. at these *w*. his heart sank
  19:22. I will judge you by your own *w*.
  19:46. driving out the traders, with these *w*.
  19:48. the people all hung upon his *w*.
  22:19. with the *w*.: 'This is my body
  22:37. these *w*., I tell you, must find fulfilment in me
  23:3. he replied, 'The *w*. are yours
  23:46. with these *w*. he died
John 1:2. the *W*., then, was with God at the beginning
  1:23. in the *w*. of the prophet Isaiah
  2:17. his disciples recalled the *w*. of Scripture
  6:14. the *w*. went round
  6:60. why listen to such *w*.
  7:26. speaking openly, and they have not a *w*. to say to him
  8:38. revealing in *w*. what I saw in my Father's presence
  8:55. I know him and obey his *w*.
  16:25. tell you of the Father in plain *w*.
  18:37. King' is your *w*.
Acts 16:40. spoke *w*. of encouragement
  17:8. these *w*. caused a great commotion
  20:2. often speaking *w*. of encouragement
  28:22. no one has a good *w*. to say for it
Rom. 6:19. *w*. that suit your human weakness
  9:7 ⎫
  15:3 ⎬ in the *w*. of Scripture
1 Cor. 1:31 ⎭
  2:1. without display of fine *w*.
  2:4. the *w*. I spoke, the gospel I proclaimed
  2:6. yet I do speak *w*. of wisdom
  2:9 ⎫
  2:16 ⎬ in the *w*. of Scripture
  10:20 ⎭
  14:3. his *w*. have power to build
  14:11. his *w*. will be gibberish
2 Cor. 7:14. every *w*. we ever addressed to you bore the mark of truth
  9:15. thanks be to God for his gift beyond *w*.

Eph. 4:9. the *w*. 'ascended' implies that he also descended
  5:31. in the *w*. of Scripture
  6:19. that I may be granted the right *w*.
1 Thess. 4:16. at the *w*. of command
1 Tim. 1:6. gone astray into a wilderness of *w*.
  1:7. without understanding either the *w*. they use
  1:15 ⎫ here are *w*. you may trust, *w*.
  4:9 ⎭ that merit full acceptance
2 Tim. 2:11. here are *w*. you may trust
Tit. 2:8. he finds not a *w*. to say to our discredit
  3:8. these are *w*. you may trust
Heb. 3:5. bear witness to the *w*. that God would speak
  3:13. while that *w*. 'Today' still sounds in your ears
  4:7. he uses the *w*. already quoted
  7:21. will not go back on his *w*.
Jam. 2:23. fulfilment of the *w*. of Scripture
  4:13. a *w*. with you, you who say
  5:1. a *w*. to you who have great possessions
1 Pet. 1:8. a joy too great for *w*.
2 Pet. 1:21. they spoke the *w*. of God
1 John 1:6. our *w*. and our lives are a lie
Jude 9. did not presume to condemn him in insulting *w*.
  15. defiant *w*. which godless sinners had spoken
Rev. 2:1. the *w*. of the One who holds the seven stars
  2:8. these are the *w*. of the First and the Last
  2:12. the *w*. of the One who has the sharp two-edged sword
  2:18. these are the *w*. of the Son of God
  3:1. the *w*. of the One who holds the seven spirits of God
  3:7. these are the *w*. of the holy one
  19:9. these are the very *w*. of God
  22:6. these *w*. are trustworthy and true
  22:7. the *w*. of prophecy contained in this book
  22:9. the *w*. of this book
  22:10. do not seal up the *w*. of prophecy

wore
Mark 6:35. as the day *w*. on
Rev. 9:17. they *w*. breastplates
  16:2. men that *w*. the mark of the beast

work-s-ed-ing
Mat. 6:28. they do not *w*.
  11:28. come to me, all whose *w*. is hard

Mat. 14:2. miraculous powers are at *w.* in him
17:12. *w.* their will upon him
20:2. he sent them off to *w.*
20:9. started *w.* an hour before sunset
20:12. late-comers have done only one hours *w.*
Mark 1:16. at *w.* with a casting-net
4:29. he sets to *w.* with the sickle
6:2. how does he *w.* such miracles
9:13. they have *w.* their will upon him
9:39. a *w.* of divine power in my name
Luke 3:23. when Jesus began his *w.* he was about thirty years old
5:5. Master, we were hard at *w.* all night
10:40. my sister has left me to get on with the *w.*
13:32. casting out devils and *w.* cures
19:43. your enemies will set up siege-*w.*
John 5:16. *w.* of this kind done on the Sabbath
6:27. you must *w.*, not for this perishable food
7:4. no one can hope to be in the public eye if he *w.* in seclusion
8:41. you are doing your own father's *w.*
Acts 1:1. in the first part of my *w.*, Theophilus
2:22. which God *w.* among you through him
6:8. began to *w.* great miracles
7:36. it was Moses who led them out, *w.* miracles
11:23. saw the divine grace at *w.*, he rejoiced
14:3. causing signs and miracles to be *w.*
15:12. the signs and miracles that God had *w.*
15:17. thus says the Lord, whose *w.* it is
19:11. God *w.* miracles of an unusual kind
19:40. charged with riot for this day's *w.*
20:35. help the weak in this way, by hard *w.*
26:9. thought it my duty to *w.* actively against the name of Jesus
Rom. 9:22. God, desiring to exhibit his retribution at *w.*
13:4. God's agents *w.* for your good
1 Cor. 3:8. whether they plant or water, they *w.* as a team
5:7. the old leaven of corruption is *w.* among you
9:6. bound to *w.* for our living
13:8. prophets? their *w.* will be over
15:10. the grace of God *w.* with me
16:9. a great opportunity has opened for effective *w.*

2 Cor. 1:24. we are *w.* with you for your own happiness
2:12. an opening awaited me for the Lord's *w.*
5:18. this has been the *w.* of God
8:6. this *w.* of generosity
8:10. a good beginning last year both in the *w.* you did
8:19. help in this beneficent *w.*
10:15. *w.* done where others have laboured, work beyond our proper sphere
10:16. *w.* already done in another man's sphere
12:12. the *w.* I did among you
Gal. 5:5. the *w.* of the Spirit through faith
6:10. let us *w.* for the good of all
Eph. 6:21. trustworthy helper in the Lord's *w.*
Phil. 1:5. the *w.* of the Gospel
1:12. the *w.* of the Gospel has been helped on
2:16. proof that I did not run my race in vain, or *w.* in vain
2:22. like a son *w.* under his father
Col. 4:7. fellow-servant in the Lord's *w.*
4:13. he *w.* tirelessly for you
1 Thess. 2:9. we *w.* for a living night and day
5:12. those who are *w.* so hard among you
2 Thess. 2:11. which *w.* upon them to believe the lie
1 Tim. 1:4. God's plan for us, which *w.* through faith
2 Tim. 4:2. the patience that the *w.* of teaching requires
Tit. 1:14. the *w.* of men who turn their backs upon the truth
Heb. 2:4. by manifold *w.* of power
13:7. the outcome of their life and *w.*
2 Pet. 3:12. the Day of God and *w.* to hasten it on
2 John 8. that you may not lose all that we *w.* for
3 John 8. it was on Christ's *w.* that they went out
Rev. 13:13. it *w.* great miracles
13:18. *w.* out the number of the beast
19:20. *w.* miracles in its presence

worker-s
Luke 10:7. the *w.* earns his pay
Rom. 16:3. my fellow-*w.* in Christ
1 Cor. 3:9. we are God's fellow-*w.*
12:28. then miracle-*w.*
Phil. 2:25. Epaphroditus, my fellow-*w.*
Col. 1:7. a trusted *w.* for Christ
1 Thess. 3:2. God's fellow-*w.*
Philem. 24. my fellow-*w.*

workman
1 Tim. 5:18. the *w.* earns his pay

world-s-ly
Mat. 5:13. you are salt to the *w*.
19:28. in the *w*. that is to be
20:25. in the *w*., rulers lord it over their
subjects
24:30. the peoples of the *w*. will make
lamentation
Mark 10:42. in the *w*. the recognized
rulers lord it
13:19. the *w*. which God created
Luke 16:9. use your *w*. wealth to win
friends
16:11. the wealth of this *w*.
21:26. all that is coming upon the *w*.
21:34. *w*. cares
21:35. wherever they are, the whole
w. over
22:25. in the *w*., kings lord it over
John 8:15. you judge by *w*. standards
Acts 19:35. the *w*. knows that our city of
Ephesus
21:21. all the Jews in the gentile *w*.
21:28. spreads his doctrine all over
the *w*.
22:15. you are to be his witness before
the *w*.
Rom. 1:13. as I have in other parts of the
w.
8:38. in the *w*. as it is or the *w*. as it
shall be
9:17. to spread my fame over all the
w.
1 Cor. 1:17. the language of *w*. wisdom
15:21. it was a man who brought
death into the *w*.
2 Cor. 1:17. my plans, frame them as a
w. man might
5:16. *w*. standards have ceased to
count
5:17. united to Christ, there is a new
w.
6:10. penniless, we own the *w*.
Gal. 3:22. the whole *w*. to be prisoners in
subjection to sin
Col. 2:18. the futile conceit of *w*. minds
1 Tim. 1:9. the irreligious and *w*.
1:17. now to the King of all *w*.
5:5. one who is alone in the *w*.
6:20. turn a deaf ear to empty and
w. chatter
2 Tim. 2:16. avoid empty and *w*. chatter
3:1. the final age of this *w*.
4:17. the Gospel for the whole pagan
w. to hear
Tit. 2:11. the grace of God has dawned
upon the *w*.
3:4. generosity of God our Saviour
dawned upon the *w*.
Heb. 9:11. not belonging to this created
w.
12:16. no one *w*.-minded like Esau
13:3. you like them are still in the *w*.
Jam. 1:1. the Twelve Tribes dispersed
throughout the *w*.

1 Pet. 4:3. the things that men want to
do in the pagan *w*.
2 Pet. 3:4. as it has always been since the
w. began
Rev. 1:7. all the peoples of the *w*. shall
lament
5:6. seven spirits of God sent out over
all the *w*.
14:3. alone from the whole *w*. had
been ransomed
16:19. the cities of the *w*. fell in ruin
17:2. men all over the *w*.
18:3. merchants the *w*. over have
grown rich
18:23. the merchant princes of the *w*.

worm-ed
Jude 4. certain persons who have *w*.
their way in

worn
Luke 8:27. for a long time he had
neither *w*. clothes
22:45. he found them asleep, *w*. out
by grief
1 Cor. 15:49. we have *w*. the likeness of
the man made of dust

worry-ing
Mat. 10:19. do not *w*. about what you
are to say
Mark 13:11. do not *w*. beforehand about
what you will say
Luke 12:11. *w*. about how you will
conduct your defence
12:29. you are not to *w*.

worse
Acts 28:5. shook off the snake into the
fire and was none the *w*.
2 Cor. 12:13. is there anything in which
you were treated *w*. than the other
congregations
1 Tim. 5:13. they learn to be idle, and *w*.
than idle

worship-ped-ping
Luke 1:74. free from fear, to *w*. him
1:75. with a holy *w*.
2:37. *w*. day and night
Acts 7:7. *w*. me in this place
10:2. joined in the *w*. of God
13:2. offering *w*. to the Lord
13:16. men of Israel and you who *w*.
our God
26:7. *w*. with intense devotion
27:23. God whose I am and whom I
w.
Rom. 9:4. the temple *w*., and the
promises
12:1. the *w*. offered by mind and heart
1 Cor. 14:26. when you meet for *w*.
1 Tim. 5:5. meetings for prayer and *w*.
2 Tim. 1:3. *w*. with a pure intention
Heb. 12:28. *w*. him as he would be *w*.

worshipper-s (continued)

Jam. 2:2. two visitors may enter your place of *w*.
1 Pet. 4:3. the forbidden *w*. of idols
Rev. 22:3. his servants shall *w*. him

worshipper-s
Acts 13:43. many Jews and gentile *w*.
  13:50. the women of standing who were *w*.
  17:17. the Jews and gentile *w*.
Heb. 9:9. cannot give the *w*. inward perfection
  10:1. can never bring the *w*. to perfection

worst
Eph. 6:13. to stand your ground when things are at their *w*.

worth
Mat. 6:26. you are *w*. more than the birds
  10:31. you are *w*. more than any number of sparrows
  12:12. a man is *w*. far more than a sheep
Mark 12:42. two tiny coins, together *w*. a farthing
Luke 12:7. you are *w*. more than any number of sparrows
  12:24. you are *w*. far more than the birds
1 Cor. 2:15. a man gifted with the Spirit can judge the *w*. of everything
  3:13. fire will test the *w*. of each man's work
  14:5. the prophet is *w*. more than the man of ecstatic speech
  16:4. *w*. while for me to go as well
2 Cor. 5:12. in outward show and not in inward *w*.
1 Pet. 2:6. a choice corner-stone of great *w*.
  2:7. the great *w*. of which it speaks

worthless
Mat. 13:48. threw the *w*. away
Luke 6:43. no such thing as a good tree producing *w*. fruit, nor yet a *w*. tree producing good fruit
John 8:54. if I glorify myself, that glory of mine is *w*.
Heb. 6:8. if it bears thorns and thistles, it is *w*.

worthy
John 1:47. here is an Israelite *w*. of the name
Rom. 16:2. a welcome *w*. of God's people
Phil. 1:27. conduct be *w*. of the gospel of Christ
1 Tim. 1:12. judging me *w*. of this trust
2 Tim. 2:15. show yourself *w*. of God's approval

1 Pet. 1:7. that your faith may prove itself *w*. of all praise
3 John 6. in a manner *w*. of the God we serve

wound-s-ed
Acts 16:33. washed their *w*.
2 Cor. 7:8. if I did *w*. you by the letter
  7:9. your feelings were *w*. but that the *w*. led to a change of heart
  7:10. the *w*. which is borne in God's way
1 Pet. 2:24. by his *w*. you have been healed

wrangle-s-ing
Phil. 2:14. without complaint or *w*.
1 Tim. 6:4. endless *w*.

wrap-ped-pings
Luke 24:12. peering in, saw the *w*.
John 11:44. his face *w*. in a cloth
  20:5. saw the linen *w*.
  21:7. he *w*. his coat about him
Acts 12:8. *w*. your cloak round you and follow me
1 Pet. 5:5. *w*. yourselves in the garment of humility
Rev. 10:1. he was *w*. in cloud

wreath
1 Cor. 9:25. to win a fading *w*.; we, a *w*. that never fades

wrist-s
Acts 12:7. the chains fell away from his *w*.

write-s-ings
Rom. 10:5. of legal righteousness Moses *w*.
1 Cor. 6:5. I *w*. this to shame you
2 Cor. 10:9. you must not think of me as one who scares you by the letters he *w*.
2 Tim. 3:15. the sacred *w*. which have power to make you wise

writer-s
Luke 1:1. many *w*. have undertaken to draw up an account

written
Rom. 2:27. your *w*. code
  2:29. not by *w*. precepts but by the Spirit
  7:6. the old way, the way of a *w*. code
2 Cor. 3:6. not in a *w*. document, but in a spiritual bond; for the *w*. law condemns to death
Phil. 3:7. all such assets I have *w*. off because of Christ
1 Pet. 2:6. for it stands *w*.

wrong-s-ed-ing
Mat. 5:39. do not set yourself against the man who *w*. you

Mat. 6:12. forgive us the *w*. we have done, As we have forgiven those who have *w*. us

6:14. forgive others the *w*. they have done

6:15. then the *w*. you have done will not be forgiven

18:21. forgive my brother if he goes on *w*. me

Mark 11:25. forgive you the *w*. you have done

Luke 11:4. we too forgive all who have done us *w*.

13:16. was it *w*. for her to be freed from her bonds on the Sabbath

17:3. if your brother *w*. you, rebuke him

17:4. even if he *w*. you seven times

23:22. what *w*. has he done

23:41. this man has done nothing *w*.

John 5:29. those who have done *w*. will rise to hear their doom

8:46. which of you can prove me in the *w*.

16:8. show where *w*. and right and judgement lie

16:9. he will convict them of *w*.

Acts 25:5. if there is anything *w*., let them prosecute

Rom. 1:17. God's way of righting *w*.

2:8. take the *w*. for their guide

3:21. God's way of righting *w*.

6:13. as implements for doing *w*.

7:8. produced in me all kinds of *w*. desires

7:19. the *w*. which is against my will

7:21. only the *w*. is within my reach

13:4. if you are doing *w*.

13:10. love cannot *w*. a neighbour

1 Cor. 7:28. if, however, you do marry, there is nothing *w*. in it; and if a virgin marries, she has done no *w*.

7:36. there is nothing *w*. in it; let them marry

13:6. love keeps no score of *w*.

Gal. 2:11. he was clearly in the *w*.

4:12. it is not that you did me any *w*.

5:10. I am confident that you will not take the *w*. view

6:1. if a man should do something *w*.

1 Thess. 4:6. no man must do his brother *w*.

5:15. see to it that no one pays back *w*. for *w*.

2 Thess. 3:2. rescued from *w*.-headed and wicked men

1 Tim. 5:15. widows who have taken the *w*. turning

Heb. 1:9. thou hast loved right and hated *w*.

11:7. through his faith he put the whole world in the *w*.

Jam. 3:2. all of us often go *w*.; the man who never says a *w*. thing is a perfect character

4:3. you pray from *w*. motives

4:16. all such boasting is *w*.

1 Pet. 2:20. when you have done *w*.

3:9. do not repay *w*. with *w*.

3:11. must turn from *w*. and do good

3:13. who is going to do you *w*.

3:17. better to suffer for well-doing, if such should be the will of God, than for doing *w*.

2 Pet. 2:15. consented to take pay for doing *w*.

1 John 1:9. cleanse us from every kind of *w*.

3:12. because his own actions were *w*.

wrong-doers-doing

Rom. 5:15. Adam's *w*. For if the *w*. of that one man brought death

5:17. by the *w*. of that one man

Gal. 3:19. to make *w*. a legal offence

1 Pet. 2:16. to provide a screen for *w*.

3:12. the Lord's face is set against *w*.

1 John 5:17. all *w*. is sin

wrote

Matt. 26:56. to fulfil what the prophets *w*.

Acts 1:1. I *w*. of all that Jesus did and taught

Y

yard-s

John 21:8. not far from land, only about a hundred *y*.

Acts 7:5. he gave him nothing in it to call his own, not one *y*.

year-s

Heb. 4:7. through the lips of David after many long *y*.

7:3. his *y*. have no beginning

Rev. 12:14. for three *y*. and a half she was to be sustained

22:2. fruit, one for each month of the *y*.

yearn-ing

2 Cor. 5:2. we *y*. to have our heavenly habitation put on over this one

Phil. 1:8. I long for you all, with the deep *y*. of Christ Jesus

1 Thess. 2:8. with such *y*. love

yeast
Matt. 13:33. the kingdom of Heaven is like *y*.
Luke 13:21. it is like *y*. which a woman took

yell-ing
Acts 21:36. at their heels *y*., 'Kill him
22:23. as they were *y*.

yellow
Rev. 9:17. fiery red, blue, and sulphur-*y*.

yield-s-ed-ing
Mat. 7:17. a good tree always *y*. good fruit
7:19. when a tree does not *y*. good fruit
13:8. it bore fruit, *y*. a hundredfold
13:23. *y*. a hundredfold
21:43. a nation that *y*. the proper fruit
Luke 8:8. *y*. a hundredfold
8:15. by their perseverance *y*. a harvest
12:16. whose land *y*. heavy crops
John 1:12. *y*. him their allegiance
Rom. 6:17. *y*. whole-hearted obedience
1 Cor. 14:9. if your ecstatic utterance *y*. no precise meaning

Gal. 2:5. not for one moment did I *y*. to their dictation
Phil. 2:1. life in Christ *y*. anything to stir the heart
1 Tim. 2:14. the woman who, *y*. to deception, fell into sin
6:5. they think religion should *y*. dividends
6:6. religion does *y*. high dividends
Heb. 6:7. *y*. a useful crop to those for whom it is cultivated
Jam. 5:7. the precious crop his land may *y*.

young-er
Mat. 10:35. a *y*. wife against her mother-in-law
13:6⎱ when the sun rose the *y*.
Mark 4:6 ⎰ corn was scorched
15:40. Mary the mother of James the *y*.

yourself-ves
Mat. 6:6. when you pray, go into a room by *y*.
Luke 22:32. when you have come to *y*.
Acts 5:39. you risk finding *y*. at war with God
Rom. 12:2. adapt *y*. no longer to the pattern of this present world
12:8. if you are a leader, exert *y*. to lead

Z

zeal
2 Cor. 8:7. *z*. of every kind

Zealot
Mat. 10:4⎱ Simon, a member of the Z.
Mark 3:18 ⎰ party
Acts 1:13. Simon the Z.